NIGHTS OF PLAGUE

Orhan Pamuk is the author of many celebrated books of fiction, non-fiction, and photography. In 2003 he won the IMPAC prize for *My Name Is Red*, and in 2006 he was awarded the Nobel Prize in Literature. He has since been described as 'that rare author who writes his best books after winning the Nobel Prize' (*Independent*). His work has been translated into sixty-four languages.

Nights of Plague

ORHAN PAMUK

Translated from Turkish
by Ekin Oklap

faber

I would like to thank my historian friend Edhem Eldem, who offered suggestions and corrections as I worked to finish the book.

First published in 2022
by Faber & Faber Limited
Bloomsbury House
74–77 Great Russell Street
London WC1B 3DA

This export edition published in 2022

Published in the United States by Alfred A. Knopf, a division of
Random House, Inc., New York

Originally published in Turkey as *Veba Geceleri* by Yapı Kredi
Yayınları, Istanbul, in 2021. Copyright © 2021 Orhan Pamuk

Designed by Cassandra J. Pappas. Typeset by Scribe.
Printed and bound by CPI Group (UK) Ltd, Croydon, CR0 4YY

A CIP record for this book
is available from the British Library

ISBN 978–0–571–35293–7

MIX
Paper from
responsible sources
FSC® C171272

2 4 6 8 10 9 7 5 3 1

At the approach of danger there are always two voices that speak with equal power in the human soul: one very reasonably tells a man to consider the nature of the danger and the means of escaping it; the other, still more reasonably, says that it is too depressing and painful to think of the danger, since it is not in man's power to foresee everything and avert the general course of events, and it is therefore better to disregard what is painful till it comes, and to think about what is pleasant.

—LEO TOLSTOY, *War and Peace,*
translated by Louise and Aylmer Maude

No writer has so far attempted to examine and compare these narratives to write a true history of the calamity of the plague.

—ALESSANDRO MANZONI, *The Betrothed*

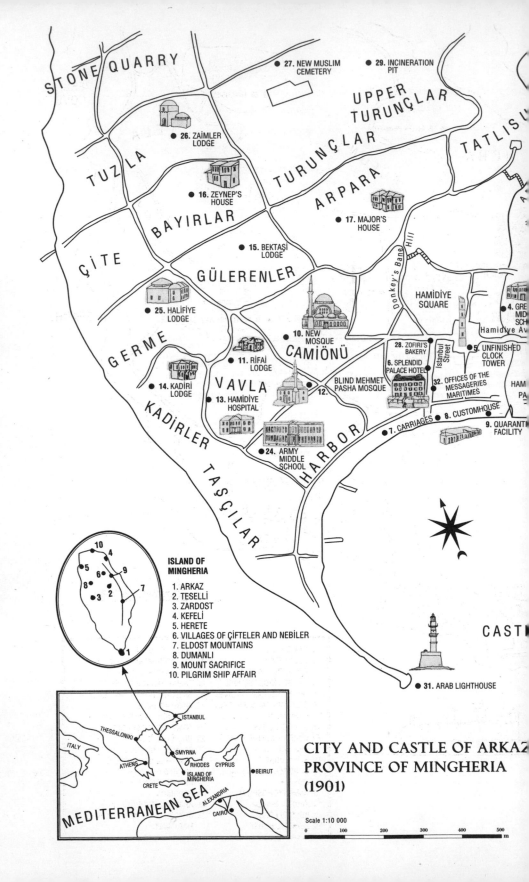

STONE QUARRY

27. NEW MUSLIM CEMETERY

29. INCINERATION PIT

UPPER TURUNÇLAR

TATLISU

26. ZAİMLER LODGE

TUZLA

TURUNÇLAR

ARPARA

16. ZEYNEP'S HOUSE

17. MAJOR'S HOUSE

BAYIRLAR

ÇİTE

15. BEKTAŞİ LODGE

GÜLERENLER

Donkey's Bank Hill

HAMİDİYE SQUARE

4. GRE MID SCH

Hamidiye Av

25. HALİFİYE LODGE

GERME

10. NEW MOSQUE

CAMİÖNÜ

28. ZOFİRİ'S BAKERY

Istanbul Street

5. UNFINISHED CLOCK TOWER

11. RİFAİ LODGE

6. SPLENDID PALACE HOTEL

32. OFFICES OF THE MESSAGERIES MARITIMES

HAM PA

14. KADİRİ LODGE

VAVLA

12.

BLIND MEHMET PASHA MOSQUE

13. HAMİDİYE HOSPITAL

8. CUSTOMHOUSE

9. QUARANTI FACILITY

KADİRLER

7. CARRIAGES

HARBOR

24. ARMY MIDDLE SCHOOL

TAŞÇILAR

10
4
5
9
6
8
7
3 2
1

ISLAND OF MINGHERIA

1. ARKAZ
2. TESELLİ
3. ZARDOST
4. KEFELİ
5. HERETE
6. VILLAGES OF ÇİFTELER AND NEBİLER
7. ELDOST MOUNTAINS
8. DUMANLI
9. MOUNT SACRIFICE
10. PILGRIM SHIP AFFAIR

CAST

31. ARAB LIGHTHOUSE

ISTANBUL

THESSALONIKI

ITALY

SMYRNA

ATHENS

RHODES   CYPRUS

CRETE   ISLAND OF MINGHERIA

BEIRUT

ALEXANDRIA

CAIRO

MEDITERRANEAN SEA

CITY AND CASTLE OF ARKAZ PROVINCE OF MINGHERIA (1901)

Scale 1:10 000

0   100   200   300   400   500
m

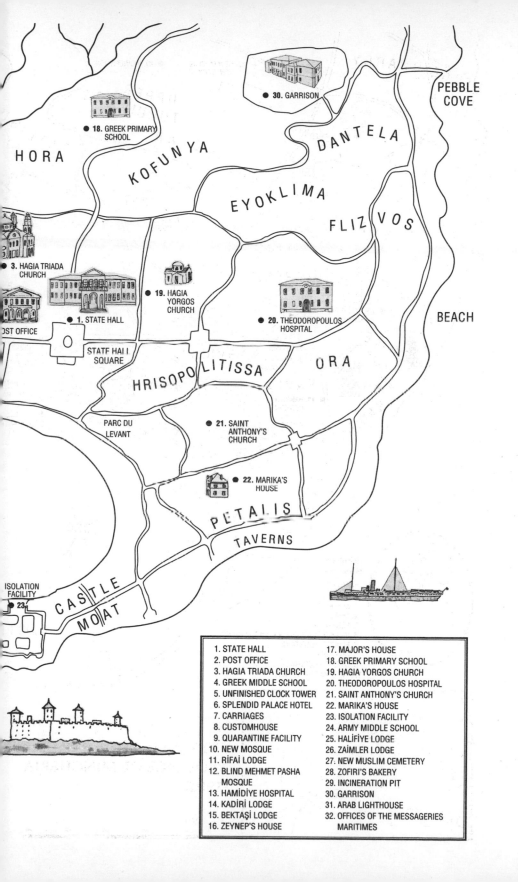

PEBBLE COVE

● 30. GARRISON

18. GREEK PRIMARY SCHOOL

HORA

KOFUNYA

DANTELA

EYOKLIMA

FLIZVOS

3. HAGIA TRIADA CHURCH

● 19. HAGIA YORGOS CHURCH

● 20. THEODOROPOULOS HOSPITAL

BEACH

1. STATE HALL

POST OFFICE

STATE HALL SQUARE

HRISOPOLITISSA

ORA

PARC DU LEVANT

● 21. SAINT ANTHONY'S CHURCH

● 22. MARIKA'S HOUSE

PETALIS

TAVERNS

ISOLATION FACILITY

● 23.

CASTLE MOAT

1. STATE HALL	17. MAJOR'S HOUSE
2. POST OFFICE	18. GREEK PRIMARY SCHOOL
3. HAGIA TRIADA CHURCH	19. HAGIA YORGOS CHURCH
4. GREEK MIDDLE SCHOOL	20. THEODOROPOULOS HOSPITAL
5. UNFINISHED CLOCK TOWER	21. SAINT ANTHONY'S CHURCH
6. SPLENDID PALACE HOTEL	22. MARIKA'S HOUSE
7. CARRIAGES	23. ISOLATION FACILITY
8. CUSTOMHOUSE	24. ARMY MIDDLE SCHOOL
9. QUARANTINE FACILITY	25. HALİFİYE LODGE
10. NEW MOSQUE	26. ZAİMLER LODGE
11. RİFAİ LODGE	27. NEW MUSLIM CEMETERY
12. BLIND MEHMET PASHA MOSQUE	28. ZOFIRI'S BAKERY
13. HAMİDİYE HOSPITAL	29. INCINERATION PIT
14. KADİRİ LODGE	30. GARRISON
15. BEKTAŞİ LODGE	31. ARAB LIGHTHOUSE
16. ZEYNEP'S HOUSE	32. OFFICES OF THE MESSAGERIES MARITIMES

Nights of Plague

PREFACE

This is both a historical novel and a history written in the form of a novel. In this story of what took place during the most eventful and momentous six months in the life of the island of Mingheria, pearl of the Eastern Mediterranean Sea, I have also included many tales from the history of this country I love so dearly.

When I began to research the events that took place on the island during the outbreak of plague in 1901, I realized that although an understanding of the subjective decisions taken by the protagonists of this brief and dramatic time could not be achieved by historical method alone, the art of the novel could help, and so I set out to bring the two together.

But readers must not think to find my starting point in these complex literary conundrums. It really all began with a series of letters I gained access to, and whose invaluable riches I have sought to reflect in this book. I was asked to annotate and prepare for publication one hundred thirteen letters that Princess Pakize, third daughter of the thirty-third Ottoman sultan Murad V, had written to her older sister Hatice Sultan between 1901 and 1913. The book you are about to read began as an "editor's introduction" to that correspondence.

The introduction grew longer, and broadened with further research, until it turned into the book you are now holding. I admit that above all else it was Princess Pakize's writing style and intelligence that captivated me. The charming and profoundly sensitive Princess Pakize possessed a narrative appetite, an awareness of detail, and a descriptive flair that few historians and novelists are blessed with. I have spent many years in British and French archives reading consular dispatches from the Ottoman Empire's port cities, on the basis of which I have com-

pleted a doctorate and published several academic books. But no consul
had ever been able to describe these events, those days of cholera and
plague, with such elegance and depth of understanding, nor could any
of them convey the atmosphere of Ottoman port cities and the colors
of their streets and markets, the squawking of seagulls and the sound of
carriage wheels, in quite the same way. So perhaps it was Princess Pakize,
and her profoundly perceptive approach to people, objects, and events,
who inspired me with her lively, vibrant accounts to turn that editor's
introduction into a novel.

As I read the letters, I asked myself: Is it because she was, like me,
a "woman" that Princess Pakize was able to describe these events much
more vividly and "meticulously" than the average historian or foreign
consul could? We must not forget that during the outbreak of plague,
the author of these letters rarely left the guesthouse in the State Hall
and only found out what was happening in the city through her doctor
husband's tales! Princess Pakize did not just describe this world of male
politicians, bureaucrats, and doctors in her letters; she also managed to
identify with these men. I too have attempted to bring that world to life
in my novel-cum-history. But it is very difficult indeed to be as recep-
tive, bright, and hungry for life as Princess Pakize was.

Of course another reason why I have been so moved by these extraordinary letters, which will span at least six hundred pages when they
are published, is that I myself am a daughter of Mingheria. As a little
girl, I would come across Princess Pakize in schoolbooks, newspaper
columns, and most of all in the pages of national children's weeklies
(Island Lessons, Learning History), which published comic strips and tales
of historic figures. I had always felt a particular affinity toward her. Just
as other people saw the island of Mingheria as a mythical, fairy-tale
land, Princess Pakize was, to me, a fairy-tale heroine. It was a magical
experience to find the fairy-tale Princess's day-to-day troubles, her true
emotions, and most important her striking personality and her integrity enshrined in the letters that had suddenly come into my possession. Eventually—as the patient reader will discover by the end of this
book—I met her in person too.

I was able to verify the authenticity of the world described in Princess Pakize's letters by consulting archives in Istanbul, Mingheria, England, and France and by reviewing historical documents and memoirs

from the era. But there were moments as I wrote my historical novel when I could not help but identify with Princess Pakize and feel as if I were writing my own personal story.

The art of the novel is based on the craft of telling our own stories as if they belonged to others, and of telling other people's stories as if they were our own. So whenever I began to feel like a sultan's daughter, like a princess, I knew deep down that I was doing precisely what a novelist should do. The harder part was empathizing with all the men in positions of power, the pashas and doctors who were in charge of quarantine measures and oversaw the battle against the plague.

If a novel is to reach, in spirit and form, beyond the scope of an individual's story, and resemble instead a kind of history that embraces everybody's lives, it is best for it to be narrated from many different points of view. On the other hand, I agree with that most female of all male novelists, the great Henry James, who believed that for a novel to be truly convincing, every detail and every event must be gathered around the perspective of a single character.

But because I have written a history book *at the same time,* I have often deviated from and indeed broken the rule of the single point of view. I have interrupted emotional scenes to provide the reader with facts and figures and the histories of government institutions. Right after describing a character's innermost feelings, I have swiftly and boldly moved on to a completely different character's thoughts, even when the first character couldn't possibly have known what they might be. Although I firmly believe that the dethroned sultan Abdülaziz was assassinated, I have also noted how some have argued that he committed suicide. In other words, I have tried to look at the dazzling realm Princess Pakize described in her letters through the eyes of its other witnesses too, and thus make my book closer to a history.

Of the questions I have been asked so frequently over the years, such as how these letters came into my possession, how seriously I take the murder mystery therein, and why did I not publish the letters first, I will only address here the second of the above. This idea for a novel found support among fellow academics to whom I spoke of the murders described in the letters, and of Sultan Abdul Hamid II's literary preferences. I was also encouraged by the fact that a prestigious publisher like Cambridge University Press was interested in the murder mystery angle, and in the history of the little island of Mingheria. Of course the meanings and enigmas of this wondrous world, which I have been recording with unfaltering enjoyment for so many years, go much deeper and further than the mere question of who the killer was. The identity of the killer is, at most, a sign. But a proclivity for murder mysteries may transform every page of this book—starting from the words of Tolstoy, the greatest historical novelist of all, and of this preface—into an ocean of symbols.

Some have accused me of disagreeing too much (though I never name names) with certain popular and official historians. They may be right. But if we have done so, it is only because we have given their much-loved works due consideration.

Introductions to history books about the Orient and the Levant, or the East and the Eastern Mediterranean, will always touch upon problems of transliteration and seek to explain how ancient local scripts have been rendered into the Latin alphabet. I am glad not to have written yet another of those dreary books. There is no match for the Mingherian alphabet and language anyway! In some cases I have used the original spelling of local names, and in others I have written them as they are pronounced. The existence of a city in Georgia with a similar spelling is a simple coincidence. But it is entirely intentional, and certainly no coincidence, that many things in this book will seem as familiar to the reader as old and nearly forgotten memories.

—Mîna Mingher, Istanbul, 2017

CHAPTER I

In the year 1901, if a steamer with black coal-smoke pouring from its chimney were to sail south from Istanbul for four days until it passed the island of Rhodes, then continue south through dangerous, stormy waters toward Alexandria for another half day, its passengers would eventually come to see in the distance the delicate towers of Arkaz Castle upon the island of Mingheria. Due to Mingheria's location on the route between Istanbul and Alexandria, the Castle's enigmatic shadow and silhouette were gazed upon in awe and fascination by many a passing traveler. As soon as this magnificent image—which Homer described in the *Iliad* as "an emerald built of pink stone"—appeared on the horizon, ship captains of a finer spiritual disposition would invite their passengers on deck so that they could savor the views, and artists on their way to the East would avidly paint the romantic vista, adding black storm clouds for effect.

But few of these ships would stop at Mingheria, for in those days there were only three ferries that made regular weekly trips to the island: the Messageries Maritimes *Saghalien* (whose high-pitched whistle everyone in Arkaz recognized) and *Equateur* (with its deeper horn), and the Cretian company Pantaleon's dainty vessel the *Zeus* (which only rarely sounded its horn, and always in brief bursts). So the fact that an unscheduled ferry was approaching the island of Mingheria two hours before midnight on the twenty-second of April 1901—the day our story begins—signaled that something unusual was afoot.

The ship with pointed bow and slender white chimneys closing in on the island from the north, stealthy as a spy vessel, and bearing the Ottoman flag, was the *Aziziye*. It had been tasked by Sultan Abdul Hamid II with transporting a distinguished Ottoman delegation from Istanbul on a special mission to China. To this delegation of seventeen fez-, turban-, and hat-clad religious scholars, army officers, translators, and bureaucrats, Abdul Hamid had added at the last moment his niece Princess Pakize, whose marriage he had recently arranged, and her husband, Prince Consort Doctor Nuri Bey. The joyous, eager, and slightly dazed newlyweds had not been able to fathom the reason for their inclusion in the delegation to China, and had puzzled over the matter at great length.

Princess Pakize—who, like her older sisters, was not fond of her uncle the Sultan—was sure that Abdul Hamid had meant her and her husband some kind of harm by putting them in the delegation, but she had not yet been able to work out what the reason might be. Some palace gossips had suggested that the Sultan's intention must be to drive the newlyweds out of Istanbul and send them to die in yellow fever–infested Asian lands and cholera-ridden African deserts, while others pointed out that Abdul Hamid's games tended to be revealed only once he had finished playing them. But Prince Consort Doctor Nuri Bey was more optimistic. An eminently successful and hardworking thirty-eight-year-old quarantine doctor, he had represented the Ottoman Empire at international public health conferences. His achievements had caught the Sultan's attention, and when they had been introduced, Doctor Nuri had discovered what many quarantine doctors already knew: that the Sultan's fascination with murder mysteries was matched by his interest in European medical advances. The Sultan wanted to keep up with developments concerning microbes, laboratories, and vaccinations and introduce the latest medical findings to Istanbul and across Ottoman lands. He was also concerned about the new infectious diseases that were making their way toward the West from Asia and China.

There was no wind in the Levant that night, so the Sultan's *Aziziye* cruise ship was making swifter progress than expected. Earlier it had made a stop at the port of Smyrna, though no such stop had been declared in the official itinerary. As the ship had neared the misty Smyrna docks, one by one the committee's delegates had climbed up the narrow stairwell that led to the captain's quarters to request an explanation and had learned that a mysterious new passenger was to come on board. Even the captain (who was Russian) had claimed not to know who this passenger was.

The *Aziziye*'s mysterious passenger was the Ottoman Empire's Chief

Inspector of Public Health and Sanitation, the renowned chemist and pharmacist Bonkowski Pasha. Tired but still sprightly at the age of sixty, Bonkowski Pasha was the Sultan's Royal Chemist and the founder of modern Ottoman pharmacology. He was also a semisuccessful business-man who had once owned a number of different companies producing rosewater and perfumes, bottled mineral water, and pharmaceuticals. But for the past ten years he had worked exclusively as the Ottoman Empire's Chief Inspector of Public Health, sending the Sultan reports on cholera and plague outbreaks, as well as rushing from one outbreak to the next, from port to port and city to city, to oversee quarantine and public health provisions on behalf of the Sultan.

Chemist and pharmacist Bonkowski Pasha had often represented the Ottoman Empire at international quarantine conventions, and had written Sultan Abdul Hamid a treatise four years ago on the precautions that the Ottoman Empire should take against the plague pandemic that had begun in the East. He had also been specially appointed to combat the outbreak of plague in the Greek neighborhoods of Smyrna. After several cholera epidemics over the years, the new plague microbe from the East—whose infectivity (what medical experts termed "virulence") had waxed and waned in time—had, alas, finally entered the Ottoman Empire too.

Bonkowski Pasha had taken six weeks to halt the outbreak of plague in Smyrna, the largest Ottoman port in the Levant. The local popula-tion had obeyed orders to stay indoors, respected sanitary cordons, and acquiesced to the various restrictions that had been introduced. They had also joined forces with the municipal authorities and the police to hunt down rats. Disinfection crews—composed mostly of firemen—had been deployed, the whole city soon reeking of the solution that issued from their spray pumps. The success of the Ottoman Quarantine Authority in Smyrna had been reported not just in the columns of local newspapers like the *Harmony* and the *Amalthea,* and in Istanbul dailies like the *Voice of Truth* and the *Endeavor,* but also in various French and British news-papers that had already been tracking this plague from the East from port to port; and so to the average European too, Bonkowski Pasha, born in Istanbul of Polish parentage, was an esteemed and well-known figure. The plague in Smyrna had been successfully curbed after just sev-enteen deaths; the port, the docks, the customhouses, the shops, and the markets had opened again, and in all the schools, classes had resumed once more.

The distinguished passengers of the *Aziziye* who watched through their cabin portholes and from the deck as the chemist pasha and his assistant boarded the ship were aware of this recent triumph in quarantine and public health policy. Five years ago, the former Royal Chemist had been conferred the honorific title of Pasha by Abdul Hamid himself. Today Stanislaw Bonkowski was wearing a raincoat whose color could not be discerned in the dark, and a jacket which accentuated his long neck and the light stoop of his shoulders, and he was carrying his ever-present gunpowder-gray briefcase that even his students from thirty years ago would have instantly recognized. His assistant, Doctor Ilias, was hauling the portable laboratory which enabled the chemist pasha to isolate cholera or plague bacteria and tell contaminated and potable water apart, which was also an excuse for him to taste and test every source of water in the Empire. Once on board, Bonkowski and his assistant immediately retired to their cabins without greeting any of the *Aziziye*'s curious passengers.

The two new passengers' silence and guardedness only heightened the Guidance Committee delegates' curiosity. What could be the purpose of all this secrecy? Why would the Sultan send the Ottoman Empire's two foremost plague and epidemic disease experts (the second being Prince Consort Doctor Nuri Effendi) to China on the same ship? When it became apparent that Bonkowski Pasha and his assistant were not bound for China at all, but were due to disembark on the island of Mingheria on the way to Alexandria, the committee delegates were able to turn their attention back to the task at hand. Ahead of them now were three weeks in which to debate how best to explain Islam to the Muslims of China.

Prince Consort Doctor Nuri—the other quarantine expert on the *Aziziye*—found out from his wife that Bonkowski Pasha had boarded the ship in Smyrna and was due to disembark on Mingheria. The newlyweds were pleased to discover they had both met the amiable chemist pasha before. The Doctor and Prince Consort had recently attended the International Sanitary Conference in Venice with the Royal Chemist, who was more than twenty years his senior. Bonkowski Pasha had also been his chemistry professor when young Nuri was still a student at the

Imperial School of Medicine, attending classes at the Demirkapı Garrison in Sirkeci. Like many of his fellow medical students, young Nuri had been captivated by the applied chemistry classes that Paris-trained Bonkowski Bey had taught in his laboratory, and by his lectures on organic and inorganic chemistry. The students had been enthralled by the professor's jokes, by his wide-ranging Renaissance man's curiosity, and by his easy command of the Turkish vernacular and of three other European languages which he spoke as fluently as his mother tongue. Stanislaw Bonkowski was the Istanbul-born son of one of the many Polish army officers who had gone into exile following defeat in their nation's war against Russia and ended up joining the Ottoman army.

The Doctor and Prince Consort's wife, Princess Pakize, gaily recounted her memories of Bonkowski from her childhood and youth. One summer eleven years ago, when her mother and the other women of the harem in the palace where she and her family were kept confined had been infected with a disease which had left them in the throes of a terrible fever, Sultan Abdul Hamid had declared that the outbreak must have been caused by a microbe and had sent his own Royal Chemist to the palace to collect samples. Another time, her uncle Abdul Hamid had sent Bonkowski Pasha to the Çırağan Palace to test the water Princess Pakize and her family drank every day. Abdul Hamid may have been holding his older brother the former sultan Murad V captive in the Çırağan Palace, watching his every move, but whenever anyone fell ill, he would always send his best doctors. As a child, the Princess had often seen the black-bearded Greek doctor Marko Pasha, who had been Royal Physician to her father's uncle the assassinated sultan Abdülaziz, in the palace and inside the rooms of the harem, as well as Abdul Hamid's own Royal Physician Mavroyeni Pasha.

"I saw Bonkowski Pasha again at the Yıldız Palace many years later," said the Princess. "He was inspecting the palace's water supplies and preparing a new report. But by then he could only smile at me and my sisters from a distance. It would not have been proper for him to play little jokes on us or tell us funny stories as he used to do when we were children."

The Doctor and Prince Consort's memories of the Sultan's Royal Chemist were more official in nature. The diligence and experience he had displayed at the Venice Conference where they had jointly represented the Ottoman Empire had earned him the Royal Chemist's respect. It might even have been Bonkowski Pasha himself, as the Doctor and Prince Consort excitedly told his wife, Princess Pakize, that first brought his abilities as quarantine doctor to Sultan Abdul Hamid's attention, for his path had crossed the chemist and pharmacist pasha's not just in medical school but also after he had graduated. Once, at the request of the Mayor of Beyoğlu, Eduard Blacque Bey, they had reviewed the sanitary conditions of Istanbul's roadside abattoirs together. On another occasion, he and a few other students and doctors had gone to Lake Terkos where Bonkowski was preparing a report on the lake's topographical and geological features and a microscopic analysis of its waters, and once again he had been impressed by Bonkowski's intelligence, dedication, and discipline. Filled with the excitement and warmth of these recollections, the newlyweds were eager now to meet the chemist and Chief Inspector of Public Health again.

CHAPTER 2

The Doctor and Prince Consort sent a cabin boy with a note for Bonkowski Pasha. Later the captain hosted them all for dinner in what was known as the guest hall. This dinner, where no alcohol was served, was also attended by Princess Pakize, who had hitherto stayed out of sight of the mullahs on the ship and taken all her meals in her cabin. We should note that in those days it was still very rare for a woman to sit at the same table as men, even if she happened to be a princess. But today we know everything about this historic dinner thanks to Princess Pakize, who later wrote her sister a letter in which she described all that she saw and heard that night from her seat at the end of the table.

Bonkowski Pasha had a pale face, a small nose, and large blue eyes that no one who met him ever forgot. When he saw the Doctor and Prince Consort, he immediately embraced his former student. He then turned to Princess Pakize with an elaborate bow, greeting her as he would a princess in some European palace, though he was careful not to touch her bare hand lest he should embarrass her.

The Royal Chemist, who nurtured a particular interest in the intricacies of European etiquette, was wearing the insignia of the Order of Saint Stanislas, Second Class, which he had received from the latest Russian czar, and his Ottoman-issue gold Imtiaz Medal, which he was also particularly fond of.

"Most esteemed professor," began the Doctor and Prince Consort, "allow me to express my deepest admiration for the prodigious triumph you have achieved in Smyrna."

Ever since the newspapers had begun to report that the epidemic in Smyrna was dying down, Bonkowski Pasha had perfected a modest smile with which he received these kinds of compliments. "I should congratulate you!" he responded now, peering into Doctor Nuri's eyes. Although he recognized that he was not being congratulated as a former student who had been working for years in the Quarantine Authority of the Hejaz (the Muslim holy land), but as someone who had married a princess, a member of the Ottoman dynasty, and a sultan's daughter, Doctor Nuri smiled anyway. Abdul Hamid had arranged for him to marry his niece because he was a brilliant and accomplished doctor; following this match, Doctor Nuri's brilliance and his accomplishments had largely been forgotten, and people were now far likelier to remember his status as husband to the Princess.

Nevertheless Prince Consort Doctor Nuri had quickly adjusted to this new state of affairs. He was so happy with his wife that he could not even feel resentful. Besides, he idolized his old professor Bonkowski Pasha, who was—to use two words that had recently entered the Turkish language from French and become extremely popular with the Ottoman intellectual elites—as "disciplined" and "methodical" as the Europeans. He decided to say something to flatter him:

"Your victory over the plague in Smyrna has shown the world the true might of the Ottoman Quarantine Authority!" he began. "You have delivered a fitting riposte to those who would call the Ottoman Empire a 'sick man.' We may have yet to eradicate cholera, but there has not been a serious outbreak of plague in Ottoman lands in eighty years. They used to say, 'The dividing line of civilization that sets Europe and the Ottomans two hundred years apart is not the Danube, but the plague!' But now, thanks to you, that line has disappeared, at least in the fields of medicine and quarantine studies."

"Alas, the plague has now been detected on the island of Mingheria," said Bonkowski Pasha. "And with exceptional virulence too."

"Really?"

"The plague has spread to Mingheria's Muslim neighborhoods, my dear Pasha. You have been absorbed by wedding preparations, of course, so it is only natural that you should not have been aware, and that you should marvel at the news, for they are keeping it secret. I regret that I was not able to attend your wedding celebrations; I was in Smyrna!"

"I have been following the effects of the epidemic in Hong Kong and Bombay, and reading the latest reports."

"The situation is much graver than what is being written," said

Bonkowski Pasha with an air of authority. "It is the same microbe, the same strain that has killed thousands in India and China, and it is the one we saw in Smyrna too."

"Yet the Indian populace is being decimated . . . while in Smyrna you beat the disease."

"The people of Smyrna and their newspapers were a great help in that!" said Bonkowski Pasha, then paused for a moment, as if to signal that he was about to say something important. "In Smyrna, the disease affected the Greek neighborhoods," he continued, "and the people of Smyrna are known for their culture and civility. On the island of Mingheria, the outbreak has mostly affected the Muslim areas, and already fifteen people have died! Our task there will be rather more onerous."

Doctor Nuri knew from experience that when it came to respecting quarantine measures, Muslims were harder to persuade than Christians, but he had also grown exasperated of hearing these truths exaggerated by Christian experts like Bonkowski Pasha. He decided not to argue. But the silence lengthened, so for the sake of breaking it, he turned to the Princess and the captain and said: "This is the eternal debate, of course!"

"You must be familiar with the story of what happened to poor Doctor Jean-Pierre!" said Bonkowski Pasha with the smiling mien of a jovial schoolteacher. "I have been told repeatedly by the palace and by Governor Sami Pasha that His Highness the Sultan regards claims of a plague outbreak in Mingheria as a political trap, and that I must therefore keep hidden from all the true purpose of my visit to the island. I have known the island's governor Sami Pasha for a very long time, of course, ever since his earlier postings to other provinces and districts!"

"Fifteen deaths are a significant number for a small island!" said Doctor Nuri.

"I have been forbidden to speak even with you on this subject, Your Excellency!" said Bonkowski Pasha, gesturing humorously toward the end of the table—as if to say "Beware the spy in our midst!"—at Princess Pakize. Then, as he used to do when the royal family's westernized princesses were still little girls whom he would meet at the theater in the Yıldız Palace, or observe from afar during the various ceremonies that marked Kaiser Wilhelm's visit, he addressed the Princess with the playful air of a friendly uncle.

"It is the first time in my life that I have seen the daughter of a sultan, a princess, being allowed to travel beyond Istanbul!" he said with a show of incredulity. "Such freedom bestowed upon its women must be a sign that the Ottoman Empire is Europeanizing!"

Those who shall read, once we have published them, Princess Pakize's letters from this time will see that she had intuited the "ironic," perhaps even derisory, tone in which these words had been uttered. Like her father Murad V, Princess Pakize was an intelligent and sensitive person. "In truth, Excellency, I would have rather gone to Venice than China," she told the Royal Chemist, and thus the conversation turned to the city of Venice, where the two men had attended international public health conferences. "Is it true what they say, sir—that in Venice one travels from one waterside mansion to the next by boat, just as we do along the Bosphorus, and that these boats can sail all the way into one's home?" asked Princess Pakize. From there the discussion moved to the speed and power and comfortable cabins of the *Aziziye*. Thirty years and two sultans ago, Sultan Abdülaziz (for whom the ship was named) had spent enormous sums on strengthening the Ottoman navy—unlike his nephew today—and having thus thrust the state into debt, he had then ordered the construction of this extravagant ship for his own use. The gilded, mahogany-paneled Sultan's Cabin—its walls covered in framed paintings and mirrors—was a replica of the Sultan's Cabin in the battle-ship *Mahmudiye*. Their Russian captain explained the ship's superior specifications: capable of carrying as many as one hundred and fifty pas-sengers, it could reach a maximum speed of up to fourteen miles per hour, but unfortunately the Sultan had not had the time in many years for even a Bosphorus cruise with his *Aziziye*. The truth was that Sultan Abdul Hamid feared an attempt on his life and thus took especial care to avoid ships and boats, but although everybody at the table knew this, they discreetly avoided the subject.

The captain mentioned that it would be only another six hours before they reached Mingheria, and Bonkowski Pasha asked the Doctor and Prince Consort whether he had ever been to the island before.

"I have not, for there have never been outbreaks of cholera or yellow fever or other infectious diseases there," Doctor Nuri replied.

"I have not been either, regrettably," said Bonkowski Pasha. "But I have researched it extensively. Pliny described in great detail in his *Naturalis historia* the island's utterly distinctive vegetation, its flora, its trees and flowers, and its steep volcanic peak, as well as the rocky coves that line its northern shore. Even its climate is unique. Many years ago I prepared a report for your esteemed uncle, His Highness the Sultan, on the prospects for rose cultivation there—in this place I have never before had a chance to visit!"

"What happened then, Your Excellency?" asked Princess Pakize.

Bonkowski Pasha gave a rueful, pensive smile. Princess Pakize silently concluded that even the Royal Chemist must at one point have suffered the consequences of the apprehensive sultan's fears and castigations, and proceeded to ask the question she and her husband had already so often discussed: Could it really be a coincidence that the Ottoman Empire's two most renowned quarantine specialists had happened to meet one night in the Sultan's private passenger ship as it sailed through the waters off Crete?

"I assure you that it is indeed a coincidence!" said Bonkowski Pasha. "Nobody, not even the Governor of Smyrna, Kâmil Pasha of Cyprus, knew that the nearest ship heading in the direction of the island would be the *Aziziye*. I would of course have liked to come with you to explain to the Muslims of China why it is essential that they should obey quarantine rules and other modern conditions and restrictions. To accept quarantine is to accept westernization, and the farther east one travels, the more tortuous the matter becomes. But our Princess must not lose heart. I promise you that there are canals in China too, just like in Venice, and indeed far-larger and longer ones, and graceful little boats that can sail all the way into people's homes and mansions, just as we see upon the Bosphorus."

The newlyweds' admiration for the chemist pasha only grew to hear that he was as knowledgeable about China as he was about Mingheria, despite having been to neither. But the dinner did not last for much longer, and at its conclusion, husband and wife returned to their cabin, which, with its French and Italian coffee tables, clocks, mirrors, and lamps, resembled a room in a royal palace.

"I fear that something has upset you," said Princess Pakize. "I can see it in your face."

Doctor Nuri had perceived a note of derision in the way Bonkowski Pasha had kept addressing him as "Pasha" that evening. As tradition dictated, Abdul Hamid had made him a pasha as soon as he had married the Princess, but Doctor Nuri had hitherto been able to avoid using the title. Hearing older, high-ranking, influential men—actual pashas, in other words—calling *him* "Pasha" flustered Doctor Nuri, who felt he did not really deserve the honorific. But they soon agreed that Bonkowski Pasha was not the kind of person who would make that sort of mean-spirited insinuation, and quickly forgot all about the matter.

Princess Pakize and Doctor Nuri had been married for thirty days now. For many years they had both dreamed of finding a suitable partner to marry, but had long given up hope that they would ever meet the right person. Only two months had elapsed between the day when Abdul Hamid, following a moment of sudden inspiration, had arranged for them to be introduced and the day of their wedding, and if they were quite so happy, the reason was evidently that they had both found so much more pleasure in lovemaking and sexuality than either of them had expected. Ever since they had set sail from Istanbul, they had spent most of their time in bed inside their cabin, and neither of them had ever thought there was anything unusual about this.

They woke up before dawn the next day when the sound of the ship, not unlike a wail, began to die down. Outside, it was still completely dark. In its approach to Arkaz, Mingheria's largest city and administrative capital, the *Aziziye* had followed the ridge of the tall, sharp Eldost Mountains that stretched from the north to the south of the island, and once the Arab Lighthouse's pale beam had become visible to the naked eye, the ship had veered west toward the port. There was a large moon in the sky and a silver shimmer over the water, so from their cabins the passengers could now see, like a phantom rising in the darkness behind Arkaz Castle, the shape of the White Mountain, considered to be the most mysterious among the various volcanic peaks that populated the Mediterranean Sea.

When Princess Pakize spotted the sharp spires of the majestic Arkaz Castle, they climbed on deck for a better view of the scene in the moonlight. The air was humid but mild. A pleasant scent of iodine, kelp, and almonds came from the sea. Like many small seaside towns across the Ottoman Empire, Arkaz did not have a large jetty and dock, so the captain put the engines in reverse in the waters off the Castle and began to wait.

There followed a strange and heavy silence. Husband and wife shiv-

ered in the thrall of the resplendent realm before them. The inscruta-
ble landscape, the mountains, the silence beneath the moonlight, were
imbued with a wondrous intensity. It felt as if beyond the silver glow of
the moon there were another source of light that had bewitched them
and that they must search for. For a time the newlyweds observed the
glorious, shimmering view as if it were the true source of their wedded
bliss. In the darkness ahead they saw the lantern of an approaching rowing boat, and the slow, deliberate motions of its boatmen. Bonkowski
Pasha and his assistant materialized at the top of the stairway on the
lower deck. They seemed to be standing very far away, as in a dream.
The large black rowboat the Governor had sent pulled up to the *Aziziye*.
They heard footsteps and the sound of people speaking in Greek and
Mingherian. The rowing boat took Bonkowski Pasha and his assistant
on board and vanished back into the darkness.

The newlyweds and a few other passengers in the captain's quarters
and on the deck stood for a long time looking out at the view of Arkaz
Castle and of Mingheria's spectacular mountains, which had inspired so
many Romantic travel writers and seemed to belong in the pages of a
fairy tale. Had the passengers of the *Aziziye* looked more closely at the
southwestern bastions of the Castle, they would have seen the light of a
torch burning inside a window. Parts of the stone-built Castle complex
dated from the era of the Crusades, others from periods of Venetian,
Byzantine, Arab, and Ottoman rule, and for centuries, one section had
been employed as a prison. Now, in an empty cell two floors beneath
the room where that torch was burning, a guard—or, in the modern
parlance, a "warden"—named Bayram Effendi, a prominent figure in
those parts of the great Castle, was fighting for his life.

CHAPTER 3

W hen Bayram Effendi had felt the first symptoms of illness
five days ago, he had not taken them seriously. He had
developed a fever, his heart rate had sped up, and he'd felt
shivery. But it was probably just a cold he'd caught that morning from
spending too much time walking around the Castle's windy bastions
and courtyards! In the afternoon the next day his fever returned, but this
time it was accompanied by fatigue. He had no desire to eat anything,
and at one point he lay down in the stone courtyard, looked up at the
sky, and felt that he might die. It was as if someone were hammering a
nail into his skull.

For twenty-five years Bayram Effendi had been a guard in the prisons of Mingheria's famous Arkaz Castle. He had seen long-serving convicts chained up and forgotten about in their cells, watched handcuffed
inmates walk in a line in the yard for their daily exercise, and witnessed the
arrival of a group of political prisoners Sultan Abdul Hamid had locked
up fifteen years ago. He remembered how primitive the prison used to
be in those days (though in truth it still was), and wholeheartedly trusted
and supported the attempts that had recently been made to modernize
it, to turn it into an ordinary prison or perhaps even a reformatory. Even
when the flow of money from Istanbul was interrupted and he had to
go for months without pay, he wouldn't rest unless he had personally
attended the prisoner count every evening.

When he was struck again the next day, as he walked through one
of the prison's narrow passageways, by the same shattering exhaustion,
he decided not to go home that night. His heart was beating alarmingly
fast now. He found an empty cell, where he lay writhing in pain on a

bed of straw in the corner. He was shivering, too, and had developed an unbearable headache. The pain was located near the front of his head, in his forehead. He wanted to scream, but he was convinced that if he kept quiet, this strange agony would somehow disappear, so instead he gritted his teeth. There was a press, a roller, upon his head, squeezing it flat.

So the guard spent the night in the Castle. He would do this sometimes—when he had a night shift, say, or if he'd had to deal with a minor riot or a scuffle—instead of going back to his house a ten-minute ride away on a horse-drawn gig, so his wife and his daughter, Zeynep, were not concerned by his absence. The family was in the midst of various preparations and negotiations for Zeynep's imminent wedding, which meant there were quarrels and long faces at home every night, with either the guard's wife or his daughter ending up in tears.

When Bayram Effendi woke up in the cell the next morning and inspected his body, he found near his groin, just above and to the left of his perineum, a white boil the size of his little finger. It looked like a bubo. It hurt when he pressed on it with his thick index finger, as if it were filled with pus, but reverted to its original shape as soon as he took his finger away. The bubo didn't hurt unless he touched it. Bayram Effendi felt oddly guilty. He was lucid enough to know that this boil was connected to the fatigue, the tremors, and the deliriousness he had been experiencing.

What should he do? A Christian or a government clerk or a soldier or a pasha in his position would go to a doctor or to a hospital if there was one. When there was an outbreak of diarrhea or contagious fever in a prison dormitory, that dormitory was quarantined. But sometimes, a defiant dormitory chief would put up a fight against quarantine measures, and his fellow prisoners would suffer the consequences. In the quarter century he'd spent in the Castle, Bayram Effendi had seen some of the old Venetian-era buildings and courtyards on the seafront used not just as dungeons and jailhouses but as customhouses and quarantine facilities (known in the olden days as lazarettos) too, so he was not unfamiliar with these matters. But he was also aware that no quarantine measure could protect him now. He could feel that he had fallen into the grip of some uncanny force, and he slept and slept, moaning and raving in his terrified, unconscious state. But the pain kept returning in waves, until he realized despairingly that the force he was grappling with was far greater than he was.

The next day he managed to briefly gather some strength. He joined the crowds at the Blind Mehmet Pasha Mosque for midday prayers. He saw two clerks he knew and embraced them in greeting. He tried with much effort to follow the sermon but struggled to understand it. He felt dizzy and nauseated, and he could barely sit upright. The preacher didn't mention the disease at all and kept repeating that everything that happened was the will of God. As the crowds dispersed, Bayram Effendi thought he might lie down on the mosque's carpets and kilims to rest for a while and suddenly realized he was drifting out of consciousness, about to faint. When they came to wake him up, he summoned whatever energy he had left to hide the fact that he was unwell (though perhaps they already knew).

By now he could sense his own imminent death, and he wept, feeling that this was an injustice and demanding to know why he had been singled out in this way. He left the mosque and went to see the holy man in the neighborhood of Germe who handed out prayer sheets and amulets and was said to talk openly about the plague and the mystery of death. But the fat sheikh whose name Bayram Effendi couldn't remember didn't seem to be there. Instead, a smiling young man in a lopsided fez issued Bayram Effendi and two others, who, like him, had come from the midday payers, a consecrated amulet and a prayer sheet each. Bayram Effendi tried to read the writing on the prayer sheet, but he couldn't see properly. He felt guilty about this and became agitated, knowing that his death was going to be his own fault.

When the sheikh eventually arrived, Bayram Effendi remembered that he had just seen him at the midday prayers. The holy man was indeed very fat and had a beard as long and white as his hair. He smiled kindly at Bayram Effendi and began to explain how the prayer sheets were to be used; at night, when the plague demon manifested itself in the darkness, one must recite thirty-three times each the following three names of Allah: Ar-Raqib, Al-Muqtadir, and Al-Baaqi. If the prayer sheet and the amulet were pointed in the direction of the demon, even nineteen repetitions could be sufficient to repel the scourge. When he realized how gravely ill Bayram Effendi was, the sheikh drew back from him a little. This did not escape the prison guard's notice. The sheikh explained that even if there was no time to recite the names of God, he could still achieve a good result by wearing the amulet around his neck and placing his right index finger over it just so. More precisely, he should use his right index finger if the plague boil was on the left-hand side of his body, and his left index finger if the boil was on the right-hand side. The sheikh also told him that if he began to stutter, he should hold the amulet in both hands, but by that point Bayram Effendi was finding it difficult to keep track of all of these rules and decided to return to his home nearby. His beautiful daughter Zeynep wasn't there. His wife started crying when she saw how sick he was. She made his bed with sheets fresh from the linen cupboard, and Bayram Effendi lay down; he was shaking uncontrollably, and when he tried to speak, his mouth was so dry that the words would not come out.

There seemed to be a storm breaking inside his head. He kept twitching and jerking where he lay, as if someone were chasing him, as if something had startled or angered him. His wife Emine wept even harder at the sight of these strange spasms, and when he saw her tears, Bayram Effendi understood that he was going to die soon.

When Zeynep came home in the early evening, Bayram Effendi rallied for a time. He told them that the amulet around his neck would protect him, then fell back into a delirious sleep. He had a series of strange dreams and nightmares; now he was rising and falling with the waves of a roaring sea! Now there were winged lions, talking fish, and armies of dogs running through fire! Then the flames spread to the rats, fiery demons who tore rosebushes apart with their teeth. The pulley of a water well, a windmill, an open door kept turning and turning, and the universe contracted. Drops of sweat seemed to be falling from the sun onto his face. He felt restless; he felt like running away; his mind alternately raced and froze. Worst of all, the hordes of rats that just two weeks ago had shrieked and wailed their way through the dungeons, the Castle, and all of Mingheria, invading kitchens and devouring all the straw and cloth and wood in their path, now seemed to be chasing him through the prison corridors. Worried that he might recite the wrong prayer, Bayram Effendi tried to outrun them instead. He spent the final hours of his life shouting with all the strength he had to make himself heard to the creatures he saw in his sleep, yet he struggled to make a sound. Zeynep was kneeling beside him now, trying to contain her sobs as she watched over him.

Then, like many who fell ill with the plague, he seemed to make a sudden recovery. His wife served him a bowl of hot, fragrant wheat soup with red chili, a recipe that was popular across the villages of Mingheria. (Bayram Effendi had only ever left the island once in his entire life.) After he'd had his soup, sipping at it slowly as if it were some kind of elixir, and recited some of the prayers the fat holy man had suggested, he felt better.

He must go and make sure they didn't make any mistakes with the prisoner count tonight. He would not be gone for long. So he'd said, as if he were talking to himself, when he had left his house for the last time without even a farewell to his family—as if he were merely heading for the privy in the garden. His wife and daughter did not believe that he had recovered and wept as they watched him go.

Around the time for evening prayers, Bayram Effendi first made his way toward the shore. He saw horse-drawn carriages, doormen, and gentlemen in hats waiting outside the Hotel Splendid and the Hotel Majestic. He walked past the offices of the ferry companies that operated routes to Smyrna, Chania, and Istanbul and around the back of the customs building. When he reached the Hamidiye Bridge, his strength ran out. He thought he might fall over and die. It was the time of day when the city was at its liveliest and most colorful, and under the palm trees and the plane trees, on the sunny streets, and among all those people with their warm and friendly faces, it seemed that life was, perhaps, quite good after all. Under the bridge flowed the Arkaz Creek, its waters a celestial shade of green; behind him was the historic covered market and the old bridge; in front of him was the Castle whose prisons he'd guarded all his life. He stood there for a time, quietly weeping until he was too exhausted to do even that. The orange light from the sun made the Castle look even pinker than it was.

With one last effort he walked in the shade of palm and plane trees down the dusty street with the Telegraph Office, and all the way back to the shore. He crossed the old city's meandering alleys, near the buildings dating from the Venetian era, and entered the Castle. Witnesses would later say they saw the guard attending the prisoner count outside the door to dormitory number two, and drinking a glass of linden tea in the guards' recreation room.

But no one saw him again after nightfall. A young guard had heard someone crying and screaming in a cell on the floor below around the same time the *Aziziye* was approaching the port, but had forgotten about it in the ensuing silence.

CHAPTER 4

Once it had dropped off Abdul Hamid's Royal Chemist Bonkowski Pasha and his assistant on the island of Mingheria, the royal vessel *Aziziye* continued at full speed toward Alexandria. The task of the Ottoman delegation aboard the ship was to counsel China's angry Muslim community against joining the surge of popular anti-Western uprisings in the area.

In 1894, Japan had attacked China, and the Chinese army, still wedded to traditional methods, had suffered a rapid and comprehensive defeat at the hands of the more westernized Japanese forces. Desperate in the face of Japan's triumphant demands, the empress dowager of China had called on Western powers for help, just as the Ottoman emperor Abdul Hamid II had done twenty years before in the aftermath of a heavy defeat at the hands of the more modern Russian army. The British, the French, and the Germans had come to China's aid. But in the process, they also acquired a series of mercantile and legal privileges (the British in Hong Kong and Tibet, the French in southern China, and the Germans in the north), dividing the country into colonial territories and deploying missionaries to enhance their political and spiritual influence.

These various developments had inflamed the impoverished Chinese populace, particularly the more conservative and religious among them, and ignited a series of uprisings against the Manchu government and against "foreigners," especially Christians and Europeans. Western workplaces, banks, post offices, clubs, restaurants, and churches were set on fire. Missionaries and Chinese people who had converted to Christianity were picked off one by one and murdered on the streets. Behind this rapidly spreading popular protest movement was a sect Westerners referred to as the Boxers, who drew their strength from the mystical allure of the traditional sorcery and sword rituals they practiced. Caught between conservatives and more tolerant liberal elements, the Chinese government was unable to defeat the rebels, and to make matters worse, the army gradually began to side with the insurgents. Finally the empress dowager herself joined the anti-foreign uprising. By the year 1900, Chinese soldiers were blockading foreign embassies in Peking while angry mobs wandered the streets attacking Christians and killing foreigners. Before the Western powers managed to assemble an allied army to send to the rescue, the German ambassador von Ketteler, who had taken a particularly aggressive stance, was killed in the fighting on the streets.

The German emperor Kaiser Wilhelm II retaliated in exemplary fashion, sending newly formed German army battalions to suppress the revolt in Peking. As he saw his soldiers off at Bremerhaven, whence they would make their way to China, he instructed them to be "as ruthless as Attila the Hun" and to take no prisoners. Western newspapers had long been filled with reports of the savagery, the primitiveness, and the murderous rampages of the Boxer rebels and the Muslims who had joined them.

Kaiser Wilhelm II also sent telegrams to Istanbul requesting Abdul Hamid's support. The soldiers from the Kansu region who had killed the German ambassador in Peking were Muslims. In Kaiser Wilhelm's view, the Ottoman emperor Abdul Hamid, caliph of all Muslims the world over, should do something to help subdue these deranged Muslim soldiers who were blindly attacking Christians. Perhaps he could add some of his own soldiers to the armies of the West that were being deployed to quash the uprisings.

It was not exactly easy for Abdul Hamid to say no to the British, who had protected him against the Russian armies; the French, who were Britain's allies in China; and the Germans and their Kaiser Wilhelm, who had visited the Sultan in Istanbul and had always treated him with warmth. The Sultan was also aware that if these great powers were to find common ground, they could easily gobble up the Ottoman Empire—what the Russian czar Nicholas I had called "the sick man of Europe"—carving out its territories among themselves and facilitating the formation of countless separate states upon its lands, each speaking its own language.

Abdul Hamid had been watching the progress of these Muslim uprisings against Western superpowers—the so-called Great Powers—with mixed feelings. From what he had been able to glean through the reports he received, he was particularly intrigued by the many Muslim uprisings that were taking place in China and by the actions of Mirza Ghulam Ahmad in India, who was leading the Muslims there in a revolt against the British. He was also sympathetic to the Mad Mullah's rebellion in Somalia and the various anti-Western Muslim-led rebellions taking place throughout Africa and Asia. The Sultan had deployed special military attachés to track these anti-Western and anti-Christian movements, and in some cases he would also surreptitiously provide them with material support, unbeknownst even to his own government and bureaucratic cadres (for there were spies everywhere). As the Ottoman Empire unraveled, losing its Orthodox Christian populations across the Balkan states and on its islands in the Mediterranean, Sultan Abdul Hamid began to warm to the notion that if he was seen to openly favor Islam (as the new demography of the Empire was already suggesting), he might be able to rally the world's many Muslim communities and nations to stand with the Ottomans against the West, and at least give the Great Powers something to fear. In other words the Sultan was beginning to discover all by himself that force which we now call "political Islam."

But the opera-loving, crime novel–reading sultan Abdul Hamid was not exactly a sincere and steadfast Islamist jihadist either. When Egypt's Ourabi Pasha had staged his rebellion against the West, the Sultan had understood straightaway that it was a nationalist uprising aimed not just against the British but against all foreigners—including the Ottomans—and he had loathed the Islamist pasha for it, secretly hoping the British would obliterate him. As for the Mahdist movement in Sudan, which had fought the British doggedly and culminated in the death of their beloved Major General Charles Gordon—a popular figure among Muslims too, who had affectionately called him Gordon Pasha—the Sultan had deemed it "a revolt of the hoi polloi" and, partly under pressure from the British ambassador in Istanbul, had sided with the British against it.

In the end Abdul Hamid managed to find a painless compromise between the conflicting urgencies of making sure he did not provoke the Western superpowers and of showing the world that he was the caliph and leader of all Muslims everywhere: he would not send any Ottoman soldiers to fight and kill Muslim insurgents, but as their caliph, he *would* send a delegation to China to tell the Muslims there: Don't wage war on the westerners!

The head of this delegation, who was currently in his cabin and struggling to fall asleep, had been personally selected by Abdul Hamid, and alongside this experienced army general, the Sultan had appointed two clerics he also knew and held in great esteem, one of whom—black bearded—was a teacher of Islamic history and the other, white bearded, a renowned and gifted scholar of Islamic law. These two clerics would sit in the *Aziziye*'s spacious central cabin, across from an enormous map of the Ottoman Empire hanging on its wall, and spend the whole day debating how best to reason with China's Muslims. One of the clerics, the historian, argued that the delegation's real mission was not to pacify the Chinese Muslims but to teach them about the true might of Islam and of its caliph Abdul Hamid. The other cleric, the white-bearded jurist, was more prudent, arguing that a jihad was only a "proper jihad" if it could count on the support of that country's king or sultan, and pointing out that by then the empress dowager of China had already changed her mind about supporting the rebels. The committee's other delegates, translators and army men, would sometimes join the debate too.

At midnight, as the *Aziziye* sailed toward Alexandria under the moonlight, Doctor Nuri noticed that the torches in the central cabin were still alight and took his wife to look at the map hanging on its wall. It was an updated map of the Ottoman Empire, first established by Princess Pakize's great-great-grandfathers six hundred years ago. Abdul Hamid had commissioned the map in the autumn of 1880—four years after he'd taken the throne aged thirty-four—in the aftermath of the Congress of Berlin, when the Ottomans, with the help of the British, had taken back some of the lands they had lost to the Russians. The Ottoman Empire had lost control of many of its territories (Serbia, Thessaly, Montenegro, Romania, Bulgaria, Kars, Ardahan) in the war that had broken out as soon as Abdul Hamid first took power. Following this debacle, the Sultan had convinced himself that it was the last time anything like this would ever happen and that the Empire would not lose any more of its possessions, and thus proceeded to dispatch trains, carriages, camels, and ships to carry the new map he had optimistically commissioned to the farthest reaches of the Empire, its military garrisons, its governors' offices and foreign embassies. The delegates of the Guidance Committee had seen this map many times before all over the Empire—whose lands stretched from Damascus to Ioannina, from Mosul to Thessaloniki, from Istanbul to the Hejaz—and each time they had looked in wonder and veneration upon the enormity of the area covered by Ottoman rule, only to remind themselves that, unfortunately, the true map continued to shrink at an ever-increasing rate.

I shall take this opportunity to note here a rumor about this map that Princess Pakize had first heard in the Yıldız Palace, and which she now relayed to her husband and later recalled again in a letter to her sister. According to this story, Abdul Hamid had entered his beloved eldest son Prince Selim's quarters unannounced one night and was delighted to find the boy—who was around ten or eleven at the time—studying a smaller-scale version of the very map the Sultan had commissioned. The Sultan noticed that some territories on the map had been colored black, the way children do in their coloring books. Upon further inspection, it became clear that the lands his son had crossed out were those that Abdul Hamid had lost during his reign, or that—though they might still fly the Ottoman flag and appear on the map as Ottoman possessions—he had handed over to the enemy without a fight, and the moment he realized this, Abdul Hamid instantly began to hate this treacherous child who apparently held his own father responsible for the Ottoman Empire withering into nonexistence. Princess Pakize, who loathed her uncle just as much, added that Abdul Hamid's hatred for her cousin—his son—intensified ten years later when a concubine that the Sultan had his eye on was found to have fallen in love with Selim Effendi.

As a child, the Princess had overheard many conversations about the various catastrophes and territorial losses that had begun in the years immediately following the deposition of her father Murad V. As blue and green uniformed Russian troops had approached San Stefano, just four hours from Abdul Hamid's palace, squares and parks and empty, burned-down plots of land in Istanbul had filled with tents the army had provided for the fair-skinned, green-eyed Balkan Muslims who'd been dispossessed overnight as they fled the Russian army, and in the space of fourteen months, the Ottoman Empire had lost most of the territories it had held in the Balkans for the past four hundred years.

The newlyweds spoke dispassionately of the other disasters they had heard discussed during their childhoods: to the east of the very island of Mingheria they had just left in their wake was the island of Cyprus, which, with its fragrant orange orchards, its groves of fruitful olive trees, and its copper mines, had been taken over as a British protectorate before the Congress of Berlin in 1878 was even over. Contrary to what Abdul Hamid's map implied, Egypt too had long ceased to be an Ottoman possession. Although it still appeared as an Ottoman territory on the map, the British had in fact invaded it in 1882, after their warships had bombarded Alexandria with the excuse that Ourabi Pasha's anti-Western uprising there was a threat to the local Christian population. (On days when Abdul Hamid's suspiciousness verged on paranoia, the clever sultan would wonder if the British had perhaps instigated this particular Islamist uprising to *create* the excuse for an invasion.) Meanwhile, in 1881, the French had taken control of Tunisia. Just as Czar Nicholas of Russia had predicted forty-seven years before, all that the Great Powers had to do to share the inheritance that had fallen from the grasp of "the sick man" and into their laps was simply to work with one another.

But as they sat beneath Abdul Hamid's old map all day, what most upset the delegates of the Guidance Committee was something the map didn't even show: those Western nations who often supported the nationalist-separatist uprisings that were initiated by the Empire's Christian subjects and constantly challenged the state's authority were far more powerful than the Ottomans—not only in terms of military capability, but from an economic, administrative, and demographic perspective too. In 1901, the total population of the Ottoman Empire across its vast geographical span was nineteen million. Five million of these people were non-Muslims, and even though they paid more taxes, they were still treated as second-class citizens, leading them to make demands for "justice," "equality," and "reform" and to turn to the nations of the West for support and protection. To the north, the population of Russia, with whom the Ottomans were constantly at war, was seventy million, while the population of Germany, with whom the Ottomans had friendly relations, was close to fifty-five million. The economic output of these European countries, and particularly of the British Empire, outstripped the Ottoman Empire's feeble efforts twenty-five to one. Moreover, the Ottoman Empire's Muslim population, who shouldered most of the state's administrative and military burdens, was becoming increasingly overshadowed by the Greek Orthodox and Armenian merchant classes whose influence was rising even in the outer provinces of the Empire. The rulers of these more remote provinces were unable to meet the demands for greater freedom made by this new and rising non-Muslim bourgeoisie of Greek and Armenian tradesmen; the only reaction local Ottoman governors were able to muster against the uprisings of their Christian populations, who demanded the right to govern themselves and only pay as much tax as the Muslim population did, was to try and wipe the rebels out, and to kill, torture, and banish them into submission.

"That evil djinn has possessed you again!" said Princess Pakize to her husband once they had returned to their cabin. "What were you thinking about?"

"That it is wonderful to be going to China and leaving everything else behind for a while!" said the Prince Consort Nuri.

But his wife could tell from the expression on his face that he was thinking of the outbreak in Mingheria and of Bonkowski Pasha.

CHAPTER 5

A s it neared the shore, the traditional sharp-nosed Mingherian pinewood boat that had picked up Bonkowski Pasha and his assistant Doctor Ilias sailed along the tall Castle walls and the island's rocky cliffs. There was no sound other than the creaking of oars and the gentle sloshing of waves against the towering cliffs that had held the Castle aloft for nearly seven hundred years. There was no light other than that of a few torches burning behind people's windows, but in the otherworldly moonlight, Arkaz—the largest city and center of the province of Mingheria—looked like a white-and-pink mirage. As a positivist, Bonkowski Pasha was not a superstitious man, but nevertheless he felt there was something inauspicious in this sight. Though Sultan Abdul Hamid had granted him a royal concession to undertake rose cultivation on the island many years ago, this was Bonkowski Pasha's first visit to the island. He had always imagined that his first trip there would be a joyous, cheerful, ceremonial occasion. It had never crossed his mind that he would have to creep up to the port in the dark of night like some kind of thief.

When the boat entered the smaller bay, the oarsman slowed down. A wet breeze was blowing from the shore, carrying the scent of linden trees and dry seaweed. The boat avoided the dock with the Customhouse, where passenger ships usually alighted, but turned instead toward the Arab Lighthouse, a relic of the time when the island was under Arab occupation, and stopped at the old fishermen's wharf. It was darker here, and secluded. Governor Sami Pasha, who had organized the Royal Chemist and his assistant's secret visit to the island under orders from the Sultan, had chosen this dock not just because it was quieter, but also because it was located farther away from the State Hall.

Bonkowski Pasha and his assistant, Ilias, passed their bags and other possessions to two municipal clerks in black coats who had come to meet them at the dock, and grabbed hold of the hands reaching down to help them off the boat. No one saw them getting into the carriage the Governor had sent to pick them up. Governor Sami Pasha had sent his secret guests the special armored landau he used on official occasions, and when he did not want to be seen by the people. Sami Pasha's fat and somewhat-anxious predecessor had taken rather seriously the threats he'd received from the romantic Greek anarchists who wanted the island to break away from Ottoman rule, and believing them capable of throwing the bombs they seemed so fond of, he had commissioned Bald Kudret, Arkaz's most famous blacksmith, to make the required sheets of armor, paying for them with money taken from the municipality's eternally underfunded coffers.

The armored landau, driven by Coachman Zekeriya, passed the hotels and customs offices that lined the harbor, their lamps all unlit, and turned left into a series of alleyways to avoid entering Istanbul Street, the city's most famous slope. Through the windows of the landau, the Royal Chemist and his assistant smelled the scent of honeysuckle and pine trees and saw in the moonlight the city's ancient, mossy stone walls, its wooden doorways, and the fronts of its pink brick homes, their windows all pulled shut. As the carriage wound its way uphill and into Hamidiye Square, they noticed the half-built but unfinished clock tower that had sadly not been completed in time for the celebrations that had begun last August for the twenty-fifth anniversary of His Excellency the Sultan's ascension to the throne (his coronation). They saw the torches burning in front of the Greek Middle School and the Post Office (formerly the Telegraph Office), and the sentries that Governor Sami Pasha had planted at every intersection since the rumors about the plague had first begun to spread.

"His Excellency the Governor is a peculiar character," Bonkowski Pasha told his assistant when they were alone in their guest quarters. "But I must say I had not expected to find the city so immaculate, so calm and serene. We must recognize this as his personal achievement, unless there is something that escaped our notice in the dark."

Doctor Ilias, a Greek from Istanbul, had been "assisting" the Sultan's Royal Chemist for the past nine years. Together they had fought outbreaks of disease in every corner of the Empire, spending nights in hotel rooms, municipal and hospital guesthouses, and military garrisons. Five years ago they had saved Trebizond from cholera by arranging for the whole city to be disinfected with the sprayable solution they had brought with them on the ship they'd arrived on. On another occasion, in 1894, they had combed the environs of Izmit and Bursa village by village to halt the spread of cholera there, sleeping in army tents at night. Bonkowski Pasha had come to trust this assistant who had just happened to have been assigned to him from Istanbul one day, and had also grown accustomed to sharing his private thoughts with him. As they hastened from city to city and port to port battling outbreaks, the Royal Chemist and his assistant, already widely known for their erudition, had come to be seen among the Empire's bureaucrats and public health officials as a pair of "scientist-saviors."

"Twenty years ago, the Sultan entrusted me with the task of fighting an outbreak of cholera in Dedeağaç Province, whose Governor at the time was Sami Pasha. His obstructive disdain for me and the young quarantine doctors I had brought along from Istanbul led to more lives being lost, and he must have realized that I would mention this in my report to the Sultan. It is therefore possible that he might be hostile toward us now."

Bonkowski Pasha had spoken in the Turkish he preferred to use when discussing matters of state, similar to the language we are writing in now. But both the Greek doctor Ilias, who had studied medicine in Paris, and Bonkowski Pasha, who had studied chemistry also in Paris, sometimes spoke to each other in French. So it was that as he felt around in the darkness of their guesthouse rooms trying to work out what was inside, what was shadow and what might be furniture, and where the windows were, the Royal Chemist said in French and as if here speaking in a dream: "I can smell the scent of misfortune!"

Later that night, they were woken up by noises that sounded like the scrabbling of rats. In Smyrna, the war on the plague had become a sort of war on rats. Now that they had arrived in Mingheria, they were surprised that no traps had been set in the guesthouse they had been brought to under the Governor's supervision. The fact that the plague was spread by rats when the fleas that lived on them bit humans had been communicated in countless telegrams from the capital to provincial governors and local quarantine offices.

In the morning they came to the conclusion that the scrabbling they had heard in the middle of the night must have been produced by seagulls landing on and taking off from the roof of the derelict wooden mansion they were being housed in. To keep them hidden from Arkaz's meddlesome journalists, gossip-spreading tradesmen, and malicious foreign consuls, Governor Sami Pasha had put up the illustrious Royal Chemist and his assistant not in the spacious guesthouse annexed to the new State Hall but in an unused wooden building that had been readied in a day by the local Director for Charitable Trusts, and to which the Governor had dispatched the requisite guardsmen and servants.

The Governor turned up unannounced at the residence that morning to apologize to his secret guests for its state. Seeing Sami Pasha again for the first time after so many years, Bonkowski Pasha suddenly felt he could trust him. In the Governor's imposing, almost stocky figure, in his not-yet-graying beard, and in the thickness of his eyebrows and nose, the Royal Chemist saw strength, and a kind of toughness.

But then, to the Royal Chemist and his assistant's dismay, the Governor said what every mayor and provincial governor the world over always said when faced with an outbreak of contagious disease.

"There is absolutely no epidemic in our city," Governor Sami Pasha began, "let alone the plague, God forbid, but we have nevertheless had this breakfast sent for you from the army garrison. They will not even eat bread fresh from the oven there without having had it disinfected first."

Bonkowski Pasha spotted a tray of olives, pomegranates, walnuts, goat cheese, and military-issue bread in the adjoining room and smiled at the Governor. "The people here, Muslims and Greeks, are all rather fond of gossip," said Governor Sami Pasha as a fez-clad servant poured coffee from the stove into the cups on their table. "They will spread all kinds of misinformation, they will claim an 'outbreak' when there isn't one, and 'no outbreak' when there is, they'll tell the papers 'Bonkowski Pasha said so' just to put you in a difficult position, as they did in Smyrna. Of course their aim is to pit Muslims against Christians, sow discord on this peaceful island, and tear it away from the Ottoman Empire, as they did with Crete."

At this point we will remind our readers that "foreign powers" had recently wrested the neighboring island of Crete from Ottoman control with the excuse of needing to quell a series of clashes that had erupted between the island's Muslim and Christian populations four years ago.

"Of course the people of Mingheria are more even tempered, so here they have had to make up this story about an epidemic!" explained the Governor Pasha.

"But, Pasha," said the Royal Chemist to the Governor who was six years his junior, "during the outbreak in Smyrna nobody cared whether you were Greek or Orthodox or Muslim or Christian! Both the Greek newspaper *Amalthea* and the Ottoman paper *Harmony* and even the merchants that make a living trading with Greece took the sanitary measures seriously and obeyed quarantine orders. It was thanks to this goodwill that we succeeded."

"Well, we do have the news and papers from Smyrna delivered here—if a little late—on the Messageries ferry. Perhaps it is not my place to say, but things did not happen quite as you have described, my dear Chief Inspector Pasha," said the Governor. "All the foreign consuls in Smyrna, foremost the Greek and French, complained every day about your quarantine measures and sowed discord by having their newspapers publish their objections. I do not allow for that kind of subversive, disruptive journalism to be practiced here in Mingheria."

"On the contrary, as soon as the people of Smyrna realized that quarantine was inevitable and beneficial, their collaboration with the Governor's Office and with the Quarantine Authority was impeccable. By the way, the Governor of Smyrna, Kâmil Pasha of Cyprus, sends Your Excellency his warmest regards. He is of course aware that I am here."

"I served as Minister for Charitable Trusts under Kâmil Pasha when he was Chief Minister fifteen years ago," said Governor Sami Pasha, fondly recalling his remarkable youthful achievements. "His Excellency Kâmil Pasha is a man of superior intelligence."

"You will recall that in Smyrna His Excellency Kâmil Pasha allowed the news of the outbreak to be made public, and he was right to do so," said Bonkowski Pasha. "Would it not perhaps be better if Mingherian newspapers published news of the outbreak here too? The populace must be allowed to worry, shopkeepers must face the fear of death, if they are to follow quarantine measures willingly once these are introduced."

"I have been governor here for five years, and I can assure you there is no cause for concern. The people of Mingheria, the Orthodox and the Catholics and even the Muslims, are at least as civilized as the people of Smyrna. Whatever the state demands, they shall heed and uphold. But to announce plagues and epidemics where there officially aren't any would create needless panic."

"But if you encourage the newspapers to publish information about the plague and its spread, about quarantine measures and the number of victims, the people of the island shall be even likelier to obey the state's instructions," Bonkowski Pasha patiently replied. "You know as well as I do, Governor Pasha, that it is a difficult proposition indeed to govern the Ottoman Empire without help from its newspapers."

"Mingheria is not Smyrna!" said the Governor. "There is no disease here. That is why the Sultan has kept your visit a secret. Of course it is also his will that if the disease *is* here, then you should introduce quarantine measures to stop the outbreak as you did in Smyrna. But the nefarious machinations of the island's foreign consuls, and the fact that it was our Quarantine Committee's Greek doctors (all colluding with Greece, no doubt) who first reported an outbreak on this island, have made His Highness the Sultan suspicious, and he has forbidden you from meeting with Mingheria's Quarantine Committee."

"That had indeed come to our attention, Governor Pasha."

"It is these old Greek quarantine doctors who have been spreading all these rumors. They will waste no time in alerting their friends in the Istanbul press. There are many men here who, urged on by the foreign consuls, would like to see this island end up like Crete: seized from us overnight. It is perhaps not my place to say, but the eyes of the world are upon us, my dear Pasha, so beware!"

Was there a threat in these words? For a moment, the three servants of the Ottoman Empire—one Muslim, one Catholic, and the other Orthodox Christian—eyed one another in silence.

"In any event, it is perhaps more appropriate for the decision on who should be writing what in Mingheria's newspapers to be made not by you, Chief Inspector, but by me, as I am, after all, the Governor of this island," said Sami Pasha, feeling emboldened. "Nevertheless, please do not let my words prevent you from including in your report your true medical and chemical findings. We have arranged for you to visit three patients today—two Muslims and the third an Orthodox Christian—so that you may collect microbial samples in time for the departure of the Maritimes Company's ferry *Baghdad* to Smyrna this evening. Also, one of our veteran prison guards passed away last night, though we had not even realized that he was ill. If you please, I shall provide you both with guards to accompany you on your visits today."

"To what do we owe the need for such provisions?"

"This is a small island; however you may seek to hide it, you shall be visiting patients in a medical capacity, and there will be gossip about your arrival," said the Governor. "Spirits will be broken, morale will suffer. Nobody wants to hear that there is an epidemic. Everybody knows that quarantine means shops boarded shut, doctors and soldiers entering people's homes, and trade coming to a halt. You know better than I do the unhappy fate that awaits the Christian doctor who tries to enter a home in a Muslim neighborhood with soldiers by his side. If you insist that there is a plague, the tradesmen whose businesses are disrupted shall accuse you of calumny, and before long they will be claiming you're the one who brought the plague in the first place. There may not be too many people on our island. But everyone here has their own particular view of things, and they are not afraid to express it."

"What exactly is the size of the population now?"

"In the 1897 census the population of the island was eighty thousand, with twenty-five thousand in Arkaz. The ratio of Muslims to non-Muslims here is approximately even. In fact with the Muslims that have come here from Crete over the past three years, one might say that Muslims are now a majority, though I would not hazard to name a figure, for it would no doubt be immediately disputed."

"How many deaths have there been so far?"

"Some say fifteen, others more. Some hide their dead fearing that the quarantine officials will come and board up their homes or their shops and burn all their belongings. Others think any death is a plague death. We have an epidemic of diarrhea here every summer, and every summer our Quarantine Master, an old man named Nikos, will insist on sending a telegram to Istanbul to claim it is an outbreak of cholera. I always stop him and tell him to wait awhile. Then out he goes with his spray pump, disinfecting the market, the ditches that carry sewage down the middle of the streets, all the poorer neighborhoods, and the public fountains, and soon enough the outbreak he was sure was cholera has already come and gone. If you report the deaths to Istanbul as cholera deaths, they'll call it an 'epidemic,' and the consuls and the ambassadors will be sure to meddle; but if you report them as 'summer diarrhea,' they will immediately be forgotten, and nobody will even notice."

"The population of Smyrna is eight times that of Arkaz, Pasha, but already the number of dead here exceeds the dead in Smyrna."

"Well then, it shall be up to you to find out why that may be," said the Governor cryptically.

"I have seen dead rats around. We had to fight them, in Smyrna."

"The rats here are not like Smyrna rats!" said the Governor with a dash of nationalistic pride. "Our island's mountain rats are much more savage. Two weeks ago they came down to the cities and the villages looking for food, raiding people's homes and kitchens. Where they couldn't find food, they ate whatever else was on their path—beds, soap, straw mats, wool, linen, kilims, even wood. They terrorized the whole island. Then the wrath of God fell upon them, and they were wiped out. But the rats didn't bring this outbreak you speak of."

"Then who did, Pasha?"

"Officially, there is no outbreak at the moment!" said the Governor Pasha.

"But, Pasha, in Smyrna too the rats were the first to die. As you know, we now have scientific and medical proof that the plague spreads through rats and fleas. So we brought mousetraps in from Istanbul. We offered one Mecidiye lira as a reward for every ten dead rats turned in. We called for help from the Smyrna Hunting Club. People were chasing rats on the streets. Even Doctor Ilias and I joined the people in their hunt, and that is how we beat the disease."

"As it happens, we were approached four years ago by the exponents of two of our island's oldest, wealthiest families, the Mavroyenis and Karkavitsas Effendis, who—taking their cue from the latest London fashions—wished to solicit my support for opening a members' club here, similar to the one that already exists in Thessaloniki, but of course this is a small island, and it simply didn't work here . . . As for a hunters' club, we certainly don't have one of those on our humble island. But perhaps you will at least teach us how to hunt these rats of yours and rid ourselves of this plague!"

The two quarantine experts were alarmed by the Governor Pasha's nonchalance, but they did not let their feelings be known. They updated the Governor on medical science's most recent discoveries on the plague and the pathogen that caused it: the discovery that the microbe responsible for killing rats was the same plague microbe that also killed humans was made by Alexandre Yersin in 1894, during the current plague pandemic. Yersin was one of a succession of doctors and bacteriologists who had built on Louis Pasteur's findings on microbes to achieve extraordinary results in the fight against contagious diseases in French colonial hospitals and in the sprawling and impoverished cities outside of the Western world. Soon the work of the German doctor Robert Koch and others in Europe would also lead to the discovery of the microbes that caused a wide range of other diseases—typhus, diphtheria, leprosy, rabies, gonorrhea, syphilis, tetanus—and the vaccines that could defeat them.

Two years ago, Émile Rouvier, another of the innovative doctors who were constantly making new discoveries at the Institut Pasteur, had been invited to Istanbul by Abdul Hamid to share his expertise on diphtheria and cholera. Rouvier had presented the Sultan with a sample he had brought from Paris of a serum to combat diphtheria, and having delivered a brief and charming disquisition on microbes and contagious diseases, the bacteriologist had then installed in the imperial laboratories in Nişantaşı a series of tools which would allow the diphtheria serum to be produced there cheaply and in large quantities. Noticing that all this information seemed to trouble the Governor Pasha, the Royal Chemist assumed a more somber mien.

"As you know, Pasha, we have seen the discovery of a number of vaccines in recent years, and indeed some of these can now be produced quite quickly in the Ottoman Empire's own laboratories, but to date we have yet to discover a vaccine against the plague," he said, clearly setting out the fundamental problem they faced. "Neither the Chinese nor the French have been able to find a vaccine yet. We defeated the plague in Smyrna with old-fashioned remedies like sanitary cordons, isolation measures, and mousetraps. There is no remedy for the plague but quarantine and isolation! Usually the best that doctors can do for plague patients in hospitals is to try to alleviate their suffering. But even that we do not know for certain. Pasha, are the people of this island prepared to follow the required quarantine precautions? This is a matter of life and death, not just for Mingherians, but for the whole Ottoman Empire."

"When they like you and trust you, the people of Mingheria, Greek or Muslim, can be the most pliable, most accommodating of all!" said Governor Sami Pasha. Then, holding in one hand a cup of coffee that had previously been refilled by one of the servants, he stood up with a flourish that suggested he had said all that he had to say. He walked up to the only window in the guesthouse, which looked out at the Castle and the city, to gaze at the beautiful view and at the sea, whose blueness filled the room like a rapture.

"May God watch over us all, and over this island and its people," he said. "Though before we even get to them and to the rest of the Empire, we must first protect you and ensure that you remain unharmed."

"Who would you be protecting us from?" asked Bonkowski Pasha.

"The head of the Department of Scrutinia, Chief Scrutineer Mazhar Effendi, will explain all that!" said the Governor.

CHAPTER 6

hief Scrutineer Mazhar Effendi oversaw the Governor's rich and tangled web of spies, informants, and plainclothes policemen. He had first been sent to the island from Istanbul fifteen years ago, tasked—upon pressure from Western powers—with the entirely unrelated quest of transforming the antiquated local law enforcement agency into a modern gendarmerie and police force. While he successfully introduced the necessary reforms (such as keeping separate and alphabetized files on each suspect), he also found time to marry into one of Mingheria's oldest Muslim families—his bride was Hajji Fehmi Effendi's daughter—and, like many who happened to settle on the island in their thirties, he fell in love with Mingheria's people, its climate, and everything else about it. In the early years of his marriage he toured the island with fellow Mingheria enthusiasts, and even set out to learn the old language of the indigenous Mingherian people. Later, when the overly apprehensive Governor Pasha who had commissioned the armored landau instituted a Department of Scrutinia (an office which existed in no other Ottoman province), Mazhar Effendi began to expand his already extensive network of informants, and the relationships he had cultivated during his early years on the island turned out to be of great use as he worked to follow, identify, and arrest the island's secessionist agitators.

When Mazhar Effendi arrived to meet them, the Royal Chemist and his assistant, Doctor Ilias, found that he was a much-less-conspicuous presence than the Governor Pasha. With his threadbare jacket, narrow mustache, and affable expression, the Chief Scrutineer was a quintessential bureaucrat. In his best bureaucratic voice, he told them straightaway that he had planted spies among the island's various religious, political, commercial, and nationalist groups in order to track and monitor all their activities. He was of the opinion that there were several factions on the island—among which foreign consuls, Greek and Turkish nationalist militant groups, and certain elements that had been inspired by the snatching of Crete away from Ottoman control—who were angling for this terrible plague and quarantine nuisance to grow and turn into an international affair. Mazhar Effendi had discovered furthermore that there were various groups of unhinged religious fanatics from village sects who were determined to cause trouble and have their revenge on the Governor Pasha for an old incident that had come to be known as the Pilgrim Ship Mutiny.

"In light of all these dangers, you shall have to undertake your patient visits in the armored landau."

"But will that not draw even more attention upon us?"

"It will. Children here love to follow the landau and tease Coachman Zekeriya. But there is no alternative. Still, you must not worry; every house and every building you will enter is being watched very closely by municipal employees, spies disguised as hawkers, and various others in our network. But I must make one humble request of you: please do not protest at every guard you see. Even if you think there are too many, and find their presence irksome, I must advise you to desist from any attempt at escaping them . . . Not that you would be able to escape even if you tried, for our spies are razor sharp, and they would catch you immediately . . . And if you should hear someone calling out to you—'Most esteemed Pasha, we too have a patient at home, might you come and see?'—do not, under any circumstances, follow their lead."

Like a carriage escorting a pair of curious European travelers, the Governor Pasha's armored landau first took the Chief Inspector of Public Health and his assistant to the prisons of Arkaz Castle, as famous as the island itself. In order to keep the mysterious visitors apart from the island's quarantine doctors, the Governor had told the Chief Prison Warden that they were the state's two new health inspectors (one of whom was also a doctor). The warden made sure to keep Bonkowski Pasha and Doctor Ilias out of sight of the convicts looking out of the peepholes that had been carved into the Castle's thick walls. They passed through various passageways and unlit courtyards and emerged onto the bastions. From there they climbed down a treacherous stone stairway overlooking a rocky cliff face crisscrossed by seagulls, and entered a damp, dark cell.

As soon as the crowd milling about the cell door parted, allowing more light inside, Bonkowski Pasha and his assistant understood immediately that Guard Bayram had definitely died from the plague. They had seen that same unearthly pallor in at least three other victims in Smyrna, those same sunken cheeks, the protruding, wide-open, astonished eyes, and the fingers clutching at the hem of the jacket as if to try and claw out the pain. The traces of vomit, the bloodstains, and even the strange smell in the room were also the same. Doctor Ilias carefully unbuttoned and peeled off the guard's shirt. There were no buboes on his neck or near his armpits. But once they had uncovered the dead man's stomach and legs, they saw the plague bubo on his left groin. It was large and prominent enough to leave no room for doubt. When they pressed on it, they found that the bubo had lost its initial firmness, which meant that it was at least three days old and that the victim must have died an agonizing death.

Doctor Ilias pulled out a needle and scalpel from his bag and sterilized them with the disinfectant solution he had also brought, while Bonkowski Pasha dispersed the throng at the door. Had the patient still been alive, they could have alleviated his pain by making an incision on the bubo and draining the pus. Doctor Ilias inserted the needle into the bubo and extracted a few drops of the yellowish, gelatinous liquid inside. Once he'd carefully transferred the liquid onto one of the tinted glass slides they had brought to collect microbial samples, and just as carefully placed it in its protective casing and into his bag, their job in the great prison was done. As the disease was definitely plague and not cholera, it was imperative that the sample should be sent to Smyrna for testing.

Bonkowski Pasha ordered the victim's belongings to be incinerated, but when nobody was looking, he picked up the scalpel and cut off the small amulet that was tied around the guard's neck. He disinfected the amulet and put it in his pocket to examine later, then walked out into the daylight. He could tell from the state of the guard's corpse that the disease would spread quickly on this island and that many more people were going to die, and the weight of this knowledge was such that he felt a pain reaching from his throat all the way down to his stomach.

As they passed through the gnarled jumble of streets in the old city, Bonkowski Pasha and his assistant Doctor Ilias saw that the coppersmiths had opened their shops, that the blacksmiths and carpenters had already got to work despite the early hour, that life in the city went on as if nothing were happening. A cafeteria that served the neighborhood's tradesmen had also ignored the rumors and opened its doors. When the chemist pasha noticed that Kotzias Effendi's pharmacy (which looked more like a spice emporium) was also open, he stopped the carriage, got off, and went inside.

"Do you have any *acide arsénieux*?" he asked the shopkeeper coolly.

"No, we're out of ratsbane," replied Kotzias, owner of the Kotzias Pharmacy. The pharmacist felt nervous, for he could tell that the distinguished-looking gentlemen who had just walked into his shop must be important people.

Bonkowski Pasha saw that in addition to selling spices, dyes, seeds, coffees, and herbal teas, the pharmacist also supplied pastes, ointments, and old wives' remedies. Even in his busiest days crossing the breadth of the Empire as Chief Inspector of Public Health and Sanitation, Bonkowski Pasha never forgot that he was a chemist and a pharmacist first and foremost. On Kotzias Effendi's shelves and tables he now saw some of the readymade medicinal products supplied by well-known pharmacies in Istanbul and Smyrna. As a young man, he would often come across pharmacists selling old wives' remedies in small provincial towns, and he would never hesitate to enlighten them on the principles of modern pharmacology. But this was not the time.

The bays and the hotels and tavernas along the shore were dotted with colorful sunshades, and the outdoor restaurants teemed with cheerful customers. The landau traveled through linden-scented backstreets and up past lavish Greek mansions until it reached Hamidiye Avenue. The peach trees were in bloom, and there was a distinctive, appealing aroma of roses in the air. They saw gentlemen wearing hats and fezzes and villagers with leather slippers on their feet walking under the plane and acacia trees that flanked the wide Hamidiye Avenue. Bonkowski Pasha and his assistant gazed uncomprehendingly at the row of houses that lined the creek all the way to the market, at the storehouses, the hotels, the horse-drawn carriages and their dozing drivers, at life unfolding on Istanbul Street as it wound its way down to the port and the

Customhouse. They saw that classes had begun at the Greek Middle School, and that the travel agencies had put new notices and advertisements for ferry companies on display. When they stopped in front of the Hotel Majestic and gazed out at the city and its mostly pink, yellow, and orange hues, the guilt caused by the knowledge that all of this beautiful, winsome way of life was about to come to an end became so difficult to endure that Bonkowski Pasha began to think that perhaps he had been mistaken.

But he would soon realize that he had not made any mistake. Bonkowski Pasha and Doctor Ilias were next led to the Hagia Triada neighborhood, to visit a stone cottage surrounded by olive trees. There they found a coachman named Vasiliy, who had been driving around the city for fifteen years, lying in a semiconscious state, dazed with pain, and with a substantial bubo protruding from his neck. In Smyrna, Bonkowski Pasha had often seen how the plague microbe's stupefying, befuddling, and wholly debilitating effects could, within a couple of days, reduce many patients to a state where they became unable to talk—if they could talk at all—in anything but an unintelligible stammer. Most patients who reached this point died fairly soon thereafter, and very few survived.

When the patient's teary-eyed wife pulled at his arm, Vasiliy seemed to come to his senses for a moment, and tried to speak. But his mouth was dry and wouldn't open properly, and even when it did, he could only manage a stutter.

"What is he saying?" asked Bonkowski Pasha.

"He is speaking in Mingherian," said Doctor Ilias. The coachman's wife began to cry. Doctor Ilias tried to apply the treatment he had used with patients in Smyrna when they had reached this stage of the illness. With his scalpel he made a delicate incision on the bubo, which was still hard and fresh, and patiently drained the pearly, yellowish pus that burst forth, wiping it off with a piece of cotton until there was no more liquid left. The patient's queer, unpredictable twitching knocked one of the doctor's glass laboratory slides to the floor. Although they were already sure that the disease was plague, Doctor Ilias still took utmost care in readying the samples that were to be sent to Smyrna for testing, diligently dabbing the liquid he'd extracted from the patient onto the slides he had prepared.

"Make him drink plenty of boiled water, sugar water too, and yogurt if he is able to eat," said Bonkowski Pasha on his way out. He personally propped open the door and the room's single small window. "Most important: you must keep the air in the room fresh and boil his clothes clean. He must not exert himself, and he must sleep as much as possible."

Bonkowski Pasha suspected that these recommendations he had so often given to the comparatively wealthy Greek shopkeepers that had been his patients in Smyrna would not be of much use in this case. Yet despite all the discoveries that had been made in Europe over the past decade on the subject of bacteria, he still believed that clean air, a peaceful environment, and a hopeful disposition could "in some measure" help a plague patient to recover from the disease.

Past the Stone Jetty (with its backdrop of steep black-and-white mountain peaks) beloved by Romantic painters, the armored landau entered the Taşçılar neighborhood and stopped outside the garden gate of one in a long row of derelict houses. The guide Mazhar Effendi had assigned them told Bonkowski Pasha and his assistant the doctor that this was the area where Muslim youths who'd fled Crete after the troubles there three years ago had now settled. This particular house was occupied by three young men who hauled cargo and worked odd jobs or skulked about in the port, and according to the guide kept causing trouble for the Governor Pasha who had so generously housed them here.

Three days ago, one of the youths had died. Another who had since also fallen ill was now beset by a fierce, agonizing headache, but his body was fighting back with sudden, forceful twitches. In Smyrna, two out of every five infected patients had died. There were also people who were exposed to the microbe that didn't fall ill or even realize they had it. Doctor Ilias felt he might be able to save this young man and set about trying to treat him.

First he gave him an injection to lower his fever. Then, with help from an older man the boys referred to as "Uncle," they took off the patient's discolored clothes. Despite a careful examination, Doctor Ilias could not see any buboes in his armpits, on his groin, or around the backs of his legs. Regularly dipping his fingers into disinfectant solution, the doctor probed the youth's armpits and the lymph nodes in his neck, but could not detect any hardening or unusual tenderness there either. A doctor who had not already been informed about the outbreak of plague would never have concluded, from observing the patient's accelerated heart rate, fever-parched skin, bloodshot eyes, and delirious rambling, that this was a case of plague.

Bonkowski Pasha noticed how carefully the rest of the household was watching the doctor and could see in the two youths' faces that, since their friend's passing, they had quite understandably been gripped by a fear of death, but this did not trouble him, for he knew that it was only this fear that would ensure people paid heed to quarantine doctors. What he could not understand was why the youths, despite having been so clearly in need of a doctor, were still using their dead friend's belongings.

In truth there was only one thing left to say now to this household and to everyone on the entire island: "Get out of here!" Bonkowski Pasha wanted to shout. "Run!" He had heard stories from European doctors of how this disease had killed tens of thousands of people in China, how in some places entire families, villages, and tribes had been completely wiped out before they had even had time to comprehend what was happening to them. That same devastation and those same horrors would soon, he feared, destroy this calm and charming island.

He could see that the microbe had "infiltrated" deep into Arkaz, that it was spreading undetected, and even disinfecting with spray pumps would be of no use in clearing houses like this one of the disease. What really needed to be done was to completely evacuate contaminated buildings and, if anyone protested, resort to the same ruthless methods that had been employed hundreds of years ago: lock people up inside their own homes and nail the door shut. In areas that were affected particularly badly, and where everyone was infected, another old and effective remedy was to burn people's homes and belongings.

In the afternoon they found buboes on the neck and groin of a fourteen-year-old barber's apprentice in a house in the Çite neighborhood. The boy was suffering from headaches and uttered such agonized screams with every fresh wave of pain that his mother would start crying too, and his helpless father would flee to the back garden, then give up and quickly come back inside. Only much later did they realize that the boy's grandfather, who was lying on a daybed in the adjacent room, was also ill. But nobody was paying him any attention.

Doctor Ilias made an incision on the hard but not-yet-swollen bubo on the boy's neck and cleaned the wound with disinfectant solution. As he was performing this procedure, he noticed the boy's father approaching with a prayer sheet, which he pointed at his son's body. Bonkowski Pasha had often seen people caught in the hysteria of an epidemic hoping for some benefit from these sorts of prayer sheets. Christians too would sometimes appeal to priests who were willing to hand out talismans of this sort. As they left the house, Bonkowski Pasha turned to the clerk that the Chief Scrutineer had assigned to them and asked him who was issuing these consecrated prayer sheets.

"The holy man whose prayers and benedictions the whole island trusts, and whose blessings are the most powerful of all, is of course the sheikh of the Halifiye sect, Hamdullah Effendi," said the clerk. "But he is not like these other unscrupulous sect leaders who'll hand out amulets to anyone who comes knocking on their door offering money. There are many who try to copy him. That must be where these prayer sheets came from."

"So people are aware that the blight of the plague is upon them, and they are beginning to take precautions."

"They are aware that there is some kind of pestilence, but they do not fully realize the gravity of the situation," their guide replied. "Sometimes people request love charms, or amulets to cure their stutter, or to protect them from the evil eye . . . The Governor Pasha has got our informants watching every sheikh, every amulet-giving holy man from the most effective to the most dishonest, and all the priests who do the same kind of thing from their monasteries. He sends them spies disguised as supplicants and disciples, and even as mystics. And he extracts information from their real acolytes too."

"Where is Sheikh Hamdullah's lodge? I would like to see that neighborhood too."

"If you go there, there is bound to be gossip," said the clerk. "The sheikh does not venture out much anyway."

"Gossip is the least of our worries now," said Bonkowski Pasha. "The plague has definitely arrived in your city, and it is imperative that everybody should know this."

Bonkowski Pasha and Doctor Ilias personally delivered the samples they had extracted that day to the Messageries Maritimes Smyrna-bound *Baghdad* and sent two telegrams to Smyrna as well. Bonkowski Pasha requested an urgent meeting with Governor Sami Pasha that same afternoon, but it was around the time for evening prayers when he finally knocked on the door of the Governor's Office.

"We had given the Sultan our word that we would keep your visit here a secret!" said Governor Sami Pasha, his manner suggesting how regrettable it was that this promise had not been kept.

"Secrecy would have been important if the unsubstantiated rumors spreading through the Sultan's twenty-ninth province had turned out to be untrue. That would have revealed this to be a political matter, and it would have been important, in that case, to prevent the spread of false information. Unfortunately, as we have observed today, the plague has spread widely here. We are certain that the disease that has struck the island of Mingheria is the same as the one observed in Smyrna, in China, and in India."

"But the *Baghdad* has only just set sail for Smyrna with the samples you extracted."

"Your Excellency," said Bonkowski Pasha, "tomorrow they will send us a telegram from Smyrna with the official results. But I can tell you now, in my capacity as the Sultan's Chief Inspector of Public Health and former Royal Chemist, accompanied here by the brightest among my doctors, and backed by forty years of experience in the field of epidemic disease, that this is plague. There is no room for hesitation in this matter. I wonder if you recall our encounter in Dedeağaç Province? It was when you were governor there, twenty years or so ago, just before the war with Russia. And that was only a bout of summer diarrhea, or perhaps a little outbreak of cholera!"

"How could I forget?" said Governor Sami Pasha. "Thanks to our sultan's resourcefulness and your prodigious efforts we acted without delay and the city was saved. The people of Dedeağaç remain grateful to you to this day."

"You must immediately gather the press and have them declare that there is plague in the city, and that quarantine measures will be announced tomorrow."

"It will take time for the Quarantine Committee to convene," said the Governor Pasha.

"Do not wait for the results from the laboratory in Smyrna; send notice now that quarantine will be declared," said Bonkowski Pasha.

CHAPTER 7

B ut the next morning the Mingherian Quarantine Committee did
not manage to gather. The Muslim delegates were ready, but the
French consul was away in Crete, Doctor Nikos—chairman of the
committee—wasn't home, and the British consul, whom the Pasha considered a friend, asked to be excused on some unexpected pretext. The
Governor Pasha summoned Bonkowski Pasha from the shabby guesthouse where he was being kept with sentinels guarding the door. "While
we wait for the Quarantine Committee to convene, I thought you might
wish to see your pharmacist friend from Istanbul, Nikiforos—your old
business partner," he continued.

"Is he here? I had no response to the telegrams I sent him," said
Bonkowski Pasha.

The Governor turned toward a corner of the room, where Mazhar
Effendi—whose presence had gone hitherto undetected—sat like a
nebulous shadow. "Nikiforos is on the island, and I can confirm that
he has received both of your telegrams!" said Mazhar Effendi. He had
no qualms about making this statement, counting on the fact that
Bonkowski Pasha would deem it entirely normal for the Governor's
spies to screen every telegram sent to the province.

"He did not reply to your telegrams because he was afraid you might
bring up the business disputes you've had with him in the past, and
the matter of the royal concession," said the Governor. "But he is at his
pharmacy right now, waiting for his old friend to honor him with a visit.
Ever since he left Istanbul and opened a pharmacy here, he has become
a rich man."

Bonkowski Pasha and Doctor Ilias walked to the pharmacy. Shopkeepers all along the little roads that led up to Hrisopolitissa Square had

pulled down their blue-and-white- and blue-and-green-striped awnings to protect the wares displayed in their windows—fabrics of every color, lace, ready-to-wear clothes from Thessaloniki and Smyrna, bowler hats, European-style umbrellas, and shoes—from the glare of the morning sun, so that the streets seemed narrower than they were. Here too the chemist and the doctor noticed something they had observed in so many other cities during the early days of an outbreak: none of the people they saw walking around seemed unduly concerned about bumping into one another and catching the disease. The women out doing their morning shopping with their children in tow, the street vendors hawking walnuts, shortbreads, Mingherian rose biscuits, and lemons, the barber quietly shaving his distinguished customer's cheeks, and the boy selling the Athenian newspapers that had arrived with the latest ship were all signs that life on the island continued as it always had. Bonkowski Pasha surmised from the relative wealth of these streets and neighborhoods, and the variety of goods and services on offer in these shops which served the Greek bourgeoisie of Arkaz, that his old friend Pharmacist Nikiforos's business must be thriving.

Bonkowski Pasha had met the Mingherian-born Nikiforos twenty-five years before, when Nikiforos owned a small pharmacy in Istanbul's Karaköy neighborhood. In the back of his shop, which stood on a side street leading to the Ottoman Bank and was adorned with a sign that read PHARMACIE NIKIFOROS, there was a makeshift kitchen—the so-called cauldron room—that he had converted into a workshop. Here, Nikiforos produced rosewater-scented hand lotions and sweet green peppermint-flavored cough pastilles and was able to sell these to some of the Empire's more distant provinces thanks to Abdul Hamid's railway expansion policies.

Their acquaintance had deepened in 1879, when—in the wake of the 1877–78 Russo-Turkish War, which had resulted in another rout for the Ottomans, and at a time when the sting of the Empire's latest territorial losses and the plight of its displaced populations were still keenly felt in Istanbul—the two young men had worked together to set up a pharmacists' guild. Soon the Société de Pharmacie de Constantinople, as it was also known, had gained more than seventy members, most of them Greek. Their organizational success and educational activities had caught Abdul Hamid's attention too, and soon the youthful sultan was entrusting young Bonkowski—whose father he knew from the army—with a variety of tasks, such as analyzing the quality of Istanbul's supplies of drinking water and producing reports on microbes.

It was around this time that Abdul Hamid had turned his attentions to the production of rosewater, as part of his broader ambitions for shifting traditional Ottoman cottage industries to workshop and factory-based manufacture. For hundreds of years families in Istanbul had been distilling small quantities of rosewater in their homes from plants grown in their own gardens and using it in jams, in baking, and in their day-to-day lives. With this kind of experience and tradition behind it, might the Ottoman Empire embark on production on a significantly larger scale, in European-style factories, and could it harvest enough roses to adequately supply such an undertaking? Soon Sultan Abdul Hamid II had commissioned the indefatigable young chemist Bonkowski Bey to prepare a report on this question too.

Within a month Bonkowski Bey had drawn up plans and a budget for a factory in Istanbul that could produce industrial quantities of rosewater, explaining to the Sultan that aside from the greenhouses in the Beykoz area, the only location that could house the vast farms that would be needed to supply the tonnes of rose petals such a factory would require was the island of Mingheria, the twenty-ninth state of the Ottoman Empire. In gathering this information, Bonkowski Pasha had of course relied upon the ideas and suggestions of his Mingherian friend Nikiforos, who made hand creams from roses grown on the island. The Sultan summoned Bonkowski Bey and Pharmacist Nikiforos for an audience at the palace, where he asked them again whether or not it really was possible—as Bonkowski's report posited—for Mingheria to supply substantial quantities of the special rose plant known for its particular fragrance, its oiliness, and its heavy yet layered and syrupy aroma, and when the two trembling pharmacists before him, one Catholic and the other Orthodox, had responded in the affirmative, he had finally left the room.

Afterward a messenger sent to Bonkowski Bey from the government had announced that the Sultan would issue Bonkowski Bey and Nikiforos Bey with a royal concession to cultivate roses in the province of Mingheria and sell their crop to the rosewater factory the Sultan intended to set up in Istanbul. The recipients of this royal charter would not have to pay any tax on this activity.

Nikiforos took this privilege the Sultan had granted them more seriously than Bonkowski did. A year later he had set up a company to produce rosewater on the island. Bonkowski, who had invested ten golden liras of his own money in the business, managed the company's relations with the Ministry for Commerce and Agriculture in Istanbul and handled its publicity activities, and in that first year they enjoyed some success in systematizing the island's cultivated rose production. Bonkowski had even found a farmer familiar with the intricacies of rose cultivation who had fled to Istanbul from the Balkans after the 1877–78 Russo-Turkish War and had sent him and his family to the island.

But these efforts and endeavors were interrupted when Bonkowski Bey suddenly fell from Abdul Hamid's good graces. His offense, it seemed, was to have pompously informed two doctors and a pharmacist in the waiting room of Istanbul's Apéry Pharmacy about the Sultan's trouble with his left kidney, and this in the presence of two dissident journalists—one of whom was a spy. (Abdul Hamid would die thirty-eight years later of renal disease affecting his left kidney.) What had wounded the Sultan was not so much that his illness should be revealed, but rather the fact that Bonkowski had spoken so casually of his kidneys.

Stanislaw Bonkowski's real crime, though, was the unforeseen success of the modern Pharmacists' Guild he had helped set up. In those days, old-fashioned herbalists selling folk remedies, spices, herbs, roots, and poisons, as well as opium and other drugs, were still able to compete with pharmacies run according to modern medical principles. Upon Bonkowski Bey's suggestion, and initially with Abdul Hamid's support, a new pharmacists' charter was drawn up which forbade herbalists from supplying poisonous, mind-altering, or otherwise noxious substances, even by prescription.

Seeing their income thus reduced, traditional herbalists, most of whom were Muslim, soon began to protest. They wrote to Abdul Hamid claiming that Muslim businesses were being persecuted and sent countless letters to the Sultan, signed and anonymous, denouncing this or that injustice. It was all part of those Greek pharmacists' wicked scheme to ensure they alone became the sole purveyors of poisons and narcotics! Abdul Hamid stopped handing young Bonkowski Bey any new assignments for a while, probably—we would argue—because he was displeased with Bonkowski's lapse in discretion, but after five years and much pleading from various go-betweens, the Sultan was finally mollified into trusting Bonkowski again and began once more to commission various reports from him, such as on the water quality in Lake Terkos or on the causes of the recurring summer epidemics of cholera in the city of Adapazarı. The chemist, now forgiven, would go on to write numerous treatises on subjects ranging from a list of which plants from among those grown in the gardens of the Yıldız Palace could be used in the production of poisons to the cheap new substances discovered in the West that could be used in disinfecting holy Zamzam water.

In the intervening five years, Bonkowski had lost touch with his old pharmacist friend in Karaköy, while Nikiforos had closed his shop and gone back to live in his native Mingheria.

As he studied the abundance and variety of wares on offer at the enormous pharmacy on Hrisopolitissa Square now, Bonkowski Pasha felt glad for his old friend. In the window, adorned with the sign NIKIFOROS LUDEMIS—PHARMACIEN, the pharmacist had placed in prominent view his fez decorated with an image of a rose. This was the same symbol he had used in his shop in Istanbul to make himself known to illiterate customers with prescriptions that needed filling. Next to the fez, they saw dainty bowls and bottles of Nikiforos's own rosewater creations, as well as jars of fish oil, camphor, and glycerin. Boxes of medicines, Swiss chocolates, bottles of Evian and Vittel mineral water imported from France, canned goods, Hunyadi Janos branded items from Hungary, English Atkinsons cologne, boxes of aspirin imported from Germany, and many more items brought in from Athens all filled the window with color.

The owner stepped out to greet the two distinguished newcomers admiring his window. Taking care not to come too close, Pharmacist Nikiforos showed his guests inside and ordered some coffee. The reunited friends paid each other many compliments as if it had not been years since their last encounter, and shared a few reminiscences.

"Governor Sami Pasha said you did not wish to see me?"

"Governor Sami Pasha is not fond of me."

"I have not been involved in the royal concession His Supreme Highness granted us all those years ago to encourage our work," said Bonkowski Pasha.

"I invite you to inspect the products of the company we established together."

Nikiforos first showed them the delicate, tasteful bottles of rosewater he arranged to have manufactured in Istanbul. Then they inspected his range of rosewater-scented hand lotions, ointments, rose-flavored soaps of various colors, and rose-scented perfume sprays.

"Our brand of ointments is second only to Edhem Pertev's products in popularity. There is much demand for our hand lotion, not just in Istanbul's Greek pharmacies, but also among Muslim housewives."

Today we know what was discussed during this encounter at the Nikiforos Pharmacy because the conversation was transcribed word for word by a spy hiding in the next room, where he had been sent by the Chief Scrutineer. Having first described his success in distributing his rosewater preparations across the port cities of the Levant, Nikiforos began to speak proudly of where most of the money he made from Abdul Hamid's concession really came from: more than half the rose farmers on the island of Mingheria sold their harvest to Nikiforos and his sons. Todoris, the elder of two sons from his Mingherian Greek wife Mariantis (whom he'd married while he still lived in Istanbul), now ran the farm in the village of Pergalo in the north of the island. His younger, Apostol, managed the Mingherian Rose company's shop in Athens.

"It is a worthy cause to be promoting Mingheria's fruits abroad and bringing wealth back into the island," said Bonkowski Pasha. "How come Governor Sami Pasha doesn't like you?"

"The rival Greek and Muslim gangs that roam around Pergalo village in the north are always fighting and battling and ambushing each other. The Greek outlaw Pavlo is very popular with the inhabitants of that mountainous region, and if he comes down to our rose farm and demands payment, my son cannot refuse him. If he tried, our farm wouldn't last three days before it got burned down or someone got killed. Everyone knows that dastardly Pavlo won't think twice about murdering Ottoman government employees, raiding Muslim villages and running off with their daughters—he claims, 'They're all Greeks that were forced to convert'—and poking people's eyes out or cutting their ears off when he really loses his temper."

"Can't Governor Sami Pasha catch Pavlo?"

"His Excellency the Governor has thought it best to fight the wicked Pavlo by backing the leader of the pious Terkapçılar lodge in the nearby Muslim village of Nebiler, and their protégé Memo the outlaw," said Pharmacist Nikiforos, with a jaunty wink to signal to his guests that he knew his words were being listened to by someone next door. "But Memo is just as bad as Pavlo, and a fanatic too, who won't hesitate to punish any restaurant that dares open its doors during Ramadan."

"Good heavens!" said Bonkowski Pasha, glancing smilingly at Doctor Ilias. "So what sort of thing does this Memo do, then?"

"Last Ramadan he horsewhipped the owner of a diner in Dumanlı village for serving food during the day, both to make an example of him and to make a name for himself."

"But what about Mingheria's own Muslim community, the government clerks, the old families—do they tolerate these kinds of abominations?"

"And what if they didn't?" the pharmacist replied indifferently. "As good, dutiful Muslims, they might disapprove . . . But it is only Memo who protects them from Pavlo, for it always takes rather a long time for the Governor Pasha to send soldiers over from the capital. The one thing the Governor does know how to do is to identify the names and locations of the insurgent Greek villages that support Pavlo's atrocities, so that in the summer he can invite the Ottoman navy's battleships *Mahmudiye* and *Orhaniye* to bomb them all. Luckily, the ships usually never come."

"It sounds like you really do have your work cut out for you!" said Bonkowski Pasha. "But at least your shop seems to be thriving!"

"You will have heard that around thirty or forty years ago there was a period of about a quarter of a century when Mingherian marble—known around the world as Mingherian stone—was very much in demand," said Pharmacist Nikiforos. "From the stone jetties we would put load after load of pink Mingherian marble onto ships headed for America and Germany. In the 1880s, the pavements lining the boulevards of many cities known for their cold winters—Chicago, Hamburg, Berlin—were

all made with stone we had carved off of our mountains, and which was
said to be resistant to cold and ice. In those days, trade with Europe was
conducted over Smyrna. But over the past twenty years, between the
decline in the popularity of Mingherian stone and the support we have
been receiving from Greece, our products are increasingly going to Athens instead. Athenian and European ladies like to use our rose-scented
cream on their hands, and treat it almost as if it were some kind of
expensive perfume. In Istanbul, meanwhile, rosewater is merely a drink
you sip on at the patisserie, and not an especially expensive one either.
But I gather you are not really interested in our rosewater concession.
So it must be true what they say, that you are here to fight the plague."

"The outbreak has spread because it was kept secret," said Bonkowski
Pasha.

"Things will take a sudden turn for the worse, just like when the rats
died," said Nikiforos.

"Aren't you afraid?"

"I know that we are standing on the verge of a tremendous
catastrophe . . . But because I cannot quite picture it, I keep telling
myself I must be mistaken, and then, my dear friend, I find I cannot
bring myself to think about it any longer. What really scares me is that
the Governor Pasha has spent so long pandering to these worthless sects
and their spoiled, ignorant leaders that they won't let him implement a
proper quarantine. These third-rate sheikhs with their prayer sheets and
amulets will do everything in their power to water down the quarantine."

Bonkowski Pasha brought out the amulet in his pocket. "I found
this on the dead prison guard!" he said. "Don't worry, I made sure to
disinfect it."

"Now tell me something, my dear Stanislaw," said Pharmacist Nikiforos. "You are bound to know better than anyone else: Is it really true
that there have to be rats and fleas around for the plague to spread? Even
if there were no rats, could it not be transmitted from person to person?
Or, say, from this amulet to me?"

"Even the wisest, most celebrated doctors and quarantine specialists
at the Venice Conference last year could not quite say that it cannot be
spread through touch or even through saliva and particles in the air.
When you cannot be sure of either of those things, your only choice is
to resort to traditional isolation and quarantine methods and to start

hunting rats. There is still no vaccine against this awful curse. The British and the French are looking for one; we will see what comes of that."

"Then may the Lord Jesus and the Virgin Mary help us all!" said the pharmacist.

The church bells began to ring for noon. "Do you have any rat poison?" asked Bonkowski Pasha. "What do people use on the island? Ratsbane, perhaps?"

"Our pharmacies stock cyanide-based products from Smyrna's Great Britain and Aristoteles Pharmacies. They are not too expensive. A single box can last you seven or eight weeks. People here used to buy their ratsbane and their arsenic from the herbalist to get rid of mice in their homes. You could also use the solution that has just been sent to the Pelagos Pharmacy from Greece on the latest Pantaleon ferry, or the one that has arrived from Thessaloniki for the Dafni store. That one's got more phosphorus in it. But you are the chemist; you'll know more about poisons than I do."

The two old friends exchanged a deep, mysterious look. In that moment Bonkowski Pasha felt as if he had grown distant from this friend from his youth, and more attached to Abdul Hamid and the Ottoman Empire, though readers of the Princess's letters will know that this was not entirely true. Even so, Bonkowski couldn't understand Nikiforos's emotions; he could not accept that Nikiforos had broken with Abdul Hamid and Istanbul completely.

"When the rats first struck, then began to die of their own accord, nobody had any interest in mousetraps and rat poison," Nikiforos continued. "But now, with this talk of a plague and these stories of people hunting rats in Smyrna, the wealthy Greek Yanboidakis family's daughter-in-law has bought herself two mousetraps imported from Thessaloniki. And the Frangiskos' gardener bought one of our carpenter Hristo's spring-loaded traps."

"You must tell Hristo to make as many mousetraps as he can!" said Bonkowski Pasha. "How long would it take to have some more brought over from Crete or Smyrna?"

"Ever since these quarantine rumors first started, there have been fewer scheduled ferries and more unscheduled ones than usual. Some wealthier families who usually come for the summer have already fled, worried they wouldn't be able to leave once quarantine starts. Some haven't even come this year. It would take a day for rat poison to get here from Crete, and two days from Smyrna."

"As a pharmacist, you must surely see that soon everybody will be infected, the hospitals will run out of beds, and there won't be enough doctors to deal with the sick nor enough undertakers to bury the dead."

"But in Smyrna you defeated the disease quickly and easily."

"In Smyrna, we got the owner of the city's biggest pharmacy, the Greek Lazarides, and the owner of the Muslim Şifa Pharmacy to sit together in the same room, and instead of blaming each other for what was happening, they rolled up their sleeves and set about fighting this scourge. Tell me, are there any supplies on the island that might serve to make disinfectant solution?"

"In the garrison they have a lime kiln where they make their own solution. The municipality imports barrels of disinfectant from Istanbul and Smyrna, while some of the hotels and restaurants source theirs from Nikolas Aghapides's pharmacy in Istanbul. The smell of lavender in certain hotels and restaurants might give the impression that the place has been disinfected, that it is clean, but I do wonder whether the concentration of alcohol in these solutions is high enough to kill the plague microbe, and whether these scented disinfectants really achieve the desired results. Mitsos, the owner of the Pelagos Pharmacy, is also a member of the Quarantine Committee and will often loosen quarantine measures on hotels that buy his solution at a favorable price."

"Do you carry copper sulfate?"

"They call that blue vitriol, here . . . If my esteemed friend can wait a day, I should be able to source enough from the other pharmacies to make some disinfectant solution. But the nature of quarantine politics on this island is such that I do not think we will be able to procure a steady supply."

CHAPTER 8

Bonkowski Pasha was impressed by Pharmacist Nikiforos's exhaustive knowledge of which substances were currently available on the island of Mingheria, and precisely where they could be found. "You too must join the Quarantine Committee, not just Pharmacist Mitsos," he said.

"You honor me with your offer, dear Pasha," said Nikiforos. "I love Mingheria. But I will not put up with those consuls who are only good for selling ferry tickets, smuggling contraband, and finding new ways of outwitting each other. Of course none of them are actual consuls; they are all vice-consuls. In any case it will be difficult to make any quarantine work as long as His Excellency the Governor continues to protect those sheikhs."

"Which of the sheikhs is the most fervent opponent of quarantine?"

"Us Greeks would never seek to meddle in the religious affairs of the Muslim community. But you must understand, this island is just like a boat, and we are all on it together. The arrows of the plague make no distinction between Muslims and Christians. If Muslims break quarantine, it is not just they who will die, but Christians too."

Bonkowski Pasha stood up from his chair to signal that the time had come for them to leave and began scrutinizing the glass cabinets in which the pharmacy's rosewater products were displayed.

"Our two most popular creations remain La Rose du Minguère and La Rose du Levant," said Nikiforos. He opened the cabinet and handed Bonkowski Pasha a small, shapely bottle of one and a medium-sized jar of the other.

"La Rose du Minguère is our rose-scented hand lotion, and La Rose du Levant is our finest rosewater. We came up with those names together one night in Istanbul more than twenty years ago. Do you remember, Pasha?"

Bonkowski Pasha did remember that night in Istanbul, and smiled wistfully at the memory. With the Sultan's royal concession suddenly and unexpectedly in hand, the two young pharmacists had sat in the back room of Nikiforos's shop in Karaköy drinking *rakı* and dreaming of the riches that would soon be theirs. First they would bottle Mingheria's special rosewater; then they would use it to make hand creams. The 1880s were the golden age of the kinds of concoctions referred to in Europe as *spécialités pharmaceutiques*. Traditional herbalists' shops with their profusion of scents and colors had fallen out of favor, and suddenly the market had come to be dominated by pharmacies with their walls painted white and their windows framed with timber, where people had their medicines made for them by prescription. These pharmacies had soon begun to import goods from abroad—stylish bottles of ready-made callus ointments and stomachache remedies, beard and hair dyes, toothpastes, and antiseptic creams. Some pharmacies in Istanbul and Smyrna even sold *eaux de toilettes* and purgatives from Europe. It was around this time that certain cannier pharmacists had begun to make their own domestic versions of these products. Even Bonkowski Bey had set up his own company for manufacturing "laxative sodas" and "carbonated fruit juice." That was when he discovered that the bottles, the lids, the luxurious boxes, and the fancy labels that many of these "locally made" medicinal drinks and preparations came with were often made in Europe—usually in Paris. In Paris, they charged you for the design they put on the label too. So Bonkowski had enlisted his painter friend Osgan Kalemciyan instead.

"Your friend Osgan drew this for our rosewater bottles. We haven't changed it since. When we started out, we got the only printer in Arkaz who specializes in labels and business cards to print a thousand copies, and we stuck them onto our bottled rosewater."

"Osgan was not only a pharmacist and chemist but also the most sought-after advertising artist of his time," said Bonkowski Pasha. "He made posters for all the best-known hotels and several famous shops—including Lazzaro Franco's—and of course drew catalog pictures and designed packaging for pharmacies."

"Come and look at this!" said Nikiforos, and having led Bonkowski

Pasha to one side, he lowered his voice to say: "The most fervent enemy of quarantine measures, the one that the Governor Pasha must really watch out for, is the sheikh of the Rifai sect. Sheikh Hamdullah secretly supports him too."

"Where are their lodges?"

"Go to the Vavla and Germe neighborhoods. Do you recall this symbol we used for the Rose of the Levant? A more figurative design. You will notice traces of the Castle's characteristic spired towers, of the White Mountain, and of the Mingherian rose."

"Yes, I remember this one, too!" said Bonkowski Pasha.

"I will send some samples of our products in the landau for His Excellency the Governor," said Nikiforos, gesturing at the two bottles of Rose du Levant he had put into a basket. "I once had the design on these bottles stitched onto a cloth to hang up in the window as an advertisement, but sadly the Governor, mistaking my intentions, had the banner confiscated and has still not given it back. I will join the Quarantine Committee on the condition that my piece of cloth is returned to me. It is an important part of the history of our company."

Half an hour later, having insisted upon a meeting with Governor Sami Pasha, Bonkowski Pasha entered the Governor's Office and immediately conveyed Nikiforos's request: "My old friend Pharmacist Nikiforos has agreed to join the Quarantine Committee," he began, "but on one condition: that we give him back his advertising banner."

"He told you about that, did he? The audacity! That Nikiforos is a vile, ungrateful little man. He has earned a fortune from his rose farms, his pharmacy, and his rosewater, and all because of the royal charter the Sultan granted him. Yet no sooner had he made his money than he turned his back on His Royal Highness and started sidling up to the Greek consul and the trade minister. If I wanted to, I could set the tax inspectors on him, issue him with a few fines and tax bills, and watch his rosewater palaces come crashing down over his head."

"You mustn't do that, Your Excellency!" said Bonkowski Pasha with an air of humble deference. "Quarantine is a labor of unity and collaboration. It was hard enough to persuade him to join the Quarantine Committee."

The Governor Pasha walked through a green door to a small room

next to his office, opened a trunk, and took out a pink-tinged Mingherian red cloth, unfurling it like a sheet.

"Look! You can see how this could easily be construed as a flag."

"I understand your concern, Your Excellency, but this is not a flag;
it is a label Nikiforos and I designed many years ago to advertise the
products of the pharmaceutical company we set up together. It is like
a badge to affix on bottles!" said Bonkowski Pasha. "Your Excellency,"
he quickly added, "please have the Telegraph Office check again!" He
had not been trying to change the subject; he just could not believe that
there still hadn't been a telegram from Smyrna. Later, Bonkowski Pasha
and his assistant walked back to the disused guesthouse where they were
staying. When they arrived, Doctor Ilias once again urged the impatient
Bonkowski not to venture to the Telegraph Office alone.

"What exactly is the danger? Why would anyone here want there to
be an outbreak of plague? This island is just like everywhere else; when
the plague strikes, all its warring factions will immediately set their quarrels aside."

"There will be those who come after you only for the glory, Your
Excellency. You will remember what happened in Adrianople, where
you toiled for a month to end that outbreak of cholera. Yet even as you
were preparing to leave the city, some individuals were still claiming that
you had been the one to bring the disease to Adrianople to begin with."

"But this is a warm, green, and thriving land!" said Bonkowski Pasha.
"People are gentler here, just as their climate is."

When there was still no word from the Governor's Office on the
expected telegrams, the Ottoman Empire's Chief Inspector of Public
Health and his doctor assistant slipped quietly out of the guesthouse.
By the time the sentries and guards stationed at the door had caught
up with them, the two men had already reached the State Hall Square.
The sky above the square on that hot spring afternoon was clear. The
lively, gleaming views of the magnificent Castle to their left and the
sheer, mythical rock face of the White Mountain to their right stirred
Bonkowski Pasha's spirit. They walked in the shade of the colonnades
around the State Hall Square. The Post Office and the chic fabric store
Dafni had each stationed someone at their door to spray disinfectant
solution over visitors. There was no other sign that there was a plague in

the city. The horses harnessed to the carriages around the square dozed on their feet, and the coachmen chattered cheerfully among one another as they waited for customers.

As they entered the Post Office, a clerk at the door sprayed them with rose-scented Lysol. Bonkowski Pasha looked around and picked out an elderly telegraph operator who was busy counting something, dipping his fingers in vinegar every now and then.

"The telegram you were expecting has arrived, and so have those addressed to the Mingherian Quarantine Committee!" said the clerk before returning to his counting.

Anxious for news, Bonkowski Pasha had also sent Smyrna's Quarantine Chief a personal telegram inquiring after the test results. So it was that he "officially" learned that there was an outbreak of plague on the island, just as he had already surmised.

"I shall quickly drop by Vavla and Germe before the quarantine meeting begins!" said Bonkowski Pasha. "A quarantine official must make sure to see everything with his own eyes."

Doctor Ilias saw that, just to their right, the door to the parcel storage room behind the telegraph counter had been left open. The door that led out of the storage room itself was also ajar, and they could see the dark green of the garden at the back of the building.

Bonkowski Pasha noticed the surprise in Doctor Ilias's expression, but paid it no heed. He stepped behind a counter to their left. He wandered around undisturbed (Postmaster Dimitris and a clerk were looking at a document and had their backs turned to him) and entered the empty storage room in the back. He kept going without slowing down, pushed the half-open door that led to the back garden, and walked right out of the Post Office building.

Doctor Ilias would not normally have left his superior alone in such circumstances. But everything had happened at once, and he had watched him as if in a trance, thinking that the Chief Inspector would come back the way he had gone.

As he stepped out into the back garden, Bonkowski Pasha basked in the gleeful knowledge that he was momentarily free of the spies and bodyguards employed by the Department of Scrutinia. He walked out onto the street and up a sloping road. Soon they would send all their men to look for him, and it would not be long before they found him.

But the venerable sixty-year-old chemist was enjoying his little escapade and was delighted to have evaded everyone's attention.

Two hours later, Bonkowski Pasha's bloodied corpse was found in the corner of an empty plot diagonally across the street from the Pelagos Pharmacy in Hrisopolitissa Square. To this day, historians of Mingheria still sometimes argue, if reluctantly, over what the Sultan and the Ottoman Empire's Chief Inspector of Public Health (and head chemist of Abdul Hamid II's personal pharmacy) did during those two hours, and over the mystery of when, how, and by whom he was abducted and killed.

The narrow, sloping road Bonkowski Pasha had wandered into and climbed in slow, unhurried steps was flanked on one side by an old wall whose plaster had long since fallen off, and whose surface was overhung with vines, weeping willows, and hackberries, and on the other by a stretch of empty land, where a group of laughing, boisterous women were hanging their laundry up to dry among the trees as their half-naked toddlers scampered around them. Farther ahead, Bonkowski Pasha saw two lizards coupling energetically among the vines. The Greek community's Marianna Theodoropoulos Girls' Secondary School had not yet closed, but only half its students were still turning up for classes. Walking along the wall and peering into the school's back garden as if he were looking between the black railings of a prison yard, the Chief Inspector of Public Health observed—as he had so often witnessed in his extensive experience of epidemics—that here too, despite the news of the outbreak, many Greek children whose mothers and fathers could not stay at home to look after them and did not have the resources to feed them were still being sent to school so that they might at least have a bowl of soup or a slice of bread to eat, and as he watched those children now, whiling the hours away as their school's population steadily dwindled, he could see the apprehension in their faces.

Bonkowski Pasha then walked into the courtyard of the Hagia Triada Church. Two funeral processions had just set off for the Orthodox cemetery behind the Hora neighborhood, and a relative calm had descended on the churchyard following the commotion of their departure. Bonkowski Pasha remembered the controversy that had accompanied the construction of this new Greek Orthodox church twenty years ago, and whose echoes had reached all the way to Istanbul. The site of the church had previously been a cemetery built hastily to house the victims of a cholera epidemic that had ravaged Arkaz in 1834. Those among the Greek community who had most prospered from the island's marble trade wanted to exorcise the memory of those terrible days of cholera by erecting a church on this same site. The Governor at the time had stalled under the pretext that constructing a new building on land where cholera victims were buried would have adverse effects on public health, until one day, during a discussion of Istanbul's supplies of drinking water, Abdul Hamid had asked the young chemist for his views on the matter, following which a permit had finally been issued for the church to be built over the cemetery. Like all Ottoman churches constructed over the previous sixty years, in the wake of Tanzimat-era reforms allowing for domes to be used in Christian architecture too, the Hagia Triada possessed an enormous dome. Mingheria's governors resented the fact that the proportions of this dome and the view of the church's belfry would give visitors approaching the harbor the impression that this was a Greek island. The dome of the New Mosque, the largest Ottoman-made building on the island, may well have been bigger, but its location was not perhaps quite as striking!

Bonkowski Pasha knew that if he stepped inside the church, he would be hounded by the fireman with the disinfectant pump and by the congregation, so he remained outside in the courtyard, walking close to the walls. One of the walls was lined with shops. In the same corner on the opposite edge there was a boys' high school funded by the church's charitable trust. It reminded Bonkowski Pasha of his days going around high schools in Istanbul thirty years ago delivering chemistry lectures to the pupils there. He would have enjoyed doing the same now, teaching these bewildered, idling students about chemistry, microbes, and the plague.

As he walked out of the courtyard, he came across an elderly, well-dressed Greek man and asked him in French if he could point him in the direction of Vavla. The stuttering old man (who happened to be distantly related to the island's wealthy Aldoni family) showed him the way, and afterward, having reported this encounter and the Chief Inspector's question to the police just two hours after Bonkowski Pasha's body was discovered, he was treated for a time as if he too were a suspect, an unpleasant experience which he would recount to an Athenian newspaper ten years later.

Once he had left the church, Bonkowski Pasha walked by several convenience stores and greengrocers—some open, others closed—and past Zofiri's almond biscuit shop, which remains in business to this day (2017 at the time of writing). As he climbed down Donkey's Bane Hill, Bonkowski Pasha stepped to one side to make way for a small gathering of mourners pulling an enormous coffin up the same slope. He was seen doing so by Barber Panagiotis, whose shop stood in the corner where the slope met Hamidiye Avenue. A series of funerals had just taken place, and in the time before the next batch was due to begin, the mosque commissioned in 1776 by former grand vizier and renowned Mingherian Ahmet Ferit Pasha stood empty and quiet. Bonkowski Pasha passed this comparatively smaller-domed mosque, stepped through the gate on the side of its courtyard that faced the sea, and walked along the thread-like, linden-scented streets nearby. When he saw the Hamidiye Hospital, which had not yet been completed but had already begun admitting patients that morning, he realized that the Chief Scrutineer might send his men to look for him there, and so he turned around and made his way first into the Kadirler neighborhood, and later into Germe.

When he entered these streets that had already lost so many lives to the disease, Bonkowski Pasha stood for a time looking at the ditches that carried sewage down the middle of the road, at the children running around barefoot, and at two boys—brothers—tussling over some indeterminate disagreement. He walked past the lodge led by the sheikh who had blessed the amulet he carried in his pocket, and which had belonged to Bayram Effendi. We know all this because it was reported by a plainclothes policeman who was permanently stationed in this area.

This policeman did not know Bonkowski Pasha. But he would later witness an encounter near the lodge between Bonkowski Pasha and a young man, and the beginnings of the conversation that took place between them, which went more or less as follows:

"Doctor Effendi, we have a patient at home, please come."

"I am not a doctor . . ."

They continued to talk for a time, but the policeman was not able to hear the rest of their conversation. Then, all of a sudden, they vanished.

The Chief Inspector of Public Health and the agitated young man walked briskly for a while until they reached a garden with a low wall and no gate. Bonkowski Pasha felt as if he were in a dream, pushing vainly against the wrong door. He kept pushing despite knowing that even if he did manage to open the door, it would be of no use.

Then the house door opened, and they stepped inside. The air was heavy with the smell of sweat, vomit, and stale breath that was the mark of plague-infested homes. Fearing that he might catch the disease too unless someone opened the windows soon, Bonkowski Pasha stopped breathing. But nobody opened the windows. Where was the plague patient? Instead of taking him there, they all stood staring at him with accusatory looks, and Bonkowski Pasha became so distressed that for a moment he thought he might suffocate.

Then, a figure with fair hair and green eyes stepped forward and said: "You have brought sickness and quarantine here again to blight us. But this time, you will not prevail!"

CHAPTER 9

Two days after dropping Bonkowski Pasha off on Mingheria in the middle of the night, the *Aziziye* reached Alexandria, where the Sultan's Guidance Committee received an enthusiastic welcome from the Consulate of the German Empire. The German consul in Alexandria, troubled and angered by the assassination of the German ambassador to China, had organized a reception and press conference to which the other Western consuls had also been invited. The aim was to get English-language papers in Egypt like *Les Pyramids* and the *Egyptian Gazette* to report on the Guidance Committee's mission, and for newspapers in India and China (particularly those serving the Muslim communities there) to pick up on these reports. In this way, Kaiser Wilhelm—who regarded the suppression of the revolt in China as an opportunity for Germany to show the world its might—could announce to the world before the committee had even reached Peking that the Sultan of the Ottoman Empire, the caliph of Islam, was not siding with the rebellious Muslims in China, but joining forces with the Western powers instead.

Princess Pakize and her husband spent their days and nights in their cabin aboard the *Aziziye*. At the sight of the barefoot, kaftan-wearing Bedouin porters who had all but stormed the deck of their ship as it docked at Alexandria's newly built wharf and begun unloading suitcases and cargo unbidden, Princess Pakize had declared herself relieved that her royal rank meant she had been forbidden from leaving the ship. The Princess was aware that the officer the palace had sent to guard the delegation, Major Kâmil, had been ordered never to leave her side in any of the ports and cities the ship happened to stop by on its journey.

As they stood on the *Aziziye* and watched the sun setting over Alexandria on their first evening there, Princess Pakize spoke to her husband about her father, the former sultan who now lived like a prisoner in the Çırağan Palace. She told him that even though the palace was small and overcrowded, there had been times during their confinement when she and her father and sisters had been able to spend some time alone, playing the piano together; that her father was a man of gentle, delicate sensibilities; that he had secretly joined the Freemasons, a fact which, despite his best intentions, had been used against him. One day they had been looking at a map of Africa in an atlas when their father had walked into the room and started telling his daughters of the time he had visited Egypt as a young prince twenty years before. Both his uncle Abdülaziz, who was the Sultan at the time, and his little brother Prince Hamid Effendi, who would eventually succeed him on the throne, had also made the trip. (Later they would also travel together to Paris, London, and Vienna.) In Egypt, the one current and two future Ottoman sultans, Abdülaziz, Murad V, and Abdul Hamid II, had journeyed by camel to see the Pyramids and had also boarded a train for the first time; "One day," they had concurred, "there will be railways in Ottoman lands too, God willing." As his daughters looked at Africa in their atlas, their father recalled how fondly the Egyptian people had received the Ottoman sultans' visit. Nineteen years ago, upon hearing the news that the British had invaded Egypt, the deposed sultan had wept with grief inside the palace where he was imprisoned.

Princess Pakize was the third daughter of the previous Ottoman sultan, Murad V. Three months after Murad V took the throne in the year 1876, some of the more influential pashas of the Sublime Porte had deposed him, claiming he was too volatile and maybe even mad, and had installed in his place his younger brother Abdul Hamid, the current sultan. Three months before Murad V was deposed, his uncle Sultan Abdülaziz—Princess Pakize's great-uncle—had also been removed from the throne in a plot led by bureaucrat pashas, and a week later he had been assassinated, with his death made to look like a suicide. Considering this horrifying precedent, Princess Pakize felt it was only natural that her father Murad V should have had some difficulty controlling his nerves. It was in the wake of all these unexpected developments that Prince Abdul Hamid Effendi—who had been second in line to the throne, and was not as well known or liked as his older brother Murad—had suddenly become sultan, and gripped by the fear that he might end up deposed and imprisoned or killed like his uncle and older brother had been, he had imposed upon his brother and predecessor Murad V a lifetime of strict incarceration.

Princess Pakize had been born four years into the captivity of her father, Sultan Murad V, which would last for twenty-eight years, and for her entire life she had seen nothing but the palace to which she had been confined. (Her beloved older sister Hatice, on the other hand, was born in the Kurbağalıdere Mansion before their father took the throne, and after her father became the Sultan, she had sat on his and her uncle Prince Abdul Hamid's laps in the Dolmabahçe Palace.) To prevent Murad V from taking back the throne or conspiring with opposition factions, Abdul Hamid had given him the same treatment he reserved for the Ottoman princes, isolating him and his family from the world outside the palace.

With the three sisters spending their lives confined to a minor palace, the question of whether they would be able to get married had long been a source of woe and concern for their father, the former sultan Murad V. Abdul Hamid declared that if his three nieces wished to be married, they must leave their father and come and live with him instead, in the Yıldız Palace; the nervous, cruel sultan did not want people to come and go from the little palace in which he kept his brother imprisoned even with the reasonable excuse of wedding preparations. Princess Pakize's father was dismayed to hear of this stipulation from his younger brother, with whom they had got on so well as children. But even as he complained to his daughters of Abdul Hamid's cruelty and spoke of separating a father from his daughters as the greatest sin of all, he also told them time and time again that getting married and having children was life's foremost joy. So it was decided that the best thing to do would be for the princesses to leave their father's side for a while, demonstrate their good faith and their improved relations with their uncle, and move into the Yıldız Palace to find grooms befitting their beauty and status.

The eldest sister Princess Hatice, who was nearly thirty, and the slightly younger Princess Fehime had both agreed to this condition, while nineteen-year-old Princess Pakize had initially refused to leave her father and mother's side. But within two years the matter had been smoothed over, with Abdul Hamid's last-minute intervention securing Princess Pakize a husband too (even if he was "only a doctor"). The three sisters had got married together at the Yıldız Palace, and in fact Princess Pakize—unlike her sisters—was happy with this sudden match (perhaps, some might say, because she wasn't as beautiful or ambitious as her sisters were).

As they passed the time in their cabin, talking and getting to know each other, Princess Pakize would look at Doctor Nuri's wheat-colored skin, at his large, plump, hairy body, and experience a delicious thrill she had never even known could exist. Watching her husband perspire as he spoke of something that excited him, or even listening to him inhale and exhale through his nose in moments when his breathing quickened, the Princess—as she wrote to her sister Hatice—was filled with a feeling of absolute bliss. Sometimes when her doctor husband got out of bed to fetch a jug of water, she would stare in astonishment and wonder at the backs of his fleshy legs, at his feet so small she couldn't imagine they could look good on any man, and at his enormous bottom.

Husband and wife spent most of their time in bed, making love. In the hours that remained they were content to lie quietly side by side in their hot and humid cabin, temporarily out of reach of any mosquitoes. If they happened to touch upon a difficult but important topic, they took care to soften the mood, afraid of how the other might react. Sometimes they would get out of bed and put on their best clothes to make conversation, but whenever any dangerous subject was broached, they stopped talking about it.

For Princess Pakize, these dangerous subjects were, of course, her hatred of Abdul Hamid and the many years she had spent imprisoned inside a palace. Prince Consort Nuri saw that his wife wanted to talk about these things and open up to him, but he was also worried that this could mar their contentment, so he reined in his curiosity and did not press the issue. Doctor Nuri also felt that if his wife was going to tell him all her most sorrowful stories, then he should tell her too of his own harrowing experiences as a quarantine doctor, of all the horrors he had witnessed in the Hejaz, and of what the pilgrims who went there were put through, even though he was concerned that these harsh tales might shock and disturb the Princess. Even so, he yearned to share his inner world with the intelligent, self-assured woman he had married. He wanted his wife to be aware of what was happening in those far-flung provinces that were slipping away one by one from under the rule of her uncle's Ottoman Empire, and he wanted her to know how the people there were being decimated by these epidemics.

The morning of their third day in Alexandria, Doctor Nuri went out into the city. He visited the Greek watchmaker from Istanbul whose shop was situated just behind the Mehmet Ali Pasha Square, in the same street as the Zizinia Hotel, where British quarantine doctors and clerks usually stayed (and which had now stationed men with disinfectant spray pumps at its entrance). After asking him for all the latest news from Istanbul, the watchmaker began as he always did to tell the curious Ottoman doctor of the day when British warships, ostensibly sent to quash Ourabi Pasha's anti-Western and anti-Ottoman nationalist uprising, had shelled Alexandria for hours. He described how terrifying the noise of those bombs had been, how the whole square had collapsed and been covered in a cloud of white dust, and how even British and French buildings had been hit. Christians and Muslims had taken up arms and started killing one another on the streets, and the watchmaker recalled how for a time it had been unsafe for Christians living in outer neighborhoods to even wear hats when they left their houses. Some time after the fires and the looting had ended, the watchmaker had met Gordon Pasha here. Having yet again told Doctor Nuri the story of how he had personally repaired and handed back to Gordon Pasha the very same Theta watch the Pasha wore the day he was killed in Khartoum by the Muslim armies of the Mahdi of Sudan, the watchmaker summarized his thinking in the following terms: "In my view neither the French nor the Ottomans nor the Germans can rule Egypt; only the British can!"

In their previous meetings, Doctor Nuri would have corrected the watchmaker whenever he disagreed with his statements. "No, the Ottomans did not hand Egypt over, they were already having trouble ruling it and the British just needed an excuse to take over!" he might have said; or he might have politely pointed out that Christians had already been beating and killing Muslims before the Arabs had started murdering Christians. But ever since his marriage a month ago to the niece of that same man whom the watchmaker had just referred to as "the Sultan" and as "Abdul Hamid," he had forbidden himself from raising these kinds of objections and indeed from expressing any kind of political opinion.

That day the Doctor and Prince Consort did not enjoy the watch-maker's conversation, nor his visit to Alexandria under quarantine. There was a new life ahead of him now, though he could not quite make out what it was going to be. He soon began to feel restless and started to make his way back to the port.

When he had gone through customs and stepped back on board the *Aziziye,* the cabin boy informed him that a Thomas Cook ship had just delivered two encrypted telegrams for him.

Just before the *Aziziye* had departed from Istanbul, a palace clerk had presented Doctor Nuri with a special codebook from the Sultan. It was the kind of codebook Abdul Hamid issued to ambassadors, local chieftains, and spies of all nationalities when he wished to establish a closer rapport and a direct line of communication outside the bureaucratic channels of the Sublime Porte.

Doctor Nuri embraced Princess Pakize and told her the news, then retrieved this codebook from the depths of his valise and turned eagerly to decoding the first telegram, letter by letter and digit by digit. But he had not done this in a long time, and as he leafed through the pages of the codebook looking for the letters and words that corresponded to each number, he found that he was struggling. His wife had been hovering around him as he worked, so he asked her to help. They soon discovered that certain commonly used words had been rendered as two-digit numbers, and after that they quickly unscrambled the telegrams.

The first telegram had come directly from the palace. It decreed that the Doctor and Prince Consort had been commissioned, upon the death of Bonkowski Pasha, to oversee the fight against the plague in the province of Mingheria and its capital, Arkaz, and ordered him to proceed immediately to the island. It also ordered the Russian captain of the *Aziziye* to take Princess Pakize, Prince Consort Nuri, and Major Kâmil to the island of Mingheria without delay. The second telegram, which also came from the palace and was expressly presented as an order from the Sultan himself, referred openly to the possibility that Bonkowski Pasha might have been "assassinated" and requested that the Doctor and Prince Consort should act "as a detective" and assist Governor Sami Pasha in his investigations to elucidate the matter.

"I told you my uncle would not allow us to enjoy this journey!" said Princess Pakize. "I have no doubt that he is the one who had poor Bonkowski Pasha killed."

"You must not be so quick to come to conclusions!" said the Doctor and Prince Consort. "Before you make your mind up, let me first tell you of the state the international quarantine establishment finds itself in."

The *Aziziye* promptly set sail from the port of Alexandria with its three passengers on board and journeyed north all night. After nightfall, as the ship's progress was slowed by a strong northeasterly *poyraz* wind, the Doctor and Prince Consort felt it was time for him to introduce in his wife's mind the likelihood that it might not have been her uncle Abdul Hamid who'd had poor Bonkowski Pasha killed, and that it was at the very least possible that some other force could have been involved. So as they sat in their cabin, he began to describe to his wife the politics of global quarantine operations.

In 1901, the British, the French, the Russians, and the Germans, who were enjoying at the time a position of global military, political, and medical dominance, believed that plague and cholera spread to Europe and the rest of the world from Mecca and Medina and that the people who brought these diseases to the West (to western Asia, southern Europe, and North Africa) were Muslims who came on pilgrimage to the Hejaz. In other words, the sources of the world's plague and cholera epidemics were China and India, while their distribution center was considered to be the Hejaz Province of the Ottoman Empire. Doctors and quarantine experts working in every corner of the Ottoman Empire, be they Christian, Muslim, or Jewish, knew deep down that from a medical perspective, this claim was sadly true. But some of them, particularly the younger Muslim doctors, also believed that Western powers exaggerated this contention for political purposes and used it toward the intellectual, spiritual, and military humiliation of the peoples and nations of the world outside of Europe. When the British declared, "If you cannot protect our Indian subjects from disease while they are on the hajj, then we will!" everyone in the Ottoman camp—including Sultan Abdul Hamid himself—knew that this was not just an expression of disdain toward the Ottomans' handling of medical matters, but a military threat too. This was why Abdul Hamid ("Your uncle!" said Doctor Nuri, looking into his wife's eyes) had spent so much money on setting up quarantine facilities in the Hejaz. He had built new quarantine stations, military outposts, and docks on Kamaran Island at the mouth of the Red Sea and sent his brightest doctors to work there.

The quarantine station set up in the Yemen Province of the Ottoman Empire, on the island of Kamaran in the Red Sea, was at the time the world's largest quarantine facility, both in terms of capacity and of surface area. As he described his first trip there seven years ago during an outbreak of cholera that had flared up at the height of hajj season, Doctor Nuri did not conceal his emotions. In those early years the suffering of the mostly Indian and Javanese pilgrims stuffed into the bowels of rotting, hulklike vessels, usually sailing under the British flag, had frequently brought tears to his eyes. In time he would see the conditions on all pilgrim ships setting sail from any Indian port become even more desperate. British travel companies in Karachi, Bombay, and Calcutta made it compulsory for passengers to purchase return tickets, but in those years one out of every five Indian pilgrims who embarked on the hajj either died there or couldn't come back.

Doctor Nuri had seen how, in spite of the high ticket prices pilgrims were charged, passenger ships on the Bombay–Jeddah route that might have been designed to carry four hundred people at most could end up sailing with anywhere between one thousand and one thousand two hundred aspiring hajjis on board, packed in like sardines all the way down to the cargo hold. Rapacious steamship captains would squeeze pilgrims into the most unthinkable spots, such as the railings around the upper deck, which were the narrowest parts of the ship, and even on the flat roof of the captain's cabin, so that those who found a spot in which to stand had no room to bend down and sit, and those who could sit or were lucky enough to have space to lie down knew that if they stood up they would lose their spot, and therefore avoided moving altogether. As he told this story, the Prince Consort imitated the manner in which pilgrims on these ships would curl up to sit.

Peering out from his quarantine officer's boat as it edged slowly toward those rusty, sunbaked ships that seemed to lose parts as they sailed and looked like they might sink at any moment, Doctor Nuri would be amazed and even a little alarmed at the sight of the multitude of male heads staring at him from decks and portholes and any other available gaps. Once he had climbed on board for his inspection, escorted by soldiers, he would quickly realize that every available surface was covered in pilgrims sitting or lying down, that there were likely to be three times as many people hidden out of sight inside the ship as there were in the doomsday throngs he could see from the outside, and that every one of these aspiring Indian hajjis was worn out and exhausted, if not already sick.

The monstrous crush of hopeful pilgrims would be so dense that there was hardly any room to walk in, and Doctor Nuri described how sometimes he would have to call upon his armed guards to help him cleave his way through to the captain. To a query from his wife he responded by explaining that most of these ferries were actually cargo ships with no seating room for any passengers. Descending into the dark and putrid bowels of the hold, he would feel in that vastness without portholes or windows the squirming and the humanity of hundreds of terrified pilgrims, hear some of them moaning or praying, and see others still watching him in inquisitive silence. These cargo holds could get so dark that quarantine doctors had been forbidden from entering them after sunset. "But I must not talk too much of these matters and distress you unduly!" said Doctor Nuri.

"Please do not keep anything from me!" replied Princess Pakize.

Doctor Nuri could see that to his wife, these people he had described seemed destitute and desperate, and faced with this misconception, he couldn't help but tell her the truth: pilgrims who undertook the hajj were, in fact, relatively wealthy in the countries they came from. Some would have sold their land or their homes to pay for the journey; some would have spent years saving up for it; some would make the journey a second time even though they knew how arduous and expensive it was. Over the past twenty years, the introduction of steamships and the fall in ticket prices had multiplied the number of yearly pilgrims to the Hejaz, bringing it close to a quarter of a million. Never in history had Muslim men from all over the world, from Java to Morocco, congregated and communicated in such vast numbers. Doctor Nuri recalled one religious festival day during which he had gazed out at a vast assembly of pilgrims' tents and parasols and thought of how this prodigious sight would have delighted "your uncle" Abdul Hamid, who was eager to harness the power of Islam and of the caliphate.

"It is sweet of you to try and make me see my uncle in a kinder light!"

said Princess Pakize. "I suppose we are beholden to him for orchestrating our meeting."

"Your uncle himself is sending us to Mingheria to solve the murder. You shouldn't say that he had Bonkowski Pasha assassinated."

"Very well, then I shall not say it again!" said Princess Pakize. "But you can tell me all your darkest and most terrible cholera stories."

"I worry that if I do, you will be afraid of me, and not love me anymore."

"On the contrary! I love you all the more for how you have toiled in the bleakest corners of the Empire. Now tell me your most dreadful story."

They walked out onto the deck together, and that was where Doctor Nuri told his aristocratic wife about the ramshackle toilets that would be constructed around the bulwarks of pilgrim ships sailing across the Arabian Sea. The few toilets that were available on these cataclysmically overcrowded vessels were either all broken to begin with or became blocked after a day's sailing due to misuse and excessive demand. Crafty European ship captains would attend to the problem by building latrines out of rickety gangways suspended over the sea, hanging from ropes down either side of the main deck. Long queues for these toilets would form on every ship sailing from India to the Hejaz, and sometimes fights would break out. On stormy nights, pilgrims doing their business on these suspended latrines would fall off and plunge straight into the Arabian Sea, there to be feasted upon by ferocious sharks. The more prudent and experienced pilgrims among those traveling in the hold would relieve themselves in buckets and chamber pots they had brought for the journey, then empty their filth out of a porthole and into the ocean. But when the sea was choppy and the windows couldn't be opened, these buckets and chamber pots would rock slowly back and forth until they spilled over. After he'd described how the stink of excrement from these pots would mix with the stench of the corpses of pilgrims who had silently perished of cholera in the darkness of the hold, Doctor Nuri fell into a long silence.

"Please continue your story!" said Princess Pakize after much time had passed.

They returned to their cabin, and Doctor Nuri began to tell his wife about the hajjis from North Africa, a subject he suspected would prove less distressing to her. Seen off with elaborate ceremonies and prayers as they set sail from ports such as Alexandria and Tripoli, these pilgrims would arrive in the holy lands via the Suez Canal and travel in greater comfort and tranquility. But Doctor Nuri had also seen how pleasure-seeking and a flippant approach to regulations could cause diseases to spread even in these pilgrim ships sailing toward the Hejaz from the north. On these relatively wealthy ships that came from west of the holy land, Doctor Nuri had watched Arab pilgrims and their coterie of attendants lay out meals of olives, cheese, and pita bread on deck, with the occasional bon vivant going so far as to have his servants set up a barbecue in a corner of the crowded deck and cook him kebabs. One time, in Alexandria, he had watched as a British quarantine officer who was inspecting a ship had ordered his soldiers to throw one such barbecue grill and other paraphernalia into the sea, and he described to his wife the riot that had ensued.

"Now tell me, my lady, who is to blame in this situation, and who has behaved inappropriately?"

"One should certainly not be consuming food and drink aboard a quarantined ship!" said Princess Pakize, who had immediately grasped where the question was leading.

"That is so, but the British officer has no right to throw anybody's possessions overboard either!" said Doctor Nuri, speaking as deliberately as a schoolteacher. "A quarantine officer cannot just introduce restrictions and rely on the threat of military force to implement them; he must also seek to persuade people to adhere to those restrictions of their own volition. The pilgrim whose barbecue is thrown into the sea shall come to view that harsh and discourteous Englishman as the enemy. He will flout the officer's rules on principle until slowly but surely quarantine will fail. In Bombay there have been riots caused by British officers' draconian and degrading methods. Rocks have been thrown at vehicles transporting the sick, and doctors have been attacked. British government officials have been killed on the streets. Now the British have even stopped saying that cholera spreads via the Ganges, lest the claim should encourage even more rebellion."

"If things are that bad over there, then once we have left Mingheria we should not stop in Bombay, but go straight to China," said Princess Pakize.

CHAPTER 10

They fell asleep in each other's arms. Toward morning, as the steady sound of the pistons pumping inside the steamship grew softer, they went out on deck together. As the first light of day rose to the right of the ship, the black shadow of Mingheria materialized upon the blue horizon. A gentle breeze picked up and made their eyes water. The island's tall dark silhouette was becoming clearer now.

The sun was rising, bringing a soft pink glow onto the row of precipitous cliffs and sharp, rugged mountains that began with the White Mountain and followed the eastern shore of the island, while the slopes that faced toward the west looked as if they had been painted a dark purple, in parts an almost crepuscular hue. As the *Aziziye* moved closer to the island, this view—the very same view which all those painters who had visited the island since the 1840s had so enthusiastically depicted, and which had been so poetically described in many a travel journal—acquired an increasingly otherworldly quality.

When the Arab Lighthouse became visible to the naked eye, the captain veered toward the port, and the view which has variously been described as "worthy of a fairy tale" and "mythical, maybe even eerie" became more clearly defined.

Now the sight of the magnificent Castle with its quaint spired towers, and the buildings and bridges behind it, all built out of the same pale pink-and-white Mingherian stone, generated an even-more-intense and more beguiling effect upon the beholder. They saw the vegetation growing over the island's rugged cliffs, and the colors of the city's red roof tiles and white walls, and felt the presence of an unearthly light hanging over it all.

Major Kâmil, the Princess's bodyguard, had also climbed on deck and was watching the view with them.

"I must say, sir, that I am quite excited, for I am Arkazian born and bred!" he said all of a sudden.

"What a wonderful coincidence!" said Doctor Nuri.

"Perhaps it is not a coincidence," said the Major, taking care to address the Doctor and Prince Consort only, in case the Prince Consort should be displeased to see another man speaking directly to his wife. "Perhaps our most compassionate sultan knows that I am a Mingherian, and maybe that is why he included me in the delegation in the first place."

"Our sultan's interests are manifold, and he never forgets what he discovers!" said Doctor Nuri.

"What do you like best about the island?" asked Princess Pakize.

"I like everything about it," said the Major diplomatically. "My lady, the best thing about Mingheria is that it is exactly as I know it and exactly as I would want it!"

They sailed south of a rocky islet housing a graceful white Venetian-era building, which was known among locals as the Maiden's Tower and had been used in the past as a quarantine zone. By now they could distinguish the hills and rooftops and pink walls of Arkaz, Mingheria's biggest and best-known city, and even see splashes of color, the green of the island's palm trees, the blue shutters of people's homes. The three domes that signaled the city's Venetian, Byzantine, and Ottoman history were also gradually coming into view, all aligned on the same plane: those of the Catholic Saint Anthony's and Orthodox Hagia Triada Churches on the eastern side of the island, and that of the New Mosque—the island's largest mosque, situated on the first hill on the island's relatively flatter western end. As our travelers approached the island, their eyes were trained on the sinuous contours of these three domes, whose silhouettes had, in recent years, frequently been portrayed by European painters. But after the White Mountain, it was the Crusaders' colossal Castle that dominated the city and its landscape. Looming across the path of any ship that happened to sail by this corner of the Levant, the pink-hued Castle reminded those who looked upon it that there had been people living and working on this island, waging war and slaughtering one another, since time immemorial, a time even older than fairy tales.

They were close enough now that they could pick out smaller structures, people's homes, individual trees, and feel life coursing through the charming streets and squares of Arkaz. They could see distinctly the colonnaded balcony of the Governor's Residence and State Hall, the new Post Office just down the road, the Greek High School, and the walls of the new clock tower still under construction. The captain turned the engines down, and in the ensuing hush, the passengers of the *Aziziye* recognized that the brightness of the sun, the green of the palm and fig trees, and the blue of the sea were of a different texture here. As she breathed in the scent of orange blossoms, Princess Pakize did not feel that they were sailing toward a city on the verge of a plague epidemic and an outbreak of bloody political strife, but rather that they were heading toward a small seaside town that had been drowsing uneventfully under the sun for hundreds of years.

There did not seem to be much activity in town in the early morning light. The mansions and houses made of pale pink stone that lined the wooded hills rising straight up from the shore had all their windows and shutters still closed. There were no vessels of note in the dock apart from two freighters, one French and the other Italian, and a handful of small sailboats. Doctor Nuri saw no quarantine flags on any of the ships, nor any traces onshore of precautions being taken to stop the disease from spreading. But on the western side of the port, to the left of the *Aziziye* as it approached the island, he did notice—and privately identified as potential epicenters of the outbreak—various abandoned and dilapidated jetties, ruined buildings, old and new customhouses, and dormitories and decaying houses where the poorer population lived.

Standing beside him on deck and looking at the turquoise waters around them, his wife was staring into the sea as if she were surveying her own memories—entranced by the rocks on the seabed, the darting, spiky, fist-sized fish, and the delicate green and dark blue flowerlike seaweed. The flat mirror of the sea returned a gleaming reflection of the city's mostly pink-and-white and occasionally orange-brown houses, its trees in their many shades of green, the Castle's spired towers, and the pewter domes of churches and mosques. The Doctor and Prince Consort and Princess Pakize could hear the ripple of the *Aziziye*'s sharp bow carving its way through the water. Then there was an interval of silence so perfect that all the way from the deck they could hear the sound of cocks crowing in the city, dogs barking at nothing, and even the braying of a donkey.

The captain tooted the ship's horn twice. Accustomed as they were to receiving one ferry a week from Istanbul and two via Smyrna, Alexandria, and Thessaloniki, the Mingherians of Arkaz were surprised and intrigued to hear the whistle of an unscheduled ferry. As always the sound of the horn echoed between the capital's two hills. The Major sensed a quickening on the streets where he had spent his childhood. A horse cart was trundling past the row of hotels, travel agencies, restaurants, nightclubs, and coffeehouses that lined the Pier Road, while farther up on Hamidiye Avenue, the street where the Post Office and the State Hall were located, an Ottoman flag billowed behind a row of trees. These two roads running parallel to the seafront were connected by the very short and steep Istanbul Street, currently peopled by the odd pedestrian. The Major was glad to see he could pick out their hats and fezzes already, even if from a distance. The signs for the Ottoman Bank and for Thomas Cook which he had seen on his last trip to the island were still there. Now the words SPLENDID PALACE had also been spelled out in giant letters on the roof of the eponymous hotel. From the port he could not see his family home where he had spent his entire childhood, but he could make out the stumpy minaret of the little mosque of Saim Pasha the Pious at the top of the sloping road that led to the market.

The port of Arkaz was a natural harbor shaped like a near-perfect crescent. The colossal Castle the Crusaders had built on the imposing promontory at the southeastern tip of the crescent had once been a town and barracks in its own right, like the castles of Malta and Bodrum. But despite the size of the Castle and the availability of a natural port, it had proven impossible to construct a dock that could accommodate the modern era's new and larger ships. The improvised jetties that had been erected thirty years before at the peak of the trade in Mingherian marble, and which had allowed the stone to be loaded onto merchant vessels that left daily for Smyrna, Marseille, and Hamburg, were not equipped to deal with the size of modern passenger liners. In any case passenger steamboats, which were growing increasingly larger in those years, had been banned from entering the port altogether seven years ago, after a small Russian vessel that had been trying to moor in one of these old jetties had ended up crashing into the rocks.

Thus, like all passenger ships that came to Arkaz, the *Aziziye* noisily dropped anchor in the waters off the port and began to wait. When he was a child, this would have been the Major's favorite moment. Every new steamship—every "ferry," in other words—that came to the island would bring with it new post, new travelers, new stories, new stock for the shops, and a sense of anticipation. As soon as an incoming ship had anchored, a bevy of boatmen and porters, each operating under the instructions of a specific foreman, would set off immediately to retrieve its passengers and their luggage and ferry them to shore. Every foreman had his own team of porters and oarsmen who were constantly competing to bring as many passengers and as much luggage ashore—and earn as many tips—as possible.

As soon as they heard the whistle of a passenger liner, Kâmil son of Mahmut, his classmates from the Army Middle School, and many other children and adults would rush to the docks to watch the ensuing commotion. The kids knew about the competition among the boat crews and would run bets among one another on which rowboat would reach the big ship first, with almond biscuits or the island's famous walnut-and-rose biscuits from Zofiri's shop for prizes. Sometimes the waves of the sea would swell to towering proportions and the little boats would disappear among them, only to resurface, to everyone's relief, on the crest of the next wave and continue on their way to the passenger ship. Back on the shore, the relatives and families of the arriving passengers, their servants and porters, and anyone else milling about would mix in a great crowd with all the people who were waiting to board the same ship and leave the island. Upon disembarking, the new arrivals would immediately be hounded by hotel clerks, tour guides, porters, and swindlers, their luggage would be picked up without their permission, and swarms of coachmen, pickpockets, and beggars would descend upon them in search of opportunity, so that, by order of Governor Sami Pasha himself, gendarmes were now also deployed to the docks whenever a passenger ship was due. But even they had been unable to instill any kind of order to proceedings, and the scuffles and havoc on the docks continued.

As he thought back to these scenes from his childhood, the Major also kept an eye on the Princess—who was, in that moment, clinging to her husband while bravely negotiating the ladder that led from the *Aziziye* to the awaiting rowing boat—and wondered whether the crowds, the dust, and the ruckus on the docks might unsettle her. No doubt there would also be packs of impertinent kids clowning about in the hopes that some European tourist or wealthy Arab alighting that day might toss them a coin. They too could trouble the Princess. But as their rowing boat neared the shore, the Major saw that the docks were in unusually perfect order and realized that a special welcome must have been prepared for the former sultan's daughter.

The Governor Pasha hadn't left the island once in three years, but thanks to the newspapers he read and to friends lucky enough to travel back and forth from the island, he was still able to learn, if a little belatedly, all the gossip from Istanbul, what foolish act had dented which pasha's reputation, which wily maneuver had earned this or that minister Abdul Hamid's approval, which of His Serene Highness's daughters was next in line to be married and whose son was to be picked out for her, what fresh neuroses Abdul Hamid had recently developed, and who had been appointed to which foreign embassy. He had therefore heard, and indeed read about in official announcements published in the newspapers, that a month ago Abdul Hamid had arranged for three low-ranking and unexceptional grooms to marry the daughters of the former sultan Murad V, Abdul Hamid's "unhinged" older brother whom the Sultan had for years been keeping imprisoned inside a tiny palace in the Çırağan complex. The Governor Pasha had also overheard that the doctor who had been wedded to Murad V's youngest daughter was apparently a gifted quarantine expert.

Governor Sami Pasha had wanted his welcome ceremony to be worthy of the first royal princess in history to have ever left Istanbul and had therefore asked the Commander of the island's military garrison to bring his brass band to the port. Most of the aging officers stationed on the island of Mingheria couldn't even read and write properly. After the infamous episode of the "Pilgrim Ship Mutiny," which had resulted from a mishandled quarantine operation, Abdul Hamid had sent to the island two battalions of infantrymen from Damascus who did not speak any Turkish. Two years ago a young army captain who had been banished to the island for some disciplinary misdemeanor had set up a brass band out of boredom, similar to the army band in Istanbul if much more modest in its ambitions, and though he had since been pardoned and returned to Istanbul, last year the Governor Pasha, busy preparing for the celebrations to mark the twenty-fifth anniversary of the Sultan's accession to the throne, had ruled that the band should continue its activities under the supervision of the teacher Andreas, who taught music at the Greek High School.

So it was that as Princess Pakize and her husband stepped onto the island of Mingheria, they were greeted first by the notes of the "Mecidiye March," which had been composed in honor of the Sultan's father, and then by the "Hamidiye March," created to mark the reign of Abdul Hamid himself. The fear of disease had been weighing on people's spirits, but the music proved to be a tonic. The idlers and busybodies and porters who had come down to the docks to see the arriving ship, the coachmen, shopkeepers, merchants, and telegraph operators who were watching the ceremony from afar, and the people leaning out of their windows and balconies, all felt momentarily heartened. In the gardens and terraces of the hotels that lined the port and the hill above it, European visitors, foreign adventurers, and wealthy islanders looked up from their cups of tea and wondered what this music was supposed to be. Then a third march began to play. This jolly melody was the "Naval March," composed at a young age by music and piano prodigy His Highness Prince Burhanettin, who was Abdul Hamid's favorite among his eight sons, and whom the Sultan always wanted by his side.

After many calm and peaceful decades, both the province of Mingheria and its capital, Arkaz, had been beleaguered over the past two years by a series of violent clashes, murders, and various misfortunes, and the latest rumors of plague had only served to heighten the general sense of malaise. When he looked at the crowds of Christians and Muslims who had come out to hear the marches and saw the tender, earnest expressions on their faces, Governor Sami Pasha's conclusion was an optimistic one: people could see that political tensions on the island were being manipulated to escalate a war between Christians and Muslims, as had been the case in some of the Ottoman Empire's other Mediterranean islands, but they had no desire for such a conflict and hoped that the Governor and the institutions of the state might step in to bring the situation on the island back under control.

Governor Sami Pasha received Doctor and Prince Consort Nuri at the dock and introduced himself. He had been unsure how to address the former sultan's daughter without arousing her uncle Abdul Hamid's suspicions, so he had decided it would be best to observe how her husband behaved, and adjust accordingly.

Marrying an Ottoman princess had quickly taught Doctor Nuri how to manage this kind of institutional pageantry and the torrents of flattery and sycophancy that came with it. As they stepped off the rowing boat swaying gently in the water, he was not too surprised to hear marches being played, despite there being no such tradition, and neither did he dwell for too long on the Governor Pasha's prolonged congratulations on his marriage. A crowd had soon gathered around them, speaking Greek, French, Turkish, Arabic, and Mingherian. The Governor had readied for their use the armored landau he had previously set aside for Bonkowski Pasha and his assistant and had even assigned them a newly assembled troop of experienced bodyguards. These menacing, mustachioed guards were a rather conspicuous presence, and as the landau left the port and rode up the Pier Road, its passengers saw hat- and fez-clad bystanders peering curiously as they passed by. It was a known and self-evident fact that in the provincial territories of the Ottoman Empire, and with the sole exception of Smyrna, Thessaloniki, and Beirut, any person seen walking around a given city—no matter how developed it may be—with a hat and wearing a shirt and tie was bound to be a Christian. This truth, which Doctor Nuri had learned through experience, his wife had grasped just then in a moment of sudden intuition. They both also realized that on this island Muslims were to be found not on the boulevards or in and around the hotels but somewhere else, somewhere in the background. Already Doctor Nuri could picture the city wrestling with disease, a stage for scenes of cataclysmic devastation, but for the time being, these visions would remain a secret he carried inside.

Through the window of the armored landau husband and wife surveyed the European-style buildings and the hotels, diners, travel agencies, and department stores along Istanbul Street. The shops on the eastern side of the street included a draper, a clothier, a shoemaker, a haberdasher, a bookshop (the Medit, the only bookseller in Mingheria, stocking books in Greek, French, and Turkish), and stores selling tableware, furniture, and textiles imported from Thessaloniki and Smyrna. To protect their windows from the glare of the sun, shopkeepers had rolled out their striped awnings as far as they would go. The city's gardens, lush with palm, pine, lemon, and linden trees, surprised the visitors with their size and with their panoply of plants and flowers. The fragrant scent of blue, pink, and purple roses was intoxicating. They could feel the lure of the narrow stepped lanes that twisted their way uphill between rocks and boulders, or down to the creek and into the city's hiddenmost corners; they were charmed by the odd mosque with a solitary minaret, by the occasional little church, by ivy-wrapped stone houses with wooden oriels, Venetian-era buildings with Gothic windows, and redbrick arches from the Byzantine period. The sight of sleepy old men and contented cats sitting in doorways and standing at windows watching life go by filled Princess Pakize and her husband with the sensation that this was a realm infinitely more familiar than what they had pictured China to be like. But there was also a fairy-tale quality to the world around them, kindled by the stillness on the streets, the smallness of everything they saw, and their dread of the plague.

The Governor Pasha had hastily arranged for the guest wing of the State Hall to be readied for the visitors. He showed the newlyweds in, informing them that he had also prepared another residence elsewhere should this one not be to their liking. But the proximity of this place to the offices of the Governor and of the state gave them a sense of comfort.

Built in 1894 with funds personally allocated and released by Abdul Hamid, and at a time when the Sultan was engaged in the bloody suppression of guerrilla attacks and uprisings among the Empire's Armenian populations, the State Hall of Mingheria was an impressive two-story building with columns, arches, bay windows, and balconies. All who strolled past it—be they wealthy, hat-clad Greek gentlemen out shopping in the city center, unemployed idlers who'd taken to loitering on Hamidiye Avenue and around the docks after the Mingherian marble quarries had shut down for good, or villagers who'd come to Arkaz—were equally awed by its neoclassical grandeur. As they looked upon its graceful, heavily embroidered and ornamented façade, at the vast balcony perfectly placed to address the crowds below, and at the white steps and columns at its entrance, they would also come away with a sense that the crumbling Ottoman Empire was still a force to be reckoned with, and an appreciation of its sincere attempts to appear at once Muslim and modern. Governor Sami Pasha, whose own residence and offices were housed in another wing of this same building, was glad to see the former sultan's daughter and her husband settled in its guest quarters.

Formed of two adjoining rooms, and smelling pleasantly—as Princess Pakize immediately noticed—of "rosewater soap and wood," the guest residence also contained a writing desk overlooking the Castle, the port, and the beautiful vistas and gardens of the city, which reminded the Princess of the promise she had made to her older sister Hatice after the many joyful and momentous events that had occurred during her last days in Istanbul, and the envelopes, the elegant letter paper, and the tasteful silver writing set that Hatice had given her so that she could keep that promise. "My darling Pakize, you are bound for China, for faraway lands and fairy-tale realms; who knows what wonders you will find there! Promise me you will write to me about everything you see and hear?" Hatice had said to her beloved sister, presenting her with the writing set while they said their farewells. "You will see that I have left you two reams of paper so that you can write to your heart's content. And you must make sure to write to your Hatice every day!" So Princess Pakize had promised to write to her cherished sister about everything she saw, heard, and felt during her travels. Then they had embraced each other, and wept.

CHAPTER 11

Meanwhile, in a storeroom two floors below the window behind the writing desk at which the Princess now sat composing her letters, Bonkowski Pasha's corpse was laid out beneath a mound of ice from the kitchens. Municipal officers had first tried to take the body to Theodoropoulos Hospital, but the hospital had turned out to be full of plague patients, and so, under new orders from the Governor, they had brought the murdered Chief Inspector's corpse back to the State Hall for safekeeping. The Governor was planning a grand funeral to intimidate those responsible for the murder and to appease the island's dissident factions, Sultan Abdul Hamid, and the palace bureaucrats.

The Governor had gone to Hrisopolitissa Square as soon as he had heard about the killing, and the sight of Bonkowski Pasha's bloodied and butchered corpse and disfigured face had so affected him that he had begun arresting people the moment he'd returned to the State Hall. In the two days that had passed until the Doctor and Prince Consort's arrival, the Governor Pasha had arrested nearly twenty suspects from three different local factions.

Before the Quarantine Committee was due to convene, and at the Sultan's orders, the Governor called a meeting in his office to confer on these matters with Chief Scrutineer Mazhar Effendi and Prince Consort Nuri.

"I am of the opinion that there is a conspiracy behind this murder," the Governor began, "and it will not be possible to quell this outbreak until we have also found out the truth about Bonkowski Pasha's death and discovered and apprehended those responsible for ordering and carrying out the killing. His Serene Highness shares this view, which is why he has called upon you to work on both fronts. Indeed the consuls here would make a fool of you if you were to disregard the political element altogether."

"Half our job at the Quarantine Authority in the Hejaz was political."

"Then we understand each other," said the Governor. "Even that which may appear at first to have nothing at all to do with politics may reveal beneath the surface all manner of plots and nefarious intentions. Allow me to digress, if you will, on a rather delicate matter which happened to land on my desk the very day that I came to this island and took this office five years ago. In those days every team of oarsmen and porters serving the ships that approach Mingheria operated under the supervision of a specific foreign shipping company. The Lloyd Company, for example, would work only with the foreman Aleko (known for his handlebar mustache); the Pantaleon Company favored Kozma Effendi's rowers and porters; and both companies only ever assigned jobs to these men. The Thomas Cook Company, among the biggest of all, is represented here by one of the island's famous Greek families, the Theodoropouloses. They would only work with boatman Stefan Effendi and his team.

"As well as acting as agents for these travel and shipping companies, each of these wealthy Greeks also served as vice-consul for several powerful foreign states. The Messageries Maritimes representative, a Cypriot Greek named Andon Hampuri, was also the consul for France and remains so to this day. The agent for the Lloyd ferries, a Cretian Greek named Monsieur Frangouli, also acts as consul for the Austro-Hungarian Empire and Germany; and the representative for Fraissinet ferries is Monsieur Takela, the vice-consul for Italy. Naturally they all insist on being addressed by the loftier title of Consul, and back then they would shun the foreman of the Muslim boat crews, Seyit, whom they deemed ignorant and vulgar, and find all kinds of excuses to avoid giving him and his men any jobs. The task of unloading those ships that came to port, whether they sailed under the Ottoman flag or otherwise, should have been shared equally among all boatmen and porters. But the Muslim boatmen were given fewer jobs than the others and found it so difficult to get by that they would sometimes be forced to sell their boats. When I intervened in defense of the Muslim porters, the consuls started sending letters to His Serene Highness and to the palace to try and discredit me. 'When the state begins to make distinctions between its subjects based on religion, and to favor one religion over another, that is when the Empire falls apart,' they wrote in their newspapers. Would you agree with that statement?"

"Perhaps a little, Your Excellency . . . It is all a matter of degrees, of course."

"But they knowingly and deliberately favor the Christians. Is it not significant that the Sultan took no notice of any reports against my conduct and kept me as governor here when so many other governors are continually being transferred between provinces? The Sultan must have deemed my refusal to bow to the consuls' pressure to be entirely appropriate, in the circumstances. The murder of the chemist pasha is manifestly a response to this, and to the unfortunate event known as the Pilgrim Ship Affair.

"It is my belief that Sheikh Hamdullah's stepbrother Ramiz and his henchman Memo the Albanian, whom he uses to raid the island's Greek villages, are behind this murder. These people will do anything to paint Christian doctors as the enemy and provoke conflict between Christians and Muslims. Nor does it ever occur to them that such conflict might make the situation for Muslims on this island worse. We will find out soon enough whose idea this murder was, whom they employed to do it, and quite what was going through their witless heads. Mazhar Effendi will have them all talking in no time, down there in the dungeons, and I am sure he will get them to incriminate others too."

"It seems you have already made your mind up on who the culprits are, Your Excellency!"

"His Serene Highness expects immediate results. It is his belief that if we do not promptly punish the planners and perpetrators of this heinous act, the state will be made to look impotent, and our quarantine measures will fail."

"It is imperative that those who are apprehended and charged should actually be guilty of having committed the murder, or at any rate planned it!"

"I can deduce through logic alone that the Greek nationalists could have had nothing to do with this murder!" said the Governor. "They would not wish to see the island's Greek population die of the plague, which means they would have wanted Bonkowski Pasha to succeed in his efforts to contain the epidemic, and it would never have crossed their minds to kill him. You are a brilliant young doctor who has won the confidence of the Sultan. I shall speak plainly, for the good of our country: first His Highness the Sultan sent a Christian chemist. Now he has been murdered. This is a stain upon my conscience. Now they have sent a Muslim doctor. I shall be taking especial care over your safety and introduce all necessary precautions. But you must heed what I say."

"You have my ear, Your Excellency."

"It is not just the consuls we must be wary of! Should any journalist, Greek or Muslim, find some excuse to approach you—at the funeral tomorrow, say—you must categorically refuse to give any interviews. Every Greek newspaper here, without exception, takes its orders from the Greek consul anyway. Greece's ultimate objective is to call upon foreign powers at the first sign of unrest and with their help take this island as their own or at least tear it away from Ottoman rule, just as they did with Crete. They will print fabrications too. If I should say 'They are peddling lies and publishing libel' and dare to demand an explanation, their consuls will run to the Telegraph Office and send off a complaint to their ambassadors in Istanbul, who will in turn relay these complaints to the Sublime Porte and to the palace. The Sublime Porte and the palace will hold them off for a little while, then send me an encrypted message along the lines of 'Set the Greek journalist free.' So even if I do close a newspaper down, it is never too long before it starts publishing again, perhaps under a different guise, but with the same staff and using the same printing press, and nothing for me to do but look the other way.

"You should know that we are not so strict here as in Thessaloniki or Smyrna or Istanbul. I am on friendly terms with these journalists, and if we run into each other on the street after they are released, I might jokingly wish them a 'speedy recovery.' Of course we have spies in all of the newspapers, including the ones that publish in Turkish. Nevertheless, if the subject should arise and you should hear some consul or other claim that Orthodox Christians are in the majority here, do please demur! The Christian and Muslim populations on our island are nearly equal in size. Indeed, it is for this very reason that your wife's late grandfather Sultan Abdulmejid decreed, shortly after the Tanzimat Edict was issued, that our island of Mingheria should go from being merely a humble district of the province of the Archipelago to a separate province of its own. While the Muslim population on every other island is outnumbered ten to one, here the numbers are almost equal. The reason for this is that our forefathers would often load the Empire's rebellious tribes and insubordinate sectarians onto ships and send them here, banishing them to the valleys and the mountains in the north. This practice of forced settlement, which persisted for over two centuries, and was frequently and periodically revived with new communities, has made its mark on our island. But with the British and the French demanding an end to this Ottoman policy of forced resettlement, Sultan Abdulmejid surprised them all in 1852 with a decree that suddenly changed the island's status. The island's population is pleased, of course, that their little outpost is now officially a province. There are slightly more Orthodox Christians than there are Muslims, but this is immaterial, for the Orthodox and Catholic communities here are native to Mingheria and spoke Mingherian until the Byzantine conquest. Many still do. It is our island's good fortune that most of its people speak Mingherian at home and out on the streets, and that they are—in the words of the archaeologist Selim Sahir Bey who once came here to extract statues from a cave—direct descendants of the ancient tribe of Mingherians who broke away thousands of years ago from their original homelands north of the modern-day Aral Sea and came to settle here. I am convinced that the instinct to turn to Greece is weak among this Orthodox community, which speaks a different language anyway. I am more concerned about those families who have clung to their Greek and Balkan identities since the Byzantine era and speak Greek at home, as well as this new generation of modern Greeks who have recently come to the island from Athens. These two groups are aligned in their views now. There are also gangs of agitators from Crete and even Greece itself who have been emboldened over the past few months by their success in Crete. They have infiltrated the Greek villages in the north of the island and have been stirring trouble there, demanding that taxes be paid to them rather than to the Sultan's tax collectors. I shall point them out to you all one by one at the funeral tomorrow."

"Your Excellency, is it true that you have sent Bonkowski Pasha's equally esteemed assistant, Doctor Ilias, to the dungeons too?"

"We have arrested both Doctor Ilias and Pharmacist Nikiforos Bey!" said the Governor. "I am thoroughly convinced of their innocence. But

Bonkowski Pasha had a long conversation with the pharmacist the day before his death. That alone is reason enough to arrest him."

"If you alienate the Greeks, we will have trouble even just announcing the quarantine."

"Doctor Ilias was with other witnesses when Bonkowski Pasha disappeared from the Post Office. He cannot be guilty. Yet he has had such a fright that if I were to release him now he would flee to Istanbul immediately. But he is a key witness. If they could get their hands on him, they would kill him too to stop him from testifying. Already they have been threatening him to try to stop him from talking."

"And who is doing that?"

The Governor Pasha exchanged a meaningful look with the Chief Scrutineer. Then he told the Doctor and Prince Consort that because the consuls had been dragging their feet, the Quarantine Committee would not be able to meet until the next day. "Of course Ottoman citizens cannot act as consuls for other nations, so really they are all *vice*-consuls—though they don't like it when I call them that. In truth they are a meddlesome, impertinent gaggle of ignorant shopkeepers who are making a fuss of this outbreak nonsense purely to spite me."

The unfinished and still mostly unfurnished Hamidiye Hospital, whose completion had been planned to coincide with last year's celebrations for the twenty-fifth anniversary of the Sultan's accession to the throne, had now been declared open by order of the Governor. He also noted in passing, as if it were a matter of little import, that Pharmacist Nikiforos and Doctor Ilias would be released in the morning. The Doctor and Prince Consort would then be able to take Doctor Ilias with him on patient visits if he wished.

CHAPTER 12

Princess Pakize was among the first to resign herself to the fact that the epidemic might make it dangerous to go outside. Since she never left the State Hall anyway, the Princess asked her bodyguard, Major Kâmil, to make sure he was always by her husband's side. As we account for the Major's ascent to the Hegelian "stage of history" on the island of Mingheria, we will sometimes repeat and sometimes correct his story as it is told in Mingherian schoolbooks.

The Major was born in 1870, and his rank was sadly lower than what his age would have warranted. He had attended the city's military middle school, whose pale pink roof tiles could be seen from the port. Having graduated third in his class of fifty-four, he had been admitted to the military academy in Smyrna. One summer he had come home to discover that his father had died. (As always the first thing he did when he arrived on the island now was to pay a visit to his father's grave.) On another visit two years later, he had discovered that his mother had married again, and he had found her new husband, the fat and shallow Hazım Bey, so irksome that he had spent the next two summers in Istanbul and not returned until Hazım Bey's death, whereupon his mother had made him swear that he would henceforth come back home every year. Until the war with Greece, for which he had received a medal four years ago, he had not done anything in particular to distinguish himself in the army. His mother had been expecting him at the start of summer as usual, so when she saw him suddenly walk across the garden and in through the kitchen door, she was startled at first, then noticed the medal on his chest and started crying.

When he was not at the State Hall or accompanying the Doctor and Prince Consort, Major Kâmil spent most of his time at home with his mother or roaming the streets of his childhood. On his first day back in the city, his mother filled him in on the past year's gossip and updated him on who was to be married off to whom, and why. As she told him these stories, every now and then she would ask her son whether he had made his mind up to get married too.

"I have made my mind up," the Major admitted eventually. "The question is, are there any suitable girls?"

"There is one!" she replied. "But of course she will need to meet you and see whether she likes you too."

"Of course! Who is she?"

"Oh darling, how lonely you must be!" said Satiye Hanım, sensing his eagerness from his questions and kissing his cheek as she sat down next to him.

Had someone asked the Major for his views on arranged marriage ten years ago, he would have declared himself firmly against the idea. Like many of his officer friends, he had graduated from the Harbiye academy an idealist and was opposed to women covering their heads and faces excessively (in the Arab way). He was repulsed by landowning hajjis with four wives and rich old men who took young women for brides. In common with many young army officers, he felt that the explanation for how rapidly the Ottoman Empire was falling behind the West after centuries of military dominance was to be found in its harmful and regressive traditions. This relatively European way of thinking was no doubt influenced by his Mingherian, Mediterranean background, and by his familiarity with Orthodox Christian culture. At the Harbiye academy the Major had also seen the declarations that revolutionary student groups had issued against the Sultan. He had read in one night the famous biography of Napoleon everyone else was reading, and he had understood—and at times sincerely agreed with—what the heroes of the French Revolution had meant when they had called for *Liberté, égalité, fraternité.*

But after so many drunken, solitary nights spent in whichever backwater town his latest posting was, full of despair and blazing with a helpless, agonizing longing to make love, he had set some of these lofty ideals aside. Like many other officers, he too had not yet turned twenty-five before he'd started to take notice when people told him, "There is a widow who would be just right for you, very respectable."

It had been on the back of one such suggestion that, at the age of twenty-three, he had married without his mother's knowledge an Arab widow in Mosul who spoke broken Turkish and was twelve years older than him. This was one of those marriages army officers and civil servants sometimes entered into knowing that all they had to do when they left the city was to say "I divorce you" thrice, and they could forget the arrangement had ever existed. The older, experienced woman the Major had married knew this too. Consequently he had not felt too guilty divorcing her when the news came that he was to be transferred to Istanbul, though in the years that followed, he had found himself pining for Aysha's big eyes, her tender, inquisitive gaze, and the pleasure of holding her lithe and vigorous form in his arms.

In those years, any lonely, unmarried civil servant or army officer transferred to a provincial town or sent to join a new garrison would make sure to learn where the available women lived, avoid potential sources of syphilis and gonorrhea, and quickly befriend the local doctors. Army officers, local government officials, and civil servants who had been posted to the provinces and whose only wish was to return to Istanbul as swiftly as possible could always immediately identify one another. The Ottoman bureaucracy was like an autonomous nation of itinerant clerks, and marriage was one remedy for that universe of solitude. Discussions of marriage aside, the Major's sense of loneliness was also sharpened with every demoralizing instance of wrongdoing, negligence, and depravity he witnessed (and there were many) across the far-flung possessions of the Ottoman Empire. His job and that of his peers was to man the ship of state, but the ship was sinking, and it was almost impossible to stop it from doing so. Of the Empire's countless subjects, people like the Major were destined to suffer the most when the vessel finally succumbed to the waves. So it was that many government and army officers couldn't even imagine the end of the Ottoman Empire, just as they couldn't bring themselves to look at the map of its former territories.

One solution was for soldiers to cultivate some source of private joy, but the Major had met very few army officers who had managed to find happiness in marriage while having to dash east to west, continent to continent, and war to war. Yet he frequently found himself yearning for someone he could share his life with (even if they weren't happy together) and make love to, and with whom he could talk openly and companionably about anything at all, just as his mother and father used to do.

For a long time mother and son sat side by side on the couch saying nothing at all. The crows flew noisily on and off the trees in the garden. (They had done so ever since Major Kâmil was a child.) When he said again that he was serious about marriage, the Major's mother explained that the girl she had been thinking of introducing him to was Zeynep, daughter of the prison guard who had died five days previously.

Satiye Hanım tended to describe any eligible young woman as "very pretty," so at first the Major did not take too seriously his mother's disquisitions on the merits of this latest among her finds. But every time he came home, his mother greeted him with a new story about Zeynep, and soon he began to feel his interest grow.

He would listen to his mother's stories, then go back to reading and daydreaming over an old book he had returned to time and time again during his summers on the island, Mizancı Murat's *The French Revolution and Liberty*, a volume that had been published in Turkish in Geneva and smuggled from there to Istanbul. He knew that to be caught with such a book in his possession could wreck his whole life, so he never left the island with it, nor did he ever share the ideas it contained with anybody else.

CHAPTER 13

As he sat aboard the Governor Pasha's armored landau on its way through the city's narrow streets toward the offices of the Mingherian Quarantine Authority, Doctor Nuri felt as if he were experiencing a perfectly ordinary day at the peripheries of the Empire, rather than the beginnings of an outbreak of plague. He heard birds chirruping over the low walls of the gardens that lined the downhill slope to the sea, caught the fragrance of bay leaves and aniseed in the air, and stared in amazement at the enormous shadows cast by trees so large he had never seen the like in any other Ottoman city.

Doctor Nuri had been working in the Ottoman Quarantine Authority for more than ten years. He had been dispatched to fight epidemics in countless provinces, towns, and small villages, often situated at several weeks' traveling distance from one another. In these outer states of the Empire, it was the local Quarantine Authority's responsibility to identify any outbreaks and alert Istanbul. But in practice this pressing and vital duty was likelier to be performed not by quarantine officers but by local Greek doctors, working in their own private practices but also receiving patients in small village hospitals, clinics, and pharmacies. After all, the officers of the local quarantine establishments were employees of the imperial government and knew the heavy burden of responsibility that came with sending Istanbul any kind of infelicitous news, so they usually preferred not to rush matters.

But Doctor Nikos, who ran the Mingherian Quarantine Authority and reported to the Governor's Office and the central quarantine office in Istanbul, possessed the sense of urgency and the determination others in his position lacked, and had been the first to warn of the outbreak on the island. Ignoring the Governor's initial indifference, Doctor

Nikos had also sent a series of insistent telegrams to Istanbul which had resulted in Bonkowski Pasha being posted to Mingheria. The Governor Pasha had found out about these telegrams and decided that the Quarantine Master—who happened to be a Cretian Greek, and was therefore, in the Governor's view, not to be trusted—was secretly a Greek nationalist who had been purposely overstating the gravity of the island's outbreaks of summer diarrhea as evidence of Ottoman incompetence.

When the elderly Doctor Nikos, with his goatee and slightly hunched back, came to greet him at the door of the landau, Doctor Nuri recognized him straightaway: "Perhaps you will recall we met nine years ago when all the soldiers in the garrison at Sinope got head lice," he said, smiling. "You also attended to the cholera outbreak in Üsküdar seven years ago . . ."

The Quarantine Master returned the Doctor and Prince Consort's greeting with an elaborate flourish. They went inside and sat for a time inside a white room with a domed ceiling. "Before coming here I worked as a doctor and served as head of quarantine operations in Thessaloniki and Crete. I was not born in Mingheria, and I do not speak Mingherian; try as I might, I have not been able to learn it. But I must say I am rather fond of this place," said Doctor Nikos.

The Public Health Office of Mingheria was a small four-hundred-year-old Gothic stone building dating from the Venetian era. It had originally been built as an extension to the Venetian Doge's palace. In the seventeenth and eighteenth centuries, during the early Ottoman era, it had also served as a rudimentary military hospital.

"How did you go about trying to learn Mingherian?"

"I couldn't really do much, in truth . . . I was never able to find a teacher. The Department of Scrutinia will put anyone who shows an interest in this language under surveillance and considers such an interest to be a sign of nationalist tendencies . . . Mingherian is an ancient but still primitive language, and a difficult one too."

There followed a spell of silence. Doctor Nuri was struck by the neatness and cleanliness of the files and cupboards around him. He remarked that it was the tidiest quarantine office he had ever seen.

In response the Quarantine Master took him to the historic mansion's backyard to show him the little botanic garden that his predecessor, a doctor from Adrianople, had set up there to pass the time.

Doctor Nikos smiled as he reminisced of those happy, carefree days before the disease when he and the groundskeeper would use a jug with a beak-shaped lip to water the garden's potted dwarf palms, date palms, and tamarind trees, and its hyacinth, mimosa, and lily blossoms. Then he brought out some carefully arranged cardboard folders. With the rigor of a true Ottoman bureaucrat, and partly because there had not been much else to do, Doctor Nikos had spent the past two years sorting and classifying by subject matter all the letters and telegrams that had been sent from Mingheria to Istanbul. This evidence of meticulousness and perseverance impressed Doctor Nuri, who had seen the wretched and impecunious state of so many provincial public health departments across the Empire, and soon he found himself reading—as if he were casually skimming the verses of an epic romance—a series of reports detailing in French all the suspicious deaths that had occurred in Arkaz and in the other towns and villages of Mingheria over the past thirty years, any deaths whose nature and cause could not be determined, cases of epidemics among livestock, and the general state of public health in the province.

Quarantine laws had been introduced to the Ottoman Empire seventy years ago, during the first great epidemic of cholera that had devastated Istanbul in 1831. The empire's Muslim population had resisted the new measures, particularly where they concerned the examination of female patients and the sanitization of corpses with lime before burial, and this had led to the spread of many unfounded rumors, as well as sparking altercations and unrest. In 1838, the westernizing sultan Mahmud II arranged for the Shaykh al-Islam (the Empire's highest religious authority) to issue a fatwa declaring that quarantine was compatible with Islamic precepts, which was then published in the official state gazette, the *Takvim-i Vakayi*, along with an article describing the benefits of the precautions being taken against the disease, and the same sultan brought in doctors from Europe too. He also worked with the Western nations' ambassadors in Istanbul to institute a special committee which would advise on the reforms he was implementing. This committee, based in Istanbul and composed primarily of bureaucrats and Christian doctors, became the Ottoman Empire's first Quarantine Council, or in other words its first Ministry of Public Health. It oversaw the creation of local quarantine departments across every province of the Empire, particularly in its ports, and in the seventy years since, a whole quarantine bureaucracy had come into existence.

Doctor Nuri was experienced enough to recognize that the venerable Doctor Nikos was the kind of servant this bureaucracy could only be proud of. He went straight to the point: "Who do you think is behind the assassination?"

"Bonkowski Pasha was killed by someone who knew the story of Doctor Jean-Pierre," the Quarantine Master replied guardedly. It was clear that he had thought about the matter and had prepared for this question. "Whoever did it, they wanted people to think, 'He must have been murdered by those benighted Muslims who oppose quarantine.'"

Every doctor involved with the Ottoman Quarantine Authority, whether Christian, Jewish, or Muslim, knew the woeful story of Doctor Jean-Pierre. The story, now half a century old, had become something of a cautionary tale warning Christian and Jewish quarantine officers and doctors of what not to do in a Muslim neighborhood during an epidemic. In 1842, following an outbreak of plague in Amasya, the young sultan Abdulmejid had sent to that small backwater town a famous doctor from Paris who could implement the modern quarantine methods that Abdulmejid's father, Sultan Mahmud II, had brought in from Europe. Doctor Jean-Pierre was a youthful Frenchman who had avidly read his way through Voltaire and Diderot and was somewhat skeptical of religion. Undeterred by their snickers and taunting jibes, he would tell the Muslim clerks accompanying him that if men were to set their prejudices aside and rely on reason alone, they would soon discover that all humans were equal and governed by the same fundamental emotions and beliefs. He was disheartened to hear people shouting "We want a Muslim doctor!" when all the Governor and his municipal officers were trying to do was to implement quarantine measures. But he did not give up. He insisted on personally examining female patients too, preaching and pontificating as he did so that "There is no such thing as Christian or Muslim when it comes to science and medicine!"

By then Amasya's Christian population and its wealthier citizens had already fled the city; shops and bakeries had shut down; and the starving, furious Muslims left behind refused to let the doctor into their homes or show him their ailing relatives. As the plague continued to spread, Doctor Jean-Pierre reluctantly began to call upon soldiers to knock people's doors down by force, separate children from their mothers, post guards outside homes suspected of infection and isolate the families therein, carelessly pour lime over the bodies of the dead, and have anybody who did not adhere to the regulations immediately arrested. He ignored the Muslim population's growing protests, noting only that he was acting under the orders and express authorization of Sultan Abdulmejid. In the end, as he was walking through an outer neighborhood of Amasya one rainy evening, he suddenly disappeared, as if he had "vanished off the face of the earth."

All quarantine doctors knew that Doctor Jean-Pierre had been killed that night, but still they would give one another bitter, rueful smiles every time they told his story, as if there were still a chance that this idealistic quarantine expert might someday resurface.

"These days, no Christian quarantine doctor in Ottoman lands would dare visit patients in a Muslim neighborhood without a revolver in his belt," said the Quarantine Master.

"Are there any Muslim doctors on the island?" asked the Doctor and Prince Consort.

"There used to be two. One of them returned to Istanbul two years ago when he became convinced that the Hamidiye Hospital would never be finished. Had they found him a wife here, he would have stayed. The other one, Ferit Bey, must be at the Hamidiye Hospital now."

Like many of the well-intentioned, European-inspired institutions that the Ottoman Empire had set up over the past century to address any given issue, only to find that they seemed incapable of solving anything at all, the Quarantine Authority too had soon itself become part of the problem. Its individual branches in the Empire's provinces were responsible for hiring the required clerks, guards, and janitors, but soon these state employees and even the local quarantine doctors would find that their salaries were not being paid in a timely fashion, and in turn the doctors would begin to bend the rules to make ends meet, seeing patients privately in pharmacies and apothecaries, and holding all kinds of other jobs too.

In the year 1901, there were 273 qualified civilian doctors in the Ottoman Empire, and most of these were of Greek Orthodox background. This meant that particularly in the predominantly Muslim provinces there never were enough doctors, and the few that were present were disinclined to battle with epidemics—the kind of task which called for unusual courage, self-sacrifice, and even a dose of heroism. As for experienced Muslim doctors who might be able to enter impoverished neighborhoods and convince pious Muslims suspicious of quarantine measures to let the bodies of their dead be disinfected and allow their wives and daughters to be examined, those were nearly impossible to find. Anyone who joined the Empire's sixty-five-year-old quarantine establishment would quickly realize that their first and most important duty to the Sultan and the Ministry of Foreign Affairs was not so much to stop outbreaks of cholera, as to stop the news of those outbreaks from spreading. It was precisely because of this geopolitical dimension that the Quarantine Authority had initially reported directly to the Ministry of Foreign Affairs.

"There have been three major outbreaks of cholera in Mingheria!" said the Quarantine Master as if to change the subject: "One in 1838, one in 1867, and a smaller one in the summer of 1886. As our island has fallen increasingly farther from the most common trade routes, the last decade's pandemics have largely passed us by, but this has also caused Istanbul to forget us. Despite all the letters we send, the Department of Public Health will not replenish our depleted supplies. Then one day they'll send a telegram announcing the imminent arrival of 'the bright young Muslim doctor so-and-so,' and we will run gaily down to the docks to greet him, only to discover the passenger we were expecting is not going to step off the Messageries ferry after all; the doctor assigned to our island has either resigned and stayed in Istanbul or leaned on his contacts at the palace and his friends at the court to have his transfer revoked at the last minute."

"You are right," said Doctor Nuri. "But as you can see, the Sultan has finally sent your island its Muslim doctor, and here I am now, off the ship and at your service."

"You may find this hard to believe, but we do not even have enough funds to buy milk of lime," said Doctor Nikos. "I have to beg the Governor Pasha to intercede with the Commander of the military garrison for some of their supplies, or we keep our quarantine tax high and try to source the equipment and medication we need *ourselves,* from our own budget."

In accordance with international law, local quarantine stations had the right to collect payment from incoming ships and passengers in exchange for their services. The logic of quarantine—a word derived from the Italian term for "forty days"—was to isolate the sick to prevent illnesses from spreading to others. Over the centuries, and after many instructive epidemics around the Mediterranean and across Europe, those forty days had been reduced first to two weeks and later to even-shorter spans of time depending on the type and location of the epidemic. Quarantine practices had continued to evolve over the past forty years in the wake of French doctor Louis Pasteur's discoveries on germs. The methods used to distinguish between clean and contaminated ports were constantly changing, as were regulations for the transport of goods and passengers, the criteria for determining which ships should be marked with the yellow flag indicating they were infected, the number of days patients had to spend in isolation, and the level at which quarantine fees and levies should be set.

Yet despite all these exhaustive prescriptions, a quarantine doctor examining a ship could also exercise a degree of autonomy in his decisions. Climbing with his entourage of soldiers aboard a Lloyd passenger ship bearing the flag of the German Empire, someone like Doctor Nikos might therefore decide, upon concluding his inspection, to turn a blind eye to a feverish passenger in exchange for a bribe, and thus effectively rescue a merchant from bankruptcy by allowing the ship to reach Istanbul five or six days earlier than it would have otherwise done; conversely, he might report on the basis of the slightest trace of suspicion that all of the passengers and even the cargo on an incoming ship were infected with disease, and thereby cause many a shopkeeper to lose their livelihoods overnight.

But a quarantine doctor could also ensure, with just one word, that a pilgrim who had saved up for years, sold his home, and embarked on the arduous two-month journey of hajj ended up being separated from his fellow travelers, taken off the ship, confined in an isolation camp, and deprived of his pilgrimage—his protests, threats, tears, and paroxysms of rage falling on deaf ears. Doctor Nuri had also seen impoverished quarantine doctors in distant coastal villages wield their power as a way of avenging their miserable lives, cowing and controlling the wealthier locals, and perhaps even punishing tradesmen whose businesses were doing too well. This same power was also what enabled many quarantine doctors to subsist.

The Doctor and Prince Consort was curious to know when Quarantine Master Nikos had last been paid, but rather than ask the question, he adopted instead that patronizing air that provincial governors often deployed when faced with civil servants and doctors complaining about the shortages they had to face and the insolvency of state institutions.

"In the Hejaz, when we ran out of lime to disinfect toilets and cesspits, we would make do with coal dust instead."

"Is that an appropriate method for our modern age?" said Doctor Nikos. "I would rather use milk of lime, diluted twenty or thirty parts to one instead of ten, if need be."

"What do you have that might serve as disinfectant solution?"

"Mingherians call blue vitriol 'Cyprus vitriol.' We do indeed have some copper sulfate in stock—I have been saving it up. Pharmacist Nikiforos will have some too. But it will not be enough to cope with an epidemic. We have a little bit of phenol and calomel, what they call white sublimate in Istanbul. Among Muslims here the understanding of microbes and epidemics goes no further than washing their coins with vinegar. The most they will tolerate is fumigation by sulfur and saltpeter. In the Çite and Bayırlar neighborhoods they sometimes light those useless fumigation sticks and rub them over their faces as if they were amulets blessed by His Holiness the Sheikh. We are going to require a great deal of disinfectant solution."

"The men who will have to spray this all over the city and the doctors who will have to enter Muslim neighborhoods are going to have a difficult task on their hands after Bonkowski Pasha's assassination," said the Doctor and Prince Consort, eager to return to the most pressing subject of all.

"I attended some of Bonkowski Bey's lectures on organic and inorganic chemistry at the Imperial School of Medicine. He was appointed Chief Inspector of Public Health and Sanitation while I was serving in Lebanon, and his reputation as a scholar grew and grew. To think that such a man should have been butchered in this manner! When you are out visiting patients, do not assume it will be enough to announce 'I am a Muslim'; make sure you take a bodyguard with you, too—like that major of yours."

"Don't worry, I will be careful. But if the aim is to 'sabotage' quarantine efforts," said the Prince Consort, using that word loaned from the French, "then you too must be careful. May I ask who this malicious actor is whom we must all be wary of?"

"The Governor Pasha did the right thing in locking up Sheikh Hamdullah's stepbrother Ramiz. Of all the island's sect leaders, Sheikh Hamdullah is the one the Governor Pasha is most wary of. So Ramiz has taken advantage. I think whoever killed poor Bonkowski Pasha is someone who knew Ramiz would end up being blamed for it."

"Yet there is an element of chance in this matter. You must have heard how everyone saw Bonkowski Pasha slip out of the Post Office of his own free will. Neither Ramiz nor anyone else could have predicted that."

"Perhaps it is so, but then someone who happened to see him afterward might have thought that if they killed him there and then, the Muslims would be blamed for it anyway. For it is true that there are Greek doctors on our island who might, on occasion, not even deign to speak in Turkish to their Muslim patients."

"The Muslim community may be right to complain about Christian doctors, particularly the more stern, tactless, and condescending among them," Doctor Nuri prudently noted. "But earlier you mentioned that Muslims can sometimes resist quarantine measures out of ignorance alone."

"They can and they do. But though they complain, they also fear the plague. They want somebody they can trust to come to them with advice on how they can protect themselves from infection. There is a world of difference between objecting to something, and objecting to it enough to be ready to kill someone over it. Bonkowski Pasha and his assistant, Doctor Ilias, visited those neighborhoods only to examine and treat patients. They did not have soldiers with them forcing people's doors open and barging into their homes. Bonkowski Pasha wasn't doing anything to hurt Muslims. Why should any Muslim want to kill him? Or why should it be assumed that it was a Muslim who killed him?

I can already tell you what is bound to be the outcome of any serious investigation!"

"What would that be?"

"I do not know the killer's name . . . But it is someone who wishes to see the Mingherian people obliterated and forgotten. I love Mingherians. I could not abide to see them suffer a fate they do not deserve."

"Would you say that Mingherians are a distinct nation?" asked Prince Consort Nuri.

"If the Chief Scrutineer heard you ask that question, he would lock you up in the dungeons and torture you with clamps and vices to get you to talk," the Quarantine Master replied. "It is true that some on the island still speak the old language at home, but if you gathered them all together, they probably wouldn't even fill up a single room."

CHAPTER 14

On his return to the guesthouse at the State Hall, Doctor Nuri ran into the Major at the door. The Major was on his way to the Post Office to drop off Princess Pakize's first letter, which she had just finished and sealed.

That night, husband and wife ate dinner on their own for the first time. The Governor's cook had left them a tray with a simple meal of *börek*—a savory pastry—and yogurt. They were both feeling uneasy, troubled by the rigors of their situation, the possibility that they might have been exposed to infection, and by the mousetraps inside their room. They could see that the joyful, carefree days they had enjoyed at the start of their marriage were over now. There was still some light around the State Hall, Hamidiye Avenue, and near the hotels and the port, where gas lamps burned until around ten o'clock. Later, when the streets outside were plunged into darkness, they stood at the window looking out at the bewitched city of Arkaz and listened to the sound of waves gently lapping at the shore, a hedgehog scurrying about the gardens of the Governor's Residence, and the singing of cicadas.

The next day, the Doctor and Prince Consort went to the quarantine office to meet with Doctor Ilias, who had been released early that same morning.

"Bonkowski Pasha was like a father to me," said Doctor Ilias. "To have treated me like a suspect, to have had me thrown into the dungeons as if I could have been responsible for his assassination—it will have given rise to all sorts of misconceptions. How could they not foresee that?"

"But you are not in the dungeons now!"

"The Istanbul dailies will have already written about it. I must return to Istanbul immediately to clear my name. Has the Sultan been informed that I am being held here?"

Before his appointment as Bonkowski Pasha's assistant, Istanbul-born Doctor Ilias had been an ordinary physician whose work had passed largely unobserved. But after becoming assistant to the Chief Inspector of Public Health and traveling with him to all corners of the Empire, he had begun to make a name for himself, and written newspaper articles on epidemics, hygiene, and health. He was paid an excellent salary too. Five years ago, he had married Despina, the youngest daughter of a fairly wealthy Greek family in Istanbul. At Bonkowski Pasha's suggestion, Abdul Hamid had even awarded him an Order of Mecidiye Medal. But this adventurous, honorable, fulfilling career would now be cut short by the brutal murder of his boss, Bonkowski Pasha.

The Doctor and Prince Consort realized that Doctor Ilias must have had occasion to accompany Bonkowski Pasha to audiences with the Sultan, and that he might perhaps have met the Sultan more than Doctor Nuri himself had done. (Though he was married to the Sultan's niece, he had only met the Sultan thrice.)

"His Serene Highness the Sultan's wish is that you should stay on the island and assist us in discovering who is behind this diabolical act."

That afternoon someone sent Doctor Ilias an anonymous letter indicating that it would be his turn next.

"This is no doubt the handiwork of opportunists, of shopkeepers who are against quarantine," the Governor remarked. Then, to reassure the terrified Doctor Ilias, he had him picked up from the derelict house where he was still staying, and to which the anonymous letter had been sent, and had him taken to the guesthouse attached to the military garrison. This place abounded with mousetraps and was therefore slightly better equipped against the plague, as well as being safely out of reach of would-be assassins.

That day, in accordance with the Governor and the Quarantine Master's plan, Doctor Nuri and Doctor Ilias took the landau to visit the hospitals first. There were two hospitals in the capital: the small and underequipped Hamidiye Hospital (named after Sultan Abdul Hamid), which had not officially opened yet and was used by soldiers and by the Muslim elites, and the Theodoropoulos Hospital, which had been built by the island's Greek community. Constructed during the golden years of the trade in Mingherian marble by the family of one Stratis Theodoropoulos, a Greek from Smyrna who had prospered from that trade, this second establishment was equipped with thirty beds. Like the Hamidiye Hospital, the Theodoropoulos Hospital often also doubled as a refuge for the poor, the helpless, and the downtrodden and was seen by Mingherians as a peaceful, perhaps even a pleasant, place by virtue of its wonderfully fragrant grove of lemon trees and its magnificent views of the Castle. As the disease continued to spread, the Theodoropoulos Hospital had also begun to be attended by Muslims who did not have the means to see a doctor privately and had nowhere else to turn.

Accompanied by the Major and the Governor's men, Doctor Nuri arrived at this hospital to find it in a state of heightened activity. There was a tense crowd outside the entrance. Since the increase three days ago in the number of plague patients turning up at the door, the hospital's largest ward had been partitioned into two halves, with a screen separating ordinary patients from those afflicted with the plague. But the plague section had soon expanded, and with that day's arrivals, it had now become entirely congested. The other patients were unsettled by the noise of the plague patients raving in their sleep, their endless vomiting, their howls of pain from the headaches they suffered, and by the way they seemed to descend, just before they died, into a state of exhausted madness. Over the past week, most of the homeless, the poor, and the elderly who had previously been staying at the hospital had already gone elsewhere. Doctor Nuri and Doctor Ilias were told by the director of the hospital, the elderly Doctor Mihailis, that fights over beds had started breaking out between the families of patients with familiar complaints like asthma and heart disease and the more panicked and desperate plague victims.

Doctor Mihailis's affable welcome to Doctor Nuri and Doctor Ilias had been followed by his admission that, up until now, he had been convinced that the disease spreading through the island was not the plague. He had been waiting for the results of the microscope tests from the laboratory, and in the meantime he had only concerned himself with those symptoms of the disease which were reminiscent of cholera—namely, fever, vomiting, variations in heart rate, fatigue, and lethargy. With a similar glint of adventure and crisis in his eye, he told Doctor Nuri that he had been in Izmit during the epidemic of cholera there seven years ago. His working manner was stern, but there was also something in his expression that seemed to say, "Don't worry, we'll sort this out," which was heartening to his patients and had earned him the trust of the island's plague victims too, so that they would scream and call out for him to come and look at the swollen and pus-filled cysts on their necks, armpits, and groins. There was also another doctor in the ward that day, a frowning young man from Thessaloniki named Doctor Alexandros.

This Doctor Alexandros told the Doctor and Prince Consort that the elderly patient who seemed to sleep all the time and would immediately start groaning and crying if he happened to wake up for a few minutes was a fisherman who had come to the hospital two days ago. (The fishermen's wharf and neighborhood was close to the jetty that had been used during the Mingherian marble trade.) The ward's janitor, meanwhile, reported that the elderly, semiconscious woman who lay quietly dying over there was not the wife but the sister of the man weeping at her bedside, that she had been vomiting constantly on the day she'd arrived, and that yesterday, like many of the other patients, she had raved and ranted without pause. Fever and delirium were symptoms common to all those infected. A patient who worked as a porter in the docks tried to stand up but couldn't walk properly, and after a couple of wayward steps he fell backward onto his bed. Doctor Ilias devoted a lot of time to this tenacious patient, pointing out the view from the window and the Castle's childlike spires as a way to rekindle his optimism, his will to live, and his zest for fresh air.

All patients seemed to exhibit bloodshot eyes and suffer from strange convulsions and unbearably painful headaches. Some experienced paranoia, irrational fears, and anxiety, while others engaged in compulsive behavior like repeatedly turning their heads from left to right (the customs officer sitting by the window, for example) or making sudden attempts to scramble out of bed (like the aging, teary-eyed master potter who had a shop on Hamidiye Avenue). Most of the patients had some kind of boil, an abscess half the size of a little finger—what the Europeans called a bubo—growing on their neck, behind an ear, in an armpit, or on their groin. But the Doctor and Prince Consort had heard from other doctors that even patients who did not have boils or blemishes of any kind could still become feverish, somnolent, and lethargic, until they suddenly dropped dead (or got better).

A remarkably thin, scrawny patient (reportedly a roofer) was suffering from dry mouth, could no longer speak, and kept obsessively stammering. Some patients complained vociferously of their various discomforts, and Doctor Nuri tried his best to understand what was ailing them. Piercing and draining patients' buboes did seem to have temporarily calming, reviving effects. Indeed every patient—even those who didn't need it—asked for this procedure to be performed on them, though it was not a cure. Patients in the throes of a seizure or a bout of delirium sometimes gripped their sweat- and vomit-stained sheets so hard in their suffering that their skin and the sheets seemed to fuse into a single entity. The patients' wailing, their agonized howls and exhausted sighs, blended into one another, like one long hum. One of the reasons why doctors often confused the plague with cholera was that some of those affected seemed to be constantly thirsty. The steam from the cauldron of boiling water outside the entrance to the hospital building mingled with the thrum and the aura of death inside.

During his time in the Hejaz, Doctor Nuri used to look at the destitution and backwardness of the pilgrims arriving from India, Java, and all over Asia, witness how the British would treat them as if they were less than human, and feel guilty about his good education and his fluent French. Now he felt guilty for having nothing but spurious words of comfort to offer patients who knew they had contracted a fatal disease and for knowing that over the coming days things were going to get much worse than they already were.

They visited the Hamidiye Hospital next and found that the situation there was the same. The Doctor and Prince Consort was struck by how Doctor Ilias put his grief and his fear to one side to examine every patient one by one and listen earnestly to their complaints.

"But this won't last," said Doctor Ilias when the two of them were alone again. "They will kill me too. Do not forget, please, that the Sultan wishes for me to return to Istanbul as soon as possible!"

Sitting on the landau later on their way to Nikiforos's pharmacy with the Major and the Governor's men in tow, Doctor Nuri and Doctor Ilias called to the coachman to slow down so that they could assess the mood on the streets. Unnervingly, the European way of life around the hotels and in the streets that led down to the port seemed to be proceeding as usual. It was eerie to see how relaxed these Mingherians were, lounging in coffeehouses and diners and sitting in their barbers' chairs, laughing at one another's jokes and making plans for their next business venture or to go fishing together. In the Vavla neighborhood, the sight of bare-foot children gaily running around the dusty, neglected streets that led to the shore transported the Doctor and Prince Consort to some hot and distant city in the East.

When they reached the pharmacy, Nikiforos immediately informed them that he had definitely not owed the Royal Chemist—may he rest in peace—any money from the activities he had undertaken under the royal concession.

"Who would you say might have thought they had something to gain from killing Bonkowski Pasha?" said Doctor Nuri, again asking the question outright.

"Not all murders are committed for gain. Some are committed out of a sense of injustice or hopelessness, and sometimes a person becomes a killer entirely by chance, from one moment to the next, and without ever having planned to. The folk from Çifteler and Nebiler villages and the followers of the Terkapçılar sect that Governor Sami Pasha rounded up and jailed after the Pilgrim Ship Affair are known to loathe doc-tors and quarantine officers. One of them might have been out selling produce—eggs, say—then chanced upon Bonkowski Pasha wandering around Vavla and decided there and then to drag him right off the street. I did hint to my dear friend that he would do well to go to Germe and Vavla to evaluate the situation there. They know this, of course, and that's why they left the body here, to try and make me look like a poten-tial suspect."

"You are indeed a suspect!" said Doctor Nuri.

"But it is a conspiracy," said the pharmacist, turning to Doctor Ilias.

"I warned Bonkowski Pasha not to venture into those neighbor-hoods alone," said Doctor Ilias. "But every time we went to investigate a new outbreak in some district capital, he would always find an excuse to go out exploring on his own if he was not satisfied with what the local governor or quarantine master was showing us."

"Why?"

"Nobody ever wants a quarantine, not governors or mayors, not shopkeepers nor the rich. Nobody wants to accept that the comfortable lives they are accustomed to might suddenly come to an end, let alone that they might die. They will reject any evidence that disrupts their usual ways, they will deny any deaths, and even resent the dead. When they see the renowned Chief Inspector of Public Health Bonkowski Pasha and his assistant appear before them, they realize that even the authorities in Istanbul have recognized the gravity of the situation. But this never happened here. They would not let us meet with anyone."

"That was a precaution requested by His Excellency the Sultan himself," said Doctor Nuri.

"More than everything else, that is what troubled Bonkowski Pasha when the *Aziziye* secretly dropped him off on our island at midnight five days ago!" said Pharmacist Nikiforos. "It will be a formidable task to prepare an island for quarantine when it hides its dead and denies there is an outbreak at all. We must also contend with the existence of forces upon this island bent on eliminating quarantine doctors. We would all do well to fear another assassination."

"Do not worry!" said Doctor Nuri. He was troubled and even a little mortified by Pharmacist Nikiforos and Doctor Ilias's fears. He had just realized that the reason why these two Greek men seemed more perturbed than Muslims were by recent events was that they were Christians. As this book is ultimately intended as a historical account, we see no reason not to mention future events here. By the time they reach the end of this book, our readers will discover that Doctor and Prince Consort Nuri's instincts were sadly accurate, and that Pharmacist Nikiforos, the painter in Istanbul, and Doctor Ilias would all be killed for political reasons.

As he enumerated the properties of the various products he was placing in a gift basket, Pharmacist Nikiforos showed Doctor Nuri the symbols that adorned the bottles of La Rose du Minguère and La Rose du Levant and brought the conversation—as he had planned to do all along—to Bonkowski Pasha's friend from his youth, the Armenian painter Osgan Kalemciyan, and to the cloth that the Governor Pasha had confiscated.

"The Governor Pasha misunderstood the significance of that piece of cloth, and thought it a flag!" he said.

When the doctors convened in the Governor Pasha's office upon their return from the pharmacy that day, Governor Sami Pasha stated crisply that he would return the confiscated cloth to Pharmacist Nikiforos as soon as the Quarantine Committee assembled. The meeting was cut short when Governor Sami Pasha received the news of the sudden death of one of the municipal government's clerks.

Bonkowski Pasha's funeral was held that evening in the small and gracious Saint Anthony's Church. Despite the Sultan's telegrams and the encomiums that had appeared in the Istanbul press, the island's Greek journalists did not turn up, and the ceremony was a small one. Because of the plague, the family of the murdered Chief Inspector of Public Health had not been able to attend anyway. Aside from a few elderly members of the island's Catholic community, the only other mourner in the church was a former Polish army officer's son; the army officer had later joined the Ottoman army, and his son now lived in Mingheria. But it was Doctor Ilias, who stood weeping outside in the churchyard beside the rose-adorned grave site, who was the most desperate and broken-hearted of all.

CHAPTER 15

At this point it will benefit this story and history for us to go back three years in time to describe the events of the Pilgrim Ship Mutiny, an incident which was still causing the Governor much political trouble and personal distress.

During the 1890s, one of the precautions the Great Powers took to halt the outbreaks of cholera that spread from India through to the rest of the world via pilgrim ships passing through Mecca and Medina was to impose a ten-day quarantine on any vessels returning from the holy lands. Empires with colonies in Muslim countries were particularly adamant about the need for this second quarantine. For instance, the French, not trusting the quarantine measures employed by the Ottoman authorities in the Hejaz, would put passengers returning from the hajj to the French colony of Algeria aboard the Messageries Maritimes *Persepolis* through a further obligatory quarantine, and only then allow them to disembark and go back home to their towns and villages.

This procedure was one that the Ottoman authorities also implemented, deeming it necessary in light of the perceived weakness of their own Quarantine Authority in the Hejaz. Soon the Quarantine Committee in Istanbul had made this "precautionary quarantine" mandatory across the Ottoman Empire, regardless of whether a ship bringing pilgrims home had raised the yellow flag or reported any sick passengers.

The journey itself was grueling and torturous enough, with many dying on the way (it was indeed considered unremarkable for a fifth of the pilgrims from Bombay and Karachi to perish in transit), and most returning pilgrims, having made it safely back home, objected to the prospect of being quarantined for another ten days. Soldiers would sometimes have to be brought in, and in many places doctors had to ask the police and the gendarmerie for help. In outlying ports and on small islands like Mingheria, where quarantine premises fell short of requirements or existing facilities were too small to contain the villager pilgrims, the authorities would hastily round up leaky old ships and barges available for cheap hire and use these as temporary holding and isolation facilities. Sometimes, as in Chios, Kuşadası, and Thessaloniki, these vessels would be towed to some remote bay or near a stretch of empty land where a camp would be set up with tents borrowed from the army.

Desperate to get home, returning pilgrims were often exasperated by this second quarantine. Some would survive the journey only to die during those final ten days. There were scuffles and arguments between the hajjis and the Greek, Armenian, and Jewish doctors who came to examine them. Having been forced to endure this mandatory quarantine, the pilgrims were also expected   to their immense frustration—to pay a quarantine levy. Some of the wealthier and more cunning pilgrims would bribe doctors and break quarantine outright, to all the other pilgrims' fury.

Three years ago, a series of blunders had led to an incident that, out of the many similar situations occurring throughout the Ottoman Empire, was to prove the most egregious of all and give rise to the most vehement anger against quarantine measures. A telegraph from Istanbul had ordered that on its return from the Hejaz, whence it had sailed under the British flag, the ship named *Persia* should not be allowed to approach the port of Arkaz. Accordingly, its forty-seven pilgrims were transferred onto a rickety old barge procured by Quarantine Master Nikos, and the barge was then towed to one of the small coves in the north of the island, where it dropped anchor. This remote bay was surrounded by rocky hills and cliffs that served as a natural cage and was therefore a suitable spot to establish a quarantine zone. But those same steep and rocky cliffs also made it harder to deliver food, potable water, and medicines to the pilgrims.

A storm delayed the setting up of the camp for the doctors who would be needed to examine the pilgrims, for the soldiers that would help the doctors, and for the storage of medical supplies. The storm raged on for five days, during which the returning Mingherian pilgrims suffered the torments of thirst and hunger. Then they were subjected to a scorching heat. The pilgrims were mostly bearded, middle-aged villagers who tended to small farms and olive groves, and had never traveled outside the island before. There were also some pious and equally bearded younger men among them who had set out to help their fathers and grandfathers on the journey. Most of them hailed from mountain villages in the north of the island, like Çifteler and Nebiler.

After three days, cholera began to spread through the overcrowded barge. One by one, the exhausted pilgrims began to die. Weakened by their journey, they had no strength left to resist the disease. But though the death toll kept rising every day, the officials and doctors who had dragged the pilgrims here were still nowhere to be seen, until even the older hajjis began to grow restless.

The two Greek doctors who had managed to climb over the mountains on horseback and finally reach the quarantine camp after a three-day journey were in no hurry to row out to the germ-infested barge and deal with the furious pilgrims. They could sense that the vessel was filthy and overrun with disease. Some of the pilgrims did not understand why they were being kept there, but knew deep down that they were dying. Faced with their imminent end, the last thing that these weary old pilgrims wanted was to have one of these Christian doctors with their goatees and strange spectacles to spray them with Lysol and disinfectant liquid. In any case, two of the disinfectant spray pumps the doctors had carried across the mountains on horseback broke on the first day. Quarrels had also begun to erupt among the pilgrims themselves. Those saying "We should throw the dead into the sea" clashed with those who replied "They are family, they are martyrs, we will bury them in the village!" and used up what little strength they had left in arguing.

At the end of the first week, with the disease still rampant, and the bodies that had been thrown into the sea not recovered and buried but left instead to be picked at by birds and fish, rebellion broke out on the barge.

The angry pilgrims overpowered the two soldiers that had been sent to guard them and threw them overboard. When one of the soldiers—who, just like the pilgrims themselves (and indeed like most of the Ottoman Empire's Muslim-majority population), didn't know how to swim—drowned in the sea, Governor Sami Pasha and the Commander of the island's garrison embarked on a disproportionately harsh reprisal.

Meanwhile the younger pilgrims had managed to pull up the anchor, but instead of grounding itself on the rocks, the run-down barge was swept farther out to sea and swayed about in the water like a drunk. After half a day at the mercy of the currents, the pilgrim ship finally crashed into another rocky cove farther west. With their barge now grounded and leaking water, the tired pilgrims were not easily able to gather their bundles and their gifts and flee back to their villages. Had they managed to do so, perhaps the whole incident could still have been forgotten, even if a soldier had been killed. But instead the pilgrims remained amassed in the barge full of increasingly foul-smelling corpses, struggled against the waves, and were unable to collect their seemingly indispensable parcels, gifts, and bottles of cholera-infested holy Zamzam water to get away from the scene of the shipwreck.

The troop of gendarmes sent by Governor Sami Pasha to follow the pilgrim ship from the shore positioned themselves some way behind the rocks and on top of the nearest cliff, and their commander instructed the pilgrims to surrender, respect quarantine regulations, remain on board the ship, and refrain from coming ashore.

We cannot say with any certainty today whether these warnings were heard. The pilgrims seemed to have been swept with an all-consuming dread: they understood that they were going to be quarantined again, and they knew that this time they would definitely die. In their mind, quarantine was a diabolical European invention designed to punish and kill perfectly healthy pilgrims and take all their money.

In the end, some of the pilgrims who still had a little strength and wherewithal left realized that if they stayed on the besieged ship they would not survive, so they staged a breakout attempt.

As these pilgrims scampered among the rocks and tried to climb up the goat tracks, the soldiers panicked and began firing. Their shooting was frenzied, as if they were fighting off enemy troops come to invade Mingheria. Some were thinking of their colleagues who had been thrown into the sea to die. It was at least ten minutes before they calmed down and set their weapons aside. Many pilgrims were hit. Some had been shot in the back. But others had headed straight for the Ottoman soldiers shooting at them on their own island, like patriotic soldiers running toward machine-gun fire.

Governor Sami Pasha banned the press from reporting or even indirectly addressing these events, and so to date we still do not have accurate information on the number of pilgrims who were shot and killed that day, and how many eventually made it back to their villages.

Following his role in this historic event, the Governor Pasha was never able to shake off the condemnation, contempt, and reputation for cruelty that it brought him. He had expected Abdul Hamid to discipline him in some way, but it was instead the elderly garrison Commander and his soldiers who were punished and sent into exile. Sami Pasha dreamed a few times of a figure with a white beard who was trying to talk to him—to ask him "Where's your conscience, mighty Governor?"—but the man in the dream never managed to speak. When people criticized him to his face, the Governor Pasha argued that sending the army in against the pilgrims to protect the island from cholera had been the right decision, adding that there was no room in his conscience to sympathize with miscreants who had seen fit to hijack a vessel of the state and to kill a soldier, but also pointing out every time that the order to shoot at the pilgrims had not come from him, and that it had been a mistake to be ascribed to the inexperience of the troops involved.

Governor Sami Pasha soon decided that his best defense would be to wait for the whole incident to be forgotten. He was therefore particularly vigilant about ensuring that news of the event did not make it into any newspapers, and for a time his efforts were successful. During this period the Governor could often be heard expounding on the idea that those who died on the hajj were to be considered "martyrs," as indeed the laws of Islam stipulated, and that there was no higher honor than this. When the dead pilgrims' families came to Arkaz to request financial compensation, he would receive them in his office, touch upon the "special place in heaven reserved for those who have tasted the elixir of martyrdom," and assure them that he would do everything in his power to ensure they were successful in their demands, but that they must not speak to the Greek journalists and sensationalize the matter.

Once the incident had begun to fade from memory, Governor Sami Pasha quietly launched the second phase of his plan: he sent gendarmes to the villages to arrest the ten pilgrims he deemed to have been the ring-leaders of the mutiny, locked them up in the Castle dungeons, and told them, in a surge of brutal, despotic excess, that they would be punished for the death of the drowned soldier and for commandeering the ship. The Governor also rejected the demands for compensation put forward by the dead pilgrims' families.

The resentments these events generated began to fuel a religiously inflected resistance against the Governor, based in Çifteler and Nebiler villages, where most of the pilgrims had come from. These villages and the Terkapçılar lodge backed Memo and his band of guerrillas, who had been sowing terror for the past two years through the Greek villages in the north of the island. Many suspected that behind this lodge was Sheikh Hamdullah himself, head of the Halifiye sect, the island's most powerful.

To add to the Governor's woes, the whole affair—which had driven a wedge between the Muslim government and the people of the island—was periodically picked at by journalists aligned with the Greek nationalist cause. For instance, the Governor Pasha had given an interview to a Greek newspaper he was on good terms with, the *Neo Nisi,* during which he had spoken of some pilgrims who had funded the construction of a drinking fountain in their village and had then been berated for referring to them as "impoverished hajjis." Ordinar-ily nobody would have taken much notice of this expression. But the Greek journalist Manolis had gone on to write a polemical piece in his newspaper arguing that the pilgrims weren't poor at all and that, on the contrary, the island's wealthy Muslims had been following the latest fashion by selling off their possessions to embark on the hajj, with many falling sick and dying on the journey. Considering how undereducated the island's Muslim population was when compared with the Orthodox community, would it not be more sensible for the wealthy rural Muslim families to band together and raise funds to set up a secondary school to serve their community, or at the very least repair the broken minarets of their neighborhood mosques, rather than frittering their riches away in faraway deserts and on British ships?

The Governor agreed with the principle that put schools before mosques, but even so, as he'd read the article Sami Pasha had felt like he might choke with rage.

He had partly been annoyed by Manolis's condescending tone in referring to the Muslim community, but the main reason for his anger was that while he had been waiting expectantly for this matter of the "Pilgrim Ship Mutiny" to be forgotten, here was yet another Greek journalist rehashing it all.

CHAPTER 16

Early in the morning on the day the Quarantine Committee was due to meet, Doctor Nuri arrived at the Hamidiye Hospital to find a Muslim family standing at the door arguing with a clerk he recognized from the Governor's Office, and thanks to the Prince Consort's intervention, the patient—a farrier—was given a newly vacated bed in an overcrowded ward.

Over the past three days, the number of patients turning up at the hospitals had doubled. In the "Cause of Death" column where doctors used to write "diphtheria" or "whooping cough," they were now noting down the word "plague."

On the second floor, the additional beds that had been brought from the military barracks two weeks ago were already nearly full. Doctor Ilias and the island's only Muslim doctor, Ferit Bey, were rushing from one cot to the next, draining patients' buboes and dressing their wounds.

A young man who recognized Doctor Nuri called him over to his mother's bedside. But the fever-ravaged, sweat-drenched, delirious old woman didn't even register the doctor's presence. Doctor Nuri opened the nearest window, wondering—as most doctors who worked with plague patients did—whether it would do any good. In their heroic efforts to alleviate their patients' suffering, some doctors would come into very close contact with the sick.

In every ward there was a corner where the sanitizing solution was kept, and the doctors, who regularly washed their fingers and hands with these substances, would often meet there and talk among themselves. On one such occasion Doctor Ferit gestured at a container full of vinegar and told Doctor Nuri with a faint smile: "I know it doesn't really work, but I still use it anyway!" He added that the young doctor from

Thessaloniki, Alexandros, had developed a fever the night before and started shivering, so Doctor Ferit had sent him home and urged him not to come in if he still had a high temperature in the morning.

At the Theodoropoulos Hospital Doctor Nuri had seen young Doctor Alexandros's selfless devotion to his patients, and how fearlessly close he would get to them when he treated them. "Doctors and janitors know how to deal with cholera, but not how to protect themselves from the plague," said Doctor Ilias. "A plague patient might cough in your face at any moment and infect you too. It is imperative that we give doctors strict instructions on this matter."

There was still time before the Quarantine Committee convened, so they crossed the city in the armored landau toward the Theodoropoulos Hospital in the Ora neighborhood, speaking not a word to each other but realizing, from the number of people they saw milling about in dumbfounded silence and from the apprehensive expressions on everyone's faces, that there must have been more cases and more deaths in these backstreets than they had previously thought. The fear of death was slowly taking over the city, but the kind of panic that the two doctors had seen during really serious outbreaks seemed not to have erupted here yet. Zofiri's bakery, famous for its almond biscuits and rose-flavored pastries, was empty. But elsewhere, restaurant owner Dimosteni was sitting on Barber Panagiotis's wicker chair for his usual morning shave.

The diners, shops, and coffeehouses on Hamidiye Avenue and Square all seemed to be open. They saw a black-haired little boy sobbing to himself in a garden down a side alley on the way to the square, and a little farther along there was a group of women on a condolence visit sitting down with their arms around one another.

Both doctors were dismayed to see the size of the crowd outside the entrance to the Theodoropoulos Hospital. It was clear to them now that the outbreak had already spread much deeper than they had thought, on top of which the assassination of Bonkowski Pasha and the fact that the Sultan had immediately sent someone new to run quarantine operations meant that there was now a kind of collective certainty around the idea that this disease really was the plague.

Doctor Nuri also observed that the hospital's wards were disorganized, chaotic, and full of new patients. The patients he had seen here two days ago—the old man who slept all day, the tired porter who worked in the docks—were already dead and buried. A Greek woman who had recently been admitted was accompanied by two other women and a man.

"We can no longer let relatives and visitors into the hospitals!" said Doctor Nuri.

Doctor Mihailis summoned every doctor in the hospital to an empty room in the basement, where Doctor Nuri explained that many doctors had died in China as a result of patients making unexpected movements, sneezing, vomiting, or spitting while they were being examined or while their buboes were being drained.

He also told a story he had heard from a British doctor at the Venice Conference: in Bombay, a dying plague patient who had been misdiagnosed with diphtheria had started coughing during a final phase of "delirium," and droplets of his saliva had reached a nearby nurse's eyes. The nurse's eyes had immediately and generously been cleaned with diphtheria antitoxin, but within thirty hours the nurse had fallen ill anyway and died four days later in the throes of a similar delirium.

The doctors now began to debate the significance of those thirty hours: Should that be considered the length of time between the moment the microbe entered the body and the onset of symptoms like tiredness, shivers, headaches, fever, and vomiting? Doctor Ilias noted that in Smyrna, the duration of this interval had depended on the patient and explained that both those spreading the disease and those being infected would not be aware of it, and so the outbreak would grow, undetected, at a rapidly accelerating rate. Very soon, all over the city, people would begin to die, just like the rats had done before them.

"This is the situation we are in, unfortunately!" said Doctor Nikos.

Once again, Doctor Nuri thought, the Quarantine Master was bemoaning the island's lackluster response to the epidemic, though this time his criticism was aimed not just at the Governor and at the authorities in Istanbul but at his fellow doctors too.

"At this point we must shut everything down—markets, shops, and all the rest," said Doctor Ilias.

"Any isolation measures we introduce now would be entirely appropriate," said Doctor Nuri. "But the microbe has already been spreading, so even if people start following the rules immediately, they will still fall ill and die in their homes. And when that happens, they will argue that the bans are futile."

"That is a very pessimistic prognosis," said Doctor Ilias.

Everyone then started talking at the same time. Readers of Princess Pakize's letters will realize that quarantine operations began in earnest that morning in the basement of the Theodoropoulos Greek hospital. All the doctors agreed that it was necessary to call upon Istanbul to send fresh supplies and reinforcements—all the better if they were Muslim doctors, of course.

By then it had become clear that the disease had spread widely, with some streets, particularly in the Vavla and Germe neighborhoods, so infected that it would be difficult to slow the outbreak there, and with these facts in mind one of the doctors asked Doctor Ilias what Bonkowski Pasha would have done in this situation.

"Bonkowski Pasha firmly believed in the importance of distancing, isolation, and quarantine procedures," said Doctor Ilias. "It was not enough to just hunt down rats. But he also knew that in places where spraying disinfectant solution would no longer suffice, the best thing to do was to send the army in to vacate the area, and then to burn it to the ground. His Excellency the Sultan himself kept a close watch over what happened during the outbreaks of cholera in Üsküdar and Izmit seven years ago, where the disease was finally defeated when the most infected houses were emptied and burned down, and entire neighborhoods reduced to ashes."

No one wanted to risk falling prey to an informant now that Abdul Hamid had been mentioned, and when a familiar silence took hold of the room, the meeting came to a close.

CHAPTER 17

The Central Post Office of the province of Mingheria had been inaugurated twenty years ago, when the Major was eleven, with a lavish and rather memorable opening ceremony. (A Greek schoolteacher had fallen into the sea and drowned during the celebrations.) Previously, the Telegraph Office had been housed inside the old State Hall, in a mysterious little room from which issued a constant clicking sound, while the old Post Office, which dealt mostly with parcels, had been situated in a run-down building by the customs office. Little Kâmil had never been to either.

But after the opening of the Central Post Office, he would constantly plead for his father to take him there, or at least to walk past it so they could look at the building's extravagant entrance. Inside there were framed charts showing postage prices, franked envelopes in different colors, blank postcards, local and foreign stamp series, various noticeboards, and a map of the Ottoman Empire one could consult to determine which rate applied to one's postage. Unfortunately the map was no longer quite up to date, and on one occasion this had caused a row between a post-office clerk wanting to charge an overseas rate, and a customer insisting on paying the domestic rate.

It had been thirty years since the Ottoman Ministry of Post had been combined with the Telegraph Department, and though the first centralized post offices had begun to be built under the rule of Sultan Abdülaziz (who was said to dislike Mingheria) at a time—the 1870s—when the Empire was much larger than its current size, the island's turn did not come until after Abdul Hamid took the throne. It would not be an overstatement to say that Mingherians loved Abdul Hamid, under whose patronage there had also been a hospital, a police station, a bridge, and a military school built in their capital.

Even today, every time he spotted the Post Office and its grand entrance in the distance, and every time he climbed up the stairs to its front door, Major Kâmil would feel the same thrill he had experienced as a child. When the Major was still a boy, the most eventful moment of the week was when the sacks of new mail were unloaded off the ferry from Thessaloniki or Smyrna and brought up to the Post Office. Distinguished gentlemen waiting for their letters, shopkeepers expecting the boxes and parcels they'd ordered, servants, housemaids, farmhands, clerks, and municipal officers who'd been sent to "have a look and see if there's any post" would all gather around the entrance. In theory, any letter that had come in the registered post was supposed to be delivered to its recipient by the Post Office's letter carriers in accordance with the address indicated on the envelope, but in practice registered post was expensive and the process of individual delivery too time-consuming, and so people preferred to send their attendants to collect their mail from the Post Office instead. (In those days people would often improvise addresses, and some might add a little prayer underneath to make sure their letter reached its destination.)

The rest of the crowd usually consisted of children and curious bystanders. Some would watch raptly as sacks and parcels brought in through the back entrance were examined by customs officers and sent out to be delivered to their respective recipients. Some of the packages might still be making their leisurely way uphill from the port on the back of a horse cart, a gaggle of children running and skipping behind it. During the heyday of the marble trade, there used to be an Italian ferry called the *Montebello* which made stops in Trieste and at several islands on the way. The Major used to love this ship, which had its own special stamp series, a chart with color-coded postage rates, and a cart for the distribution of mail to distant villages all over the island.

Often the Post Office's elderly Greek clerk would step onto the porch—where Abdul Hamid's seal hung—to call out people's names and hand them their letters and parcels, and once he'd repeated a few more times and in a louder voice the names on the envelopes he was left with, urged the assembled audience to "let those people know they've got mail and they should send someone over to pick it up," and told those who'd been left empty-handed, "There's nothing here for you today, come back on Thursday morning after the ferry from Thessaloniki arrives," he would return inside the building.

Ever since the outbreak had grown, there had been an attendant stationed at the door to the Post Office to squirt Lysol over any visitors. The moment he stepped into the building that day, the Major was transfixed by the sight of the giant Theta wall clock hanging in its usual place.

As he listened to the echo of his footsteps in the cavernous hall, his eyes roamed over the counters where documents, letters, and parcels were being exchanged. Along the high tables where tall customers leaned their elbows, someone had placed bowls of vinegar that were now spreading a pleasant aroma throughout the hall. The Major had heard from the Doctor and Prince Consort that this was a precaution usually taken against the spread of cholera. It appeared to be the single most important provision in place here. (We should like to point out to our readers that as he reflected upon this matter, the Major happened to be standing in *precisely* the spot where Bonkowski Pasha himself had stood before he'd slipped out through the back door and disappeared.)

Like everyone else in the capital, Postmaster Dimitris Effendi knew that the Major had arrived on the *Aziziye,* and he was familiar with all the gossip concerning Murad V's three newly married daughters. He was particularly careful as he weighed the heavy, sealed envelope, for he could tell from the writing upon it that it must contain a letter from a sultan's daughter, from one Princess to another.

The Major had frequently posted letters to Istanbul from port cities across the Empire. To send an ordinary letter from one port to another, it was enough to stick a stamp worth twenty *para* on the envelope. The tiny, one-room post offices found in the train stations of more distant provinces (places like Athos, Veroia, Elassona) might not have twenty-*para* stamps available, in which case the attendant clerk would dutifully cut a stamp worth one *kuruş* down the middle and stick that onto the envelope instead. Having consulted the table of postage rates and made his calculations for Princess Pakize's letter, Dimitris Effendi requested, in addition to the usual fee, one *kuruş* each in additional fees for registered mail and proof of delivery.

The Major sincerely believed that the epidemic would soon be under control, and that they would quickly be back on the *Aziziye* and on their way to China. He later shared these thoughts with Princess Pak-ize in explaining to her why he had decided against paying the addi-tional proof of delivery fee. The Major's admission shall prove to anyone who will have the pleasure of reading the Princess's letters that, in that moment, the young officer had not even an inkling of the decisive role that history would soon thrust upon him.

Major Kâmil took a brush from inside a bowl of glue, holding it near the bristles, and used it to affix the one *kuruş* stamps—each decorated with the seal of Abdul Hamid, exquisite blue engravings and a star and crescent—onto the envelope. Once Dimitris Effendi had stamped the Mingherian postmark twice onto the envelope, the Major turned away and looked at the clock hanging on the wall.

The Major silently conceded, as he walked toward the enormous Theta wall clock, that it had always been the object that had most drawn him to the Post Office, and that when he was far away in some distant city and reminiscing about Mingheria, it was always the first thing he thought of. Even he was not entirely sure why. The first time his father had brought the Major here twenty years ago, he had respectfully shown his son the seal of Abdul Hamid hanging near the entrance and then taken him to examine the Theta clock, pointing out with similar feelings of gratitude and reverence that it too had been a gift from the Sultan, and showing Kâmil how it was marked with both Arabic and European numerals, just like Ottoman postage stamps were. That day his father had explained to him that unlike Muslims, Europeans did not refer to the hours of dawn and sunset as "twelve," but that instead their clocks pointed to the number twelve at noon, when the sun was at its highest in the sky. This was a fact little Kâmil already knew from hearing church bells ring, but he did not know that he knew it, and perhaps this was why it brought out in him what we might describe as a kind of "meta-physical apprehension." Could two different clocks both mark the same moment in time but use different numbers? If the Sultan, who'd had clock towers built in every provincial capital of the Ottoman Empire since taking the throne, wanted all of his clocks to show the same time no matter where they were, then why did they bear both Arabic and Western numerals?

These feelings of metaphysical disquiet he had experienced as a child returned now while he distractedly leafed—as he did every summer—through the frayed, loosened pages of the old volume on the French Revolution and liberty. On his way from the Post Office to the State Hall, where he was due to join the meeting of the Quarantine Committee, Major Kâmil passed the clock tower that had been built to mark the twenty-fifth anniversary of the Sultan's reign but had not yet been completed, and wandered through the streets around it as if he had lost his way, unconscious of where he was going, and mesmerized by his surroundings.

CHAPTER 18

The inaugural meeting of the Mingherian Quarantine Committee, attended by its president and nineteen other members, began at two o'clock on the first day of May. As there had not been any serious epidemics on the island for twenty-five years, this was the first time that this committee, which had hitherto existed only on paper, had convened for a formal meeting. Bushy-bearded Constantinos Laneras, head of the Greek Orthodox congregation and bishop of Hagia Triada, and the permanently breathless Stavrakis Effendi, bishop of Hagia Yorgos, were both present, wearing their lushest cassocks and miters and bedecked with their ceremonial stoles and enormous crucifix pendants.

All of the delegates except Doctor Ilias and Doctor Nuri already knew and recognized one another from their involvement in the life of the island. Whenever disputes arose between different communities over the marriage of one of their girls, the Governor would summon their representatives to this same room, listen to everyone's side of the story, deliver a few rebukes, and resolve the matter amicably without having to put anyone in jail. Or if he felt it was essential for the whole island to contribute to the expense of sourcing timber for new telegraph lines to the villages in the interior, he would gather them around the meeting room's ancient wooden table and treat them to a poignant panegyric on the subject of loyalty toward the Sultan.

The leaders of every religious community, the pharmacists, the consuls, the army men from the garrison, the Governor Pasha, and every other delegate present that day believed that the disease had spread widely through the Muslim neighborhoods on the hills that rose to the west of the port and spoke openly of their conviction that in order to stop it spreading even faster, the neighborhoods of Germe, Çite, and Kadirler would have to be cordoned. Death rates in these neighborhoods had reached around five or six a day by now, yet people who were potentially infected were still being allowed to roam freely around the city.

Another topic that the delegates softly confabulating before the start of the meeting generally agreed upon was that Bonkowski Pasha had fallen victim to a political murder. This was certainly what was being *implied* in most of their exchanges, though nobody was openly pointing the finger at any particular group. The exception was the French consul Monsieur Andon, who had shared with the other consuls, the clerks, and the religious leaders waiting for the meeting to begin his view that the killing must have been the work of crazed fanatics hostile to science, medicine, and the West. The Governor Pasha, the outspoken French consul had added, must act fast to apprehend the planners and perpetrators of this murder, and any delay in doing so could only be interpreted as a direct challenge to the nations of Europe.

The Ottoman Ministry of Public Health in Istanbul had already sent a telegram overnight to the Quarantine Committee of the province of Mingheria with an itemized summary of the measures they were supposed to introduce. Istanbul itself received these ever-changing lists (to which new measures were added every day) by telegram directly from the International Quarantine Agency. The Mingherian Quarantine Committee's task was to discuss how to adapt these directives to the island's specific circumstances and then to formally announce and implement them.

It was agreed that all schools would be closed. This measure was not even put up for debate. Most parents had already stopped sending their kids to school anyway. The only children left roaming the playgrounds and schoolyards now were the delinquent offspring of indifferent and unhappy families. As far as government offices were concerned, it was left to the heads of each individual department to decide whether they should operate as normal or cut back. It was further decided that, starting first thing in the morning two days after the date of this quarantine meeting, all vessels arriving from Alexandria, the northern shores of Africa, the Suez Canal, nearby islands, and the East would be subject to quarantine. These ships would be considered "fully contaminated," and all their passengers would be quarantined for five days before being allowed to enter Mingheria. It was also agreed that any ships departing the island would be quarantined for five days too.

The process of drawing up and voting on the list of substances that were to be banned from the island and its shops took a long time. "We are pulling out all the stops with these bans, Your Excellency," said the normally taciturn German consul Frangouli, "as if we believed that the more things we ban, the sooner the epidemic will end."

The Governor raised his eyebrows at this comment, for he suspected that deep down, like most of the bureaucrats and civil servants he had encountered in his life, so too the members of this committee took pleasure in banning things. "Don't you worry, Frangouli Effendi!" he said. "Once we have turned this list into a sign and put copies up all over the city, people will be so terrified that we won't even need soldiers or gendarmes to secure their compliance."

There was some debate over a provision dictating that the bodies of the dead were to be disinfected with lime and their burial monitored by municipal authorities. The elderly Greek doctor Tassos Bey pointed out that it would be especially difficult to implement this measure among the poorer and more fanatically religious Muslim population, that there were sure to be altercations, and that it would be wise to deploy soldiers from the Mingherian military garrison to escort Muslim doctors when they ventured into those kinds of areas, rather than relying on the ordinary guards employed by the quarantine office. This was how the possibility of soldiers being called upon to protect doctors first came to be mentioned. For his part, the Governor Pasha felt that a government that couldn't even sterilize an infected house or exercise enough authority to disinfect a corpse would never be able to stop an epidemic, so he did not raise any objections.

As instructed by Istanbul, it was then agreed that the belongings of those who perished from the disease were to be sterilized immediately. The price of the corrosive sublimate solution that was to be used as a disinfectant would be fixed by the municipal authorities, and its sale on the black market would not be tolerated. It would be forbidden to touch, take, use, or sell victims' belongings and to visit a house where somebody had died without the prior authorization of a public health official and before the building was disinfected. All junk shops would be sterilized and shut down.

The skeptical, weary consuls and doctors did voice the occasional question—"Do we even have enough firemen, clerks, disinfectant, and Lysol to deal with all this?"—but by now the Governor had more or less stopped paying heed to objections and was simply instructing his clerks to make a formal record of each provision. It was decreed that the public would be encouraged to hunt rats; that traps and rat poison would be brought in from Smyrna, Thessaloniki, and Istanbul; and that there would be a reward of six *kuruş* paid out for every dead rat handed in to the municipal authorities.

Noting the doubtful expressions on some of the delegates' faces, Doctor and Prince Consort Nuri reminded them that "the first thing to do is to stop the movement of rats." He explained in great detail how in India the speed at which the disease had spread inland had not been determined by the movement of people fleeing from it but by the pace at which rats had swarmed from one village to the next. Where there were railway lines, these rats and their fleas would travel on trains too, and the outbreak would spread even faster. But when people took deliberate precautions to avoid rats and worked with the municipal authorities to drive them away, and when incoming ships were cleared of vermin before they were allowed to dock, the spread of plague was seen to slow down until it stopped altogether.

Doctor Nuri next reminded them all of something they already knew: although the microbe that caused the plague had been discovered, there was no effective vaccine against it yet. That year some patients in hospitals in Bombay had been injected with different doses of a plague serum, but this had produced no noticeable improvement in their conditions. In other words, anyone who became infected with the microbe either survived (some never even fell ill) or perished within five days, and the outcome depended solely on the strength of their constitution. It had also occasionally been observed that even where there were no rats, the disease could still spread between humans through saliva, phlegm, and blood. This unexplained and disquieting phenomenon, combined with the absence of a known cure, forced even the most forward-thinking and knowledgeable of quarantine doctors to resort to traditional lazarettos of the kind the Venetians had invented four hundred years ago; quarantine facilities that the Ottomans called shelter stations; isolation wards; and ancestral folk remedies. So it was that even as the British announced, back home in London, that isolating patients and imposing cordons was "pointless," they still relied on those same methods in Bombay, using the army to enforce them.

By this point, Doctor Nuri could see that his audience was becoming thoroughly confused and thought it wise to introduce a visual aid. The Governor Pasha had just been using an old fumigation stick to disinfect a letter a clerk had brought in from the Post Office. The implement was passed around the table until it reached Doctor Nuri, who demonstrated its usage. He had bought himself a sleeker version of this very same model many years ago in Paris from the famous Galerie Colbert.

"You see, just like everyone else, I too sometimes fumigate documents I've received in the post, or the newspaper I've bought, or the loose change in my pocket," he said. "Yet at the last Quarantine Conference in Venice it was agreed that even if they have come from a contaminated source, there is no need to disinfect or sanitize things like paper, letters, and books. Even so, you will never hear me telling plague patients and those poor souls who gather in hospital corridors, desperate for a glimmer of hope, that fumigation is useless. I urge you not to do so either, gentlemen! Otherwise they will no longer bother with sanitization measures either." ("These people only believe in prayer sheets and amulets anyway!" someone muttered in French.)

To elucidate how frighteningly vague the medical community's understanding of the plague was, Doctor Nuri told the delegates a striking anecdote from Hong Kong: a Chinese doctor in Hong Kong's Tung Wah Hospital, declaring his hospital to be "perfectly clean," had spent the night sleeping in the same ward as his plague patients as a demonstration of how firmly he believed that the plague could only ever be spread by rats and fleas, yet despite there being no sign of any such vermin in the building, he had died of the plague three days later.

Doctor Nuri noticed the fear and despair this story had instilled in his audience. "I do not believe there is any benefit to washing metal coins in diluted vinegar," he continued. "But I have heard that some doctors in Hong Kong will still dip their fingertips in vinegar before taking a new patient's pulse. These precautions are not altogether ineffective, and indeed they can give hope to doctors and patients alike. Where there is no hope left, you may draft in as many soldiers as you wish, but you will still not be able to implement any restrictions, and once you have failed to persuade people of the benefits of such restrictions, you will find that you are unable to enforce quarantine at all. Quarantine is the art of educating the public in spite of itself, and of teaching it the skill of self-preservation."

"Do you mean to say, sir, that there might as well be no soldiers at all?" said the German consul in a derisory tone. "Do you really expect the masses to obey without soldiers to make them?"

"If it weren't for their fear of the army, these people would never comply with any restrictions," said the French consul. "Forget about cordons and regulations; any Christian doctor who sets foot in neighborhoods like Çite, Germe, and Kadirler is likely to be attacked on sight, unless he's remembered to hide his doctor's briefcase first. You did well to lock Ramiz up in the dungeons. Don't ever let him out."

The Governor exhorted the assembled dignitaries not to entertain preconceived notions (he spoke the words "preconceived notions" in French) regarding any lodge, sect, or individual, and assured them there was no cause for alarm, as all necessary precautions would be taken.

"Then we must immediately ban all movement in and out of the Kadirler, Çite, and Germe neighborhoods," said the French consul. "There are still people there who will visit a home where someone has died and come out wearing the victim's clothes, sauntering up and down Hamidiye Avenue, back and forth across the bridge, into the markets, the shops, the docks, and anywhere else where there's a crowd. Unless we immediately institute a cordon to stop these people, within a week there will not be anyone left on this island who has not been exposed to the plague microbe."

"Perhaps we are all infected already," said Bishop Stavrakis, then pulled out a crucifix and began to pray.

"We know for a fact that Sheikh Hamdullah does not hand out amulets and consecrated prayer sheets, nor is he one of these charlatans who will paint incantations onto the hands and chests of sick and desperate people," said the Governor Pasha.

The consuls were momentarily pacified to thus learn that the Governor, by his own admission, was secretly monitoring the sheikh. "You will soon see for yourselves that tomorrow, once these measures are officially announced, our people shall be more than willing to observe them," the Governor declared when the debate resumed. "Six people died yesterday, five of them Muslims and one of them Greek. But our policies shall bring these numbers down. So it was in Smyrna too."

"What will you do if the people do not yield and submit to the decrees, Your Excellency? Will your soldiers shoot them like they did the pilgrims?" said the French consul.

In slow, deliberate gestures, Governor Sami Pasha finished fumigating a message he had just been handed, and although he would have much preferred to keep its distressing contents secret, he announced with a note of heartfelt sorrow:

"Gentlemen, it is with great sadness that I must inform you that our popular and well-respected young Thessalonikian doctor Alexandros Bey has fallen ill and died. The cause of death is—"

"Plague, of course," interjected Quarantine Master Nikos.

"If you had been willing to admit from the start that it is plague we are dealing with, perhaps Doctor Alexandros, whose death you're mourning now, might have survived after all," said the French consul.

"Let us be clear, gentlemen, that the plague is not to be blamed on the state!" said the Governor.

But among the members of the committee, the argument continued, and so the Governor Pasha, thinking it best to bring proceedings to a close before the agitation could settle, declared the meeting adjourned until the morning, "given the circumstances," then sprang to his feet and walked out through the main door with his characteristic short, brisk stride.

CHAPTER 19

As he walked out of the meeting hall, the Governor Pasha first turned his attention to the activity in the adjacent room. Having anticipated that the meeting would run late into the night, the municipality's footmen had lit gas lamps and were now setting out petite, pear-shaped watermelons they'd carved with decorative flower and leaf motifs and preparing to serve olive-and-thyme-flavored bread that the garrison Commander had ordered in from the army kitchens. Clerks, gendarmes, consular staff, guards, journalists, soldiers, and young priests had gathered in the inner courtyard at the foot of the stairs. Some were sitting on chairs and benches along the walls, most of them were standing, but all of them reeked of the carbon chloride solution that had been liberally sprayed over them by a team of overzealous firemen.

Sitting in his office and reading the messages his clerks had left on his desk, the Governor soon learned that the island's wealthier Muslim and Christian residents were expecting him to secure them places aboard the ships scheduled to leave the city. He realized with some degree of consternation that all the tickets must have already sold out, and there was an exodus underway from the island. A bevy of footmen, servants, doormen, and other supplicants were waiting in the courtyard and outside his door, sent by their wealthy employers to petition the Governor for tickets on their behalf.

The Governor looked at the telegram on his desk and divined its contents without having to resort to the services of the municipal code breaker: it was a message from his wife informing him that she was on her way to the island again. Had news of Bonkowski Pasha's assassination and of the epidemic on the island perhaps not reached the family home in Üsküdar yet? Or was his selfless wife suggesting that she would not leave her husband alone in his hour of need? Her tender, forbearing expression briefly flashed in the Governor's mind.

Sami Pasha had been appointed governor of Mingheria five years ago. Born of an Albanian family, in his youth he had by chance landed in Egypt, where he had distinguished himself at the Khedive's court with his competence in a variety of roles, including as clerk, aide-de-camp, and translator (he spoke French), and having risen through the ranks there he had traveled on to Istanbul and entered directly into the service of the Ottoman state as district and county chief, and later state governor, of various imperial outposts, such as Aleppo, Skopje, and Beirut. His acquaintance with Kâmil Pasha of Cyprus had won him a government role during Kâmil Pasha's first stint as grand vizier fifteen years ago, but he had been relieved of his ministerial duties for reasons he had never been able to fathom and dispatched as governor to various far-flung provinces of the Empire. The Governor Pasha believed that whatever fault had caused his dismissal would eventually be forgotten by Abdul Hamid and that he would soon be recalled to Istanbul for a more prestigious role, and every time he was relieved of one duty and sent to another part of the Empire on a new assignment, he—like many Ottoman governors who were frequently shuffled from post to post—would interpret it as a sign that Abdul Hamid had not forgotten about him, rather than an indication of any kind of dissatisfaction with his performance in his previous role.

When he was appointed governor of Mingheria, Sami Pasha's wife, Esma, did not go with him. Their lives had been made miserable in recent years by his frequent transfers, and by all the times they had gone through the expensive trouble of moving their home to his latest posting only to find as soon as they had settled down that he was to be dispatched elsewhere after all. The strain of relocating, of furnishing a home, and of having to live—often in isolation—in some faraway town where people hardly even spoke Turkish had eventually worn Esma Hanım down, and rather than go to Mingheria, she had decided to stay behind in Istanbul, thinking, "By the time we get there they'll probably decide to send him somewhere else anyway." But with the Pasha's posting in Mingheria lasting an unprecedented five years, the distance between husband and wife had grown deeper, and finding himself unable to cope with the loneliness, the Pasha had begun a "secret" affair (which many on the island speculated and gossiped about) with the widow Marika, who taught history at the Greek High School.

The Governor arranged for an encrypted telegram to be sent to his wife and two married daughters telling them he missed them all very much but that under no circumstances must they come to the island. He waited awhile until it became completely dark outside. The port area was full of people looking for tickets and a way out of the island. When he was sure that the crowds in the State Hall Square had dispersed and that all the horse-drawn cabs were gone, he walked out of his residence through the back door. The streets smelled of fresh horse dung (a smell the Governor, like most locals, quite liked). The reliably unreliable municipal staff had yet to light the oil lamps along the main roads, though even if they had done so, it would still have been too dark for anyone to recognize him.

The Governor Pasha watched women ushering their children home, beggars pleading with passersby in the market square, people walking and talking to themselves, and old men weeping inconsolably. Outside the Dafni emporium was a sign saying that the mousetraps from Smyrna had arrived, but the shop had not opened at all that day. The Governor was not surprised at all by the unlit, locked-up storefronts he saw, for he had received reports from his informants that the canniest among the city's butchers and greengrocers had followed the carpet sellers and quilt makers' lead and made sure to empty their shops and hide their stock away before the quarantine officers turned up. But the diners reeking of meat stew and fried olive oil were still open, and the city's elderly and unemployed had congregated near the port to watch people come and go. People seemed to be behaving as if nothing unusual were going on. Or perhaps they were afraid and worried, and it was just that the Governor Pasha didn't notice. Eventually he spotted bodyguards behind him and knew that someone must have recognized him. He had always enjoyed wandering around the city in disguise, and often he wouldn't even wait for nightfall but venture out as soon as the light began to fade.

The municipality's elderly coachman Zekeriya was waiting for him, his nondescript phaeton parked in a dark corner in Hrisopolitissa Square. That detestable Nikiforos's pharmacy was closed. The Governor was sure there was a plainclothes policeman stationed somewhere in this square, but where could he be? Chief Scrutineer Mazhar Effendi was a capable and loyal bureaucrat who had trained all of his spies and police officers well. The Governor knew that if the somewhat-unusual fact of his affair with Marika had not become a political issue or caused a diplomatic incident yet, he owed it to Mazhar Effendi's efforts to silence any who dared gossip about it. The Governor would sometimes picture Mazhar Effendi sending telegrams to the palace on the matter, if not perhaps to the Sultan himself.

The Governor Pasha stepped onto the carriage in the little square. There was no real need for him to be driven to his destination, which was not at all far. But he did not feel he could turn up at the widowed history teacher's door with dirty boots during the winter, when it rained and the streets became mud baths, and eventually taking a carriage to see her had become a habit that extended into the summer. As usual they took the turn opposite the gardens of the villa where the historically wealthy Greek Mimiyannos family lived and wound their way through the backstreets of the Petalis neighborhood, but rather than alighting at the usual dark recess concealed by horse-chestnut trees, this time the Governor got off at a square where a cluster of tavernas overlooked the sea.

He noticed that the Romantika and the other two tavernas on the square were quiet that night, and that customers were being sprayed with Lysol at the entrance of the Buzuki restaurant. He began to walk toward his lover Marika's house, ignoring the stares of those who recognized him.

The seriousness of the plague epidemic and the proximity of death had led the Governor Pasha to the sudden realization that it was unnecessary and indeed demeaning to sneak around like a thief over this "secret" liaison which everyone seemed to know about anyway. He walked through the gate in the back garden as usual, feeling upon him the eyes of the hens in their coop who had first clucked in terror at the thought that he might be a fox, then fallen silent. As he approached the kitchen in the back of Marika's single-story home, the door opened quietly of its own accord, as it always did. A moist and mildewy kitchen smell and the scent of wet stone hit the Governor Pasha's nostrils as it did every time he walked in there. In truth, it was the smell of love and guilt.

They embraced each other longingly and found their way in the dark to the room next door, where they began to make love. The Governor Pasha felt that his tendency to give himself over unreservedly in their lovemaking was perhaps unseemly and would usually try, like a conscientious statesman, to slow things down every now and then and show that he was still in control. But today he held Marika as if he were a child who had lost his mother in a crowd and only just found her again. After a day filled with dire news, he was less afraid of opening up than he was of being alone. He made love to Marika again and again that night without inhibitions.

Later, when they sat down to eat, Sami Pasha said: "Lots of families from Ora and Flizvos and the other neighborhoods up there are packing up and leaving. The Angeloses who come every spring and Naci Pasha's lad visiting from Smyrna had already instructed their butlers to ready their houses in Upper Turunçlar, but then sent telegrams to cancel. Now they're asking for tickets for their nephews. Sabahattin the stone merchant is trying to leave too, looking for a ticket if he can get it."

Marika told him what had happened to the daughter-in-law of the Karkavitsases, a family from Thessaloniki who had made their fortune in stone mining and had a house two blocks away. The woman had arrived as she did every year before Easter to stay at the family's palatial mansion, readied especially for her visit, and had gone with her sister and the butler to her beloved Old Market to shop for spices, visit the renowned herbalist Arif's famous store, and buy bread from Zofiri's bakery. But as she walked by a poultry shop, she had spotted its owner inside lying in a drowsy stupor and with a conspicuous bubo on his neck, at which point she had immediately gone back to her neighborhood, had the house boarded up, and taken the first ferry back to Thessaloniki that same morning.

"She didn't," said the Governor Pasha. "They couldn't find any tickets for the Lloyd's ferry, or for the unscheduled Maritimes ship, so they came to me to see if I could help. It is odd, for these families are much better connected with the consuls than I am."

They were quiet for a time. As Madame Marika presented the Pasha with the plate she had been preparing for him, she explained that the chickens and the plums were from her own yard, and that the flour had come from the garrison bakery ten days ago. "They bake the most delicious buns at the garrison," she said. "Do you think the plague can be passed through food, Pasha?"

"I don't know," the Governor replied. "But I do wish you hadn't slaughtered that chicken!" he added, as if to imply he had seen enough bloodshed for the day. Then, surprising himself with his own frankness, he spoke to his lover of a plan he had only just concocted.

"Our quarantine will start in a few days' time. Even if it doesn't, the British and the French will be sure to put a five-day isolation order on all passengers and cargo coming in and out of our port. By then it will become much more complicated and expensive to leave the island. On top of that, once quarantine is in place the ferry companies will reduce their services. Those who have foreseen all this as I did have already flocked to the travel agencies and bought every last ticket available. But I have three places reserved for you, your brother, and your nephew on tomorrow's Messageries Maritimes ship to Thessaloniki."

It was not quite true that the Governor had specifically booked three tickets for them, but he did know that a few tickets had been set aside for him to use at his convenience.

"What do you mean, Pasha?"

"Madam Marika, if you don't think you can be ready by tomorrow, I expect the last ship to depart before quarantine will leave the day after. If you wish, I can easily get you tickets for that Pantaleon ferry instead."

"But what about you, Pasha? When will you leave?"

"What a thing to say! I shall remain here as the lord and Pasha of this land until this scourge has been eliminated."

In the silence that followed, the Governor tried to see the expression on her face, but it was dark and he couldn't make it out.

"My place is by your side."

"This is serious!" said the Governor Pasha. "They've killed Bonkowski Pasha—*Bonkowski Pasha*!"

"Who do you think killed him?"

"It may have just been an unfortunate coincidence, of course. But clearly the same people who got rid of Bonkowski Pasha, who want the plague to spread even farther so that they can pit Muslims and Christians against each other and take advantage of the situation, are now threatening Doctor Ilias too. The poor man didn't feel safe in the guesthouse."

"I won't be afraid with you by my side, Pasha."

"You should be!" said the Governor, resting his hand on his lover's knee. "The consuls, the tradesmen, our own holy men, are going to resist every measure we come up with. The epidemic will grow, I can see that already. We will have to deal with that and dodge assassins at the same time."

"You mustn't think such lugubrious thoughts, my Pasha. I shall follow all your instructions, and I shall be careful with what I eat. I will keep my door locked and won't let anyone in, and all will be well."

"What about the people who deliver your bread and your water, what about your brother and your nephew, and what if someone comes by to sell you plums or cherries, and, if not them, the neighbor's kids you feel sorry for—won't you let them in either? Won't you let *me* in? I could be the one to bring the plague into your home."

"Whatever disease you may catch, I should like to have it too, my Pasha. I would rather die than turn you away when you are most in need."

"It may end up looking like Judgment Day out there," said the unrelenting pasha. "The Koran says that on Judgment Day mothers shall turn away from their sons, daughters from their fathers, and wives from their husbands . . ."

"If you continue in this vein I shall interpret your insistence as a personal slight."

"I knew you would say that," said the Pasha.

"Then why do you persist in breaking my heart?"

The Pasha was relieved to sense that she had not uttered these words in real anger, but rather as a prelude to one of those little flirtatious tiffs they sometimes liked to engage in. Had Marika converted and become a Muslim, he might have been able to do what other governors did and take her for a second wife without even informing his first wife in Istanbul. But the Pasha held an important rank in the Ottoman bureaucracy. More important, in recent years foreign consuls and ambassadors had taken to claiming that Christians were being made to convert to Islam "under duress," and their increasingly vociferous protests had turned into a political headache that discomfited Istanbul and had dissuaded the Pasha from that course of action.

"Oh my darling Pasha! What will happen now? What have we done to deserve this? What must we do now?"

"Do as I say, do as your government says, obey the rules. Don't believe the rumors. The authorities have the matter under control."

"If only you knew what people have been saying!" Marika exclaimed.

"Let us hear it, by all means!" said the Governor Pasha with an air of formality.

"They say it was Bonkowski Pasha who brought the plague in the first place, and now that he has been killed, the plague is wandering the streets like a lost and orphaned child. And they say that others too will die."

"What else?"

"Sadly there are still people who say there is no plague. Even among the Greeks."

"Not for much longer, I should think," the Pasha. "Then what?"

"Some people say the plague arrived on the *Aziziye*! With rats that got onto the rowboat."

"And what else?"

"They say that the old sultan's daughter is very beautiful!" said Marika. "Is that true?"

"I wouldn't know!" said the Pasha, as if he had been asked to reveal state secrets. "But anyway, there is no one more beautiful than you."

CHAPTER 20

When the Quarantine Committee convened again the next morning, Governor Sami Pasha showed them the small room next to his office which had been prepared following the previous day's discussions. As the discipline of epidemiology dictated, any house which was known to be infected or where someone had died would henceforth be marked on the map that hung inside this little room, and decisions on which streets and neighborhoods should be cordoned would be made on that basis.

Pharmacist Nikiforos very courteously asked the Governor if his advertisement banner might finally be returned to him. "After all, I have attended your committee meetings and voted in accordance with your wishes," he said.

"What a persistent man you have turned out to be, Nikiforos Effendi," said the Governor Pasha, opening the only cupboard inside the little room. "Behold!" he said as he took out the cloth and showed it to the delegates.

The Doctor and Prince Consort, the Major, the Chief Scrutineer, the bishops, and everyone else now examined the reddish-pink cloth on which the image of a Mingherian rose had been skillfully embroidered. The Governor Pasha watched their reactions closely.

"Your advertisement banner is proving popular, Nikiforos Effendi," said the Governor.

"It was Bonkowski Pasha who came up with the idea," the pharmacist replied.

"Then you will certainly have your banner back, and indeed we have kept a record of it in our ledgers. I may not be able to return this to you right now, but when the plague is over and we are celebrating its defeat,

I shall stand before our people and hand it to you; let these esteemed professors, their excellencies the bishops, and these army officers be my witnesses."

"As you feel is best, Your Excellency," Nikiforos replied.

"The banner is yours, of course . . . But the Mingherian rose belongs to the entire nation."

Historians would later debate whether Governor Sami Pasha's expression "the entire nation" had been a reference to the people of the island alone, or of the Ottoman Empire as a whole.

After he had placed the cloth back in the cupboard, Governor Sami Pasha took his usual seat at the quarantine meeting table to work briskly through the list of measures he had drawn up with Doctor Nuri and Doctor Ilias earlier and put each item to the vote. These included turning parts of the Castle—specifically one of its more spacious courtyards and a large building inside the complex—into isolation facilities, selecting new burial grounds outside of the city, and determining the kinds of provisions that would be put in place to protect vacated homes. Many such decisions were made in quick succession that would later shape the course of the island's history and change some neighborhoods of Arkaz beyond recognition. Of all the prohibitions agreed upon that day, the one that was to cause the greatest consternation when it was announced to the public was the ban on crowds and on "gatherings of more than two individuals."

"Will Friday prayers and public sermons from the more popular preachers also be banned?" said the Russian consul Mihailov.

"We do have the authority to ban them, but we shall not do so for the time being," said the Governor. "In any case, what doctor, what pretext, could possibly stop a worshipper who comes to the mosque by himself, performs his ablutions, and says his prayers without touching or bothering anyone else?"

"Those dirty old carpets must be a breeding ground for all sorts of diseases," someone pointed out in a tone half scornful and half aggrieved.

"The Greek Orthodox community could suspend Sunday Mass," said its leader, Bishop Constantinos Effendi. "Our flock would understand."

Churches had been somewhat quieter since the outbreak had started. In mosques, however, there appeared to be more people than usual, and funeral services in particular had been attracting large crowds.

"If the disease is all the way over by the Stone Jetty in the huts where the migrants from Crete live, why should the quilt maker in my neighborhood of Eyoklima have to shut up shop?" asked the French consul Monsieur Andon.

"Because you're right by the garrison!" someone replied, but nobody else said anything further on the matter.

During the proceedings of the quarantine meeting, the consuls relied on clerks to bring them regular updates on their business activities in the city and on the progress of the disease. Consequently everything the committee delegates discussed that morning immediately found its way to the local tradesmen and from there spread to the rest of the city, embellished with misunderstandings, resentments, and unsubstantiated rumors, and seasoned with all sorts of accusations and reminiscences.

Much of the debate that day concerned the claim that there had been many more deaths than reported, but that people   and particularly the poor, Muslims, and migrants from Crete—were hiding their dead for fear that the quarantine officers would turn up, board their homes shut, and confiscate or perhaps even set fire to the stock in their shops.

"Muslims are very particular about their dead and—as you have all observed—will not compromise when it comes to funerals," said the Governor in response to these allegations. "It is simply inconceivable that the people of this island should skulk about in the middle of the night to bury their loved ones without bothering to wash their corpses first, or giving them a proper funeral service, or saying the right prayers."

"Perhaps his Excellency the Governor should ready his armored landau so that I might take him right now to the Old Stone Jetty near the Army Middle School!" said the French consul.

"It has indeed come to our attention," replied the Governor, "that you were in the area last night together with the Greek vice-consul Leonidis. But there are no locals there, only immigrants."

"Tell us, did you spot the Cretian roaming around at night holding a basket full of dead rats and spreading the plague around?" said the British consul Monsieur George, who was known for never letting the opportunity for a joke slip by. (Unusually, he was actually British, and a genuine consul.)

"There are so many people who believe in that sort of thing that even I am tempted to start believing it."

"We knew about the plague-spreading devil, but we did not know he was from Crete!"

"In the olden days," said Doctor Nuri, "when the plague struck in Florence or in Marseille and the local prince, the governor, or the state were not equipped to cope with the situation, the citizens themselves, from the youngest to the eldest, would take matters into their own hands and go from door to door to track the outbreak. There are heroes like that on this island too, people who are ready to make sacrifices not just to save their own lives, but to save the whole city."

"People like Doctor Alexandros from Thessaloniki, you mean?"

"It's true that we might have people here willing to risk their lives for the good of the island. But no one is going to volunteer when there is so much hostility in the air."

"No matter what the Governor might say, these days you will be hard-pressed to find a Muslim ready to sacrifice himself for a Christian, or a Christian for a Muslim. Let those who have brought this division upon us reflect on what they have done."

"Muslim youths could volunteer in Muslim neighborhoods, and Greek youths in Greek neighborhoods," the British consul responded.

"The alternative is to do what the British are now doing in India, and successfully too."

"I must say this is the first I've ever heard of the British making any kind of progress against the plague in India."

"Where no one volunteers or understands why they need to volunteer . . ."

". . . the army will *make* them volunteer!"

"Not quite," said Doctor Nuri, smiling at Russian consul Mihailov. "When that's the case, you forget about volunteers and send soldiers door to door instead."

There was a brief silence. "The Arab soldiers we have would not be able to set foot inside any home here," said the Russian consul.

In the aftermath of the Pilgrim Ship Affair, Abdul Hamid had relieved the island's four army divisions and their respective commanders of their duties and sent them off to serve in other parts of the Empire, replacing them with two divisions from the Fifth Army stationed in Damascus and composed of Arab soldiers who did not speak any Turkish. Their commander was under strict orders to remain uninvolved in the island's political and quarantine matters and to concentrate on chasing after the Greek guerrillas in the mountains.

"Let us not be so pessimistic!" said the Governor Pasha. "There is no need for soldiers to physically enter every home and mansion that is being checked. All that will be required of them is to guard the streets and break up any fights. Though we will equip them with gunpowder and ammunition too!"

"What if these soldiers who speak nothing but Arabic should accidentally end up shooting at the people again?" said the French consul.

"His Royal Highness the Sultan has sent Major Kâmil all the way from Istanbul to ensure that the volunteer Quarantine Army recruited from within the province of Mingheria itself shall adhere to the high standards of the state's military establishment," said the Governor, gesturing toward the Major. "And now this brave young officer is here among us!"

Major Kâmil, who was sitting with the clerks and soldiers in a row of chairs lined up against the wall, quickly stood up and greeted the Quarantine Committee, his face flushed with embarrassment. (He thought for a moment of how his rank was lower than his age warranted.) By the time he'd sat back down, he had become commander of the special division that was to be assembled to enforce quarantine in the province of Mingheria. Given the urgency of the matter, it was also decided that recruitment for this division should begin immediately.

"The government in Istanbul has already allocated funds to cover the volunteer army's wages," said the Governor, telling another lie.

"You know we will never see that money!" the British consul Monsieur George bravely replied. In some ways his observation put into words what everyone at the meeting was collectively feeling. For although nobody would say it openly, they all sensed that the authorities in Istanbul, and sadly the Sultan too, were putting their own interests above those of the island. Faced with these stirrings of despondency and insecurity, the Governor Pasha reached for something to say that might help overcome them. "We must remember that it is our whole island's moral duty to try and prevent those who will soon be boarding company liners and unscheduled ferries to flee Mingheria from taking this disease with them to Istanbul, to the Ottoman Empire, and indeed to the whole of Europe too," he said.

Even as he spoke the words, the Governor could almost hear the silent objections from those assembled around the table. Their misgivings had secretly found their way into his own heart too. The primary function of these Istanbul-mandated quarantine protocols was clearly to safeguard the state from disease, not Mingherians.

This veiled anger toward Istanbul was now being projected onto the Governor Pasha. But despite the consuls' and the doctors' insistence, even that second meeting of the Quarantine Committee did not prove enough to place a strict quarantine cordon around the Muslim neighborhoods and the most infected streets where all the migrants from Crete lived. As the delegates of the Quarantine Committee had intuited, the reason for this was that the Governor, having already thrown Sheikh Hamdullah's brother Ramiz into jail, now feared the sheikh's anger and the possibility that the holy man might try to sabotage quarantine efforts.

Another measure Istanbul had suggested was that houses that were too contaminated for normal disinfection to work should be burned to the ground. To make a fair assessment of the amount of compensation owed to people whose homes and possessions were thus destroyed, the Governor was to nominate a committee of seven composed of community leaders and Mingherian treasury officials. This committee's decisions on the compensation owed for each home would be nonnegotiable.

"Of course this all assumes there's enough money left in the coffers to pay those wretched souls who'll lose their homes!" said the German consul.

"I would be amazed if a government too timid to even enforce a quarantine cordon could ever be bold enough to burn down a Muslim mansion," added the French consul.

"As our dearly departed Bonkowski Pasha's assistant, Doctor Ilias, explained to us yesterday morning: the Sultan is well aware that the only thing that defeated the outbreaks of cholera in Üsküdar and Edirne seven years ago was to burn to the ground those entirely contaminated neighborhoods that the outbreaks originated in."

"You did say that it is our sultan's preference to burn infected locations, and that His Supreme Highness had personally expressed this view to Bonkowski Pasha!" said Doctor Nikos, looking at Doctor Ilias.

"That is not what I said!" Doctor Ilias replied.

"You did, and now you are denying it. What are you afraid of?"

"It is not a question of courage, but of balance," said Doctor Nuri, coming to Doctor Ilias's rescue. "To stop the disease in villages around Bombay it may be sufficient today to incinerate scraps, refuse pits, and infected homes. But just ten kilometers to the west, in the large tenements at the center of Bombay where the epidemic is at its fiercest, the only way to thwart the outbreak is to cordon the whole street and neighborhood."

Doctor Nuri paused for a moment, studying the delegates' expressions to see what effect his words had wrought, then resumed: "Every measure is relative to its context. The practice of burning the belongings of the dead and any other contaminated items is still common in Arabia and in the Hejaz, and now in China and India too. Burning down grimy, impoverished neighborhoods during outbreaks of cholera has been regarded in some cases as a chance to clear docks and city centers of loiterers, vagrants, and petty criminals, and an opportunity to engage in a little urban planning—opening up new, modern areas within cities, and creating public parks to benefit the health of all citizens."

"We will not stand for that here!" said the Governor.

"But this epidemic might not be like those little outbreaks of cholera we've had in the past that simply disappeared of their own accord by the time the summer was over," said Quarantine Master Nikos.

"Your Excellency, why do you think the situation in India has escalated into open conflict between the British and the native population? Is it really true that the locals there have been slaughtering British officers and doctors on the streets?"

"Sadly the intransigence of British colonial officers is to blame. They send mounted troops to look for the sick among ignorant village folk who know nothing of microbes and plagues, and all this with an unfortunate disregard for religious sensibilities regarding female modesty. They split families up, isolate those suspected of carrying the microbe, and send the sick off to the hospital without even deigning to explain where these people are being taken, and what for. So the locals have begun to suspect hospitals of poisoning people, that the plague is an excuse to cut and carve their bodies open."

"But we must of course remember that the natives, in their ignorance and atavism and their hostility toward the British, will *sabotage* anything," said the Quarantine Master. "Haven't you heard the kinds of things they've been saying over there? 'The mosque is our hospital!'"

"Do you condone such remarks?" said the Russian consul Mihailov. "Should doctors abandon the tenets of medical science when they are dealing with a benighted populace that rejects science?"

"At one stage the Indians were so livid that they would kill any Europeans or white men they saw on the street, whether or not they were doctors. So the British decided to loosen quarantine measures. This subdued the unrest, but caused the plague to spread faster. Eventually the British, wary of causing further turmoil, began to reason along the following lines: if the locals are going to resist quarantine measures, we might as well sit back and do nothing at all until they come to us themselves to ask for help . . . But this approach favored the outbreak of plague in Calcutta, for example."

"If I may please say a few words," said the leader of the Greek Orthodox community and bishop of the Church of Hagia Triada, Constantinos Effendi. His Excellency the Bishop had not spoken much over the past two days, and now everybody gave him their full and respectful attention. The bishop proceeded to deliver a speech he had prepared in advance. "Gentlemen, our Mingheria is not India! This comparison is misguided. The good people of our island, be they Orthodox or Muslim, are enlightened and civilized, and in this time of crisis they shall remain disciplined and adhere to the rules that our sultan has dictated and that the Governor Pasha is striving so valiantly to execute."

"Hear, hear!"

"When you hesitate to follow recommended medical procedures out of fear the fanatics will object and violence will ensue, that is when disaster is bound to strike," the bishop continued. "The Greek community is fleeing the island; the epidemic has frightened us. You will even hear some claim: 'This story about an epidemic was concocted to drive as many Greeks as possible away from the island and reduce us to a minority here so that we cannot demand independence.'"

"Gentlemen, our island is neither an Ottoman colony nor anybody else's dominion," said the Governor Pasha. "The people of Mingheria, more than half of whom are Muslims anyway, are an integral part of the Ottoman Empire, and whether they are Christians or Muslims, they shall remain loyal to the end to their beloved sultan."

But the debate on whether or not Mingheria was "like India" continued for a time as if the Governor hadn't spoken at all, and Doctor Nuri intervened to point out that when Bombay was in the throes of the plague three years ago, a full third of its nearly one million inhabitants abandoned the city to seek refuge elsewhere.

"Unless you quarantine the infected lodges in Germe and Kadirler, the Greek community will start leaving the island too—perhaps abandon it altogether," said the bishop of the Church of Hagia Triada. "Lamentably the exodus of Greeks from our island has already begun."

CHAPTER 21

As the meeting of the Quarantine Committee drew to a close, travel agents along Istanbul Street and near the port learned through clerks passing information on to those outside that starting at midnight on Sunday, all passengers aboard ships leaving the island would be subject to a five-day quarantine. There were only two ships officially scheduled to depart the island before that deadline. But in the three and a half days left until then, people would attempt to leave the island en masse.

The island's travel companies had immediately cast about for vessels to rent and sent telegrams calling for more ships. A substantial crowd began to assemble on the shore, composed of people looking for tickets, families who had boarded up their homes as soon as they had heard, those who preferred to see for themselves first what was happening at the docks, and others still (a significant presence) who were determined not to leave the island but had come down anyway, purely out of curiosity. Those who had already closed down their homes and packed their bags and trunks as if they were ending their seasonal sojourn on the island a little earlier than usual were mostly the island's wealthier Greek families, for instance the Aldonis, who had grown rich during the golden age of the trade in Mingherian marble; the new olive oil magnates the Hristoses; and the owner of the Dafni department store Tomadis Effendi, who imported the choicest embroidered coverlets, petticoats, and cross-stitched tapestries from Thessaloniki. (He had boarded up his shop overnight, smuggling his stock to his home outside the city to save it from disinfection.)

The scions of a handful of the island's foremost Muslim families had also come to the port, like Fehim Effendi, descendant of Blind Mehmet

Pasha, who was a clerk at the customs office, and Celâl son of Ferit, who normally lived in Istanbul but had come to oversee some repairs to the family home on the island. But most of the island's Muslim population had remained unmoved by this early agitation. We will not suggest, as Orientalist historians often do, that their attitude was a product of Muslim "fatalism" in the face of disease. Rather, compared with the island's Christian population, the local Muslim community was poorer, less educated, and more disengaged from the rest of the world.

A thunderstorm broke out just as the Quarantine Committee was dispersing, drenching the delegates. Black clouds hung so low in the sky that they brushed against the Castle towers, and each clap of thunder was like an omen of death. A bolt of green lightning fell upon the waters off of the Arab Lighthouse, and seemed, to the inmates who saw it from the prison battlements, like the image of a distant memory. There followed a rainfall which some remember as "the deluge," and to which they have ascribed a symbolic significance.

As the waters released by the thunderstorm wound their way toward the port, flowing through gutters, down walls, and into sewage drains dug into the middle of the street, municipal clerks delivered the list of quarantine provisions to two newspapers—one published in Turkish and the other in Greek—for typesetting. The words PLAGUE and QUARANTINE ran in large type right through the middle of these announcements, which were printed at the same printing press and affixed to every wall in the city. A handsomely illustrated poster declared that the municipal authorities would pay six silver coins for every dead rat.

Quarantine Master Nikos and the Governor had received intelligence that many shopkeepers had been hiding their goods to prevent them from getting damaged in disinfection operations and that nearly half the shops in the Old Market now lay empty. Doctor Nuri sent his most capable, brawny, and determined spray-pump operators to disinfect two junk shops near the Saddlers' Gate at the Old Market. These junk dealers stored their stock behind their shops, in empty lots cleared by fire and otherwise used as rubbish dumps, and had been selling all manner of objects—old pocket watches, religious icons, cigarette holders—that had belonged to dead plague victims, as well as victims' suits, trousers, and bedsheets and plague-infested mattresses and woolen fabrics. There were also cheaper articles available, supplied by thieves who had robbed and ransacked vacant homes until there was nothing left to steal and then injected their loot of contaminated clothing, carpets, quilts, and woolens into a deadly stream of commerce. The Governor had always regarded these junk shops, run by gregarious, sharp-witted Cretian Greeks, as hotbeds of disease, filth, and squalor, and the reason he had not shut them down before was that he had always been wary of the backlash this might cause.

A team of masked and gloved quarantine officers had soon cleared out the two junk shops and the smaller stores a few streets down, loading every object and item of clothing they had seized onto a wagon. They drove the wagon along the creek and slowly up Dikili Hill, where municipal authorities had been excavating two vast pits in which all the filthy, infected, disease-ridden cloths, woolens, and linens they gathered, and any other object that carried the plague microbe, were to be incinerated and sterilized with lime.

This policy, reminiscent of epidemics from bygone eras, was one that could be reasonably justified. Rather than use up the island's already limited supplies of carbolic acid and Lysol to painstakingly disinfect dead people's belongings handed over by the victims' fearful relatives, it was much easier and cheaper for quarantine officers to simply destroy them.

The island's quarantine officers were mostly unmoved by the tearful pleas of miserly shopkeepers, though we know today through the many letters of complaint from this time that some tradesmen were given preferential treatment. Some shopkeepers made no trouble at all when their shops were emptied out and whitewashed, for the treasury clerks sent by the municipality's damages committee to accompany these operations could sometimes decide on unexpectedly generous compensation payments. But elsewhere, such as among the shoemakers and leather dealers near the Old Bridge, there was more resistance, though there was not much these merchants could do other than complain vociferously. Everywhere, the general refrain was as follows: "This quarantine is being used to mistreat the island's Christian population; it's the Muslim pilgrims who brought the disease here in the first place."

In their bulky masks, their oilskin ponchos, and with their spray tanks strapped to their backs, the decontamination crews made for a rather unnerving sight. Destined to become fixtures of local children's dreams and nightmares for years to come, the first nine men recruited into these crews were in fact ordinary firemen who had received special training to operate the disinfection pumps. Years ago, when sprayable disinfectants were first introduced to the island and required people capable of operating the apposite pumps, the obvious solution had been to enlist Mingheria's firefighter crews, who were already affectionately nicknamed "siphon-men," and who had thereafter become the first to be called upon whenever there was a decontamination operation to be undertaken, or a job that required disinfectant solution to be sprayed. Ever since the discovery of the existence of bacteria, known in the popular parlance as microbes, there had been a vogue for haphazardly spritzing and sprinkling things with antiseptic solution and for inventing stylish implements commonly referred to as "sprinklers." Kiryakos Effendi, owner of the luxury store Bazaar du Île, had already placed an order in Thessaloniki for two separate models of disinfection pumps for domestic use.

Since the start of the outbreak, government clerks had been dispatched to stand outside municipal buildings to spray disinfectant carbolic acid solution, Lysol, or some other mixture into the air, just as the valets outside the Hotels Splendid and Levant were also doing. These initial precautions, which we now know to be largely ineffective, encouraged the public to remain cautious and mindful of hygiene but also fostered the illusion among those constantly reassuring one another with cries of "Don't worry, we'll be just fine!" that the epidemic was a minor threat easily defeated with spray pumps and remedies that could be sprinkled into the air like perfume.

In Arkaz too, during the outbreaks of diarrhea that erupted every summer, particularly in Germe and Çite and in the hovels near the port, people had become accustomed to seeing an elderly siphon-man trudging through their neighborhoods, disinfecting lavatories and filthy, mosquito-infested puddles with a dark green liquid. Children were not afraid of this endearing old man who'd been sent to stave off diarrhea and would follow him up and down the street. If the elderly siphon-man asked them to open up a door or show him some hidden spot or hole in the ground, local residents and shopkeepers immediately obliged, and everyone gladly helped out with disinfection operations.

But now nobody seemed to want to go anywhere near the spray-pump wielding firefighters. Could this changed disposition have been due to the new, larger cut of their black masks, or to the blinding gleam of their oilskin uniforms when they caught the evening sun, or to the fact that they never seemed to travel to any part of the city in groups of fewer than five? This time around, children didn't even think of playing with these mask-wearing officers but ran from them in sheer terror, as if they'd come face-to-face with the cyclops who was known to carry the plague and smear it all over drinking fountains and doorknobs. The city's grocers, butchers, snack vendors, sherbet makers, and café owners, meanwhile, did not even consider collaborating, but thought only about how best to protect their shops and their stock.

But not everyone was quite so "wily." A fruit seller at the bazaar had imagined that he would be spared if he just swore on the crucifix around his neck that the lettuce and cucumbers arranged upon his stall had come directly from his own garden. At the sight of two firemen clad in black oilskins pouring disinfectant all over his wares, the fruit seller had become so incensed that he had fainted. (He would later be revealed, through torture and interrogation, to have links to the Greek nationalists.) The amiable Kostis Effendi, who ran Arkaz's favorite sherbet stall, had also thought that a similar display of good faith might suffice. When the quarantine officers in their dark masks and the doctors turned up at his famous shop, much revered by children too, Sherbet Master Kostis theatrically poured himself four glasses in four colors of each of his rosewater-, orange-, bitter orange–, and sour cherry–flavored sherbets and drank them all in succession, as if to announce "My sherbet is clean!" But within moments quarantine officers and the crew of firemen had emptied the sherbet out of every jug on the shelves and thoroughly disinfected the shop with carbolic acid. A second team had followed in their wake to whitewash the place, have the door nailed and sealed shut, and declare the shop debarred from doing any further trade until the epidemic had passed.

"Let every drop you have spilled be my gift to you! But tell me, how will we put food on the table now, how will we survive?" said Sherbet Master Kostis.

When the Governor Pasha, who was following every development from his office (just as Abdul Hamid ruled his whole empire from the Yıldız Palace), heard what the sherbet maker had said, he sent another telegram to Istanbul to plead for assistance. Since all of the Governor's

telegrams tended to say the same things in the same tone and word-
ing every time, his code breakers hardly even needed to consult their
codebooks to find the numerical equivalent of a given phrase and would
often compose the message from memory. The terms most commonly
used in these telegrams to Istanbul were "disinfectant solution," "tent,"
"sterilizing oven," "cash," "doctor," and "volunteer."

The Doctor and Prince Consort knew from his experience of epidemics in other cities how quickly the firefighter crews could slip from
the tactful, solicitous manner of Istanbul's historic siphon-men into a
brutish ruthlessness. Some firemen sprayed disinfectant solution with
gentle, delicate gestures, as if watering a flower. Some looked almost
apologetic when approaching shopkeepers. A plea to sprinkle "anywhere
but there, sir, for the love of God!" could soften the heart of even the
most seasoned siphon-man and persuade him to shift his target. But
the opposite could also happen. Standing at a side entrance to the Old
Market, Doctor Nuri had watched a quarrel unfold between a quarantine officer and a local tradesman: drawn into a shouting match with the
shopkeeper, the officer, holding his hose almost as if it were the barrel
of a gun, had proceeded to vindictively drizzle disinfectant over rows
of plucked and singed chickens and quails, their skins all pink and yellow, stacks of chicken thighs, bits of offal, and bloodstained chopping
boards, as well as on the butcher himself and his apprentice. Having frequently had to settle quarrels between Ottoman soldiers and Arab grocers and camel drivers across the cities of Arabia, Doctor Nuri knew that
for quarantine to succeed and for the city to be saved, it was imperative
for these kinds of rows to be managed before they became too serious.

The Governor Pasha took particular care over the disinfection of
Sheikh Hamdullah's lodge, and began the operation by having his spies
draw up a map of the premises. The spray-pump crew was briefed in
advance by the Governor's clerks on where Sheikh Hamdullah slept
and where he delivered his sermons (both locations to be assiduously
avoided), where the guest rooms and wool-carding stations were situated, which room the lodge's treasured wool was stored in, and where
the kitchens, the privies in the garden, and the dervishes' cells were.

"Do not request permission to enter," said the Governor Pasha, "but
simply present them with the list of quarantine measures and proceed
immediately to your target and initiate the decontamination procedure.

Should anybody grab you or try to use force against you, do not fight back, but retreat immediately to the garden. Whatever may happen, do not allow yourselves to be drawn into arguments and recriminations."

Twelve burly-looking infantrymen from the Fifth Army were also standing at the ready, their rifles resting against their shoulders as they waited in the courtyard at the back of the State Hall. Their uniforms were old and faded, but clean. They had been selected from among the rare soldiers on the island who spoke at least a few words of Turkish, and placed under the command of an officer from Sinope who was, like his men, illiterate.

With its troop of armed, hulking soldiers, its mask-clad spray-pump crew, and its group of clerks carrying the municipality's gift of ten newly made mousetraps, the delegation made for a rather impressive quarantine patrol. Following closely behind them was the Major, who had been sent by the Doctor and Prince Consort as a kind of observer. We now know every detail of what happened in the lodge that day thanks to what the Major reported to Doctor Nuri, and what Doctor Nuri, in turn, told Princess Pakize:

The disinfection team entered the lodge as if they were staging a raid. By the time the gatekeepers standing in the lodge's garden, the dervishes, and the disciples scattered about the grounds had even begun to grasp what was going on, the spray-pump operators had already reached the first of their meticulously planned targets, subjecting the wool-carding room, the kitchens, and the entrance of the courtyard that led to the cells to a heavy, pungent shower of Lysol.

The scuffles began when they turned toward the little mosque and the cluster of cells that were among the oldest buildings on the lodge grounds. The guardsmen and gatekeepers tasked with protecting the lodge pushed an elderly fireman to the floor and set upon him with wooden bats that had been cut and prepared in advance. Alerted by the shouting and screaming, the disciples leaped to their feet, the dervishes stepped out of their cells, and all of them ran straight into the garden to join the fight—some of them only half dressed, some with their heads bare, and some holding pickaxes they had grabbed along the way.

Understanding that open battle was about to break out in the lodge's gardens, the Arab soldiers' commanding officer disregarded the Governor's repeated warnings in favor of his military instincts, and ordered his men to fight.

In that same moment, Sheikh Hamdullah spoke, his voice heard by all those present. "Welcome, welcome, we are glad to have you!" he began. His devotees, who had believed their sheikh to be unwell and asleep, stopped fighting as soon as they heard him speak. The sheikh then addressed the soldiers of the Fifth Army with a few words in Arabic. He was reciting the verse from the Koran's Hujurat *surah* that said "believers are but one brotherhood," and although no one understood him at first, the fact that he was talking in Arabic, and the sincerity in his voice, immediately convinced everyone around him that all of this fighting was altogether needless.

But in the meantime, a group of industrious firemen had continued to spray Lysol into the lodge's cells. Some have argued that what most enraged Sheikh Hamdullah was not that his stepbrother Ramiz had been arrested as a suspect in Bonkowski Pasha's murder (it was said that the sheikh wholeheartedly believed his stepbrother's name would soon be cleared), but rather the fact that even though everybody at the lodge that day had stopped fighting when they'd heard his conciliatory speech, these spray-pump operators had unceremoniously broken into the room where the lodge's secret fortune (its "hidden treasure," to quote the Hadith)—its wool—was kept, and ruthlessly sprayed reeking Lysol all over it.

The spraying of Lysol onto the "hidden treasure" was an offense so intolerable to the lodge that when they heard about it, some of the island's elders furrowed their brows as if they had been told a slanderous lie and declared that such an act could not possibly have taken place. The Governor too emphasized the same message for fear that the situation might otherwise escalate. But others were convinced that there had been an affront against the lodge, and that the sacred temple had been defiled with Lysol. Some gossipmongers (particularly the Greek newspapermen) and the foreign consuls, on the other hand, argued the exact opposite, suggesting that the Governor had given the lodge preferential treatment and should really have pushed for more Lysol to be sprayed. These claims were supported by the account of an elderly fireman who had been present on the scene.

This fireman had reported that during the disinfection operations, he had spotted two plague-afflicted disciples lying in a cell, the buboes on their necks and the stupefied, deranged expressions on their feverish faces making the nature of their ailment clear. Some foreign consuls seized upon this story to send telegrams to Istanbul and pressure the Governor into implementing a quarantine cordon, not just around the lodge, but over the whole neighborhood too, but the Governor, predicting that such a measure would incense Sheikh Hamdullah, decided that the best course of action would be to practice patience, let some time pass, and make sure to silence the gossipmongers, just as he had done after the Pilgrim Ship Affair. The other outcome of this episode was the universal consensus that the Arab soldiers from the Fifth Army in Damascus who spoke neither Turkish nor Mingherian could not be used to enforce quarantine.

So the Governor and Doctor Nuri told the Major he must redouble his efforts to turn the recruits that had been selected to support the quarantine effort into a new force—a little army of its own, perhaps. Over the past three days, and despite all the complications he'd had to deal with, the Major had managed to accomplish two weeks' worth of work and successfully recruited fourteen "soldiers" to the small Quarantine Army whose command he'd been assigned by the Quarantine Committee. It was decided then that this army should be headquartered in a small building near the garrison bakery, and operations to clear this space—which had hitherto been used as a depot—began that same morning. The main room at the entrance of the Mingherian Army Recruitment Office's small building by the docks was also provisionally handed over to the Quarantine Division. The Major would be given his own desk here, and this would be where volunteers were registered. Quarantine Master Nikos remarked that the people of the island were fond of this charming Venetian-era building, and that many among them—Greek and Muslim alike—were sure to volunteer for this temporary army, so long as their wages were paid and they were allowed to return to their own homes at night.

"Given that its Headquarters are to be housed within our garrison, the recruitment of soldiers to this Quarantine Army must follow Ottoman military conventions and be conducted solely from among the island's Muslim population," declared the Governor Pasha. "The Sultan has already introduced all of the reforms he promised to the Great Powers, starting from the French and the British, and just like his uncle and grandfather before him, he has been so earnest and determined in his efforts to remove all inequalities between his Christian and Muslim subjects that today the Ottoman Empire's Christian population has surpassed its Muslim community in terms of wealth, education levels, and craftsmanship skills, as indeed is the case on the island of Mingheria too. The only matter on which our sultan will not yield to the wishes of the Great Powers is allowing Christians into the ranks of the army. We've gathered here informally today to discuss and deliberate the most effective way to enforce quarantine measures; let us not start arguing among ourselves now as if we were having to deal with the foreign consuls too."

CHAPTER 22

As the editor of the *Adekatos Arkadi* was currently locked up in the Castle prison, the Governor summoned the editor of the island's other Greek-language newspaper, the *Neo Nisi,* to tell him word for word how he was to report on the decontamination of Sheikh Hamdullah's lodge. The Governor offered the young and idealistic journalist—whom he'd arrested in the past, and whose newspaper he'd withdrawn from circulation a few times—a plate of dried figs and walnuts, and some coffee, claiming both falsely and needlessly that everything had "just been disinfected in the sterilizing oven," as if it were an epidemic of cholera that they were dealing with. Later, as he saw the journalist out, the Governor spoke of the scale of the turmoil and calamity they were facing and of how anxiously Istanbul and the rest of the world were following events, and explained with a menacing smile that it was the duty of the press to support the state, so he had better make sure he didn't print the wrong thing lest he should get himself in trouble.

The next day the registry clerk brought in a copy of the new issue of *Neo Nisi* fresh from the printing press. The municipal translator read out to the Governor the column he had carefully translated from Greek to Turkish.

The report made explicit references to what Sami Pasha had told the journalist he must not "under any circumstances!" write about, describing in overblown terms and for the whole island to read how the siphon-men and the dervishes residing in the lodge had gone at one another with wooden bats and with their fists, and how the lodge's secret treasure—its store of wool—had been soiled and covered in noxious fumes. The Governor knew that the rumors generated by this report would spread thoroughly among the Muslim community. The charlatan sheikhs who'd been handing out amulets and the rural folk who believed in their powers, the angry young migrants from Crete, and indeed every Muslim on the island, including the more "enlightened" ones, would be moved to resist quarantine measures and grow resentful of the Governor.

The Governor and Manolis, the journalist responsible for the story, had had disagreements before. There had been a period three or four years ago when the courageous Manolis had sought to undermine the Governor and the Ottoman bureaucracy with his reporting on problems in the municipal government, the filthy state of the city's streets, allegations of corruption, and the laziness and ignorance of the local government clerks. The Governor, whose patience had long since run out but who had nevertheless been putting up with the situation lest he should be accused of intolerance, had eventually sent his intermediaries to threaten to shut the newspaper down unless it changed its position, and for a while the journalist had softened his tone.

But after some time, the same newspaper had undertaken a "planned and systematic" attack upon the Governor and the Quarantine Authorities, publishing a series of articles blaming them for the Pilgrim Ship Affair and compelling the Governor to find some pretext to lock Manolis up in the dungeons—although he had been forced to set the prisoner free eventually, under pressure from British and French consuls and from the telegrams he kept receiving from the palace.

What pained the Governor most now was to discover that all the warmth he had shown Manolis in their meetings after he'd had him released from prison seemed to have been for nothing! Once, when they had run into each other at the Hotel Splendid, the Governor had praised Manolis for his reporting on the war between the coachmen and the porters, congratulated him on his sources, and offered to pay him upfront with cash from the municipal purse to publish the piece and two future columns in the municipality's own Turkish-language newspaper, the *Arkata Times*. Another night, when they both happened to be dining at the Dégustation restaurant, the Governor had behaved very amicably toward Manolis in front of all the other patrons, inviting the journalist to his table, offering him some onion-and-mullet soup, and telling him openly and loud enough for everyone else to hear that his newspaper was by far the finest in the Levant.

Reflecting on these antecedents, the Governor now resolved to have the ungrateful Manolis thrown back into the dungeons, treating him to a fresh dose of its freezing, damp cells to find out under whose orders he had written his latest article and all those older pieces on the incident with the pilgrim ship. The plainclothes officers who'd been dispatched to capture Manolis did not find him at the offices of the newspaper whose copies they'd taken from circulation, nor at his home in the Hora neighborhood, but hiding at his uncle's house, where they caught him reading a book (Hobbes's *Leviathan*) in the garden, and hauled him straight to prison. Following a last-minute twinge of conscience on the Governor's part, the journalist was put in the more comfortable western wing of the jailhouse, which was also farther away from the areas worst affected by the plague.

When he went to see Marika that night, the Governor Pasha made love to her more out of habit than of any real desire, and afterward he listened to her account of all the latest gossip. This time Marika began by recounting the most improbable rumor of them all:

"They say there is a gang of Greek and Muslim orphans who go around at night knocking on honest, kindhearted people's doors. If you hear them knocking at your door, you are supposed to give them food, for it is said that those whose doors they knock upon and who give out food will not die of the plague."

"I'd heard this story before, but the knocking on doors is new!" said the Governor.

"It is said that the plague has no effect on these children. They will not fall sick, not even if they've been sleeping curled up with their dead mothers and fathers."

"And what about that man you said you saw from your window, the one who walks around at night carrying a bag of dead rats and scattering them about; has anyone else come across him?"

"I really did see that demon, my Pasha, but upon your advice I no longer believe that such a creature exists. In any case there has been less talk of him now that the masked disinfection crews have appeared."

"I see how it is: our siphon-men must have driven the demon away!"

"This will upset you, I know, but people are more and more convinced now that the plague arrived on the ship that brought the old sultan's daughter here."

"And you choose to believe this flagrant lie just to hurt me," said Sami Pasha with a degree of rancor even he was surprised to feel.

"Can a person really deceive themselves into believing something they know to be untrue?"

"So are you saying that you actually believe this lie?"

"Everyone believes it!"

"They believe it out of spite," said the Pasha. "The Sultan turned his own China-bound ship around to bring his most valued quarantine doctor here and save the people of this island, and in response these Greek nationalists think it fair to insult His Supreme Highness and the Ottoman Empire by saying it was that ship which brought the disease here. You must not allow them to manipulate you in this way!"

"Forgive me, Pasha . . . There are also those who say it was the rebel pilgrims who broke quarantine that brought the plague."

"It was cholera that those pilgrims carried three years ago, not plague!" the Pasha replied.

"It seems some of the State Hall clerks have been telling shopkeepers that 'for just five gold liras' they can issue them permits to keep their shops open."

"Those bastards!"

"Some children in the Kofunya neighborhood have seen people squatting in vacant homes. The children's fathers reported this to the authorities, but nobody came to check, no government clerks, no gendarmes nor guards."

"But that is nonsense; why should they not come?"

"There have been rumors that clerks and gendarmes have been too afraid for their lives to turn up for work, and that there have been cases of insubordination."

"What else?"

"It is said that there are several ships ready to come and pick up those who want to leave the island, but that you will not allow them to do so."

"And why would that be?"

"To make the disease spread farther so that all the Greeks will run away . . . Twice now I've heard stories of British and French soldiers landing in the north, near Kefeli."

"There is no reason why they would go north to Kefeli when they could come straight here."

"What do you mean, Pasha?"

"Seven people have died today!" said the Governor.

"Pasha, my brother's business partner has not been able to find any tickets on the Messageries *Baghdad,* nor on the next *Persepolis* ship. He holds you in the highest regard, and truly admires you. He is a proud man too, and he would never have come to me if it had not been a matter of vital importance."

"Will that Pantaleon ferry with the red chimney actually turn up, I wonder? These greedy agencies have been selling three tickets for every seat, and even so I've not said a word against them."

"There is another rumor going around, but I did not want to speak of it in case it should anger you. Perhaps it is not a rumor at all."

"What is it?"

"They say that the siphon-men who went to disinfect Sheikh Hamdullah's lodge got into a fight with the dervishes. With the rumor out that the Muslim sects will not follow quarantine procedures, and that the outbreak will never be controlled, it seems that some Greeks have begun to leave the island. But, Pasha, this island cannot be without its Greeks—just as it cannot be without its Muslims!"

"Of course," said the Governor. "But don't you worry, we will soon put that sheikh in his place. Though truthfully, he is a gentle soul."

When he convened with Doctor Nuri and Doctor Ilias the next morning to mark on their map the location of the homes of the previous day's seven victims, as well as any spots where they might have been exposed to the microbe, the Governor went straight and unhesitatingly to the point. "As long as Istanbul keeps protecting and pandering to Sheikh Hamdullah, we will have a hard time enforcing a serious quarantine here and ensuring that Muslims abide by its provisions," he began. "And when they see Muslims repeatedly violating quarantine protocols, Christians will stop respecting them too, and this plague will continue to kill and deplete us for years to come, just like in India. My dear doctor, how would you explain the fact that everything and everyone seems suddenly to have turned so dismally against us?"

Doctor Nuri noted that the first day of quarantine had in fact been relatively successful. The only unsavory incident had been the arrest of the owner of the large hay barn that served the island's coachmen;

though regrettable as the whole episode had been, the man had left the authorities with little choice. Having spent several agonizing days howling in pain as he battled the plague, the hay dealer's young apprentice had finally died, to the anguish of all those present, at which point the quarantine doctors had decided that it would not be sufficient to disinfect the haystacks, and that they would have to be burned instead. When the wagons that were supposed to carry the confiscated hay arrived, the owner of the barn had seen fit, in a moment of rage, to throw himself over his contaminated goods and bales of hay, and had attempted—with some success—to set himself on fire. He had subsequently been arrested for attacking the quarantine officers and trying to infect them with the disease.

But in the Governor's view, the real problem lay in getting people to "submit" to quarantine measures. Sheikh Hamdullah's brother Ramiz would be put on trial that same afternoon. "When Ramiz and his two murderous coconspirators are hanging from their necks in the State Hall Square, even the most unruly and impertinent will understand who really holds the reins of power on this island."

"Gentlemen, none of us are consuls here, and we need not argue about whether the state treats all its subjects equally, Christians and Muslims alike!" said Quarantine Master Nikos. "But our charming island has never seen anybody hanged in its State Hall Square in warning, as they do sometimes in Europe, so although I am sure that it would prove an effective deterrent for misbehaving children, I am less sure that it would be of any benefit to quarantine operations."

"It would be of no benefit at all, Your Excellency," said Doctor Ilias, addressing the Governor. "Bonkowski Pasha always used to say that hanging, beating, or locking people up is never the way to secure a successful quarantine or to modernize and westernize a nation."

"You are so scared you hardly leave the garrison anymore, and yet here you are defending the very people, these fanatics, who threaten you."

"Ah, Pasha! If only I could be so sure that they were the ones threatening me!" said Doctor Ilias.

"I am sure. I am also sure that if anything were to happen to any of us, it would undoubtedly be the work of that Ramiz and his men."

"If you are perceived as making unfounded accusations or perpetuating injustice of any kind, it will only encourage rebellion and disobedience among the populace!" said the Quarantine Master.

"It amazes me to see how many supporters this shameless, impertinent gangster seems to have gained just by virtue of his older brother being a sheikh," said the Governor, glancing at the Major.

But the Major did not say a word. When the Doctor and Prince Consort found the Governor alone in his office an hour later, he immediately addressed the matter that had been weighing on his mind.

"As you are aware, His Excellency the Sultan did not just send me to the island to institute quarantine provisions, but to find Bonkowski Pasha's killer too."

"Of course."

"Neither I nor the inquiry committee I head possess any evidence to suggest that Ramiz is the guilty party. In the time that passed between the moment Bonkowski Pasha walked out of the back door of the Telegraph Office to when his body was found in Hrisopolitissa Square, numerous witnesses saw Ramiz in the park behind the fishermen's jetty, then at Barber Panagiotis's (where he got a shave), and later with his friends in the garden of the clubhouse at the Levant Hotel."

"You would not be in such a hurry to come to these conclusions if you stopped to think for a moment why a man like Ramiz, who is normally so rarely seen, should be at such pains to parade himself in the city's best-known and most crowded areas precisely around the time that Bonkowski was killed," said the Governor with a derisory smile. "You'll see, when the gallows go up in the State Hall Square, nobody will dare take our quarantine lightly!"

CHAPTER 23

The Major always listened closely when the Governor mentioned Ramiz, but never said anything himself, lest he should reveal his own emotions. For under the effect of the stories his mother told him every time he came home, he had begun to develop an interest in Ramiz's former fiancée, Zeynep. More than all his mother's praise for the girl, the Major had been most impressed in those early days by how headstrong Zeynep seemed to be, and by the fact that she had broken off her engagement with Ramiz.

Zeynep's father the prison guard had already negotiated a marriage settlement with Ramiz, promptly sharing some of the ensuing payment between his two sons, and arranged every detail surrounding the nuptials—down to preparations for the wedding party itself—when all of a sudden he had died of the plague, and within two days his daughter Zeynep had called the wedding off. There was a possibility now that the matter might escalate, for Ramiz was related (if not by blood) to Sheikh Hamdullah, head of the island's most powerful religious sect and Ramiz's stepbrother.

According to the Major's mother, Zeynep might find a way out of the situation she was in by quickly marrying someone else and leaving the island altogether. The thought of this possibility and potential opportunity had entered the Major's mother's mind the moment she had seen her son, who had seemed to her—despite his good looks and officer's rank—so lonely and dejected.

We too shall now devote a few pages of this book to what is perhaps the most controversial—and consequently also the most fondly remembered and most frequently embellished and misrepresented—romantic love story in the history of Mingheria. In doing so we shall attempt to separate the historical facts of the Major and Zeynep's love from its romantic details. For the more romantic a historical account is, the less accurate it tends to be, and—unfortunately—the more accurate it is, the less romantic.

The varying interpretations of this love story rest on the possible reasons behind Zeynep's decision to call off her wedding to Ramiz. The account the Major's mother gave her son was that Zeynep had changed her mind about the wedding when she had discovered at the last moment that Ramiz already had another wife (some even said he had two) in Nebiler village in the north of the island. The Major really wanted to believe this explanation, but there were also those of a more polemical bent who claimed that Zeynep had known about this other wife from the start, and had been too afraid of her father and her brothers to oppose the match. When her father died, she had simply used something she had known all along as an excuse to break off the engagement. The real reason for her decision was that her father had bequeathed her bride price to his twin sons, Hadid and Mecid, but the two brothers had not shared any of it with their sister Zeynep. This had inflamed the young woman's rage, and she had become obsessed with the idea of leaving the island and going to Istanbul (a place she had never even seen before). We should point out, at this juncture, that it was a sign of remarkable temerity for a seventeen-year-old Muslim girl from a provincial town to even dream, in 1901, of doing such a thing, and this too proved irresistibly alluring to the Major.

Those on Ramiz's side, on the other hand, claimed that Ramiz and Zeynep had been madly in love but had been forced apart by Governor Sami Pasha for political reasons. The Governor Pasha's objective was to humiliate Ramiz so as to show Sheikh Hamdullah who was really in charge, and—as one male historian has put it—to use the Major's "charisma and authority" to strengthen his own political position.

Zeynep's mother, Emine Hanım, and the Major's mother lived in different neighborhoods, but had been friends for five years. Satiye Hanım had known Emine Hanım's fetching daughter since she was just a twelve-year-old girl. Even back then she had already been beautiful, but would the Major like her, and would Zeynep warm to the Major? After all, they hadn't even met each other yet.

But Zeynep and her family were still in mourning, and the threat of contagion loomed—if still somewhat vaguely—over the city; it was not perhaps the most appropriate moment to be discussing marriages and suitors again. Accordingly, the Major's mother had determined that the best course of action was for her son to call upon the bereaved family for a belated condolence visit. Zeynep's mother, Emine Hanım, believed that the only way for her daughter to salvage her own and her family's honor was to flee the island. It had been her idea, even before Zeynep had thought of it, that her daughter might find a route to Istanbul by marrying the handsome, decorated army officer and hero of the Greek War sent to their island by the Sultan himself, and she was the one to sow the first seeds of doubt and possibility in her daughter's mind.

But Ramiz really was madly in love with Zeynep, and the Major knew that, which was why he was feeling a little uneasy that day as he went, clad in his Ottoman officer's uniform, to meet Zeynep. It was not the first time the Major had gone to see a girl at his mother's suggestion. No sooner had her son graduated from the academy in Harbiye than Satiye Hanım had arranged a meeting with a girl whose family she referred to as "our relatives from the island" and who lived in a crumbling wooden house in the Vefa neighborhood. That girl had not been pretty. Hanging on one of the walls of her family home there had been a framed painting of the sea, something Kâmil had never come across in any house in Istanbul and which he would not forget for many years.

Zeynep's family lived just past the Muslim cemetery in the western edge of the Bayırlar neighborhood. When he was a boy, children from this neighborhood would fight turf wars with the kids from the Arpara neighborhood, where the Major lived. They would use slingshots to fire stones and unripe figs at one another, and sometimes they would pick up sticks and fight at close quarters like soldiers in the trenches. Sometimes the kids from the two neighborhoods would join forces to form a united Muslim front and descend like raiders upon the Orthodox neighborhoods of Hora and Hagia Triada across the Arkaz Creek, stealing plums and cherries from the enemy's gardens. In winter, when it became harder to ford the creek, everyone would retreat to their own streets and neighborhoods.

The Major watched a funeral convoy climbing up from the Bayırlar neighborhood toward the cemetery. It was a group of fifteen to twenty men, all walking in silence. Half of them wore fezzes and the other half were children; there was also a dog trailing behind them. Near the entrance to someone's garden, a child wept quietly, looking mortified. The Major caught the guarded, fearful glances of people peering out at the street from behind their garden walls. But the fantasy of marrying a beautiful girl seemed to shield him from their fear.

Major Kâmil and his mother had come up with a simple plan, in accordance with which the Major would begin to walk up the hill as soon as the tinny bells of Hagia Triada Church rang for noon.

At the same moment, his mother—who would, by then, already be in Zeynep and her mother's sitting room—would remark on "how terribly hot" it was, open the small bay window, call the girl and her mother over on some pretext, and show them her son walking along the street below the window. At that point she might even call out to the Major to come upstairs.

The Major had proudly convinced himself that he would not allow his heart to break even if he was rejected. He was wearing his uniform—which always had an effect on women—with its buttons polished to a shine, and his medals and badges were on display. But as he climbed the hill, he was astonished to feel his heart beating faster. There was his mother standing at the window where the sunlight shone. She saw her son and turned to speak to someone inside. The Major slowed his steps.

Just then the front door opened and the Major looked hopefully inside, thinking he was about to see beautiful Zeynep.

Instead a little boy showed him into the building. Upstairs, the Major found his mother, Satiye Hanım, and Zeynep's mother, Emine Hanım, sitting on the sofa. Emine Hanım cried a little. Once she had regained her composure, she said how well his officer's uniform suited him, God bless him. They talked about the rats for a while. One morning ten days ago the women had woken up to find the street that led to the neighborhood below so covered in dead rats that it had become impassable. Zeynep's mother then relayed with total conviction some of the rumors that had been circulating about the plague, rumors that neither the Major nor his mother (under her son's influence) believed in the slightest. The plague had been brought by a priest with bloodshot eyes, a black cape, and a black goatee who crept in every night from the Christian neighborhoods with a sack full of dead rats to strew across the streets and gardens of the Muslim quarters, and a plague-infested paste to smear onto fountains, walls, and doorknobs. A child from the Kadirler neighborhood who had run into him one night had discovered that the priest was a cyclops, and he'd had such a fright that he had stuttered for two days straight. Emine Hanım told her guests that if you could get yourself an amulet blessed by Sheikh Hamdullah and hold it toward the one-eyed plague demon, it would immediately retreat without taking any dead rats out of his sack.

The beautiful girl the Major's mother had told him about was not there. Like a child fed up with the grown-ups' talk, the Major gazed out of the window at the dark blue sea, the last few houses along the edges of Arkaz, and the sparse groves of olive trees. He was so nervous that he felt parched with thirst, like a patient in some hospital in the desert.

His mother somehow sensed his thirst. "If you go downstairs, Beşir will give you water," she told him.

The Major climbed down the stairs to the graveled yard and entered the unlit kitchen adjoining the barn.

Just as he had begun to think he would never find the water jug and its ladle in that darkness, a gas lamp briefly flickered to life before quickly going out again. In that single breath of light, a woman, a shadow, whispered in Mingherian, *"Akva nukaru!"*—"The water's over here!"

But it was Beşir who lifted the wooden lid off the water jug and ladled water out for the Major. The Major drank the water (which tasted of dust) and returned upstairs, and it was only then, when he noticed the strange expression on his mother's face, that he realized that the girl he had seen in the kitchen must have been Zeynep. Shortly after that, he began to think that she was rather beautiful. Zeynep did not come upstairs to sit with him.

This is all that Princess Pakize's letters tell us of the two lovers' first encounter. We believe this version to be true. The story that the couple had a long conversation in Mingherian that day was a myth later introduced and encouraged by the Major himself. These inventions were also popularized by official histories, school textbooks, and the ultranationalist right-wing press of the 1930s, influenced at the time by the policies of Hitler and Mussolini. But in truth, in 1901 the Mingherian language was not sufficiently developed to allow for the complicated, profound utterances the couple was later rumored to have exchanged, such as "We could have met much sooner!" or "Let us rename everything in the language of our childhood!"

It must also be noted that in 1901, an Ottoman officer from the provinces of the Empire who wanted to impress a girl was much likelier to speak to her not in their local language, but in Turkish, the language under which he had made a name for himself. The same was true of Zeynep too. The two words she had spoken in Mingherian *(akva nukaru)* had not been planned, and had come out of her mouth unbidden. *Akva* (meaning "water") is the oldest and most beautiful of all Mingherian words, and has spread—starting of course with Latin—from Mingherian to all the languages of southern Europe.

CHAPTER 24

As in every part of the Ottoman Empire, in Mingheria too court cases involving foreign citizens were dealt with by the island's consulates. A financial dispute between Monsieur Marcel, French citizen and owner of the island's Medit bookstore, and a British citizen (the consul Monsieur George), had been handled by the French consulate, as the plaintiff in the case in question was Marcel Effendi. Cases involving both foreigners and Ottoman citizens were tried in the Ottoman courts, but consuls were allowed to attend as translators and intervene as needed. The only cases in which the Governor Pasha could legitimately interfere and exert his influence to ensure the most appropriate outcome were disputes between Muslims over debt, property, and minor incidents of bodily harm, but he enjoyed wielding what power he did have, and would always readily share his views with the judge.

Cases involving charges of murder or abduction and elopement against subjects of the Ottoman Empire tended to be more complicated and inevitably attracted the attention of the Istanbul press, as a result of which they were usually moved to the courts of the imperial capital by order of Abdul Hamid himself, who was always eager to exercise direct control over all matters. Three years ago the trial of the bandit Nadir, charged with kidnapping a Greek girl and murdering two people in the process, had attracted a great deal of attention outside the island thanks not only to the efforts of the local consuls but of the foreign ambassadors in Istanbul too. The case had conveniently served as evidence for those who argued that the Ottoman Empire may have introduced a whole host of reforms on paper but that, in practice, it persisted in its old despotic ways. Eventually, and before the Governor could interfere in the verdict, the bandit had been taken to Istanbul, there to be quietly and discreetly hanged in the gloomy prison wing of the Selimiye Barracks. Another case that had caught Istanbul's attention the previous year and been moved to the courts there was that of the insolent, recalcitrant Ramos Terzakis, who had been caught—thanks to a tip-off from the archaeologist Selim Sahir—trying to smuggle out a sculpture of Venus, and who had used forged documents to claim he was a consular employee when he was, in actuality, an Ottoman citizen. (In the end Abdul Hamid had not only pardoned the smuggler, but also rewarded him with gold and a medal of the Order of Mecidiye, Third Class, as was his wont with former enemies turned informants whom he thought he could recruit to his service.)

But although Bonkowski Pasha's death had been widely reported in the Istanbul papers, Abdul Hamid had not sent any orders for the trial to be held in Der-i Saadet. The Governor Pasha assumed this must be because of quarantine regulations, and a concern that the plague might spread to military vessels. Having thus surmised that what the Sultan wanted was for the perpetrators to be quietly punished and for the whole matter to be forgotten as soon as possible, the Governor summoned the President of the Court to his offices and informed him that it was the Sultan's command that the court should proceed to trial without waiting for the Investigative Committee's report and immediately sentence the three defendants to death.

That same afternoon, an armored vehicle sent from the garrison transferred Ramiz and his two associates to the holding cell in the basement of the State Hall. After being kept in that dark, fetid room for two hours, the prisoners were then led to the courtroom. Despite the torture he had endured during his interrogation, Ramiz had never admitted to the crime he was accused of (a rare occurrence), and his proud, dignified comportment in court was received by the presiding judge—who had arrived on the island from Istanbul two months ago—both with respect and with a measure of irritation. Unlike most people, tall, green-eyed, good-looking Ramiz had not been turned ugly by the torture he had been subjected to.

The charges had been drummed up with reference to the files compiled over many years by spies and detectives employed by the Department of Scrutinia to record Ramiz's crimes against the Governor and the Ottoman Empire. Ramiz's ties to the exasperated villagers involved in the Pilgrim Ship Affair, his confrontations with the gendarmerie, and his support for the marauder Memo, responsible for countless raids upon the island's Greek villages (and whom the Governor himself also secretly sponsored), were all cited in the case files as evidence that Ramiz's nature and disposition pointed to his having arranged for the assassination of Bonkowski Pasha, with the fact that his whereabouts at the time of the killing were accounted for being no indication of his innocence. According to the indictment, Ramiz's men had been lying in wait for the famous Royal Chemist in and around the neighborhoods where the island's religious sects were based and where consecrated prayer sheets were most commonly to be found. Ramiz's motive for organizing the assassination was to undermine the quarantine and precipitate unrest upon the island. This would give the Western powers an excuse to intervene in Mingheria too, as they had already done in Crete, and tear the island away from Ottoman rule. Ramiz—who supported the island's highway bandits in their raids on Greek villages for precisely the opposite reason—did not even deign to respond to these accusations. When he was asked if he had any final words for the court, he said:

"None of these falsehoods nor the torture I have been put through have anything to do with politics. I am being framed for this crime because of a woman. This is a matter of love and jealousy."

"He must have been talking about Zeynep!" said Princess Pakize when her husband relayed Ramiz's words to her. "Was the Major there?"

Prince Consort Nuri told her that the Major had been present at the deliberations over the verdict, but had not been seen at all during the trial itself. It was especially the Princess who was interested in the Major's infatuation with Zeynep. But Ramiz's eloquence had surprised them both, for he had mostly been described to them as little more than a bully and a boorish thug.

The Princess and Prince Consort sat in their quarters discussing the latest developments in the search for Bonkowski Pasha's killer. Under pressure from the Governor, the officers of the Investigative Committee were concentrating their efforts on Ramiz's entourage, the disciples of the Terkapçılar and Halifiye sects, and the merchants who were known to frequent these lodges, but so far they had not uncovered any conclusive evidence.

The Doctor and Prince Consort's view was that the Governor's polit-

ical preconceptions were preventing him from considering other pos-
sibilities, and that he lacked any interest in facts and details—that his
method, in other words, was also wrong. By the Governor's logic of political inquest it could indeed just as easily be concluded that the man
behind Bonkowski Pasha's murder must be the Greek consul Leonidis,
who wanted the outbreak to keep spreading! Or perhaps it could have
been a different consul, acting on the general assumption that people
like Ramiz would ultimately get the blame.

Emulating the characters of her uncle's beloved detective novels,
Princess Pakize devoted much of her time during this period to puzzling
with her husband over the mystery of Bonkowski Pasha's murder. But
sometimes she would let her anger toward her uncle get the better of
her, her emotions clouding her judgment in a way that Sherlock Holmes
would certainly have frowned upon, and leading her to the sudden and
impulsive conclusion that the assassination must have been carried out
under orders from her wicked uncle Abdul Hamid. Once she even let
slip to her husband that she found his refusal to accept the truth of her
uncle's involvement in the assassination, and his willingness instead to
run around the island investigating on the Sultan's behalf, to be both
foolish and demeaning.

"I must confess it amazes me that you are unable to see how this is
evidently all his doing, and that he is now merely shifting the blame
onto others, just as he did after the assassination of Mithat Pasha!" she
said. "You really are naïve."

Feeling, for the first time in their marriage, hurt and heartbroken
by something his wife had said, Doctor Nuri hurried out of the room.
Whenever he was lost in his thoughts, he liked to walk aimlessly around
the city, lending his ear to the mysterious silence of its streets and wanting to see for himself the symptoms of the disease, the signs of the
spreading outbreak, and the kinds of remedies people were coming up
with. It was clear now even from the way the trees rustled in the breeze
that everyone had begun to feel afraid. Some homes appeared to have
their front doors shut and sealed, but a glance at their second-floor windows would reveal that there were still people inside. There was a heavy
air, almost a kind of aura, weighing over the streets now, under which
the spread of the disease seemed to coalesce with the actions of the killer.
Some people had piled their pots and pans, their travel trunks, and their

earthenware out in their yards, and in another garden Doctor Nuri saw a harried father and son rushing to complete some kind of carpentry work. Perhaps they were making preparations in case the outbreak worsened, and planned to barricade their home from the inside. As he surveyed this world of ordinary objects, of well sweeps, doorknobs, locks, gas lamps, and kilims laid out under the sun, Doctor Nuri hoped that he might understand something about the disease and the epidemic that no one else had noticed before, but that was, in fact, perfectly obvious once you knew it was there.

He would have liked to explain to the Governor Pasha the remarkable similarity between solving a murder and stopping an epidemic. But when he visited the Pasha in his office again that evening, all he could do was question him on what he considered to be the most unconscionable aspect of that day's trial.

"Your Excellency, is this person really the killer? Or might he perhaps have 'confessed' under duress?"

"The telegram sent by the palace directly to your esteemed self and the royal directives that I have received can leave no doubt in either of our minds that His Royal Highness the Sultan wishes above all else for the killer to be identified without delay!" said the Governor Pasha. "That is why they have sent you here, of course. If a murder is committed in a province of the Empire and matters get so out of hand that the authorities in Istanbul and the Sultan feel the need to intervene, there is no longer anything the local governor can do. In the olden days, if I had come out and said I was looking for the killer but hadn't found him yet, my words would have been taken as a declaration of inadequacy and a sign that I had lost my grip over the province, and I would have been relieved of my duties posthaste. Some of those old sultans might even have interpreted such an admission as a nefarious plot to challenge their authority and collude with the enemy, and have me beheaded for it!"

"But things have changed now. After the reforms of the Tanzimat era, it is no longer communities but individual citizens who are held responsible for their actions. That is why the Sultan sent me here."

"On a matter as significant as this, it should be the state that decides who is responsible for what," the Governor replied. "Otherwise the Christian minorities that control some of the smaller matters upon this island, and its commercial activities too, shall no doubt seek to take advantage. In any event, we have apprehended the killer, and he has confessed unequivocally to his crime."

"This is not how the Sultan wishes for Bonkowski Pasha's killer to be caught."

"You speak as if you had some special understanding of what His Supreme Highness wants and how he wants it."

"I do," said the Doctor and Prince Consort. "His Serene Highness wishes for us to find Bonkowski Pasha's true killer just like Sherlock Holmes would—that is, by examining the details of the murder and building a case based on evidence, not on beatings and torture."

"Who is Sherlock Holmes?"

"He is a British detective who collects evidence first, then goes home and unravels the mystery by using logic to analyze all the clues. Sultan Abdul Hamid wants us to solve this murder like Europeans would, finding the killer by following the clues that will lead us to him."

"Our sultan may recognize the accomplishments of the British, but he takes no pleasure in them. You should consider that in your logic too."

We will note here, in a tantalizing nod to our readers, that there was an element of the prophetic in these final words from the Governor that evening.

CHAPTER 25

B ut what did Abdul Hamid mean by the phrase "like Sherlock Holmes"? Doctor Nuri had first heard the expression shortly before his marriage, and directly from the Sultan himself. For our story to be more readily understood, we shall remind ourselves now of a fact about Sultan Abdul Hamid known by all historians specializing in the history of the Ottoman Empire during the second half of the nineteenth century: Abdul Hamid, the last great Ottoman sultan, was a fan of murder mysteries. Wary of ever leaving the confines of the Yıldız Palace, Abdul Hamid subscribed to the world's principal newspapers and magazines and sought to keep up with new books and ideas. The clerks of the Translation Bureau he'd had set up in the palace translated political treatises for the Sultan's perusal, as well as any newspaper articles and books on the latest developments in science, technology, engineering, and medicine. Most recently, for instance, they had translated three books from French: a volume on the Russian military, a life of Julius Caesar, and a study of infectious diseases. But most of the time, the clerks of the Translation Bureau were busy translating detective novels.

Sometimes the Sultan would discover a new writer (Eugène Bertol-Graivil, Edgar Allan Poe, or Maurice Leblanc, for example) and wish to read all of his other books too; or perhaps his ambassador to Paris, Münir Pasha (whose duties also included, as he later revealed in his memoirs, purchasing underwear for the Sultan from the Bon Marché department store), would notify him of a new book by one of the authors the Sultan already knew and loved (such as Émile Gaboriau or Ponson du Terrail), so that the palace's translators could get to work the moment the book in question—swiftly dispatched by express post—arrived in Istanbul. Princess Pakize's older sister and frequent correspondent Princess Hatice was by then already engaged to be married, and her future husband, a palace clerk, had sometimes worked on these rushed translations too, all in a bid to ensure the novel the Sultan wished to read that evening would be ready in time. The Sultan also had English translators at his disposal. When an article on Abdul Hamid had appeared in the *Strand Magazine* (calling him, among other things, the Bloody Sultan and a tyrant), the translator who had rendered it into Turkish had, in a moment of intuition, also translated the Sherlock Holmes story ("The Adventure of the Engineer's Thumb") that had been printed on the other side of the same page, and having read and enjoyed the story, the Sultan had begun following its author Arthur Conan Doyle too.

When the palace's own translators could not turn things around quickly enough, professional translators would be brought in, their services secured through any one of Istanbul's famous booksellers. So it was that during those years many Young Turks, revolutionaries, liberals, and journalists inadvertently translated novels for Abdul Hamid, a man they despised. Opponents of the Sultan, who claimed he was a tyrant capable only of banning things and locking people up, and French-speaking Greek and Armenian medical students, who called him the Bloody Sultan, ended up serving as his translators, and although some might have had an inkling of the truth, most of them thought they were merely working for the Armenian bookseller Karabet. Sometimes Abdul Hamid would also commission unabridged translations of classic novels like *The Three Musketeers* and *The Count of Monte Cristo* for someone to read out to him in the evenings, and if he deemed any of their contents inappropriate, he would take it upon himself to censor the whole book or some of its pages. These translations were reissued after the foundation of the Turkish Republic, billed as "translations commissioned by Abdul Hamid," and missing the sections he had censored.

The publication in France of the world's first murder mysteries and detective novels, their growing popularity in England, and their spread across the world through translations into foreign languages coincided with the period of Abdul Hamid II's rule, so that it would not be inaccurate to describe the Sultan's collection of five hundred translated volumes, currently held at the University of Istanbul, as a little library of the early years of crime fiction.

More than a hundred years later, at a time when the Turkish Republic's ruling politicians were naming hospitals after Abdul Hamid and extolling his virtues as an autocratic but also a patriotic and pious leader beloved by the masses, historians were able to study the collection of novels amassed by the Sultan they idolized and thus determine his specific taste in crime fiction. The last great Ottoman sultan, who was to rule for thirty-three years, did not appreciate melodramatic coincidences in his detective novels (such as in Eugène Sue's *The Mysteries of Paris*), nor did he enjoy tawdry romances that interfered with the plot and relegated logic to the background (such as in the works of Xavier de Montépin). The stories that pleased him most were those where the clever detective, working in harmony with the state and the police, would carefully read through every report he received, then use his superior intellect to identify the culprit and solve the puzzle.

Abdul Hamid would not read these novels himself. A palace clerk, usually a seasoned courtier who had gained the Sultan's confidence and was known to possess a pleasant speaking voice, would sit at night behind a folding screen near the Sultan's bed and read the books to him. For a time, the chosen reader was the Master of the Royal Wardrobe, whose chief role was to dress the Sultan, and later the task was assigned to reliably loyal palace pashas. When he was tired Abdul Hamid would call out, "That will do," then promptly fall asleep. Or sometimes the trusty palace reader would infer from a lengthy silence that His Highness the Sultan, pillar of the world, had dozed off, and so he would tiptoe out from behind the folding screen and leave. Every time a novel was finished, the clerk would write "Read" on the last page, just like that Chinese emperor who stamped landscape paintings he liked with a red seal. For like all people prone to paranoia and rancor, Abdul Hamid had a prodigious memory, and once, when a clerk had accidentally started reading him a novel the Sultan had already heard seven years before, Abdul Hamid had first banished him from the palace, and later exiled him to Damascus.

Doctor Nuri Bey already knew most of these stories when he went to meet the Sultan for the first time at the Yıldız Palace. As he waited to be seen, he heard once again from Princess Pakize's sister Princess Hatice's husband-to-be that—just as Doctor Nuri had presumed—Professor Nicolle and Professor Chantemesse, the two Frenchmen who taught at the Imperial School of Medicine, and Professor Bonkowski had all three spoken highly of him in the past, that it was on these grounds that Doctor Nuri had been authorized, with His Supreme Highness's approval, to enter the harem and examine the former sultan Murad V's elderly wife (who was afflicted by a stubbornly persistent ailment), and that, following his encounter with Princess Pakize there, and after a thorough vetting of his background, it was not only agreed that he should be permitted to marry the Princess, but that the match should be actively encouraged. The Sultan had personally requested lengthy reports at every stage of this process, and had been impressed by what he had heard of Doctor Nuri's expertise in microbiology and laboratory practices.

As he received Doctor Nuri at the palace on the day set for his audience with the Sultan, Princess Hatice's husband-to-be carefully explained that contrary to popular credence, His Supreme Highness very rarely accepted visitors, that even grand viziers, field marshals, and the most distinguished foreign ambassadors could be kept waiting for hours outside his door, and that the doctor should regard the time afforded him today as a great honor. Even so, Doctor Nuri was made to wait inside a room in the palace for half a day. At one point he was told that he would be accompanied to the Imperial Guesthouse, for the Sultan would not be able to receive him until the next day after all, and in the meantime it would be more expedient for Doctor Nuri to spend the night at the palace. Doctor Nuri's mind was mostly preoccupied with thoughts of Princess Pakize and the prospect of marrying a sultan's daughter, but at the same time he was also thinking that he could be arrested at any moment, like so many young doctors before him who'd been summoned to the Yıldız Palace for an audience with the Sultan and kept waiting. Indeed nobody—not his mother, his relatives, or any of his doctor friends—would have been surprised if, having turned up at the palace with dreams of marrying the former sultan's daughter, Doctor Nuri had ended up being taken captive and put into prison instead.

But later a palace clerk showed up and informed the doctor that His Supreme Highness would see him now. Doctor Nuri followed the hunchbacked clerk up a lightly sloping path to a single-story structure on the palace grounds. There was a crowd of aides, clerks, and eunuchs assembled inside. But the only other person present in the room where he met Sultan Abdul Hamid was the palace's Chief Secretary, Tahsin Pasha.

The young doctor found that looking at the Sultan for too long was tiring and even a little frightening. A substantial portion of his mind had now been taken over by the single refrain that he was "here, now, in the exalted presence of the great and all-conquering sultan Abdul Hamid," and he could not really think of much else. Having bowed all the way to the floor in obeisance, he kissed the Sultan's small, warm, bony hand. The room, fitted with thick curtains and carpets the color of dark naphtha, was only dimly lit. When the Sultan spoke, Doctor Nuri listened without thinking of anything else, except to remind himself he must make sure he didn't do anything wrong.

Abdul Hamid was very glad that both his brother's consort and granddaughter had recovered, and even gladder that this had been achieved through the knowledge and resources of the Imperial Bacteriology Institute in Nişantaşı, but he was especially pleased that her illness had proven "conducive" to an altogether-different, happier occurrence. It was a speech that Princess Pakize would later often ask her husband to repeat. For according to the Princess, these remarks proved that by arranging for the third of his older brother Murad V's captive daughters to be married too, Abdul Hamid had cleared his conscience—which showed just how little guilt he must have felt to begin with for having kept them all imprisoned inside a tiny palace for twenty-five years.

Once he had satisfied himself that everything was in order with the three sisters' bridal trousseaus (then on display at the palace) and all of the other wedding preparations, the Sultan had turned to the topic he was most interested in, and began to ask Doctor Nuri a series of searching questions on the workings of the Quarantine Authority in the Hejaz. Having devoted five years of his life to this very subject, Doctor Nuri responded with a candid account of his experiences. Abdul Hamid had assumed a demeanor designed to encourage sincerity. The Sultan's expression was placid, and he looked tired, but his interest and attention were undivided. Doctor Nuri's nervousness had subsided; his heart was still beating fast, but he was no longer afraid. He began instinctively to tell the Sultan about the misdeeds of the captains of the British ships that brought pilgrims from India. Unable to stop himself, he then described in unsparing detail the difficulties the Quarantine Authority had had to deal with in trying to bury those who had died from cholera, and pointed out that the dormitories the Sharif of Mecca and his clan offered for the pilgrims' use were rife with disease. It briefly crossed Doctor Nuri's mind that having previously considered Abdul Hamid to be the principal cause of all these evils, he was now appealing to the same man as if he were the only person in the world who could possibly rectify them, but just as he was about to mention two more problems that needed urgently to be solved, the Sultan interrupted him.

"I have oft been apprised of your impeccable conduct and qualities," said the Sultan and pillar of the world. It was as if all of the horrors that had just been described to him only mattered insofar as they provided the Sultan with a reason to commend the young doctor. "Now tell me all the knowledge you possess on microbes."

The doctor replied that "every disease comes from microbes." As he knew how much money the Sultan was spending on all the quarantine and cholera experts he had brought to Istanbul, and how proud he was of his Imperial Bacteriology Institute in Nişantaşı, Doctor Nuri made sure to speak of that institution as one of the world's leading scientific laboratories, second only to the one in Paris. The Sultan responded with a satisfied half smile. Doctor Nuri added that the Empire's doctors and medical students had "learned so much" from Professors Chantemesse and Nicolle, the two French doctors who taught there. Finally, knowing that three days ago the Sultan had been read a book (translated from French) on infectious diseases, that he had asked for some passages to be read out to him over and over again, and that he had always been interested in the sciences and in all the latest scientific and medical discoveries, he said: "Your Highness, the secret to defeating diseases like cholera, yellow fever, and leprosy lies, of course, in microbes and bacteria. However, the science of bacteriology"—Doctor Nuri pronounced that last word exactly as he thought a Frenchman would—"is no longer sufficient in fighting outbreaks, and the British have now also invented something called epidemiology, a new and vital science of infectious disease."

With the Sultan appearing to be engrossed in his explanation, and the expression on Tahsin Pasha's face reassuring him that he was not doing anything he shouldn't be doing, Doctor Nuri continued to talk, describing how the science of epidemiology had first been discovered forty-five years ago during an epidemic of cholera in London. During this outbreak, while every doctor was busy combing the city street by street to try and have infected homes cordoned off and the belongings of the dead incinerated, one doctor did something different: he began to mark all of the information coming out of London upon an enormous map of the city. "They soon realized by observing the disposition of the green marks made by this doctor that homes nearest to the city's major water fountains were likelier to be infected with cholera," Doctor Nuri explained with breathless excitement. A closer look at the map had revealed that "whereas everyone on one street seemed to have fallen ill, the beer factory workers who lived on the next street had been entirely unaffected. The doctors begin investigating why this might be, and discover that the beer factory workers do not collect their drinking water from the municipal fountain, but from the beer factory's own supply, which is boiled clean. That is how they realize that the source of the epidemic is not, as they had previously believed, the humid, filthy air of this or that neighborhood, or the sewage system, or even people's private water wells, but the city's own contaminated water network, which supplies the public fountains. All of this to say, Your Highness," the prospective groom concluded, "that an epidemiologist could uncover the mystery behind an outbreak without examining a single patient—all by sitting in his office and studying a map!"

"Just like Sherlock Holmes!" said Abdul Hamid, who never set foot outside his palace.

The Sultan had of course made this remark, which is of central importance to our story, under the influence of the detective novels he was, in those days, so fond of having read out to him. What he was referring to was the idea that even the thorniest of problems could be solved from behind a desk, off the field and from a distance, solely through the power of logic.

Just after he had spoken these words, His Royal Highness was approached by Chief Secretary Tahsin Pasha, and at the same time another clerk informed Doctor Nuri that the audience had terminated. So it was that the Sultan's remark took on a whole new significance. Doctor Nuri exited the chamber, walking backward and improvising a series of salutations. The encounter he had just experienced would continue to affect him for a very long time.

What had Abdul Hamid meant when he'd said, "Just like Sherlock Holmes"? Busy with their wedding celebrations, Doctor Nuri and Princess Pakize had not found much time to stop and reflect upon the weight of the Sultan's words. Perhaps the Sultan had only wished to make a quip, knowing that one of the palace clerks who translated his detective novels was engaged to marry Princess Pakize's older sister and correspondent Hatice, and that he and the third sister's suitor would therefore soon be brothers-in-law.

But the Doctor and Prince Consort had often thought of that phrase "like Sherlock Holmes" since he had been sent to Arkaz with the task of curbing the outbreak and finding the culprit behind the death of the Royal Chemist. He had come to the conclusion that what Abdul Hamid wanted was for his cherished Royal Chemist Bonkowski Pasha's killer to be apprehended through the same methods Sherlock Holmes employed.

Yet Doctor Nuri often found himself having to argue with the Governor Pasha over the implications of the expression "like Sherlock Holmes," both in general terms and in relation to the assassination of Bonkowski Pasha—that is to say not just on a conceptual level, but in its practical applications too. The crux of these arguments was that the approach the Governor Pasha had taken to the search for Bonkowski's killer, and the "method" he had applied, were wrong. By using torture, the Pasha had managed to force a confession from one of the men he'd had arrested along with Ramiz. Having been beaten with sticks, tortured with pliers, and deprived of sleep, the suspect—by this point already half dead—had done what most people in his position would have done: confessed his guilt, accepted the fabrication that he had acted under Ramiz's orders, and hoped that in doing so he might be pardoned by the Governor. But even if the prospect of a special pardon hadn't been dangled before him (and in truth the Governor had no idea that the torturer had made such a promise in his name), the prisoner had by then been reduced to such a wretched state that he would have been ready to admit even to being the person walking the streets of the capital at night spreading the plague into mosque courtyards and water fountains, along the city walls, and all over doorknobs too.

Princess Pakize's early letters to her older sister had already been replete with teasing remarks about the Governor and mocking references to his officious, affected airs, yet they had also revealed a measure of respect for his diligence and his responsible, statesmanlike manner. But soon Doctor and Prince Consort Nuri began to worry that the Governor might arbitrarily decide to execute Ramiz and his men without checking with Istanbul first, and that this would turn Sheikh Hamdul-lah into a sworn enemy of quarantine and Governor both.

Having grown increasingly westernized under the influence of the world's Great Powers, by 1901 the Ottoman legal system dictated that every death sentence handed out in the Empire had to be sanctioned by the high court in Istanbul. In practice there were many exceptions made to this rule, whether due to war, rebellion, problems in communication, or a lack of time. With imperial troops constantly fighting on this or that front and busily hanging rebels as a way of suppressing separatist movements, governors across the Empire would arrange rapid, exemplary executions almost as a matter of course, and without waiting for Istanbul's consent. Where a death sentence was likely to be rejected by the authorities in Istanbul, governors would sometimes carry out the execution anyway—in the middle of the night and without telling anyone—and put the high court in Istanbul in the position of having to approve the verdict retroactively to avoid giving the impression that the state disagreed with itself. With so many Greek, Serbian, Armenian, and Bulgarian separatists (the Arabs' and the Kurds' turn had yet to come), as well as anarchists and highwaymen thus put to death without Istanbul's official approval, Abdul Hamid would placate the British and French envoys who besieged him with their talk of minorities, human rights, freedom of thought, and legal reform by saying that the cruel and unwarranted sentence had been carried out without his endorsement, and that he would be sure to immediately dismiss the Governor in question. But actually the Sultan preferred it when executions took place without his and Istanbul's prior knowledge.

In the Empire's more distant provinces, where Ottoman functionaries and soldiers were always outnumbered by the locals, death sentences would be carried out quietly and discreetly in some prison courtyard or in the barracks jail, with the general populace and more prominent citizens only informed after the fact. But perhaps because he felt elated and secure in the knowledge that Muslims constituted a majority on the island, Governor Sami Pasha had begun talking openly now of having three gallows erected right in the middle of the State Hall Square. Many commentators have pointed out that under these plans, the first people due to ever be hanged on the island would all be Muslims. Every time he heard that the Governor was planning to have a special balcony built from which the consuls could view the public executions, Doctor Nuri would find some excuse to bring the matter up with the Governor again and warn him that he was making a mistake.

"How curious," the Governor might reply with a note of derision in his voice. "The whole city knows that we have caught Bonkowski Pasha's killer. Now tell me, if we were to follow the methods of this English detective, this Sherlock Holmes, and set the culprit free, how could we expect anyone to ever take the Governor and all these quarantine regulations seriously again?"

CHAPTER 26

There were so many people out by the port that last evening before the quarantine on ships was due to begin that the shops on Istanbul Street did not shut until midnight. Some historians have argued that it was among these crowds that the first stirrings of a "Minghcrian identity" began, but this is an overstatement. By Princess Pakize's account, the dominant mood at the docks that evening was not one of "national consciousness," but of uncertainty and trepidation. By now the island's Greek community as well as its more educated Muslims were all profoundly aware that they were standing on the edge of some kind of catastrophe.

But there were also those whose imaginations were too weak for fear. According to Princess Pakize, who had spent twenty-one years of her life fantasizing about the world outside, these people had comparatively little talent for picturing their future and feeling joy or disappointment accordingly. As they pondered these philosophical questions, husband and wife would look out of their windows at the crowds gathered at the port. There were a great many people out in the streets leading down to the docks and to the shore, far more than just those who were preparing to leave the island. Having glimpsed the magnitude of the cataclysm they faced, people simply couldn't bring themselves to stay at home.

"Just look at these people!" the Governor Pasha exclaimed when he next saw Doctor Nuri in his office. "I am more certain than ever now that the only thing that will bring this lot to heel is a good old-fashioned hanging!"

That evening the island was divided between those who were fleeing it, and those who were staying. Greek or Muslim, those who stayed were the *true* islanders. The others were deserters abandoning the battlefield for the safety of their homes.

The Governor Pasha put Doctor Nuri and his guard Major Kâmil into the armored landau, and together they set off on a tour of the city. Initially their intention was to observe, measure, and try to understand the anxious multitudes that had assembled at the port.

The most eminent among the wealthy old Greek families who lived in the Ora and Hrisopolitissa neighborhoods—the Aldonis who'd made their fortune through the stone trade, and the Mimiyannoses, who had their own village in the north of the island and frequently contributed to the running of hospitals, schools, and other philanthropic operations—had already left the island. (Their shutters were all closed.) The landau and its trail of guards wound their way down Hamidiye Avenue toward the Customhouse. There were long queues outside the offices of the shipping companies, and the dock and the streets that led to it were in a state of commotion, but there were still people sitting and reading old newspapers on crowded hotel terraces and in Western-style coffeehouses. The largest of Arkaz's three pharmacies, the Pelagos, had closed because it couldn't keep up with demand, and its owner Mitsos did not wish to be dragged into rows with angry customers. The Hotels Splendid and Levant were spraying antiseptic over the clean-shaven men in Western hats and the various fez-clad notables who passed through their doors. They saw the same disinfectant sprays outside the Bazaar du Île, which sold cigarettes, chocolates, and furniture imported from Smyrna on the Marseille ferry, and at the entrance of the expensive Istanbul Restaurant too. The situation in the more secluded neighborhoods was the same. Some shops hadn't even opened, and some families had boarded up their homes and run away.

Families who had planned to shelter in their homes or repair to some isolated hideout had begun to hoard crackers, flour, chickpeas, lentils, beans, and any other supplies they could get their hands on, so the island's grocers and grain dealers had no complaints. The Governor had been informed that some shopkeepers and bakers had taken to stockpiling goods, while others were hiking up their prices. It could not be said that there was anything unlawful yet in these price fluctuations, but the passengers aboard the landau all acknowledged the inevitability that a black market would soon begin. What had really brought a sense of impending doom upon the streets was the closing of the city's schools. The Governor had also heard that there had been an increase in the number of Muslim children left orphaned and unsupervised by the outbreak. As Coachman Zekeriya's landau climbed slowly up a steep slope, they heard someone playing Chopin on a piano; through the windows they caught fleeting, ephemeral glimpses of Mingherian roses in midbloom, cyclamens, and pine- and mildew-scented ivy.

In the five years he had ruled over the city, the Governor Pasha had never seen it look so forlorn. That joyful, animated mood that usually took over in spring, when the orange trees blossomed, the streets were fragrant with the delicate scent of honeysuckle, linden, and rose, when birds and insects and bees suddenly emerged and seagulls mated frantically upon the rooftops, had now been replaced with a kind of silence and unease. There was not a soul in sight on those street corners from where vagrants and loiterers normally harassed passersby, in the roadside cafés where well-dressed men sat tittering and gossiping, on the pavements where Greek housewives and servants would take children dressed in sailors' outfits for their daily walks, or in the two European-style parks the Governor had opened, the Hamidiye Park and the Parc du Levant. As the landau crept across the city, its three passengers discussed questions ranging from how to stop black-market traders to how best to guard the city's new isolation facility. There were orphaned and abandoned children to look after, there were burglars breaking into empty homes, the Major's unit needed volunteers, and it was important to understand just what the French consul was so angry about. Every home had to be searched; quarantine posters that had been defaced with swear words in Turkish and Greek had to be covered up; any dead rats had to be disposed of immediately in the lot behind the State Hall; people turning up for Friday prayers and other popular services should be disinfected as they entered the mosque itself, not its courtyard; and it would be wise to have that bad-mannered spray-pump operator people kept complaining about suspended from the job.

But the greatest danger of all lay in the extremes to which people resorted that day in their desperation to get onto any one of the last few ships that would be permitted to leave the island without being quarantined first. Today we can say that the frantic actions of the frightened crowds waiting at the port that evening were entirely justified: in

1901, at a time when antibiotics had not yet been discovered, the most sensible thing anyone caught up in an outbreak of plague could do was to flee. But when combined with the travel agencies' mercantile frenzy, this understandable impulse generated a strange kind of mood, a state of mind that could be summarized as "It's every man for himself!"

The representatives of the major shipping companies all held seats on the Quarantine Committee through their role as consuls, and by engineering—supposedly on humane considerations—for quarantine to begin a day later, they had secured precious additional hours in which to schedule more ferries and make more money. The agents of the Messageries Maritimes, Lloyd, Hidiviye, the Russian Steam Navigation Company, and every other ferry service that operated on the island had sent telegrams to all nearby ports requesting additional vessels for those who wished to leave the island, and in many cases they had begun selling tickets for these services before they'd even received a response to confirm they could be arranged. In truth no ferry company wanted its ships to be quarantined on a plague-infested island and have its name associated in the newspapers with that kind of story.

Some families had decided to wait at home for their ships to arrive. Others had camped out at the port and refused to budge. Two Greek Orthodox families had been so sure of the tickets they had bought for the ferry that would take them to their relatives in Thessaloniki that they had closed down their respective homes in Flizvos and Ora and loaded every household item and piece of furniture they would need for the summer, as well as mattresses, curtains, and several sacks of walnuts, onto a cart bound for the docks, and when they had later learned that the ferry they were supposed to take had been "delayed," they had decided to wait in the new park the Governor had opened next to the Customhouse rather than go back to their closed-up homes.

Others were queuing up with their trunks and suitcases where the boatmen who carried passengers out to anchored ships had set up their booths. Porters and boat crews angling for tips compounded these people's agitation with all sorts of blithe assurances that any minute now the ships that had been sent to ferry customers off the island would come into view from behind the Castle. Some waited in the cafés that lined the wharf; others kept thinking of the homes they were leaving behind, sending the maidservant back to fetch a teapot they might have forgotten to pack. Amid all this confusion, a few people were still foolishly doing the rounds of the travel agencies in search of a ticket. Others despairingly bought tickets from every company there was, just to be on the safe side.

But apart from wealthy, educated Greeks, the overwhelming majority of the island's population made no attempt to leave. Most Muslims were staying—even the few among them who understood how contagious the plague could be. Would it be fair to look back upon their behavior today, one hundred and sixteen years after the fact, and explain it as a function of factors such as poverty, lack of opportunity, indifference, fatalism, recklessness, religion, and culture? It is not the purpose of this book to try to "interpret" this peculiar phenomenon, but it must be said that the few Muslims who did leave the island during this time were those who happened to have jobs, homes, and families to go to in Istanbul and Smyrna. One of the main reasons why so many people stayed on the island is that they were not expecting and could not even imagine the horrors that they were about to face and that we will faithfully describe in this book. Their failure to foresee the disaster that would soon befall them ensured, in turn, the inevitability of that same disaster, and caused history to take the turn it did.

The landau passed through the narrow lanes of the Old Market, where they saw that the junk dealers and fruit sellers had dismantled their stalls. In the Tatlısu neighborhood, children were still playing outside at dusk; in the alleyway behind the Bektaşi lodge, the smell of linden trees mixed with the stench of carrion; out on the streets, the patrols that had been created by special order of the Governor to protect vacant homes from looters were already doing their rounds; and as the landau passed the Greek Middle School on its way down to the wharf, the Major told the Governor that he had begun to arm the Quarantine Regiment. There was much to do still, but the Governor felt he ought to pay a visit to the garrison anyway, to inspect the Major's recruits firsthand and show his wholehearted support for this newly formed division.

It was still possible to convince oneself that this was as bad as things were likely to get, that this outbreak too, like every outbreak before it, would eventually fade away, and that one could get through it all unscathed by hiding out in some quiet, private corner, and avoid going out for a while.

We know from several published memoirs from this era that a number of people who fled Arkaz despite not having any homes, friends, or acquaintances to go to in the island's rural regions were quickly driven away by locals who accused them of having the plague, and ended up—along with a few others who hadn't even attempted to seek refuge in the villages—living on hills and mountains and in forests, a little like Robinson Crusoe.

Of the ferries scheduled for that evening, only the *Baghdad* arrived on time, and took on board one thousand two hundred and fifty passengers—exactly two and a half times its capacity of five hundred. None of the next five ships that had been previously announced turned up at the expected time, though supposedly they were on their way. Meanwhile, an unidentified vessel had approached the port, dropping anchor at some distance from the shore. The Governor instructed the landau to turn onto Hamidiye Avenue and stop at the corner of the square. He peered through the small carriage window, trying to follow the action at the docks. A heavily loaded rowboat was making its way swiftly toward the anchored ship, loaded with passengers and luggage. The crowds on the shore were shouting and jeering. The boatmen ignored the spectators' protests and slowed their oars down to stop just past the Arab Lighthouse, where the boat, swaying in the waves, began to wait. Shortly thereafter, a carriage loaded with trunks, baskets, and suitcases hurtled from the direction of the Castle toward the port carrying various hat-clad members of a Greek Orthodox family with their many children (girls and boys), servants, and maids in tow, all of whom moved with such leisurely calm upon disembarking from the carriage that one might think they had only just found out that there was a plague on the island. An approaching siphon-man sprayed disinfectant all over them. Soon a row broke out, with coachmen and porters also involved.

"Doctor Ilias has been very insistent about his wish to leave the island," said the Governor, his eyes still fixed on what he could see through the window. "He cannot seem to accept that the peril we face goes far beyond securing ferry tickets or managing quarantines. His Supreme Highness wants him to stay, of course. But Doctor Ilias is too afraid to even step out of the garrison. We must make sure to give him some encouragement at your men's swearing-in ceremony tomorrow morning."

"We are still a little short on numbers and equipment, so we might not be quite ready for an inspection yet," said the Major sheepishly. The swearing-in ceremony—to which he himself had invited the Governor—had been his idea; he had thought it might help to motivate the inexperienced Quarantine Regiment.

"Didn't I send you Sergeant Hamdi Baba yesterday?" the Governor replied. "That man alone is worth a whole army."

The landau turned toward the city's almost wholly deserted back-streets and threaded its way through narrow sloping alleyways. In some streets there was not a single person in sight, and in two others they spotted two fresh rat corpses, one at the foot of a garden wall, and the other lying in the middle of the dusty road. How had they been over-looked by the same children who were usually so efficient in gathering and selling to the municipal government all the rats that died from eating poisoned bait?

"How would you explain this?" the Governor asked Doctor Nuri.

"If the rats and the plague return with a renewed vigor, then who knows what could happen!"

They made their way through the empty streets back to the State Hall. The uproar in the port continued until midnight. Doctor Nuri and Princess Pakize could easily hear from their guesthouse, as could the Governor from his office, the scuffles that broke out every time a rowboat set off from the shore toward one of the last ferries, and the shouting and swearing among the boatmen. When the Lloyd ferry failed to materialize, a group of furious ticketholders marched over to the company's offices to shout at the clerks who worked there and demand an explanation. The gendarmes eventually intervened, after one of the Lloyd's employees was beaten up and his new spectacles from the Essel store in Thessaloniki were broken.

There was also a disturbance at the ticket stall for Messageries Maritimes, whose ferries were the island's most regular visitors, and whose orange-and-red booth displayed black-and-white photographs of distant exotic realms all over its walls. The agency's owner, Monsieur Andon, an ambitious tradesman who belonged to one of Arkaz's oldest Greek families and was also the island's French consul, arrived on the scene and bravely addressed the angry, restless mob. What he told them, in French, was something along the lines of: "The ship is on its way; it's the Governor's Office that won't let it dock!"

It is difficult to describe here the emotional collapse some of these families experienced that evening, having spent the past two days making plans to flee to Crete, Thessaloniki, Smyrna, or Istanbul with their trunks and boxes. Nobody wanted to go back in the middle of the night to homes whose doors they'd locked up and whose windows they'd nailed shut the day before. To make matters worse, having assumed they would be leaving the island, they had not made any of the preparations other people had made, such as filling their kitchens as well as their linen closets and any other storage areas the rats couldn't reach with biscuits, dried noodles, pasta, cured trout, and salted sardines.

For the island's illiterate poor, these were comparatively calmer days, for they were either oblivious to what was happening or had not yet experienced fear and the presence of death with sufficient intensity. Let no one criticize us, then, for devoting so much attention to the island's wealthier families who owned most of its land and property (and many of whom usually left their Mingherian possessions in the care of a housekeeper and spent most of the year living in Istanbul or Smyrna). Of the families that had been left with no other choice after the events at the port that evening but to trudge dolefully back to their homes in the early morning, the argumentative Pangirises and the Sifiropoulouses had lost most of their members to the disease, and there had been several deaths among the Cypriot Faroses too.

As the night wore on, the allegation that the Governor was not allowing the additional ferries for which tickets had been sold to enter the harbor transformed into a rumor that quarantine measures would be postponed by a day so that the delayed ships could dock. Around this time, a quiet, unassuming man who had been standing on his own watching what went on, and whose lack of any trunks or baskets, a ticket, or any clothes appropriate for travel suggested that he was unlikely to be a passenger, had caused a small commotion when, having sat on the ground in a spot between the Customhouse and the area where carriages waited, he had nearly fainted from the effects of a headache. The lantern lights were dim, and it was hard to see properly. The siphon-men who had been wandering among the throngs rushed to the sick man's aid, and the crowd briefly dispersed. Others thought that the man who had brought the plague to the city and scattered dead rats around at night must have finally been caught, and rushed over to watch the lynching.

When he heard that a small group had gathered at the Austral Coffeehouse on Istanbul Street to draft a petition demanding that the quarantine be pushed back until the last ships had arrived, after which they planned to go around collecting signatures in the middle of the night from the heads of the island's leading families, the owners of its travel agencies, its consuls, and ultimately anyone who was hoping to leave the island, before finally marching to the Governor's Residence to deliver the petition to the Governor himself or perhaps even to the Doctor and Prince Consort, the Governor had dispatched a group of siphon-men to the café to disperse the meeting with a pungent dose of Lysol. The enterprising young man who had acted as the group's ringleader was later arrested, along with his uncle, and thrown into the Castle dungeons.

Around eleven o'clock, as the ferment in the port—influenced in part by this incident—continued to intensify, something happened that raised everybody's spirits: the *Persepolis,* the last ferry which the Messageries Maritimes had been officially authorized to send to the island, came into view in the waters off of the Castle. It wasn't possible to see the ship clearly from the port, but the quivering light of its lamps was just about visible if one looked hard enough. Everyone ran to fetch their boxes, their trunks, and their families. Before long the first of Foreman Lazar's rowboats had set off toward the ship, loaded with passengers and their belongings. Whoever else wanted to escape the island then charged toward the second boat, leading to struggles and scraps between those who were particularly vociferous and insistent in their efforts and the customs officers, policemen, and siphon-men who were present on the scene. But soon, Foreman Lazar's second boat was also gone, swallowed into the darkness.

It was a moment of petrifying loneliness. Everyone at the docks—we estimate around five hundred people in total—understood with piercing clarity that the last ferry would soon be gone, and that they had been left behind, alone with the plague. Some families, having come to believe the rumors they themselves had concocted, waited until dawn for more ships to arrive. Others waited because they thought it would be too difficult to go back home in the middle of the night. But most people loaded their belongings onto wagons and quietly returned home, and if there was no carriage available, they walked instead. (Strangely, nobody that night seemed to encounter the man with the sack who was said to throw rats around and spread the plague across the city.) It was a cold, shivery night, for the start of May. The wind whistled through the city's empty homes.

CHAPTER 27

As it sailed away from the island after midnight, the Messageries Maritimes *Persepolis* blew its horn twice, producing a mournful, muffled sound that echoed against Mingheria's rocky peaks. The Governor Pasha was still in his office, meeting with the Chief Prison Warden and the Chief Scrutineer to discuss in greater detail how the death sentences that had been issued against the gang of murderers should be carried out. He was still hesitant about hanging Ramiz, as executing him without waiting for Istanbul's explicit authorization could easily lead to even-greater political complications. The warden and the Chief Scrutineer reminded him that the man who had agreed to carry out all three executions, Tuzla neighborhood's resident burglar Şakir, might not be entirely trustworthy, was always drunk, would perhaps not even show up at the prison at the appointed time, and was even demanding to be paid for his services upfront.

"So summon him to the Castle tomorrow and lock him up before it gets dark!" said the Pasha. "You can give him his wine after midnight. Which shop does he buy it from anyway?" It was in that moment that they heard the whistle of the *Persepolis,* and all three walked up to the wide window overlooking the port. Though its lights were only faintly visible, everyone could see that the ship was sailing away from the island and feel the fateful significance of that moment.

"So it is just us and the plague now!" said Governor Sami Pasha. "We had better continue tomorrow morning."

To those present at this meeting, the Governor's sudden decision to adjourn to the next day did not come as a surprise, so they quickly put the matter in question out of their minds, as they knew the Governor would want them to do, and locked the door of his office behind them, making sure to leave the gas lamp on inside. In times of crisis the Governor liked to think that if the lamps inside the State Hall and his own office burned until the morning, people looking up at the building's windows would be left with the impression that the state never slept, and any assassin planning an attempt on the Governor's life would never be able to find him.

When they heard the *Persepolis* blow its horn, Princess Pakize and Doctor Nuri, like many others who were on the island that night but had not gone down to the port, went to the windows of their guesthouse bedroom to look outside, but while so many others contemplated the same view with the fear of death in their minds, a feeling of abandonment, and an odd sensation of regret, the couple's emotions took a rather more romantic turn. Everywhere was dark; only the Castle was visible. To Princess Pakize, the vision of the lights of the *Persepolis* gliding away into the velvet night seemed a sign that she and her husband were truly alone for the first time. Doctor Nuri did not consider himself a potentially "infected" person, for like all doctors he was constantly washing his hands, neck, and arms with disinfectant. It is with a historian's eye for accuracy, then, that we shall note now that the couple joyfully made love that night.

Doctor Nuri woke up before dawn. As he got dressed, he watched his sweetly sleeping wife and at the same time kept thinking that the rumors must be true, that the Governor Pasha must be planning to do what governors usually did in emergencies, and execute Ramiz and his two henchmen without waiting for approval from the high court in Istanbul.

He walked down the stairs followed by the respectful glances of the guards on night shift and made instinctively for the inner courtyard; most executions were carried out in the inner courtyards of government buildings. But there was nobody there. The overgrown sheepdog that was always tethered to the railings on the kitchen windows, and barked relentlessly every night, had vanished at the start of the plague outbreak.

In the darkness, there was not even a single shadow to be seen. He walked past the columns of the domed gallery and felt like a ghost. As he slowly circled the square, he kept thinking that any moment now he would run into someone, but the night was like a dark, two-dimensional room; no matter how many steps he took, he could not find his way out of that black box, but sometimes the shadow of a tree or a faded color would drift silently past him. He passed the quarantine notices and the shuttered shops, then turned into an alleyway and walked in the dark for a long time across the never-ending streets of the plague-ridden city.

He was greeted in every neighborhood by a different pack of dogs howling frenetically as he neared the center of their territories, but none of them ever came close enough for him to hear their panting or their low growls. Sometimes when he entered a narrow street or walked down a sloping road he would smell the scent of seaweed coming from the shore and hear the squawking of seagulls, then instinctively take a right turn and find himself climbing up another slope, surrounded this time by the scent of roses. He heard a man and a woman giggling and whispering to each other in Greek inside a garden; he listened to an owl hooting persistently at unseen clouds, and later he found he could no longer even hear the sound of his own footsteps. What street was this with sand scattered all over the ground? He walked down a stairway and passed the Hotel Mingher, then got lost again. When the shuttered windows of a dark stone house appeared before him, he realized that he was not walking on a street, but inside someone's garden. He followed the sound of frogs in the distance, their croaking like the ripple of a waterfall, and as he approached them the frogs hopped one by one into the water, though in the darkness he could discern neither the gleam nor the coolness of the pond.

At one point he thought he heard a burglar and backed away into a corner, but he couldn't see anyone in the darkness that cloaked the world like a heavy, coal-black fog. He walked up a hill he thought would lead him back toward the State Hall Square, but soon realized he was moving farther away, and it took him longer than he expected to return to his wife's side.

When morning finally came, Doctor Nuri told his wife about how he had gone out in the night to the State Hall Square because he had been worried about the executions.

"My uncle prefers it when his exiled enemies are executed by his loyal and efficient governors of their own initiative and volition. He would never issue a death sentence himself, especially not against a Muslim; he is far too cunning and cautious for that."

Princess Pakize listened to her husband's account of his metaphysical experience of getting lost in the dark streets of Arkaz, and later that day she sat down at her desk to begin writing it all down word by word upon a fresh sheet of paper, under the heading "Nights of Plague." Earlier, they had spoken about how this new letter would not reach her sister Hatice in Istanbul anytime soon, since the last ship off the island had already left the port. "I cannot explain why, but I have this yearning to describe it all in even-greater detail," said Princess Pakize now. "Please, tell me everything you saw!"

Afterward, as a clerk used a green pen to mark the epidemiology map with the locations where yesterday's eight victims had died, the Governor told the Doctor and Prince Consort that it would be just the two of them that morning, as Doctor Ilias and the Major had remained at the garrison for the swearing-in ceremony. Having then expressed his great admiration for the Major's diligence, competence, and discipline, the Governor added that it would be very good for the island if the Major married Zeynep.

The Governor knew every one of the eight people who had died the day before. A clerk at the Department of Charitable Trusts who had announced as soon as the outbreak had started that he would be returning to his village had, in fact, not gone anywhere at all, but shut himself and his family up in their villa in the Çite neighborhood. The house had since been vacated and disinfected after two people had died there yesterday. A farrier who lived in the Stone Quarry neighborhood, and the Turunçlar neighborhood's popular, loquacious barber, Zaim, had both died in their homes without even making it to the hospital. The Governor had also been informed of the deaths of an old farmer who had been brought to the Hamidiye Hospital yesterday, an elderly mother who had wept for her children as she died, a victim who had been found in the morning lying in the garden of the Theodoropoulos Hospital, and a Greek waiter who worked at the Petalis restaurant. The waiter's demise had reignited the debate among the island's doctors on whether the plague could be passed on through food. Banning the sale of watermelons and cantaloupes, as well as other fruits and vegetables, was usually a precaution taken against the spread of cholera.

"Doctor Ilias always says—like our dearly departed Bonkowski Pasha used to—that the plague does not spread through food," said Doctor Nuri. "We can ask him again when we see him at the garrison later."

"How would you assess the current situation on the island?" said the Governor.

"It is still too early to see the results of quarantine provisions."

"It had better be!" said the Governor. "Otherwise we would already have had to conclude that they are of no use at all."

"Your Excellency, quarantine provisions are usually rendered ineffective by the same people who refuse to take them seriously. And in the end, those people die too."

"Well said!" exclaimed the Governor Pasha in a burst of inspiration. "But we will not die! I keep hearing that the Major's Quarantine Regiment is exceptionally capable and determined, a force to be reckoned with."

As they boarded the landau, the Governor Pasha told Coachman Zekeriya not to take the hilly road through Kofunya, but to go instead by the slower route along the shore. They passed Saint Anthony's Church, followed the wall that abutted Marika's back garden and her chicken coops (how lovely to see her shutters wide open now!), and meandered at a leisurely pace all the way down to the coast. Beyond the clatter of horses' hooves, the creaking of the landau's wheels, and Zekeriya's voice calling "Brrrr" as he pulled on the bridles so that the carriage would not go too fast down the hill, there was not a single sound to be heard. The Governor realized that they couldn't even hear the seagulls and the crows. The silence seemed to have even dimmed the color of the sea, which they could glimpse in the gaps between the seaside hotels and tavernas.

"Everyone went away with that last Maritimes ship, and now there's no one left!" said the Governor with a childlike sorrow. An expression of wide-eyed innocence came over his face; Doctor Nuri found it endearing.

Once it had passed the row of hotels and restaurants, the landau continued on its way, following the steep cliff to the right-hand side of the road. How close and how white the sea looked below them now! This route, which went down and back up and then down again as it turned and twisted northward along the coast where the Ora neighborhood met the sea, was one of the Governor Pasha's favorites. Tracing the edge of every cove, and lined with palm trees on either side, it would always fill the Pasha with a sense of peace. He liked the smell of roses wafting from the rose gardens of the rich, the new beach resort and its cabins with their white-and-blue-striped umbrellas, the little dock, and the rose farms. Lately the island's newest rich had been moving here; the Governor had kept close watch on the construction of their homes.

"When I first arrived here, I told the senior members of the island's oldest Muslim families and all the wealthy Muslims who live near Hamidiye Square over and over again: 'Do what the Greeks are doing, start from the Kadirler neighborhood and build your way north with villas and palaces and mansions and move your families there, for it is the future of this city to grow northward along its two shores!' Maybe it is because I told them to 'Do what the Greeks are doing' that they chose not to listen. It turns out these patriarchs, these doddering grandfathers who pray five times a day, wanted nothing more than to live somewhere close to the Blind Mehmet Pasha Mosque or to one of the other historic mosques! So the areas around the Old Stone Jetty, the stone merchants' offices, and their workers' dormitories remained empty and were, for a time, the domain of wastrels and spiders. Then the migrants from Crete arrived and settled there. I must confess I was initially in favor of having these impoverished refugees, these idle, unemployed youths going to live there—in fact I encouraged it. Not only would they find shelter there; they might also bring new life to the neighborhood. But all they did was loaf around, make mischief, and plot revenge against the Greeks. If we used the plague now as an excuse to drive them all out of there, that would mean burning the whole neighborhood down. But we can't even do that, because the stone merchants' offices were all built out of the best Mingherian stone, and they would never catch fire. But listen to me, talking about burning things! To think that I had started off wanting to tell you about the island's idyllic seaside road . . ."

Once they had passed the empty beach, the road sloped uphill again. To their left was the Flizvos neighborhood, home to many wealthy Greek families whose immaculate mansions the Governor Pasha had always regarded with respectful, even admiring, approval. With their overhanging roofs, spired towers, and panoramic sitting rooms (all influenced by the architecture of the Castle) facing the empty, boundless waters of the Levant, the view from these homes of the morning sun rising from the sea was truly a spectacle to behold. The Governor Pasha knew some of these wealthy, westernized families personally and had occasionally been invited to the receptions they held in their palatial homes. He had even turned a blind eye to the gambling that took place at their members' club, the Circle du Levant, which the Governor had helped them set up and which Muslims never frequented (except by special invitation), but when he had found out that the games of tombola and the raffles that the club organized around Christmas were being used to raise money for the outlaw Pavlo, who was known to raid Muslim villages, or for the Greek nationalists locked up in the Castle dungeons, the Governor had arrested the foppish dandy who organized the club's fundraising activities, and whose father owned the Bazaar du Île, under the pretense that his family's shop was selling contraband goods, put him in the prison's worst cell, and terrorized him for a couple of days with the screams of other inmates being tortured. That was how the Circle du Levant stopped supporting anarchist insurrectionists through games of tombola—without the club ever needing to be shut down or a single diplomatic telegram having to be sent. Chief Scrutineer Mazhar Bey was very adept at silencing these kinds of troublemakers without provoking political scandal.

As their carriage followed the curve of the bays that dotted the shore of the elegant Dantela neighborhood, the Governor Pasha looked up toward the garrison at a little white house on top of a hill and surrounded by fields. Once he'd relinquished all his duties—that is to say, once Abdul Hamid had removed him from his post—the Governor did not intend to return to Istanbul, but to settle here, where he could spend his life cultivating Mingherian roses and befriending the Greek fishermen who moored in the bay below.

Outside the window of the landau, the line of the horizon had disappeared into the misty sea, and to the Governor it seemed as if the island had come undone from the rest of the world and was now entirely alone in the firmament. The silence and the sunlight evoked a strange feeling of loneliness and insignificance. Through the open window on the right-hand side, whose leather sunshade Doctor Nuri had pulled down against the heat, a noisy, irascible bee flew in, growing even more incensed when it banged into the opposite window, and flustering the two men. The bee finally escaped from the same window it had come through in the first place, but in the meantime the passengers had made such a ruckus that Coachman Zekeriya had grown concerned and slowed the horses down.

"It was only a bee, Zekeriya, but the rascal's gone now; take us to the garrison!" said the Governor Pasha.

The carriage began its slow ascent up the narrow, stone-paved lane that connected Pebble Cove with the garrison. The horses' shoes and the landau's wheels clanged against the cobblestones made from rough-hewn Mingherian marble. This road, which led from the garrison down to the shore, had been built sixty years ago so that reinforcements sent to the island from Istanbul to help quash hypothetical nationalist guerrilla uprisings against the Ottoman Empire would be able to reach the garrison quicker and without having to go via the Castle, but so far it had never been used for that purpose. Lavish mansions and old manor houses were scattered across the verdant hillside. They gazed at green tree branches reaching out beyond the confines of their gardens, with tiny lizards scuttling up and down the length of the wood, they saw strange, thorny, pointed leaves, and they listened intently to the singing of impertinent parrots and the rare chirping of sweet-toned, bashful little birds. They filled their lungs with the moist, fine air that hung over the cool and shaded hill.

"Stop, Coachman, stop!" the Governor Pasha exclaimed as he looked out of his window at a lush, shadowy garden.

The carriage stopped, slipping slightly backward down the hill. As always, the Governor Pasha waited in his seat. Once the guard who sat beside Coachman Zekeriya had come down and opened the door for him, they looked to where the Governor was pointing and saw, peering out at them from between the hanging fronds of a willow tree, two dark-haired children in pale, faded clothes.

One of the children hurled a stone at them, while the other tried to hold him back, his gestures seeming to say, "Don't do it!" The next moment they had run away, out of sight. They hadn't made a single sound; it was as if they'd come out of a dream, and perhaps they were imaginary after all.

The Governor told the guards to run after the children. "That house must have been robbed and looted after it was left empty!" he said once they were back inside the carriage. "They'll soon be coming here from outside the city and from the villages too, you know. Truth be told, there are so many of these criminals and lowlifes around that it is an impossible task to monitor and discipline them all!"

"If Doctor Ilias were here, he would tell us what Bonkowski Pasha would have had to say on the matter."

"Don't you think Doctor Ilias is a little too afraid?"

Garrison Commander Mehmet Pasha had organized a small welcome for the guests attending the swearing-in ceremony. A group of forty men selected from among the Arab soldiers of the Fifth Army paraded for the Governor Pasha, saluting him as they marched past. Then the Governor spoke to Sergeant Sadri, commander of the artillery unit that had fired twenty-five blank shells last year to celebrate the twenty-fifth anniversary of Abdul Hamid's ascension to the throne. "I've got enough gunpowder to fire a hundred more shots if we need them!" the Sergeant boasted to the Governor. Afterward they sat down to a meal the garrison Commander had especially arranged. The latest issue of the municipality's newspaper the *Arkata Times* was on the table, as well as those of the still-circulating *Island Star, Neo Nisi,* and *Adekatos Arkadi.* Doctor Ilias was there too, wearing a petrol-green frock coat.

"We missed your analysis while we were studying the map this morning!" the Governor told him. "The death rate is rising, and all the Muslim neighborhoods and half the Greek ones are infected. Is it prudent to be eating these things?"

Doctor Ilias's eyes followed a soldier who brought an enormous bowl of black fruits picked from the grand old mulberry tree that grew on the grounds of the garrison. Next to the berries was a freshly baked tray of Mingheria's famous walnut-and-rose biscuits.

"Trust me, Pasha, there's nothing to worry about," Doctor Ilias replied cheerily. "I'll have a taste first before you do. I don't know about the mulberries, but the biscuits have just come out of the oven."

There was a sudden clamor. In the same moment a bay horse galloped past them, bit between its teeth. Two soldiers who were running after the horse and had been preparing for the swearing-in ceremony stopped when they saw the Governor and the other dignitaries at the table and gave an unpracticed, embarrassed salute. The Governor, who had grown restless in the heat, stood up to see where the horse was going. He spotted nearby the soldiers of the Major's new Quarantine

Regiment getting ready to be sworn in, and gladdened by the sight, he walked toward them without waiting for the coffee to arrive. Various guards, municipal clerks, and officers who had come for the ceremony followed behind him.

Over the last two days the Major had recruited another seventeen soldiers to his quarantine unit. His primary "adviser" in the selection of these recruits had been Hamdi Baba. Nobody knew how old the bearded and mustachioed Hamdi Baba was. Having completed his period of compulsory military service, he had decided to stay in the army, and despite being hardly able to read and write, he had risen to the middle ranks of the Ottoman army and fought in numerous battles. Being of Mingherian origins, Hamdi Baba had eventually been deployed to the island and managed to stay there ever since. From Arabs to Greeks, from Mingherian-speaking native islanders to Turkish-speaking families and civil servants, Hamdi Baba knew the most proper way to address them all and could charm and cajole anyone into doing anything.

The Governor watched solemnly as Hamdi Baba led his men through elaborate drills and lined them up in rows of four. Hamdi Baba had found his first "volunteers" for this unit, whose recruits were paid upfront, among his acquaintances in the Bayırlar and Gülerenler neighborhoods where he'd grown up—people he loved and that he could trust. As many historians of Mingheria have noted, this meant that the quarantine unit was effectively enlisted from among those who spoke Mingherian in their homes. But contrary to the general misconception, this decision was not one initially made by the Major.

For three days now the Major had been coming to the garrison in the afternoons to "train" the new soldiers. But more than advancing their military training, he was teaching them to observe quarantine rules, to be magnanimous, to always wear their protective gear, to make sure they disinfected themselves, and to listen to what the doctors said, though ultimately they must of course always defer to their commander. Doctor Nuri had attended one of these sessions once, where he had been introduced to the soldiers and later accompanied them and the Major on an expedition to the neighborhoods of Kadirler and Upper Turunçlar. There they had successfully deterred two different households that had come out in open defiance of the new rules and cordons. They had also managed, through a combination of gentle reasoning and veiled threats about "the Sultan's orders," to suppress a minor revolt instigated by a young man who was insisting on being buried with his wife, who had died while pregnant.

The Governor thought that the Major had chosen his "quarantine troops" expertly and trained them well in the little time he'd had at his disposal. These new soldiers understood the character of the streets that had been most blighted by the plague and knew, of any given person who lived there, if they would turn out to be hostile and whether they were more or less inclined to follow instructions. It was mostly thanks to their efforts that some of the island's Muslim population (though admittedly still a minuscule number), and particularly those among them who could not read or write, had been persuaded over the past two days to begin following quarantine protocols. Whenever a new case was reported by a quarantine officer overseeing a particular neighborhood or by one of the municipality's ubiquitous informants, the first to arrive on the scene was always Hamdi Baba. People were likelier to submit to the rules when confronted with a man who wore a soldier's uniform but styled his beard like they did and spoke their language too.

Thus heartened to see how adeptly the Major's soldiers and this cer-emony had been organized in just five days, the Governor Pasha was moved to deliver a personal address to the troops. The Ottoman army, he said, was the sword of Islam, but this time, the sword would not be used to behead infidels, but for the far-holier and more humane purpose of cutting the plague demon into pieces.

The sky above was blue and flecked with thick white clouds. The Governor Pasha was just in the middle of reminding the soldiers that they must be careful not to fall ill themselves, and of how lucky they were to be serving under such a brilliant commander, when the Chief Scrutineer came up to him and unceremoniously whispered into his ear. Everyone understood at once that the matter must be serious if it warranted interrupting Governor Sami Pasha and collectively held their breaths.

"Doctor Ilias has been taken ill, Your Excellency," Mazhar Effendi had whispered to the Governor.

If the outbreak had reached the garrison, it would no longer be pos-sible to contain it. The Governor wanted to finish his speech, though much of his mind was now occupied with considering the ramifications of this latest development. Doctor Ilias might have caught the disease at the hospital down in the city and brought it here with him; it had been a mistake to put him in the garrison. But it also occurred to the Governor, with a strange twinge of guilt, that he might have brought the plague himself in his landau. He continued with his speech anyway, explaining to the recruits watching him exactly why there could be no greater fortune or happiness in life than to serve as a soldier in the army of His Highness the Sultan, pillar of the world. But at the same time he was thinking to himself, "Doctor Ilias can't have died of the plague, can he? For wasn't he standing right here behind me only a minute ago?"

CHAPTER 28

A few moments earlier, Doctor Ilias had been observing proceedings with a benevolent smile and the feeling of security that came with being inside the garrison and among the scattered crowd standing behind the Governor. At the same time he had been nibbling on a warm Mingherlan biscuit he had surreptitiously tucked into his pocket. Now he was just a hundred meters away, lying on his bed in the garrison guesthouse, writhing in unbearable agony. The pain in his stomach was so piercing that he thought he was going to faint, and yet he couldn't faint. At first he had tried with all his strength to resist the nausea, for he had been looking forward to watching the Governor's inspection of the troops, but moments after scrambling back to his room and throwing himself onto the camp bed therein, he had begun to vomit uncontrollably. He felt as if it wasn't him but someone else who was throwing up. Soon everything he had eaten for breakfast that morning had come back out in white and yellow chunks.

Then the diarrhea began, sharp as a corkscrew. He walked out into the high-ceilinged corridor in search of a toilet. On his way back, he nearly fell over, dazed with pain. A soldier spotted him and helped him to his room. Soon a small crowd had gathered at his door. Doctor Ilias thought that they would see him now as the person who had brought the plague, the devil among them, and even he wasn't sure what sickness it was that ailed him.

When the tremors started, he began to imagine he was falling into a well. The garrison doctor was trying to unbutton Doctor Ilias's shirt, taking care to touch it only around the edges. Doctor and Prince Consort Nuri, who had meanwhile rushed over to the guesthouse, noticed that Doctor Ilias's face had taken on a cold, bluish hue and wondered if this might not be the plague at all but something else altogether. The patient was shaking, vomiting continuously, and seemed to be approaching a state of delirium, but with the plague, these symptoms tended to appear at a later stage of the illness. Doctor Nuri checked for buboes on the neck and armpits. But he was unable to look inside the patient's malodorous mouth, for Doctor Ilias would not stop vomiting. The plague could easily spread through particles suspended in the air.

The patient tried to say something, but his mouth couldn't seem to produce proper words, and all that came out was a series of peculiar noises. Doctor Nuri stared into his stricken eyes, willing him to speak. Then Doctor Ilias took a piece of biscuit out of his pocket, and suddenly everything fell into place.

Doctor Nuri bolted out of the room and ran toward the table that had been laid out for the ceremony.

The army officers, the municipal clerks, and the garrison Commander were about to sit back down. For the Governor Pasha, having swiftly decided that the news of the plague reaching the garrison must be kept secret, had ordered everyone in his firmest voice to not do anything rash, and to return to the table where they had been sitting earlier. In the meantime, the Major had led his soldiers away. The Governor had sat down first, to set an example. The others had joined him too now, if somewhat disconcertedly. One of the experienced soldiers who worked in the kitchens brought out a beaked coffee jug made of brass and began pouring out cups of richly aromatic coffee, serving the Governor first, then everybody else, and the garrison Commander's aide-de-camp bit into a walnut-and-rose-flavored biscuit.

"Stop! It's poisoned!" Doctor Nuri called out in that very moment. "Don't eat or drink a thing. The coffee and the biscuits are poisoned!" he said, trying to catch his breath.

Tests would later show that the coffee itself was of the finest Yemeni kind, and the water had been sourced from the island's own Pınarlar spring just north of Arkaz, and that it was, therefore, perfectly clean.

As for the walnut-and-rose biscuits, it was decided there and then that they must have been laced with arsenic, which was often used in rat poison, and was known colloquially as ratsbane. In 1901, there was of course no laboratory in this distant province of the Ottoman Empire equipped to test a person's blood or their gastric juices for signs of arsenic poisoning, but over the past fifty years many on the island had perished under the effects of rat poison, and these old ancestral methods were as vividly familiar to people as their own most private memories could be.

The Chief Scrutineer and Doctor Nikos watched garrison Commander Mehmet Pasha's aide-de-camp throw one of the biscuits at a short-tempered shepherd dog chained to an oak tree just past the guest-house, and within a few minutes the dog was dead.

Gripped now by a strange fury and fear of death, and having thus dispatched the rowdy, unruly dog he had long been wondering how to get rid of, garrison Commander Mehmet Pasha proceeded to feed another biscuit to the same bay horse that had taken the bit between its teeth earlier and apparently nearly caused a soldier's death, but as the creature's front legs buckled beneath its weight, and as it twisted and writhed on the ground in the throes of death, the Commander couldn't bring himself to watch, and fled the scene. We should clarify for our readers that the garrison Commander's actions were not motivated by any particular hostility toward animals (though it could not be said that he was a friend to them either), but rather by the need to measure the severity of this plot to poison the entire upper echelons of Mingheria's governing classes. Half the flour in the Mingherian biscuits had been replaced with ratsbane. This substance, which indeed closely resembled flour, could be found in some herbalists' shops sold out of sacks like those used for flour and was a scentless poison whose taste was almost impossible to detect—just like flour.

But of all the cases of arsenic poisoning reported in the Ottoman Empire during the nineteenth century, none had been as acute (involving enough poison, in other words, to immediately knock a person dead) as in this incident at the Mingherian garrison, or openly manifested as an attack of such remarkable political audacity and arrogance. From the Governor to the Quarantine Chief, from the Doctor and Prince Consort to the garrison Commander, the island's entire governing hierarchy had been targeted at its highest levels. They retaliated with equal force.

The eight soldiers who worked in the garrison kitchens were arrested straightaway, along with their sergeant. Then came the turn of the five privates who usually waited on officers and had laid out the table that day, as well as the garrison's provisions master and his two assistants. The Governor sent the higher-ranked suspects to the Castle prison and had the kitchen staff locked up in separate cells at the southern end of the garrison grounds, where torture and interrogations were normally carried out. To make sure the new recruits didn't notice anything, Mehmet Pasha arranged for the prisoners to be transported not in the vehicle traditionally employed for that purpose but in the van the garrison used to distribute the bread and pastries from its bakery. Afterward the bread van had to be disinfected, and this, combined with the striking appearance of the two spray-pump operators who had been summoned for the purpose, gave rise to a general and erroneous impression that the soldiers who worked in the kitchens had been arrested because they had brought the plague to the garrison. This misapprehension was also aided by the fact that plague victims were so often treated as if they had committed a crime, and that those infected were confined almost like prisoners to the isolation facility in the Castle's prison wing.

For such illustrious personages from Istanbul to be picked off like sitting ducks on the island whose every inch the Governor was supposed to rule and control was an act of defiance aimed not only at the Ottoman Empire and at quarantine provisions, but clearly at the Governor too. But instead of mounting any kind of counterattack, Sami Pasha decided that the priority should be to conceal from Mingherians the truth about Doctor Ilias's poisoning. He told the Quarantine Master that, if necessary, he should add one more to the tally of plague cases in his next telegram to Istanbul. Besides, Doctor Ilias hadn't died yet, though he occasionally became disoriented and delirious, talking about his wife back in Istanbul before another spell of tremors similar to those that afflicted plague patients plunged him back into exhausted silence.

When Princess Pakize's letters are published, historians will discover that the debate on the question of method that took place between the Governor and the Doctor and Prince Consort in the meeting that was held an hour later at the State Hall gave rise to some noteworthy philosophical and political paradoxes. The Governor and the Prince Consort once again compared the relative merits of studying the available evidence to reach a conclusion (inductive reasoning), a process which—influenced by Abdul Hamid—they referred to as "the Sherlock Holmes method," versus those of applying a thorough and comprehensive political logic to establish the identity of the culprit from the outset and locate the supporting evidence accordingly (deductive reasoning).

"They stood in that very kitchen shamelessly pouring rat poison into the biscuit flour. It's clear who did this—and neither I nor the Sultan back in Istanbul need any help from Sherlock Holmes to work out who must have supplied them with the poison. This afternoon the state prosecutor and his clerk will be questioning the kitchen staff held in the garrison prison. The Department of Scrutinia and the prosecutor will get those Greek nationalist guerrillas talking in no time, you'll see."

"Your Excellency, I am convinced that this is the work of one person alone," said Doctor Nuri. "Do we really need to torture fifteen people to try and get to one?"

"Indeed we do not," said the Governor. "Even the prospect of being tortured has got them so afraid that they have already started talking; they have been telling us things we haven't even asked about yet. Tell me, could your Sherlock Holmes have done it so fast?"

In Minghcria, prisoners held on suspicion of theft or organized criminal activity would typically be interrogated in the Castle prison, where the soles of their bare feet would be beaten with sticks until their agonized screams could be heard in the Castle's southern wing. In the garrison, the same torture was inflicted upon Greek nationalist militants and guerrillas caught trying to ambush Ottoman troops. The Governor knew that soldiers tended to be more lenient compared with prison guards and the prosecutor's men, so he had sent the Chief Scrutineer to join the team leading the investigation at the garrison. The Chief Scrutineer was particularly skilled at formulating precisely the kinds of questions that could most effectively disorient prisoners already stupefied by the beatings they had suffered to their feet, and pick at the inconsistencies in their statements until they caved altogether. The Governor had ordered him not to leave the garrison until he had conclusively determined who among the cook and his assistants was to be blamed for this act.

But despite having their feet beaten and some having their nails torn off with pliers, none of the kitchen staff produced a sufficiently compelling account. Not one of the tortured prisoners was able to say convincingly enough: "Yes, I saw who did it: it was bald Rasim who mixed rat poison in with the walnuts and the rose-scented flour!" For they all knew that whatever they said, the officer interrogating them in the garrison would take them to the kitchen and expect to be shown exactly where they had seen it happen. In other words it was not possible to lie one's way out of the foot whippings. There wasn't even any proof yet that the arsenic had come from rat poison. The Governor Pasha was vexed that the torture carried out in the garrison jailhouse had not yielded the desired outcome, but he did not lose hope. The biscuits had been prepared and baked that morning in the garrison kitchens. Evidently the provisions master, who had been sent to the Castle prison earlier, or one of the elderly garrison waiters must somehow be involved.

So it was that the Governor Pasha decided to make another of his customary nighttime visits to the prison and sent word to Prison Warden Sadrettin Effendi accordingly. He also wrote Istanbul another telegram requesting that a support vessel be sent with additional doctors and supplies on board. An appeal made on behalf of a four-person family whom the Quarantine Regiment had put into the Castle's isolation facility that afternoon following the swearing-in ceremony had been passed up through the ranks until it had finally landed on the Governor's desk. He decided to ignore it.

The Governor then busied himself for a time with everyday matters that had nothing to do with the outbreak: he read and sent back to the Chief Scrutineer a report from an informant stating that there were twenty-five revolvers hidden inside the crates of cherries and strawberries that the deputy of the consul who ran the local Lloyd agency had arranged to have delivered directly to his seaside home without going through a customs check, declaring them to be for "personal consumption"; there had been a request from Istanbul (coming most likely from inside the harem) for a pair of Mingheria's native green-speckled, garrulous parrots to be caught and sent to the palace; money was needed to repair the Maviaka Bridge in the north after it had been damaged by rain. Another problem that, fueled by a stream of informers' reports, had grown increasingly urgent over the past few months, centered on allegations of misconduct around the municipal kitchens. To stop municipal employees from trading rumors over lunch, the Governor Pasha had made these meals the responsibility of individual department heads. So the Chief Secretary and his clerks, the Chief of Charitable Trusts and his assistants, and the Chief Archivist and his men all had their lunches in their respective offices. The municipality provided each office with an allowance and with food supplies for this purpose. But the department heads were known to take some of these supplies home with them, particularly when their salaries from Istanbul were delayed, or even to do what Chief Scrutineer Mazhar Effendi unabashedly did and pilfer beans and lentils from the municipal storehouse to fill up their own family kitchens. The British consul Monsieur George had helpfully suggested that one way to stem this hemorrhage of public funds might be to adopt a table d'hôte system (as was beginning to be done in some military bases in Istanbul), but it would have been unwise to introduce such a measure now, for it was bound to cause the plague to spread even faster and to antagonize the department heads. Some clerks, particularly those with influential friends, only came to the office to eat lunch.

The Governor was also thinking about his upcoming night trip to the prisons. When Chief Scrutineer Mazhar Effendi returned from the garrison, the Governor outlined his plans for this visit. Three separate gallows were to be erected that night side by side to carry out the exemplary punishments of the three villains—starting with Ramiz—who were guilty of Bonkowski's murder. Şakir would be more than enough to deal with these three cowards, but his working alone could also pose a problem; the executioner would have to carry out each sentence in turn, and that could take a long time.

CHAPTER 29

Shortly after dark the Governor looked out of his window to see that the gallows really were being erected in the State Hall Square, and prompted by an urge he could make no sense of, he walked to Marika's house. As always, the sight of her dark eyes and her thin, delicate nose filled him with joy, and he was able to forget his political preoccupations for a while. The first new rumor of note that Marika relayed to him that night was that Doctor Ilias had caught the plague at the garrison. This was being regarded as yet more evidence that the plague had been brought to the island by Bonkowski Pasha.

"Doctor Ilias is hiding in the garrison because he is afraid, not because of the plague," said the Pasha.

Marika had also heard that despite pressure from foreign consuls, the Sultan was going to intervene to stop Ramiz's hanging.

"How strange!" said the Governor. "I wonder where they got that from."

"But neither the Greeks nor the Muslims think Zeynep is going to wait for Ramiz while he is locked up in the dungeons. Pasha, is it true that the old sultan's daughter's guard is in love with Zeynep?"

"It is!" said the Governor.

As he walked back through the silky night toward the State Hall, without a carriage and without guards, the Governor was stopped by the night watchmen, who did not recognize him at first. He looked again at the gallows rising in the darkness.

Three telegrams had arrived that evening, and a secretary had placed them on the Governor's desk after arranging for the municipal code breaker to decrypt them. The first telegram requested that the executions of the suspects in the Bonkowski murder be put on hold until they were approved by Istanbul. The second was in response to the telegram the Pasha had sent that morning: it said that the supply ship *Sühandan* would soon be on its way. The third telegram suggested that if the killers were to repent and confess, they might be granted the Sultan's pardon, but there would have to be some justification provided and information supplied to support such a decision. The Governor was not in the least surprised by any of these three telegrams. He sat at his desk for a long time, staring at the Castle lanterns burning in the distance.

When the Governor wished to silence and browbeat his opponents and any journalists into submission, he would intimidate them with beatings, prison sentences, and solitary confinement but also ensure that he provided these treacherous snakes with gaps through which they could slither back to their old lives, using municipal clerks and mutual acquaintances to present them with gifts and offers of collaboration. (The Governor liked to think of this dual approach of his as a form of "merciful cunning" learned from Abdul Hamid.) He particularly enjoyed making secret trips to the prison in the middle of the night to visit prisoners in their cells and propose alliances. It was the kind of grand entrance that could impress even the most disconsolate of inmates. The Pasha usually undertook these expeditions whenever pressure mounted from Istanbul for a particular prisoner to be released.

The Chief Prison Warden had come to the State Hall to deliver his report. As they made their way back to the Castle together in the armored landau, they discussed the state of its prison wing. Among politicians and intellectuals of that era, the Arkaz Castle Prison, also known as the Mingherian Dungeon, was one of the most-feared penitentiaries in the Ottoman Empire, its reputation surpassed only by the prisons in the castles of Fezzan, Sinope, and Rhodes. Conditions in the island's prison were worse than those in other similar establishments across Ottoman lands. The prison dormitories, where petty thieves and unfortunate victims of calumnious accusations lived shoulder to shoulder with hardened killers and inveterate swindlers, were veritable criminal academies where even the most innocent of prisoners quickly learned all kinds of tricks and longed for a chance to put their new skills into practice.

Like many other reform-minded Ottoman statesmen, the Governor harbored a particular interest in prisons. Whenever Hüseyin Pasha, a retired brigadier general who now served as the Chief Inspector of Prisons, came to visit the island, the Governor and the Prison Warden would always have long talks with him on the subject of "prison reform." What was the surest way to discover and deal with insubordination in the dormitories, overly permissive guards, and unruly inmates? Should the openings on cell doors be moved a little higher, and should the dormitory system be replaced with individual cells?

Another cause for embarrassment was the pervasive misconduct of the prison staff. Some would seize the money and belongings handed over by inexperienced new arrivals; others would collect regular levies from selected victims and even hold out the promise of a pardon or a more comfortable confinement in exchange for "gifts." Some wealthier and more powerful inmates would bribe the dormitory chiefs, the warden, and the guards and spend most of their days and nights in their own homes, paying only the occasional visit to the prison. The Governor Pasha would sometimes remark that when destitute prisoners were left to rot in dank cellars for having stolen a piece of bread while these far-more-culpable local celebrities wandered freely on the streets, people's faith in the concept of justice was bound to be eroded. In these moments the municipal secretary, Faik Bey, who considered it his duty to enlighten the Governor on the facts of life even when the Governor knew those facts already, would remind the Pasha that the prison guards had not been paid in five months, and that Master Emrullah, who was mostly serving his sentence at home, had not only been providing several prison guards with financial assistance, but that he had also paid for glass windows to be installed in the dormitories that overlooked the port, that every time he came to the prison he would hand out jugs of olive oil, dried figs, and eggs he had brought from his village, and that he had engaged his own men out of his own pocket to repair the broken wall near the main entrance.

"He could at least avoid going out into Hamidiye Avenue with his entourage when it's busy!" the Governor would reply. "Everyone thinks he's locked up in the dungeons!"

After midnight, as the landau with the Governor Pasha and the Prison Warden on board descended toward the shore, it crossed paths with a quiet, unassuming Greek family. Though it was completely dark, the father, who was carrying the family's belongings on his back, recognized the Governor Pasha from his voice. Speaking slowly in rudimentary Turkish and a strangely sentimental manner, he told them that an infected person had visited their home. The Pasha was able to understand that one of the man's children had developed a fever and fallen sick too. But was it the plague, or was it something else? The man's wife began to cry. After the family had vanished into the darkness, the landau continued down the slope. They passed through narrow, crooked streets once lined with Janissaries' shops, lorimers, leather dealers, saddlers, and small eateries. The Pasha experienced that same sensation of having been admitted into a boundless, mysterious, ancient realm that he and everybody else felt whenever they passed through the gates of the Castle.

Before going into the prison, the Pasha wanted to see the courtyard where people who had been exposed to the plague were being kept in isolation. The Castle was a convoluted network of walls, towers, and assorted structures built over hundreds of years, and the partially covered isolation facility was situated in the northeastern section of this vast complex, facing the port. Those who were being held in isolation there were visible from the city across the bay. Far from the Venetian- and Byzantine-era buildings in the southeastern section that had served for centuries as prisons, and from the Venetian Tower, famous for its damp dungeon cells, the isolation area was bordered along its southern edge by the Janissaries' Barracks, built in the time of Blind Mehmet Pasha. From his chair in his office in the State Hall, Sami Pasha could look across the bay and see the windows of this most elegant of all the Castle buildings, and watch the bored and weary people held in isolation sitting and waiting on the rocks by the sea. Now, in the middle of the night, he found himself looking at the same place up close, and from the opposite vantage point.

More than half the people currently in isolation came from the city's Muslim neighborhoods. They had been brought here because someone in their house had died, and it was therefore believed that they too might be infected. Most were angry at having been forcibly removed from their homes and families. But they were also trying to reason with themselves and accept the necessity of quarantine. In the first five days since the beginning of quarantine, a total of thirty-seven people had been put into isolation. The Prison Warden told the Governor that initially these "suspects" had been furious at their predicament, but that they had eventually calmed down. They were being given the same food that was fed to the convicts in the Castle prison, but even so the warden could not refrain from petitioning the Governor for an additional allowance.

As they climbed to the second floor of the barracks, they crossed an empty landing where the Governor felt the presence of the port and the darkness and the chill of the sea. The Castle gave everyone rheumatism. In the two months that he had spent here locked up in the Venetian Tower writing satirical odes to Sultan Abdulmejid, the famous stuttering poet Saim of Sinope had been driven half mad with rheumatic aches. The warden noted that there weren't enough beds, so most of the plague suspects were having to share mattresses. Ever since the discovery of Guard Bayram's corpse fifteen days ago, the Governor and the Prison Warden had been extremely concerned that the disease might spread across the Castle, and had accordingly taken extensive precautions to prevent this.

There had been mousetraps installed in every corner of the Castle. The rats killed by these traps were picked up with tongs, as the warden was at pains to note, and delivered to the municipal authorities. But so far none of the rats that had been caught in the Castle had died as the plague-infested ones in the city did, with blood oozing out their mouths and noses. A murderer shackled in his cell had become feverish and delirious, vomiting occasionally, but a second convict who shared the same cell did not seem to be sick at all. The Pasha strongly suspected that the murderous scoundrel didn't really have the plague and was just pretending. The Prison Warden should have known that the only way to deal with a man in that state was to give his feet a good beating until he admitted he wasn't sick, but the warden was probably worried that his men might catch the plague themselves while administering the necessary torture. It had also occurred to the Governor Pasha that if that beast really were to die of the plague, the definitive solution would be to dispose of his corpse in the middle of the night, throwing it into the sea unbeknownst to all, and before any rumors could start about an outbreak in the prison. Would the sharks who ate the corpse also die of the plague?

They walked across the spacious courtyard between the Castle's first wall, built by the Crusaders, and its second wall, built by the Venetians, and listened to the sound of their own footsteps before they entered the prison through its side gate.

The Pasha went to the door of the second dormitory first, where gangsters and felons were housed. The father and son who had been convicted during the pilgrim ship trial and had been serving their sentences ever since slept in this dormitory too. The Pasha glanced through the window on the door as if he could see into the darkness, then walked away. He had been thinking of finding an excuse to release the pair early, as he was worried that something might happen to them while they were inside.

Occasionally the Prison Warden would complain so much about a particularly unmanageable dormitory chief that the Governor, running out of patience, would instruct him to serve some kind of exemplary punishment, and the inmate in question would be given a thorough beating by the prison guards. It was imperative to the smooth running of the Ottoman Empire that the prisoner should never discover where the order that had resulted in his punishment had originated. After the beating, the convict would be taken from his dormitory, which the Crusaders, the Venetians, and the Byzantines had perhaps once used as a refectory or an armory or as sleeping quarters, and be transferred to the prison tower on the rocky cliff along the Castle's southwest wall, where he would be thrown inside a frigid cell overlooking the sea. Also known as the Venetian Tower, this tall construction with thick walls had originally been built as an observation tower, but a mere one hundred and seventy years later it had begun to be utilized as a prison, and now, four hundred years on, this first seed of what had since become the much-larger Castle prison still served that same function under Ottoman rule. Healthy prisoners who were locked up in this tower, and particularly in the smaller cells on its lower floors, would soon fall ill, while older, sicklier, wearier prisoners would usually die within a year or two. The one relatively salubrious cell in the tower faced a narrow courtyard. Here, after being tormented all day by rats, cockroaches, and mosquitoes, and surrounded by the presence of so many others slowly dying with him, the prisoner would look out into the courtyard as the evening sun began to set to see inmates shackled and weighed down like galley slaves, pacing back and forth outside, and realizing then that things could get far worse for him than they already were, he would be moved to reflect upon his actions.

Governor Sami Pasha stepped onto the gloomy stone-paved landing next to the cell where Manolis, editor in chief of the *Neo Nisi,* had been locked up. A prison officer who had been waiting for the Governor to arrive told him that the interrogation was ongoing, but the exhausted suspect had fallen asleep. The Pasha's orders were to do whatever it took to discover who had made Manolis write the column where he had brought up the Pilgrim Ship Mutiny again. He was convinced that whoever had been responsible for that must have also organized Bonkowski Pasha's assassination. But this was not a theory he felt he could share with Doctor Nuri, who believed in the fanciful notion that a series of unconnected clues would eventually lead him to the killer. The Governor also didn't want anybody to know that he was having the Greek journalist tortured. The Pasha hated when the uppermost tiers of the Ottoman ruling classes had their underlings do their dirty work for them, then acted as if they didn't know anything about it, almost as much as he hated people who pretended to be more westernized than they really were. Often those who did that dirty work on some mysterious superior's bidding would then strenuously and wholeheartedly deny that the order had originally been given by the highest authority in the land. It was Abdul Hamid who had arranged for the Ottoman bureaucracy's brightest and most westernized minister and governor, Mithat Pasha—the man whose actions had led to Abdul Hamid's older brother being deposed and Abdul Hamid himself taking the throne in his place—to first be banished to the Ta'if prison in the Hejaz and later be strangled in his cell, but all this the Sultan had organized in such a way that nobody had been able to tell who had planned it. The Governor Pasha had come across many naïve and simpleminded Ottoman bureaucrats who revered the memory of the reformist and parliamentarianist Mithat Pasha but could not bring themselves to believe that he had been assassinated on Abdul Hamid's orders.

Apart from Manolis, there was another prisoner in the tower where the Governor Pasha usually put any Greek guerrillas, suspected criminals, and journalists he did not immediately wish to see beaten. The Prison Warden reminded the Governor about Pavli Bey. The Governor had had him locked up in the tower for penning false reports about a plague in the city, then forgotten that he had done so. Or perhaps he had not forgotten him altogether, but everything had been happening so fast that the Pasha hadn't quite known what to do with him.

The iron door opened noisily, and two guards stepped inside, carrying torches.

"Ah, Pasha . . . ," said the journalist, sitting up on his bed of straw. "So the outbreak is real after all!"

"Yes, Pavli Bey; that is why we are here. You were right. We have begun quarantine procedures."

"It is too late, Your Excellency!" said the journalist. "It has reached the prison too, and soon we will all be dead."

"You mustn't despair!" said the Pasha. "The state will sort everything out."

"You're the one who put me in prison because I said there was an outbreak . . . ," the journalist replied. "And now people are dying, killed by that same outbreak!"

The Governor reminded the journalist that he had been put in prison not because he had reported the truth, but because he had not followed the Governor's instructions.

"Don't think you'll be set free now just because you were right about the outbreak!" he continued sternly. "They might decide to try you for treason. I can stop that from happening, but Chief Scrutineer Mazhar Effendi will need your help."

"We have always been the municipality's and the sultans' staunchest supporters, and prayed for their success," said the journalist.

"We know that the rebel Haralambo, who has set up camp near Menoya Bay and in the Defteros Mountains, receives support from Arkaz, and we know who from," said the Governor Pasha. "Let me make it very clear to you that you must stay away from these people!"

"They are up in the mountains, and I've had nothing at all to do with them . . ."

"They have friends in Arkaz, places to stay and people who support them. We know all this, Pavli Bey. I am informed that Haralambo comes to Arkaz sometimes, and that when he does, he stays in the Hora neighborhood."

"I don't know anything, Pasha," said Pavli the journalist, giving the Governor a look that seemed to say that even if he did know something, he wouldn't tell.

The Governor stormed out of the cell and told his clerks to send a note to the prison the next morning and see to it that both "this one" and Manolis were set free. Then he followed the Prison Warden toward the wing of the prison where Ramiz and his associates were being held.

As they walked across flagstones and up stairways to the sound of their own footsteps, the Governor could tell from the silence around them that the prisoners had heard the sound of the Castle's main gate, the doors to its courtyards, and the entrances to its prison buildings opening and closing in the middle of the night, and that they were waiting expectantly to discover the reason for this unannounced visit—perhaps an execution to be carried out in the inner courtyard, or a dormitory search that would result in a round of bastinado. The clerk behind him was carrying a torch, and the Governor enjoyed watching its black shadow cast upon the walls and stone floors of the prison.

That afternoon, in preparation for the Governor's visit, Ramiz had been taken to a room in the prison's administrative offices where they had served him a plate of mullet stuffed with vegetables and some bread on the side, told him that his sentence might be commuted if he behaved himself and elicited the Governor's trust, made sure he was aware that gallows were already being erected in the State Hall Square without waiting for Istanbul's approval, and finally sent him back to a more comfortable cell.

As he always did in these nighttime visits, the Governor strode into Ramiz's cell and coolly delivered the speech he had prepared.

"It is my belief and that of the judicial committee that has convicted you that you are guilty of this crime, but against the scourge of plague we must practice forgiveness and obedience, not conflict. Thus, if you answer my questions truthfully and honorably, confess to your crimes, and provide a written statement expressing your heartfelt remorse, the authorities in Istanbul may order you to be released on the condition that you never set foot in Arkaz again."

Ramiz was completely drained after three days of intermittent torture and hardly any sleep in his cold and preternaturally damp cell, but the Governor saw a glimmer of life in his eyes. Was it righteous anger, or the confidence of having friends in very high places? The Governor Pasha asked Ramiz a long list of detailed questions about Haralambo, the Greek consul, and the rumors that the Pantaleon Company's ferries were being used to smuggle weapons to the island. He even intimated that the Pilgrim Ship Mutiny had been provoked by the British. But, he added, Istanbul would ensure these enemies of the Sultan received the punishment they deserved. He warned Ramiz not to get complacent just because the army was fighting the Greek guerrillas in the northern villages, and ordered him to leave the prison guard's daughter Zeynep alone. The whole island would be better off if she married the Major, said the Governor Pasha, stating openly that "the girl" was in love with the army officer anyway.

"If that is true, then I should rather die!" said Ramiz, looking at the floor. He really was more handsome than the Major.

The Governor Pasha made a show of being angry and disappointed with this declaration, then left the cell. The next morning, after half a day's journey on an army rowboat, Ramiz and his men were released in one of the coves in the north of the island. Ramiz had no consuls to protect him, so the Governor had judged it sufficient to set him free in this manner. As proof of his repentance and confession, they had also had him sign a piece of paper with half a page of hastily scribbled text on it. Ramiz had been released on the condition that he must never return to Arkaz again, but both sides knew that this was a promise that would never be kept.

CHAPTER 30

Doctor Nuri, Doctor Nikos, and two Greek doctors tried to look for an antidote and make the patient regurgitate the poison, but their attempts proved fruitless. After vomiting blood, Doctor Ilias fell into a coma and later died in Theodoropoulos Hospital, one day after ingesting the rose-and-walnut biscuit. To prevent the kinds of discussions that would be harmful to the quarantine effort, the true cause of death was concealed from the whole island, so that only the doctors knew that it had been poisoning, and Doctor Ilias was buried with the plague victims.

The "exposition"—as Princess Pakize herself called it—of this murder-and-poisoning plot features prominently in the Princess's correspondence from this period. Adopting in some ways the same logical approach her uncle Abdul Hamid favored, Princess Pakize, "like Sherlock Holmes," sat at her writing desk and sought, together with her husband, to unravel and chronicle the secrets of this hidden assassination from a distance.

When her husband had first described to her how Doctor Ilias had been poisoned by a biscuit and told her of the dog and the bay horse that had also been poisoned and killed by the same biscuits, Princess Pakize had remarked: "Once again, everything comes back to my uncle and to the line of succession." Sultan Abdul Hamid may have been the single topic she and her husband most frequently discussed, but the second was surely the palace's proliferating population of indolent princes. Our readers must not think that we are straying too far from our story if we too take a moment now to examine the reasons behind this phenomenon.

Any man who wedded a sultan's daughter, a princess, would soon find that because he had married into the royal family, his life would inevitably come to resemble the lives of the idle, aimless princes of the Ottoman dynasty. Doctor and Prince Consort Nuri had no intention of giving up his profession, yet he couldn't help but feel that no matter how hard he tried to resist, he would eventually be compelled to lead the same hollow, vacuous existence those princes led.

Abdul Hamid had already awarded the title of Pasha to the husbands he had found for the three sisters—his nieces—he'd separated from their father, gifting them each a mansion on the shores of the Bosphorus and arranging for them to receive generous stipends. Like her sisters' and Abdul Hamid's daughter's waterside mansions, Princess Pakize and her husband's too was in Ortaköy. Her sisters' husbands had already reduced their duties at the palace. Soon they would give them up completely. Their newfound position in the dynastic order made it awkward for them to be given orders or tasks or be assigned any other kind of duty. It was a strange quandary, and one that derived, of course, from centuries of Ottoman history.

During the first five hundred years of Ottoman rule, there were three main avenues for the edification of Ottoman princes: the palace school, the army, and provincial government. But with both academic and military training growing increasingly westernized, the administration of local provinces shifted away from an older system to a new order where these roles were assigned to salaried governor pashas selected from among specially trained army officers and bureaucrats, and careers in the army and in local government were no longer available to Ottoman princes. During the early years of the Ottoman Empire, the throne was supposed to be passed on from the father to eldest son. But sometimes one of the other sons, ruling perhaps over Trebizond or Magnesia, would try to upend the order of succession and take the throne for himself, gathering his armies to march to Istanbul before his older brothers could get there. This tradition often led to civil war, so that eventually princes began to be kept in Istanbul. But this in turn led to certain incidents that would later be considered cause for great shame, most notably Sultan Mehmed III's order—on the day he ascended to the throne—to have every single one of his nineteen brothers strangled to death, until it was eventually decided that sultans would no longer pass on the throne to their son but to their eldest male sibling instead. But like Abdul Hamid, most sultans were suspicious by nature, and so in an effort to prevent not just their one or two siblings who were closest in line to the throne but all their other brothers and their nephews too from meeting with dissenters and becoming involved in coup attempts, they took to physically confining their rivals to so-called princes' quarters inside royal palaces, all in a concerted effort to sever them altogether from life beyond the palace, Istanbul, and the rest of the world.

Throughout the course of Ottoman history, one of the most famous of these confined princes was Princess Pakize's older brother, forty-year-old Prince Mehmet Selahattin Effendi. Just three months after happily watching his father Murad V take the throne, the then fifteen-year-old Mehmet Selahattin Effendi was imprisoned along with his deposed father. For twenty-five years since, he had been stuck inside the same palace, living a life of captivity. Like his father and sisters, he played the piano. He filled journal after journal with aphorisms, memoirs, and theater scripts. Unlike other princes, he was neither lazy nor uneducated. He enjoyed reading, if only occasionally—just like his father, whom he venerated. With Princess Pakize, he was always amiable and loving. The Princess, who knew that he was not like those other idle, spoiled princes, would sometimes see from the expression on his face as he stood surrounded by his captive sisters, other princesses, footmen, and servants, just how desolate he was, and she would feel sorry for him. In the palace that served as his prison, the Prince had his own harem (more than forty beautiful women of varying ranks and titles, each vying for his attention), and seven living children.

Princess Pakize was particularly concerned that her husband should not become "anything like" one of these isolated, ignorant, and lazy princes. One reason for this was that she was proud of her husband's quarantine achievements and of the fact that his name was known—if not too widely—in the international medical community. What her enemies also noted was that the Princess, who was not nearly as beautiful or striking as either of her two sisters, was merely being realistic and preparing herself for what would most likely be a fairly plain and unextravagant existence. The third reason for her concern was the tales Princess Pakize had heard from her sister about the princes of the Ottoman dynasty.

Her two older sisters Hatice and Fehime had both left their father's home before she had and entered the harem in the Yıldız Palace, where they had made friends with their uncle's unmarried daughters and been introduced from a distance to the princes themselves. The royal dynasty's daughters and princesses of marriageable age would gossip freely about these princes, just as they did about the sons of pashas and viziers. After the supposed abolition of slavery and in the wake of the gradual western- ization of Ottoman court customs and harem life, most of these princes and potential future sultans were no longer interested in following the many centuries of tradition which might have seen them wed a Circas- sian or Ukrainian slave girl brought in from some distant province and expected instead to marry women who had been given European-style piano lessons in palace harems, spoke French, and read novels. On the other hand, these sophisticated young women, with their good breeding and westernized education, found those pampered princes to be coarse, uninformed, and dull witted. (Indeed even in that period very few "mat- rimonies" took place between sultans' daughters and Ottoman princes.) Teaching these princes anything was very difficult; to strike a young man who might one day sit on the Ottoman throne and become the caliph of four hundred million Muslims was unthinkable, and the Ottomans were only just beginning to discover how to discipline students without beating them.

Princess Pakize's sisters would often laugh and occasionally bristle with fury as they traded stories about these princes, who had, like them, spent their lives confined inside royal palaces, and who (so the sisters believed) were too afraid of Abdul Hamid to propose to them. Here was Osman Celâlettin Effendi, seventh in line to the throne, who had locked himself up in his mansion in Nişantaşı and devoted twenty-three years of his life trying to figure out how to "be himself," an endeavor which he considered to be more important than seizing the throne, and which finally cost him his sanity. Prince Mahmut Seyfettin Effendi, who was rather close to the front of the line of succession, had lived for twenty-eight years without once setting foot outside his quarters in the Çırağan Palace, so that when he saw, for the first time in his life, a sheep standing in the palace's central courtyard, he shouted "Monster!" and summoned his guards. (Others told similar stories about the sisters' own brother, Mehmet Selahattin.) Then there was Prince Ahmet Nizamettin, who was not only exceptionally vain, but had also taken out substantial loans by promising, despite having no chance of ever sitting on the throne, that he would soon pay the lenders back with interest, until there had been so many complaints about his failure to do so that he had had to be reprimanded by the Sultan. But the most feared and the most odious of all the princes was of course Abdul Hamid's fourth-born son, Mehmet Burhanettin Effendi. Composer of the official "Naval March," which he had created at the age of seven, Burhanettin Effendi had for a time been the Sultan's favorite son, always sitting next to him in the royal carriage during public processions to Friday prayers, and Princess Pakize's sisters, who were much older than he was, dreaded this spoiled young princeling's practical jokes and cruel impertinences, suspecting the boy's father to be behind these provocations. Meek and timorous Mehmet Vahdettin Effendi reported in writing to Abdul Hamid with information on the other princes (his brothers and cousins) in exchange for gifts of money, land, and houses (and would end up on the throne himself seventeen years later). Then there was the acutely sensitive and introverted Necip Kemalettin Effendi, who loved art and had no interest in romancing women. Finally there were those like Mehmet Hamdi and Ahmet Reşit Effendi, who were close to the bottom of the order of succession and free to roam around Istanbul as they pleased, but were nevertheless all too quick to feel aggrieved and claim that the Sultan was following their every move. Even these princes who knew they would never have the opportunity to sit on the throne insisted that the Sultan might still attempt to poison them and studiously avoided shopping at the Yıldız Palace Pharmacy.

"Did you ever go to that pharmacy?" asked the Doctor and Prince Consort.

"I stayed at the Yıldız Palace for a month before our wedding. We rarely left our quarters," said Princess Pakize. "Anyway there was a second pharmacy at the palace only for our and for my uncle's use. You see, my uncle too was afraid he might get poisoned, just like those princes were. Of course no one knew more about this subject than Bonkowski Pasha—may he rest in peace—for he was the one who ran this private pharmacy, the laboratory, as my uncle sometimes called it."

"Pharmacist Nikiforos might know something about it too!" said her husband.

It was almost midday before Doctor Nuri had the opportunity to discuss the matter with Bonkowski Pasha's old friend Pharmacist Nikiforos.

He had first seen him that morning among the doctors and other pharmacists gathered around Doctor Ilias's bed in the Theodoropoulos Hospital. Every now and then Doctor Ilias would lift his head from his pillow and cry out for his wife in Istanbul: "Despina!" He had just been given an antidote whose formula had been devised jointly by the doctors and the pharmacists. The consensus at the time had been that the antidote seemed to be bringing the patient some relief.

They met five minutes later at the Pharmacie Nikiforos, just a few steps from the Theodoropoulos Hospital.

"You once told me that a long time ago Bonkowski Pasha prepared a report for our beloved sultan on the kinds of herbs he might be able to grow in the Yıldız Gardens and use for making poisons!" said the Doctor and Prince Consort, getting directly to the point.

"I thought of that too when I found out that Doctor Ilias had been poisoned," said Nikiforos. "The Sultan was always most afraid of ratsbane, which could be administered gradually over a long time and in doses so small that he wouldn't even notice them in his food. The British newspapers always wrote about that kind of thing. But these people have done just the opposite with the arsenic they've used on poor Doctor Ilias."

"How do you know it was arsenic?"

"That is a very good question, and the Governor Pasha would be especially pleased to hear you ask it, for it puts me in a rather suspicious position. Allow me, then, to provide you with a detailed response, so that I might eliminate any trace of suspicion that may have come to rest upon me."

"That's not why I asked."

"I must beg your pardon for what may turn out to be a needlessly elaborate disquisition, but as you know, we pharmacists can't help ourselves: even our words must be weighed and measured. The island of Mingheria has certainly never experienced any cases of ratsbane poisoning comparable to those we have seen in Europe, where they have often captured the popular imagination and been investigated by public prosecutors and regional and national inquest committees. But in the time that I have been running my shop here, the locals have learned that rat poison can be used to slowly kill a person and leave no trace. Twenty-two years ago, when his first wife passed away, the still-childless eldest son of the wealthy Greek Aldoni family spent a lot of effort and vast sums of money trying to find a young and beautiful Mingherian girl to take as his second wife, and eventually married Tanasis's daughter, whose father runs one of the seaside tavernas in Ora. Not too long after the wedding, the groom came to me complaining of stomachaches and vomiting and asking for medicine. The doctors could not seem to come up with a diagnosis. The skin on his hands and face had darkened, and there were sores on his arms and fingers. But unless they read French novels, nobody would have been able to put those things together and come to any kind of conclusion. In just one year I saw that forty-year-old man waste away and die. At his funeral, which we all attended, his young widow cried more than anyone else, so much so that nobody could really think there had been any kind of wrongdoing. But when that same widow sold all that she had inherited from him and ran away to Smyrna with her young lover just three months after the funeral, people began to say, 'They killed him.' It was Pharmacist Mitsos (who is known to enjoy reading French novels in Greek translation) who first told me it might have been a case of arsenic poisoning. But by then the horse had long since bolted. We are all of us Ottoman citizens. Never mind twenty years ago, even today our Ottoman courts are still not equipped to investigate this kind of murder as the European courts would do, using scientific methods to uncover a case of poisoning. No wonder people were so impressed with the fictional doctors (and jealous of them too) that they read about in these detective novels that are so popular in Europe, and that are translated and serialized in our newspapers. Then, as now, rat poison—sold under the name white arsenic—was readily available to purchase from any herbalist's shop. This particular incident was not reported in the island's newspapers, but our Greek and Turkish papers did write about these sorts of poisonings sometimes, and always with a tone that seemed to say, 'Look at the terrible things that happen in Europe.'

"Our other notable case of poisoning—and one that was also never properly investigated—involved a half-mad but beautiful sixteen-year-old girl from the poor Tuzla neighborhood who, in my estimation, poisoned more than forty people. Over the course of a year, as her family sought to sell her into marriage and entertained a series of old matriarchs, prospective grooms, and matchmakers come to appraise her, as well as go-betweens, relatives, and prying acquaintances, she mixed small, non-fatal, and indeed initially imperceptible doses of ratsbane into their cups of coffee, and poisoned them all. But nobody realized. In any case, the Governor at the time had banned newspapers from reporting on cases of murder by rat poison. The idea that a person could slowly be poisoned with small doses of flourlike white arsenic is an insidious thought. But it is certainly not prevalent on our island. The cook's apprentice must either have been given a bag of poison by someone, or he must have heard about this method somewhere. We did try to ban traditional herbalists from selling ratsbane in their shops here too, just as we did in Istanbul through the Pharmacists' Guild."

"Why do you think you were not able to succeed?"

"Just a moment longer, Doctor Pasha, and I shall explain . . . Sometime after our current Governor took up his position, he lifted the ban on the story of the beautiful, cursed girl with arsenic in her pocket. This was supposed to help establish the notion that 'the old governor was incompetent.' The old story was quickly picked up by the newspapers, particularly Greek ones, who used it to ridicule the delegations that lecherous men sent to approach marriageable girls on their behalf, and hint at the enduring backwardness of Muslims who still seemed incapable of getting married unless there was a matchmaker involved. As I said, arsenic poisoning is not known on our island because nobody here reads French novels. Sometimes they bring people to me who have become unhinged with romantic heartbreak and swallowed fistfuls of rat poison; I know from these cases that people who have ingested rat poison will exhibit small, whitish, soil-like particles in their vomit. When they are close to dying, they also tend to regret their decision, and reveal what poison they took. That is indeed one of its more unusual symptoms . . . It is an agonizing death." There was a silence. Then: "The famous French novel's immoral, unstable heroine Madame Bovary also committed suicide in the same manner," said Bonkowski Pasha's learned friend, correctly surmising that Doctor Nuri would not know who she was.

There was a glass cabinet between them, and from where they were sitting, they could see inside it a number of pill jars, small, colorful boxes of imported medicines, bottles of all shapes and sizes containing mostly dark-colored pastes and preparations, and various packages. In the room next door were gas lamps, alembics, scissors, brushes, and mortars. Three customers came into the pharmacy, carefully studying the goods on display, and lingering over their shopping as if there were no plague in the city.

"Twenty-two years ago the Sultan commissioned Bonkowski Pasha to write a treatise on how to extract poison from the plants in the Palace Gardens."

"Yes!" said Pharmacist Nikiforos. "I knew you would remember and ask me about it, so I have been thinking very hard indeed and sifting through my memories. What I have concluded is that this is ultimately the story of the development of modern Western-style pharmacies in Istanbul and on the island of Mingheria."

On the one hand there were young, Western-educated pharmacists like Bonkowski and Nikiforos, returning from their studies in Paris and Berlin with an unwavering commitment to the notion of "scientific pharmacology" and supported by a faction of angry "radicals" demanding a ban on the sale of poisonous (or otherwise harmful) substances and on the provision of drugs without prescription. Another faction included the big pharmacies clustered around Istanbul's Beyoğlu and Beyazıt neighborhoods and selling all kinds of products, local and imported. Like the first faction, they too were mostly Christians. Everyone in Istanbul frequented the Reboulss's pharmacy or the British-run Kanzuk. These establishments also sold products usually found in herbalists' shops, as well as ready-made and continually evolving European drugs, medicinal pastes that came in boxes and dainty bottles, syrups, creams, and assorted luxuries ranging from European chocolates to canned foods.

Abdul Hamid knew from his spies and informants that several Ottoman princes, worried that they might be poisoned if they shopped at the palace pharmacy, would make their purchases from these big Beyoğlu pharmacies instead. The Sultan understood that even those princes who were lowest in the line of succession were so wary of him that they felt safer shopping in Beyoğlu, while others did it purely to show off, but what he really wanted to know was whether the princes ever bought any substances from these pharmacies that could later be used to produce poison. As our readers will be able to glean from Princess Pakize's letters, the Sultan had requested an exhaustive report on this subject from Bonkowski Pasha.

As well as checking on the poison trade, the Sultan had also wished to find out what conversations the doctors who saw each other at the Apéry Pharmacy in Istanbul's Galata neighborhood were having. (In this operation, he was successful.) All of the major pharmacies also had doctors' clinics and waiting rooms on their premises. But Apéry had turned the waiting room of his pharmacy in Galata into something more akin to a reading room. He had taken out subscriptions to numerous European medical journals and brought in all the latest textbooks. Every doctor in Istanbul, Greek or Muslim, frequented this reading room, and not just to peruse its journals, but also to meet and talk with colleagues.

The Sultan was especially protective of Muslim-owned establishments and their locally produced wares and wished to see these pharmacies—places like the Hamdi Apothecary, the Istikamet (meaning "righteous path"), or Edhem Pertev's—join Bonkowski Bey's guild too. But the single largest group that Abdul Hamid wished both to support and to regulate was that of family-run herbalists, who often sold powders, medicines, rat poison, and cinnamon all in the same shop, and who made their own pills and ointments too. It was among these old-fashioned herbalists that the proportion of Muslim shop owners was the highest, and Abdul Hamid wanted both to support them because they were Muslims and to ban them from selling poisons, two objectives that he knew to be contradictory.

"My impression is that as with all subjects to which the Sultan dedicates his undiluted attention, he must have had conflicting feelings on this matter too," Pharmacist Nikiforos told Doctor Nuri. "Twenty years ago too His Supreme Highness was championing Muslim pharmacies one day and burdening them the next—all in the name of 'reform and betterment'—with extensive prohibitions and demands that they introduce modern European practices, which these Muslim pharmacists were ill equipped to implement. But whenever a new rule that the Sultan has introduced upon the insistence of the European powers, and that even he doesn't believe in, turns out to be deleterious to his Muslim subjects, he will not follow it through. Did he not indeed dismiss the parliament for precisely the same and entirely warranted reason—namely, that these new liberties were proving unpropitious to the Empire's Muslim population?"

The Doctor and Prince Consort briefly wondered if the reason the pharmacist seemed so comfortable making such controversial assertions was that he had rehearsed them beforehand, and upon his return to the municipal guesthouse, he shared this thought with Princess Pakize. What they quickly realized, with the benefit of Princess Pakize's insight too, was that Pharmacist Nikiforos had spoken that day like a man with a secret connection to Abdul Hamid—like someone whom the Sultan might have issued with a special codebook.

Fifty days before, in a quiet moment during a wedding function teeming with horse-drawn carriages and liveried servants, Princess Pakize's sister Princess Hatice's much-older husband had turned to Doctor Nuri and said: "Beware those who have the temerity to openly malign our sultan! They are all *agents provocateurs*. If you agree with them, they will immediately denounce you to the Sultan. You must ask yourself: 'How can this person come here and say to my face things that most people would be too afraid to even think about?' The answer is that they are informers, and they have nothing to fear."

CHAPTER 31

What is the role of "personality" in history? To some, this question is immaterial. They see history as a colossal wheel much greater than any individual. Yet some historians have sought explanations for historical events in the personalities of the protagonists and key figures of the period. We too believe that a historical figure's personality and temperament can sometimes alter the course of history. But these individual traits are, in turn, shaped by history itself.

It is true that Sultan Abdul Hamid was of such a suspicious disposition as to warrant Europeans calling him "paranoid." But what made him so suspicious were the things he had seen and experienced—that is to say, history itself. In other words, Abdul Hamid had perfectly reasonable justifications for his anxieties.

In 1876, Abdul Hamid was an unremarkable but respectable (thrifty, earnest, pious) prince, aged thirty-four and second in line to the throne. The Sultan was his uncle Abdülaziz. That year Abdülaziz was removed from the throne and replaced with Abdul Hamid's older brother Murad V in a nighttime coup jointly carried out by Mithat Pasha and General Hüseyin Avni Pasha (commander in chief of the Ottoman army). Abdülaziz died shortly thereafter, either assassinated or driven to suicide. Through it all—as the Fifth Army's Arab soldiers besieged Dolmabahçe Palace, and as the overthrown sultan was carried away in a rowboat only to be found dead four days later just a few palaces down the same shore, killed by slashes to his wrists or perhaps by his own hand in a burst of suicidal fury—an increasingly dismayed Abdul Hamid, now next in line to the throne, had sat in his quarters trying to follow and make sense of the events unfolding in the rooms and palaces around him. He was still struggling to come to terms with his uncle's death—how terrifying to think that even in these modern times, it was still possible to remove and assassinate a sultan!—when, just three months later, Mithat Pasha and the other army bureaucrats who had ousted Abdülaziz did the same to the new sultan, Murad V (Princess Pakize's father). Murad V had also been greatly disturbed by his uncle's death (he had, in fact, lost his marbles), and now he too had been deposed. So it was that Abdul Hamid went from being second in line to the throne to sitting on the throne in just four months, during which time he had the opportunity to observe how powerful Mithat Pasha and the other pashas who had orchestrated everything truly were, and come to understand that they could easily do to him what they had already done to the sultans who had preceded him.

But Abdul Hamid had experienced these kinds of fears even before his ascent to the throne. If Ottoman princes in 1901 were afraid they might be poisoned by Abdul Hamid, Prince Abdul Hamid himself and his brother Crown Prince Murad had been afraid thirty years before of being poisoned by their uncle Abdülaziz. For regardless of what Ottoman laws of succession dictated, Sultan Abdülaziz was determined that he should be followed on the throne by his son Prince Yusuf Izzettin Effendi (whom he had promoted to the rank of general, aged fourteen, and appointed as commander of the armed forces).

Tensions between Sultan Abdülaziz and his nephews—the Crown Prince and his brother—intensified during a trip that the Sultan, his above-mentioned son, and his two nephews took to Europe together in the summer of 1867. Usually Crown Prince Murad would spend most of his time in his own residence in Kurbağalıdere rather than in the heir's designated quarters in the Beşiktaş Palace (known today as Dolmabahçe Palace) precisely to distance himself from these kinds of tensions. According to a letter Princess Pakize wrote to her sister following the death of their father many years later, and to the stories she and her brother and sisters had heard directly from Murad V, the first significant confrontation during this trip to Europe occurred during a ball they all attended at the Élysée Palace in Paris, where Crown Prince Murad was reprimanded by his uncle the Sultan for conversing in French with a group of revealingly clad French ladies he had gathered around him, and for dancing the quadrille with one of them.

According to the Sultan's nephews, their uncle had also felt "jealous" and angry about the warm welcome that Queen Victoria and her heir, the dull-witted Prince Edward (whom she did not trust with any state secrets), had given the young Ottoman crown prince Murad and his brother Prince Abdul Hamid during a reception at Buckingham Palace in London. The next day Abdülaziz's aide-de-camp had knocked on Prince Murad's door and walked into his room in Buckingham Palace bearing a plateful of grapes and conveying "His Excellency the Sultan's kindest regards." Murad started eating the grapes immediately, but shortly afterward, he was struck by stomach cramps, whereupon he became alarmed and ran crying into his brother's room next door. Young Abdul Hamid (aged twenty-five at the time) always carried a bezoar stone with him wherever he went, and was able to save the Ottoman heir to the throne by quickly grinding some of the stone into a glass of water for his older brother to drink and calling for doctors to help. When Queen Victoria heard about all this, she sent her heir Prince Edward to relay the message to Crown Prince Murad and his brother Abdul Hamid that if they *truly* believed that this had been a *planned* poisoning attempt, they need not return to Istanbul at all and could wait in England for their turn on the throne. (In later years, both Prince Edward and Murad would become Freemasons—the latter in Istanbul—and exchange several letters, with Edward taking the English throne the same year in which our story is set.) The two Ottoman princes, both future sultans, knew that whole episode—which might not even have been as sinister as they had thought it to be—could have serious political ramifications, and they could also imagine how it would be construed by the press (members of the Ottoman royal family were poisoning one another in the corridors of Buckingham Palace!), so before their uncle the Sultan could hear about it, they decided to forget it had ever happened and began to think that perhaps their suspicions regarding the plate of grapes had been unfounded after all.

But by the time they returned to Istanbul, news of the scandal had already reached Abdülaziz, and the Sultan, choking with rage, had banished Crown Prince Murad—guilty of "humiliating us all"—from Dolmabahçe Palace for a time.

In later years, after the foundation of the Turkish Republic, a different and completely false version of this story would be published across the history pages of national newspapers, according to which Queen

Victoria was alleged to have offered the princesses of the British royal family in marriage to Abdul Hamid and Murad while they waited in London to inherit the Ottoman throne. The fact that a British princess would never be married to someone—no matter who he was—who already had four wives and countless concubines he slept with and mistreated, and that the Queen would not consider matching any members of her own family with men who tried to poison one another and didn't even speak any English, will be obvious to any person with even the slightest trace of common sense and, like us, they might struggle to understand why the many followers of these history columns still so thoroughly believe and so greatly enjoy reading and rereading the various iterations of this fabrication that recur every three years or so under different headlines ("The Year Queen Victoria Offered Her Daughter to Abdul Hamid") on the pages of Turkish newspapers.

Abdul Hamid took the throne nine years after this trip to Europe (following his uncle's assassination and his older brother's bout of insanity), and in those nine years he must surely have learned that, from a scientific perspective, the soft bezoar stone carried by many kings and rulers throughout the course of history (particularly in the East) could have had no effect at all that day in London. One of the first reports he commissioned from Bonkowski Pasha after he became sultan was on the subjects of which plants growing in the gardens of the Yıldız Palace could be "scientifically" employed to produce poisons, on new poisons without known antidotes, and on poisons that did not leave traces.

The Sultan had first heard of Bonkowski Bey through the activities of the Société de Pharmacie de Constantinople (also known as the Pharmacists' Guild of Der-i Saadet), which Bonkowski had founded with Pharmacist Nikiforos. This organization was at war with the other pharmacists' guilds, and championed a cause it hoped the state would back. At the center of this cause was the demand for traditional herbalists who stocked spices, powders, pastes, plants, and roots of all kinds to be banned from selling poisons and other hazardous materials. Substances like arsenic, ratsbane, wormwood, phenol, codeine, cantharidin, ether, iodoform, sabadilla, coal tar (or creosote), opium, morphine—nearly one hundred in all—must be banned from herbalists' shops and sold only in modern, European-style pharmacies, which should in turn be subject to regulation and regular inspections and only supply these items when presented with a doctor's prescription.

Abdul Hamid must have learned about ratsbane and how it could be used to slowly and almost imperceptibly poison people from the murder mysteries he had recently started reading. The Sultan would pay particularly close attention to those passages that described how to use poison and how to avoid leaving traces, and he would ask for some sections to be read out to him twice. As for his interest in cultivating toxic plants in the palace gardens, our readers should look at it this way: like all modern Eastern emperors, Abdul Hamid viewed his palace's gardens as a version of the world in miniature. So really the Sultan's question to young Bonkowski Bey was a simpler one: Which plants could be used to make effective poisons?

Bonkowski Bey had been in the middle of writing his report to Abdul Hamid on this subject when he was put in charge of the private pharmacy—sometimes known as the chemistry laboratory—on the grounds of the Yıldız Palace. This was also the same period when Bonkowski Bey was very busy with the Pharmacists' Guild and its crusade against traditional herbalists, so his conversations with the Sultan inevitably touched on poisons and how easily they could still be obtained.

Abdul Hamid knew that most of the poisons that had been used on his ancestors—such as the kind which had gradually killed Mehmed the Conqueror four hundred and twenty years ago, and left no trace—could *still* be obtained from any one of the hundreds of herbalists' shops scattered all over Istanbul. The Yıldız Palace archives tell us of the many varieties of poison that palace clerks dispatched for this purpose were able to find in shops in the Yeniçarşı, Beyazıt, Kapalıçarşı, and Fatih neighborhoods and bring back to the palace laboratory.

Doctor Nuri got back to the State Hall from his meeting with Nikiforos at midday, and the Governor called him to his office.

"To stop any rumors about poisoning, I have ordered him to be buried with the plague victims and have lime poured over his corpse," he began. "If we acknowledge that Doctor Ilias, like Bonkowski Pasha before him, has fallen victim to a nefarious assassination plot, it would be tantamount to admitting that the organs of the Ottoman state are powerless on the island of Mingheria—and that is something neither I nor Istanbul will allow. Should the Sultan find out that Bonkowski Pasha's assistant has been killed too, and that neither you nor I have yet been able to find the culprit, he might even conclude that we are doing it on purpose."

"Do you think that the people who did this are the same people who killed Bonkowski Pasha?" asked Doctor Nuri.

"We have not been able to find out, as you know!" said the Governor. "Though if Istanbul had insisted, we would have done what needed to be done and found someone to confess to having put rat poison into the biscuits eventually. But now this task falls to you. Since you will be conducting your investigation using the Sherlock Holmes method, there will be no torture and no foot whipping either. You will find the culprit by questioning herbalists and pharmacists, just as His Excellency the Sultan's favorite detective would do. Good luck to you. The herbalists are expecting you; the necessary precautions have been taken! Let us see what they say this time."

The garrison kitchen's cook, his helpers, and everyone who had been questioned and tortured so far, had each been taken to the principal herbalists' shops and shown to the owners, their assistants, and their errand boys, but nobody recalled seeing the suspects or anybody else come in to buy rat poison.

Doctor Nuri first went to a small store in the Eyoklima neighborhood. It reminded him of those pleasant-smelling shops run by Jews in Istanbul's Mahmutpaşa neighborhood. In front of the counter were sacks containing different-colored powders and spices. There were jars full of spherical objects, fruits, and medicines. Herbs and bundles and all sorts of strange, spongelike substances hung on pieces of string tied up to the ceiling. But the physician who would usually be waiting for patients—as was customary in shops in Istanbul too—wasn't there, and the only person in the shop was its owner Vasil Effendi, who had been warned by the State Hall clerks to prepare for Doctor Nuri's arrival.

Having bowed all the way to the floor to greet his visitors from the palace, Vasil Effendi repeated the statement he had already made to the authorities. Neither the cook nor his helpers had been to his shop, and sales of rat poison had been slowing down now anyway as the number of rats in people's homes and on the streets was less than it had been in the early days. Besides, the municipal government was pouring rat poison over the streets for free. Vasil Effendi explained in his broken Turkish that it was much easier these days to procure large quantities of rat poison from municipal supplies. Every time the Doctor and Prince Consort peered or sniffed at any one of the powders, boxes, tins of colorful spices, measuring instruments, herbs, and glass containers filled with sweet-scented roots displayed in bags, bottles, and jars all over Vasil Effendi's shelves, the herbalist would interrupt his account to point out what they were: mustard, jasmine, rhubarb, henna, coca, menthol, cherry-seed powder *(mahleb)*, lice-bane, cinnamon. The herbalist also showed Doctor Nuri the bag where he kept the ratsbane powder, noting that he was careful about whom he allowed near the poisonous substances and that he was always there, in his shop, whenever prescriptions were issued and medicinal pastes were made. He told the story of an herbalist in Smyrna who had sent his apprentice instructions for a prescription from home, but the apprentice had accidentally mixed in three dirhams of the wrong white powder (from the bag on the right-hand side of the counter instead of the bag on the left), and the patient had died. He had heard about this from his business partner, whose shop was on the same street as the herbalist's in Smyrna, and who sent Vasil Effendi spiced sausages on the Messageries ferry. Vasil Effendi's shop was the only one on the island where you could get sausages sourced from Smyrna.

The herbalist then set about creating a special preparation for Doctor Nuri. First he ground eight cedar seeds and a slice of ginger and mixed them together. To this concoction he added juniper tar and dried chickpea powder, proudly inviting the Doctor and Prince Consort to sniff the bags they were stored in, then crushed and stirred everything into a paste. Using a mold in the manner of a spoon, he started scooping up the mixture and shaping it into pills. "If you have diarrhea, take one on an empty stomach, and it'll sort you out right away," he declared with an air of satisfaction.

Doctor Nuri saw similar sacks of dye, coffee beans, sugar, and spices when he visited two other herbalists' shops. Vasil had put an ostrich egg in front of his shop so that prescription holders who did not know how to read or write would still be able to find it. Another shop in the Old Market had a small model of the Arab Lighthouse at its door, while the herbalist in Vavla had put up a sign with an enormous pair of scissors on it. In these two other shops too, the most frequently requested products were laxatives, hemorrhoid creams, cough pills, lotions for wounds and rheumatic pains, and stomachache treatments. Doctor Nuri discovered that some of the medicines and ingredients—like bitter almond oil, black juniper, sabadilla, and devil's snare—that Pharmacist Nikiforos had pointed out to him, and that pressure from pharmacists in Istanbul had ensured could no longer be sold by herbalists there, were still readily available in all of these shops. Doctor Nuri also made a note of the fact that chamomile, fennel, aniseed, and love-in-a-mist were all substances commonly used in the preparation of stomachache remedies, in the hope that this kind of detail might eventually help in finding the perpetrators of the plot against the quarantine doctors. The herbalist with the enormous pair of scissors in front of his shop told Doctor Nuri that the ointment they most commonly prescribed to the sheikhs who gave out consecrated prayer sheets and talismans was made out of sulfur, beeswax, olive oil, and rose petals, and he gave Doctor Nuri a bottle to take away.

Back in the guesthouse, Princess Pakize teased him about trying some of these salves and mixtures out, but her husband forbade it. After some arguing and sulking and playful flirting, the bottles were set aside. But Doctor Nuri never gave up on visiting Arkaz's herbalists.

CHAPTER 32

The news of the death of a passenger aboard the *Odityis*, which had set sail for Athens before quarantine measures had been imposed, was quickly picked up by all the main newspapers in Greece, whereupon European newspapers began to write that the Ottomans had failed to contain the epidemic that had come to the West from China and India via the Hejaz and Suez, and that Europe would have to step in. The trope of "the sick man of Europe," which had often been repeated in the pages of Paris's *Le Petit Journal* and *Le Petit Parisien* and in London's *Daily Telegraph*, was thus revived once more. The ports of western Europe began to treat any ship coming from Arkaz as if it were flying the yellow flag, and passengers were put in isolation for at least ten days when they reached their destinations.

There was also a punitive character to these quarantine precautions. The leading Western nations complained to Abdul Hamid about the Governor of Mingheria, who seemed incapable of implementing quarantine rules as they should be, and sent the Ottoman Empire the same warning they often did during outbreaks of cholera in the Hejaz. They said that unless the Governor of Mingheria quarantined departing ships properly, they would have to intervene with their warships and do the job themselves, and they sent word through their ambassadors to the Sublime Porte that they already had vessels at the ready in the Mediterranean.

The Palace and the Sublime Porte would inform the Governor of all these developments, the Governor would discuss them with the Doctor and Prince Consort, the Prince Consort would share them with his wife, and finally Princess Pakize would write to her sister to report what she had learned.

"There haven't been any mail boats coming in, which means your letters must be piling up in a basket somewhere in the Post Office!" her husband had once remarked. "I wonder if it might be more prudent to keep them here for the time being?"

"I have to send out the one I am writing before I can start a new one!" Princess Pakize had replied. "Do you think the Major might bring me twenty more of these postcards?"

She was holding seven black-and-white (that is to say, not hand-painted) postcards printed in Istanbul. Princess Pakize liked to amuse herself sometimes by reading out their captions in French as if she were reciting a poem: "Citadelle de Mingher," "Hôtel Splendide Palace," *"Vue générale de la baie," "Phare d'Arkad et son port," "Ville vue prise de la citadelle," "Hamidié Palace et bazaar," "Église Saint-Antoine et la baie."*

Princess Pakize had often read aloud to her father in French, and also read romances to pass the time. Through her husband's accounts, she was following the Major's story as if it were a novel, and writing to her sister about what she heard. Although her grandfather, her uncle, and her father—all current or former sultans—had each had half a dozen wives and a harem full of concubines, Princess Pakize did not think it was right for men to be allowed to marry more than one woman at a time. Her sisters and most of the other princesses also felt the same way. This would have been due partly to the Western-style education they had all received in the harem. But mainly it was because of the rule that stated that anyone who married the daughter of a sultan, a princess of royal blood, was not allowed to take any other wife.

From the moment she had discovered that Zeynep, the Major's bride-to-be, had given up on a previous match with a suitor her father had chosen for her when she'd realized that the prospective groom already had another wife back in his ancestral village, Princess Pakize had held the younger woman in the highest regard, and dismissed any other reasons Zeynep might have had for her decision. Two days later Princess Pakize learned from her husband that Major Kâmil and Zeynep had met, and that this encounter had sparked a mysterious attraction between them. As readers of Princess Pakize's letters will discover, this love story so cherished by the people of Mingheria rested on many small coincidences.

On his way back from the Post Office that day, the Major took a longer route, crossing the creek and wandering around the neighborhoods where Muslims were in the majority. In a shady garden that gave onto a quiet street in the Bayırlar neighborhood, he saw three boys crying under an olive tree, one of them in tearing sobs, the other two without a sound. Two gardens down, he heard some middle-aged, headscarf-wearing ladies arguing among each other: "You brought the disease here." "No, you did!" In the Tuzla neighborhood he watched a dockworker who knew what precautions to take against contagion failing to persuade the women he was talking to. On the same road he discovered that a holy man from the Zaim sect was giving out charms against the disease, and that if you stood waiting silently in his garden, crossed your arms diagonally over your chest, and bowed thrice while repeating the words "I have come to pay my respects to His Holiness," then he would let you into his lodge.

In one street he would feel the hush of death and fear and the helplessness of the doctors and bureaucrats, but by the time he had walked on to the next street and the next garden, he would find himself back in the dusty, sleepy alleyways of his childhood, and his fear would abate.

He was walking down a street with a rivulet of sewage streaming through the middle when he spotted Zeynep among a cluster of around eight to ten women and girls coming toward the same street farther ahead to his right. For a while he managed to follow the group of women, who were wearing colorful dresses and white headscarves, without anyone noticing that he was watching them. But this did not go on for very long.

Zeynep and the others suddenly vanished. The Major tried to find them again, wandering into empty, unkempt gardens, through tall grasses, and along walls covered with creepers. A woman in a headscarf was hanging laundry on a line in her back garden as if it were the most ordinary day in the world, while her two young, barefoot sons wrestled each other nearby.

He emerged onto a shabby backstreet which he thought he recognized from his childhood. He was like someone in a dream now, watching himself from the outside. But as soon as he became aware of this, he also realized he had lost the girl, and he decided to return to the State Hall.

When he saw his mother that afternoon, he knew that he would no longer be able to hide that he had fallen in love. Already his mother's demeanor seemed to imply there could be no other subject to talk about. "I heard you followed her," she said. "She liked that."

The Major was amazed and rather pleased by how fast the news had traveled to his mother, and if he hadn't been worried about alarming her with his impatience, he would have told her then and there to "start making arrangements." But his mother understood anyway just by looking at her son's face. "She is an exceptional girl," she said evenly. "Every rose has its thorns, but this is the kind of opportunity that presents itself only once in a lifetime, and the fact that you can recognize its worth shows that you do have some sense in you after all. Are you ready to do anything for her?"

"What do you mean?"

"After all these troubles, the girl will want to go away to Istanbul and be free of this Ramiz once and for all. It is certainly true that her brothers did not return the gold their father received from Ramiz, or at least not all of it. So that shameless Ramiz is still bothering her, for he knows he can rely on his brother Sheikh Hamdullah for support."

"I'm not afraid of Ramiz, but there's a quarantine now, so we wouldn't be able to go to Istanbul yet. Tell her I will take her to China first with the old sultan's daughter!" said the Major.

"If you tell her, 'I will take you to Istanbul,' it will be much more believable, and much more effective, than any talk of China!" his mother replied. "What does your Lami think?"

The man his mother had referred to as "your Lami" was a childhood friend of the Major's who knew all the gossip in the city. The Major strolled across sunny, rose-scented streets and under the shade of blooming linden and magnolia trees until he reached the Splendid Palace Hotel. He and Lami sat on a pair of wicker chairs in the hotel terrace, under the shade of its orange-and-white-striped sunshades, at a table with a view of the docks. They could smell roses, thyme, and Lysol. Thin-faced Lami had been born to an Orthodox mother and a Muslim father. When his father died, that side of his family had left the island, and Lami had been raised by Greeks. Now he was the manager of the Hotel Splendid, whose red-and-brown linen uniform he was currently wearing. The hotel's spacious lobby and terrace were frequented by Italian businessmen who had run the island's stone quarries until ten years ago, by wealthy Greeks, Ottoman bureaucrats, ostentatious and more or less influential Muslim gentlemen, government clerks, soldiers in civilian dress, and occasionally even by the Governor himself, so that anything of any importance that ever happened upon the island was bound to be discussed there.

Lami knew it was Zeynep who had broken off the engagement, and warned the Major that Ramiz might exploit his brother's standing to retaliate in some way. Ramiz was known for his erratic behavior, and it was a good thing the Governor had put him in prison. When he learned that Ramiz had since been released, under orders from Istanbul and on condition that he never set foot in Arkaz again, Lami said, "The Governor should put him right back in the dungeons!" though he also conceded that this might not be so easy to do.

"Why is that?"

"The Governor Pasha is not fond of Sheikh Hamdullah, but he also knows it would be difficult to enforce quarantine without his approbation."

Some historians have argued that for an important functionary of the Ottoman Empire like the Governor Pasha to be so wary of Sheikh Hamdullah and so fearful of doing anything that might vex him was a sign of inexplicable "pusillanimity" on the Governor's part, as there was no reason for an Ottoman governor pasha with a whole garrison stationed in his province to be so intimidated by a sheikh. Pashas in Mingheria had always wielded more power than sheikhs, as they would in the soon-to-be-established Turkish Republic too, and indeed this is the foundation that modern Turkish and Mingherian secularism both rest on. But today we might perhaps view the Governor's attempt at persuading the populace to follow quarantine restrictions by taking a softer line as the more realistic and expedient political approach.

"The whole island was after this girl, you know," said Lami. "You've got your work cut out for you."

"Yes. I've fallen in love."

"She has two older brothers, Hadid and Majid," said Lami. "They are twins; they used to own the Twins' Bakery, but it's shut down now. You should have them volunteer for your Quarantine Division . . . They're not the brightest, but they're honest people. The best bread the Splendid Palace kitchens ever got was from the Twins' Bakery!"

"I love this girl so much that I refuse to believe her brothers could have done anything wrong!" the Major proclaimed.

This conversation eventually led to plans being made for the Major, Zeynep, and her two brothers to meet in the city. But it was another three days before they were able to come together at the Hotel Splendid's half-covered terrace on Istanbul Street. Afterward the Major would speak frankly to Doctor Nuri of how excited he had been when he had arrived and seen Zeynep there.

The brothers had shaved their beards and worn clean shirts in an effort to appear more attuned to city life, but it was obvious from the fezzes on their heads and from their constant fidgeting that they did not feel comfortable there. Their mother and the Major's mother had already agreed on a bride price and on the gifts and jewelry to be exchanged, so that subject was not broached at all. The already tattered and faded quarantine announcement that hung on a wall in the restaurant of the empty hotel looked like an ancient relic, and somehow that detail made the plague seem even more frightening.

"We have put ourselves in danger by gathering here . . . ," the Major began. "According to quarantine regulations, it is forbidden for more than two people to meet at a time."

"We are in God's hands!" said Majid. "You mustn't fret; our destinies are already written, and it is not for us to worry about what is to come!"

"You will have even less reason to worry if you embrace quarantine restrictions and volunteer for the Quarantine Division. Eleven more people have died from the disease just yesterday and this morning. Some are still hiding their dead."

"Believe me, Major Kâmil Bey," said Zeynep, "I am less afraid of catching the disease and dying young than I am of growing old on this island without ever having lived at all."

"To know so clearly what you want is a quality to be admired," said the Major.

They were sitting across from each other, their faces so close that they could not look directly at each other for too long. The Major realized he was at risk of falling rather acutely in love with this dark-eyed girl, and as he imagined the agony of pining for her during lonely nights in remote military outposts, he knew there was nothing he wanted more than to marry her.

Satiye Hanım, who had already begun negotiations behind the scenes with Zeynep's mother and brothers over the wedding party and other matrimonial arrangements, now quickly settled everything and moved matters forward. The Major had also secured the Governor Pasha's support with any obstacles that should arise against the nuptials. Ramiz's entourage had been spreading rumors about Sheikh Hamdullah being upset and angry about his brother's treatment. People were convinced that Ramiz would return to the city and cause some kind of fracas.

The Governor made it a point of honor that the Major should be able to marry the girl he had chosen to marry, and celebrate however he wanted, without having to fear anyone. As for where they should live, it was agreed that the safest and most fitting home for a newly married Ottoman officer would be the Hotel Splendid. So it was that the Major, in consultation with his future wife, decided to take up residence in a room on the top floor of the Hotel Splendid, like some wealthy European gentleman.

The Governor Pasha, who was keeping track of every detail, advised the Major to get his wedding day shave done by Mingheria's most famous barber, Panagiotis, in his shop at the foot of Donkey's Bane Hill. It was noon on Tuesday, the fourteenth of May, and having begun by boasting that, over the past twenty years, every man getting married in Arkaz—Christian or Muslim—had come to him for his wedding shave, Panagiotis said: "You seem concerned, Commander; I've noticed you looking at my little shop and all my tools and wondering, 'Are they infected?' But you see," he went on, "I've followed the quarantine doctors' advice and boiled all my scissors and razors and tongs. I'm not afraid for myself, but I still do it because I know that more refined customers, like you, expect me to."

"Why aren't you afraid?"

"We are all in the hands of our Mother Mary and Jesus Christ!" said the barber, glancing into a corner of his shop.

The Major couldn't see the icon that was the source of the barber's fortitude, but spotted an assortment of brushes, bowls, mortars, knives, razors, jugs, and sharpening stones. The barber told him that he knew that the doctor who was married to the old sultan's daughter had come to the island to stop the outbreak, and that the Major whose cheeks he was shaving now had been tasked with protecting them. Then he began to speak of how devoted Mingherians were to their sultan. Every winter and spring for nearly forty years now, there had been insurrections upon the Ottoman Empire's islands in the Levant. These uprisings were organized by the islands' Greek populations, who wanted to be ruled by Greece and—as in Crete—wished to break away from the Ottoman Empire. Every summer the Ottoman navy's battleships—perhaps the *Mesudiye* or the *Osmaniye* or the *Orhaniye* with its newly fitted gun battery—would bomb the Greek villages on these rebellious islands based on information gathered by regional chiefs and local spies. Sometimes the Ottoman soldiers stationed there would follow up by raiding those same villages and putting any suspicious individuals in prison. Bombarding the Greek towns, villages, and ports on these islands was, in effect, a kind of punishment. But not once in the last twenty years had the *Orhaniye* and its new gun battery come to Arkaz and started shelling its Greek villages!

"Why is that? Because Abdul Hamid knows that the people of this island, Christians and immigrants too, are all loyal to him! Because fifteen years ago Mingheria was the wealthiest island in the whole of the Levant, and nearly half of its population were Muslims. Look at this, Commander," Panagiotis Effendi continued. "There won't be more than one or two barbershops in the whole of Istanbul where you can find this mustache oil and these beaked hair tongs. I had this bottle sent from Berlin a good ten years ago, and I've taught every lord and gentleman in Mingheria, Greek and Muslim, how to use it. Back then they thought that to style a mustache like Kaiser Wilhelm's, straight and thick at the sides and sharp at the tips, all you had to do was trim the middle short and twirl the ends as thin as you could. But when you are twisting the mustache into shape with the hot curling iron, it is just as important to rub some of this beeswax lotion in, slow and steady so that it gets properly absorbed."

The barber studiously performed the steps he was describing. The most vital point was this: the hairs on the cheeks and along the cheekbones must never ever be used to bolster the mustache. That was unsightly and vulgar, though regrettably there were still some barbers in Berlin and Istanbul who did it. But experienced and modern-minded barbers knew that any hair on the face must be shaved twice over before the grooming began. The French company that produced the beeswax glue which gave Wilhelm his special mustache, upright and sharp as a knife at the tips, and whose recipe they guarded as if it were an elixir, still sold its wares in its shop in Berlin. But even when the bottle he'd got from Germany had run out, the Mingherian barber Panagiotis had achieved the same results by grinding raw acorns and Mingherian pine resin in a mortar, mixing in rosewater made from the same plants that the murdered chemist had first brought to the island with Abdul Hamid's permission, and adding some dried chickpea powder he'd bought from Vasil the herbalist. If the Major wished, the barber could style the tips of his mustache even sharper and stiffer, though they wouldn't want to alarm his dainty and headstrong bride-to-be.

On his way back to the State Hall with his sharp-tipped Kaiser Wilhelm–style mustache, the Major walked down the near-deserted Istanbul Street and came across a plague-crazed madman. During his childhood, there had always been a few lunatics in Arkaz whose presence was widely tolerated. The Major himself had been quite fond of most of them. Children would tease them; Greek ladies and elderly citizens would pity them and give them alms. Everybody knew of the Greek madman Dimitrios who always wore women's clothing, and Chained Servet who would burst suddenly into shrieks and howls in the middle of crowded shopping streets. When these two crossed paths in the market, on a bridge, or by the docks, they would hurl all manner of indecencies at each other in a mixture of Greek, Mingherian, and Turkish, before finally coming to blows. Children and adults alike enjoyed their antics. But after the outbreak of plague, these time-honored lunatics had vanished, to be replaced by even-crazier and more obsessive plague lunatics whose presence tended to provoke not pity so much as loathing and fear.

The most famous of these new lunatics wandering around the city's neighborhoods was Ekrem from Erin. Said to have been educated at a religious institution in Istanbul, this man was a clerk at the Department of Charitable Trusts, and before the outbreak had started, everything about him had been entirely ordinary and unremarkable except for his love of books. But when his two wives with whom he had been so happily married had both suddenly died, he had thrown himself into reading the Koran and immediately concluded that the "apocalypse" was upon them all.

When Ekrem Effendi saw the Major in his army uniform with his medals and badges, he stopped abruptly in the middle of the road as he always did and began, with a series of theatrical gestures, to recite the Resurrection *surah,* the chapter of the Koran which described Judgment Day. His voice was deep, even guttural at times, sincere, and a little tearful. The Major stood in front of this tall man with a dark frock coat and purple fez and politely listened. When the lunatic reached the sixth verse of the *surah* and asked, *"Yasalu ayyana yawmu al-qiyamah?"* (When is this day of judgment?), the look he gave the Major was like a threat. When sight is dazzled, when the moon darkens, and the sun and the moon are joined, that is the day of judgment! Then the madman stretched one long arm and finger toward a point in the heavens. The Major couldn't see anything out of the ordinary in the spot that Ekrem Effendi was showing him; only a limpid, immaculate Mingherian sky. But he pretended that he could, for he did not wish to quarrel.

The lunatic clerk then recited several other verses to the effect that there was no refuge beyond Allah. These were the same verses that preachers and holy men would inevitably cite whenever any outbreak grew large enough, so all Muslim doctors and quarantine officials were perfectly familiar with the words, always gave them their full and respectful attention, and made sure to demonstrate the knowledge they'd acquired to their patients too.

Once, while quoting these verses, old Ekrem had also openly criticized quarantine measures, and when the Governor had heard about it, he'd briefly considered locking him up—though he had ultimately desisted. As he left the lunatic behind and went on his way, the Major thought again of how happy and how exceptionally fortunate he was. We have remarked on his happiness here because we are telling the story of a very small country where the emotions and decisions of individuals could often change the course of history.

The Major's wedding was supposed to be held at the Hotel Splendid, but concerns over security (notably the presence of Ramiz's men in that area) meant that it was moved to the large assembly room in the State Hall. The guests, unsettled by the change of location, were made to wait for a time in a Lysol-soaked corridor on the ground floor of the State Hall, after which they were quickly taken to the second floor and ushered into the large meeting hall for the wedding ceremony. Everybody was elegantly dressed, spotless, and full of cheer. Zeynep was wearing a traditional red Mingherian bridal gown. Her two brothers had put on boots and frock coats. The Major watched the ceremony from the outside, and felt as if he were dreaming. While the imam of the Blind Mehmet Pasha Mosque, Nurettin Effendi, was busy writing their names in the register, the bride and groom eyed each other from afar.

The Major answered the Imam Effendi's questions first. As custom dictated, he declared the amount of money he would contribute (except for the bride price and land purchases) when they married. He also stated how much money he would give this woman if they were to separate. Through it all, he kept looking at his bride in her red gown with awe and longing, and couldn't quite believe that the aching loneliness that had afflicted him for all his life was about to end. The two witnesses were the Major's friend Lami and Chief Scrutineer Mazhar Effendi—the latter at the insistence of the Governor Pasha, who wished to keep a close watch over the event. The Pasha himself, for reasons unknown, had gone back to his rooms at the last moment, and stayed there throughout the proceedings. Halfway through the ceremony, a little door opened up at the opposite end of the Main Meeting Hall, on the side that faced the docks, and in walked Princess Pakize with the Prince Consort. Though the couple stood far apart from the crowd of families, relatives, neighbors, and children wearing their best clothes and fezzes, everyone was thrilled that the old sultan's daughter had come to the wedding.

The imam began to say a lengthy prayer, at which point everyone understood that the marriage was now official. The Major presented his wife with a gold bracelet his mother had given him. He shook hands with the witnesses and with some of the guests. But the fear of disease meant that nobody was really greeting and embracing each other properly, and most people were eager to return to their homes as swiftly as possible.

Without the bowing and curtsying and hand-kissing that usually took place on these occasions, the wedding turned out to be a brief affair, and soon the ecstatic bride and groom were on their way to the Hotel Splendid with Coachman Zekeriya driving them in the Governor Pasha's landau. The Governor, on the other hand, remained perturbed, expecting Ramiz and his men to attack at any moment. In a highly personal and candid letter to her sister Hatice dated the fourteenth of May 1901, Princess Pakize, who had watched the newlyweds leaving the State Hall that day, drew particular attention to the fact that "despite the sense of calamity all around them, the couple could not keep the soft smiles and the expressions of utter felicity from their faces."

CHAPTER 33

The Major and Zeynep's bliss had reminded Princess Pakize of her own and her sisters' wedding in Istanbul, the derisive looks and allusions they'd endured, and the rancor she still felt.

"Instead of considering the injustice we have suffered, locked up in harems like caged birds, they mocked us and dared to laugh at us for knowing nothing of the world outside!" Princess Pakize had lamented in one of her letters. "But perhaps all of these people are right to find satisfaction in our misery and invent all kinds of tales and drolleries about us!" she'd continued in the same passage. (When they were relocating from the Çırağan to the Yıldız Palace, from their father's side to the uncle—Sultan Abdul Hamid—who was going to arrange their marriages, Princess Pakize's sisters had been appalled by the sight of the filthy, ugly buttocks of the horses drawing the carriage they'd been sent from the Yıldız Palace.)

"To those who ridicule us, I should like to say one thing," Princess Pakize had written in another letter. "When his father died, our great-great-grandfather Mehmed III (a contemporary of William Shakespeare's), wishing to avoid a war of succession, had his own brothers executed—nineteen hapless, blameless princes, five of whom were still children—but as our darling father has pointed out, he left the princesses (for he must have had just as many sisters too) unscathed, and not only that, he arranged for the daughters of a previous sultan, Selim II, to be married off with small dowries to low-ranking palace attendants—just as Abdul Hamid has done with us. As Father says, the fact that the Royal Biographer Mehmet Süreyya's *Sicill-i Osmânî* does not even mention these sisters' names, the fact, in other words, that even the daughters of a *sultan* are not considered worthy of notice in the Ottoman dynasty, may have saved our lives at times. These sultans' daughters would have daughters of their own, princesses of royal blood, and because such great care was taken to match them with worthy husbands, their lineage would survive, and they would lead relatively untroubled lives. If they were able to make particularly strong matches, these princesses and princesses' daughters would follow their husbands in their postings to various states and provinces and end up learning that way about the outer edges of their 'homeland,' those regions which used to be known as the 'periphery.' That is why our uncle Abdul Hamid has always treated princesses Seniye and Feride as if they were Sultan Mahmud II's daughters rather than his granddaughters, showing them the greatest regard, inviting them to functions at the Yıldız Palace, gifting them waterside mansions in Arnavutköy, and viewing them—given their age—as equals to any sultan's daughters. As princesses, we often end up married off to some vizier or pasha, so the fact that we know nothing of the world outside is neither significant nor relevant. But when a prince is expected to inherit the Ottoman throne and rule over the nations and lands and islands and mountains of an empire too vast for any map, and yet that same prince, constrained by Abdul Hamid's suspicions, has never seen anything or been anywhere beyond a handful of palaces surrounded by soldiers and spies, so that when he looks out of the harem window one day and sees a sheep for the very first time in his life he mistakes it for a monster and summons the palace guards, then surely—and with the continuance of the Ottoman Empire at stake—that prince's condition is a far-more-pressing concern than the situation we Ottoman princesses are in?"

Princess Pakize's sisters Hatice and Fehime had moved to the Yıldız Palace first. Their uncle Abdul Hamid had treated his two nieces well, inviting them as if they were his own daughters to many of the ceremonies and gatherings—some significant, others minor—that took place in the Ottoman court during this period, not only to keep them from getting too disheartened, but also to ensure that they could be seen and approved by potential suitors or by these men's mothers and aunts, and thus be able to marry. In the two years that Princesses Hatice and Fehime spent at the Yıldız Palace, they attended a great number of functions and entertainments, and made many different female acquaintances. But unfortunately there seemed to be not a single suitor interested in marrying either of these exceptional sisters. The truth was that any potential grooms and their families were terrified of Abdul Hamid. Given the intricacies of the situation, the fact that no son of any wealthy pasha had emerged as suitor to Abdul Hamid's nieces, whose father's daily movements were spied upon by the Sultan, was perhaps understandable, regardless of how beautiful and cultured they were. Even so, the sisters were left feeling profoundly dismayed.

The anger that the three sisters harbored against some of these sons of pashas and potentially suitable princes was no doubt also determined by how rude, uncouth, philandering, and superficial so many of them were. We have reported all of this here to note that, regrettably, the exquisitely beautiful thirty-year-old elder sister Princess Hatice's prediction that they might be able to find worthy husbands if they moved to the Yıldız Palace was never realized. Since nobody was asking for their hand in marriage, it ultimately fell to the Sultan himself to find them the best and most suitable husbands available.

Abdul Hamid thus began to select his favorites from among the palace's brightest and most obedient officials. Around the same time, there also came the news of another outbreak of illness in the palace in Çırağan to which Murad V was confined. So the Sultan decided to send the expert quarantine doctor he'd heard spoken of so highly to survey the sanitary condition of this residence (a stone-built construction which, for many years after the foundation of the Turkish Republic, housed the Beşiktaş High School for Girls). But there are many who claim that Abdul Hamid purposely sent Doctor Nuri to this building—which was, at the time, still part of the Çırağan Palace complex—so that the doctor would be able to see the youngest of the three sisters, Princess Pakize, who had refused to get married and still lived in Çırağan with her father. Some have even claimed that in his eagerness to find a suitable match for his third daughter, Murad V himself had agreed to this plan with his "little brother" Abdul Hamid, communicating through secret intermediaries.

At the age of sixty, Murad V had long since abandoned the fantasies he had nurtured in the early years following his overthrow, when he had thought he might yet get his throne back if there was a coup or if he were smuggled out of his confinement, and had come to accept that "perhaps it just wasn't meant to be." He spent his time in the afternoons conversing with his son and best friend, Prince Mehmet Selahattin (the age gap between them was twenty years), and with each of his four daughters (one of whom would die of consumption), reading books, and playing and composing music for the pianoforte, and in the evenings he drank vigorously. Father and son were both hearty drinkers.

Every morning the former sultan would go to "pay his respects" to his mother, Şevkefza (who, as mother to a sultan, had been given the official title of Valide), visiting her in her rooms whose entrance was right across from the door to his own quarters in the middle floor of the palace. In earlier years, his mother—an ambitious woman of Circassian birth who was set on her son taking back his throne—would concoct all kinds of plans (dressing him up in women's clothing, smuggling him off to Europe) and plots (including one that would involve using the palace's water supplies), and mother and son would sit alone together, furtively discussing them all. After his mother's death, some of her now-vacant rooms were taken over by the more favored of the harem girls who were fed up with living on the palace's overcrowded ground floor and had developed rheumatisms from their rooms being so close to the sea.

Living on the ground floor were forty-five female servants of varying rank and authority attending to Murad V and his forty-year-old son, Prince Mehmet Selahattin (who had six daughters and two sons of his own). When a group of rebels led by the political activist Ali Suavi had stormed the Çırağan Palace in 1878 to try and free the former sultan and put him back on the throne, Abdul Hamid had sent his trusted general Mehmet Pasha to fend them off, and it was the quarters of these servant "girls" that Mehmet Pasha had famously barged into by mistake, finding himself face-to-face with nearly forty beauties—some older, others in the prime of youth—in various stages of undress against the summer heat, a sight which had left him momentarily paralyzed and leaning on his sword for support. Murad V's beloved concubine Filizten, who had endured twenty-eight years of captivity beside him, witnessed every facet of life in the last of the Ottoman harems, and described it all with her own incomparable candor, noted in her memoirs—as compiled by the popular historian Ziya Şakir—that the harem girls would often reenact Mehmet Pasha's statuelike pose and laughed about it for many years after the event.

Doctor Nuri was taken through these same chambers, usually thronged

with women and girls, "without encountering anyone," and led to the
floors above. In one of the sea-facing rooms of the palace's middle-
floor living quarters, he was examining the strange red rashes that had
appeared on an elderly female servant and on one of Murad V's granddaughters, Princess Celile, when the door opened up and he briefly came
face-to-face with Princess Pakize. When another elderly attendant told
Princess Pakize that her father wasn't here, the Princess left. But for a
long moment, the harem's youthful princess and the doctor had looked
"straight into each other's eyes," as might have been described in an early
Muslim novel. When she was asked the question two days later, Princess Pakize agreed to marry this handsome doctor and to move to her
uncle's court in the Yıldız Palace as her sisters had already done.

The fact that the husbands Abdul Hamid had found for Murad V's
charming and strong-willed daughters were such singularly modest and
undistinguished individuals has been extensively remarked upon. (These
discussions usually pertain to the two eldest daughters and their husbands.) In later years, many newspapers and their history pages would
write of how the chosen husbands were simple palace clerks (and therefore not really wealthy), somewhat "old," and not even particularly
handsome. Even one of the greatest among Turkish novelists, Halid
Ziya Uşaklıgil, who eventually became assistant to the Sultan's Chief
Secretary, would later comment in his memoirs *Kırk Yıl (Forty Years)* on
the age of the two grooms, and go so far as to point out that they had
been educated In the Darüşşafaka school for fatherless children—the
implication being that on top of everything else, they were also rather
poor. Worst of all was the rumor circulating widely among the people of
Istanbul that Princess Hatice supposedly found her husband so repulsive
that she wouldn't even allow him to enter her bedroom after their wedding. "Our uncle has found handsome, wealthy husbands for his own
ugly daughters, whereas we, on the other hand . . ."—these were the
kinds of words falsely attributed to the sisters by the Turkish press in the
years following the foundation of the republic. But in the letters in our
possession, there is not a single indication that Murad V's daughters had
ever called their uncle's daughter (their cousin) Princess Naime "ugly."
They had been brought up far too well to say such a thing anyway!

We have drawn attention to these matters here to lead us indirectly
to another theme we have brought up before: the contention that Prin-

cess Pakize was not at all "pretty" when compared with her sisters Hatice and Fehime—or at any rate that she was not *as* pretty as they were. This perception would ensure that Princess Pakize was insulated from the sharp tongues and barbed remarks of the palace's many critics in Istanbul. It was their belief that when Abdul Hamid had failed to find his youngest, rather plain-looking niece a husband in the palace, Princess Pakize herself—who was not as ambitious or as striking as her older sisters—must have agreed to settle at the last moment for a doctor of much-lower "ranking" than a palace clerk, and having thus promptly forgotten all about her, they inadvertently shielded her from the worst of the vicious gossip that was to mark the last days of the Ottoman court.

On the three sisters' wedding day, the carriages streaming with their bejeweled passengers out of the Yıldız and other Istanbul palaces, and from viziers' and pashas' residences, had eventually arrived at the waterside mansions that the Sultan had gifted to his nieces along the stretch of coast between Ortaköy and Kuruçeşme. Earlier, the Sultan had taken the opportunity to host princes and foreign ambassadors at a vast diplomatic banquet at the Yıldız Palace's Main Pavilion. Abdul Hamid deplored all needless expenditure, so he had not spent too much on the day's celebrations, and contrary to what he had done two years before during his daughter Princess Naime's wedding, he had not waited at the foot of the great staircase, flanked by his sons-in-law and by palace dignitaries, to welcome the arriving guests.

The Sultan, who—partly in a bid to emulate the celebrations that had taken place for Queen Victoria's sixtieth-year jubilee—had only recently lavished significant sums on marking the twenty-fifth year of his rule, was no longer able to set aside as much time and money for official ceremonies, receptions, and parties as he used to do in the early years of his reign. Although he was often generous with his nieces, appearing to make no distinction between them and his own daughters, Abdul Hamid had nevertheless been rather slow to equip them with the two-horse carriages their station required. Whether it was the Sultan being excessively parsimonious, or the palace clerks who'd been assigned to the task wanting to spite the two grooms, Princess Pakize's correspondence tells us that her two older sisters were left wholly unsatisfied with the special carriages they were eventually given. Princess Pakize, who was the least demanding of the three sisters, and whose expectations were the humblest too, was already on her way to China and later in Mingheria in the early days of her marriage, so she had not had the opportunity to evaluate the quality of the carriages she and her husband had been assigned.

Princess Pakize's letters do contain several derisive remarks on four of the princes who had weaved in and out of the crowds that had gathered at the Yıldız Palace and in the mansions in Ortaköy on the three sisters' wedding day. Abdul Hamid's son Mehmet Abdülkadir Effendi, who was known for his improprieties and for noisily playing his violin at every gathering, was described as "witless"; Prince Abid Effendi, meanwhile, was termed "a fool." Another of Abdul Hamid's sons, Seyfettin Effendi, whom the Sultan had wanted to marry to Abdülaziz's youngest daughter Princess Emine, was a "rake," which explained why the Princess had rejected him. As for "squat little Burhanettin Effendi," whose "Naval March" (which he had composed at the age of seven) the passengers of the *Aziziye* had heard as they alighted in Mingheria, Princess Pakize had found him a "spoiled brat."

Princess Pakize began to read her letters aloud to her husband, starting—before she sealed the envelope—from that seventh letter to her sister. This way, she would not only participate in her husband's investigations in the manner of Sherlock Holmes, but also indirectly acquaint him with palace life, the only existence she had ever known.

CHAPTER 34

Doctor Nuri listened attentively to his wife's descriptions of the ceremonies she had attended, the schemes she had watched unfold, and her moments of anger and wistfulness, but did not comment on what she told him, and replied with his own disconcerting quarantine stories instead. He also told her about the scenes he had witnessed while looking after patients in Arkaz's hospitals every day.

Not only was he constantly toing-and-froing between homes and hospitals to examine the sick, he would also always turn up wherever there were problems with quarantine measures to see if he might understand why, and perhaps help in some way. People who'd been told to evacuate their homes would often try to resist, arguing and fighting with officials, and it was not easy to find an appropriate and sensible-enough solution that could work in every situation. Some would demand one last day to spend with their families; others would lock themselves up inside; some would go completely mad after losing their wife and daughter in the space of three days; others would feign insanity and attack the guards and the soldiers of the Quarantine Regiment who had come to lock them up in the Castle. As the outbreak deepened—there were more than fifteen deaths every day now—people either withdrew even further into themselves, or became angrier than ever before, if not outright belligerent. All the stories and rumors going around and the endless funeral convoys had drained everyone of any logic or composure they might have had left. Over the last three days, more and more people had come forward to collect their reward of five golden liras in exchange for information on families who were hiding their sick. Three out of every five such cases reported turned out not to be related to the plague at all. But even so, the Muslim population's response to the plague still consisted largely of fear and finger-pointing, with little instinct for self-preservation.

By this point there seemed to be only one thing left that the whole city agreed on: whether they believed the disease was spread by rats or caught from other people, no one really went out onto the street anymore unless they had to. The city's eastern neighborhoods and the port were already nearly empty anyway, as much of the Greek population had left. Others had stocked up on crackers, flour, raisins, and grape molasses, stored them in their homes and courtyards in sacks, baskets, barrels, and empty olive oil jugs, then sealed every lock they had—as if in preparation for a horde of foreign invaders—and began to wait for the epidemic to pass. But the rats and the fleas they carried simply slipped under people's walls and snuck right into their homes.

The emptiness of the streets was eerie, but even more frightening was the novel experience of looking over a wall to see a group of people gathered in a garden. For that could only mean that someone else must have died, and that behind that door over there was another corpse. Quarantine officials could arrive to evacuate the house at any moment, and the mourners huddled inside would soon start arguing and falling out over whether "to tell them now or wait a little while." Some people got so caught up in their terror that they would dream up all sorts of improbable rescue scenarios and detail their plans to anyone who would listen, while others did the opposite, turning away from the world and sinking into a wordless "fatalistic" resignation.

Most of the men who had shut themselves inside their homes quickly grew bored, and in their restless curiosity they propped their bay windows ajar to peer at their surroundings and call out to anyone and anything they saw. Others opened their windows as wide as they would go, like Christian households did, and spent all day staring at the people who happened to walk past. In the afternoons and anytime he was not with the Quarantine Regiment, the Major would do as Princess Pakize had asked him to, watching over the Doctor and Prince Consort and keeping him company. People looking out at the street from their windows were often impressed by the sight of the Major walking past in his uniform, and felt that they could trust him. "Excuse me, young soldier!" an old man—who was Greek and couldn't make out the Major's rank—had called out to him from a shuttered house one morning as he was accompanying the Doctor and Prince Consort through the hilly, sweetly fragrant streets of the Eyoklima neighborhood. "Can you tell me whether the Maritimes ferry has arrived?"

During this time, Doctor Nuri witnessed things he had never seen or heard before in any cholera outbreak. Gangs of thieves were breaking into homes where elderly people lived on their own and stealing anything they could carry. Sometimes they would enter what they thought was a vacant house only to stumble upon the corpse of someone who had died of the plague, and when they tried to hide the body so that the quarantine officials wouldn't turn up, they would catch the disease themselves and end up in the hospital, where they would finally confess everything to Doctor Nuri. Other gangs were taking advantage of the general atmosphere of chaos and lawlessness to squat in the homes they broke into. This kind of thing was more likely to happen in the Greek neighborhoods at the edges of the city, like Dantela and Kofunya, where the Quarantine Division and the police weren't always present.

Doctor Nuri, assisted by a younger Greek doctor, spent nearly two hours tending to patients at the Theodoropoulos Hospital. He gave them pills to alleviate their pain and strengthen their constitution, dressed their wounds, and tried to soothe them by making incisions on their buboes. Again and again he patiently instructed them to keep their windows open and make sure that their rooms were properly ventilated.

When he returned to the State Hall and walked into the guesthouse, he saw that his wife was writing a letter. There was also a message informing him of an encrypted "royal decree" that had arrived for his attention.

The news electrified Doctor Nuri, so much so that his uncommonly perceptive wife, realizing that her husband was wondering about the possible contents of this telegram even as they were still embracing, couldn't quite hold her tongue. "Go on then," she said, her eyes full of reproach. "Go and see what it says!" (A "royal decree" was an order issued directly by the Sultan—by Abdul Hamid himself.)

"It saddens me to see that your loyalty to the Sultan far surpasses your commitment to me," said Princess Pakize.

"They are two entirely different kinds of loyalty. One is a bond that comes from the heart," said Doctor Nuri with an innocence that even he immediately felt to be excessive. "The other is a bond that runs in the blood."

"I suppose it is me your heart is bound to. But what has your loyalty to Abdul Hamid got to do with blood? The Sultan is my uncle, not yours."

"My loyalty is not just to your uncle, our great lord and ruler Sultan Abdul Hamid. It also extends to the exalted institutions that his illustrious position represents—the state, the Ottoman dynasty, the Sublime Porte, our whole nation, and the Quarantine Authority too."

"I am astonished that you still believe there is a Sublime Porte, a state, a nation beyond Abdul Hamid," said the Princess. "The pashas and the clerks who make up that thing which you call the 'state' are merely there to do my uncle's bidding, and *his* idea of justice is that everything should be done precisely as he wishes. If there had been any other kind of justice, how could they have imprisoned me, my father, my brother, and my sisters in the Çırağan Palace for twenty-four years, caged like birds? If there really was a 'nation' quietly watching over the state, over justice, over what the pashas say and do, how could it have been so easy to call my father insane and push him off his throne? And what exactly is this 'nation' you speak of anyway?"

"Is that a serious question?"

"It is serious, yes, so tell me please."

"Those people that your cousins and all those other foolish princelings you have told me about would watch from their palace windows, those crowds walking from Kabataş to Beşiktaş—that is the nation."

"You are right. You should go and read your telegram now," said Princess Pakize tetchily. There was an odd expression on her face that her husband had never seen before. She had been trying to look condescending.

The Prince Consort was not quite sure how to respond. "You must not go out until we have fully grasped the extent of the outbreak, and understood how and where it is spreading," he declared, purely for the sake of saying something that sounded strict.

"Don't worry, I am quite used to not being allowed outside!" the Princess proudly replied.

Doctor Nuri took out his codebook and withdrew to a corner of the guesthouse to decipher the contents of the special telegram. Eventually he worked it out: it was merely a message confirming receipt of his own telegram to the palace asking them to expedite the ship with the support and supplies they had requested.

CHAPTER 35

O n Thursday, the sixteenth of May, ten days after the last ship
departed the island at midnight on Monday, the sixth of May,
nineteen people died. As they recorded these new deaths on
the epidemiological map the next day, the Governor and the Major
concluded that the quarantine campaign was proving "ineffectual," and
expressed their doubts during that morning's meeting.

Doctor Nuri wasn't quite so pessimistic. It was perfectly possible
that by the next morning, the measures they had taken could suddenly
slow the outbreak. It was all a matter of degrees. Rather than panicking
and making misguided decisions, they should follow all developments
closely and think about the possible causes of the resistance they were
facing.

By now the Quarantine Regiment always accompanied doctors in
their visits to Muslim homes where a patient had just died, helping to
confiscate the victim's belongings and to make the necessary arrangements for the corpse to be disinfected with lime at the New Cemetery.
Doctor Nuri saw these as the more successful elements of the quarantine
effort. But as the city's neighborhood supervisors kept reminding them,
even measures as simple as quarantine cordons were not taken seriously
sometimes. In the neighborhoods of Turunçlar and Çite, the restrictions
had precipitated a kind of indifference and contempt that occasionally
manifested as anger. The clearest expression of this mood had been articulated by a ten-year-old boy named Tahsin, who had claimed the plague
couldn't hurt his father because they both had "one of these." He was
proudly showing Doctor Nikos a consecrated prayer sheet covered in
minuscule handwriting. In response, Doctor Nikos had confiscated the

thick, yellowing piece of paper, and when the boy wouldn't stop crying, he'd had to call other doctors and quarantine officials to the scene.

The "Tahsin incident" was seized upon by the Governor and by many of the delegates of the Quarantine Committee as a convenient response (tradition, religion, sheikhs, the ignorant masses!) to the question of why the same measures that had been so successful in Smyrna did not seem to be taking hold on the island of Mingheria. Abdul Hamid's Pan-Islamism, as well as a wariness of the Muslim uprisings that were taking place in Africa and Asia against European colonial rule, and many other historical prejudices also played a role in promoting this simplistic explanation. Yet this view was not exclusive to the island's consuls and Greek doctors but was also held in some measure by Princess Pakize, who had received a more westernized and "rational" education in the harem than they'd had, as well as Doctor Nuri, who'd received his medical training from European doctors, and the Governor Pasha too.

The Governor Pasha had someone examine the prayer sheet the Quarantine Master had confiscated and learned that it had been issued by the sheikh of the Rifai lodge in the Vavla neighborhood. These devotional artifacts often served as a comfort to people, but what harm might they cause to the quarantine effort?

Doctor Nuri had often debated this question with the Arab sheikhs and British doctors he had encountered while fighting cholera epidemics in the Hejaz. Of course consecrated prayer sheets and amulets of this sort were of no "scientific value," but when circumstances were particularly dire, they could prevent the public from slipping into despondency, and even bring them strength. To oppose the use of prayer sheets outright would only serve to estrange the public from quarantine doctors altogether, and compound their hostility and aversion to quarantine measures. On the other hand, the more they were left to trust in these tokens, the more wholeheartedly did people and shopkeepers embrace the idea that everything would be "just fine," until they began to think that their affiliation with a particular lodge or a sheikh allowed them to transcend the laws of medicine and imbued them with superior powers.

"I could easily have that quack who runs the Rifai sect arrested, give him a good scare, and have his whole lodge, his home, and every last one of his people pumped full of Lysol, but believe me, there would be consequences!" the Governor had said. Doctor Nuri recalled that the Pasha had once spoken in a similar manner about Sheikh Hamdullah too. "Someone would immediately complain to the Sultan that we are harassing the lodges. The next day we would find a telegram from Istanbul telling us to let the sheikh go."

The following morning the Doctor and Prince Consort set off to return the prayer sheet that the sheikh of the Rifai sect had issued to protect against the plague demon, and that Quarantine Master Nikos had taken from Tahsin. He was received warmly by the family, and saw no traces of the disease in their home. There was a strange white light in here, a sense of tranquility and of trust in divine providence. The boy's father sold plums, quinces, and walnuts on a sloping road that led to the docks. The Prince Consort realized that Tahsin knew he was Murad V's son-in-law—married to the fairy-tale princess who was the old sultan's daughter.

During this period, both the Quarantine Committee and the epidemiology team in the State Hall wasted several days over an audacious theory Doctor Nikos had developed in relation to the outbreak. One morning, as he studied the map hanging in the Epidemiology Room, Doctor Nikos had made a discovery: the rats that had brought the disease from Alexandria and the local rats they had infected were still only to be found in the western half of the city.

"There are plenty of green dots in the Christian neighborhoods too!" the Governor Pasha remarked.

"Those are mostly people who catch it when they go down to the port, and when they die in their homes later, we just assume their neighborhoods are infected too."

"I have seen with my own eyes the dead rats in the forestlike gardens of the great mansion in the Petalis neighborhood where the Karkavitsases from Thessaloniki live."

Our readers will be bemused to learn of how much time the Governor Pasha and Doctor Nikos spent debating this question. Doctor Nuri could understand how this bold idea had originated, and although he didn't agree with it, he did not object to it either. Meanwhile, despite the Governor's insistence that rat corpses were still being discovered in the city's Christian neighborhoods, and the fact that even that same day some Greek children had come to the State Hall to hand in dead rats in exchange for their reward, Doctor Nikos—who had more experience with cholera than plague—never strayed from his conviction that he had made some kind of discovery. A clerk and two young Greek doctors named Philippos and Stefanos spent three days trying to find out how far the plague had spread into the Christian neighborhoods just across the Arkaz Creek, but their investigations proved inconclusive.

On the other hand, it was certainly true that some impoverished Greek children had been known to collect dead rats from Muslim neighborhoods and hand them in to the municipal authorities for money. This was a group of three boys who had run away from their respective homes when their parents had died. It was to be the first of the children's gangs. The Governor had also heard that in the Hora neighborhood Muslim and Christian children had been warring over rat corpses. The bishop of Hagia Triada even considered whether to reopen the two schools affiliated with the church and have classes resume as a way of keeping Greek children away from street fighting and microbes.

This scheme never bore fruit (a third of the schools' teachers and janitors had already fled the island), nor did any of the various other creative solutions that were dreamed up during this time, but we have reported them here to demonstrate not only the general sense of hopelessness that reigned in the State Hall, but also the mood that had taken hold among some of the island's more erudite and distinguished personages. In that age when everyone believed that scientific discoveries could transform human life, and supported the increase in wealth that colonial pursuits had brought to Europe, it was the duty of society's comparatively better-educated upper classes to come up with clever discoveries—like Samuel Morse, who devised the telegraph, or Thomas Edison, who invented the light bulb—to solve the world's problems, or indeed to catch murderers as Sherlock Holmes did in his moments of investigative inspiration. Filled with these hopeful visions, many a Mingherian patriarch whiled his days away experimenting with vinegar steam, incense sticks, and hydrochloric acid from Nikiforos's pharmacy, and various powders sourced from the island's herbalists, to try and concoct a homemade cure for the plague.

The first fully effective and reliable plague vaccine would be discovered only forty years later. Back in the 1900s, doctors in Bombay and Hong Kong were still using blood serum to administer the plague microbe to patients, practicing, in their desperation, an experimental approach similar to what we have described above. But the failure of all these haphazard efforts demoralized both the Governor and the public, and poisoned the determination and optimism that were essential to the successful implementation of quarantine measures.

With Doctor Nikos's epidemiological hypothesis leading nowhere too, any hopes that Bonkowski Pasha and his assistant's killers could be found using the latest European methods also began to fade. "European ways do not always take root on Ottoman soil!" the Governor Pasha had once said in the middle of an unrelated conversation. Doctor Nuri had sensed a note of insinuation in the Governor's words, but though he knew that it was not going to be easy to solve the murder in the manner of Sherlock Holmes, he continued to make frequent trips to talk to the city's herbalists in search of clues.

Two days later the Governor received a telegram from his wife. With reports of the outbreak of plague on the island multiplying, an increasingly agitated Esma Hanım had written to say that she would be coming on the first succor ship that sailed to Arkaz. The Governor Pasha had already surmised from incoming telegrams that such a ship was being prepared, but so many schemes of this sort had been abandoned halfway in the past that he had forgotten all about it. Even just the idea of his wife—who hadn't been to the island once in five years—emerging from such a ship with her brother by her side was completely bewildering to the Pasha. His first thought was this: in the five years he had spent apart from his wife, the Pasha had become a different person. He did not want to go back to the person he had been before. Even if the government in Istanbul were to change so that Kâmil Pasha of Cyprus became grand vizier and offered him a position as minister again, he might still not be willing to leave Mingheria and return to Istanbul.

Another strain on the Pasha's morale was a new disagreement that had recently arisen with the authorities in Istanbul. Ever since the quarantine had begun, it was forbidden for any ship to leave the island without undergoing a period of isolation first. (This was an order the Pasha had been successfully implementing.) But whenever he went to visit his lover Marika in the evenings, he would look at the little bay near the spot where the carriage dropped him off, and at the coves and beaches farther along the shore, and see boatmen busy smuggling passengers and their belongings to ships waiting out at sea. Quarantine was being broken every night under cover of darkness. On the first day that quarantine measures were introduced, all the ferry companies had done this.

For political reasons, over the next few days the Pantaleon Company's ships continued to accept passengers even if they hadn't been quarantined, as did smaller companies like Fraissinet. The nights were windy and the sea was rough, and the Greek boatmen who rowed out to these ships in the dark had a difficult job to do. The Governor Pasha eventually learned through his spies that the foreman Kozma and his team, as well as the Italian consul's protégé foreman Zachariadis, had been making a fortune out of these activities. But Foreman Seyit, who was under the Pasha's protection, had not been involved in the smuggling at all.

Having found out so belatedly about these illicit activities, the Pasha became understandably concerned that the Sublime Porte and the Sultan might judge him to have been negligent in the matter, if not downright complicit. He felt as if he had completely lost his bearings, and could not seem to make the right decisions. For a while, he fantasized about sending a telegram to Istanbul asking for the battleship *Mahmudiye* to come and bomb the smugglers. After all, the boats now smuggling people off the island were the same ones that had brought Greece-friendly separatist guerrillas onto Mingheria's northern shores just two months ago. He even considered rounding up all the heads of the ferry companies, from the smallest to the largest, and declaring that they were all under arrest for having contravened quarantine regulations and international travel protocols. But that would have been excessive. In the end, the Pasha spent a lot of time not being able to decide what to do.

In any event, as soon as they reached the countries, cities, and islands to which they were headed (places like Crete, Thessaloniki, Smyrna, Marseille, and Ragusa), all ships carrying passengers from Mingheria were now being confined to makeshift quarantine stations in remote, secluded bays, a measure readers will recall from the incident with the rebellious pilgrims which we recounted at the start of our history. The failure of Mingheria's quarantine was embarrassing Ottoman diplomats and bureaucrats, and the Sultan himself, in front of the whole world.

Sometimes the Governor Pasha could feel the unstoppable force of the plague bearing upon him like a vast, transcendent wave, but having found the composure and faith required to stay afloat, he would internally congratulate himself as well as Doctor Nuri and the other quarantine doctors for their courage and firmness in the face of adversity. But at other times he would focus obsessively on trivial squabbles with the island's consuls, on diplomatic and political schemes that were of no use in stopping the advance of the outbreak, and on pointless reports and editorials published in newspapers nobody read, expending time and energy on previously unnoticed paradoxes and on trying to expose the consuls' duplicitous behaviors.

The Messageries Maritimes representative Andon Hampuri, for example, kept demanding special privileges and concessions for his company, complaining that quarantine was damaging their profits by preventing them from carrying people who wished to flee the island, only to quietly note elsewhere that "the French government demands that no one is allowed off the island until they have gone through a period of quarantine and isolation first!" Aware that the two positions were incongruous, he would only speak of them at different times, and smile at the Pasha in abashment. Sami Pasha himself was a regular practitioner of this kind of deceit, and fully aware of how complicated politics could be. "All Ottoman citizens are equal now, and there are no more infidels in the eyes of the law!" he would daily proclaim in his enthusiasm for the range of westernizing reforms the Empire had recently introduced; yet at the same time he would favor Muslims at every opportunity, or at least believe wholeheartedly that he should do so, and feel guilty when he didn't.

Nevertheless, the Governor Pasha couldn't tolerate the consuls' duplicity. On paper, the representative of the Messageries Maritimes Company and his two secretaries were consular employees, so the Governor couldn't touch them. But one morning he had the agency's offices raided, locked its other employees up in the dungeons, and had the shop and its ticket stall sealed shut. The agency offices were full of excess ticket stubs and other criminal evidence. When Lazar Effendi, foreman of the Greek rowboats, was sent to the dungeons, the Governor Pasha remembered his early years on the island when he had felt instinctively protective of the Muslim boatmen. You really couldn't solve a problem in the Ottoman Empire without throwing *someone* into prison.

But the next day, primarily upon the insistence of the French ambassador in Istanbul the Marquis de Moustier, and after receiving several telegrams from the palace and the Sublime Porte too, the Pasha was forced to release the agency's clerks. When one of these clerks died soon after—having caught the plague while he was locked up in the dungeons—the Governor Pasha reiterated a point he would often make in those days: if it hadn't been for all these telegrams coming in, he could have stopped the outbreak of anarchy and disease upon the island within two weeks.

In a telegram whose tone indicated an awareness of all the latest medical and bacteriological advances, the palace had meanwhile reminded Quarantine Master Nikos Bey that the plague could not be transmitted through the exchange of prayer sheets and amulets, and ordered him to avoid any kind of action that would provoke unrest and turn the public against quarantine. As this telegram had come from the palace rather than the Ministry of Public Health, the Governor Pasha soon became convinced that Abdul Hamid's message had actually been meant for *him*.

The experience of being constantly interrupted by telegrams from Istanbul had caused a kind of fatigue in the Governor Pasha, who soon began to feel that it was futile to try and implement quarantine measures in a just manner. As a result, the nighttime curfew dictated by Istanbul to stop people smugglers was never fully enforced. Of course there were some areas of the city where it really was forbidden to walk around at night with torches and lanterns, and nobody did go out. It eventually became clear that these same restrictions made it easier for thieves to transport the goods they had been stealing from vacant homes. But didn't all these objects—these stolen desks and mattresses and household items—only spread the disease farther?

"The Governor Pasha didn't really mind the Greeks leaving the island by boat to flee the outbreak!" some Greek historians have argued. It meant that the island's harder to govern Orthodox population, and its wealthy, powerful Greek families, would decrease in number, and Mingheria's Muslims would become a majority on the island. But there were also some Muslim commentators who pointed out that once the disease had scythed through the Muslim population that had stayed on the island, and significantly reduced their numbers, the Greeks who had left would all return, and having thus established a substantial demographic majority, they would first demand independence, and later request to be taken over by Greece. The truth—as some others have rightly noted—was that Greeks were already a majority on the island, and had no need for such plots anyway.

If there is one veiled emotion we should be aware of for this historical account to be better understood, and that we have attempted to uncover here as a novelist would, it is Governor Sami Pasha's disenchantment with Abdul Hamid. The Governor simply could not make peace with the idea that the Sultan was less concerned with saving Mingherian lives than he was with preventing the disease from spreading to Istanbul and Europe. This emotion can be interpreted within a traditional Ottoman context as the manifestation of a classic form of heartbreak experienced by the lonely subject who feels forgotten by his own father and insufficiently loved by those in positions of authority. Indeed, Mingheria's Muslims would periodically convince themselves that the government in Istanbul did not love them enough. But surely the fact that Sultan Abdulmejid had chosen to promote this far-flung island outpost to the status of full province as a diplomatic maneuver against Europe was proof enough of the Ottoman dynasty's interest in and fondness for the island.

CHAPTER 36

The Major was usually either busy training the Quarantine Regiment, leading it on neighborhood patrols and in dealing with infected, recalcitrant households, or following Doctor Nuri on his patient visits and his strolls across the city, so that during the day he rarely got a chance to stop by the hotel. When he did manage to spend some time with Zeynep in their spacious quarters, the newlyweds talked and laughed and made love, and hardly ever left their room. After making love, they would fall asleep in each other's arms. There was a tranquility in this that neither of them had ever experienced before. The Major would listen to Zeynep breathing in and out, and marvel at how she could just drift off in his arms, at how comfortable and safe she must feel. They were both a little bashful, and kept the Italian shutters on the room's two tall windows closed.

It was the first time in her life that Zeynep had given herself fully to a lover, and within three days she had grown to trust the Major as if they'd known each other for twenty years, talking to him as fast—and sometimes just as loudly too—as she did with her brothers. So far the only trait the Major didn't like in his wife was the volume of her voice. Zeynep loved to talk noisily about going away to Istanbul.

In the afternoons, when the light filtering through the shutters threw a shadow like a grille on the floor, the Major would hold his wife close and know that he would never forget the bliss he felt in that moment, nor the shape of that shadow. They were going to be happy together for fifty years. Sometimes they lay side by side in bed without talking. The Major would hold her and cradle her pear-shaped breast. Sometimes his wife would put his hand in the palm of her own, and they would lie still. From their bed they would listen to the soft sounds of the docks, of

Istanbul Street, and of the surrounding alleys trickling through the gaps in the shutters. The city was quieter than usual; apart from the distant din of the docks and the passing of the occasional carriage, there were no other sounds. When the city and everything in it was shrouded in the heavy hush of plague, they could hear sparrows chirping on the pine trees in the hotel's back garden.

To Major Kâmil, it was a kind of happiness that was nearly impossible to believe. But their euphoria had also reminded the couple of the significance of their fears and of their lives. They could see that because they were happier than everyone else, they could sometimes be more afraid than everyone else too.

But despite this fear, their marital joy did occasionally induce them to act "imprudently." The trousseau that Zeynep's mother had assembled over the years in preparation for her daughter's wedding, and the gifts that the Major's family had presented to the bride, were all being kept in Zeynep's family home. Zeynep liked going there to look at her wedding gifts and at her trousseau, the hand-embroidered tablecloths, the porcelain coffee set from Italy, the lamps, and the (now-slightly-blackened) silver sugar bowls. One day the Major went with her to his mother-in-law's house. On their way back they came across a plague lunatic to rival Ekrem from Erin. "Walking together is banned, haven't you heard?" shouted this heavy, stocky figure neither of them had ever seen before. The Major wanted to forbid his wife from going outside unless it was strictly necessary, but Zeynep kept reminding him that he was the one who was out on the streets all day, in and out of sick people's homes.

"I'm not that worried," Zeynep said one day. "If it's meant to happen, it will."

The Major was surprised to hear his own wife so candidly express the same fatalism that quarantine officials were always fighting against, but he was so happy with Zeynep that he did not take issue with it, and soon forgot. He was more preoccupied with how he would keep his wife on the island once the ferries started working again.

The Major had begun to intuit that life on the island would never allow him to leave again. As he went to and from the State Hall, the hospitals, and people's homes, he would roam the streets of Arkaz. He would distinctly perceive on these walks the discrepancy between the atmosphere in the city and his own state of mind, but he was too joyful to feel guilty about it. The little Quarantine Division (sometimes he called them his Quarantine Regiment) he had established, the fatherly warmth the Governor had shown him, and his friendship with the Doctor and Prince Consort also gave him confidence. The Major would have liked to tell the Governor Pasha that he need not be so apprehensive about the sheikhs. Every sheikh and every Muslim in Mingheria was perfectly aware that if ever there should erupt one final, bloody battle with the Christians, the only force that would protect them was the Ottoman army, as indeed was the case on every other Ottoman island too.

Every time the Major walked from the hospital to the State Hall in his Ottoman army uniform, people would taunt him, or tease him, or pretend to be respectful only to sneer at him the next moment, and when he got home later, he would always tell his wife about these amusing encounters.

"Don't tell anyone you saw me here!" a terrified stranger said one day when the Major, out on one of his strolls, came across him in the outhouse of an empty garden.

Another time a man the same age as the Major called out to him from a second-floor window: "Soldier!" The man was a Muslim, and spoke with a Mingherian accent. "What do you think is going to happen?"

"Whatever God wills," the Major replied. "You must obey quarantine restrictions."

"We do, we do, but then what? We're like prisoners here! What's happening down by the docks, what's going on in the squares?"

"Nothing's going on! You stay at home!" said the Major imperiously. In his urge to reprimand people for their foolish, simpleminded behavior, he would often end up bickering with them and raising his voice in confrontation. Princess Pakize had very clearly diagnosed this feeling of "modern loneliness" he was saddled with.

But there were also times when the Major would spot someone peering out—more or less unobserved—from their window at the street below, and even if he happened to catch their eye, he would say nothing at all. There was a strange, almost mesmerizing quality to these protracted stares.

"What the hell are you looking at!" somebody had yelled at him once.

By now the fear of death, which even in the staunchest Muslims had

rapidly turned into panic, had begun drawing people out of their existing patterns and dispositions, and molding them into something different. The outbreak had made everyone more cowardly, more stupid, and
more selfish than they really were, thought the Major.

In the terraced homes near the center, most doors had been pulled
shut and back doors bolted up as if they would never open again, but
still the neighborhood children and anybody who was in a hurry to get
somewhere would slip through into the neighbor's garden and through
the cordon, telling themselves it was "just this once." Neither Doctor
Nuri nor the Greek quarantine doctors knew how habitually the rules
were being broken in this way. They also had no idea that people had
been returning to evacuated homes, or escaping in rowboats at night
from the Castle's isolation facility. "It's because they weren't born and
raised on this island like I was!" the Major concluded. If the island were
being looked after by quarantine doctors and soldiers who were actually
from there, the outbreak would never have grown so much.

Every morning before he went to the garrison, the Major dutifully
attended the meetings that took place by the map inside the Epidemiology Room. Through Doctor Nuri's efforts, this alcove where the map
of Arkaz was displayed had been turned into a sort of command center
where all the information on the outbreak was being collected. Over the
past twenty-five days, many of Arkaz's mansions, wealthy homes, empty
lots, lodges, mosques, churches, fountains, bridges, squares, schools,
hospitals, police stations, and shops had been marked on the map. Even
after so many people had fled, abandoning the city and the island, the
number of deaths had still not fallen. There was no doubt that the disease was continuing to spread, and with it a growing sense of collective
agitation.

The disease had entered Arkaz through the Old Stone Jetty. Using
the map, Quarantine Master Nikos had tracked the advance of the
microbe and established that the ship that had brought the plague must
have been the Greek cargo barge *Pilotos* which had come from Alexandria. (These flat-bottomed cargo vessels could come all the way into the
harbor and moor on the wooden jetties there.) Having arrived to the
island upon this ship, the disease had then nestled in the nearby Muslim
neighborhoods, particularly in Vavla, Kadirler, Germe, and Çite. The

deaths that had occurred here had been the first to be recorded on the map. The fact that the still-unfinished Hamidiye Hospital was being built in Vavla could be regarded as a blessed coincidence. Maybe it was, but we will choose not to dwell on this particular coincidence, for this was a time when people were more inclined than usual to see signs, meanings, prophecies, and omens everywhere they looked.

Yet matters had indeed come to this: analyzing coincidences and the disposition of the stars in the sky, seeing portents and signs in the shapes of the clouds and the direction of the wind—and these were things that *everybody* was doing. Even young doctors with an unerringly positivist faith in science, even Governor Sami Pasha and Doctor Nuri, would notice these kinds of details sometimes, and perhaps believe in them too. If anyone asked, they would smile and say, "I don't believe it means anything—though it is certainly strange," and they wouldn't hesitate to enact the necessary measures that science and medicine dictated, but at the same time, in some other corner of their minds, they would readily accept all kinds of nonsense (such as the idea that if a purple cloud appeared on the horizon at sunset and if the storks had migrated earlier than usual—as indeed they had done that year—there would be fewer deaths the following day).

Even the most "enlightened," when gripped by despair, were known to fixate on these kinds of signs. Princess Pakize gave them enough credence to still disappoint us today. We have made room in this book for some of these inventions and falsehoods because they could sometimes shape the course of history. But it is also our view that the public's inclination to look for the future in the stars and in their coffee grounds, or even Sheikh Hamdullah's search for answers and signs about the plague in his ancestors' writings and in the Hurufis' Lettrist manuscripts, did not greatly influence how people reacted to the plague. None of these rumors had as much of an effect on the course of the Mingherian plague epidemic as nationalist prejudices did. Even though everyone present at the quarantine meeting would talk (some laughingly) of this kind of fortune-telling, it was really the map and all the notes upon it that they anxiously consulted as they tried to work out how the disease kept spreading and how they could survive it. The rats that had arrived from Alexandria on the ship named *Pilotos* had first infected a porter who lived in a small wooden house behind the Blind Mehmet Pasha Mosque.

Since no one had been thinking of plague when the porter died, his death had gone largely unnoticed. Diphtheria, pneumonia, and many other diseases had similar symptoms too.

That day the Doctor and Prince Consort used the map to show the other doctors and the Governor how the outbreak had spread from the harbor to the rest of the city at the same velocity as the advance of the rats. They could see from the map that the path of the disease had taken it over the Army Middle School the Major had attended. The Army Middle School had been temporarily shut two days before quarantine was officially announced, so the quarantine officials hadn't put any of its students in isolation. Doctor Nuri supposed that the infected students would reveal themselves when some of them gradually began to fall ill. The military command in Istanbul was following matters closely, and upon their instructions, two educated officers who had been coming down from the garrison in the northeastern part of the city to teach classes at the army school, and thus round up their income too, had been immediately ordered to return to their regiments after quarantine was announced. This was interpreted as fresh evidence that despite how extensively the plague had spread, Abdul Hamid remained determined—in the wake of the fiasco that was the Pilgrim Ship Mutiny—not to embroil Ottoman soldiers in Mingheria's quarantine efforts, and that he continued to put the needs of the Ottoman Empire before those of Mingheria and its inhabitants.

An incident that took place on Tuesday, the twenty-eighth of May, in the neighborhood of Germe serves as a useful illustration of the indecision which paralyzed the state and its quarantine officials. The house at the center of the day's events belonged to a Muslim man who grew barley just outside the edge of the neighborhood. The farmer's twelve-year-old son had died the day before. That morning the doctors had confirmed that the man's eldest daughter was also infected and decided that she should be taken to the hospital while the parents were to be sent to the Castle for isolation. They had also found two fresh rat corpses near the house with blood around their snouts. But the mother and father whose blue-eyed son had died the day before simply couldn't bear to hand over their blue-eyed daughter—who was most probably dying too. The mother's relentless sobbing had already woken up the whole neighborhood, which was accustomed by now to attending a new funeral every day. The quarantine officials on the scene, unable to scare off the children who kept obstructing their path, had felt compelled to ask Doctor Nikos "What shall we do?" and he in turn had not been able to obtain any clear orders from the Governor. What should have been a swift evacuation procedure had ended up consuming the neighborhood for the whole day and turned into a noisy, tearful, bad-tempered affair.

The French consul had been informed immediately of the episode, and sent a telegram to Istanbul using the phrase *les maladroits* (the incompetents). The Governor Pasha had been furious with Monsieur Andon for this, but in Doctor Nuri's opinion, the Governor was definitely to blame.

CHAPTER 37

There was now a growing problem—particularly among the younger population—of people who had been infected or were suspected to be, or even those who were already sick, running away from their homes and families and from quarantine officials. One of the principal reasons for the increase in the number of these fugitives was the deplorable state of the Castle's isolation area. This special zone within the Castle complex had become a place no one ever came back from. All the latest international statutes stipulated that plague quarantine should last for five days, meaning that if someone was put in isolation, they should be let out after five days as long as they weren't sick. Yet twenty-eight days after quarantine was announced in Mingheria and people first began to be put in isolation, our calculations indicate that there were one hundred and eighty suspected cases being held in the Castle's Isolation area. More than half of these had been in the Castle longer than five days despite showing no signs of illness.

By this point, the idea of being quarantined, of being singled out by doctors and taken away by the police to be thrown into isolation inside the Castle, had come to be seen by the island's Muslim population as a fate similar to being sentenced to life imprisonment inside the dungeons. In the old days it was magistrates and traditional *kadı* judges who would send you to those dank, dark recesses with no hope of return; now it was the doctors. That was really the only difference. To make matters worse, the "isolation" facility was tucked away in the part of the Castle that looked into the harbor, while ordinary prisoners were kept in the windswept Venetian Tower and in Ottoman-era cellblocks that faced south toward the open sea.

Another problem that had yet to be solved was how to prevent people who had been put in isolation as a precaution from coming into contact with undiagnosed plague carriers and catching the disease from them. In the beginning, there had been plans to divide the isolation area into courtyards, zones, and sections, and grouping its occupants according to how many days they had spent there and how infectious they were, but it had quickly become apparent that this kind of prison discipline and dormitory system would not work here. Even maintaining the heavily shaded women's enclosure at the back of the facility had become a challenge, as men worried about their wives and children, and were not satisfied unless they could see their loved ones with their own eyes. Eventually it was deemed most beneficial to gather family units together and allow people to congregate in groups. It made it easier for Doctor Nikos to supervise the various courtyards, and quarantined inmates were happier when they could spend their days with their families. But as this solution inevitably accelerated the spread of the plague, the numbers of those held in isolation began to increase conspicuously, until the Castle's isolation facility, which had started off as a place where the disease would be vanquished, gradually turned into an overcrowded site of infection. With claims that people "were fine when they went in, so they must've caught the disease in isolation" and other justified rumors spreading through the city and compromising both the isolation policy and the quarantine effort as a whole, the Castle's isolation facility was soon on its way to becoming a "prison city."

The Governor Pasha and the Quarantine Master sent two more telegrams asking for additional doctors to be sent from Istanbul. As the population's fear of imprisonment gradually took the form of quarantine defiance, the island's doctors and municipal authorities alike began to think that it would be *politically* expedient to empty the isolation facility, so long as the necessary medical precautions were not neglected. There weren't enough rooms, beds, mattresses, chairs, or blankets anyway. For a time, and given the urgency of the situation, the garrison had sent crackers, broad beans, and bread from its own supplies. But garrison Commander Mehmet Pasha of Edirne was not convinced that the disease could only spread when there were rats around, would not send his soldiers and cooks to help in the State Hall and the hospitals, found all sorts of excuses not to make his kitchen's resources available to the Castle's quarantine services, and refused to deviate from Abdul

Hamid's politics of keeping the army "out of quarantine matters." From his office across the bay, the Governor could see the growing congestion in the Castle's isolation area, and would sometimes sit and watch the men lining up by the water to do some fishing and while away the hours.

Eventually, at the Governor and the garrison Commander's insistence, it was made easier for people to be "discharged" from the now severely overcrowded isolation premises. But although a lucky few found their families exactly as they had left them, most of those returning to their homes caused all sorts of problems of their own. In some neighborhoods, people newly released from isolation were treated as if they were sick and infectious, and sometimes the fact that they had been allowed to leave while others who had gone into isolation had never resurfaced was enough to mark them as suspicious, or interpreted as evidence that they must be informants conniving with the Governor. The biggest problem was that a significant proportion of those who returned from isolation would find that their homes and families were gone. Most of these people had been forced into isolation in the first place because someone in their house had died or fallen sick. They would thus come home to discover that much of their family had passed away, while others would find that their loved ones had fled, leaving behind an empty house. Some people came back to discover that in their absence, strangers had moved into their homes. Some would challenge these new guests, but others would find some form of compromise, and maybe even feel relieved that they had found a new family to ward off their terror of being left kinless and completely alone.

Among this multitude of sorry tales, the Governor had been saddened most of all to hear that six people who had gone home from isolation to find there was nobody there, and who had no sympathetic relative to turn to nor any money to spend, and couldn't find anywhere else to go either, had eventually returned to the Castle and requested to be put back into isolation.

Two days later, as the most recent deaths were being recorded on the map of the city, all those present glumly observed that the outbreak—far from slowing down—had now reached the city's quietest, remotest Christian neighborhoods, and each recognized the truth they had struggled to admit even to themselves: the quarantine effort they had so bravely and selflessly toiled to set up was too slow and too weak to cope with the speed and power of the plague itself, or keep up with the number of people it had infected. There were still many contaminated homes whose doors had not yet been knocked on and whose existence had not yet been discovered, and their numbers were increasing by the day. Of the infected homes that had been visited, only a third had been evacuated so far. This was such a grave and terrifying problem that nobody could bring themselves to identify it as we are doing in this book today, one hundred and sixteen years after the fact. It was like being a believer who couldn't picture God, and couldn't even begin to imagine him. The horrifying truth was clear to see from the map in the Epidemiology Room. But people thought that if they put a name to the horror, things would get even worse—just like they did in nightmares—and so they either kept quiet or told themselves lies to allay the gravity of the situation.

It could be difficult to go on with daily life when one carried at the forefront of one's mind the knowledge that the outbreak was only going to grow fiercer, so people would often tell themselves lies they'd made up and find temporary solace in those. Doctor Nikos's theory from two weeks before that the rats were only dying in the Muslim neighborhoods was one such lie, and for a few days it had even given hope to the Governor, though he did not believe it was true. Some mornings they would take a reduction in the number of deaths in a particular neighborhood, or some mischievous pattern in the figures, as their cue to make up another lie which they themselves would be the first to believe. Another falsehood they were convinced was true was the notion that the ship bringing help from Istanbul was allegedly already on its way, though at least in this case the delusion was sustained by the telegrams coming in from the capital. Whenever something turned out to be untrue, people always made sure they invented some other story with which to give themselves hope.

Doctor Nuri was experienced enough to know that during an outbreak, when matters were really desperate, even the most learned and European-minded of individuals each had their own consolatory fantasies to believe in. These didn't necessarily have to be religious in nature. "How strange! It's the third time I've seen that carriage driving past today," the Governor Pasha remarked one day, and it was clear to Doctor Nuri that the Governor believed it must mean something, and saw it as a positive sign.

When a person couldn't find enough reassurance in these everyday lies and in the interpretation of signs, an overwhelming feeling of resignation would quickly take over. Doctor Nuri, who had discussed this state of mind with his wife too, considered it to be an emotion similar to "fatalism" in nature, but in our view this wasn't fatalism at all. A fatalist might be cognizant of the danger they faced but wouldn't take any precautions, relying on Allah for protection. A person who had "lost all hope" and was "completely resigned" to their fate, on the other hand, would behave as if they weren't even aware of the danger they were in, and would neither trust nor take refuge in anyone. Sometimes, after they had worked all day, Doctor Nuri would see that the Governor Pasha was thinking "There is nothing more we can do." Or perhaps there was something else that could be done, but the person who was meant to do it did not have enough strength left, or had simply given up. At that point, as the Governor Pasha, the Major, and Doctor Nuri all knew, the only logical thing to do was to lie in the half-light by your beloved's side, and find a moment's joy and respite in their arms.

CHAPTER 38

Sami Pasha was already spending his days and nights trying to safeguard the authority of the state and the Ottoman Empire's presence on the island against the perils of the plague, and he was growing tired of also being questioned, in a steady stream of admonishing telegrams from Istanbul, on why their latest instructions had not yet been fulfilled. He could also see that the power he wielded as a representative of the state was gradually diminishing. Many of the State Hall clerks had fled the city. Others never left their homes anymore, and wouldn't come in for work. He couldn't even rely on the soldiers that were stationed in the garrison to help with quarantine measures. Yet despite all this the palace still expected the Governor Pasha to use force.

Istanbul's first concern was that all attempts at stopping people from leaving the island in defiance of quarantine rules—that is to say without undergoing a medical examination and a period of isolation first—had so far been unsuccessful. The Governor had put certain measures in place near the Stone Jetty and by the docks, deploying some of his limited numbers of gendarmes and clerks to those spots from where the smugglers' rowboats were likely to set sail. The authorities in Istanbul had sent word that boatmen and smugglers were also operating from coves situated farther north on the island, so the Pasha had asked the garrison Commander for assistance. The Commander had replied that his soldiers, who were already fighting guerrillas in those northern battlegrounds, would only intervene in quarantine-related matters if they were explicitly ordered to do so by a telegram from Istanbul.

Historians of Mingheria have offered differing explanations for why the Governor Pasha did not adopt the kinds of measures that would have placated Istanbul and the European nations and put a stop to the activities of nighttime people smugglers. In our view this was his way of saying: "If you don't give me soldiers from the garrison, then I can't chase smugglers from the coves and rocky beaches in the north." But Princess Pakize's letters also tell us that during this period the Governor Pasha was dragged with astonishing speed into the struggle for profit and dominance that had erupted between the island's boat crews. The Governor Pasha had temporarily cowed the consuls who ran the travel companies by raiding their offices under the pretext that they had sold too many ferry tickets. But it was those same travel companies and the boat foremen we mentioned near the start of our history who were now smuggling people off the island from the northern coves. The Governor had them all taken to court for breaking passport and travel regulations.

Some wealthy families who had initially underestimated both the outbreak and quarantine restrictions, and never made their minds up to flee, had now finally decided (perhaps because their cooks and servants had either died or run away) that they should probably leave the island after all. The Governor knew from his informants' reports that the boat crews were charging these people exorbitant sums. Once they reached the ships that were waiting in open waters to smuggle them away, these desperate passengers, already running for their lives, would then have to pay again for a "ticket." These ships usually belonged to small Greek and Italian companies, and half the cost of this ticket would have been paid in advance through the travel agencies on Istanbul Street. When the Governor found out about all this, he began to think that at least this time he should help the Muslim boatmen as much as he could.

That the Governor, in his wish to support Muslims, had either broken or planned to break the quarantine he himself had established was a fact officially recorded by the clerks of the Mingherian municipal government, which may explain why it has caught the attention of so many archive-loving historians. The other reason why this story has generated so much interest is, of course, that it embodies the intrinsic dilemma faced by the Ottoman bureaucracy. If a governor pasha, an Ottoman bureaucrat whose priority was supposed to be the welfare of the nation as a whole, chose, in these types of situations, to side with his Muslim subjects and put their interests first, it would be harder for him to carry out any modernizing reforms, and to employ modern methods and techniques in governing his province. But if that same governor pasha earnestly embraced modern European methods and reforms, the Empire's Christian bourgeoisie—already growing thanks to increased freedom, equality, and access to technological developments—would be much better equipped to take advantage of any new opportunities, and as the nation became ever more Europeanized, its Muslim population would lose its ascendancy.

With growing numbers of people fleeing the island at night on boats heading toward the West and to Crete, the European nations, worried that the outbreak might spread, began to look for remedies of their own. Eventually the French and the British, who were the most concerned of all, and had experience with epidemics through the large Muslim populations that lived in their colonial possessions, realized that rather than catching smugglers' boats one at a time and having them quarantine in some remote location, it would make more sense to surround the whole island with warships. Even as the matter was still in discussion with the Sublime Porte, the British sent their battleship HMS *Prince George* and the French their ironclad *Amiral Baudin* to the Levant, their presence in the waters around Mingheria serving as a form of psychological preparation.

It was at this point that the British ambassador in Istanbul suggested that an Ottoman warship should also join the cordon around the island. We can see from the archives and letters of the foreign affairs office that Abdul Hamid initially sought to delay this decision and to propagate the idea that "the outbreak is neither serious nor worthy of note." But in the wake of all the episodes of people smuggling, the raid on the ferry companies' offices, and the arrest of the island's Greek boatmen, the Sultan finally succumbed to international pressures.

The news that the Ottoman navy's *Mahmudiye* would supposedly sail out on Thursday, the sixth of June, to join the Great Powers in their efforts to stop the boats that carried people fleeing the plague was communicated to the Governor Pasha the day before through his bureaucrat friends in Istanbul. Although the Pasha didn't believe it could be true, he still felt profoundly mortified. Their quarantine had not succeeded, they had failed to stem the outbreak, they couldn't even stop people from fleeing with the disease and carrying it to the West, and now the whole world was upset. The Pasha felt guilty for being "the sick man of Europe." It had always enraged him when people used that expression. But now, faced with the Governor's incompetence, even the Sultan had felt he had no choice but to join the Europeans and deploy the *Mahmudiye* against the island, as if his own people were the enemy.

These latest developments in the political and military landscape felt so overwhelming that the Governor Pasha couldn't quite believe or think about them, just as he couldn't believe or think about the plague. Later that afternoon, after watching a court usher who had been walking along the first-floor corridor with no sign of anything out of the ordinary suddenly drop dead as if the angel of death had tapped him on the shoulder, the Governor Pasha retired to his office and sat at his desk, staring motionlessly out of the window for a long time.

But soon he was interrupted by the latest reports from his spies on the island. As expected, Ramiz had not stayed put after his release, but found sanctuary in the villages where the ringleaders of the Pilgrim Ship Mutiny lived. After the events of the Pilgrim Ship Mutiny, the father and son who'd led the revolt had moved from their home village of Nebiler—which the army kept finding excuses to punish—to the neighboring village of Çifteler, thus hoping to evade a new tax that had been levied upon them. Their new home had established its own guerrilla army to fight nationalist militants from Greece. It was a traditionalist and conservative village, and after the Pilgrim Ship Affair, its inhabitants had become stricter and more truculent, recruiting their own militias to rival the Greek guerrillas. Just as Greek gangs raided Muslim villages, so these Muslim guerrillas raided Greek settlements, occasionally going as far as to kill people and sack their property. The Governor Pasha regarded these gangs as a kind of civilian army that could be mobilized against the Greek guerrillas when needed, so most of the time he turned a blind eye to their activities (as he did with the outlaw Memo, for instance). But sometimes—egged on by hardened criminals who were not from the area—these Muslim guerrillas would take things too far, setting Greek villages on fire and prompting admonitory telegrams from Istanbul, whereupon the Governor Pasha, aided by garrison Commander Mehmet Pasha, would intervene to fend them off.

The Governor Pasha already knew that over the past two years Ramiz had sometimes taken shelter in these Muslim guerrillas' villages, sent financial aid to the militias, and even supported the foundation of a small religious lodge there. When he found out that Ramiz, accompanied by his followers from these villages and by various other thrill-seeking rogues, had not only returned to Arkaz in the middle of the night, but had also brazenly gone back to his house in the Çite neighborhood and taken his men with him, the Governor, encouraged by the Chief Scrutineer, arranged what would prove to be a fruitless raid upon the property that same evening. As Ramiz's empty home, looked after by a butler and a servant, was being searched, the Governor had ordered the confiscation of as many suspicious objects, papers, and documents—as well as books and newspapers, if any—as his men could find. Though no quarantine-related crime had been committed, the Quarantine Regiment also participated in this raid.

The anger that the Quarantine Regiment and the island's Mingherian-speaking population had been feeling toward Abdul Hamid and the authorities' failing quarantine measures had now also begun to fan the flames of Mingherian nationalism. For the time being, the Governor and the Chief Scrutineer limited themselves to recording and keeping track of this burgeoning nationalism. The Ottoman bureaucracy's principal enemy was of course the nationalism of the Christian populations (Greek, Serbian, Bulgarian, Armenian), but as they watched the Empire fall apart before their eyes, these bureaucrats had also started monitoring the first stirrings of nationalism among those Muslim populations who weren't Turks (such as Arabs, Kurds, and Albanians). (We should note that back then, the word "nationalism" was not as commonly used as other expressions like "the national question.") According to the Governor, the most important thing was that the soldiers of the Quarantine Regiment (whether they spoke Turkish or Mingherian) must all be Muslims. As Muslims, they would be able to better understand people's concerns. The Doctor and Prince Consort was not quite so optimistic, though when he heard about how diligently the brothers Majid and Hadid—whom the Major had recruited—were working at the incineration pit, he wondered if there might be some merit to the Governor's policy after all.

CHAPTER 39

The idea of digging a pit where they could burn rat corpses and any objects infected with the plague microbe had come from Bonkowski Pasha, who had suggested it to the Governor the day he'd arrived on the island. In his view, having contaminated woolens, bed frames, linen clothes, wicker furnishings, mattresses, and any other items that needed to be destroyed gathered together and incinerated—as used to be the custom long ago—in a place where everyone could see and take note would also serve to educate the populace on the importance of quarantine and cleanliness. The use of incineration pits had also been recommended in the treatise that Bonkowski Pasha had prepared for Abdul Hamid on the plague from the East.

The assassination of Bonkowski Pasha had caused operations for this kind of incineration pit to be deferred. But as the Major's "Quarantine Regiment" successfully evacuated more and more people from their homes, the beds, quilts, kilims, and all kinds of other objects the soldiers confiscated began to accumulate in vast heaps. It was dangerous to burn these filthy and infected items inside the wooden homes themselves. It would also be difficult to destroy everything in the city's old courtyards, which the fear of plague had emptied out entirely. The owners of the confiscated items would have preferred for their belongings to be thoroughly disinfected with Lysol and stored away (to be returned to them someday), but there was neither the time nor the space to do that. Anything that wasn't immediately incinerated would probably end up being sold to junk dealers anyway. So upon the Doctor and Prince Consort's advice to the Quarantine Master and the Governor, the municipal government's men began to use two currently unutilized pits situated in the hills just behind the city on a stretch of flat land between the New

Cemetery and the back edge of the Upper Turunçlar neighborhood. The single drawback to this location was that it could only be reached through a long, uphill road that twisted and turned its way through the backstreets of the Old Market and the neighborhood of Arpara, where the Major's family home was situated.

The Governor had the first fire set one day in the late afternoon. This fire, which took place a whole twenty days after quarantine was initially declared, was watched with great interest by a large and enraptured audience. Expanding in enormous, bright red waves, pulsating with radiant yellow fireballs, and painting its surroundings in purple and dark blue hues, this pit fire—fed perhaps by the kerosene that was poured onto it—burned well into the night, and was observed not only from within the city itself, but from across the rest of the island too. Over the next few days, the same pit was regularly used to destroy people's clothing, their beds, and many other objects, and for as long as the outbreak lasted, the appearance of black smoke clouds during the daytime became a source of distress for the people of Mingheria. The black plumes made them feel that the angel of death was nearby, that they were at God's mercy, and even (for whatever reason) that they were alone. As Princess Pakize notes in her letters, these were the same emotions people also felt every time they saw the belongings of the dead and any items that didn't conform to quarantine regulations being gathered from all over the city and taken with relentless regularity up the hill to the pit.

Zeynep's brothers Majid and Hadid had devoted themselves fully to their tasks in the New Muslim Cemetery behind the Turunçlar neighborhood. But not even in Mecca, where foreign observers and Christian doctors weren't allowed to enter, had the disinfection of corpses with lime before burial—one of the cardinal rules of plague quarantines—caused as much trouble as it would initially do on the island of Mingheria. Quarantine Master Nikos's explanation for this phenomenon was that there had not been a serious outbreak of disease on the island for a long time and that, regrettably, people hadn't yet fully grasped the importance of quarantine measures. Even the genial warmth of the universally popular quarantine sergeant Hamdi Baba hadn't been enough to solve the problem, for the harrowing particulars of the matter had ultimately repulsed and exhausted him too. But once the brothers Majid and Hadid began, upon the Governor's suggestion, to take shifts at the New Cemetery, a number of uncomfortable issues—not only the need to cover the faces of female corpses when they were being disinfected and to ensure that neither their intimate regions nor their naked bodies were ever glimpsed (or if they were glimpsed, that it was not for too long) but also the suggestion that it was improper for the lime to be "shoveled in" so roughly, and the importance of making sure none of this substance should find its way into a corpse's open eyes, its mouth, or its nostrils—were quickly resolved before they could get out of hand and turn into serious political incidents.

The horse cart that was used to carry infected items to the incineration pit had previously belonged to the garrison, and had been gifted to the municipality. As this old, broad wagon covered in tin carried its load up the winding road that led to the incineration pit, it was often attacked by pickpockets and thieves, as well as all sorts of troublemakers and fools. These people's purpose was mostly to steal any old kilims, mattresses, bedsheets, and clothes they could grab, either for their own use, or to hand them out to others, or to sell them to those junk dealers who were still operating in secret. Though their numbers had declined from the first days of the outbreak, there were still many people who were stubbornly using the belongings of the dead despite all the times the Quarantine Authority had warned them against it. There was, in this misguided behavior, a sort of challenge to the state, to westernization, to modern medical science, and to the international community, a kind of defiance and disdain, and even an element of senselessness.

Some believed that this unreasonable behavior resulted from the excessive attention and indulgence shown to the island's sheikhs and holy men. Eventually the Governor Pasha assigned two of his most intimidating guards to escort the wagon. This ruthless pair was equipped with whips and wouldn't let anyone—not even children—anywhere near the cart. Soon, the curses, shouts, and profanities that used to be heard every time the cart drove past began to fade, to be replaced by the gloomy silence the island had slowly grown accustomed to during those days of plague. Sometimes the wagon would go unnoticed in the quiet, empty roads. As it inched forward through the streets, elderly onlookers would mistake it for the junk dealer Foti's cart. But sometimes bands of bold, unruly, impertinent kids would evade the whips and clamber on top of the wagon anyway to clown around with their friends and see if they could steal something. In later days, whenever the wagon passed through neighborhoods like Bayırlar, Kadirler, and Germe, the locals would flinch as if they'd seen a funeral hearse; people would jeer and shout, "Get out," children would throw stones, and the neighborhood dogs would bark with a rage more frenzied than usual—their protests undeterred even as they leaped to avoid the guards' whips.

Doctor Nuri was the first to notice that these skirmishes between the whip-wielding guards and the populace were turning into a kind of obduracy against quarantine, and the first person he warned was the Governor, not the Major. Perhaps the wagon shouldn't be out in the streets at all in the daytime.

As the outbreak continued, unidentified corpses began to appear in the wagon's path. These bodies, which had to be removed immediately, were usually put there by people who had taken up residence in vacant homes. They worried that their new homes might start to smell and that the quarantine officials might come along to disinfect everything and board all the doors up. The most sensible thing to do when the wagon carrying items confiscated for incineration encountered one of these corpses was to take them to the cemetery on the opposite hill, decide what faith they must have followed based on the neighborhood they'd been found in, and bury them accordingly, with a coating of disinfectant lime and without too much ceremony or prayer. But this too required tact, expertise, and experience.

The Governor had been following matters closely, and proposed that the brothers Majid and Hadid should be put in charge of burying the abandoned corpses that were being left for the Major's wagon to collect. The Major had been unsure, but the Governor had insisted, noting how well liked and even well respected the two brothers were, particularly in those areas of the city where people still spoke the old Mingherian tongue. Known to be a little ingenuous, the brothers Majid and Hadid, who had once run their own shop and had some savings and land of their own, were popular within their community, and everyone agreed that this kind of work was, in fact, inappropriate for men of their social standing. Dragging corpses off the street and loading them onto the quarantine cart was the kind of job better suited to destitute, foolhardy

youths and oafish hoodlums from Crete, who would be willing to perform this duty, and with enthusiasm too, in exchange for a large enough
payment.

Nevertheless, the brothers Majid and Hadid agreed at first to take
on the task, recruiting assistants to help. Perhaps they thought that the
Major, now married to their sister, was bound to reward them with gifts,
money, or compensation of some other sort. But instead they quickly
became the main targets of the fury people harbored toward the cart
that carried plague victims' belongings to the incineration pit. Unlike
their predecessors, the brothers did not carry whips. Their conciliatory
remarks went uncomprehended, even though (or, some say, precisely
because) they were spoken in Mingherian. The Governor, who could
foresee that the work of guarding the cart would soon wear the twin
brothers out, quickly issued a new directive: from then on, any items
removed from vacated homes, shops, and barns were to be piled up outside the building's front door or garden with a pair of sentries stationed
to make sure nobody stole anything, until Majid and Hadid's wagon
could come at nightfall to quietly pick everything up and take it to the
incineration pit in the dark.

At night the city was even more deserted, with an eerie, deathly darkness enveloping the streets as if a strange blue fog had descended upon
them. The gas lamps that had been used for a time to illuminate the
docks and Hamidiye Avenue at night were no longer lit as they used
to be in happier days. Some homes were still occupied, but no torches
burned in their gardens, nor were there any lights or shadows at the windows. There may or may not have been people hiding inside. In some
houses, Mingheria's wise, surly owls had begun to roost on the roofs and
in the trees in the gardens. Sometimes people would burn oil lamps at
the door to give the impression that an empty house still had people living in it, and keep bandits and thieves away.

One week later, on the second Friday of June, the twins told their
sister that they wished to be relieved of their current duties. The brothers' protests heightened the Major's uncertainty on the matter. Within a
week of their wedding, Major Kâmil had fallen ardently and irremedi-
ably in love with his wife; he was sure that they would be tremendously
happy together. But meanwhile, every day Zeynep spoke loudly and
with growing insistence of how she wanted to go away to Istanbul at

the first opportunity, reminding her husband of the promise he'd made her and talking as if there were no plague or quarantine to think of. The Major didn't quite know what to do. When he heard from Zeynep that her brothers had asked to be transferred from their duties with the cart and at the cemetery and given new jobs as office clerks instead, he reacted sternly and told his wife that until replacements were found, her brothers and their assistants must continue to guard the cart.

As for Istanbul, the Major had twice promised his wife that they would indeed go "at the first opportunity." Through the clouds of indecision now gathering in his mind, he could sense that the true problem was something else: the Major's word did not seem to hold enough sway over his wife and her two brothers. This thing called marriage he'd so often heard his mother praise had generated at least one unforeseen outcome: the fear of failing to satisfy his wife's demands and losing her forever!

It was around this time that as they sat in their room in the Splendid Palace one day, looking out at the magnificent view, the Castle, and the dark blue of the Mediterranean Sea, Zeynep told her husband about the important news she had just heard from her brother Majid, and which, despite her excitement, she now relayed in slow, methodical fashion. Majid had informed his sister that for the past two days Foreman Seyit and his men had been ferrying passengers to ships waiting in the waters off the island at night, and that if one made the right arrangements, it was possible to reach Smyrna within two days, as vessels flying the Ottoman flag were taking fugitives directly to the port of Chania in Crete, from which they could then proceed to Thessaloniki or to Smyrna. This route had only just been established, and it could close at any time. They must hurry up.

We will remind our readers that Foreman Seyit, who was now also smuggling people off the island, was the Muslim foreman that Governor Sami Pasha had been protecting against the Greek boat crews. The Major suspected that Governor Sami Pasha's spies would quickly find out about this new route, and sensing that his wife did not have much patience, he decided that Zeynep should flee to join her relatives in Smyrna that very same evening.

These events—which do not feature in any history of Mingheria—are described in Princess Pakize's letters through the eyes and words of those most closely involved. Yet even we have not been able to understand what the Major might have been thinking in that moment, and perhaps it is here most of all that we have sought to take a novelist's approach. We know, as does the whole Mingherian nation, that Major Kâmil did not envisage a life outside the island and that he had decided to devote himself to serving his people. The only logical conclusion we are left with is that Major Kâmil did not really wish to smuggle his wife off the island.

"My brothers told me that if we want to go, Foreman Seyit can row us out to a ship to Crete which will be waiting tonight," said Zeynep, staring right into her husband's eyes.

Was his wife suggesting that the Major should leave with her? The moment they had decided that she should go, they had also realized how happy they were together. Lovemaking and conjugal companionship had entranced them with pleasures neither of them had ever experienced before. They loved each other, and they would smile and giggle "like children," talking in a childhood language they had invented together. They were not—as some official historians and greedy journalists have claimed—discovering "the enchanting, all-embracing beauty of Mingherian." It is true that the history of the Mingherian language dates back to the ancient Mingherian people, with roots among those tribes that originally lived in the hidden valleys south of the Aral Sea. But by 1901, under pressure from Crusaders, Venetians, Byzantines, and now the Ottomans, the Mingherian language had largely been confined to a handful of neighborhoods in Arkaz and to the villages in the island's mountainous north, without ever having the opportunity to develop the depth, the tools, the spirit, and the conceptual range of the contemporary world in which it existed, and of Catholic, Orthodox, and Islamic cultures.

As she packed her bags in their room at the Splendid Palace, Zeynep cried a little. Ever since she was a child, she had always carried with her a comb with a mother-of-pearl handle—made on the island and gifted to her by her aunt—which she had just realized she must have left at her mother's house. It saddened her to think that she would be parted from this object—one she believed to be a source of good luck—for so long. The Major offered to quickly send one of the sentries, who constantly kept watch at the hotel door for signs of Ramiz, to pick up the comb from his mother-in-law's house, but in the end, husband and wife just stood there and embraced each other in silence. They were worried that this separation would be a long one.

They made love one last time, feeling more sorrow and melancholy than passion or pleasure. His wife's tearful eyes troubled the Major's resolve. What should he do? He tried to tell himself that at least this way they could be sure his wife survived, that he could pick her up from Smyrna as soon as the outbreak was over, that it was a good thing she would be able to escape the plague and the deranged Ramiz's threats. But he knew that as soon as Zeynep was gone, he would remember these days and hours, and the look in her eyes, and fall back into the loneliness he'd experienced in the Hejaz and in the backwater towns of the Empire. He looked at his wife now so that he could store up the sight of her and never forget what she looked like. Yet readers of the Princess's correspondence may suspect that the Major's feelings in that moment were not perhaps entirely truthful.

Once darkness had fallen, the Major put on civilian clothes and a hat he had borrowed from Lami. Both Majid, who had organized the boat, and Foreman Seyit had specifically requested the hat. Zeynep handed the Major the bag in which she had packed everything she needed. They walked through the Hotel Splendid's modern kitchen and left through the back door. It seemed the plague had blackened the night as thoroughly as it had emptied the streets. They moved like ghosts through alleyways and dark, deserted streets, listening to the soft rustle of trees in the wind. They saw that many people had locked up their garden gates, that there were no gas lamps or candles burning in people's homes, that there was no light at all. Yet the dominant thought in both their minds was not the plague, but the fear of being apart. Even as they made their way toward the place where Foreman Seyit's boat was supposed to pick Zeynep up, it was as if they could both somehow sense that in the end they would not have to part after all. Otherwise they might never have set out to begin with.

The fishermen's hut at the edge of Pebble Cove, three bays to the north of the little cove with the tavernas, had been there since they were children. It took them longer than they'd expected to walk there. The improvised jetty just behind the hut was barely discernible in the light of a half-moon. The sound of waves gently breaking on the rocks and the whisper of leaves in the faint breeze gave the impression that there was somebody else there, but there was not a single person nearby. Husband and wife withdrew to a secluded corner, held each other, and began a long, silent wait. Below them the foam from the waves lapping at the pebbles shone like a white smudge.

"I will telegraph you in Smyrna every day," said the Major.

Zeynep began to quietly cry. The sea before them was like a dark wall. Majid and Hadid were going to meet them there, after which they would all walk together to the jetty where Seyit himself (not one of his men) was supposed to pick them up in his boat, but a long time went by and nothing happened. Much later, when they realized nobody was coming, the mountains seemed for a moment to be bathed in a soft light. Red, orange, pinkish flames flickered strangely over the pit where people's old belongings were being burned. The Major saw tears rolling down Zeynep's cheeks.

"Nobody's coming; we won't be parted!" said the Major.

They could see in each other's expressions that they were both secretly relieved. After their long wait, they walked out of sight through the city's backstreets and returned to the Hotel Splendid. As he held his wife's hand on the way, the Major sensed that deep down Zeynep was pleased.

As a historian, we have no proof or documentary evidence of this attempted escape beyond the account we have found in Princess Pakize's correspondence. Mingheria's nationalist historians deem the whole incident to be a taboo subject, and never even mention it. For that night, the man whose actions would soon alter the destiny of the whole island had briefly considered sending his wife away and separating his own family's fate from that of the wider population.

Lami found them shortly after they reached the hotel. "There are warships cordoning the island," he told them tensely. It was almost as if he'd just announced, "The Sultan has died!"—such was the shock in his voice. "Now that the whole world is getting involved, they'll definitely stop the outbreak. In fact Robert Effendi, who'd checked out of the hotel yesterday, has asked for his favorite room thirty-three again."

The Major understood straightaway that this blockade arranged by the world's Great Powers meant that the island had now effectively been left to its fate. But he pretended to believe Lami's more encouraging conclusion. His wife too was immediately convinced by this statement of unwarranted optimism. But the true reason for their jovial mood was that they had not been separated after all, and that they would soon be alone in their room upstairs, free to make love for as long as they wanted to.

CHAPTER 40

Europe's foreign powers had taken the decision to cordon the island together with Istanbul—or at any rate they had pressured the Ottoman government into agreeing. Years later, archive researchers studying diplomatic correspondence from this period would discover that the British ambassador in Istanbul had advised that unless the Sublime Porte also sent a ship of its own, the cordon would inevitably be interpreted as an operation targeted at the Ottoman Empire itself. But—argued Sir Philip Curry—if an Ottoman vessel were to join the operation, this would spare the Ottoman Empire a great deal of global embarrassment, as the cordon would be seen to specifically target the Governor of Mingheria and the local Quarantine Authority who had failed to properly preside over the island. The *Osmaniye* was once again undergoing repairs, so at the navy minister's suggestion, Abdul Hamid ended up deploying the warship *Mahmudiye*.

The decision to set up a maritime cordon was communicated to Governor Sami Pasha and to the Mingherian Quarantine Authority by telegraph the next morning. Given that the blockade was framed in these telegrams as a measure the province of Mingheria itself had requested in order to help protect its fellow Ottoman citizens from the plague, the Governor surmised that an official statement must have already been made to the international press.

By midday, the whole of Arkaz knew that the island had been surrounded by British, French, and Russian warships—as well as the battleship *Mahmudiye* with its star-and-crescent Ottoman banner—to stop people from trying to flee the plague without heed to quarantine rules, isolation measures, or doctors' instructions. Mingherians understood that their island was being mentioned by name in newspapers across the world, but this knowledge brought them no pleasure. For they were not being spoken of in positive terms. Not only had they failed to stop the plague, they were now also spreading it to the rest of the world.

The island's local newspapers soon took to listing the characteristics of the foreign warships at every opportunity (and with undisguised satisfaction at their island being deemed worthy of such attentions): the French *Amiral Baudin,* launched in 1883, was one hundred meters long; the British HMS *Prince George,* launched in 1895, was excellent in artillery. As for Kaiser Wilhelm, he hadn't sent a ship at all, concerned about possible diplomatic repercussions and wary of hurting Abdul Hamid's feelings. The citizens of Arkaz could not see the warships with the naked eye. They were only visible on clear, windy days from the island's mountain villages, monasteries, and rocky promontories. Whenever the weather turned hazy, the ships would vanish from sight altogether, their mysterious disappearance prompting baseless rumors that they had sailed away, or that they had never really been there in the first place.

As ordered by Istanbul, the municipal authorities prepared a statement explaining the reason for the blockade, and hung it all over the city on posters similar to those that had announced the outbreak of plague and the introduction of quarantine regulations. The statement explained that the maritime cordon was not aimed at ordinary Mingherians, but had been established to stop gangs of lawless criminals from smuggling people away on their boats.

The cordon left everyone on the island feeling heartbroken and dispirited. To the people of Mingheria, this decision was a further sign that quarantine provisions had failed, and that the whole world was telling them: "Fend for yourselves, and stay away from us!" The Orthodox Greeks, who had always felt they could rely on Europe and Russia for protection, now realized that the European nations would always put their own interests first. But the island's Muslim population too felt that Abdul Hamid had abandoned them. People soon began to invent stories with which to deceive themselves and gloss over the unpalatable truth. The Sultan's personal ferryboat *Suhulet* had been converted into a relief ship, and was on its way now with soldiers, supplies, and medicines on board; the number of deaths was actually decreasing; the British in India had discovered a vaccine which could stop the outbreak with a single injection, just like the rabies shot, and the true purpose of the cordon was merely to buy some time until the vaccine could be introduced. As for those who mostly spoke Mingherian at home, and trusted in the island's lodges and holy men, their anger was limited to the British and French for blockading the island. They assumed sympathetically that Abdul Hamid must have been forced to send the *Mahmudiye*, and did not hold this against him.

But from time to time, the Muslim population's hostility against Christians could also turn into a kind of rage against the Ottoman bureaucracy, the Governor, and the army. There was one fundamental sentiment nearly everyone on the island shared: after fifty years of reforms brought in to curry favor with the European powers, after all the adjustments and reorganizations that had been carried out—partly under pressure from Europe, and partly with genuine conviction—in the name of equality between the Empire's Christian and Muslim subjects, here was Europe turning its back on the island in its hour of greatest need. As there were many people who felt this way, and as their feelings were provoking a growing disregard for quarantine regulations, the Governor Pasha was more worried about them than he was about the Greek population. In a way, given how much the quarantine effort relied upon collaboration between the island's doctors (most of whom were Greeks), the Quarantine Authority, and the Governor, the outbreak of plague had brought Minghcria's well-educated Greeks and its well-educated Muslims closer together, when they had previously had no interest in each other's lives beyond the realms of commerce and bureaucracy. The Governor did not think there was any kind of political plot beneath this newfound closeness either, as the Greek government was genuinely concerned about the health of the island's Greek-speaking population.

It rained for three days. Every spring, these downpours would not only revive the island's abundant flora and its population of slugs and magpies but also cause floods, and that year too the Arkaz Creek burst its banks, sending mud flowing through the city's alleyways and turning the water by the docks a yellowish color and a consistency similar to that of the fermented wheat drink *boza*. The Governor Pasha sat at the bay window in his office watching the sea become a greenish blue off the Castle and a deeper blue beside the Arab Lighthouse, observing the Castle vanish from view under another sudden spell of rain and whiling away the hours as he tried, perhaps for the hundredth time, to think his way through the main problem they were facing.

"If we send more soldiers out on the streets and throw more people into the dungeons or in isolation, we'll soon have a revolt on our hands," the Governor had told Doctor Nuri one day. "Already we're locking up fifteen to twenty people in the Castle every day, between suspected plague cases and all these delinquent, opportunistic thieves, looters, and hoodlums breaking quarantine left and right!"

After the rains stopped, the Governor Pasha and Doctor Nuri began going on daily walks in the neighborhoods of Çite, Germe, and Kadirler, where the disease had spread the most. They were joined by the Pasha's own guards as well as by the Major and the soldiers of the Quarantine Division, and these twenty- to twenty-five-minute excursions quickly became an occasion to assess the latest conditions in the city and witness firsthand the troubling arguments and disagreements that had been breaking out in its most infected streets.

The city was calm and smelled of Lysol. The army had limewashed tree trunks, stone and wooden walls, and the first floors of people's houses, and at times the Governor Pasha thought the city looked like some other place altogether. This strange sensation was complemented by the emptiness of the streets. No one walked side by side or in groups of more than two anymore. Looking out at the market from the Hamidiye Bridge, which he had crossed at least two or three times a day for the past five years, the Governor Pasha would see that half the stores were shut now, and he would shudder at the sight every time.

Whenever he saw people standing around by the docks or on the boulders along the edge of the creek with nothing else to do but stare into the water, or came across shopkeepers who'd had to close their stores, or spotted someone sitting and waiting in some secret cranny as if they were hiding from the world, the Governor's unease would grow. Even a stranger to the city would have realized that most of the population had taken shelter inside their homes, protected by thick walls and closed shutters, and ensconced in their turrets, bay windows, and court-yards. The rains had ended now, and on Wednesday, the nineteenth of June, a day in which seventeen deaths were recorded, the Governor Pasha noticed that many of the shops that were closed had also been boarded up. Some of these barriers had been erected by the authorities themselves to prevent shopkeepers from returning to the premises after they had been disinfected—and to stop thieves and microbes. But a month and a half on from the introduction of quarantine provisions, many of the measures that had been so eagerly adopted at first were no longer being implemented, and every day brought new challenges and incongruities to deal with.

Boarding up vacant homes and shops may not have been strictly necessary in the age of microbes and epidemiology, but for a time these measures had also served to counter the growing problems of theft, squatting, and looting. To cover timber and labor costs, a tax was levied from people whose property was being boarded up. This ill-advised provision was later abandoned, and eventually, fewer and fewer homes were boarded up at all. The gradual loosening of certain quarantine provisions was a subject of frequent discussion between the Governor and Doctor Nuri. Most of the time, the Major would listen quietly to their deliberations, impressed by how they would weigh up the "intensity of quarantine" in making their strategic calculations. Readers of Princess Pakize's letters will find that the Governor was particularly disgruntled about having to constantly ease quarantine regulations in the wake of misconceived telegrams from Istanbul.

In the five days after the cordon was established, eighty-two people died. It is interesting to note that despite these numbers, people were still shocked when garrison Commander Mehmet Pasha himself died of the plague. Only a poet—not a novelist, and certainly not a historian—would be able to describe the despair that began to seep through the city toward the middle of June. It was a hopelessness that hindered people from acting with prudence, exercising their common sense, and taking the required precautions. It was a feeling that seemed to say, "We're done for, anyway." They might not all be dead just yet, but everyone felt that they were trapped on the island, and no matter what they did, one day death would inevitably come for them too.

It wasn't just the Greeks now, but a significant proportion of Muslims too who regretted not fleeing the island before quarantine measures were introduced. With all official routes suspended under the international blockade, small cargo ships and large fishing boats had returned to linger in the waters around the island, and the island's boat crews had once again started smuggling people out to these vessels in the middle of the night. The foremen of these crews, who were making huge profits from this new phase of smuggling, soon began to spread all sorts of lies and rumors, alleging, for example, that the British HMS *Prince George* and the French *Amiral Baudin* had withdrawn from the cordon completely, or that they were retreating to the port of Chania in Crete every night—making a crossing by sea possible after all. It was true, however, that one boatman, helped along by a fair wind and favorable currents, had managed to row a family of three all the way to the shores of Crete in just two days, though this news never did reach the island. Anyone interested in finding out more about this adventure may wish to read the extraordinary memoirs later penned by the child who had made the crossing on that boat, published in Athens in 1962 under the title *The Wind Was in Our Oars*.

In the beginning, these new smuggling methods were carried out in total secrecy. But when neither the Governor nor the Quarantine Regiment intervened, it seemed everything could continue as it had before, and soon the frequency of these attempts increased. It was during this period of heightened activity that a boat with too many passengers on board sank in the choppy seas one night. Or perhaps it was quietly, deliberately sunk—drowning more than fifteen Mingherian Greeks with it.

The incident was initially described as an accident, but right from the start, the people of the island sensed an element of "malicious intent" in the sinking of the refugee vessel. Having come to the realization that they had been abandoned to their fate, Mingherians were looking for someone to blame for their predicament. In the 1970s, Soviet historians would eventually find a series of documents proving that the boat—which was named *Topikos*—and the seventeen refugees on board had been hit that night by a shell fired from the Russian warship *Ivanov*. Seeing that attempts to illegally escape the island were not diminishing, the foreign powers, encouraged by Britain, had decided they should set an example by sinking one of the refugee boats. The plan had been to rescue its shipwrecked passengers from the sea and return them to the island, but instead, there had been some kind of disturbance. The refugee boat had advanced of its own accord toward the Russian warship in the middle of the night. The Russian foreign ministry refrained at the last moment from issuing a statement purporting that the *Ivanov* had been forced to defend itself when it had been attacked by a vessel "with infected people on board." Many aspects of this disaster, which had such a profound impact on Mingherians' emotions, remain obscure to this day. In the days that followed, the sight of the victims' corpses washing up on Mingheria's shores instilled a different kind of terror in its inhabitants, and left them with the inescapable sensation that they had become like prisoners shackled to their island.

CHAPTER 41

As of Saturday, the twenty-second of June (a day when twenty-one people died), the Major's Quarantine Regiment numbered sixty-two trained and active recruits. More than half of these came from the neighborhoods of Turunçlar, Bayırlar, and Arpara. Growing up, most of them would have spoken Mingherian at home with their families or on the street playing with their friends, and some of them still spoke Mingherian in their own homes today. But the soldiers of the Quarantine Regiment believed it was their childhood friendships and neighborhood connections—rather than their ethnic identity—that had secured them these new jobs they felt so fortunate to have been given. Most of them were in their thirties, though the Major had also recruited a father and son from the Bayırlar neighborhood. Thanks to funds especially allocated by the Governor, they had all received their first salary payment upfront.

Every morning after attending the meeting by the map in the Epidemiology Room, the Major would take the Governor's armored landau to the garrison, where he would lead the Quarantine Regiment through a series of drills and inspect the state of their uniforms. Some of the new recruits loved their uniforms so much that they hardly ever took them off, and wore them—if only for effect—even at home and around their neighborhoods. After their morning drills, the soldiers would be dispatched to various locations to perform their tasks for the day, as decided in consultation with Doctor Nuri and Doctor Nikos. Hamdi Baba and his two men might be sent to pacify the numerous residents of a recently vacated house near the Stone Jetty; if they were not busy manning the quarantine cart, the brothers Majid and Hadid might go to the tent clinic in the gardens of the Hamidiye Hospital to cover a porter who had died and another who'd run away; the father and son who had been recruited to the division might be tasked with evicting two people who had broken into the building site for the new clock tower (a job which would have normally fallen to the gendarmerie, had it not been discovered that the two individuals hiding out at the top of the tower were both infected and already feverish).

In Doctor Nuri's view, the fact that no one in the Quarantine Regiment had yet fallen sick was clear evidence that the plague microbe was transmitted primarily from rats to humans rather than directly between humans. Upon Doctor Nuri's advice, the Major had arranged for a dormitory to be set up for the Quarantine Division in the garrison, where they would be more distanced from the disease. Many of these soldiers normally lived in neighborhoods where the outbreak was at its most severe, and where they were at risk of contagion. But they would still have much rather slept in their own homes—with their wives and families, or under their fathers' roofs—rather than spending the night in that primitive garrison dormitory, and even though the Major had learned that some of them would break ranks and slip away at night, his special troops were otherwise performing so admirably that he had decided not to intervene and dampen their spirits.

That morning, after sending more than half the Quarantine Regiment out to various tasks in different neighborhoods, Major Kâmil gathered his twenty most trusted men and gave them three bullets each from the munitions supplied by the garrison Commander. Then he told them to load their rifles. They were all a little perturbed by this, but they followed his orders and noisily loaded their guns. The Major had put Hamdi Baba in charge of the squad. He had also assigned Mustafa, a recruit from the Bayırlar neighborhood, to assist Majid and Hadid, whom the Major had finally given new desk jobs just a couple of days before. For two days he had been preparing this select team for the task they were about to perform, but feeling the need to say a few more words now, he told them once again that the mission they were embarking on would help to fight this accursed disease, that they had nothing to fear, and that they probably wouldn't even have to shoot, though they might perhaps have to fire one or two bullets once they got to the Post Office. He had already spoken to them all individually to explain that they were going to protect the Telegraph Office and that this operation was essential to stopping the outbreak. At the last moment, as he was running through what they were each supposed to do one more time, he lied and told them that the Governor Pasha was aware of the plan too.

With the Major leading the way, the quarantine squad marched right out of the garrison's main entrance (the sentries had opened the gates and saluted them as they passed) and walked in loose but orderly formation down the steep road that would come to be known many years later as Hamdi Baba's Hill. They were quiet as they walked among Eyoklima neighborhood's purple bougainvillea and its verdant Lysol-and-honeysuckle-scented gardens, and they could hear bees buzzing. They filed through the back entrance of Hagia Yorgos Church, crossed its main courtyard—that familiar place whose disinfection they had witnessed time and time again, and which now smelled of death and almonds—and continued slowly toward the shore. The front of the church was often thronged with coffins and quarrelsome crowds of mourners and cemetery visitors, but that day there was only a pair of dejected beggars sitting on the stairs, and a handful of dark, shadowy figures watching the soldiers with eyes full of dread.

The soldiers marched down the same Lysol-soaked streets they would walk through several times a day, crossed the State Hall Square without slowing their step, and emerged onto Hamidiye Avenue, and within two minutes they had reached the Post Office. Not many people saw them, and those who did assumed they must be on their way to attend to some quarantine dispute.

As planned, the brothers Majid and Hadid and three other soldiers surrounded the courtyard outside the Post Office's back door. Seven others, including the Major, climbed the steps at the front entrance of the building and onto the landing. Meanwhile, in the little square outside where people used to gather and wait for their parcels back when mail boats came less frequently, the other eight soldiers of the squad stood guard with their backs turned to the Post Office, their stance a signal to curious onlookers that they were there to keep watch over some sort of military operation. There was no crowd outside just yet, but anyone walking along Hamidiye Avenue could see the soldiers of the Quarantine Regiment stationed by the Post Office, and soon people began to gather to try and find out what might be going on.

The Major entered the building. It was still early in the day, and there were only five customers inside. Some were servants dispatched from wealthy households; others were gentlemen in frock coats. They had come to send telegrams to places like Istanbul, Smyrna, and Athens. The Major had seen them many times before when he had come to drop off Princess Pakize's letters. Most of their telegrams either said "We're fine" or "Everything is terrible, but we never go outside." (When someone died, those who lived in the same house wouldn't even get the chance to send any telegrams, as they would be taken by the Quarantine Regiment and put into isolation right away.) The Major realized that there were no Muslims around that day. This was the kind of detail he had only recently begun to notice.

The Major was just about to approach a frog-faced clerk he had become acquainted with from posting Princess Pakize's letters, when the Postmaster came down. He had seen from his office upstairs that there was something out of the ordinary going on.

"Have you brought us a new letter from the Princess?" he said with an amiable smile.

Over the course of his frequent visits to the Post Office, the Major had developed a friendship with Postmaster Dimitris Effendi. Dimitris had been sent to the island from Istanbul twelve years ago. He was not from Mingheria. He was a Thessalonikian Greek who had worked in the Ottoman Empire's oldest telegraph offices, continued his training at the Imperial Academy for Advanced Telegraphy in Istanbul's Çemberlitaş district, and developed, over the course of many years, a capillary knowledge of the intricacies of wiring telegrams in French and Turkish. In the early days of the plague, as Princess Pakize's heavy envelopes were weighed to work out postage fees, and Post Office clerks picked out the right stamps, Dimitris Effendi would often start talking to the Major about Istanbul; he would tell the Major about the classes he'd attended with telegraph engineers who had taught in French, describe the way Istanbul used to be back then, and ask him what it was like now.

"I have no letter this time!" the Major replied. "Today I have come to take over the Post Office."

"What do you mean?"

"The Post Office is closed now."

"There must be some mistake," said Dimitris Effendi.

The confidence in his manner—as if he were merely correcting the number of characters and symbols in a telegram, or pointing out some technical error—irritated the Major.

"You must not resist!" he said, as if he were sharing a secret.

"But the circumstances necessitate explanation . . ."

The Major stepped away from the counter—where someone had placed a precautionary fumigation kit which would not have been out of place forty years earlier—and walked back to the main entrance, bringing in Hamdi Baba and the other two soldiers who had been standing at the threshold. He was deliberately exaggerating every gesture he made, as if to show Dimitris Effendi and the Post Office staff that they had better toe the line when the Major and his men were around. The clerks were already familiar with Hamdi Baba and the other soldiers, whom they crossed paths with in the city streets every day, and knew how eager they could be to pick fights, use force, and even fire their rifles if need be.

For several days now, the mess inside the Post Office—the tables covered in clutter, the envelopes piling up on top of mailbags, desks, and boxes—had been bothering the Major. When he was a child, the Post Office was as spotless as the framed postcard samples on its walls, and as tidy as an industrious housewife's kitchen. The reason for its current state of disarray could not have been the introduction of quarantine measures, for after the latest international public health conference, the practice of disinfecting mail and newspaper deliveries had been abandoned, and there were no impediments to sending or receiving post. If the Post Office's activities had slowed down, it was because visits from mail boats had become more infrequent, and some clerks, fearing they might catch the disease, had renounced their positions and run away. When the Major barred access to the second floor and sent one of his soldiers to stand guard at the foot of the stairs, everyone in the Post Office understood that he had planned this move in advance.

In that same moment the Postmaster was approached by a man whose embroidered waistcoat identified him as a Mingherian of old stock. This man had sent out a valuable package to Istanbul through registered mail a month ago on the Messageries Maritimes *Guadalquivir*, but he had not yet received any "proof of delivery." The Postmaster had already twice explained on each of the man's last two visits what procedure he should follow if he wished to find out definitively whether his package had arrived. In the past week, the old man had been coming by every other day, arguing with the clerks and brandishing a new document he'd had ratified by the State Hall which stipulated that any sealed bags of returned mail should be opened up and searched through until his valuable package was found and given back to him.

With the Postmaster and the old man's exchange in Greek turning into another prolonged quarrel, the Major thought this would be a good opportunity to declare his intentions.

"That's enough; let us put an end to this discussion now," he said in Turkish. "From this moment on, all Post Office operations shall cease!"

He had addressed the whole room with this pronouncement, and spoken loud enough for everyone to hear. The Postmaster told the man with the embroidered waistcoat something in Greek and sent him away. The other customers, disquieted by the presence of the soldiers, had also begun making their way toward the door.

"Exactly which 'operations' are you referring to?"

"You will halt all transactions. You will neither send nor accept any telegrams," said the Major.

The Postmaster signaled with his eyes at the notice hanging on the wall. Drawn up in consultation with the Quarantine Master and with the Governor's approval a week after quarantine was officially declared, the notice detailed in Turkish, French, and Greek the new rules that Post Office customers would now have to follow: they would only be let in one at a time, and no two people would be allowed to stand next to each other. Post Office clerks were not to be touched; clerks were authorized to use fumigation sticks, and no objections would be tolerated to disinfection spray operators. The proportion of literate Mingherians, particularly among the Muslims, was no more than one in ten, but even so the Governor and the Quarantine Master had insisted on posters like this one being put up in many of Arkaz's shops, hotels, and restaurants, and even in open spaces and on the walls of certain buildings.

"Are telegrams being banned too?" said Dimitris Effendi. "What do they have to do with the disease?"

"They will not be banned. They will be subject to structure and scrutiny."

"This kind of measure can only be taken under the Governor Pasha's orders. Do you have an official decree with you? You are a bright young man, and your future is even brighter. But you must be careful."

"Hamdi Baba!" the Major called out to the older quarantine soldier whose face everyone knew.

Hamdi Baba lowered his Mauser infantry rifle from his shoulder. Though he knew that everyone was looking at him as he released the safety catch and pushed the bullet into the barrel, his gestures remained composed. The clatter of his rifle silenced the Post Office. Everyone watched as Hamdi Baba rested the rifle against his shoulder and slowly, carefully took aim.

"That will be sufficient. I understand now," said Postmaster Dimitris.

Hamdi Baba opened the eye he'd screwed shut for better aim, glanced at the Major, and understood that he must continue as they had planned in advance.

A telegraph delivery clerk who had been standing near the barrel of the gun now stepped away. A man with a hat and a secretary who had been close to the door quickly walked out.

Hamdi Baba pulled the trigger. There was a loud explosion. Several people threw themselves to the floor. Some tried to hide under tables and behind desks.

Hamdi Baba fired two more shots, as if he had got carried away for a moment.

"Cease fire!" said the Major. "Slope arms!"

The first two shots had hit the Swiss-made Theta clock on the wall, shattering its glass cover. The last bullet had struck the clock's wooden casing and disappeared inside, so that the witnesses in the Post Office assumed it must have magically vanished. The Post Office's spacious entrance hall smelled of gunpowder now.

"That is quite enough for us too!" said Postmaster Dimitris. "Please do not shoot again in here."

"I am glad you understand," said the Major. "We have some proposals you will wish to argue with."

"I would never argue with the government's armed infantry," said Dimitris Effendi. "Do come upstairs to the Postmaster's office. We shall make note of your commands there."

The Major thought there was a hint of derision in the Postmaster's tone. He sent Hamdi Baba outside to handle the people who had gathered there when they'd heard the sound of gunfire. The brothers Majid and Hadid, stationed at the door, told anybody who asked that on the

Major's orders, the Post Office's telegraph operations had been suspended. Letters and parcels would continue to be mailed out and distributed to their recipients as normal whenever any mail boat arrived. It was only the telegraph service that had been terminated. As nobody seemed to believe this, an announcement in Turkish, Greek, and French was put up on the door. But most of those who turned up through the rest of that day still thought they might be able to send their telegrams out anyway.

CHAPTER 42

The events we have just described came to be known in the history of Mingheria as the Telegraph Raid. This designation was somewhat inexact, as the raid had technically been conducted on the Post Office. The historical and official consensus is that the Telegraph Office Affair, as it was also sometimes known, marked the beginning of a "national awakening" on the island. In the one hundred and sixteen years since, the island has celebrated the twenty-second of June as Telegraph Day, closing schools and government offices for the occasion. During these commemorations, elderly telegraph clerks in flat caps re-create the Quarantine Regiment's walk from the garrison down the hill to the Post Office. Have those living on the island today really forgotten that the "troops" that came down from the garrison that day were soldiers, not telegraph clerks? Some official "historians" have argued that the reason the event is now remembered as a joyful experiment in "modernity," rather than a military operation where bullets were fired and force was used, is that the Mingherian people are naturally averse to violence.

Having made sure that the Postmaster would continue to follow his orders for at least some time after the raid, the Major went back to the Hotel Splendid Palace to be with his wife. He did not leave the room for two hours. Much later he would tell journalists that in that brief pocket of time, he had experienced a state of incomparable euphoria.

When the bells of the Hagia Triada Church rang for one o'clock, the Major exited the Hotel Splendid Palace through the kitchen, and walked toward the State Hall. The Hamidiye Square, the area around the unfinished clock tower, and even the environs of the Hamidiye Bridge, usually teeming with idlers, hawkers, and plainclothes policemen disguised as flower or chestnut vendors, were now completely empty. As he passed by the Post Office, the Major saw that the soldiers he had stationed to guard the door were still in position. We can say that during this walk, the Major was edging closer than ever before to that which we would now call history.

The Major entered the State Hall full of confidence and purpose. He felt as satisfied as a chess player who had just made a brilliant and unexpected move. He was immediately shown to the Governor's Office. Doctor Nuri was there too.

"Please explain why you have done this, what you expected to achieve, and how you propose to rectify the matter," said the Governor, fuming. "In the midst of an outbreak, we now find ourselves cut off from the world."

"But, Your Excellency, you yourself have always said that 'if only they would stop sending telegrams from Istanbul for a couple of days' you would be able to very quickly end any resistance to quarantine."

"This is no laughing matter!"

Doctor Nuri intervened. "Your Excellency, if you wish we could have the telegraph line repaired right away and start receiving orders from Istanbul and from the palace again within half a day. Or we might take a more . . . leisurely approach to repairs. Then nobody would be able to interfere for a few days—just as you wanted . . ."

"We do not let *anybody* interfere in our affairs," said Governor Sami Pasha. "You are under arrest," he said, turning to the Major.

Two guards entered the room, and the Major did not resist. As they took him to be locked up in a cell on the first floor of the State Hall, the Governor assured him that he would arrange for Zeynep to be looked after by her brothers. He was impressed by the Major's poised, resolute manner.

The Major's confidence undoubtedly derived from the feeling that his Telegraph Raid had been a success. Right from the start, and before it had even acquired its official nomenclature, the Telegraph Raid had become a source of hope. Everyone was afraid now—even the "fatalists" whom the Europeans misguidedly belittled, even those who were so hard-hearted and so foolish as to mock other people's fear. The international blockade and the sinking of the refugee boat had burdened them all with the feeling that they were trapped with the disease. People used to feel grateful, whenever they opened the newspapers to reports of the latest terrible events taking place elsewhere, that God had put them on this remote island, far from all those wars and disasters and global entanglements. But now the sense of distance that their island provided suddenly seemed like a horrible curse.

The light that always spread over the city around the middle of June—sometimes a soft yellow, sometimes pale and colorless—now gave everyone the feeling that they were stuck in their own unique version of hell. It was as if the plague itself were a yellow presence hanging in the sky, constantly stalking the people of Mingheria and casually deciding which life to extinguish next.

A substantial contingent who believed that the disease had been brought in from "outside" were genuinely convinced that the foreign powers that had supposedly snuck the illness in were the same ones who were now shamelessly blockading the island with their warships. These views were held by some Christians too.

The Governor Pasha recognized this strange mood sweeping through his subjects before anyone else did. He soon learned from his informants that the Major, whom the Governor had imprisoned inside the State Hall, was becoming an increasingly well-known figure among Muslim shopkeepers and gangs of angry troublemakers in the Vavla and Kadirler neighborhoods, and even with those in the Greek community who loathed the Governor.

"No one can interfere with you now," said Doctor Nuri as they sat before the epidemiology map that same day.

Governor Sami Pasha replied by recounting a fond personal memory: "Back when we were young, those of us who worked in the department headed by the dearly departed Fahrettin Pasha (whose villa used to neighbor ours for a while) would sometimes meet in the evenings with our colleagues from across the street in the Translation Bureau after we were done with our tasks for the day and tell each other our dreams for the future of the nation. During one of these nighttime conversations, our friend Necmi from Nazilli challenged us to answer this question: If we were to become grand vizier today, and hold all the power in our hands, what would *we* do to secure the welfare of the nation?"

"What did you reply, Pasha?"

"There must have been spies and informants among us, so like everyone else, I recited some lengthy prayers for His Highness Sultan Abdül-aziz's health and offered a few banalities. I have always regretted how ordinary my suggestions were! I said, 'I would give greater precedence to science and education, I would close religious schools, I would establish European-style universities.' For years afterward, I wondered what I might have said instead, what would have been a more interesting, a more fitting response . . . One does wonder sometimes if we should just give all these rascals and reprobates out there the punishment they deserve! Sometimes it is the mullahs I am angry at, who do nothing but weaken our quarantine effort, and these charlatan sheikhs who write up prayer sheets against the plague. The consuls here have always infuriated me too. But do you know, I have recently come to think that the best thing for this island now would be to banish every last Christian from it."

"But why, Pasha? And what if they didn't want to go? What would you do then—kill them all?"

"Certainly not! We couldn't do that even if we wanted to. Most of them are good, intelligent, capable, hardworking people. But it is a source of great personal distress to be unable to do anything at all while so many people are dying out of sheer indiscipline, insubordination, stubbornness, and ignorance. Now each and every one of these despicable consuls is going to come up with some complaint, some threat, some lie of his own, and demand that the Post Office is opened once more. Perhaps the time has come to put them in their place."

"You mustn't do that, Pasha. They would start opposing quarantine too, out of spite. Perhaps you could say that there is a fault at the Telegraph Office and that our line with Istanbul is broken. You could tell the consuls that you have jailed the Major, and that you couldn't possibly countenance such an outrageous incident."

"In fact our connection to Istanbul isn't broken at all!" said the Governor. "The telegraph line at the Post Office is ticking away. I have asked the municipal code breaker to keep deciphering any messages that might arrive."

The Pasha had already read the two latest telegrams from Istanbul. One advised that the relief ship *Sühandan* was on its way, and called for the required arrangements to be made in preparation for its arrival. As for the contents of the second telegram, the Governor Pasha decided to share them then with Doctor Nuri. "The Quarantine Committee in Istanbul has requested that from now on, any medical examinations conducted on the roads that connect Arkaz to the island's other cities, Zardost and Teselli, should also include checking travelers' temperatures with the aid of a thermometer. But we do not have enough thermometers. Why are they asking us to do this?"

Doctor Nuri explained that this kind of measure had been adopted in India, where the disease spread through rural areas, in Kashmir, and in inner Bombay. "All Istanbul cares about is whether the disease will spread to the rest of the island," they muttered to each other. The next day the Governor silenced the consuls' furious protests by telling them that he had arrested the Major, but he did not restore the telegraph line.

CHAPTER 43

On the morning of Monday, the twenty-fourth of June, the Governor dispatched a municipal clerk to the British consul George Bey's residence—a house with famously magnificent views—in the neighborhood of Ora and invited the consul to his office. The British consul, whom Sami Pasha had purposely placed on the Quarantine Committee, was not currently well disposed toward the Governor.

The Governor was very fond of George Bey, and favored him over all the other consuls. George Bey wasn't there to represent a ferry company or any British commercial interests, but purely out of love for the island, and given that he was British by birth, he was a proper consul too, rather than a mere vice-consul. Fifteen years ago, he had gone to Cyprus as a young engineer to work on the British protectorate's public infrastructure projects, and having married a Mingherian Orthodox girl he'd met there, he had left Cyprus and moved to Mingheria nine years ago. Unlike the consuls who were native Mingherians, he did not brazenly exploit consular privileges and customs exemptions for his own personal gain.

The Pasha also nurtured a heartfelt respect toward George Bey for the way he treated his wife as an equal: George and Helen were often spotted together, they traveled and took picnics together, they were always discovering the island's best panoramic spots, and they confided in each other all the time. They had introduced the Governor Pasha to Marika's husband (who would later pass away) even before the Governor had met Marika herself. In those early years, whenever he sat in the consul's house having a glass of wine and enjoying the spectacular views, the Governor would boast to George and his wife Helen of how he would rather die than give in to those cowards who wanted to take this beautiful island of Mingheria, pearl of the Levant, away from the Ottoman Empire, and he would vow to fight them all until his dying breath. Though he could sense that they regarded his views on love, marriage, and life as somewhat rough and high-handed, and though he sometimes suspected (perhaps unfoundedly) that they might be secretly making fun of him, the Governor Pasha still treasured George Bey's conversation and friendship.

It was, sadly, a dispute over books that had now driven them apart, as well as an argument over freedom of speech that had turned unexpectedly fraught. Under the reign of Sultan Abdul Hamid II, any book mailed to Mingheria from abroad was first sent from the Post Office to the State Hall, where it would have to be reviewed and deemed "suitable" before it could be released and delivered to its intended recipient. George Bey, who was writing a history of Mingheria in his spare time, would often find that the monographs and memoirs he would order from London and Paris were confiscated for dangerous content, or handed over to him only after many months had passed. These difficulties were caused by the three-person committee tasked with evaluating incoming books. (The members of this committee were ordinary municipal clerks who happened to speak a little French.) George Bey had finally asked his friend the Governor if he might intercede with the Review Committee to speed things up, and for a while, this approach had proven effective. But soon the time it took to retrieve his books had begun to lengthen once more, and George Bey had started using the French Post Office of Mingheria—that is to say the Messageries Maritimes offices on Istanbul Street—as his mailing address.

To the Governor Pasha, Monsieur George's solution felt like a political conspiracy as well as a sly and devious personal affront, but he was also afraid of what might happen if the palace's informants on the island started reporting to Abdul Hamid that dangerous books were circulating freely in Mingheria, and it was in this state of heightened agitation that he had managed two months ago to impound a trunk containing a new shipment of books for George Bey.

This operation had mobilized considerable investigative resources. It began with the Governor Pasha's spies reporting that Consul George had been boasting to his friends about a new shipment of books he was expecting from Europe, whereupon the Governor instructed his informants in the docks and post offices to be on the alert for this delivery so that he could have the trunk tracked all the way to the so-called French Post Office. Later, as the books were being transported to the consul's house, the police stopped the cart and confiscated the trunk on the pretext that the Muslim coachman was wanted by the authorities for theft. Once the trunk was opened and its contents revealed, the Governor Pasha had the books sent to the State Hall's censorship committee for evaluation. Behind the Governor's actions that day lay a long-standing argument he and George had been embroiled in: the question of "how to shield the state and the public from dangerous books" was one the Pasha had always enjoyed debating, though he now regretted having let this particular discussion go on for as long as it had.

When he saw the expression on George's face as the consul walked into his office that morning, the Pasha realized that their days of gentle sparring and convivial badinage were definitively over. Speaking in the rudimentary French they always used with each other, the consul, his manner now rather reserved, asked when the Post Office would open again and when normal telegraph services would resume.

"There has been a technical issue," said the Governor. "The Major overstepped, and he is in prison now."

"The consuls think you encouraged him."

"For what purpose and whose benefit would we do such a thing?"

"They are calling him a hero in Çite and Vavla neighborhoods. Everyone is scared of the Quarantine Regiment now. You know better than I do how many people believe that the disease was brought here deliberately to cause harm and wrest the island away from Ottoman rule, just like Crete . . . These people are pleased about the Telegraph Raid. We are seeing now the one thing Abdul Hamid most wished to prevent in Rumelia and on his islands: Greeks and Muslims turning against each other."

"That is indeed unfortunate."

"Your Excellency, in honor of our friendship, I must warn you," said Monsieur George, his French improving as it always did whenever he became emotional. "Britain and France will no longer tolerate this illness hovering so close to European borders. The Great Powers have never been able to stop the plague in India or China because those places are too far away. These kinds of things can be very onerous there, and the locals are ignorant and intractable. But the outbreak here must be stopped, for it is starting to turn into something that could threaten Europe too. If we do not do it ourselves, they are fully prepared to send their own soldiers to eradicate the disease, and even evacuate the whole island if need be."

"Our sultan would never allow that," said the Governor, losing his temper. "If the British came here with their Hindu troops, we would not hesitate to deploy the Arabs from our garrison, and you can be sure we would fight to the last man. I would fight too."

"My dear Pasha, as you are aware, Abdul Hamid has long since been prepared to give this island up, just as he did with Cyprus and Crete," said Monsieur George with a smile.

The Governor Pasha shot him a hateful glare. But he knew that all of this was true. After they had helped him take back some of the Balkan territories he had lost to the Russians in the war of 1877–78, Abdul Hamid had practically gifted Cyprus to the British, only asking in return that the Ottoman flag should continue to fly over the island. The Governor Pasha was reminded of the writer Namık Kemal's famous words: "the state would never give its castles up!" It was a line from the play *Vatan yahut Silistre (For the Homeland and Silistria),* spoken by the sweet and innocent soldier character Islam Bey. But the Ottoman state had been retreating for one hundred and fifty years now—one castle, island, nation, and province at a time.

With a surge of confidence and vigor even he couldn't explain, the Governor Pasha coolly and sardonically posed Consul George the following question: "So what would you suggest that we do?"

"Only yesterday I met with His Excellency Constantinos Effendi, leader of the Greek congregation . . . ," said Consul George. "The most appropriate move would be for the island's Muslims and Christians, its priests and sheikhs, to issue a joint statement so that we can forget old rivalries and fight side by side against this scourge. Of course the Telegraph Office should immediately open again too . . ."

"If only everything were as simple as you have so benevolently put it!" said the Governor. "Come and let us go with Coachman Zekeriya to the most infected, malodorous spots, and perhaps you will change your mind."

"We all know the corpse that was spreading that terrible smell all over the Çite neighborhood has finally been found now," said the consul. "Whose negligence was that? But of course it would be the greatest honor to join you in your landau for an inspection, dear Pasha."

Usually when the British consul began to speak to him with the excessive courtesy of a diplomat rather than as a friend would do, the Governor Pasha would begin to worry and suspect that George Bey was secretly scheming against him, but on this occasion he was mostly just pleased that they would embark on this excursion together. Having gone into unnecessarily lengthy detail with the coachman about which route he should take to get to Çite this time, the Governor had Monsieur George sit beside him rather than in the seat across, and opened the landau's windows.

As they advanced toward the New Mosque, the emptiness of the streets seemed utterly strange to the Pasha. Even without the plague, it would have been dispiriting not to see a single person outside.

They saw that most of the shops along the creek were closed. In the market quarter, there were two barbers still open (nobody came in for shaves anymore except for a handful of "fatalistic" old men; as for Panagiotis, his shop was closed that morning), and a few blacksmiths who would have probably starved if they stopped working. The Quarantine Regiment had harassed so many shopkeepers—Greek and Muslim—for resisting their authority and breaking quarantine prohibitions, and locked so many of them up in the Castle prison, that most of these shop owners had stopped opening their stores altogether, and never came down to the market anymore either. The Pasha had been against this at first, insisting that there should be some semblance of order to how the shops were closed, but by the time any system could be put in place, the shopping district was already empty and completely silent.

With the collaboration of Doctor Nikos and the local Greek community, and the help of the municipal authorities and the gendarmerie, a food market had now been set up in the Greek Middle School, stretching across its playground and up to the first floor (where mousetraps lay at every corner). Supervised by quarantine doctors and regularly spritzed with Lysol by a team of spray-pump operators, this market sold eggs, walnuts, pomegranates, herb-flavored cheeses, figs, raisins, and other similarly "safe" products brought in from the countryside. The Governor had started this quarantine bazaar to help people who had been slowly starving because they wouldn't leave their homes and couldn't find food, and he was eager for Consul George to see how well it was working and how useful it was. But as the consul pointed out, he had been coming here himself every day, for there was nowhere better than this market to give one a sense of how people were coping. These brave market vendors who came down once a week and underwent medical examinations before they entered the city to confirm they did not have a fever would also inform Monsieur George of all the latest developments, not only in the northern parts of the island, but also in the villages just outside Arkaz. (At this, the naturally suspicious Sami Pasha couldn't help but wonder if the consul was secretly gathering intelligence in preparation for a military landing in the north of the island.)

CHAPTER 44

The armored landau turned into Istanbul Street. Two months ago, this sloping road had been the island's most vibrant, boisterous spot, but now it was completely empty. The agents of the travel companies (Messageries Maritimes, Lloyd, Thomas Cook, Pantaleon, Fraissinet), the notary Xenopoulos's office, and photographer Vanyas's shop were still open, but there was nobody around. The landau rounded a corner, and they saw a young Greek boy holding his mother's hand and staring at the place where the street vendor Luka—who had died of the plague—used to sell the dried-chickpea snack *leblebi*. When she saw the Governor's landau, the wan-faced, black-robed mother (whose name was Galatia) froze for a moment, then hurriedly covered her son's eyes so that he wouldn't look at the Governor's carriage. The eleven-year-old boy was Yannis Kisannis, who would become Greece's foreign affairs minister forty-two years later, be accused of treason and collaboration with the Nazis, and pen his memoirs, entitled *Ta Viomata Mu (What I Saw)*, where he wrote wistfully of his childhood days and with frank intensity about the horrors of the plague of 1901.

By now both the Governor and Monsieur George had so often witnessed how the plague could drive people to think and behave in strange and inexplicable ways that they did not take much notice of the black-clad mother's actions. On the other hand, they were later quite startled by a man who threw himself onto the dirt road in front of the armored landau and demanded—undeterred by the guards' batons—to be told where his wife and sons had disappeared to. The Governor was determined that anyone who openly defied the doctors' and Quarantine Regiment's instructions, and did the opposite of what they were told to do, should be punished for it. There should be no mercy shown to

people who protested when their homes were being disinfected, evacuated, or boarded up, nor to anyone who attempted to attack the doctors
or purposely infect them.

Suddenly, they were shaken by a deafening bang. They quickly surmised that someone must have thrown a large rock or a block of wood
at the roof of the landau. The experienced coachman Zekeriya sped the
horses up before turning left into Rose Fountain Road and coming to
a stop. There was a silence. They listened to the horses' rapid breathing.
The Governor did not step out of the carriage this time. A few days
earlier, they had been passing near the Rifai lodge in the Vavla neighborhood when some children had thrown rocks at the carriage and run
away before the guards in the carriage behind the landau could catch
them. In his five years as governor, it was the first time anything like this
had ever happened.

"That is what you get when you associate with sheikhs and holy
men," said Consul George knowingly.

When the patients and doctors in the gardens of the Hamidiye Hospital spotted the Governor Pasha's landau, with his guards riding in the
carriage behind it, they waited expectantly for it to stop, but instead
the horses hastened past, as if to escape from that most ravaged and
contaminated area of the city. At the fork in the road approaching the
Germe neighborhood, Coachman Zekeriya chose the wider upper road.

"I heard that Chef Fotiadi of the Hotel Regard à l'Ouest died after
running away to his village," said the consul, as if he were speaking of
an old friend.

The news saddened the Governor. The consul and the Governor used
to have lunch once a month at Fotiadi's hotel restaurant on a rocky cliff
past the Stone Quarry, amicably talking their way through the island's
various afflictions. They would discuss all kinds of issues together, from
the city's lampposts to its limited and constantly overflowing sewage
system (which seemed to do as much harm as it did good), from the
illegalities taking place at the docks to the Greek consul Leonidis's minor
swindles, from the trade in Mingherian stone to the complexities of rose
cultivation. During this time, the Governor's admiration for the British
consul had grown enormously.

That had been three years ago. Back then, the island—so far removed
from wars, epidemics, and nationalist struggles of any sort—was such a

peaceful place that the kinds of friendships and political discussions we wouldn't even dream of having today were perfectly possible there.

On their way to the Çite neighborhood, a young man whose purple gown identified him as a disciple of the Halifiye sect stepped to the side of the road when he saw the landau approaching, and held the amulet he wore around his neck toward the carriage, tweezered between his middle and index finger just as the sheikhs always instructed. As the landau drove past, the consul and the Governor saw the young man's lips twitching, and understood that he must be reciting some kind of prayer.

They first noticed the smell just after the landau had overtaken the young man in the purple gown. It was the smell of corpses, which even after nine weeks the citizens of Arkaz had not yet become accustomed to. It wasn't always there. Sometimes it could be so pungent that it would burn in people's throats. Other times all they could smell was the scent of roses. Only when someone died inside a house or a garden or somewhere unexpected, and their body lay undiscovered for a time, would the smell of the corpse waft through the air, and even then it depended on what direction the wind was blowing from. The doctors who examined those corpses that were found only because of the stench they had been emitting would sometimes find that the person had died somewhere else before their body was moved there, or that they hadn't died of plague at all but had been beaten or stabbed to death. People would die alone while hiding from the plague and the world in some invisible, untraceable recess they had so proudly made their own, and only be discovered when their corpses began to reek. Cooks, maids, watchmen, and married couples would break into empty homes that had been boarded up and abandoned after their owners had fled the outbreak, and die in there with no one finding out for days.

As they entered Çite, they saw a boy sobbing his heart out. He seemed completely disinterested in everything around him, including the Governor's landau. It was such a heartrending scene that the Pasha was tempted to stop the carriage and console the child. The consul felt the same sorrow too. The Greek community had recently converted an empty neoclassical building behind the Marianna Theodoropoulos Girls' Secondary School into a kind of orphanage housing seventeen children (according to the latest numbers the Governor had learned) whose parents had died of the disease. In the Muslim neighborhoods of

Çite, Germe, and Bayırlar, more than eighty children had already been orphaned. They were usually taken in by uncles and aunts and any other family and relatives they might have in the city, or even by neighbors and acquaintances.

But there were also some children from the Muslim community with no relatives who could foster them after their own families were locked up in the Castle's isolation facility as confirmed or suspected cases, and so the Governor had ended up placing nearly twenty Muslim children in the care of the Greek orphanage too. A week later, the Governor had been enraged to learn from his informants stationed near the Kadiri lodge that the disciples of that sect had drawn up a petition protesting the Christianization of Muslim children in the Greek school. The Governor ordered the Kadiri dervish who had authored the petition—a strange, bespectacled young man—to be put in prison for infringing quarantine regulations. But in the meantime, the bespectacled dervish had disappeared, and upon suggestion from the Chief of Charitable Trusts, Doctor Nuri had proposed that the old Venetian-era building on Sapling Street in the Camiönü neighborhood be converted into a home reserved for orphaned Muslim children. This had left the Pasha feeling even more unsure about what to do, for like all Ottoman bureaucrats, and especially all Ottoman governors, he had always stood by the "unquestionable axiom" that the moment the state began to make distinctions between Christians and Muslims when providing the services and protection it owed all its citizens, it would be the beginning of the end of the Ottoman Empire. With preparations for the Muslim orphanage taking longer than expected, the Pasha ended up sending even more children to the Greek orphanage.

These children's fight for survival, hiding in empty homes and living off stolen walnuts and lemons and oranges they plucked off the trees, is a subject as vivid as it is poignant. The elementary- and middle-school textbooks published on the island now tend to describe the touching adventures of these plague orphans in an idealized light influenced by a kind of romantic nationalism, and although most of the kids in these children's gangs would perish in the outbreak, their stories are told today as if the plague never touched them at all. Schoolbooks in the 1930s would portray these poor children as the oldest, purest, and truest descendants of the Mingherians who had arrived from the environs of the Aral Sea thousands of years ago. They would come to be known colloquially as the "Immortal Children," a name which was later adopted by the Mingherian Scouts Association until, at the request of the World Organization of the Scout Movement, it was changed to the "Young Roses."

The children who had attacked the landau were protesting the fate of one of their peers, who, despite having no buboes, had been put into isolation because he had developed a fever and had eventually caught the plague in the isolation facility itself. For these children, the most horrifying aspect of the plague was not even the fact that it could kill their mothers or fathers or both at the same time, leaving them completely alone in the world. Rather, according to the reports the Pasha had received from both Muslim and Christian neighborhoods, it was when they saw the disease transform their sweet, loving mothers into wretched, desperate, selfish animals that these children truly lost their minds. Some of them would give up on the world altogether and run as far away as they could, as if a demon had taken possession of their bodies.

As the landau veered up and to the right into the Turunçlar neighborhood, the coachman did what the soldiers of the Quarantine Regiment always did and pressed a cloth against his nose. The Governor closed the window. The stench had become so bad over the past three days that some local families had left the neighborhood and gone to stay with friends. A soft, tentative breeze blowing from the west had been carrying the smell all over the city and right into people's nostrils, including the Pasha's when he sat in the Governor's Office (and Princess Pakize's as she busied herself with her letters), and people were getting exasperated. There was even a rumor that the smell was coming from a secret mass grave, though there was no truth in this at all.

The carriages stopped when they spotted a group of municipal officials and soldiers from the Quarantine Regiment gathered in the distance. When Doctor Nuri—who was there too—saw the guards form a ring around one of the carriages, he deduced that the Governor must be inside it and was taken aback, when he hopped on, to find the amiable face and rotund figure of the British consul sitting in there too.

The Governor was aware that they already knew each other, but he made the usual introductions anyway. They listened to Doctor Nuri's news: they had just searched an old wooden home where they had discovered two people, who must have died in each other's arms at least twenty days ago, wedged in the beams between two stories. It was hard to tell whether they had been a married couple or lovers or something else. With so many people believing that the disease could spread through smell as well as touch, the task of retrieving the corpses had fallen to a brave young recruit to the Quarantine Regiment named Hayri.

When the news spread through the city that the bodies of two unidentified young people had been found inside an empty house, anyone who had been looking for a missing sibling or a son began to flock to Turunçlar. The Doctor and Prince Consort took the Governor to the house's back garden, sheltered from the sun by lemon trees. The stench made the lemons with their corrugated skins look like dead fruit hanging among the leaves.

"A sanitary cordon will not be enough to guard this place, Pasha, nor will sentries and soldiers. We need to burn it to the ground!" said Doctor Nuri in a burst of uncontrollable emotion. "There is no amount of phenol that could disinfect it now. Even I think the plague can spread from this kind of place regardless of whether there are rats and fleas around."

"You said Bonkowski Pasha was murdered because he was planning to have some streets burned down."

"I was merely speculating about the killer's possible motive," said Doctor Nuri. "We have no other choice here if we want to get rid of this contamination swiftly."

Some historians have since argued that it had been "wrong," if not even futile, to burn this building down. But when the same pandemic had spread across India, in Bombay, and particularly in the countryside, many of the ramshackle homes, the crumbling buildings, the hovels, and the dumping grounds where the plague had taken hold had been burned to the ground without a moment's hesitation. Quarantine officials in Kashmir, in Singapore, and in China's Kansu region would burn down buildings, whole streets, and even entire villages to prevent the outbreak from reaching the bigger cities. Indeed, in these places, the sight of the red and yellow flames and black smoke of a fire rising over wide plains and arid, destitute vastnesses would often signal the approach of plague.

The Governor Pasha went to speak to Quarantine Master Nikos, ordering him to vacate the surroundings of the wooden building and carefully burn it all down. They decided that the best people for this job would be the valiant firemen and Quarantine Regiment soldiers who were on duty at the incineration pit and had them summoned down to the Turunçlar neighborhood from the hill above it. They kept close to the armored landau, where they could talk more freely. Some among the crowd assembled farther down the street had spotted the Governor and were trying to approach him.

The Governor got back into the landau and sat across from the consul. The smell had seeped into the carriage too. It was impossible for two corpses to be causing such a stench. Just as the carriage was about to set off again, the door opened. They took Doctor Nuri back on board too.

As the armored landau gently swayed toward the State Hall, Consul George, the Governor, and Doctor Nuri were silent for a time. The Governor had crossed his arms over his chest and was looking down at his hands as if to say he had seen enough for the day. The consul was gazing at the streets outside the window, but the expression frozen on his face seemed to exclaim, "I cannot believe the scale of the calamity I have just witnessed!"

The landau was on the stretch of road between the Rifai lodge and the New Mosque when the sea appeared between the streets through the window on the vehicle's right-hand side, and the Governor briefly squinted at the water as if he might be able to spot one of the warships there. "Your opinion is of exceptional value to us, Monsieur George!" he said. "What must we do here on the island for these European warships to withdraw from our seas and lift the blockade?"

"As I submitted to you in your office earlier, Your Excellency," the consul began, speaking like an old friend and a humble diplomat, "the passage of plague patients to Europe must stop."

"We have taken every precaution Istanbul asked for, and even some they didn't ask for. You should tell your people that we are doing all that needs to be done, and with the utmost integrity and commitment, but still the number of deaths is not slowing," said the Governor.

"Should you consider opening the Telegraph Office again, the help and support you need will come. But there is another matter I would like to speak of. That purple-robed young man in the Çite neighborhood . . .

Why is he so hostile to you and to us all, Pasha? It is plain to see that if it were up to him, he would flout every quarantine rule, and even destroy us if he could."

"That is Sheikh Hamdullah's fiery young disciple Halil!" said the Pasha. "They are the worst of the lot. Everyone is always talking about other charlatan sheikhs and their inconsequential prayer sheets. Why won't anyone come out and say that it is really Sheikh Hamdullah who is behind all of this? Why do they never speak his name in public? The Quarantine Regiment is displeased that I have put their commander in prison!" This was the first time in the history of Mingheria that someone had used the word "commander" in this way. "But they are the only ones who can subdue the sheikh and his men. That is why I must set the Major free now and let him return to his soldiers," the Governor continued.

"You will have heard that the sheikh has caught the plague!" said Consul George, not objecting to the plan to release the Major.

"What?" said Governor Sami Pasha. "Sheikh Hamdullah has the plague?"

As soon as he had returned to the State Hall, the Governor freed the Major and had him summoned to his office, where he advised him to be careful not to let the people's support go to his head, to stay out of sight, and not to stray too far from his soldiers.

CHAPTER 45

The Governor was surprised and even a little shaken to hear that Sheikh Hamdullah had caught the plague. During his early years as governor, he had developed a friendship with the sheikh, whom he held in far greater esteem than the needy, faithful throngs who gathered around him. It is possible that he secretly believed in the sheikh's wisdom and transcendence too. Having probed around for more information and learned that the sheikh was rumored to be afflicted by some kind of illness but was refusing treatment, saying he had surrendered his life "to fate and divine providence," the Governor sent the sheikh a letter. He wrote that he had heard about the sheikh's illness, but that the Sultan's most esteemed plague doctor was in the city now and could immediately examine and treat him. To act as intermediary, the Governor summoned the old Ottoman Urgancızâde family's eldest son Tevfik, who owned a ship company, and whom the sheikh and the Governor used to spend time with when they became friends five years ago.

The next morning an old dervish with a round white beard and a tall felt hat (his name was Nimetullah Effendi, but he insisted on being addressed as "Regent") came down from the lodge and delivered the sheikh's response to the State Hall clerks. The Governor had come to his desk early that day, and when he read the sheikh's note informing him in perfectly neat handwriting that he would be glad to accept the offer and honored to receive the Doctor and Prince Consort's visit, he felt as exhilarated as if he had won the final, decisive victory against the plague.

But the sheikh did set one condition. The soldiers of the Quarantine Regiment who had sullied the Halifiye sect's sacred (the sheikh had used the word "pristine") treasure of wool and felt must never set foot inside the lodge again.

The Governor accepted this condition. He discussed the matter with Quarantine Master Nikos and Doctor Nuri, who had just arrived.

"Now that he realizes he might die, the sheikh has understood how foolish it is to avoid doctors," said the Governor.

"Not everyone who becomes infected is bound to die!" replied Doctor Nuri.

"If that's the case, then why did he write back to us?"

"Pasha, I have witnessed all kinds of self-proclaimed sheikhs troubling governors and local chiefs in our provincial towns only to make a name for themselves. These people will actively provoke confrontations with the authorities, make a great fuss, then make a ceremonious show of reconciliation, all for the sake of showing their benighted disciples how exceptional and important they are. There are many sheikhs, many lodges and sects around. It is essential for them to make sure their names are heard and their presence is known."

There were twenty-eight Muslim sects in Arkaz alone. This was a lot for a city with a population of only twenty-five thousand—half of whom were Christian. In the years following the Ottoman conquest of the island, these religious sects could be effective in converting Christians to Islam, and so the imperial government in Istanbul had provided nearly all of them with some measure of support.

From venerable scholars to utter scoundrels, there were all sorts of sheikhs in Mingheria now, some pious, some book-loving, some unerringly dour, and all wearing a different color of robe. When a Mingherian-born soldier managed to rise through the ranks in Istanbul and become a pasha or even a vizier, he would often endow the proceeds from his holdings across the Ottoman Empire to one of the sects on the island (as the Mingherian Mahmut Pasha—who had financed the construction of Arkaz's New Mosque—had also done). Sometimes people who happened to harbor a fondness for the island, and who had managed to distinguish themselves in a particular field until they became quite wealthy, would send gifts and gold from Istanbul to Mingheria for the sheikh of whichever lodge the government felt most aligned to, or perhaps donate the income from an olive oil press or two Greek fishing villages or the rent from a couple of shops in the city to fund the construction of a new lodge or the conversion of a disused mansion into new dervishes' quarters. But when the Ottoman Empire began to lose its possessions in Europe, the Balkans, and around the Mediterranean Sea, these sources of income from beyond the confines of the island dried up. Left to fend for themselves, some of these lodges became impoverished and soon turned into sanctuaries for homeless people, paupers, and even thieves and ruffians, until eventually the Governor and the Chief of Charitable Trusts would have to step in to ensure they did not fall into a state of total disrepair.

Shortly after taking the throne, Abdul Hamid—who knew how influential the religious sects and dervish lodges scattered all over the Empire could be, and monitored their activities closely—had presented the Mevlevi lodge, the island's wealthiest, oldest, and most powerful sect, with a Theta wall clock, but not long after that, he fell out with the Mevlevis' leader in Istanbul (guilty, in the Sultan's eyes, of being too friendly with the reformist statesman Mithat Pasha), and sought to assuage his anxieties by endorsing other sects too, such as the Kadiri and the Halifiye.

It was thanks to this support that the sheikh of the Halifiye sect now had enough power and popularity to either bolster or undermine the quarantine effort. Before Doctor Nuri went to see the sheikh, there was a meeting held in the Governor Pasha's office. The Major, whose confidence had only increased after the raid on the Telegraph Office and his spell in prison, eagerly supplied an account of how the lodge—which he had so frequently visited as a child—had come to be established. He told Doctor Nuri a long story of how thirty years ago he had sat on a previous sheikh's lap and pulled at the old man's thick white beard.

In that moment, the Governor, who had been watching the view of the city from his window, pointed out that there were clouds of black smoke rising from the hills in the distance, near the New Mosque as well as the Bektaşi and other lodges. They all gathered around the window to try and work out what might be happening. A clerk then informed them that this was the house in Turunçlar which they had decided to burn the day before—the one where the pair of welded corpses had gone to hide. There was so much smoke that it looked like the whole neighborhood was burning rather than just one small building (even if it was made of timber). The wood was so dry that it had burned up quickly, making

Nights of Plague

crunching sounds, sending flames towering into the sky, and issuing an expanding cloud of black smoke that everyone would later interpret as a bad omen.

The people of Mingheria had become accustomed to seeing plumes of blue smoke rising periodically from the incineration pit on the hill, but these new yellow and orange flames—glowing to the west this time—with their dark shadow of smoke indicated that things had taken a turn for the worse. Finding it difficult to believe that a single house could generate so much smoke as to cover the sun and darken the sky, the Governor concluded that the fire must have spread, and stepped out of his office and onto the terrace. He was sure the smoke must also be visible from the warships the Great Powers had sent to besiege the island. The whole world must be looking at them now with the same pity and condescension it reserved to the rest of the Ottoman Empire—these poor Mingherians who couldn't reply to telegrams, couldn't stop the outbreak, and couldn't even put a fire out.

As a historian we should like to note that in this case Governor Sami Pasha's intuition was correct: thanks to a journalist stationed on the *Amiral Baudin,* the ship the French had sent to join the blockade, the news that the island of Mingheria—already surrounded by a maritime cordon and trapped in the jaws of the plague—was now also aflame was reported in the following week's edition of the Parisian publication *Le Petit Parisien,* accompanied by a romantic and fantastical full-page illustration.

When he arrived at the Halifiye lodge, Doctor Nuri was greeted at the entrance by the regent with the felt hat and led to a two-story wooden construction near the edge of the compound. There were no scholars or disciples around. The door to the wooden building opened up, revealing a stocky man with a distracted look on his face. There was something he was trying to remember, but he couldn't, and so he wore an odd smile instead. Doctor Nuri understood that this must be the sheikh. He looked pale and tired, but there was no bubo on his neck.

"I should like to kiss your blessed hand, Sheikh Effendi, but I must desist in light of quarantine regulations."

"That is as it should be!" said the sheikh. "Like His Royal Highness Sultan Mahmud, your wife the Princess's great-grandfather, I too have great faith in quarantines. I shudder at the mere thought that I should be responsible for passing the disease on to anyone, let alone a royal consort such as yourself. Three days ago I was sitting in this very room—just like this, Your Excellency—when I fell down and fainted. I myself was quite delighted with what I saw of the spiritual realm while I remained unconscious, but my dear dervishes were worried, overcome with anguish at the thought that their sheikh might be ill, and so the rumors began to spread, and people started saying, 'The sheikh has caught the plague.' But I did not alert the doctors. Though I am currently in the midst of a solitary contemplation exercise I began ten days ago, I must say I am nevertheless profoundly moved by His Excellency the Governor Pasha's insistence that you should visit me. I have offered many grateful prayers to the almighty Allah, our holy Prophet Muhammad, the Sultan, and our governor for sending the Ottoman Empire's most renowned quarantine doctor—and a Muslim too!—right to my doorstep. But I have one question, and one condition."

"Certainly, Your Excellency."

"What is the meaning of having a house only two streets away from our lodge burned down like kindling, ostensibly for quarantine purposes, with so much smoke that even the sun is obscured, and all of this happening just before you come to visit me here?"

"That is a coincidence."

"Was this place not burned down by the same Quarantine Regiment who sprayed Lysol on us, and the army major who commands them all? If the purpose was to say 'You have the plague too, so you'll be next,' I am sure the Governor Pasha's clerks could have told us as much."

"Of course not . . . The Governor Pasha's regard for you knows no bounds."

"Be that as it may, before you begin your medical examination I should like to acquaint you with our lodge's one-hundred-year history, so that you may understand why we will never be infected with this monstrous pestilence, and why you will never have reason to burn us to the ground," said Sheikh Hamdullah. "The Halifiye lodge in Mingheria was founded by my grandfather Sheikh Nurullah Effendi, who was sent here from the Kadiri lodge in Istanbul's Tophane district," he declared, starting at the very beginning. The people who had invited the sheikh's grandfather to the island had intended for him to take charge of the Kadiri dervishes in the Kadirler neighborhood and push out those devotees who were flouting the sect's teachings by sticking spikes and skewers all over their bodies in accordance with Rifai rituals. But when the Rifais, backed by the Governor at the time, refused to give up their rituals, Nurullah Effendi and the dissenters who had brought him to Mingheria decided to leave the lodge altogether and established a new sect of their own in nearby Germe.

Sheikh Hamdullah continued with his story: Just like his father before him, he had grown up right here, in this lodge and on these streets. He had gone to Istanbul to study at the Rumelian Mehmet Pasha Mosque madrasa, which was where he had first developed an interest in religious matters, poetry, and history. Despite his father the sheikh's exhortations, he did not return to the island for many years. In Istanbul he married the daughter of a poor family of migrants from Rumelia, taught at a small madrasa, published a poetry collection entitled *Aurora*, and worked for a time at the Karaköy customs office. He even caught a distant glimpse of Abdul Hamid at the Yıldız Palace once, during one of those public processions that were held every time sultans attended Friday prayers. (At this point the sheikh paused in his account to recite several lengthy prayers for the Sultan's health.) When he returned to Mingheria seventeen years ago to settle his late father's estate, he sensed on his first night back that he was there to stay, and having had his books and other possessions sent down from Istanbul, he had since devoted himself to worship, spiritual contemplation, and the affairs of the lodge he had come to lead.

It had been an animated account, and now the sheikh was tired. "Come, let me show you our most secret treasures!" he said.

Doctor Nuri followed the sheikh—who could only walk if he was leaning on one of his disciples—out into the garden, which had darkened in the shadow of the smoke. As they approached the lodge's main building, the doctor saw that his visit was being meticulously observed by the whole lodge, from its newest acolytes to its oldest dervishes, with the same suspicion with which they were watching the fire burn a few streets away. The sheikh showed his illustrious guest the sleeping chamber (which he'd requested be painted blue) to the left of the sitting room, where the lodge's sacred one-winged Mingherian beetle was held captive. Just like those Mingherians who could never leave their island, this beetle would not escape even if you left the door open. After this they went to view the seclusion chamber. The sheikh told the story of a dervish who had dreamed, on the last night of his forty-day solitary retreat there, of a ship that had sunk to the floor of the ocean, only for the same ship to appear the next day in the waters off the Arab Lighthouse to take the dervish to China, where he would go on to establish the newest branch of the Halifiye sect.

The sheikh showed off his grandfather's staff made out of date palm, which looked "just like our holy Prophet's staff," and his father's staff, "as hard as steel" and decorated with mother-of-pearl inlays along the handle.

As they crossed a row of cells, each with its own young dervish—some bald, some with very pink lips, some rather pale, some looking stern and others more gentle—standing like a sentry at the door, Doctor Nuri realized that the plague would spread quickly around here.

They walked underneath a walnut tree as tall as four men would be and entered the lodge's newest building, which smelled of timber and varnish. The sheikh opened a wooden trunk in a corner of the room and showed Doctor Nuri the green, purple, and gray hats—also known as crowns—his predecessors had worn, their yellow-and-blue-striped ceremonial *tanoura* skirts, the "submission" stones they had broken off Mount Sacrifice in the north of the island for the dervishes and the sect's disciples to carry as badges around their necks, and the twelve-knotted belt every sheikh could wear as he wished. These were the sect's most sacred heirlooms, and if even so much as a drop of black Lysol and quarantine poison were to touch them, they would die. Everyone else would die with them too—down to the last dervish and disciple.

As he described each object, the sheikh spoke in constant overstatements and double meanings, and even though it was obvious that he was not really upset or particularly angry, he made such an elaborate show of being upset and angry that Doctor Nuri began to feel that same hopelessness and guilt he usually experienced when faced with uneducated patients in rural villages who did not even know how to explain their symptoms.

They entered a room full of books and smelling of lemon blossoms, where the sheikh spread out a few volumes, some handwritten scrolls, several pages of old, yellowing papers, and various pamphlets, and introduced the main topic he wished to discuss, informing the doctor that he had begun to compose a poem in rhyming couplets wherein he hoped to address the most commonly asked questions about the plague, and to discuss and explain what the most appropriate Islamic approach to the disease should be.

"On the subject of plague and infectious diseases, there are two views within the Islamic tradition that to this day remain vehemently at odds," said the sheikh. "The first of these postulates that the plague is brought about by Allah, and not only is it futile to try and escape it, it is as difficult and dangerous as trying to escape one's fate. Indeed our Prophet Muhammad did say, as do the Hurufis, that 'those who proclaim that the plague is contagious are no better than people who look for signs in the movements of birds and owls and snakes and hope to find some kind of meaning.' When the plague arrives, the best thing you can do is to meekly withdraw and wait for it to pass, without showing yourself to anyone, and without letting your soul be tainted. Europeans will misguidedly call these people fatalists. The second view accepts that the plague is contagious. If they wish to survive, Muslims and Christians alike must escape from that disease-ridden place, get away from that air and from those people. This conclusion is supported by our Prophet's words as reported in the Hadith: 'One should run from the leper as one would run from a lion.' But once the plague is among us, it is no good locking doors or trying to flee. At that point there is nothing else to do but to seek refuge in the mercy of Allah."

There were six or seven people hanging around the door and listening to their conversation. The Doctor and Prince Consort could see that every word that was said here would soon be repeated—accurately or otherwise—among shopkeepers in the Old and New Markets, between consuls, clerks, and journalists, and in the reports the Sultan's informants sent to Istanbul.

"Come and look at this room, now!" said the sheikh, pushing another door ajar.

The Doctor and Prince Consort saw three young disciples sitting at a weaving loom, surrounded by different-colored skeins of spun wool and several types of fabric.

"As instructed by my grandfather Sheikh Nurullah, founder of this lodge, we make all our own underwear, shirts, jackets, cardigans, and skullcaps using wool we spin ourselves and our own fabrics and linens, all cut and sewn the way our forefathers did, and dyed using roots and Mingherian herbs and powders from China."

A young disciple who had been listening to their exchange opened various wardrobes and linen cupboards where the Doctor and Prince Consort saw shirts, jackets, pillows, heaps of raw wool, and fabrics in many colors. Struggling to catch his breath, the sheikh continued:

"Now tell me, what conscience is this that could countenance coming here, pouring Lysol all over our precious wool, and turning our most sacred patrimony into a pile of mud?"

Doctor Nuri did not reply, for he could tell that these words had been spoken mostly for the benefit of those who had gathered around to listen, and that the sheikh made it a habit of half jokingly and half seriously scolding everyone around him.

"Even the Muscovites in the War of Ninety-Three wouldn't stoop so low as to come at us with Lysol!" he added in a burst of genuine fury, then suddenly doubled over and cried "Oh, God!" He would have fallen to the floor if not for the two disciples who had immediately rushed to his side.

"I'm all right!" he snapped at the men who had linked their arms with his, but although he had spoken again in his sternest voice, it did not escape Doctor Nuri's notice that the sheikh was clearly used to walking with a pair of dervishes he could lean on.

They returned to the first door, and as Doctor Nuri prepared for the medical examination, the sheikh readily removed his gown, shirt, and undergarments, and began to wait.

"Did you experience any vomiting before or after your fall?"

"No, Doctor."

"Any fever?"

"No."

Doctor Nuri took the pharmacist Edhem Pertev's bubo ointment from his bag and pulled it out of its box, then fingered the metal container where he kept his syringes. He picked up a small green bottle to check that the purple opium pills were still there. He aimlessly opened and closed the jar of tincture he'd sourced from the Istikamet Pharmacy and a box of Bayer aspirin (first introduced ten years before) he had bought in France and only used if it was really necessary, then took out the concentrated Lysol he kept in a purple bottle like some kind of elixir, rubbed it meticulously over his fingers with sterilized cotton balls, and finally approached the sheikh.

He could see that the sheikh was uneasy lying there naked. His bare arms, narrow chest, and slender neck were startlingly white and childlike.

Doctor Nuri examined the sheikh from head to toe as if he were an old man who couldn't articulate his woes. His bright, pink tongue showed no signs of the discoloration often seen in plague patients. Using a spoon to push the restless muscle down, he checked the sheikh's tonsils. (The plague always "struck" the tonsils in some way, and at first many doctors who could not recognize the disease would mistake it for diphtheria.) There was no redness in his eyes. Doctor Nuri checked his pulse twice; it was normal. He did not have a fever; there was no sweating nor any sign of confusion. Doctor Nuri used his stethoscope to listen carefully to the sheikh's tired chest. His heartbeat was erratic; his lungs were full. Every time the cold, metallic surface of the stethoscope touched the sheikh's pale skin, Doctor Nuri noticed that he would shiver a little.

"Take a deep breath, please!"

After peering inside the sheikh's hairy ears, the doctor pressed his fingers slowly and gently over the glands in his neck to check for any pain or hardness. He examined the patient's armpits in the same way too, carefully probing them with his fingertips until he was satisfied there was no swelling or hardening there either.

After he had poked and prodded at the naked sheikh's groin area too, the Doctor and Prince Consort went back to his bag, and as he disinfected his hands, he said: "Everything is fine. You are not ill."

"Allaahumma innee as'alukal-af wal'aafiyata wal'aakhirati!" the sheikh intoned. "Tell our Governor Pasha and all the consuls that I am in good health, and that our lodge remains clear of disease. The rumors about my supposed illness are being spread by those who seek to sow discord between me and the Governor Pasha. These people want to see our whole lodge quarantined; they want us all taken away and locked up in isolation in the Castle's courtyards; they wish us nothing but harm."

"The Governor Pasha would never wish harm upon you or your lodge."

"I am sure that is true!"

"But there are some whose behavior provides excuses for those who do. The sheikhs of the smaller sects, these people who concoct false prayer sheets and wave them around to hold off the plague demon . . . That is the kind of thing which erodes the public's trust in quarantine measures and people's willingness to submit to restrictions."

"Not every sheikh will listen to me," said Sheikh Hamdullah. "Some are mere acquaintances, and most of them wish me ill."

"Your Holiness, I am also here in the capacity of ambassador for our Governor Pasha. He would like you and the leader of the Greek congregation, Archbishop Constantinos Effendi, to come out onto the State Hall balcony and send a message to the whole island that they must obey quarantine rules. The Pasha has released Ramiz."

"Archbishop Constantinos Effendi is a poet, like me," said the sheikh. "I had promised to present him with a copy of *Aurora* once it is printed in Mingheria too. I would gladly participate in the Governor Pasha's assembly! But I have one condition."

"Whatever it is, I shall relay it to the Governor immediately and insist upon its acceptance," said Doctor Nuri, picking up his bag.

"I must deliver the sermon at the New Mosque this Friday! The Chief of Charitable Trusts and the authorities in Istanbul have already confirmed their approval. But if the Quarantine Committee were to issue a ban, for fear the mosque should become too crowded, that would break many Muslim hearts and turn them against quarantine officials."

"There is nothing we fear more than Your Holiness and his supporters turning against quarantine."

"Doctor Nuri, do you know why, more than anything else, I would like to see your quarantine effort succeed?" said Sheikh Hamdullah, frowning. He had put his underwear, shirt, and jacket back on, as well as his sect's special skullcap. "For the past four hundred years, the introduction of quarantine regulations has been protecting Christians in Europe from disease; if Muslims continue to reject quarantine and refuse to embrace modern methods, they will die in ever-greater numbers, until they are left alone and outnumbered in this world."

CHAPTER 46

T he Governor was delighted to learn that Sheikh Hamdullah had
agreed to join the leaders of the island's Muslim and Christian
communities in addressing the public from the State Hall balcony, and immediately began negotiating the timing and other details
of this event.

The sheikh was represented in these talks by the dervish with the
felt hat, Nimetullah Effendi. The negotiations were intense, with the
Governor Pasha noting that Nimetullah Effendi was "more consummate
a diplomat" than even the consuls were, and indeed "a tougher nut to
crack," for unlike the consuls, who were motivated purely by greed and
self-interest, the dervish with the felt hat was an "idealist." At the same
time the Governor was also busy arguing with the consuls over when the
Post Office would open again, and trying to work out whether the Great
Powers really were planning on sending their soldiers to the island under
the pretext of stopping the outbreak.

Ever since the telegraph lines had gone down, the consuls had lost
much of their influence and authority. Every day the Governor saw how
the interruption of telegraph services had provided an invaluable opportunity to enforce quarantine properly and bring some form of discipline
to the city. Cases of insubordination against the Quarantine Regiment
had also diminished since the raid. Even inveterate agitators who normally questioned the authorities' every decision had since gone quiet,
waiting to see what would happen next.

The Governor eventually settled on a mutually acceptable plan
for the public events and gatherings set to take place two days later:
on Friday, the twenty-eighth of June, after Friday prayers and Sheikh
Hamdullah's sermon, the sheikh and his congregation would convene at

the State Hall Square, whereupon the sheikh would join the Governor and the other community leaders on the balcony to address the crowds, urging them to respect quarantine measures and making statements of fellowship and unity. Once these two assemblies were concluded, there would be a further ceremony at the Post Office, after which the telegraph line would be restored.

Not once in his five years as governor had Sami Pasha ever spoken to the public from the State Hall balcony, though there had been moments when he would have liked to. Abdul Hamid did not approve of governors who felt they were important enough to put themselves between the Sultan and his subjects. The public address was not a political convention the Ottomans were particularly familiar with either. The Governor instructed the registry clerk to make posters announcing the assembly, with the same format and font size they had used in their notices informing the public of quarantine regulations. As they feverishly planned the details of how the crowds should gather when he addressed them from the balcony on Friday, and where and how far apart the consuls, the journalists, and the photographers should stand, the exhilarated Governor stepped out onto the terrace.

By the time he had walked back inside, there was a new telegram waiting on his desk. The municipal code breaker had deciphered it and, realizing that it was important, had immediately placed it on the Governor's desk.

The Governor couldn't help but notice that the telegram was from the palace. His heart sped up. It could be bad news. Perhaps he shouldn't even look at it! But he couldn't stop himself and read the telegram's deciphered contents anyway.

The first thing he learned was that he had been relieved of his duties as governor of Mingheria. He held his breath. He had been given a new position as governor of Aleppo. A sudden pain took hold of his chest. They were giving him just ten days to go directly to Aleppo without passing by Istanbul. He read the telegram again, his heart beating even faster. The message implied that there was some kind of unrest taking place in Aleppo.

It was only when he read the telegram for the third time that the Governor realized he was being punished. His new salary was to be two-thirds of his current one. This despite the fact that Aleppo was a much-larger and more populous state, with the provinces of Urfa and Maraş tied to it too.

What would become of Marika? He had thought about this so many times; even if she agreed to convert to Islam and marry him, it would cause a diplomatic scandal, with all the ambassadors and consuls protesting that even after the Tanzimat reforms, Ottoman pashas were still forcing the prettiest Christian women in the states they governed to convert to Islam so that they could take them as their second and third wives and lock them away in their harems. In any case, Marika couldn't possibly come with him to that distant, scorpion-infested land!

The more he read the telegram, the more Sami Pasha (we are not sure whether to call him Governor anymore) realized that he could not accept the truth. Istanbul must have made some kind of mistake! It was impossible for him to get to Aleppo that quickly anyway. That alone was proof that this transfer (and dismissal) was an error. Did those who expected him to travel to Aleppo within ten days not know that nobody was allowed off the island without quarantining for five days first? What would become of Marika?

He tried to look positively at the decision: yes, he had been removed from his current post, but he had also been given a new one at the same time. At his most aggrieved and mistrustful, Abdul Hamid had been known to teach dismissed governors a lesson by leaving them in limbo and without salary for a time, only announcing much later where they were to be posted next. This had not happened now. Tyrannical though he might be, Abdul Hamid had refrained from putting Sami Pasha through that. He remembered how ruthlessly everyone in the Sublime Porte had laughed at the story of poor Mustafa Hayri Pasha, whose very heart had stopped beating the day he had finally received the telegram he had been expecting for years, dismissing him from his post. At least Sami Pasha's situation was not quite as bad.

Sami Pasha soon concluded that the best course of action was to accept the new appointment but delay its execution. One day, when they realized that he had heroically stayed behind to continue his fight against the plague, they would reward him with a First-Class Order of Mecidiye. As an avid reader of journals like the Ottoman *Malûmat* or even the French *Moniteur des Consulats* which arrived on ships from Istanbul and published the details of every diplomatic posting, he was aware that new appointments *could* sometimes be canceled, that such a miracle was in fact possible. People with special connections to Abdul Hamid and the palace, and friends in the highest places, could arrange this kind of thing. Sometimes a governor would turn up at his new post only to find that the old governor had already been reinstated, and never left at all. With some luck, he might manage to do that too.

He pondered for a time whether Doctor and Prince Consort Nuri might telegraph Abdul Hamid or even the palace about him. But we know from Princess Pakize's letters that Sami Pasha never did manage to set his pride aside and make this request of Doctor Nuri.

Sami Pasha understood then that if he acted for a while as if nothing had happened, everything could remain exactly as it was. The only person on the island who knew he had been dismissed from his post was the municipal code breaker. If this clerk saw the Pasha's collected, unruffled demeanor, he might even think the order had been rescinded. Maybe the best thing to do in the two days until Friday was to pretend everything was normal. But immediately thereafter, Sami Pasha did the opposite of what he had been thinking and summoned the municipal code breaker to his office, where he told him that the encrypted telegram he had deciphered contained state secrets, and that if he were to betray those secrets, both Istanbul and Sami Pasha would see to it that he received the harshest possible punishment.

That day Sami Pasha saw neither Doctor Nuri nor Major Kâmil. Doctor Nikos came by, but the Pasha refused to meet him, and shut himself in his office. He felt that as long as he didn't see anyone, nobody would know that he had been dismissed. As a wedding present, his wife Esma's father Bahattin Pasha had given his promising son-in-law a pocket watch with two dials, one showing the time the European way and the other the Ottoman way. Whenever he felt lonely or dejected, Sami Pasha would hold this Belgian-made watch and feel in the palm of his hand that the world was a more bearable place. But as he sat in his office that day, he couldn't even muster the strength to do that.

The moment he'd read the telegram, he knew that he would only find serenity again by Marika's side. As Coachman Zekeriya drove him across the city, Sami Pasha looked at the dark, gloomy streets outside the carriage window and was nearly moved to tears, but managed to collect himself by reasoning that giving in to melancholy would be the same as

conceding defeat. He stepped off the carriage and walked with a dignified stride up to Marika's back door.

Inside her house, he was as poised and judicious as usual, behaving
with what he liked to think of in its melodious French form as *autorité*.
How beautiful Marika was; and not only was she beautiful, she was honest too. The Pasha immediately forgot about his dismissal.

Everyone was still talking about the two young people who had been
found dead in each other's arms and the black smoke that had risen
when the house had been burned down. "They're saying there must have
been other bodies in there for so much dark smoke to come out," said
Marika.

"People are always so quick to come up with these inventions."

"They say the fat in corpses will release black fumes."

"It does not befit you to speak of such horrors, and it afflicts me to
hear it," said the Pasha. But seeing that Marika had become upset, he
thought to make amends by telling her about a strange story he had read
a year ago in a translated article published in the journal *Servet-i Fünun
(Wealth of Knowledge),* and which he had miraculously recalled in that
very moment: "I heard that in some Asian faiths, they can judge how
sinful or innocent a person was, how virtuous or diabolical, by examining the color and thickness of the smoke from their burning corpse."

"You know so many things, my Pasha."

"But the things you know are more important! What else?"

"Ramiz is back in the city, Pasha. You must have heard about it too.
He has sworn an oath to exact revenge against those who have taken
Zeynep from him. It seems he is still madly in love with her. He did not
take this oath with his brother the sheikh, but in Sheikh Rıfkı Melul's
Rifai lodge instead."

"The Rifai lodge has had a peculiar resurgence during this
plague . . . But I suspect nobody else knows about this gathering."

"It seems that people are not being allowed into the Çite neighborhood unless they are carrying one of those rose-pink prayer sheets that
cross-eyed Şevket, sheikh of the Zaim lodge, has been issuing against the
plague. Migrant youths from Crete will stop you on the street and ask to
see your prayer sheet, and if you don't have one, they won't let you in."

"All very sensible!" said Sami Pasha. "Though that kind of thing
could only happen if we were not present in the area. There have been

one or two unlawful incidents of this sort, but we have nipped them in the bud. My spies and gendarmes would never let those curs get away with it."

"Darling Pasha, please don't be angry at me for telling you about these rumors. I am not the one who started them, and I don't believe most of them either."

"But there are a few that you do believe!"

"I always tell you when I do . . . Sometimes you believe them too, but you never say so because you're ashamed that you believe them, yet continue to do so anyway. Every time I report these rumors to you, I can tell which ones you believe just from the look on your face. They have begun smuggling people to Crete from the bays farther north of Pebble Cove."

"That I can believe. But I wonder how they have been evading the warships?"

"Some people are saying that Sheikh Hamdullah will not participate in the assembly at the State Hall on Friday, Pasha . . ."

"Why would that be?"

"Everyone knows the rumor that the sheikh has plague, and they've heard that the Prince Consort came from the State Hall to visit him."

"Let them hear it . . ."

"There's another rumor too. After the Prince Consort had come all that way to see him, it seems Sheikh Hamdullah imperiously told him 'The plague could never touch me.' This story is especially popular with children, but everyone else secretly believes it too. Children also love the Telegraph Raid and the Major."

"Do you know why all these rumors come about, Marika? Because the Greeks don't know the Muslims, and the Muslims don't know the Greeks. They don't even know what they do inside their churches and mosques. If we are to be one people, these rumors must end."

"There is also the question of the Prince Consort's visits to the herbalists. They are all scared of him. They're worried that he'll hand them over to the Chief Scrutineer, that they'll have their feet whipped in the dungeons like the cook's helpers and be taken to court for selling poison."

Sami Pasha quickly realized that of all the rumors he had just heard, the only one that had lodged itself in his mind and soul was Sheikh Hamdullah saying, "The plague could never touch me." He had first heard the claim that the sheikh was ill with plague from Consul George, and he had believed it immediately. Now he wondered if he had been caught in a trap. He thought dispiritedly that Doctor Nuri must have tricked him too, and thus been instrumental in this conspiracy. If he could somehow get back at Sheikh Hamdullah and Consul George for this plot, perhaps the decision to have him dismissed from his post would be reversed!

"I would like to think happier thoughts today, Marika. Let us stop talking about the plague now."

"As you wish, my lord, but that is all everyone talks about."

"One day this damnable plague will pass. When it is gone, I will plant trees all over our beautiful Mingheria, particularly palm trees, Bosphorus pines, and acacias. I shall begin making arrangements for a proper wharf to be built where passenger ferries can dock, even if we do not receive any grant from Istanbul. We must be sure to raise the requisite funds not just from the Greeks but from the Muslims too. If we manage to secure the support of the Theodoropouloses and the Mavroyenis, then the Kumaşçızades from Smyrna and Tevfik Pasha's descendants will be sure to offer donations too."

"No one loves this island more than you do, my darling Pasha," said Marika. "How sad it is that they blame you for everything."

What a wonderful person this Marika was! The Pasha couldn't imagine life without her. Her loving, compassionate expression was the perfect mirror to her soul; there was not even a single drop of insincerity in this clever woman, and that was another reason why he loved her so much. Sometimes the Pasha would daydream that she was Muslim, and teasingly share his fantasies with her, to which she would playfully respond by pretending she was a harem concubine, arousing and amusing the Pasha with her seductive figure and enormous breasts.

Sami Pasha was beginning to feel restless now with the knowledge that only making love to Marika would rid him of the aching despair and loneliness he was feeling. Of all his traits, his impatience to make love was the one Marika most disliked. But the Pasha did not think he had the strength that evening to entertain Marika with his half-peeved, half-ironic accounts of the municipal government's latest misadventures.

Eventually, after a long silence, Marika realized this too, so she smiled and moved toward the bed. The Pasha could not have been more grateful. As they made love, his feelings alternated between thankful-ness and wonderment. But at the same time he was letting the animal inside of him do as it pleased. Though he hadn't drunk anything, he felt intoxicated. He had always been particularly engrossed by Marika's right breast, and now his mouth latched onto its nipple. Tenderly, she stroked his head and his thinning hair, and the Pasha was reminded of his mother and of his childhood. He loved it too when Marika's soft breasts rubbed against his thick beard. They made love for a long time; the Pasha sweated profusely, and did not notice the mosquito that had landed on his back until the end.

"Something has happened to you today, but I will not ask what," said Marika later on. "In fact there is something I must tell you about."

"Please do."

"They found a bloodied rat corpse in our back garden today," said Marika. "Last night the fiendish creatures were scuttling around beneath my bed."

"God damn them!" the Pasha replied.

The Pasha stayed up until dawn to guard Marika's room. Whether he was dozing on the edge of the armchair, or getting into bed, he managed to stop the rats from attacking Marika. When he got back to the State Hall the next morning, he called upon the municipality for assistance and dispatched two clerks to set up mousetraps and pour rat poison in Marika's house. The thought that Marika—and indeed he himself—should be made to quarantine, or at least be examined by a doctor, did not even cross his mind.

CHAPTER 47

An average of twenty to twenty-five deaths were being recorded every day during this period, though the bleak consensus was that the true figure must be even higher. Some families were hiding their dead to avoid a visit from the Quarantine Regiment. When there was no prominent bubo on the victim's neck, people would tell themselves that the patient hadn't died of the plague at all, but of something else altogether. These same people would go on to spread the disease to others in their neighborhood—at least until there was a second or third death at home.

The morning after the sleepless but happy night he had spent guarding Marika's home from rats, Sami Pasha learned that the *Sühandan* had stopped in Smyrna to load medicine and tents and was now on its way to the island. A telegram addressed to the Quarantine Master explained that the ship was bringing supplies, soldiers, and volunteers, their exact numbers listed with the Ottoman registrars' customary care and precision. At the end of the telegram, Sami Pasha saw another piece of information which destroyed whatever hopes he might have had left: a new governor had now been assigned to Mingheria, and he too was on the *Sühandan*. This was Ibrahim Hakkı Pasha, a man Sami Pasha had briefly befriended, and whom he considered to be both mediocre and simple-minded. Ibrahim Hakkı Pasha used to work as a clerk in the translation department, which was how Sami Pasha had met him. He would do nothing all day but flatter Abdurrahman Fevzi Pasha, who supervised the clerks. His rank was probably equivalent to that of a major general. So how was he supposed to give orders to the new commander who would come to take over the garrison? Evidently there must be no one left at the palace or in the Sublime Porte with the wherewithal to give these intricate matters of status and rank the thought they deserved. Or maybe they were doing all of this just to spite him!

When reason prevailed over anger and agitation, and he realized that the news of his dismissal must have spread by now and that the decision would not be revoked, Sami Pasha came up with a new plan.

Later that morning, after they had put their green dots on the map in the Epidemiology Room to mark the dead as they did every day, Sami Pasha announced: "Gentlemen, I am sorry to inform you that a handful of palace clerks who believe our quarantine is not succeeding have decided to transfer me to Aleppo." (In truth, as everyone knew, governors were always appointed directly by Abdul Hamid himself.) "This decision will be reversed. But even if it is not reversed, I shall continue to fulfill my duties with the usual dedication until the new governor is formally installed, and I shall deliver my speech in the State Hall Square on Friday. Let us not forget that those aboard the relief ship must quarantine for five days before they can alight on Mingheria."

"Travelers coming from ports to the north and west are not subject to quarantine," said Doctor Nikos.

Was this an innocent remark, or was Doctor Nikos implying that he would no longer follow the Pasha's orders? The Quarantine Master had seemed to react rather coolly to the news of Sami Pasha's dismissal.

"These new doctors and this new governor who have no idea what's going on and don't know the people of our island will brush our quarantine efforts aside and introduce all sorts of new methods and restrictions," said Sami Pasha. "More time will be wasted, and of course none of these new measures will work either. Many more people, hundreds more, will die for nothing."

"Whereas a five-day quarantine would give us the opportunity to prepare for the new measures His Highness the Sultan requests!" said Doctor Nuri.

There is widespread agreement among historians that in that moment, by expressing his support for Sami Pasha's suggestion to quarantine all passengers on the *Sühandan,* Doctor Nuri effectively altered the island's destiny. Some have suggested that he must have been influenced by Princess Pakize's "suspicions" about Abdul Hamid's relief ship and by her hostility toward her uncle. Those with a special interest in the history of medicine will note that as far as the integrity of quarantine was concerned, the Doctor and Prince Consort was right.

Ever since quarantine had been introduced, and regardless of whether they were running a fever, all passengers on ships flying the yellow flag and coming to Mingheria from infected ports were being made to isolate for five days in the Maiden's Tower on the rocky islet near the Arkaz docks. But ships coming from Alexandria and other southern ports were few and far between now. Most of the people in the Maiden's Tower were quarantining so that they could board a ship leaving Mingheria. Every morning and evening, a little boat would set off from the docks to the isolation facility on this islet, ferrying guards, doctors, and the quarantine officials responsible for the plague suspects who were confined there.

Having decided that the Maiden's Tower would be the ideal place to keep the passengers of the relief ship *Sühandan* away from Arkaz and under observation, Sami Pasha summoned the boat foreman Seyit—who had already been tasked with collecting those same passengers—and gave him long and detailed instructions on what he was supposed to do.

The *Sühandan* was six hours late. Some particularly suspicious historians have been known to imply and at times even openly suggest that this delay was the result of some kind of international conspiracy. In reality the aging ship had been caught in a storm near Rhodes, and one of its weary engines had given out. As soon as the ship was first sighted from hilltop neighborhoods like Upper Turunçlar and Kofunya, people began flocking to the docks to await its arrival. Within an hour, a curious, hopeful crowd had gathered all along the harbor, and especially around the Hamidiye Bridge, the Hotel Majestic, and the Customhouse. A few old men who had come down from Vavla and Turunçlar were pleased that the Sultan had finally sent help from Istanbul. But these were people of that particularly impressionable sort who would shout "Long live the Sultan!" no matter what they endured. Everything that had happened on the island so far was a product of the authorities' indifference, incompetence, and lack of concern for the public, so most people's expectations of the relief ship—as indeed of quarantine measures—were low. Some particularly incensed citizens had gone to the docks not because they thought there might be help for them too, or at least a glimmer of hope against the plague, but only to stir up trouble and shout, "What took you so long!" Sami Pasha had sent every single one of his gendarmes to the port. On the Major's orders, sixteen Quarantine Regiment soldiers under Hamdi Baba's command had also been stationed at the jetty where the rowboats moored.

When the relief ship *Sühandan* reached the waters off the Arab Lighthouse, it tooted its horn just as scheduled passenger ferries used to do in the good old days, and the high, plaintive sound echoed twice between the jagged mountains around the capital. Foreman Seyit, who had been waiting near the Customhouse for this signal, and had been told what to do by the Governor, now began rowing out to the ship. His rowboat—whose undulating progress toward the *Sühandan* was keenly observed by the crowds gathered at the port—carried Quarantine Master Nikos, the young doctor Philippos, four soldiers of the Quarantine Regiment, and a spray-pump crew with tanks full of Lysol on their backs.

Although the *Sühandan* had sailed from the safe ports of İstanbul and Smyrna, and was not flying the yellow flag, its Italian captain Leonardo raised no objections when he saw who was on the rowboat. He was aware of the terrifying proportions the outbreak had reached upon the island, and that twenty or more people were dying every day. He let the doctors and the Lysol sprayers board his ship.

But Ibrahim Hakkı Pasha was perturbed. "Far be it from us to complain when even Kaiser Wilhelm can be quarantined!" he said when Quarantine Master Nikos came to see him in his cabin, though it should be noted, he continued, that His Supreme Highness did not wish to see these quarantine procedures cause any delay in the new governor taking up his position. (It was customary for the Sultan to meet with every governor and ambassador he appointed before they traveled to their destinations.) It wasn't long before the group who had just boarded the ship realized that their new governor had arrived with it. The most appropriate response would have been to acknowledge that all jurisdiction now rested with the new governor—even if he did have to quarantine in the Maiden's Tower—and act accordingly, but that is not what happened.

As the passengers on Seyit's rowboat climbed onto the relief ship, the crowds watching them from the docks began to sense that there was some kind of disturbance happening on the *Sühandan*. The new governor Ibrahim Hakkı would not leave his cabin, and was understandably refusing to be put in quarantine. When he had been given his latest orders in Istanbul, he had been told of a fault at the island's Telegraph Office and of the old governor's ineptitude, but he had not anticipated that there might be—in the words of conspiracy-minded historians—"a more sinister plot at work." In the meantime the team with their Lysol pumps had already begun disinfecting the ship. The deck was open and breezy, but there were many other spots shut away behind closed doors that now needed to be sprayed with disinfectant.

It was during this operation that Quarantine Master Nikos noticed signs of illness in one of the volunteers aboard the *Sühandan*. As would later become apparent, the young man—Yannis Hadjipetros, a first-year student at the Imperial School of Medicine who had volunteered for the mission because his grandfather was Mingherian—actually had diphtheria. But just as some plague patients with buboes on their bodies could still recover from the plague without so much as a raised temperature, others who had no buboes in either their groin area or their armpits had been known to develop sudden fevers and be dead within a couple of days. Yannis Hadjipetros's fever was thus interpreted as a symptom of plague, and his "diagnosis" served as an additional excuse to quarantine the *Sühandan*'s passengers for five days before they were allowed to land on the island.

The new governor did not argue with Quarantine Master Nikos or the soldiers who were brutally soaking his cabin in Lysol. His deputy, Hadi, later admitted in his extraordinarily candid memoirs, *From the Islands to the Motherland,* that Ibrahim Hakkı Pasha's only thought amid the chaos and the flurry of disinfection activity going on around him was how to get his luggage and trunks unloaded onto the rowboat without any items going astray. As far as he was concerned—and as he had been wrongly informed in a telegram from the palace—the old governor Sami Pasha had left the island and was already on his way to Aleppo.

The volunteers—three Greek doctors of Mingherian ancestry, two young Muslim doctors who had just graduated from the Imperial School of Medicine and had been forced to go on Istanbul's orders, and a few other inquisitive, adventure-loving souls—clambered down the *Sühandan*'s rope ladder and onto Foreman Seyit's bobbing, swaying rowboat. They had spent most of their journey in a state of boisterous companionship, as if they were going on holiday rather than to battle a gruesome disease, but before they had even stepped off the *Sühandan,* the smell of Lysol and the brusqueness of the Quarantine Regiment had silenced and cowed them. (Two of the three young Greek volunteer doctors and one of the Muslim doctors on that rowboat would die of the plague within a month.)

Once he had made sure his suitcases and trunks had all been unloaded, the new governor also got in. When he realized that Foreman Seyit was directing his oarsmen not toward the docks, but in the opposite direction, toward the islet with the Maiden's Tower, Ibrahim Hakkı Pasha stood up from his seat to object: if it really was necessary to quarantine the *Sühandan's* passengers, could this not be done by the Customhouse in the port, or somewhere else in the city? Quarantine Master Nikos Bey frightened him with a reminder that Arkaz was "dangerous" right now. Some commentators have claimed that the new governor only agreed to get on the rowboat because he assumed he would be taken to the city, and had he known that he was going to be locked up in the Maiden's Tower for five days during such a historic moment, he would have first cleared the matter with Istanbul by telegram. Some see the whole incident as part of a scheme concocted by Britain and the West, or perhaps even by the Greeks. Others may be right in their observation that the new governor—who had served many years before as the Mayor of the Mingherian town of Zardost—was probably a little too afraid of the plague.

These fanciful interpretations are of dubious value in helping us conjure a more vivid impression of the day's events. But what we can be sure of is that many people (including those who had no intention of attending) were now waiting expectantly for Sheikh Hamdullah's Friday sermon and for the meeting set to take place afterward on the State Hall balcony.

CHAPTER 48

For centuries, Friday sermons in Mingheria's Pious Saim Pasha and Blind Mehmet Pasha Mosques had always been delivered by resident preachers approved by Istanbul. But in special, historic circumstances, the leaders of the island's major lodges would also be allowed to preach at the New Mosque, and when times were difficult, people would turn out in large numbers to hear these famous sheikhs talk. Dispensing all sorts of advice to their audience, and translating Arabic prayers into simple, day-to-day language, some of these sheikhs told such affecting parables, and could be so adept at frightening their congregation or moving them to tears, that they would be invited to preach in Istanbul's biggest and best-known mosques, and thus enter the pantheon of famous Mingherians.

Sheikh Hamdullah had only ever given two sermons in the mosques of Arkaz, both many years ago. He had covered familiar topics like faith, how to resist the temptations of the flesh, and the traps laid out by the devil. He had not addressed or even alluded to events on the island. In other words, the sheikh's previous sermons had been strictly academic, and as they had not spoken to the Muslim population's everyday fears and tribulations, they had not left much of a mark. Although the sheikh's renown on the island had increased in the twelve years that had since gone by, his reluctance to become involved in any affairs of the pulpit which required approval from the Department of Charitable Trusts and from Istanbul meant that he had never delivered a sermon again. There was therefore much curiosity now—not just among the island's pious Muslim community, but among its consuls and the heads of its Christian congregations too—regarding the sermon he was set to give on the subject of the plague.

Sami Pasha had arranged to have the sheikh followed in secret. He was worried that after the sermon, the sheikh might find some pretext to avoid the meeting at the State Hall, and that his absence could transform the whole event into a protest against quarantine—the opposite of what was intended.

That Thursday's angriest and most determined protagonist was Ramiz. After a telegram from Istanbul had set him free, Ramiz had gone north to the villages of Çifteler and Nebiler. We will not indulge here in any protracted account of his confrontations with people fleeing the plague in Arkaz, and of how he extorted money from Pharmacist Nikiforos's eldest son. But Marika had been right to warn Sami Pasha: a week ago, Ramiz and his new gang of seven henchmen he had recruited from Çifteler and Nebiler had slipped back into Arkaz. The men were armed with knives and hunting rifles (supposedly to shoot rats with). Meanwhile, Ramiz had been going around telling people that the Great Powers would only withdraw their ships and lift the blockade once the new governor was installed in his seat and took charge of the garrison and the Arab divisions stationed therein.

As there weren't enough coffins anymore, most bodies were now being buried without. Some of the dead had no one to perform the proper burial rites for them—either because their whole families had died too, or because they'd fled the city—and with Majid and Hadid no longer involved in these matters, and the villagers and Cretian troublemakers who had been recruited in their stead soon abandoning their posts too, this had become a significant issue. At the same time, with the number of municipal employees too afraid to come to work increasing every day, it had become harder for Sami Pasha's men to be able to track Ramiz's whereabouts in the city.

On Thursday night, Ramiz secretly sailed to the Maiden's Tower in the rowboat owned by Lazar Effendi—the foreman who operated under French consul Andon Hampuri's protection. Ramiz was accompanied by ten armed men, three of whom had joined his entourage in Arkaz. Ramiz and his men stepped quietly onto the Maiden's Tower's makeshift jetty. Here, they were attacked by two furious dogs who took their guard duties over the rocky island more seriously than most, until eventually some sentries showed up. The raiders displayed their rifles, and after announcing that they had come with Sami Pasha and Doctor Nikos's blessing to protect against a group of guerrillas who planned to kidnap the new governor that night, they relieved the sentries of their weapons and tied them up.

Persuading the new governor Ibrahim Hakkı Pasha proved a little more difficult. As his deputy would entertainingly recount in his memoirs *From the Islands to the Motherland,* the new governor had reacted to Ramiz and his men like a crown prince hiding away in his harem in fear of the daredevil rebels who had come to install him on the Ottoman throne. (Murad V had been similarly alarmed when the organizers of the coup that was to overthrow his predecessor, Abdülaziz, had arrived to retrieve him a day earlier than he had expected them to.) For a while, Ibrahim Hakkı Pasha refused to let Ramiz into the room where he was being quarantined. Already he thought it inappropriate that he should be detained in the Maiden's Tower under so-called quarantine regulations, and in this state of heightened mistrust, he could sense there was some kind of plot at work. He took out his Nagant revolver and loaded it with bullets.

It was already past midnight when—having finally understood that Ramiz and his gang had taken control of the Maiden's Tower, that nobody from the city was coming to the rescue, and that he was, in other words, Ramiz's captive—the new governor stepped out of his room holding his Nagant. Ramiz declared that, as the one true governor, Ibrahim Hakkı Pasha had every right to carry that revolver, and after making all sorts of other earnest proclamations, he led Ibrahim Hakkı Pasha to the large room at the entrance of the Maiden's Tower. Upon Ramiz's instruction, the new governor's deputy, Hadi Bey, and his clerk, both of whom had followed Ibrahim Hakkı Pasha from Istanbul, as well as the volunteers and everyone else who had arrived on the ship were also brought to this spacious hall. After journeying all the way from Istanbul to battle the outbreak on the island, the *Sühandan*'s impatient volunteers were rather displeased about the senseless quarantine they had been subjected to, and just as most of them had begun to think that they must have been brought here in the middle of the night so that they could finally be ferried from the Maiden's Tower to the city itself, Ramiz had all the gas lamps in the room turned on, and once he had made sure that everyone had looked around and seen one another, he bowed before the new governor Ibrahim Hakkı Pasha and kissed his hand as if he were swearing allegiance to a new sultan who had hastily been placed on the throne. Ramiz then announced that, in accordance with his Royal Highness the Sultan's orders, he and his men recognized Ibrahim Hakkı Pasha's sole authority as Mingheria's new governor, and that they would escort him to the Governor's Office the next day.

Ibrahim Hakkı Pasha's deputy, Hadi, makes it clear in his memoirs that the Pasha did not believe a word these hoodlums were saying but pretended to go along with their plan so as not to anger the bandit Ramiz. The Pasha's real intention was to escape at the first opportunity and locate Sami Pasha (who, as he had just found out, was still on the island) so that they could assess the situation together.

Ramiz, on the other hand, was buoyed by the success of his night-time foray into the Maiden's Tower. At daybreak on Friday morning, the new governor and his retinue were ferried to the island in the fore-man's rowboat and entered the city through the Old Stone Jetty. As they looked toward the unfailingly romantic, mysterious silhouette of the Maiden's Tower and saw Foreman Lazar's boat slowly approaching the city, the Greek fishermen who had sailed out at dawn glumly concluded that it must be carrying bodies for burial. The outbreak was not slowing, quarantine measures were not working, and perfectly healthy people were catching the disease in the same places where they were being holed up for quarantine purposes.

After dropping off its numerous passengers at the Old Stone Jetty, the rowboat returned quietly to its usual place in front of the Custom-house. Sami Pasha's spies had already spotted the boat, but by the time they got to the Old Stone Jetty, Ramiz and the new governor's men had already entered Vavla. Had they needed to, they could have easily over-powered Sami Pasha's spies, his night watchmen, and any other guards that might try to stand in their way. But nobody saw them or tried to stop them as they vanished into the neighborhood's alleyways.

CHAPTER 49

Sheikh Hamdullah spent his Thursday evening surrounded by the same books and pamphlets his grandfather and great-grandfather used to consult during outbreaks of plague in Istanbul. These texts sought to unravel the mysteries of the plague through the interpretation of omens, the predictive powers of the Abjad numeral system, and the mystical attributes of the alphabet as codified in the Lettrist Sufi doctrine of Hurufism. The outbreak of plague that had struck Istanbul ninety years ago had been such an appalling ordeal that the most pious Muslims had turned away from the world and placed all their remaining hopes on cryptic signs, talismans, and consecrated prayer sheets. Given their interest in this kind of esoteric knowledge and in the secret properties of the alphabet, Sheikh Hamdullah's forefathers had found some consolation in these ancient writings. They had even composed verses and texts of their own, replete with allusions and double meanings. But in this new age when all everyone talked about were microbes and Lysol, Sheikh Hamdullah could see that these old pamphlets would be of no use at all. There was no advice in there about how to quarantine, nor any kind of cure.

After midday prayers on Friday were over and the time came for him to deliver his sermon, Sheikh Hamdullah realized the moment he stepped onto the pulpit that the teeming, disconsolate crowd before him had no interest in his own doctrinal quandaries or in the sophistications of complex religious precepts, and that all they wanted was to mourn and weep and tearfully call upon Allah for consolation. The sheikh had climbed twelve steps to reach the pulpit, and now he felt like he was standing far above the restless, anxious, frightened worshippers gathered below him. Usually when he talked to his disciples and to those who came to him with their problems, eager to unburden themselves, the sheikh liked to be able to look into their eyes from up close. That nearness was what allowed him to forget his own self and meld with the self of the person sitting before him. But even all the way up on that pulpit, the sheikh could sense that what his audience wanted most from him was not advice but a new mood and a new frame of mind they could embrace. He also intuitively understood that they expected him to provide some kind of remedy against fear and death. He had not realized any of this back at the lodge. Whether he told them that everything would happen as it was fated to, or claimed that the Holy Koran itself prescribed quarantine measures, it would not make any difference to these people now. The tense, apprehensive worshippers in the mosque were not in a composed-enough state to grasp that kind of distinction. They paid the sheikh most attention when he mentioned the Almighty and spoke of how great and how merciful he was, and every time the name of Allah was spoken, their faces lit up with the spark of epiphany and consolation. The sheikh quickly realized that rather than reasoning about quarantine and fate, he would do better to simply lead the congregation in prayer.

"Rabbanaa wa laa tuhammilnaa maa laa taaqata lanaa bih!" he proclaimed, following his instincts. This was a verse from the Baqarah *surah.* As the sheikh explained in simple Turkish, it translated to "O Lord, do not burden us with more than we have the strength to endure!" He then shared some spontaneous reflections on the notion of endurance: "The only way to endure is to seek refuge in Allah," he began. Since everything happened according to his will anyway, there could be no other solace for believers than to turn to Allah. He spoke in the confident manner of a man having the final word on a particular subject and clearing the matter up in everyone's minds. Sure enough, the crowd came to the conclusion that there must be some profound message enshrined in his words, though they remained as exhausted and preoccupied as ever.

Sheikh Hamdullah knew most of the tired, bearded men listening intently to his heartfelt words. He had met them in the early days of the outbreak, standing in mosque courtyards, gathering around biers, and searching for available burial plots. He had spent those first few days rushing from house to house and funeral to funeral. That fair-haired man over there who now sought reassurance in the sheikh's words could easily have lost his mind following the deaths of his wife and two daughters, but instead he had behaved with great dignity. Over here was the farrier Rıza, who seemed to die himself every time any one of his neighbors did. Then there was this young migrant from Crete who had become accustomed to other people's deaths but hadn't even been able to think of his own, and although he had turned up to listen to the Friday sermon that day, he had really been running away from everything else. But perhaps these cases were anomalies. Most of the three hundred people assembled in the mosque that day had come there to be like everybody else, to feel closer to God, to avoid being alone, and to be surrounded by other people who were just as scared as they were. Soon the mood of the sermon began to turn of its own accord into one that favored sects, holy men, and sheikhs over the quarantine effort.

At the start of the outbreak, and before he had retreated to his cell in contemplation, Sheikh Hamdullah had been called to many different households, where he had provided comfort—some might even say a reason to carry on living—to people who had been so stunned by the unstoppable force of the plague that they had begun to doubt their faith. He had also attended to the bathing and burial of numerous corpses, dispensing advice and consolation to bereaved relatives driven half mad with grief. During those days spent visiting homes, gardens, graveyards, coffin makers, and mosque courtyards, the sheikh had become completely immersed in the lives of these dependably open, honest people. When they learned that their sheikh had fallen sick, those same people were overcome with despair—and when they heard that he had apparently recovered, and that he was somehow immune to the poisoned darts of the plague, they believed those stories too. The sheikh saw that they were now expecting him to reveal the secret of his powers, or at least lead them in prayer so that they could avail themselves of his immunity too. He wanted with all his heart to bring some consolation to these people whose grief and dread he had so closely been involved in.

The greatest consolation was of course to be a Muslim and die a Muslim. The sheikh recited in Arabic from the Surah An-Nisa to remind everyone that embracing Allah at the last moment was not enough to rescue lifelong infidels from the pits of hell; and just as Allah could kill the living, he could also bring the dead and even the earth itself back to life. Those who feared death should vanquish their fear by thinking of life after death. If they had sinned, they were probably right to be afraid . . . But if they hadn't, then being so afraid of death would only make them lose their minds. "That very death you fear so greatly, and are so desperate to escape, will always find you and catch up with you one day," said the sheikh. "You can hide inside the strongest castle, and still it will find you."

As the French consul would later point out, these remarks "clearly undermined quarantine." The old governor Sami Pasha, who was waiting at the State Hall to start the meeting that would take place there after the conclusion of the sermon, had hoped that the sheikh might at least say a few words to criticize the prayer sheets, amulets, and made-up incantations that had sprung up against the plague, but that didn't happen either. Instead, the sheikh spoke of the interpretation of dreams, of the shadow that fell from the owl's wings, and what it meant to see two falling stars in the same night sky. But he felt that the congregation understood him best when he described what it felt like to stand and mourn next to someone's coffin.

There were some neighborhoods of the city whose inhabitants had spent their last few days running from one funeral to the next. Were the citizens of Arkaz and all those who had remained on the island regretting their decision not to flee? Had they made an error of judgment in not following those who had gone to hide in faraway mountains, villages, and caves? Who was more deserving of divine consolation—those who had fled on rowboats even at the risk of drowning, or those who had come to the mosques to find refuge in Allah?

The congregation felt that the sheikh was delivering an exceedingly profound and meaningful sermon, and that he was very knowledgeable and wise. They were ready to listen to whatever he had to say about the fear of God and fear of the plague, and to find solace in his words. Sensing their enthusiasm, the sheikh recited in Arabic from the Surah Yusuf and led the congregation to repeat after him: "O Lord, Creator of the heavens and of the earth," he said, "let me die a Muslim, and place me among the righteous!"

Near the end of his lengthy sermon—frequently interrupted by cries of "Amen!"—the sheikh referred to the passage in the Surah Al-Anbiya which said that "every living creature shall have a taste of death" and spoke with such fervor that some people began to cry. For they knew they were all dying too, and they hadn't even been able to come together in that collective spirit required to battle death. The sheikh could see in their expressions that this was why they were going to the mosques and lodges in the first place. He felt regret and a pang of guilt for having retreated to his chambers over the past few days, from where he had been unable to comfort these suffering multitudes.

As his speech went on, the sheikh occasionally paused to peer into his listeners' eyes. Most of them were troubled, frowning, aghast. But there were also elderly worshippers who seemed as serene and oblivious as if this were an ordinary Friday sermon in normal times; people who were sitting there marveling at the scenes around them as if they couldn't quite understand what was happening; and others who were optimistically nodding their approval at the sheikh's every word. The sheikh himself kept nodding too, as if to say, "Yes, it is incredible, is it not?" Some people averted their eyes from the sheikh's every time there was a moment of silence. The sheikh had also noticed Sami Pasha's spies among the crowd. He had known from the very beginning that there would be a political aspect to his sermon, and from the very beginning he had wished he could forget about it.

Just then an old coachman who had been listening reverently to the sheikh from near the front of the congregation felt so dizzy with emotion—or was perhaps so ill—that he had to lie down, and shortly after that he began to shiver and moan. The man looked like he was having a plague seizure, and soon the sheikh had to interrupt his sermon so that he could join the congregation and help.

The crowd, who had already been on tenterhooks, now sprang into motion. Some regarded this as the end of the sermon. Those who got up and left straightaway, or didn't notice the shivering, delirious coachman near the front, assumed that the usual agitators must have caused some kind of disruption. Sami Pasha and the consuls had also been expecting Ramiz to show up at his brother's sermon to make trouble, and indeed Sami Pasha had made sure to put precautions in place in the area around the New Mosque and at the entrances to its courtyard.

But it quickly became apparent that this was not the work of hostile mischief-makers. Most people knew or at least recognized the sweet, elderly coachman who had fallen ill, and to see this beloved figure suffer so much and so visibly was immensely dispiriting to everyone present.

In their analysis of these various fast-paced developments, some historians have suggested that if the old coachman had not fallen over and writhed in pain at the end of Sheikh Hamdullah's sermon, the history of Mingheria might perhaps have taken a different course.

For the upshot of this all was that in the end, and for a variety of reasons, the multitudes who had attended the sheikh's sermon did not head on to the meeting at the State Hall Square as Sami Pasha had imagined they would. Sheikh Hamdullah hadn't been able to direct them there, and he had neglected to even mention the important event about to take place in the State Hall Square. Having just told his audience that there was nowhere left to turn to except for Islam, that there never had been anywhere else to turn to in the first place, Sheikh Hamdullah was reluctant to be seen standing with the bishops of the Christian congregations half an hour later. The announcement they had planned to make at this event, banning entry to mosques and churches, would directly contradict the contents of the sermon the sheikh had just delivered. Though he had given his word to Sami Pasha, the sheikh couldn't bring himself to move toward the State Hall, and he was still lingering at the mosque and letting his many admirers kiss his hand in total disregard for quarantine regulations when a team of guards specially selected and instructed by Sami Pasha came by to "extract" him.

Sami Pasha had already thought of the possibility that Sheikh Hamdullah might stall after his sermon and try to avoid joining the assembly at the State Hall balcony. He had also predicted that there might be people on the route between the mosque and the State Hall who would try to block the sheikh's way or cause a disturbance and had prepared accordingly by readying Coachman Zekeriya as well as six of his most loyal bodyguards. Sheikh Hamdullah was still having his hand kissed after the conclusion of his sermon when these men suddenly appeared, took him by the arms, and casually escorted him out of the mosque's side entrance, through its courtyard, and onto the armored carriage waiting in the shade of a linden tree. Sami Pasha had told his men that if the sheikh tried to put up a fight, they must drag him away and force him onto the carriage if they had to, and under no circumstances must they let the crowd take him, but when the moment came, the sheikh (and everyone around him) mistook the disguised guards for his own men, did not resist at all, and quickly walked away without saying goodbye to anyone, stepping into the armored carriage that had been waiting to pick him up.

Meanwhile Ramiz and his men, who had smuggled the new governor, his deputy, and his secretary out of the Maiden's Tower that morning, had crept through the city's backstreets and taken shelter in a derelict house in the Vavla neighborhood. They stayed there until midday prayers. Their hiding place was the ruin of an old Ottoman mansion in the shadow of the Blind Mehmet Pasha Mosque and across from the courtyard of the Army Middle School. The pupils of the army school believed this house was cursed and haunted, and would use it as a secret meeting spot, as well as a place where they could drink wine and organize wrestling matches. During the outbreak of plague, a vast number of dead rats had been discovered there. Two corpses had also been found in the garden on two separate occasions over the past fortnight, their presence revealed in each case by their stench. One was a Muslim man who had lost his mind after his wife and his mother had both died and run away and disappeared before their funerals had even taken place. His now-vacant house was close by, so clearly he had not been able to get very far before he too had passed away.

The other corpse was a more suspicious case, for it belonged to a youth from Flizvos. Since no Greek resident of the wealthy Flizvos neighborhood would ever come to Vavla to die, the two municipal clerks who had investigated the matter had suggested there might be foul play involved, though the resulting inquiry had since been abandoned. In any case, the Quarantine Regiment had banned access to the building and its garden just like they had done with many other locations throughout the city. As this seemed to be one of those rare prohibitions that people were actually respecting, Ramiz and his men knew they would be safe inside the crumbling mansion.

The Governor's deputy, Hadi, who would later drolly describe all of these incidents in his memoirs, tells us that Ramiz was propelled purely by love and vengeance, and that it is senseless to seek more complex motivations behind his actions. Ramiz simply believed that the best way to exact revenge on the Major who had taken his betrothed from him, and on the old governor Sami Pasha who had supported the Major in this endeavor, was to help the new governor take up his duties without further delay. It was only proper that the new governor should be there when the island's leading figures addressed the public from the balcony of the Governor's Residence half an hour after midday prayers. Later, during his trial, Ramiz would repeat again and again that it had all been his idea—not the consuls', nor his brother's, nor anyone else's.

There would have been no one better placed to attest to the confusion in Ramiz's mind than the municipal caretaker Nusret, who often passed information on to Ramiz and had once been loyal to the Chief Scrutineer and Sami Pasha too—but Nusret would be killed later that day. Ramiz had relied on Nusret, who came from Çifteler village and worked as a janitor in the State Hall, to keep him updated on what was happening in the city. In fact Nusret had long been spying for both sides, revealing to Sami Pasha the whereabouts of Muslim guerrillas (not all of them, of course—only the ones he hated) who were attacking Greek villagers, and providing extremely valuable information on the Greek guerrillas too.

Shortly before Sheikh Hamdullah had begun his sermon, a carriage took half of Ramiz's men to the State Hall. Nusret had disguised them as a team newly assigned to work in the building. This first group hid for a time inside the woodshed opposite the State Hall kitchens.

Half an hour later the same carriage picked up Ramiz, the new governor, and three others, and brought them to a side door near the main entrance. This second group, including Ramiz's visibly armed men, were able to enter the State Hall without difficulty. Nusret met them at the side entrance, took them through several long, narrow hallways, and up the staircase at the back of the building.

Sheikh Hamdullah was just beginning his sermon when Nusret led the group with Ramiz and the new governor up the back staircase, across the room next to the large meeting hall that had been readied for the day's guests, and from there quietly and furtively locked them up inside the Outbreak Room (the little office with the map on the wall that we have sometimes referred to as the Epidemiology Room). As Sami Pasha and all his spies were focused on securing the environs of the New Mosque, no one was paying much attention to what might be happening at the State Hall, though, later on, this degree of negligence would come to be seen as a form of collusion.

Sheikh Hamdullah's sermon was still going on when the consuls, the journalists, and other guests who had been invited to Sami Pasha's balcony ceremony began to arrive. People were keeping their distance from one another, preferring to exchange greetings from afar. As usual the consuls had gathered in their own separate group. Journalists and various other curious invitees were milling about along the edges of the room, where they began waiting patiently for this meeting Sami Pasha had insisted on, and which they probably thought was largely pointless, to begin and end as soon as possible, and hopefully without too much incident.

CHAPTER 50

We shall begin this chapter with a question historians of Mingheria have so often asked: When he wore his officer's uniform that morning, why did the Major choose to pin to his chest the medal he had been awarded after the war with Greece four years ago, and his Third-Class Order of Mecidiye badge, when he was about to embark on what would turn out to be such a historic challenge to the authority of the Ottoman state? Let us now resolve this conundrum which has baffled the island's historians for all these years: neither the Major nor Sami Pasha had any inkling yet of the significance and the ultimate outcome of the events that would take place that day. They had heard that the new governor had been snuck out of quarantine in the Maiden's Tower, and they were furious at Ramiz. The Major had a feeling that his beloved wife's former fiancé might attack the State Hall, disrupting the quarantine effort and the public assembly Sami Pasha had so meticulously organized. Understandably, he thought that his Ottoman-issue medals and his military uniform might act as deterrents.

In their room at the Splendid Palace that morning, Zeynep told her husband that as well as his medal and badge, she was finding his whole manner that day to be somewhat alarming.

"Don't worry, we will survive this," said the Major. "And believe me, there will be salvation for the people of this island too! I'm taking this with me," he added, showing her his Nagant revolver, but Zeynep seemed to take no interest in it. It was as if she were less worried about possible scraps and gunfights than about some other more spiritual, metaphysical menace.

According to Sami Pasha's orders, once Sheikh Hamdullah had been put in the carriage and a soldier had waved a white flag to signal this to the State Hall and the Hotel Splendid, the armored landau would set off for the State Hall through the city's steep and sloping backstreets, avoiding the main road. Sami Pasha expected the armed fugitive Ramiz to make trouble at the first opportunity, and was concerned that he might intercept the carriage and get in with his brother, causing havoc on the way or perhaps even attempting to escape with the sheikh. But if the landau went past the Splendid Palace and picked up the Major on its way, Sheikh Hamdullah would understand how serious the matter was and behave accordingly.

When he saw the white flag waving, the Major went to his wife and put his arms around her. Zeynep told her husband that she was afraid Ramiz would try to harm him, and that he must be careful. They embraced again.

The Major slowly made his way down the stairway of the empty hotel. Four armed soldiers from the Quarantine Regiment had been stationed in the lobby in case Ramiz should attack. The Major glanced at his reflection in a large mirror with a gilded frame and listened to one of his soldiers reporting on a dispute between two Muslim families in Çite that was having negative repercussions on quarantine too, so that by the time he stepped outside, the armored landau was already approaching the hotel. There was another carriage behind it, full of guards.

When the tired, sweat-drenched horses pulling the armored landau stopped in front of the hotel, the Major saw that Nimetullah Effendi, the dervish with the felt hat who was Sheikh Hamdullah's most trusted deputy, was also sitting in the carriage. We shall take this opportunity to inform our readers that despite his modest and unassuming appearance—or perhaps because of it—Nimetullah Effendi would come to play a crucial role in the history of the island.

Sheikh Hamdullah had not been aware that the Commander of the Quarantine Regiment was going to join him in the landau. His feelings toward the Major, who had taken his stepbrother's fiancée, and whose Quarantine Regiment had bullied the residents of his lodge and sprayed Lysol everywhere, were understandably less than positive. But when he saw him proudly standing in his officer's uniform with his medals and his gun, the sheikh smiled as if he were meeting a fan or a new disciple.

"I had heard you were a hero," he said. "But I did not know you were so young. That medal really suits you!"

The Major settled in across from the sheikh and Nimetullah Effendi, then leaned forward and humbly thanked the sheikh.

"His Holiness the Sheikh gave a wonderful sermon!" said Nimetullah Effendi. "Everyone cried, and felt reassured, and they wouldn't let him go until they had all kissed his hand." There was an interval of silence, after which Nimetullah Effendi added: "Thanks to the sheikh's sermon, the congregation has understood the great importance of observing quarantine rules."

Our attentive readers will know that this was not true. But the Major had not heard the sermon himself.

As Coachman Zekeriya slowly and steadily drove the carriage through empty alleyways and sloping streets toward Hamidiye Square, they passed by a garden, where they were startled to see a gathering of people who had come for a condolence visit, a boy eating grapes on the floor, and his little brother crying next to him. The Major sensed that this was the perfect moment to say what he had decided to say to the sheikh during this short seven- or eight-minute carriage ride.

"Your Excellency, the whole island holds you in such regard that if you had given the doctors and quarantine officials your full support from the start, there would not have been so many deaths, nor so much sorrow and suffering."

"We are servants of Allah and of his Prophet. We must do as Allah commands. We cannot just 'leave it to the doctors' and turn away from our religion, our beliefs, and our past."

"We are all servants of Allah," said the Major. "But are the beliefs and history of a nation more important than the life and future of its people?"

"There is no life or future for a people without a religion, beliefs, and a history of their own. What exactly do we mean by 'the nation' on this island anyway?"

"Anyone who is from the island. The natives of this province."

As the carriage crossed the Hamidiye Bridge, its wheels started making a different sound, and as if on cue, everyone fell silent and looked out of the windows. To the right were the Castle's pale pink walls and the blue of the port, and to the left were rows of pine trees and palm trees and the Old Bridge.

Shortly afterward, they saw the gendarmes Sami Pasha had stationed—

if somewhat sparsely—along Hamidiye Avenue. Despite all the posters that had been put up, the announcements printed in newspapers issued especially for the occasion, and the municipal officials' exhortations, the city's main boulevard was not conspicuously busier than usual. "They'll come!" said Nimetullah Effendi, realizing that everyone was thinking the same thing. "The congregation is only just leaving the mosque." He stuck his head out of the window and looked behind. But he did not see any people arriving for the event, only the carriage carrying the guards who were following the armored landau. People had become accustomed to the sight of Quarantine Regiment soldiers and gendarmes standing outside the Telegraph Office. But stringent security measures had also been put in place in the State Hall Square, where there was now a small crowd composed of travel agency clerks, shopkeepers, and some municipal employees whom Sami Pasha had told to attend. Sami Pasha, who had cracked a window open to survey the scene below, had hoped that they might stand in the middle of the square, but most people were waiting in the shade of the almond and palm trees that lined its edges.

All eyes were upon the armored carriage as it entered the square and approached the entrance to the State Hall. By the time the visibly sweating horses had come to a stop, a crowd of guards, gendarmes, and clerks had already gathered around the carriage. It was a while before the sheikh managed to step off (using a mounting block the doormen had deftly placed before him), slip away from his numerous well-wishers, and walk in through the State Hall door.

"I must perform my ablutions!" said the sheikh to Nimetullah Effendi and his felt hat as soon as they were in the shade inside.

There was a European-style lavatory at the foot of the main staircase, complete with running water and designed specifically with Western guests (and particularly consuls) in mind. Some historians have posited that the rather long time the sheikh spent in this toilet (we estimate ten minutes) would end up altering the course of Mingherian history, a theory which has generated all manner of inaccurate and sensational interpretations of this incident.

We shall put these unabashedly political exaggerations to rest here by providing our own explanation: the only reason the sheikh went into this "ablution room" and spent so much time in there was simple curiosity. For when the new State Hall had been inaugurated seven years before, every newspaper, starting from the *Arkata Times,* had written at length about how European, how new and modern, the building's offices, guesthouse, and balconies looked, and there had been a great deal of talk too among the island's more educated Muslim population, particularly in the context of broader conversations around westernization and the growing wealth of the Christian community, about the quintessentially European character of its toilet bowls purchased from the Stohos shop in Thessaloniki.

CHAPTER 51

While Sheikh Hamdullah was busy in the lavatory, Major Kâmil climbed up the State Hall's wide staircase, coated in pinkish-white Mingherian stone and known to everyone on the island. He felt the usual mixture of pride and embarrassment he experienced whenever he wandered around with his medals and badges pinned to his military uniform, and tried not to draw too much attention to himself. But in that place and in that moment, this was impossible to do. As he walked up the steps, he could feel the janitors' and the clerks' and everyone else's nervous, apprehensive eyes upon him and did his best to avoid their gazes by studying the quarantine posters (some of which were two months old) affixed to the walls as if it were the first time he had ever seen them.

He arrived at the Main Meeting Hall. This room tended to be dimly lit, as it had been even during the Quarantine Committee's meetings, and most of its curtains were usually drawn shut, so when he walked in that day to find it bathed in the most brilliant light, the Major wondered for a moment whether he had come to the right place. He saw that Doctor Nuri was talking to Monsieur Andon (whom the Major couldn't stand) in a patch of sunlight beside the balcony, so he walked toward the green door of the Epidemiology Room.

When he tried to open the door, he found that it was locked; he was just about to head back to the balcony when he heard a noise from behind the door, and the sound of someone talking. Perhaps there was a clerk still in there, marking deaths on the map. Locking the door seemed a sensible precaution, and whoever was inside would probably come back out soon.

The Major joined Quarantine Master Nikos and the elderly Quarantine Committee delegate Doctor Tassos, who were talking about another raft of rat corpses in the gardens and backstreets of Kofunya and Eyoklima. Most of these rats appeared to have died recently, and others had been found coughing up blood. That morning, the brawny, strapping son of the old Greek Mavroyenis family had been taken to the hospital in a state of delirium, and the family's much-frequented haberdashery store hadn't even opened.

As he listened to their conversation, the Major—like everyone else in the meeting hall and on the balcony—was also watching the people beginning to arrive from Hamidiye Avenue to the State Hall Square. A group of about fifty to sixty had now assembled in the middle of the square, where they were waiting for the balcony speech to begin. But it was clear now that no matter how long they waited, the vast crowds of hundreds and hundreds of people that the Pasha had been dreaming of were never going to turn up.

The Major approached a clerk he had often seen with Sami Pasha and in the Pasha's office and asked him to unlock the door of the Outbreak Room.

"Nusret Effendi has the key," said the clerk, who had a brushlike mustache. "You will find him in the Pasha's office," he added, glancing at the door that led from the meeting hall to that office.

Just then, that same door opened up, and Sami Pasha, the registry clerk, and Nusret Effendi all walked out into the meeting hall. Their demeanor was calm and resolute.

In that moment the Major also noticed some activity by the main entrance at the opposite end of the meeting hall and realized that Sheikh Hamdullah must have come up the stairs and into the room. Just as the Major and the clerk with the brushlike mustache arrived to stand outside the Epidemiology Room, a hard, insistent knocking began from the other side of the door. The knocking soon sped up and took a fiercer turn.

As if he had been waiting for this to happen, Nusret stepped away from Sami Pasha and went to open the door. But it was rattling so much from all the banging that the caretaker couldn't even get the key in the lock.

"Do not open that door!" cried the French consul (whose exclamation would, predictably, go down in history). It seemed everyone was expecting some sort of ambush.

The guests assembled in the meeting hall and on the balcony had begun to feel uneasy. When the Major saw two of the guards who had accompanied the sheikh moving forward with their rifles at the ready, he stepped away from the door and took cover on the ledge of one of the meeting hall's tall windows.

By this point everyone in the Main Meeting Hall had realized that some kind of trap had been set. The perpetrators of the would-be attack were caught inside the Epidemiology Room, whose door was stuck. People were trying to figure out what exactly was going on, and the nature of the attempted raid. Was it all Sami Pasha's work? Governors of far-flung Ottoman territories would often lay these kinds of traps as a way of frightening Christian minorities and other perennially dissatisfied troublemakers into submission. But Mingheria was a proper province of the Ottoman Empire, and there were journalists here watching everything unfold.

As Sami Pasha's guards encircled the Epidemiology Room, some of the guests slipped outside or onto the balcony. They could hear noises coming from inside the Epidemiology Room. Those who knew his voice heard Ramiz shouting, "Open the door!" Was there a scuffle or an altercation of some sort going on inside?

Everyone was trying to work out what to do next, when the green door of the Outbreak Room finally opened, and out stepped one of Ramiz's associates, a man from Nebiler with a bald head and a handlebar mustache. He was pointing his rifle toward the petrified guests still left inside the meeting hall, though he wasn't aiming at anyone in particular.

From the corner of the room where the Greek journalists and notables were hiding, Kiryakos Effendi—owner of the Bazaar du Île—called out "Please keep calm!," his Greek-accented Turkish giving voice to the emotions and fears of every single person in the room. They were all thinking the same thing: "For God's sake hold fire!" But most of them could also sense that this would not be possible.

Someone else cried, "Don't shoot!"

Ramiz then stepped forward and came to the door. His manner, his pink face, his expression, were all perfectly calm. It might even be said that he looked inexplicably confident.

"It would be more appropriate for this ceremony to take place after the new governor Ibrahim Hakkı Pasha has taken office!" said Ramiz.

As Sheikh Hamdullah was surrounded both by his own men and by the new governor's entourage, neither Sami Pasha nor the consuls were able to see how he reacted to his stepbrother's audacious outburst. Perhaps he would have put him in his place if he'd had the chance, as some would later argue. As if it weren't enough that this hoodlum whose fame rested solely on the fact that his brother was the sheikh of the island's most popular lodge, and who had no official role or qualifications, had nevertheless taken it upon himself to smuggle the new governor out of quarantine, here he was adopting this imperious tone in the presence of the old governor.

Ottoman and Turkish commentators, Mingherian nationalist historians, and the rest of the world all have different theories on where the first shot had come from. In these kinds of situations, it is sometimes possible to identify the willing instigator who fired the first bullet or the terrified fool who pulled the first trigger. But this was not the case at noon that day in the Main Assembly Room of the State Hall. Instead, everyone seemed to start firing at one another at the same time, as if they had all been simultaneously ordered to shoot. Their fingers had already been poised on the triggers of their guns and their rifles. Ibrahim Hakkı Pasha's deputy would later write in his memoirs that he had realized there was going to be a skirmish the moment the door had opened, and so he had immediately pulled his Nagant revolver from his waist and opened fire himself.

There was also a "second front" formed by a group of Sami Pasha's men who had forced their way into the Epidemiology Room through a door that opened onto a back corridor. Based on the last-minute intelligence he had received from the informant and provocateur Nusret, Sami Pasha had stationed armed guards along the State Hall staircase and around his own office. When the skirmish began, Governor Sami Pasha had eighteen armed men inside and around the entrances of the meeting hall. Some of these men were municipal guards who carried their weapons openly. Others had come to the hall in disguise, dressed as clerks, servants, or shopkeepers. (Yusuf, who had taken cover behind the same column as the Major, was one of these men.) The moment they heard the first shot—and in accordance with the instructions they had already received from Sami Pasha—they picked up their own weapons and immediately started firing at the enemy.

Sami Pasha had warned the men he had summoned to the State Hall and to the State Hall Square that a handful of reprobates might seek to "sabotage" the historic quarantine meeting planned for that day, or even mount an assassination attempt, so they must be ready to shoot these traitors down without hesitation. (In other words, when the shooting began, Sami Pasha's men were firing in the Sultan's name, rather than for an independent Mingheria.)

When he had first found out about the planned attack, Sami Pasha had imagined—perhaps naïvely—that he would be able to catch Ramiz's men one at a time, and quietly arrest them all without compromising the security of the balcony ceremony. This plan rested on ambushing the ambushers themselves at the door of the Epidemiology Room.

But in our view it was precisely this aspect of the plan which caused the shooting to begin in the first place, and led to the mad "skirmish" that ensued. Within moments, everyone was firing at the "enemy," using tables, columns, armchairs, and potted plants for cover.

For the first eight to ten seconds after the first shot was fired, the battle was not too fierce. The guests inside the meeting hall and all the people who had assembled for the ceremony did not quite understand what was going on. Their attention had been elsewhere, for His Holiness the Sheikh and Sami Pasha had both just walked into the room. This might explain why the first gunshot initially caused such havoc and bewilderment. Then, shortly after that first bullet, almost everyone began shooting at once. The sound of gunshots bounced between the thick curtains and wood-paneled walls of the cavernous meeting hall, but even outside people could hear their eerie, powerful, intermittent din.

The infernal cacophony they were forced to endure during those few minutes of incessant fighting nearly drove the guests in the meeting hall mad. They would remember the things they saw and heard during that brief interval of time, and the terrifying sound of those gunshots, for the rest of their lives. They might even have been more frightened of the deafening noise than of the sight of soldiers, clerks, and bandits being struck down before their eyes.

Some guests crawled under the wide wooden table where the Quarantine Committee had held its endless meetings; others ducked behind cupboards, chairs, and writing desks; the majority threw themselves onto the floor.

Most of them had already realized that they were not the targets here—but what did that matter when there were so many guns being brandished? There was a kind of fury in the air; anyone could be its victim, and everyone could understand where it came from. It was as if the bullets were being fired at the plague itself. According to eyewitness accounts and historians' investigations, nearly one hundred and fifty shots were exchanged over those next few minutes.

Against Sami Pasha's team of eighteen well-drilled men, Ramiz had ten shooters with him, most of whom were more concerned with protecting themselves than they were with killing anybody else.

Some of Ramiz's men— even those who'd already been wounded—had tried to return fire during the early moments of the battle, taking cover behind anything they could find. Thanks to their grit and determination, their attempts were briefly successful, and they were able to hit many in the crowd around them. But soon their guns fell quiet. They had been quelled by the relentless volley of bullets from Sami Pasha's men, coming particularly from the main entrance of the meeting hall, and one by one, they'd begun to die.

Two bullets had hit Ramiz in the arm and shoulder mere moments after his presumptuous outburst, and forced him to retreat. But he had quickly realized that he would not be able to escape through the back door of the Outbreak Room either. Sami Pasha had sent three guards over to that side too, and they had been shooting without pause. Realizing that any attempts to break the siege were bound to end in failure, Ramiz returned to the green door and started shooting at the guards who were firing at him from the meeting hall. Within minutes, he was the only one left still returning fire from the Outbreak Room.

"Everyone hold your positions!" said the old governor Sami Pasha.

There was a prolonged silence. Two seagulls shrieked and bickered furiously as they flew over the square. Though all the shooting had happened inside, the noise had reached the farthest edges of the city and echoed against the mountains.

The silence that followed was even more eerie. While some of the guests snuck out through the door, others stayed put, lying on the floor or cowering in their hiding places. They could hear the wounded groaning and whimpering around them.

The Major emerged from behind the column he had been using for shelter and walked into the devastated Outbreak Room. He saw straightaway that four of Ramiz's men and the caretaker-provocateur Nusret had all died. There was blood everywhere, taking an unusual crimson hue on the slabs of Mingherian stone. Ramiz had fallen over, but he was still alive, twitching and moaning where he lay.

The Major spotted one of the municipal guards writhing in pain, and thought that at least he might survive. Among the attackers was a young man with a white, childlike face whom the Major had never seen before and who had made it through the whole encounter without a scratch. The youth was quaking with fear, but the realization that he was still alive had also brought a peculiar tinge of elation to his face. When he saw the Major walking toward him with his gun, he put his hands up in surrender.

The fighters clustered around the other door of the Outbreak Room hadn't faced quite as much fire. The new governor, Ibrahim Hakkı Pasha, had been killed by a bullet to the forehead. The Major saw the new governor's deputy, Hadi, sighing over his master's dead body, and watched as the rest of Ramiz's team handed themselves in to the municipal guards.

Four bullets had struck the map where every morning for the past two months the Governor Pasha and Doctor Nuri had placed green marks to signal plague deaths and infected homes and locations. Another bullet had made a hole in the window panel of a large black display cupboard whose paint was flaking off, though the rest of the glass remained intact.

But the glass windows of the walnut cabinet right beside it had shattered in the commotion. When the Major saw Sami Pasha's men and the gendarmes approaching the Outbreak Room, he eased out the trunk that was stored in the walnut cabinet's bottom compartment, prized open its unlocked lid, and retrieved from beneath two folded kilims the old crimson-and-pink banner embroidered with the emblem of La Rose du Levant, featuring the distinctive spires of Mingheria's Castle, the White Mountain, and the Mingherian rose, and so reminiscent of a flag.

In the dimly lit room around it, the red flag with its pink rose seemed to be reaching for a place where it might come alive. The Major took a couple of steps toward the balcony, and as the guests in the hall looked on, still shocked by the terrifying tumult they'd had to endure, the cloth seemed to find the gleam it had been searching for, and in the next moment, the whole meeting hall was bathed in a brilliant red glow.

The newspapers of Mingheria and future history books too would produce many eloquent accounts of how the apprehensive guests gathered in the meeting hall that day were left spellbound by the radiance of the flag in the Major's hand. We are now at a point when nationalist fervor blurs the lines between history and literature, myth and reality, colors and their significance. Let us therefore proceed to take a closer and more pondered look at events.

CHAPTER 52

T here have been many oil paintings depicting the Major as he walked from the Outbreak Room to the balcony across the meeting hall with his Nagant revolver in one hand and the red linen flag in the other. Most of these are based on an illustration that the Greek painter Alexandros Satsos—a relative of Lami's from his mother's side—would later prepare for the newspaper *Adekatos Arkadi* in celebration of the first anniversary of the "revolution." This image was in turn clearly influenced by Delacroix's *Liberty Leading the People,* a painting to which every freedom-loving revolutionary in the world has always harbored a somewhat-romantic attachment. Indeed, as we have penned this history, it has been impossible to ignore the feeling that similar events to those we have described had already unfolded before in a place not too far away. Decorative trinkets, lamps, and other objects inspired by Delacroix and Satsos's revolutionary *Liberty* would be sold in the island's shops all the way through to the late 1930s.

The Major was about to cross the threshold of the balcony when Doctor Nuri reached out to stop him. In a heartfelt, instinctive gesture, he placed his hand on Major Kâmil's shoulder. He had seen him shooting at the attackers, and now felt the urge to embrace him. He couldn't do so, as the Major was still holding the flag in one hand and a gun in the other. But Doctor Nuri did spot something that neither our readers nor the Major himself had noticed yet.

"Are you hurt?"

"No!" said the Major. Then he looked down at the hand in which he was holding the flag and saw blood and a gunshot wound near his wrist. Though he did not feel any pain, it was true that he had been hit, and that he was bleeding heavily. "I hadn't even noticed, Pasha," he said, addressing Sami Pasha who had just walked up to him too. "But no bullet can stop us now from doing what we must do for our people."

The Major had made sure everyone could hear him, his voice growing louder as he spoke. The assembled guests had been listening attentively to every word, and now waited to see how the Pasha would respond. But Sami Pasha was uncertain, and remained quiet.

"Pasha, unless we all go out there together and declare that mosques and churches are to be shut, it will be impossible to make quarantine work. If we do not reach out to the people now, especially in the wake of this ambush, never again will they listen to anything you or the Quarantine Regiment tell them to do."

Even the Major was surprised to find himself speaking so forcefully to the Pasha. A photograph taken in that moment shows him pointing his gun toward the Pasha. Sami Pasha had dispatched some of the island's photographers to the square so that they could photograph him as he addressed the public from the State Hall balcony, and so that he could later have those images published in newspapers and magazines. The photographer assigned to the meeting hall itself was Vanyas, Mingheria's first-ever professional photographer. In his painting inspired by Delacroix's *Liberty*, the artist Alexandros Satsos would copy some of the details of the Major's uniform and pose from that first photograph Vanyas took.

Near the edge of Vanyas's second photograph, we find Sheikh Hamdullah standing, his back straight and his demeanor solemn. We do not know if he was aware that his stepbrother had just been shot and wounded in the raid (not to mention that everyone assumed Ramiz was dead). But he was experienced enough to understand that from a political perspective, they had no choice but to go ahead with the ceremony. By now the guests had regained some measure of composure and reached a collective consensus that Ramiz's attack had been an attempt to sabotage the quarantine measures that were about to be announced. Everyone gathered in the State Hall—Muslims and Christians alike—agreed that the thing to do was to proceed with the ceremony as intended, send out a message of unity and solidarity, and tell the public that mosques and churches would henceforth be shut.

There was also a shared sense in that historic moment that the person most fit to articulate this position would be Major Kâmil (rather than

Sami Pasha, who was still reeling from his dismissal). It has also been remarked that the Major seemed in a jubilant mood as bishops, community leaders, and journalists started filing out onto the balcony. The expression on Sami Pasha's face when the Major informed him that the new governor Ibrahim Hakkı had been killed by a bullet to the head told the young officer that the news had thrown the Pasha into a state of despondency.

"No one is going to listen to us now!" exclaimed Sami Pasha in a burst of candor.

"On the contrary, Your Excellency," began the Major, improvising a response that would soon become famous: "If we take a step forward now and announce the revolution, Mingheria's progressive-minded people will take not one but two steps forward with us."

It has always been difficult for nationalist and conservative Ottoman and Turkish historians to understand the context within which words like "progress" and "revolution" might have been used on the island in the year 1901. Unable to accept that the island may have wanted to sever itself from Ottoman rule because of the Empire's inadequacies, and because there really was such a thing as a Mingherian nation, they have also come to see it as their mission to insinuate at every opportunity that there must have been other, more mysterious reasons for what transpired, and all sorts of hidden forces at work. These people believe that the moment in which the "revolution" took place could simply never have happened "as described." The proof, as they see it, is that as a relatively low-ranking officer, and one who had, moreover, just been imprisoned for insubordination, the thirty-one-year-old Major would never have spoken to the "old" governor—a seasoned bureaucrat, a pasha, and a man more than twenty years his senior—in such an authoritative manner.

Of course one of the main features of any revolution is that things that have never happened before, and that no one ever thought or even dreamed could happen, will start happening one after the other.

The Major had nothing to rely on but his own experiences, his conscience, and his sincere devotion to the people of the island. It was his innocence and integrity that moved him to act in spite of all the pressures he faced, the fear, and the Ottoman medals and badges pinned to his chest. As the guests began to take their places on the State Hall bal-

cony in accordance with the Pasha's plan, the Major turned once more
to Sami Pasha and delivered a heartfelt speech he made sure Doctor
Nuri and everyone else could also hear:

"Your Excellency, as long as His Royal Highness Sultan Abdul
Hamid remains on the throne, both you and I will find that any roads
that might lead us safely back to our old lives and to Istanbul are forever
closed."

He had once again spoken loud enough for all to hear, and having
made this declaration—which would come to hold a "prophetic" significance for Princess Pakize and her husband for many years to come—the
Major raised his voice again and continued with increased rhetorical and
poetic flourish:

"But you must not be disheartened, Pasha, for there is one consolation. We are not alone. The Mingherian nation stands with us. Everyone
upon this island, the whole of the Mingherian nation understands that
as long as we continue to receive our orders by telegram from Abdul
Hamid, any roads that might lead us safely away from this plague will
too remain forever closed."

It was the first time in the history of the island that anyone had spoken publicly of a "Mingherian nation" and in open defiance of Abdul
Hamid. This alone was enough to frighten everyone present.

The Major had now reached the balcony railing. "As soon as we stop
waiting for telegrams from Istanbul and start governing ourselves, this
quarantine will end, the outbreak will subside, and we will all be saved,"
he said, his manner like that of a consummate politician.

Then, he turned toward the square and shouted as loud as he could:
"Long live Mingheria! Long live Mingherians! Long live the Mingherian
nation!"

The square had finally begun to fill up. There must have been one
hundred and forty to one hundred and fifty people there. Most of
them had gathered a little earlier, scattered when the gun battle had
erupted, and then returned, intrigued, to find out what might have happened. Meanwhile, all the coachmen, the guards, and the street hawkers
who had previously taken shelter in the shops, behind the columns,
and under the trees around the State Hall Square had also emerged,
drawn by the sight of Sheikh Hamdullah and Archbishop Constantinos
Effendi standing on the balcony beside the old governor and the Prince

Consort. To give everyone more time to gather, the Major turned again toward Sami Pasha and—as confirmed by witness accounts and by Princess Pakize's letters—uttered the following historic words:

"Your Excellency, we would never have come this far without your exemplary guidance. You are the greatest governor we have ever had. God bless you! But you are no longer the Sultan's governor now; you are the people's governor! From this moment on, our committee declares Mingheria independent. From this moment on, our island is free. Long live Mingheria, long live the Mingherian nation, long live liberty!"

In the square below, the crowd kept growing and the photographers kept taking pictures. Their rather hopeful shots of the island's various dignitaries all standing together on the balcony would end up illustrating several news reports chronicling the day, the twenty-eighth of June 1901, when the island of Mingheria finally stepped onto the stage of world history. The images would be published in hundreds of newspapers across five continents and later be reproduced in countless books, in encyclopedias, on postage stamps, and in historical monographs.

The first of these photographs to be published was a shot taken by Arhis Bey, carried to Crete and from there to France with the assistance of the French consul and one of the fishing boats that was still smuggling people off the island, and printed three days later, on Monday, the first of July 1901, alongside a report on the second page of Paris's principal conservative right-wing newspaper *Le Figaro:*

Revolution in Mingheria (Révolution à Minguère)
The little Ottoman island of Mingheria, situated in the Eastern Mediterranean and famous for its marble and roses, has declared independence. For the past nine weeks, the island, whose population of eighty thousand is split evenly between Christians and Muslims, has recently been gripped by a terrible outbreak of plague. With the island's local Quarantine Authority failing to control the outbreak, the international community—encouraged by the Ottoman Empire—had sent four warships to blockade the island and prevent the plague from spreading to Europe. Three years ago, pilgrims returning to the island from the Hejaz had revolted against harsh quarantine regulations, with seven pilgrims and one soldier

killed in the resulting clash. There are reports of gunshots having been fired in the city during the revolution, and Ottoman soldiers have been seen marching on the streets.

That last sentence had been somewhat exaggerated. We have not given much room in this book to correcting this kind of misinformation, and we will not spend any time on this particular fabrication either, except to note that the French might have included it in their report in order to give the impression that the island remained under Ottoman control.

Another interesting theory around this falsehood is that it might have been designed as an attempt to trick the Sublime Porte and even Abdul Hamid himself. The Ottoman government in Istanbul did not quite know what was happening in Mingheria. With telegraph lines down, and the only reports from the island coming through smugglers—most of whom were of Greek origins, and whom Abdul Hamid could not easily infiltrate with his network of spies—even Istanbul was not sure of who was currently in power there.

Arhis Bey's photograph of the gathering on the balcony had taken up a quarter of a page in *Le Figaro*, with the caption: "The moment Mingheria declares independence from the balcony of its Ottoman State Hall." A week later, the French magazine *L'Illustration* would publish an engraving based on the same photograph, including a similar description below. Of course the French press had no idea who any of the people in the photograph were. We have therefore listed their names here for the purposes of our history: Sheikh Hamdullah; head of the Orthodox Christian congregation, Archbishop Constantinos Laneras; former governor Sami Pasha; Doctor and Prince Consort Nuri; all of the consuls; Chief Scrutineer Mazhar Effendi; five municipal guards; and two others whom we are not able to identify today. (The new governor's deputy, Hadi, had been locked up in the cells in the State Hall basement, along with Ramiz and his surviving henchmen.)

A day later, *The Times* published the same photograph together with a caption that would prove so popular with historians that they would end up repeating it over and over again until it turned into one of those hackneyed statements people make without giving them much thought:

"The island of Mingheria declares independence with an announcement from the Ottoman State Hall building made jointly by the leaders of its Christian and Muslim communities."

Abdul Hamid and the Ottoman government in Istanbul would find out about this declaration of independence when their ambassador in Paris, Münir Pasha, and their London ambassador, Costaki Anthopoulos Pasha, sent telegrams detailing the reports they had read in foreign newspapers. Some mean-spirited and overblown rumors have also alleged, among other things, that Abdul Hamid couldn't quite believe the news, and wanting to see the respective issues of *Le Figaro* and *The Times* with his own eyes, he had dispatched special sleuths to the port of Sirkeci, where mail coming from Europe to Istanbul was first unloaded. As Mingheria was not responding to any telegrams, it is not surprising that both the Sultan and the bureaucrats of the Sublime Porte should have been eager to find out how this nationalist uprising had started and, more important, who its ringleaders might be.

CHAPTER 53

There was a brief silence after the Major's announcement in Turkish that Mingheria was now free and independent. In that moment, a man named Haşmet, the oldest of the State Hall's caretakers, took the "flag" from the Major's bloodied hand, deftly tied it to a heavy staff he had armed himself with in anticipation of an attack, and passed it back to the Major.

So it was that this caretaker who had never left the island in his life and hardly even knew how to read and write came to be remembered for a time as an important historical figure. Many years later, the new nationalist government, which took power in Mingheria after the end of the Italian occupation of the island, would name a new school in Haşmet's ancestral village in his honor, calling it the Flagbearer Haşmet Primary School. Several painters would also immortalize the moment the elderly caretaker had secured the flag to the staff. But eventually, after the education ministry decided it would be more appropriate for the images on the island's banknotes to show two young women handing the flag to Commander Kâmil, rather than some elderly janitor, depictions of Haşmet became increasingly rare, and by the 1970s, he had been forgotten altogether. Today he is only remembered in his own village.

The aging caretaker's "gesture," whose significance so many painters would also grasp, had prompted the Major into action too. He put his gun down, grabbed the flagpole with both his blood-soaked and his clean hand, and began to wave it, holding it out horizontally so that the whole square could see. His wound was aching, and the banner and pole were heavy, but Commander Kâmil managed to wave the flag right and left three times. When he was satisfied that everyone had seen the color of the flag and how it billowed in the air, he handed it over to Haşmet and repeated the words he had just said in French too:

"Vive Minguère, vive Les Minguèriens! Liberté, égalité, fraternité!"

"Long live Mingheria, long live Mingherians! Liberty, equality, fraternity!" he added in Turkish.

"The Mingherian nation is a great nation," he continued. "The Mingherian people shall vanquish the plague and advance under the direction of our esteemed committee and of our governor toward liberty, progress, and civilization. Long live Mingheria, long live Mingherians. Long live our soldiers, long live our quarantine officers, and long live our Quarantine Regiment!"

Most of the dignitaries gathered on the balcony felt the Major had overstepped. But they also believed this must all be a performance orchestrated by Sami Pasha, and as its purpose remained ambiguous, they had decided to wait patiently for its conclusion. The most valuable account we have on this subject is a passage penned by the daughter of Archbishop Constantinos Effendi—leader of the Greek community—in her memoirs *Winds of Mingheria*, published in Athens in 1932. According to his daughter, Constantinos Effendi made it clear later that afternoon that he was not at all happy that the island was being plucked away from Ottoman control. On the contrary, he was dismayed and perturbed. While the balcony speeches were still going on, the bishop had found out that Governor Sami Pasha had been dismissed from his post two days ago, that the new governor, İbrahim Hakkı Pasha, had just been killed, and that his deputy had been wounded, and at home that day, he had spoken again and again of how they were on the verge of a great catastrophe and of how Abdul Hamid would not let this senseless act of rebellion go unpunished. The bishop knew very well that whenever revolts of this kind happened on other islands, it was never too long before one of the Ottoman navy warships was deployed to indiscriminately bomb towns and villages and anything else they could reach.

But as his daughter also wrote in her memoirs, her father was somewhat reassured by the fact that the island was still surrounded by the Great Powers' warships, and that when it came to the handling of the plague-infected island of Mingheria, there was therefore an open political partnership between Abdul Hamid and the Western governments. Abdul Hamid wouldn't dare break the blockade on his own and send the *Mahmudiye* or the *Orhaniye* to bomb the island. According to the bishop, the former governor must have cunningly evaluated all of these factors before coming up with these claims of freedom and independence. In other words, his answer to Abdul Hamid and Istanbul's question "Who is the instigator and ringleader of this revolt?" would have been the old governor Sami Pasha.

After the Telegraph Raid and his subsequent arrest, the Major had gained fame and stature among those in the Muslim community who had grown resentful of Istanbul and the Governor. Even wealthy Greek families who had no interest in what went on in the Muslim neighborhoods knew who he was. By now, people were finding it increasingly difficult to believe that this brilliant officer, clearly destined for greater things, could have accidentally ended up on the island because he'd been tasked with guarding a sultan's daughter and some obscure delegation supposedly traveling to China to counsel the Muslims there, and in their hopelessness they slowly became convinced that the Major must actually be there on some other, secret mission.

The Major's wrist, hand, and fingers were now completely covered in blood from the wound he had suffered to his left forearm during the skirmish. In later years, the various Muslim notables, guards, and municipal clerks, and indeed the Christians present on the balcony that day, would be forced to speak—some sincerely, others with feigned enthusiasm—about the way the Major's blood had seeped into the flag. In the 1930s and 1940s, when the idea of Mingherianness came to be perceived and firmly established as "a question of blood," this detail would be remembered as one of the most dramatic moments of the island's "freedom struggle," and many would argue that the thing which had spurred Mingherians into action was the sight of the blood of the founder of the state pouring out of his wrist, over his fingers, and onto the flag, before dripping down to the square and the earth below.

This was the blood of the noble Mingherian people, who had migrated to the island thousands of years ago from south of the Aral Sea, and possessed a special, inimitable language of their own. The Major's hand and wrist were soaked in red, and when he put the flag down for a moment, Doctor Nuri took the opportunity to roll his sleeve up, and examine his wound. On his visits to field hospitals in the farthest reaches of the Empire, the doctor had seen plenty of soldiers and officers come back wounded from the front, and helped to treat them too. With a few skillful gestures, he exposed the Major's still bleeding wound, and determined that the situation was perilous.

It has been suggested that in that moment the Doctor and Prince Consort's intent was to subdue and silence the Major. This is not true. From a medical perspective, Doctor Nuri had to intervene, and had to do so immediately. For as we will see over the next few pages, the Major's injury could well have proven fatal. By leading him away from the balcony, Doctor Nuri might have temporarily severed the heavily bleeding Major from the rest of the day's political developments, but he was also able to give him some initial treatment to stem the loss of blood.

When the Major was taken inside, there was a stir among the small crowd of curious observers gathered in the square below. "Hooray for the Major!" cried a couple of fez-clad onlookers—foolish, inattentive types who had dismissed the gunshots, and assumed everything was unfolding just as Sami Pasha had planned. But from the sound of gunfire and the silence that had followed it, most people had realized, even before the Major had emerged to deliver his speech and wave the flag, that something extraordinary was going on. Some had been genuinely moved by the sight of the glorious flag billowing "proudly and delicately" over the assembled crowd.

To this day we do not know who it was who chose in that moment to shout:

"À bas Abdul Hamid!"—"Down with Abdul Hamid!"

Sami Pasha and everyone else on the balcony made their disapproval of such insolence clear. The voice had come from somewhere underneath the balcony, near the entrance to the Governor's Residence, but the Muslim leaders, the soldiers, and the gendarmes nearby pretended not to hear it, while the consular clerks and journalists standing close to the entrance did not reveal who had shouted. The fact that we still have no conclusive information on the subject leads us to wonder whether this provocation had even been uttered at all. In any event, the chance to express their distaste of this disrespectful, impertinent outburst against Abdul Hamid went some way toward alleviating Sami Pasha and the rest of the balcony's shared fear of "how furious the Sultan would be." Everything about Sami Pasha's demeanor seemed to say, "Someone shut that man up!"

The message from the balcony to the journalists and to the Sultan's spies was this: "We are not doing anything against Istanbul or the Sultan." (This would not last long.) Most of them still believed that despite the attempted raid and the Major's immoderate conduct, the Governor had so far succeeded in carrying out the meeting as he had intended to. As historians, we know how common it is for those who have initiated the world's great upheavals, revolutions, and devastations to have done so while fearing the consequences of their own actions, and convincing themselves that they have set out to do the exact opposite of what they will end up achieving.

This was precisely the attitude which guided Sami Pasha's actions from the moment the Major stepped away from the balcony. Addressing the crowd before him (which was not even a tenth of the size he had imagined it would be), he announced that in order for quarantine measures to work, entrance to mosques and churches would be temporarily forbidden. There would be no need for calls to prayer or bell ringing either. After all the blood that had been spilled in the skirmish earlier that day, and with the smell of gunpowder and the whimpers of the wounded still hanging in the air, he did not feel like launching immediately into the flowery, elaborately worded oration he had prepared. He proceeded to add that, henceforth, the only people who would be given access to monasteries and lodges would be those who already lived there. As soon as these announcements were concluded, clerks from the State Hall would be dispatched to these places to identify and enumerate their residents, and nobody else would be allowed in. The Governor Pasha regarded the work of these census clerks as the most delicate aspect of the new ban on places of worship and had thus devoted significant attention to the matter, working feverishly with the registry clerk to draw up detailed instructions for the municipal staff to follow. He set great store by these instructions, which he now began to read out from a piece of paper. This in turn led to him finally reciting the speech he had so meticulously prepared.

Yet neither the people on the balcony nor those gathered in the square were able to listen to Sami Pasha's speech properly—both because the old governor's voice wasn't strong enough, and because everyone was too busy talking to one another and trying to understand what was going on. There was nothing incongruous about the cries of "Long live the Sultan!" rising from the more elderly audience members and a few Abdul Hamid enthusiasts among the crowd, for there was not a single word in Sami Pasha's carefully constructed oration that could be interpreted as being against Istanbul and the Sultan.

As Sami Pasha delivered his speech, the Chief Scrutineer instructed Vanyas to photograph the scene inside the Outbreak Room. Behind its green door, this room was fairly small, and the injured, dying bandits had ended up falling on top of one another, their blood mixing and their corpses becoming entangled. Desks had been overturned, coffee tables knocked down, lamps upended, and glass shattered, and every surface was covered in holes, but the epidemiology map on the wall remained in place. It would not be an exaggeration to say that the bullets had fixed it even more firmly onto the wall.

Three days later, these photographs with the map of Mingheria in the background and bloodied corpses in the foreground would fall into the hands of the Athenian press, and would be published in the newspaper *Efimeris* with the headline "Abdul Hamid's Counterrevolutionaries Defeated in Mingheria!"

The daily *Acropolis*, meanwhile, would caption their photograph of the blood-soaked bodies on the floor as follows: "The new governor and the guerrillas deployed by Abdul Hamid to quell the Mingherian Revolution meet their terrible fate!"

The publication of these images and news reports in the Greek and European press effectively signified that there could be no stopping the forces of revolution and independence on the island now, and no way back for Abdul Hamid to consider. The government in Istanbul could not even hope that after they'd removed the Ottoman flag and handed power over to someone else, they might eventually get Mingheria back through other means.

It has been suggested that Sami Pasha must have given the photographs to the Greek press himself, and that his purpose in doing so was to show the Muslims and Christians on the island who were wary of independence and terrified of how Abdul Hamid might retaliate that the point of no return had long since passed. We do not share this view. Just as Sami Pasha had not planned any of the Major's actions that day, he also sought throughout to calm things down rather than inflame the situation any further. But even if those photographs had never been published, the Pasha knew that Abdul Hamid would still consider him responsible for the new governor's death as soon as he heard about it, and that he would be blamed even more for having ignored the order dismissing him from his post. Before the quarantine speeches on the balcony had even concluded, Sami Pasha had already understood that not only was there no way back to Istanbul for him now, but no life anywhere else within the borders of the Ottoman state either.

As the Pasha had planned, the balcony ceremony ended with the various community leaders, religious figures, politicians, and doctors all praying together and in accordance with their own faith for quarantine to succeed and for God to banish the plague from Mingheria. The photographs that captured this scene—symbolic of that feeling of secular fellowship so typical of the island (and that we have always defended)—would sadly come to be misrepresented in later years as depicting "the founders of the state of Mingheria praying for the state to thrive long into the future, and bring happiness and serenity to all."

Once the balcony ceremony was over, the curious, fearful guests went back inside, pausing every now and then to look at the corpses that the municipal guards and caretakers had begun to remove. Even Archbishop Constantinos Effendi, head of the Greek Orthodox congregation, couldn't contain himself, and before heading out of the main entrance, he walked toward the Outbreak Room and stood there for a while with his crucifix in his hand, staring at the bloodied corpses and at the new governor with his bloodstained face and the bullet hole in his forehead, until someone eventually had to drag him out of the room. As Sami Pasha walked the bishops and the sheikhs and his other esteemed guests to the staircase, he thanked them all for their support of the quarantine effort. He saw them off with hopeful platitudes, as if everything had gone according to plan, there had been no raid at all, and no one had been killed.

Doctor Nuri was by the door to the Governor's Office, where he was working to stem the Major's bleeding. He was being helped by the elderly gossipmonger Doctor Tassos, one of the delegates of the Quarantine Committee.

When he returned to the meeting hall and saw the consuls waiting for him there, a sense of exultation and assurance took hold of Sami Pasha. He could feel the power of the old governor Sami Pasha coursing through him, the man who had always been in control of everything around him. He was the island's sole ruler now, and he could see it in the consuls' eyes.

"Know this, gentlemen: nothing in Mingheria will be the way it was before!" said Sami Pasha, addressing the consuls in a stern, condescending tone he would not have used under ordinary circumstances. "Anyone involved in backing this nefarious attempt on the life and property of the people of Mingheria will be punished," he continued. "It is clear that these vermin took advantage of consular privileges to walk right through the front door. From this moment on, any authorizations we have issued for consuls to enter the State Hall shall be revoked. All other consular privileges shall be subject to review. Whichever consul is behind this attack shall absolutely be punished. The Minister of Foreign Affairs will provide you with further information in due course."

Though no one had the chance to request any clarification, all the consuls and journalists clearly heard Sami Pasha announce that a duty that would have previously been performed by the Chief Intelligence Secretary was to be carried out by a new "Minister of Foreign Affairs." Clearly "Governor" Sami Pasha too must be backing the Major's words and supporting the notion of a separate state.

"Mingheria belongs to the Mingherians," said the Major in that same moment. But he was too fatigued and in too much pain to say anything else, so he fell silent and leaned back on the pillow someone had placed behind him.

The Major's strained, stuttering gestures, and the way he seemed to be angrily muttering to himself, were likened by some observers to the behavior of a plague victim. These people were realists who thought that antagonizing Istanbul would inevitably lead to catastrophe. They wanted to believe that the Major had "gone mad," in the way plague patients sometimes did.

At the Doctor and Prince Consort's initiative, Major Kâmil was carried away through the crowd in the meeting hall on people's hands and shoulders. There is an exquisite oil painting of this scene, made in 1927 by Alexandros Satsos. This magnificent work is held in the private collection of an alcoholic Texan oil baron, so unfortunately the people of the island are not familiar with the original, and only know it through rough black-and-white reproductions published in newspapers and magazines.

We find this depiction of the founder of the Mingherian state and hero of its freedom struggle—holding his gun and the flag, his supine form imbued with an almost feminine fragility, his eyes noticeably closed, his skin pale—to be a wonderfully fitting evocation of the moment. But the consensus among most historians of Mingheria is that Major Kâmil was soon back on his feet and pushing the revolution forward.

As everyone made their way toward the door, Sami Pasha briefly crossed paths with the French consul, and decided to display his renewed sense of confidence specifically for Monsieur Andon's benefit.

"You will have to give up this habit of telegraphing your embassy in Istanbul to complain about me every time you are caught abusing your position. Though I suppose you've had to give it up already, thanks to our commander." (He was referring to the Major and his Telegraph Raid, as he made clear by glancing at the door through which the Major was currently being carried out.)

This was the second time Governor Sami Pasha had referred to the founder of the state of Mingheria, the man our readers have come to know as Major Kâmil as Commander Kâmil, the title that Mingherians have gratefully and exultantly called him by for one hundred and sixteen years. We too shall refer to him as "Commander" from now on, though occasionally as "Major" too so that our readers do not forget.

CHAPTER 54

In his diplomatic memoirs *Europe and Asia,* the retired ambassador and inveterate dandy Sait Nedim Bey framed the fact that the Sublime Porte had to read French and British newspapers to find out it had lost the island of Mingheria as a classic example of the utter incompetence of the Ottoman bureaucracy during the declining years of the Empire. We do not agree with this observation. With telegraph lines down, and their network of spies hindered by the plague and by a naval blockade, it was only natural that Abdul Hamid and the Empire's bureaucrats in Istanbul should not have news from the island. As the consuls hadn't been able to send out their usual reports, the British and French ambassadors in Istanbul were not aware of the situation either. In any case, after the declaration of freedom and independence (two exalted principles which would henceforth almost always be mentioned together) in the State Hall Square, the consuls had all but fled the building, and knowing that Sami Pasha would seek to punish them somehow, they had decided not to open their shops and travel agencies for a while, and gone straight to their homes to wait and see what would happen.

Sami Pasha had understood by now that, in the circumstances, independence was both a historic imperative and the only possible outcome, so he was not affected by the indecision that some of his municipal clerks and bureaucrats were experiencing. On the other hand, a few historians have suggested in their articles on the "loss" of Mingheria that Sami Pasha might still have been hoping that things would unfold as they had when Abdul Hamid had handed Egypt and Cyprus over to the British twenty years ago but kept the Ottoman flag flying there as a symbol of its presence and of the possibility of a return—and that he was therefore still very much the Sultan's man.

The point all historians agree on is that Commander Kâmil really had been on the verge of death that night. As there is no medical certificate detailing the precise nature of the wound the founder of the Mingherian state suffered on that day of such national, dramatic significance, there have been many extravagant and conflicting reports on the subject. The most reliable account, in our view, is the one Princess Pakize received from her husband, and which we shall therefore relay here: the bullet had hit the Major's left forearm, and caused serious damage there. Doctor Nuri and Doctor Tassos—who had both rushed to his aid—had concentrated at first on stemming the copious bleeding. They had both immediately realized that the courageous commander risked hemorrhaging to death. As one of them pressed his hand upon the wound, the other wrapped a rough cloth tightly above the Major's elbow, and secured it with a knot.

Once the bleeding had stopped, the Major was carried away from the scene in a state of semiconsciousness. Doctor Nuri thought the quickest and most suitable place to start treating him would be in the State Hall guesthouse, and he had a room readied for this purpose. Princess Pakize covered her head with a shawl and retreated to a small room in the back. The Major was helped onto a European-style couch right by the entrance, of the kind the Sultan sometimes sat and read his novels on. The capacious guesthouse room was about to be invaded by prying onlookers when the Doctor and Prince Consort pulled the door shut.

The recumbent, semiconscious Major would occasionally prise his eyes open to watch what was happening around him, and even ask a few questions. (He'd already asked about Sami Pasha, for example.) But Doctor Nuri wouldn't even let him speak, and had forbidden anyone from asking him anything. The Commander's face was wan, his eyes were closed. The doctors were relieved when the bleeding finally stopped.

The first quarter of the 1900s was, comparatively speaking, a particularly brutal time in human history, during which people shot more bullets at one another than ever before or since. This was a result of the simultaneous discovery and rapid spread of automatic machine guns and of patriotic nationalism—whose adherents were willing to run straight into the line of fire. What happened that day was quite different from the many accounts we have read in the medical handbooks from that period, but although Commander Kâmil had only been hit by a stray bullet to his left forearm, it must have pierced an artery, for he had lost a huge amount of blood anyway.

It wasn't yet dark outside when Princess Pakize emerged from the room in the back of the guesthouse where she had been hiding to come and watch what was going on. Although she had no inkling of his plans to establish a new state, she thought there was something romantic in the sight of the founder of the Mingherian nation covered in blood and lying on the couch in his Ottoman uniform, his medals, his badges, and with the flag right beside him. She was aware that several people had been killed inside the Outbreak Room. The smell of gunpowder was everywhere. She wished she could show this heroic soldier who had guarded her and her husband the same solicitude with which Doctor Nuri was treating him now, but she was not sure how to do that. At Princess Pakize's suggestion, it was decided that the Major's wife Zeynep and his mother should be informed of the situation and invited to come to the State Hall.

Zeynep arrived just as the cloth around Commander Kâmil's upper arm was being tied up again, having been loosened for a time to prevent gangrene in his hand. When Zeynep saw her husband lying there, pale and half conscious, she let out a soft wail and fell to her knees, wrapping her arms around him. Everyone else stepped back, and suddenly Princess Pakize was able to see them both from a mere six or seven feet away—a moment she would remember forever.

According to Princess Pakize, who had spent her whole life in royal palaces, the most powerful evidence of the love between a man and a woman was not just in the positive, sympathetic emotions they shared, but in the depth and sincerity of those feelings too. It seemed to her that this was precisely the nature of the Major and Zeynep's bond. Clearly Zeynep had realized in those first forty-five days of their marriage that she simply could not live without Major Kâmil. Readers interested in reading Princess Pakize's full description of this scene between the founder of the nation and his wife—a text which will one day undoubtedly be taught in schoolbooks—will be able to do so once we have released her correspondence, which will follow the publication of this novel.

In her enthusiasm, Princess Pakize also said a few words with which she expressed her support—knowingly or otherwise—for those working to wrest the island of Mingheria away from Ottoman control:

"Bravo, Commander!" she said. "You have proven yourself to truly belong to this island."

"Mingheria belongs to the Mingherians," the Commander replied, struggling to speak.

Princess Pakize was also there when Commander Kâmil was put into the armored landau and taken to the garrison, where it was deemed he would be safest. The State Hall clerks had flocked to the landau as it waited outside the door. Despite the horrors of the armed skirmish they had just witnessed, this glimpse of salvation and the thought that they might actually survive had filled them all with hope.

The evening of the day the revolution was carried out and freedom and independence first declared on the island was captured by the artist Tacettin in a painting now famous throughout the island, and which shows the State Hall's armored landau advancing in the middle of the night through the city's empty streets. In this remarkable painting, there is no one sitting in the coachman's seat of the armored landau, for just one day after independence was declared, the plague had struck that part of the city where all the coachmen usually gathered, and quickly spread to them all. Coachman Zekeriya had not been present at the time, so he had been spared, but after four of Arkaz's beloved contingent of courteous, elderly veteran coachmen all died on the same day, no one could even get hold of a carriage anymore. Affected by the deaths of their coachmen, the people of the island had imagined the landau without a driver that night, and it was this mood that the painter Tacettin had captured.

The day freedom and independence were declared, sixteen people died of plague in Arkaz. This was a little lower than the daily average. Seven of the deaths had occurred in Kofunya and Eyoklima. As the armored landau carrying the Commander to the garrison went down a narrow street between those two neighborhoods, a group of mourners who had come to offer their condolences at a house where a father and his daughter had just died watched as the torches burning on the carriage seemed to illuminate the entire neighborhood.

The shadows of all the ordinary people, the sick, the thieves, and the sinister roamers out on the streets stretched like phantoms upon the walls. Some people claimed they saw the city's plague-ridden, blood-spewing rats, its djinns, and the man who smeared plague-infested fluid on drinking taps all recoil from the light shining from the flag attached to the landau's flagpole. The news of the island's declaration of freedom and independence had given everyone hope.

The next day the old governor Sami Pasha was back in his office, but despite all the pressure upon him and all the questions people kept asking, he refrained from taking any drastic decisions. He spent most of his time standing on the balcony or having the remaining traces of the previous day's battle cleaned up from the meeting hall next door.

Later, Sami Pasha received a visit from the journalist Manolis. "Given that we have our freedom now, we shall assume the press to be free too!" the journalist boldly proclaimed, but Sami Pasha stalled.

"The press is free in free Mingheria," he said. "But in this historic, momentous time for this nation, I would advise you against publishing whatever may cross your mind without checking with us first. Your words, composed with nothing but enthusiasm and the purest of intentions, could easily be exploited by our enemies, by these hoodlums and guerrillas"—he continued, pointing at the Outbreak Room—"and turned against the cause of freedom and independence. We will announce a new government shortly, and new quarantine regulations with it!"

Sami Pasha personally arranged for the wounded attackers (starting with Ramiz) to be sent to prison as soon as they were discharged from hospital. The new governor's entourage had escaped with minor wounds, but although they had requested a meeting with the Pasha, he had put Deputy Hadi and all the rest of them in a boat and had them sent back to the quarantine facility in the Maiden's Tower, rejecting their request to attend the fallen governor Ibrahim Hakkı Pasha's funeral simply because it was easier to do so.

On that first day, Sami Pasha was mostly busy dealing with the small, lesser-known Asr-ı Saadet lodge (named after the "Golden Age" of Islam during which the Prophet Muhammad was alive) and its disciples, the so-called Golden Agers. They were a withdrawn and somewhat-impecunious lot. They did not meddle in politics or commerce, and had no relations or associations with any other group. They had decided entirely of their own volition to defy the ban on worshipping in mosques, and were prepared to fight for this if they had to. It was really only a small group that frequented this lodge, and their sheikh, Sajid Effendi, who lived in Tatlısu, was half mad.

Nevertheless, the Pasha was determined to teach them a lesson, and thus show everyone the unswerving will of the new regime. Before the Golden Agers could make the first move, he sent a group of his own most trusted guards to the small Asr-ı Saadet lodge. The mood at the lodge was angry and defiant (the Governor's men had assumed the disciples would be meek and peaceable, and that they might have to be goaded into action), and initially, the Governor's team was turned away on some pretext. When they realized someone must have tipped the Governor off about their plans to conduct prayers at the mosque, the Golden Agers became even more enraged. Before even a day had passed from when "Commander" Kâmil had declared the Free State of Mingheria, the first clash between the new state and the people of the island had already taken place. The Asr-ı Saadet's band of idlers, shirkers, and devout believers went at Sami Pasha's guards with bats and firewood.

The Governor's men fought back for a short while before retreating. The bravest and brawniest of the guards, Swarthy Kadir, suffered a cut on his eyebrow, and another guard was almost knocked out. Sami Pasha had to wait until the afternoon before he was able to call upon the Quarantine Regiment for reinforcements and mount a renewed attack. Some historians have pointed to this slowness and lack of means as an indication of the true extent of the "authority" and helplessness of the newly founded state.

Before the sun set that evening, Sami Pasha took his armored carriage to the garrison. Commander Kâmil—with Zeynep by his side—was lying on a couch in the guesthouse there, and when he saw the Pasha, he made as if to sit up, but then lay back down immediately. The Commander had already rallied somewhat, the color had come back to his cheeks, and his expression had softened. He had removed his Ottoman badges and medals but had kept his military uniform on. It gave his presence a handsome, impressive, poetic quality. We should like to note here that in that moment our hero was haloed by that special light which always falls upon people when they are about to step onto the stage of history. Zeynep and her brothers, the doctors, the clerks, and everyone else now left the garrison guesthouse. Sami Pasha closed the door. The two men spent exactly thirty minutes alone inside that room. (Doctor Tassos had asked the Pasha not to spend more than half an hour with the injured commander, so as not to wear him out.)

It has often been claimed that during those thirty minutes, these two men—the Commander and the last Ottoman governor—would discuss and determine the shape of the island's future for fifty years to come. Until the day of their not-too-distant deaths, neither the Major nor the former governor Sami Pasha would ever speak a word to anyone else about what they had said to each other inside that room. Nevertheless, there have been countless articles produced on this subject.

As Sami Pasha's landau left the garrison, Sergeant Sadri fired the first of twenty-five blank shells announcing the independence of the island of Mingheria. The sun had just set. A light that existed nowhere else, colored somewhere between purple and pink, had appeared on the horizon, and two rows of clouds—one red, the other orange—were merging with another bank of shadowy, darkening clouds above them.

On his ride back to the soon-to-be-renamed Governor's Residence, with the cannon firing in the background, Sami Pasha knew that the only way he would be able to soothe the turbulence in his soul was by talking to Marika about it, but as he had already decided that he was not going to reveal any state secrets until at least the next day, he did not go to see her after all. As the cannon continued its salute, he gazed out of the window of his office in the State Hall and tried to see the city in the dark.

The booming of the cannon left the whole of Arkaz shuddering with a fearsome roar that only seemed to get louder every time it echoed on the rocky cliffs. Years later, when people whose childhood in Arkaz had coincided with the outbreak of plague were asked what had scared them the most, many of them would recall—often smiling as they did so—the sound of these blank shells. For at first almost everyone on the island had assumed that these must be the warships firing their guns, and that the Great Powers must have decided to attack.

But as the shells were being fired one at a time, and at lengthy, regular intervals, people soon realized this must be something else altogether. It took nearly two hours for the single cannon to fire its twenty-five shells. Afterward, the city and the port returned to that preternatural hush that had prevailed ever since the mosques and churches had been closed, and church bells and calls to prayer silenced.

The next morning, by the time the landau sent by Sami Pasha (with Coachman Zekeriya driving in his smartest uniform) had brought Commander Kâmil back to the State Hall Square, most people had understood that the shells from the night before had been fired to announce Mingheria's independence to the world. When Commander Kâmil—a native son of the island and bringer of its newfound independence—stepped out of the armored landau, the garrison's brass band began to play what they knew best: the "Hamidiye March," which had been composed in honor of Abdul Hamid. Gendarmes and soldiers from the Quarantine Regiment were standing at attention at the entrance to the State Hall.

"We need a new national anthem composed by a Mingherian!" Sami Pasha remarked when they were alone in his office.

He inspected the Major's bandaged arm, which was in a sling, and his uniform, which looked austere and all the more majestic now that he had removed his medals and badges.

"They're all here now . . . You must sit at the head of the table. But I should walk in first!"

"Let us both go in together. There is no need for ceremony."

With these words, Commander Kâmil followed Sami Pasha into the large meeting hall next door. Already sitting in the chairs around the main table were some prominent quarantine officials, several members of the Quarantine Committee, neighborhood representatives, heads of various municipal departments, Doctor Nuri, Doctor Nikos, and a few other doctors. They were all sitting as far apart as possible.

"We would have liked to invite more people to this meeting . . . But it is not possible," said Sami Pasha. "Please do not cough in each other's direction. Everything we have done so far has been to stop the outbreak, save Mingherian lives, and secure our survival. As you all know, we have only taken this step because we had no choice but to declare independence."

As Sami Pasha continued to talk, it became clear to all assembled that they were about to be faced with the onerous task of drawing up or perhaps approving a constitution for the new sovereign state of Mingheria. Two clerks sat at the edge of the table, ready to transcribe the articles of the constitution as they were read out.

"One: The Mingherian people live on the island of Mingheria, in the state of Mingheria," Sami Pasha began. "Two: Mingheria belongs to the Mingherians. Three: The free and sovereign state of Mingheria is governed by the Republic of Mingheria on behalf of the Mingherian people. The government rules in the name of the Mingherian people. Four: The people of Mingheria are governed under the rule of law, which shall apply to them all. A detailed constitution will be drafted. All Mingherian citizens are equal. Five: The Mingherian people shall have full jurisdiction on all decisions pertaining to court affairs, property deeds, the official registry, taxation, the military, customs regulations, postal services, port access, agriculture, trade, and any other matters, and unless otherwise indicated, and until alternative provisions are announced, the old Ottoman regime's records, its banknotes and coins, and its ranks, hierarchies, and honors shall remain in effect." Once these first five articles had been written down, and he'd had the document signed by what he had now begun to call the "parliament"—those forty people who were gathered in the room, a vast majority of whom were Muslims rather than Greeks—Sami Pasha turned to the subject of the composition of the new government and other organizational matters.

The Chief of Charitable Trusts was to become the Minister for Charitable Trusts; Quarantine Master Doctor Nikos would be the new Minister for Public Health (and, as an exceptional measure, Doctor Nuri would be made the new government's Quarantine Minister); the Head of Customs would be appointed Customs Minister, and the chief of the gendarmes would become the new Minister for Internal Affairs. By this logic, nobody in the State Hall—henceforth to be called the Ministerial Headquarters—would even have to move offices. In any case, what mattered most was to get things done, and make sure quarantine regulations were implemented properly. Titles were not that important. From now on the island would decide for itself.

By the end of this long speech, everyone had understood that Sami Pasha saw himself as the "Chief Minister" of this new regime. The Pasha did not spend any more time on titles and positions; it hadn't even been two days since the Major had stood on that balcony and waved the flag of Mingheria in front of the people. He decided he should say something to forestall any overt objections from those who were displeased with the thoroughly sensible decision to declare independence and break away from Istanbul and Ottoman rule.

"As you all know, we are living through extraordinary times," said Sami Pasha, preparing to bring his speech to a close. "The great people of Mingheria are battling the plague in a bid to preserve their very existence. While we have supervised this battle, we have also become unwitting spectators to the Mingherian people's entrance into the realm of civilized nations. Commander Kâmil has been our leader throughout this struggle. I propose that he is elevated to the rank of General, and given the title of Pasha, and suggest that we take a vote. The motion is passed. I now nominate Commander Kâmil Pasha for the position of president of the Republic of Mingheria. Those who agree please raise your hands. Commander Kâmil Pasha has been chosen as the first president of Mingheria. The ruling shall be announced this evening with twenty-five cannon blasts."

Everyone looked at the Commander.

"I would like to thank this distinguished parliament, which represents the will of the Mingherian people!" said Commander Kâmil. He stood up to dispense a series of elaborate bows, though he kept smiling throughout. "I too would like to propose an article for our constitution, and one that should be included right at the start: 'The language of Mingheria is Mingherian, which is the native language of the island of Mingheria and of the Mingherian people! Turkish and Greek shall temporarily be the official languages of the state.'"

There was a moment of silence. The Major noticed that Sami Pasha looked displeased.

The Greek doctor Tassos clapped and said, "Bravo!"

As Greek was not an official language of the Ottoman Empire, the inclusion of this clause in the Mingherian constitution would certainly help to secure support for the new sovereign state among the island's Greek population. Until that moment everyone in the meeting had felt as if they were living in a scene from a fairy tale or a dream, but now matters had suddenly taken a more calculated turn, entering the domain of what we might perhaps call *Realpolitik*. At any rate it seemed likely that Greek too, like Turkish, would eventually be pushed aside to enable the Mingherian language to develop faster. This nationalistic, linguistic vision of Mingherian as the sole language of the island seemed a little too fantastical to the group who had gathered that day to solemnly deal with quarantine issues, so they did not take it too seriously. As for the Muslims in the delegation, the only thing that bothered them was that Greek had been made an official language too.

Commander Kâmil could sense their irritation. "For hundreds of years, we have lived as brothers on this beautiful island," he said. "It follows that the Quarantine Authority and the state must behave like a fair-minded father who maintains an equal distance from all his children. The first thing we must do if we wish to defeat this plague is to treat each other like brothers."

Commander Kâmil fell silent for a moment, as if to make sure his audience understood they were about to hear words they would never forget. "I am a Mingherian!" he said. "I am proud of being Mingherian—some might say excessively so. I regard myself as an honored and equal member of the international brotherhood of nations, and for that I feel immensely fortunate. But I yearn, too, for the international brotherhood of nations to recognize the magnificence of my Mingheria, of my island, and of my language. When my son is born, he will speak Mingherian at home, just like everyone else on this island. We must take these measures now so that when our children grow up and go to school, they will not feel ashamed of the words they speak at home and forget they ever learned them, and so that this plague may not destroy our Mingherian nation while the world watches on."

To this day, these are words that are fondly remembered—and tearfully recited—by every Mingherian citizen and anyone who has gone to school on the island. Most of the island's population will take enormous and rather joyful pride in proclaiming "I am a Mingherian!"—especially when they come across each other abroad. But even the slightest questioning of the obvious contradictions contained within this speech is strictly forbidden; one is simply not allowed to ask why the Turkish and the Greek and even the Italian and Arabic that our ancestors have spoken for hundreds of years should be considered inferior to the Mingherian language, especially if we were all supposed to be brothers. In 1901, only one in five children born on the island spoke Mingherian at home; neither could it be said that most of them grew up speaking Greek or Turkish. In any event, Commander Kâmil's improvised yet deeply poetic speech was unfortunately cut short when one of the municipal clerks who had been standing in the room suddenly slumped onto a chair and, unable to conceal his agony, begun to shiver and moan with the familiar, excruciating symptoms of plague fever.

CHAPTER 55

aving immediately put in place the requisite arrangements for his new role as Chief Minister, and quickly adjusted his manner and rhetoric accordingly, Sami Pasha got to work that same afternoon even as discussions over the new constitution continued in the large meeting room next door.

He decided first of all that the seven Golden Agers whom the Quarantine Regiment had arrested after a second confrontation with the lodge the night before should now be locked up in the Castle prison, with another group twice that size put into the Castle's isolation facility. Meanwhile the sheikh of another small sect—a man nicknamed Curly after the corkscrew curls in his hair and beard—had reportedly been heard claiming that "you can't be a true Muslim if you don't go to mosque, and using the plague as an excuse to close down mosques is a heartless affront to Islamic sensibilities," so Sami Pasha had him taken into custody too until he came to his senses. When Curly began to show signs of remorse, the Pasha let him go without resorting to the Castle dungeons. In preparation for the trial of Ramiz and his coconspirators, Sami Pasha also authorized a series of raids on several homes in the neighborhoods of Taşçılar and Kadirler, but not in Germe, where the targets would have been too close to the location of the Halifiye lodge.

Sami Pasha was paying particular attention to relations with the Halifiye lodge. He did not feel there was any fundamental disagreement with the lodge, and he wanted to make sure his actions were not misconstrued. It was a good thing Ramiz hadn't died when he had been wounded in the raid. Not only would this keep the Commander angry and alert, they would also be able to use Ramiz as leverage against Sheikh Hamdullah. The Halifiye lodge had been left rattled and dispirited by the news that their sheikh's brother had ended up injured and imprisoned after leading a bloody ambush that had cost many people their lives. Chief Minister Sami Pasha couldn't even find out which building and which room Sheikh Hamdullah had withdrawn to in contemplation. He did not consult with the Commander on how they should approach the disciples of the Halifiye sect. But he did send orders for Ramiz and his men to be tried and sentenced as soon as possible, and told the Commander what he had done.

"The state of Mingheria must be fair and just!" Commander Kâmil replied.

The former governor and new Chief Minister Sami Pasha soon worked out which matters were worth bringing to the Commander's attention, and how best to present them. The Commander was not too interested in administrative details around the roles of government clerks and employees, nor in questions of bureaucratic protocol. On the other hand he was quick to grasp the intricacies of topics like departmental budgets, money, government salaries, troop numbers, and how to use the garrison's Arab division to maintain law and order, and closely followed every development on these various fronts. There were also a number of issues in which he was more personally invested, and he would regularly bring these up for the government to resolve.

One of these related to a new series of postage stamps to mark the foundation of the state of Mingheria. The Commander had given Post Minister Dimitris Effendi direct orders in this regard. But when the minister told him that there were no printers on the island, or even in Smyrna or Thessaloniki, who were worthy of such a task, and that the stamps would have to be ordered from Paris, the Commander was not pleased. He insisted that the minister find some technical solution using whatever resources were available on the island. If the printers had all fled because of the plague, then the Minister for Internal Affairs should be told to find them . . . Sami Pasha quickly realized that the President's main concern was to see his own likeness and the landscapes of Mingheria reproduced on these postage stamps.

Another matter the Commander personally looked into was the distribution of gifts—similar to the rewards newly enthroned sultans would dispense to the Empire's military and bureaucratic cadres—among the members of Mingheria's government and parliament. He knew that there was very little money left in the coffers of the State Hall—that is to say, the new state treasury. So he came up with a creative solution to their predicament. All officials who supported him would be issued with a signed document certifying that they had been gifted a sizable plot of land on the island, and that this land was exempt from any tax on agricultural production. Today, one hundred and sixteen years later, anyone wishing to confirm the validity of these gift "deeds" and tax exemptions with Mingheria's land registry must first submit a detailed court application.

The blank shells fired late that afternoon to announce the Commander's presidency of the Mingherian state were greeted more warmly this time. The number of deaths was not falling, and finding food was becoming more difficult, but the people of Arkaz were fond of their young, daring commander who had organized the Telegraph Raid and married the girl he'd fallen in love with on the island. As it would have been fanciful to even think of organizing another official ceremony just three days after the deadly battle in the State Hall, it was decided to print posters instead, similar to the first quarantine announcements, and as soon as the last shell was fired, these signs were hung up on every street in Arkaz to declare that Commander Kâmil Pasha had been proclaimed president of the free and sovereign Republic of Mingheria, and that everyone must respect quarantine regulations and obey the instructions of the island's new government.

During the days of the "Mingherian Revolution," only half of the State Hall's permanent and salaried staff were turning up for work. Some were no longer leaving their homes; some had fled to their villages; and some had died. Most of the clerks who were still reporting to the former State Hall and new Ministerial Headquarters were only doing so for the free lunch, and to make sure their salaries were not snapped up by someone else. The State Hall's long list of tasks was therefore being handled almost entirely by a handful of middle and high ranked officials who had originally come from Istanbul and were motivated by a strong sense of responsibility. When they saw the signs on the walls on their way to work the next morning, these Ottoman bureaucrats were dismayed to realize that if what the posters said was true, they would effectively be expected to choose between the government in Istanbul and the new Mingherian state. They all knew by now that Istanbul had removed Governor Sami Pasha from his post, but that the new governor dispatched by Abdul Hamid had since been killed.

Had there been a revolt of this sort in any Ottoman city or island where a young Sami Pasha might be serving as a mayor or a local chief or a middle-ranked bureaucrat, and had he been forced—as was the case now—to make a choice between the island and Istanbul, he would of course have chosen Istanbul. Whatever their excuse, he too would have regarded any government official who did not do the same as a "traitor." So he could easily understand why some of the island's bureaucrats—such as the Chief of Charitable Trusts Nizami Bey (who had just got married, and whose wife was back in Istanbul) or Deputy Treasurer Abdullah Bey (who had never quite warmed up to the island, and didn't like it here)—wished to return immediately to Istanbul. As for those officials like the Chief Scrutineer (whose wife was from a wealthy family from the island) and the Municipal Codebreaker Mehmet Fazıl Bey whom Sami Pasha assumed would be unsure about what to do, he had put them in the committee charged with drafting the constitution specifically so that their staying on the island might help set an example to others.

The clerks who were of Greek origins, or who had been born and always lived on the island, had no serious objections to the declaration of freedom and independence, and enjoyed the excuse to forget about the plague and quarantine for a few minutes to talk and laugh with each other about the new positions and titles (minister, director, etc.) they had suddenly been given, if only on paper. Would Istanbul retaliate? Would they still be able to draw their salaries? What new titles would there be on the signed land deeds they were going to be gifted? What about the salaries Sami Pasha had promised them?

The clerks who were loyal to Istanbul and the Ottoman state, on the other hand, were disinclined to make any jokes, did not take their new titles seriously, and hardly thought about money at all, and even though they considered the situation to be rather delicate, they kept their misgivings to themselves. Sami Pasha knew every single one of these loyal, disconcerted clerks, and could see in their eyes and in their dour, dejected demeanor the terror they felt at the prospect of whatever punishment Abdul Hamid might one day mete out, and the fear that they might never see their wives and children or be able to go home again.

"The state of Mingheria is judicious and compassionate," he'd told them, smiling as he spoke. "We have no intention of keeping anyone here against their will, or of holding anyone hostage. We have summoned only a few of you here, so please do pass this message on to your colleagues. We are ready to help anyone who does not wish to be involved with the revolutionary government, and even those who prefer to leave and return to Istanbul. The Mingherian state is a friend of the Ottoman Empire. Everything will be fine, as soon as we no longer have this plague to deal with."

His manner had been amicable, as if he were discussing a mere bureaucratic hitch.

"If this goes on for much longer, we'll be betraying the motherland, the Sultan, and Islam itself," said Rahmetullah Effendi, the Mayor of Teselli.

"These are groundless suppositions!" said Sami Pasha. He hardly knew this man and had only invited him at the Commander's ill-advised suggestion, which he now realized he should never have heeded. For he had hoped this would be a meeting where expressions like "treason" and "What will His Supreme Highness think!" would never be used. "Ultimately, I'm not from this island either . . . ," said Sami Pasha uncertainly. "But there is no need for you to worry. If we were to harm you in any way, they would use that as an excuse to try and invade the island."

"The island already belongs to the Ottoman Empire and to our sultan, so it would be wrong to call that an invasion!" said Rahmetullah Effendi.

"If we let you and the others who've chosen Istanbul go back, they'll have you spying against us."

"Your Excellency, there are fifteen to twenty people dying every day. As long as this outbreak continues, no one would even think to invade the island. So there would not be any need for spies either."

"Those who continue to fulfill their duties shall soon be paid any overdue salaries accrued under the previous regime and receive their new salaries too. Those who resign from their posts in fear of betraying the Ottoman Empire shall receive their old, accumulated salaries only after the others have all been paid."

If anyone was thinking, "Is this the time to be talking about salaries?" they kept their thoughts to themselves. An ashy light was coming through the window, and the green of the pine trees had turned lead gray. With no calls to prayer and no church bells ringing, the clouds above the city hung heavier, and both the blue of the sky and people's resolve seemed to have wilted.

Some commentators have rightly remarked that by the end of these prolonged discussions, Sami Pasha had not only managed to sow division in the ranks of the Ottoman contingent who were in favor of returning to Istanbul immediately, but had also secured—by succeeding in keeping them on the island—the support of a powerful faction who had no choice but to take his side against the Greeks. These people, all of whom spoke Turkish in their homes, had decided the best thing to do was to keep a low profile until the plague was gone and Ottoman soldiers and warships could finally come to their rescue. That evening, Sami Pasha had Mayor Rahmetullah Effendi, Chief of Charitable Trusts Nizami Bey, and Deputy Treasurer Abdullah Bey—the angriest and most vocal of the Ottoman clerks who wished to return to Istanbul—picked up from their homes by a team of gendarmes and Quarantine Regiment soldiers and sent to the Maiden's Tower. With each passing day, the little quarantine island with its charming white building would become more like a prison where the Mingherian state could lock up mostly Turkish-speaking Ottoman citizens (there were only two Greek speakers there) who remained loyal to Abdul Hamid.

That night, as the boat with its loyal Ottoman bureaucrats on board sailed silently from the bay toward the Maiden's Tower, Sami Pasha stepped onto the balcony of his office in the Ministerial Headquarters. It was the first time he had come out here since Friday afternoon, the day of the revolution. As frogs croaked and cicadas chirped on the banks of the Arkaz Creek and in the hidden nooks of the city, he stood there and tried to hear the soft splash of the rowboat carrying the Ottoman clerks away.

CHAPTER 56

The happiest couple on the island during this time was undoubtedly President Kâmil and his young wife Zeynep. As they were treating the Major's wound, Doctor Tassos had taken one look at Zeynep and announced that she was pregnant, transforming the newlyweds' lives.

Zeynep had been feeling like a prisoner at the garrison guesthouse, where she didn't even get to see her mother. Ramiz and his men were in jail now, so there was nothing to fear from them. Besides, the garrison guesthouse was not an appropriate home for the head of state, nor was it a suitable base from which he could attend to his duties. They decided they would return to the Splendid Palace.

As soon as they were back at the hotel, the Commander wore his military uniform, put on the epaulettes and collar patches that showed he was a pasha (and which had been readied for him in just two days), and went to visit his mother. The photographs taken that day of the Commander's mother in her headscarf, weeping as her son bent down to kiss her hand, are familiar to every Mingherian, endlessly reproduced in schoolbooks, on banknotes, and on lottery tickets, and a staple of the Mother's Day celebrations that have become increasingly popular on the island since the 1950s. The copy of Mizancı Murat's volume on the French Revolution and liberty (written in "old Turkish" using the Arabic script) currently displayed in the museum in Major Kâmil's childhood home is another important artifact, and the subject of many visiting schoolchildren's homework assignments.

The Major allocated the first floor of the Hotel Splendid to the Quarantine Regiment, while the second floor would house his own office (smaller than Sami Pasha's, as it was effectively a large hotel room) and that of his deputy, Chief Scrutineer Mazhar, whom Chief Minister Sami Pasha had sent along with a clerk, and whom we can now also call the Chief Secretary of the President of the Republic. The Major and Zeynep had also rearranged their private quarters upstairs and already decided where they were going to put the baby's crib.

To ensure all these rooms were furnished to the highest standards, the state requisitioned all the furniture from the wealthy Greek Mavroyenis family's magnificent four-story mansion (complete with viewing turret) overlooking today's Flizvos beach, an act which has since been widely criticized. To the Greek community, this incident was a sign that when it came to mistreating Christians, the new regime was no better than the Ottomans.

The Major (whom we cannot after all call President of the Republic every time) had already made up his mind that his child was going to be a boy, and sent word to the archaeologist Selim Sahir requesting a list of old Mingherian boys' names. He was convinced that his son was going to be a very special person. The first words the child heard and spoke would of course have to be in Mingherian. Accordingly, he had been trying to spend more time alone with Zeynep so that they could talk to each other in Mingherian, but this was not easy to do amid the abundance of day-to-day duties the president of a new state inevitably faced.

Husband and wife both knew that they owed their intimacy and their enduring happiness amidst the calamities unfolding around them to the seclusion they enjoyed in their living quarters on the top floor of the Splendid Palace. Sometimes they would open one of the windows as they held each other, and listen to the motionless, unstirring, death-soaked silence of the city. Sometimes they would gaze through a cloud of black smoke rising from a burning house and across the bay at the sick, the suspected cases, and the hapless, idling figures assembled in the Castle's isolation courtyard.

They had also invented a sexual game they would play in bed together: they would fix their eyes upon some spot on the other's naked body (though not their most private regions), touch the belly button, the nipple, the ear, the finger, or the shoulder they had focused on, and find a fruit, an object, a bird, or some other animal to compare it to. They could both see how this game had helped them grow more comfortable with nakedness, with sexual intimacy, and with each other.

When they brought their eyes and noses close to some spot on the other's skin, they would notice the mosquito bites and insect stings, the scratches, the bruises, the moles, and strange spots on there too. As they were constantly being stung by mosquitoes, their necks and legs were covered in red welts. Sometimes these rashes and lumps they found on each other's bodies would make them uneasy. "What's this!" a horrified Zeynep had exclaimed one day when she had found a small swelling somewhere between the Major's armpit and his back. But to their relief, they were able to conclude from its good-natured itching and from the pore at its center that it was only a mosquito bite rather than a potential plague bubo.

In the two months he had spent on the island, the Major had seen firsthand how the fear of death could rise like a demon and come between husbands and wives, mothers and sons, fathers and daughters. Back when he was still guarding Doctor Nuri, he had become furious with a married couple he had seen in Theodoropoulos Hospital who could not look after their children anymore because they had both caught the plague at the same time. In a house near the sea in the Kadirler neighborhood, they had found a boy with an enormous bubo on his neck, but only when his father had fallen sick too and could no longer muster the strength to argue with the Quarantine Regiment had they finally been able to wrest the child away from his family and take him to the hospital. Whenever any member of a family developed a plague bubo, all the others would naturally pay much-closer attention to any redness, insect bites, and lumps they might find on their own bodies. In those moments, the Major would see in their faces the signs of that loneliness which made the thought of death so intolerable.

The day they moved from the garrison back to the Splendid Palace, he was running his hand over the bandage around his wound when he felt a hardness near his right armpit. Making sure Zeynep didn't see him, he took out a handheld mirror to check, and saw a fairly large red welt. But unlike with plague victims' buboes, it didn't hurt when he touched it—only itched a little. Nor was the President feeling any of the fatigue, fever, or other symptoms he had observed in plague patients with developing buboes. That said, he had occasionally been coughing for the past two days. In some cases, the disease had been known to start with a cough.

If he were to catch the plague, would he recognize the signs straightaway, and would he be able to accept what they meant? More than anything else, Major Kâmil hated cowards.

Ever since the young Ottoman officer Kâmil had become president and commander, he had noticed that his deepest and most private thoughts and emotions, and even his dreams, had all begun to change. This was not a painful shift, but it did surprise him. He was more "idealistic" now, more unselfish, and more determined than ever before to dedicate his life to the island, to his son, and to the people of Mingheria. Every time these feelings took hold of him, he understood the joy of being a better person.

After his unexpected rise to the position of President-Commander of Mingheria, the Major had also begun to feel that he had been destined for this. Could it really be just a coincidence that he was now the President of a whole nation, of the beloved island of his birth and childhood, when just three days ago he had been but a low-ranked army officer (though admittedly one who'd been awarded a medal after the war with Greece)? At the military academy in Harbiye, the Major had always thought he was fortunate that none of the other Mingherian students had grades as good as his. But he realized now that there had been no coincidence there either, and wanted everyone else to see that too. When his son grew up, he would learn about what kind of person his father had been in his youth and student days.

He was delighted to receive the next morning a letter from the archaeologist Selim Sahir responding to his question about old Mingherian names for boys. He had been sitting at his desk in his office, gazing out of the second-floor windows of the Splendid Palace at the view through the tops of the acacias and pine trees, and thinking how mournful the empty harbor and docks and the deserted sloping road to the shore all looked.

The contents of the letter—which is now held in the Presidential Archives of Mingheria—troubled Commander Kâmil, who summoned his deputy and former Chief Scrutineer Mazhar and had him carefully read the handwritten missive aloud.

"Have you ever heard any of these names before?" he asked Mazhar Effendi.

After he'd been sent to the island, the former Chief Scrutineer had ended up getting married and staying there, but he was not from a Mingherian family, and he had spent his childhood in Istanbul. Having apologetically explained all this to the Major, he went on to say how much he loved Mingheria, how happy everyone—and especially the island's Muslims—were about their newfound freedom and independence, and finally confessed that he had never heard a single one of these old Mingherian names before.

"Neither have I!" said the President, without concealing his disappointment.

They summoned the clerk and had him look at the letter too. The clerk stumbled over the pronunciation of a couple of words in French and of the names listed in Mingherian. The letter was mostly written in Turkish using the Arabic script, with the list of Mingherian names and a few flowery expressions in French spelled out in the Roman alphabet. Perhaps it was out of nervousness that the clerk, who had been born and brought up in Mingheria, couldn't quite work the names out either. The President was also annoyed that the archaeologist had addressed him—somewhat derisively—as *commandant,* purposely using the French word for "commander."

"Archaeologist Selim Sahir Bey must study our history better!" he said. "You will work with the post and customs ministers to draw up a series of regulations around this."

The President had become accustomed to his new office very quickly. He was kept up to date on the number of deaths by a clerk who brought news from the Ministerial Headquarters twice a day, and had stopped going to the Outbreak Room in the mornings. He was no longer in charge of the Quarantine Regiment either. He had handed that duty over to Hamdi Baba, in a modest ceremony during which he had presented the Sergeant with the first military badge ever to be issued in Mingheria.

Most of the island's best tailors, who were all Greeks, had fled to Smyrna and Thessaloniki on the last ships to leave the island, but the President still managed to have Yakoumi Effendi tracked down, and ordered a set of new civilian suits for the winter and for official functions after the plague, requesting to be shown fabric samples and possible designs in advance. Later that day, Doctor Nuri arrived to discuss the newest death toll and the latest developments on the epidemiology map.

Around twelve to fifteen people were dying every day. The death rate was mostly stable now, but things remained far more difficult than they had hoped for. Unfortunately, people were still regularly flouting quarantine measures, some out of stubbornness and defiance, others through thoughtlessness and a kind of misguided courage.

Commander Kâmil addressed the Doctor and Prince Consort—the man whose protection he'd until so recently been assigned to—as respectfully as he had always done. "Her Highness Princess Pakize is under the protection of the new state of Mingheria," he told him. Doctor Nuri had arrived in Sami Pasha's landau. He proposed that they use it now for a tour of the city, so that the Commander could assess the situation too.

"I'd rather go out on foot and see for myself, rather than peer out of an armored carriage!" replied Commander Kâmil Pasha.

As they strolled through the streets, Commander Kâmil could tell how loved he was from the way people behaved around him, the way they looked at him, and mostly from the things they said—shouting "Hurrah!" from their windows as he walked past (this had happened seven or eight times in the last three days alone). He wanted to turn their love into an abiding hopefulness, a shared faith that would shield the island not just from the plague but from every other kind of misfortune too. It was his God-given duty to protect all these good people who gave him hopeful smiles when they recognized him on the street, and to ensure they made it through the outbreak alive.

The Commander had requested two hundred Mingherian flags (even small ones would do) to be procured and paid for with money from the government's budget, but with most of the island's tailors, drapers, and cloth merchants having long since fled, and with no possibility of importing linen from abroad, this was no easy task. Perhaps that was why so many of the families who had been hiding from the plague at home did not yet know there was a new flag and a new state. There were plenty of others, too, who were simply indifferent or uninformed . . . It was hard work bringing this nation to heel. But President-Commander Kâmil did not despair. He was sure that this country would survive for much longer, perhaps for hundreds of years more, than anyone currently living and breathing upon the island. Everyone was saying that the creation of the new state had given people hope, and convinced them that the outbreak could be stopped. It was a hope that came from seeing

Major Kâmil out on the streets, from his determination, his enthusiasm, his fervor. The young commander's connection with Princess Pakize had already associated him in people's minds with Istanbul, the palace, and the sultanate; his actions during the Telegraph coup had earned him their esteem; and when he had waved that flag in challenge to the whole world, they had happily followed his lead.

Sometimes Commander Kâmil would think that being a Min-gherian by birth was a blessing from Allah. When he caught people's eyes as they looked out of their windows, and they smiled at him as they were doing now, he saw gratitude in their expressions. It was because he reminded them of how blessed they really were. They were fortunate to have been born here.

Those among the island's poorer population, and who had not taken the outbreak seriously nor prepared for it in any way, were now suffering the most, and slowly beginning to starve. The Commander felt a sense of responsibility toward them. Anyone who didn't have an orchard, a field, some land, or friends outside the city had soon run out of food. Their plight could be blamed on the previous Ottoman government, which had failed to properly educate them on the seriousness of the outbreak. In fact, at first Governor Sami Pasha had protested that there was no outbreak at all! He really was a fool, that Sami Pasha.

Flanked by a pair of guards, and followed by several more, the Commander emerged onto Hamidiye Avenue (all of these old Ottoman street names would have to be changed too). He ventured into the alleyways between the Hagia Triada Church and the Arkaz Creek, where there was a high concentration of grocery stores. In their fear of the plague and of being fined by the Quarantine Authorities, and exhausted by all the restrictions they faced, more than half the shops that stocked staples like flour and potatoes had stopped opening their doors, and now traded their goods elsewhere, if not directly from their owners' homes. All food—from olives to cheese (if it could even be found), from walnuts to dried figs (said to be dangerous)—had tripled in price. Even cheaper items like onions, leafy vegetables, and potatoes, which were usually readily available from market stalls, had all but disappeared. The baker-ies were producing half their usual quantities of bread and buns. But the Commander was not too worried about that yet, for he had heard from Sami Pasha that there was a reserve of flour in the garrison, set aside at Abdul Hamid's insistence. Butchers and poultry dealers were selling cuts to customers through their back doors, charging three or four times their usual prices. Deemed to be unsanitary, most poultry dealers, fish-mongers, and offal vendors had already been forced to close, and the cats that used to roam around their shopfronts had disappeared.

With so many people fleeing or dying every day, the population of the island kept falling, but the market and the shops were emptying at an even faster rate, and could no longer feed people. Conscious of this problem, Sami Pasha had looked to the food market that had sprung up and developed of its own accord in the Greek Middle School while the island had still been under Ottoman control, and tried to make sure, in his new role as Chief Minister of the state of Mingheria, that it contin-ued to operate as a place where the poor could find something to eat. The Commander and his retinue now turned left toward this market and into a series of alleyways. But it could be dangerous to walk beneath the bay windows that hung over these narrow streets. Most of the men in the city had nothing to do now but to sit at their windows all day and wait for time to pass.

The only way for trade to resume, and for Arkaz to be fed, was to allow a serious breach of quarantine regulations. There were guards sta-tioned around the edges of the city whose task was to stop people from wandering in as they pleased. Anyone wanting to leave the city on foot either had to show the Quarantine Regiment a permit bearing a profu-sion of stamps and signatures, or do what many people did and wait until nightfall to walk in total darkness through the empty, rocky, wind-swept fields behind Upper Turunçlar and Hora. If you could avoid the stray dogs, bandits, deranged plague victims, rats, and the plague demon himself, it was perfectly possible to slip out of the city in the middle of the night and flee into the surrounding countryside. But if you wanted to come in and out three times a week to trade your wares, you needed a special permit and protection. The new government hadn't done any-thing about any of these issues yet.

The decision to keep the market in the Greek Middle School open had reminded Doctor Nuri, as well as Sami Pasha and Commander Kâmil, of the fundamental contradiction (as in the Pilgrim Ship Affair) that afflicted any quarantine effort. Of course it was necessary to be strict for quarantine to succeed. But if you took that strictness too far, the same people who were looking at the Commander now with smiles full of hope could just as quickly turn their backs on the revolution, and on freedom and independence too.

No one in the city was dying of hunger yet, but the poorest and most bereft—those who'd lost everything and everyone they had in the outbreak—had turned to begging. At first Sami Pasha had sent gendarmes and police to scare these guileless, inexperienced beggars off the streets, and even locked a few of them up on some pretext with the petty criminals in the Castle prison, but when he realized that many of these desperate, destitute people actually preferred the prison dormitories and the free soup they would get there to the hunger and death they'd have to face out on the streets, he decided the best thing to do would be to let the quarantine soldiers deal with the matter. Hamdi Baba and two of his men were now limiting themselves to moving these beggars off the main roads, citing quarantine laws. This measure had already been introduced two weeks ago when the island had still been under Ottoman control, but the same policy continued to be applied now.

The Commander soon made a habit of going out at least once a day on long walks through the streets of Arkaz, so that he could see for himself what was happening in the city. He would turn up where quarantine measures were causing quarrels and clashes and disagreements, and encourage people to submit to the Quarantine Regiment. Sometimes he would go somewhere in order to learn as much as he could about a particular problem. In these cases, someone already familiar with the matter in question might be invited to join the Commander on his walk.

It was in this context that on Saturday, the sixth of July, the President took the baker brothers Hadid and Majid to visit a new "villagers' market" on the banks of the Arkaz Creek, and discuss possible solutions to Arkaz's growing food shortage. When they arrived at their destination, they saw fresh-faced village youths selling mullet and trout, and old Greek women in headscarves offering mallow, nettle, and other similar plants.

Ever since two children who'd been driven mad by dread and loneliness had decided to run away from home, then come back and reported that they had survived on the mallow they had found in the highlands outside the city, this strange plant that grew on the mountains and could be eaten raw or in soups had begun to be sold in the few shops that were still open, and especially in these new street markets.

We should note that even by this point, most Mingherians were still managing to feed themselves, one way or another. In a bid to stop people smugglers, Chief Minister Sami Pasha had banned fishing boats for a time, but he had since lifted that ban, for he could see that the island subsisted on fish. The daughter of Constantinos Effendi, bishop of the Greek congregation, wrote in her memoirs about those days of plague that in neighborhoods like Çite, Germe, and Kadirler, where the outbreak was at its strongest, children would go on fishing expeditions to feed their families. Creeping through people's back gardens, they would slip out of the city and move in groups across fields, secret paths, and hidden passageways, picking blackberries, wild strawberries, and mallow on their way, and within two hours they would reach the tall, rocky cliffs of the Damıtaş Valley, where the Damıtaş Creek flowed into the Mediterranean Sea. I would like to reassure those readers who might be feeling overwhelmed by our novel's somber mood that as they stood in those shallow waters, their trousers rolled up as they hunted for fish with baskets and nets tied to sticks, these children were really quite content. In her abovementioned memoirs, Constantinos Effendi's daughter writes in a "nostalgic" vein of how these children had heard the cannons announcing the *révolution* and the news of the Commander's presidency while they were wading in the mouth of the creek, nets in hand and trouser hems folded up to their knees as they looked for green-scaled mullet fish to catch.

I should point out here that I have always been greatly affected by a drawing I once saw in one of the old Mingherian magazines I used to leaf through as a little girl, where a group of these heroic children—who would effectively feed and sustain their families and neighborhoods—is shown with nets and traps in hand, fishing for green trout. Had I lived one hundred and sixteen years ago, and been born a boy instead of a girl, I could have been among those children too. With this in mind, and as we approach the end of our novel-cum-history, I suppose I should finally reveal that I am a direct descendant of one of this novel's principal characters.

There was a new market in a Greek primary school in the Hora neighborhood selling mullet fish as well as sorrel, mallow, and other similar plants. The President went with Hadid and Majid to visit this building where Greek children used to go to school before the plague began. Old quarantine posters still hung on the walls, and inside, in its gloomy classrooms set up with mousetraps and smelling strongly of Lysol, they saw that there were Muslim vendors too, selling consecrated prayer sheets against the plague. The plague had blurred the lines—both real and imaginary—that separated Arkaz's Muslims from its Christians.

Commander Kâmil and the brothers Majid and Hadid had been talking among themselves and taking stock of the situation as they stood among the many traders who had clustered in the courtyard of this tiny, charming little school, when they were approached by one of the boys who had come there, fishing boots still on their feet, to sell their catch from the creek.

The guards were about to intervene, just in case of any possible danger, when the Commander stopped them.

"In these troubled times, there is no one more deserving of our respect than these young heroes whose fishing exploits have rescued our free Mingheria from starvation," said Commander Kâmil. "Let him speak to his commander, whatever his petition may be!"

When the guards stepped aside, the sweet-looking, fez-wearing, pimply, unshaven boy—who was actually sixteen—took a few steps forward, pulled out a gun from the wide sash around his waist, and started shooting at the Commander's chest and face.

CHAPTER 57

The first bullet that emerged from the young man's revolver made a hole in the shoulder of the Commander's uniform, but did not touch his flesh and did not even leave a scratch.

Majid had already begun to suspect there was something wrong before the shot was fired, and when he saw the youth pull out a gun, he moved toward him. Some witnesses would describe seeing Majid trying to grab the weapon from the young man's hands, while others said that he had stepped in front of the Commander and shielded him with his own body.

The second shot hit Majid's heart, and the third landed right by his spine. Majid stumbled backward under the force of the bullets, then collapsed to the floor face-first and died on the spot.

The fourth bullet broke one of the primary school's windows, made with glass imported from Thessaloniki. The young man—whose name was later discovered to be Hasan—had pulled the trigger again while wrestling with the guards who were trying to take his gun, and hadn't been able to take aim.

Before he could fire for the fifth time, Hasan was finally and thoroughly overpowered, at which point he fell into an enduring, determined, and mysterious silence. Everyone was as confounded by his silent resolve as they were astonished and perhaps even a little incredulous to see young, handsome, strapping Majid drop dead the way he had. After all, this humble little market (visited mostly by children, curious passersby, and the unemployed, all of whom came to browse the stalls rather than to buy anything) was situated in the relatively sparsely populated neighborhood of Hora, far from the dangers and the atmosphere of violence that hung over the city center, the docks, and the area around the Castle.

Everyone in the market had scattered as soon as the first gunshots were heard, and the villagers and children who had been trading there did not return to their stalls and their baskets of fish for a very long time. The Commander had remained composed in the face of the sudden attack, thinking only—as he would later recount—of death, his wife, his unborn son, and the motherland.

The guards tied the young attacker's hands but did not have to hit him or rough him up, for sixteen-year-old Hasan didn't even try to resist when they led him to one of their carriages (which had swiftly turned up at the scene), took him to the former State Hall (still Sami Pasha's domain), and locked him up in the second of three narrow, empty cells across from the interrogation rooms in a corridor on the lowest floor of the building.

The attack on Commander Kâmil, hero of Mingheria's independence, had taken place around the time of midday prayers (though there was no call to prayer anymore). The President had wanted to visit the market before it closed for the day. But the only people who had known that the Commander would be there at that time were his deputy and the clerk on the second floor of the Splendid Palace. Could it all have been a coincidence? After all, Bonkowski Pasha had been killed in a similarly random encounter too.

Four hours later, a meeting on the second floor of the Splendid Palace attended by Chief Minister Sami Pasha and Deputy Mazhar resulted in a series of "radical" decisions which were put into action that same evening. Nationalist historians who enjoy drawing parallels between the humble Mingherian Revolution and some of the most significant events in world history have likened the days that would follow to the French Revolution's Jacobin Reign of Terror. There was indeed a resemblance, both with regards to the use of court trials and executions to subjugate the populace, and in the emergence of a political will based on the conviction that the "ideals of the revolution" would only succeed if their opponents were met with violence.

Sami Pasha had not invited Doctor Nuri—who always counseled moderation—to the meeting in the Commander's office. The Commander didn't ask after the Doctor and Prince Consort either, nor did he send anyone to fetch him. (Perhaps they considered him too much of an Istanbul man, and too close to the Ottoman regime.) The absence of Quarantine Minister Doctor Nuri not only contributed to harsher measures and decisions being made, and to a greater number of death sentences being issued, it also deprived Princess Pakize—and us too—of a source at the heart of events. In writing about the Mingherian Revolution's phase of "Jacobin Terror," we have therefore relied less on Princess Pakize's letters than we have on other witnesses' accounts.

Sami Pasha learned that although the young assassin continued to maintain his silence in spite of all the pressure he was under, it had nevertheless been quickly established that he came from a family that had arrived from Crete three years ago. Hasan's family had settled in Nebiler village in the north of the island, where they worked on a rose farm. The villages where Ramiz and his men had taken shelter were in the same area. The boy was bound to confess everything soon anyway, but in any case Sami Pasha had no doubt that Ramiz must be behind it all.

If Doctor and Prince Consort Nuri wished to follow Abdul Hamid's instructions and look for more clues and evidence "in the style of Sherlock Holmes," he was free to do so. But according to Sami Pasha, they must not let anything stand in the way of justice this time, for they had all seen Ramiz last week, gun in hand, leading the raid where six people had lost their lives—including some of Ramiz's own men, the caretaker and provocateur Nusret, and the new governor from Istanbul. In the eyes of the public, that alone would be more than enough to justify having Ramiz and his men hanged. In addition, it was probably Ramiz who was behind the barbaric murders of the Ottoman Empire's Chief Inspector of Public Health Bonkowski Pasha and of President-Commander Kâmil's brother-in-law and champion soldier Majid Effendi, all with the intent to cripple the quarantine effort and destroy the Mingherian people. The Ottoman administration's failure to punish this brute who'd made a habit of having people killed had been seen as a sign of fragility.

"If we show this unrepentant thug any mercy now, it could lead to even more deaths, and ultimately cost us our own lives too."

The President's deputy, Mazhar Effendi, said that the trial for the raid on the State Hall could begin as soon as Ramiz and his men's statements had been collected, with the resulting sentences carried out the next

morning. Everyone at the meeting on the second floor of the Splendid
Palace that day understood that there would have to be other executions
too, along with Ramiz's. It was the majority's unspoken wish that this
should happen immediately. It would later be claimed that the President
had been instrumental in pushing these tough decisions through, but
that he did not wish for this to be known.

It was agreed that six lodges—including the Rifai and the Zaim—that
had been causing trouble for Sami Pasha, the doctors, and the Quarantine Regiment, should now be turned into hospitals. Soldiers from the
Quarantine Regiment and neighborhood representatives would be sent
into the buildings and grounds of these lodges to set up facilities where
plague patients could be taken in and treated, and some lodges might
have to be vacated completely. Harsher punishments would also be
introduced for anyone obstructing the work of the quarantine soldiers,
or caught defying quarantine restrictions, and a house in Taşçılar—a
neighborhood densely populated with migrants from Crete—would be
burned down together with the rubbish dump beside it, given that all
efforts to disinfect it had so far proven fruitless.

Sami Pasha also ordered two streets in the Çite neighborhood—where
the outbreak was at its worst and the number of deaths just wouldn't
drop—to be cordoned off. Some have suggested that the measures
decided upon that day and later enforced by armed soldiers would end
up compounding the island's already catastrophic situation, and to an
extent they may be right. It was certainly a thoroughly ill-conceived and
indeed primitive move to ban all villagers' markets from Arkaz simply
because that was where the latest assassination had taken place. This
same decision would fuel the widespread hunger and rage that eventually followed. But we can also understand why the rulers of the island
might have begun to feel there was nothing else they could do now but
resort to state-sponsored violence and brutality.

The detail that everyone agrees on is that the Commander's wife
Zeynep was distraught over the killing of her brother Majid. She must
have put significant pressure on Commander Kâmil to take revenge on
her former fiancé.

One reason Sami Pasha was willing to exhibit a degree of ruthlessness
in this period to which he had not resorted even during the Pilgrim Ship
Mutiny was that the tiny new state of Mingheria could no longer count

on the security that the Ottoman Empire had always provided—even as "the sick man of Europe." Mingheria might be a free and sovereign state now, but it was also completely on its own . . . Forget the British or the French; if an ordinary pirate ship were to land two hundred armed men on the island's northern shore and march its makeshift army over the mountains and down to Arkaz, Sami Pasha and the untrained, inexperienced troops stationed in the garrison would have trouble stopping them even with their vastly superior numbers, and the newborn state of Mingheria would be destroyed and wiped off the stage of history before it was even a month old, with nobody left even to remember there had ever been such a thing as a "Mingherian nation." Sami Pasha believed that if quarantine failed and the outbreak continued to spread, it was very likely that something like this could happen soon.

During his trial, whose outcome was of course preordained, Ramiz claimed that he had only been trying to help the new governor take office, that he had done this because he believed it to be essential for the survival of the people of the island—he would later use the term "Mingherians" too, adapting to the prevailing nationalist mood—and their submission to quarantine rules, that neither his brother nor any foreign consul had given him instructions of any kind, and that he had done what he did solely out of personal conviction. He had never intended to serve the Ottoman oppressor. Ramiz and his entourage were so comfortable with the idea of killing in the name of the causes they believed in that to them there was no ethical dilemma in this at all—particularly if it was Christians they were murdering. They had raided and looted countless villages in the mountainous north and killed plenty of people there already.

The court sentenced Ramiz, organizer of the raid on the State Hall, and each of his surviving men to death, with the sole exception of the youngest who had surrendered at the end of the battle. The judge (and former *kadı*) who would have ordinarily conducted the trial was Muzaffer Effendi, sent from Istanbul to handle important cases involving murder, serious injury, the abduction of young women for marriage, and blood feuds, without these having to be referred to the courts in the Empire's capital, but Muzaffer Effendi was currently in the Maiden's Tower, having been sent there by rowboat in the middle of the night along with the insufficiently revolutionary mayor of Teselli, Rahmetullah Effendi, so instead Sami Pasha had the elderly Christofi Effendi of the rich Yannisgiorgis family, whom he knew through the French consul, and who happened to be the only person on the island who'd studied law in Europe (specifically in Paris), brought to the former State Hall and current Ministerial Headquarters in his armored landau, instructing him upon his arrival to kindly produce a judgment "in the European style." These were the same killers who had conspired to assassinate the island's brave doctors and quarantine officials, all so that they could plunder its resources, its precious minerals, its fish, and its rose oil, exploit its people, and deepen the outbreak of plague which had paved the way for foreign powers to intervene. The judgment, Sami Pasha noted, should put all of that in the language of the law. Christofi Effendi had assumed he must have been summoned to compose the judgment in French, but when he found out that the new state's official languages had provisionally been declared to be Greek and Turkish, he produced a magnificent text in modern legal Turkish, which he had learned after many years spent practicing in Istanbul as a lawyer in commercial disputes between "foreigners." He had long, slender fingers, and delicate handwriting.

The Chief Minister and former governor Sami Pasha dispatched a clerk and a messenger to the Splendid Palace with the execution orders for Commander Kâmil's signature, but two hours later, these were returned to him unsigned and with an accompanying note. The note pointed out that according to the constitution currently being drafted for Mingheria, the authority to approve death sentences rested with the Chief Minister, not with the President of the state. In other words, it was Chief Minister Sami Pasha's signature that would be required before the executions could be carried out, not President Kâmil's.

Sami Pasha didn't blame the President for protecting himself and expertly shifting the final responsibility for the death sentences onto the Pasha; on the contrary, he understood why this was necessary. The only way they would all come out of this alive was if he—their bright young hero—was loved by everyone on the island. But wary of all the ire he would have to face, and because he still had some mercy left in him, Sami Pasha commuted three of the death sentences to life imprisonment and signed execution orders only for Ramiz and two of his accomplices.

With the clear conscience of a man who had just spared three people "the noose," Sami Pasha set about doing whatever he could do to ensure that the other three—including Ramiz—were executed at once.

Ramiz and his coconspirators knew that with Mingheria now an independent country, death sentences no longer required Istanbul's approval, and that they could therefore be executed at any moment. What might they have been thinking? Sami Pasha had always delighted in hearing stories and reminiscences about "a convict's last night on earth" from prison wardens across the Empire. Prisoners heading for execution wouldn't sleep all night, hoping for a pardon from Abdul Hamid, and in most cases their sentences would indeed be commuted to life imprisonment.

There was a moment when Sami Pasha felt the nearly uncontrollable urge to summon the armored landau to take him to the Castle for a nighttime visit to Ramiz. But he could also see that if he succumbed to his instincts and pardoned this spoiled hoodlum, nobody would ever take the new state or its quarantine effort seriously, and not only would he offend the Commander, he might also fall out of his favor, just as he had fallen out of Abdul Hamid's.

He didn't sleep all night. At one point, Commander Kâmil's deputy, Mazhar, charged into his office.

"Sheikh Hamdullah's regent with the felt hat is here—Nimetullah Effendi!" he said. "The sheikh has sent a letter asking for his brother to be spared, and counts on your mercy!"

"What is your view?"

"The President agrees we will have no peace until we are rid of these scoundrels . . . But Nimetullah Effendi is a reasonable man . . . It would be wise to receive him."

"Where is that felt-head, then?"

It was long after midnight when Sami Pasha stepped out of his office, walked down the wide staircase where a fading gas lamp threw long, eerie shadows, found the Halifiye sect's second-in-command, Nimetullah, sitting with his felt hat just inside the entrance of the former State Hall and current Ministerial Headquarters, and told him that, as sorry as he was, there was nothing he could do, for the courts in free Mingheria were independent now.

"His Holiness the Sheikh does not defend Ramiz's actions . . . But you should know that if you execute him, those who love the sheikh will no longer love you."

"Love is an affair of the heart . . . ," said Sami Pasha in a moment of inspiration. "Sheikh Hamdullah, ruler of so many hearts, is right about this, as he is about everything. But do not forget that even Abdul Hamid was unable to prevent Mithat Pasha from being killed. You must also remember that unlike His Holiness the Sheikh, my duty is not to rule over people's hearts, but to keep the ship of state afloat and guide them through this storm alive. In difficult times, it can be more useful to frighten people than to try and win their hearts."

As if he were a simple clerk rather than the Chief Minister, Sami Pasha walked Nimetullah Effendi and his felt hat all the way to the door, sending his regards to Sheikh Hamdullah. He was about to climb back up the stairs when Mazhar Effendi informed him that the carriage with the sentenced prisoners had just left the Castle and was on its way to the State Hall Square. Şakir, the executioner, had already arrived that afternoon, drinking his wine in silent resignation. Sami Pasha realized that even if he went back to his quarters and tried going to bed, he would not be able to sleep, so instead he returned to his office. Had he been with Marika, he could at least have sipped on some cognac until dawn.

The three convicts had carefully performed their ablutions and prayed for the last time in the little mosque inside the Castle. Gathered under the trees and by the shopfronts in the State Hall Square were guards and gendarmes sent by Mazhar Effendi on behalf of the new government, and several clerks, some of whom Sami Pasha had summoned so that they would witness the executions and announce them to the public. The drunk hangman's clumsiness in tying up the prisoners' hands and dressing them in their white execution gowns (which his own mother had sewn) was such that by the time everything was ready, it was already daytime, and the gendarmes had to block off the roads that led to the square. There were no carriages around anyway since the plague had struck the city's coachmen, nor anyone with business so urgent as to require one. The dark, ominous clouds hovering low over Arkaz seemed to have driven everyone away, and plague or no plague, the streets were completely empty.

Although Mazhar Effendi had told him Ramiz should "go first," the hangman insisted with inexplicable obstinacy on leaving him for last.

When Ramiz finally realized that he was not going to be pardoned, he let out a cry—"Zeynep!"—that no one in the square that day would ever forget, then tumbled off the stool he had been struggling to balance on, and swung through the air. He writhed and twisted for a time, and only when he died did his dangling body finally fall still.

CHAPTER 58

The gallows had been erected in the center of the old State Hall Square. (Today, the spot is home to a park where Mingherian roses bloom in many different colors, and most people with an interest in the island's more recent history are not aware that men had once been hanged there, their corpses displayed for all to see.) If you stood by the unfinished clock tower or even as far back as the New Mosque or Barber Panagiotis's shop, and looked straight down Hamidiye Avenue, lining your gaze up with its row of linden trees, you would see the three bodies hanging like pale blots in the State Hall Square.

The bodies in their white gowns were left to swing for three days. As a southerly wind blowing from the Castle spun them slowly around the thick, oiled hemp nooses tied to their necks and ruffled the hems of the black trousers they had worn under their white shirts, people were as affected by the sight as Sami Pasha had hoped they would be, and told themselves they would definitely pay more attention to quarantine regulations now. The only description we have of this grisly scene is in Yannis Kisannis's book *What I Saw*. We learn from this account that although little Yannis couldn't actually see the white smudges in the distance, they became even larger and more terrifying in his imagination. There is a lot of useful information in Kisannis's book, though regrettably it is also replete with anti-Turkish and anti-Islamic sentiment, with numerous observations to the effect that the island's new government had taken on the mantle of Ottoman oppression, and that the only thing the Ottomans knew was how to hang people.

On windless days, the capital smelled even more intensely of death, corpses, and honeysuckle, and soon the hush of plague had also taken over, its presence even more noticeable in the dark of night. People hiding inside their homes and sitting all day behind locked doors spoke only in whispers now. Gone were the sounds of horns and engines echoing among the jagged peaks by the harbor as steamboats came and went from the city, the noise of anchors splashing in and out of the water, the clattering of carriages and of horses' hooves. It had been a long time since any of the torches around the docks and in the hotels nearby, along the jetty, and on Istanbul Street had last been lit. As smugglers preferred to use Mingheria's secluded rocky coves for their activities, even the island's boatmen and adventure-seekers had stopped frequenting the port. Nighttime raids conducted on the homes of various sect members had left people feeling scared and intimidated. Most of them no longer left their homes after dark. The melodious groaning of carriages, ox carts, and phaetons as they strained over bridges and around the corners of steep sloping roads had also disappeared. So had the rushed, merry chatter of people closing their doors and going home for the evening. The sound of children could still be heard every now and then, but even their joyful racket seemed muted. It was a silence too deep to be explained solely by the absence of church bells and calls to prayer.

The only people to be found on the streets after dark now were solitary hooligans, roving burglars, quarantine breakers, people running away from doctors and hospitals, and all sorts of lunatics and madmen, so the city's guards and sentries would usually arrest—and sometimes beat up—anyone they came across at night, and those they locked up wouldn't be let back out until at least a couple of days had passed.

Princess Pakize's husband did not wish to scare her, so he had not told her about the executions or mentioned the three dead bodies hanging from the gallows outside their door. The guesthouse windows did not face the square, looking out instead at a view of the Castle, the port, and the sparkling blue sea. Even so, Princess Pakize could tell from the stillness around her that something extraordinary must have happened. From her room in the guesthouse, she could hear the sound of drunken wails punctuating those otherwise silent nights of plague. During one of her sleepless nights, she wrote of how even the cry of the nearby rooster that usually woke her up in the morning seemed to have gone quiet. This was two days after the executions. Princess Pakize had noticed that even on the calmest days when there was no breeze at all, the soft, soothing splash of water on fine sand would continue unabated. The night's other sounds came from the city's dogs, crows, and seagulls. As she dozed through the night, Princess Pakize too, like so many others in Arkaz, could feel the presence of hedgehogs, snakes, and frogs moving in the dark from one garden to the next.

Through the years she had spent confined to the palace harem, the Princess had learned how important it was to observe every object, plant, cloud, insect, and bird she saw. During her stay at the guesthouse of the Mingherian State Hall, she had taken "especial" notice of a crow that had been coming "regularly" to her window. When they were children, Princess Pakize and her sisters used to divide people into "crow lovers" and "seagull lovers." Princess Pakize preferred seagulls—admiring their freedom and their white, elegant forms—and disliked crows, which might have been more intelligent, but were also noisy, impertinent, and ill tempered. Yet she had quickly grown fond of this "solemn, majestic creature" that had been appearing at her window in the evenings, and liked to sit and watch it perch. The crow would come to Princess Pakize's window every day, and stare right back at her.

Sometimes the feathers on its enormous head glimmered in the sunlight. It never cried out in that hideous, shrewish way all the other crows had; most of the time, it was silent. Its feathers were pitch-black in places and ashlike in others, and its dark pink feet were so ugly they made Princess Pakize uncomfortable. As the Princess wrote her letters, the crow would stand with its head completely still, staring in apparent wonder at the tip of her pen, at the ink seeping letter by letter into the paper and leaving words and sentences in its wake. Perhaps Princess Pakize had fallen in love with the black crow. Every time Doctor Nuri walked into the room, the big, dark bird would vanish.

But one day it stayed behind, "almost as if" it wanted to show itself to the Prince Consort. When he noticed the amorous glances the crow kept giving his wife, Doctor Nuri coolly remarked: "This is the same crow that always comes to Sami Pasha's window!"

"That must be some other crow!" Princess Pakize replied, bursting with jealousy.

Our readers should know that the Princess told her sister the rest of the story of this crow in a letter she wrote much later. For by now, Princess Pakize had understood that even though her husband was a minister in the island's new, makeshift government, every letter she wrote to her sister would still be intercepted and read by someone else first.

The next time she was alone in the guesthouse, Sultan Murad V's third daughter got dressed, covered her head, and left the room, walked down the State Hall's wide staircase, followed the second-floor colonnade that encircled the inner courtyard, and stopped at a window that gave out onto the State Hall Square, peering outside in the hope that she might spot Sami Pasha's crow.

But rather than the solemn, majestic bird she had been expecting to find, she saw instead three gallows with three corpses hanging in their white gowns, and although she had never seen anything like it before, she knew immediately who those people were.

As soon as she was back in the guesthouse where she had been sequestered for the past two and a half months, Princess Pakize threw up, and briefly wondered whether she might be pregnant, but when she realized that her body must be reacting to death rather than to any child in her womb, she sat down and cried. Later, she understood that it wasn't just the corpses that had caused her so much sorrow, but also the feeling of having spent so much time away from her father and sisters, and from Istanbul.

"Shame on you!" she told her husband when he returned to their quarters. "Here is this terrible thing right outside our door, and you have been hiding it from me all this time. Even my uncle wouldn't have gone so far."

"Indeed, your uncle very rarely agrees to executions in any of his territories. He even commuted Mithat Pasha's death sentence to life in prison. Though strangely he did then give the order for the imprisoned Pasha to be assassinated in Ta'if fortress."

"I'd rather be in Istanbul and live in fear of my uncle than stay here under the rule of a governor capable of such horrors."

"I understand why you miss Istanbul so much, my dear Princess!" said her husband respectfully. "But even supposing the plague ends soon and quarantine is lifted, I wonder if we would be able to return to Istanbul whenever we wished to do so? Surely we would first have to obtain permission from your old bodyguard—our new president. For it is not the Governor you mentioned earlier who holds power here now; it is Zeynep's husband."

"Then let us escape from this place together. Take me away from here."

"You know how keenly my sense of responsibility binds me to this island and its people," said Doctor Nuri. "I know you feel the same way too. You are fond of the Turks and Muslims who live here—and not just them, but the Greeks and all the others too—and you want to help them in some way, just as I do. Besides, even if we didn't have a humane obligation to these people, it would be rather difficult for us to return to Istanbul now. After all, I myself have been collaborating—if only with humanitarian and medical considerations in mind—with a sovereign state that has seceded from the great Ottoman Empire. I do not think your situation would be too different either. When this is all over, your uncle the Sultan will have to forgive us first before we can even think of returning to Istanbul."

Now that the subjects of "treason" and of their own helplessness had been broached, Princess Pakize began to cry. Doctor Nuri hugged her, kissed the astonishingly soft skin behind her ears, and breathed in the sweet scent of her hair.

This made the Princess cry even harder. She looked in her bag for the handkerchief that one of the old ladies in her father's harem had intricately embroidered with flowers, and used it to wipe the tears from her plump cheeks and girlish eyes.

"Then I suppose we are prisoners here . . . ," she said.

"You were a prisoner in Istanbul too . . ."

"Why are you even getting involved in these people's political intrigues? My uncle sent you here to stop the plague, not to set up a new state."

"But why did your uncle send you to China with me? Why did he send you and the Major from Alexandria to this plague-infested island?"

This had been their favorite topic of conversation ever since the day they had found out they would both be sent to China with the Guidance Committee, and they discussed it again now, managing not to hurt each other's feelings. When Doctor Nuri pointed out that the other reason her uncle had sent him to the island was to find out who had committed the murders there, Princess Pakize replied: "The real murderer here is the person who had those men hanged!"

After noting in response that it was really her old bodyguard who had been behind the executions, and that Ramiz had not exactly been an angel either, Doctor Nuri reminded his wife that her uncle had issued his first death sentences after the journalist Ali Suavi and his entourage had stormed the palace one night in a failed attempt to restore her father Murad V to the throne. Princess Pakize hadn't even been born then. Earlier that same year, a group of Freemasons had been caught plotting to break into Dolmabahçe Palace through underground passageways and put Murad V back in power. Having brazenly announced in his own newspaper that he was planning some kind of operation the next day, Ali Suavi (whose every move was being shadowed by Abdul Hamid's spies) had sailed to the Çırağan Palace with more than a hundred armed, stick-wielding men, breached its defenses, and managed to get all the way to Murad V, who had been informed of the rebels' plans and already changed his clothes in readiness for the moment when he would finally take back his throne. But in the end, Abdul Hamid's guards had responded to the attack with a counterattack of their own, and Ali Suavi and most of his men had been killed. Ali Suavi's body had been beaten with sticks and filled with bullet holes. Almost all of the raiders had been destitute Balkan refugees from Plovdiv who had lost their homes and land in the 1877–78 Russo-Turkish War and been forced to flee to Istanbul. If Princess Pakize's father were to regain the throne, the Ottomans would declare war on Russia and Europe again, and when they took back all the territories they had lost due to Abdul Hamid's incompetence, the Balkan Muslims who now filled the streets of Istanbul would be able to return to their ancestral homes.

"My poor father knew nothing of that plot!" said Princess Pakize. "But it is because of those raiders that we were all banished to the mansion where I was born, and the restrictions on our lives tightened enough to prevent my dear father and my brother the Prince from ever meeting with anyone outside."

In truth it annoyed Princess Pakize when her husband criticized the Ottoman dynasty and spoke of them in the same derisive tone she herself used whenever she talked about Abdul Hamid, and she felt the urge now to put the Prince Consort in his place—for, after all, those same Ottomans had allowed him to marry into their family, and matched him with a sultan's daughter.

"If it is going to be that difficult for us to return to Istanbul, then I suppose it no longer matters whether we follow my uncle's bidding and find out who killed Bonkowski Pasha and his assistant, so we might as well stop trying to mimic Sherlock Holmes and his frivolities once and for all!" she said, managing at last to break Doctor Nuri's heart.

One positive outcome of their lengthening discussion was that, in keeping with the promise he had made his wife, Mingheria's new Quarantine Minister requested an audience with Chief Minister Sami Pasha in which he argued that it would be beneficial to their attempts to stop the outbreak if the gallows and corpses were cleared from the State Hall Square.

"Is that the conclusion you have come to?" said Sami Pasha.

The number of people visiting the Halifiye lodge to offer their condolences to Sheikh Hamdullah for the death of his brother had been growing. These pious believers were not afraid of catching the plague, and would queue up for hours outside the lodge, most of them returning to their homes without having caught so much as a distant glimpse of the sheikh. Sami Pasha suspected that all the people who had refused to come to the State Hall Square to see the corpses displayed there for their benefit were making a point of going to Sheikh Hamdullah's lodge instead.

"Commander Kâmil Pasha often speaks—and rightly so—of the honor and dignity of the Mingherian people, and of the respect they deserve from every other nation," said Doctor Nuri. "But if we continue to parade these hangings to the world, Mingherians will come to be seen as a wicked lot, and far too fond of the noose."

"So when a hundred years ago the French guillotined their kings, the rich, and anyone they happened to pick up off the street, that was all fine, but when we start punishing inveterate murderers and treasonous separatists who seek to sabotage our quarantine, somehow we're in the wrong . . . ," said Sami Pasha.

The camaraderie that had developed between Sami Pasha and Doctor Nuri over the past two and a half months prevented their disagreement from turning into an argument. Doctor Nuri explained to Sami Pasha that crows and seagulls that picked at abandoned corpses and dead rats could spread the disease without getting sick themselves. Sami Pasha had indeed seen his own crow nibbling at the eyes, noses, and ears of dead bodies; but what he did not understand was how it was possible for these birds to fear scarecrows without being afraid of human corpses too.

CHAPTER 59

At different times during the day, Commander Kâmil Pasha would walk around the streets of Arkaz with his bodyguards in tow. Apart from these excursions, he never left the Splendid Palace anymore, and had also stopped attending the quarantine meetings in the old State Hall. After each daily conclave in the Outbreak Room, Doctor Nuri—also followed by bodyguards—would walk from the Ministerial Headquarters to the Splendid Hotel to discuss all the latest news with Commander Kâmil. Two weeks on from the declaration of freedom and independence, the number of deaths was still not falling; if anything, it kept increasing.

Just as they'd done in times of Ottoman rule, Doctor Nuri and the Commander conducted their daily assessments over a map of the city. But this was a different map. They had obtained a copy of the one in the Outbreak Room and spread it over an elegant walnut desk in the Commander's office. The other item on the desk was a candlestick they'd taken from the hotel's "clubhouse." Before they started marking up the homes where new plague victims had been found, Doctor Nuri would briefly explain where the outbreak was at its worst. But since a glum-faced clerk had already been coming by twice a day to inform the Commander of the latest and constantly rising mortality figures, the President wouldn't really learn anything from his meetings with Doctor Nuri that he didn't already know, nor would he ever offer any suggestions or advice on how the outbreak might be stopped.

The consuls and bureaucrats who had been observing events from afar thought it perfectly appropriate that the Commander—unlike Sami Pasha before him—should leave the job of battling the plague to the island's doctors and quarantine officials. Doctor Nuri would later disapprovingly report to his wife of how, as his own small hand skimmed over the map and hovered over the Germe neighborhood or Hamidiye Avenue, the Commander would seem more interested in fantasizing about all the new names he was going to give these places. He had thought at first of changing the name of the State Hall Square into Free-dom Square, but after Ramiz and his accomplices had been left out' for the crows to peck at, and people had stopped going there altogether, he'd thought of naming it Independence Square instead, until finally, he had decided on Mingheria Square. As for Hamidiye Avenue, Com-mander Kâmil wanted to rechristen it Boulevard Mingheria. He had rejected his deputy Mazhar Effendi's suggestion to go with Commander Kâmil Pasha Boulevard, saying that he would always remain a man of the people, and insisting that he would never allow for such a thing to happen—"certainly not while I'm still alive . . ."

Official chronicles of the early period of the Mingherian state will boast of the two hundred and seventy-nine streets, squares, avenues, and bridges that Commander Kâmil renamed during those days and nights of plague. The Commander also gave new appellations to all manner of tiny squares and narrow alleyways that had never had a name before the island's declaration of freedom and independence. Post Minister Dimitris Effendi had been telling everyone how useful it would be for registered mail services and in the delivery of letters and packages for these previously nameless places to finally be called something, and how wonderful it was that although this had never been done under Otto-man rule, it was finally happening under the new regime, when first his wife and then the Postmaster himself had ended up in Theodoropoulos Hospital with the plague, forcing these activities to be put on hold for a time (during which several old Greek street names were also changed) and prompting the Commander to form a new committee to deal with the matter. Upon Dimitris Effendi's death, the Commander requested that a large photograph of the old postmaster be put up next to his own portrait in the Post Office's cavernous central hall. The fact that this photograph, shot by Vanyas, remains in precisely the same spot where it was first hung up in the Post Office building one hundred and sixteen years ago is further proof of how attached Mingherians are to their his-tory and identity.

Readers of Princess Pakize's letters will note that contrary to what

Mingheria's official historians would later do, it would be wrong to overemphasize the Commander's supposed "republicanism" during this period. Commander Kâmil experienced the great revolution and transformation he had brought to Mingheria as a highly personal source of joy, and as he continued in his efforts to remodel his country in the spirit of modernity and nationalism, he would earnestly and perhaps even a little naïvely tell everyone around him that he was doing it all for his son (he was sure the child would be a boy). He was going to give his son a pure, authentic Mingherian name. The choice of this name was extremely important, for it would play a central part in Mingherian history even after the Commander's death, and serve as a perfect example of sentimental nationalism.

Every now and then the Commander would go upstairs to see Zeynep, elaborating on his dreams and ambitions, and anxiously asking if she was well and whether everything was going smoothly with the baby. Pregnancy had tempered Zeynep's anger at the world, made her skin brighter, her smile more luminous, and her face even prettier than before.

Having rejected archaeologist Selim Sahir's initial list of traditional Mingherian names, the Commander had organized a meeting with several individuals known to have nurtured an interest in the old Mingherian language. Some of them were neighborhood friends from his boyhood, while others were people the Chief Scrutineer had kept tabs on during his time at the head of the island's intelligence department, treating them as Mingherian separatists, and bringing them to heel with threats of imprisonment. (The Chief Scrutineer had always been much more ruthless in his treatment of Greek separatists.) Afraid of being inculpated and of having their collections confiscated, these people who had spent years of their lives assembling old Mingherian words and objects with a childlike, folkloristic enthusiasm were somewhat timid at first, but soon they had come up with a lengthy list of words, names, and potential street names. With Hamdi Baba's help, the President also gathered suggestions from the Quarantine Regiment, and that was how, for the first time in its history, one of Mingheria's streets came to be named after someone who lived on the island—Hamdi Baba himself.

The President also set up a series of meetings with the island's Muslim herbalists and Christian pharmacists (including Nikiforos), its Greek fishermen, and with the owners of its diners and restaurants to create a written record of the Mingherian names for the island's medicinal herbs and pharmaceutical preparations; its seafood, mussel species, and rowing and seafaring terms; and all its local dishes. These discussions would later serve as the basis for future Mingherian-Turkish, Mingherian-Greek, and Mingherian-Mingherian dictionaries, the first of which would be published thirty years later, and for the *Encyclopaedia Mingheriana,* the world's first and only encyclopedia devoted entirely to the culture of a single Mediterranean island.

The designated venue for these meetings on Mingherian language, history, and culture was the London Club, a room on the ground floor of the Splendid Hotel where consuls and journalists used to drop by in the evening for a bit of gossip, and whose grand back door opened onto a garden covered in pink Mingherian roses. Another idea Commander Kâmil had during this time was to use the Quarantine Regiment to find young people who spoke Mingherian at home, and bring them together with scholars of Mingherian language and culture. As is widely known among those who have sought to revive the spoken Mingherian language, the Commander also tasked his men with locating the gangs of orphaned children that had formed during the plague, all so that their language could be studied. It is also true that he made plans for the Quarantine Regiment to "rescue" these children from their new homes in the hidden valleys behind the island's steep peaks and nearly impassable crags, and thus ensure their unspoiled language was preserved for posterity, but the uncanny rise in the number of daily deaths eventually made it impossible for these impassioned schemes to ever be fully realized.

During the most arduous days of Sami Pasha and Deputy Mazhar's battle with the lodges, the President asked the minister and former registry clerk Faik Bey to help him find a name for his son from old Mingherian legends and fairy tales by organizing two poetry competitions, and had the Chief Minister set aside seventy Mecidiye liras of prize money. The first competition would be for a poem about freedom, independence, and the island, and the winning entry would be set to music and turned into the Mingherian National Anthem. The winner of the second competition would be read out during the celebrations set to take place on the day the Commander's son was born.

Regrettably, his meetings with the archaeologist and expert on ancient Mingherian history Selim Sahir were overshadowed by the young commander's dislike of snobs and sons of pashas. Selim Sahir and his French wife had moved to Mingheria two years before. The archaeologist's father and grandfather had both been pashas in Abdul Hamid's court, and he constantly said things like "as my late father and my late grandfather used to say . . ." He had studied law and history of art in France, worked at the Imperial Museum in Istanbul, and taught at the university there, and recently his late father's friends had persuaded the Grand Vizier in Istanbul to entrust him with the task of bringing Ottoman museums back "to the level of national museums elsewhere." In other words, he was one of a new generation of advisers recruited by Abdul Hamid and the Ottoman Empire in their quest to use museums to present a more modern, Europeanized image of themselves to the world. At first Abdul Hamid had not quite understood the value of the ancient Greek and Roman ruins scattered across the Ottoman Empire and would often give them away for free to his friends in Europe. Only later had palace bureaucrats and well-educated sons of pashas like Selim Sahir managed to convince him of how important those rocks and stones really were.

Armed with an official permit from Abdul Hamid, Selim Sahir had arrived on the island aboard the army cargo ship *Fazilet (Virtue)* two years ago and had begun digging around an archaeological site that stretched all the way to the sea in one of the coves just northeast of Arkaz. This location had been suggested to him by his friends on the island. The object he was looking for was the statue of a woman, a milky-white sculpture hidden in the depths of a vast, tenebrous cave, which could be accessed only by water. He would have liked to extract this statue, transport it to the Imperial Museum in Istanbul, and make it famous, just as the museum's director Osman Hamdi Bey had done fifteen years ago with the sarcophagus he had discovered in another ancient cave in Sidon and immediately (and erroneously) declared to be the tomb of Alexander the Great. The Ottomans still considered themselves a global power and were regarded as such by the rest of the world too. But given how quickly our archaeologist's plans for this statue "fell through," we might conclude that "the sick man of Europe" was no longer capable of setting up any kind of museum.

Maybe the necessary funds hadn't arrived from Istanbul, or maybe someone had said something to arouse Abdul Hamid's suspicions, but for whatever reason, the cranes and rail systems needed to pull the statue out from its underwater cave had been greatly delayed, and the whole operation had soon come to a standstill. The Governor, who had followed these developments through his network of informants, had always been eager to get along with Sahir Bey and would join the consuls and the island's wealthy notables at the parties the archaeologist periodically threw in his rented villa. (It was at one of these parties that Sami Pasha first tried Mingheria's famous panfried freshwater mullet.) The Governor could tell from the generous and punctual salary the Ottoman Bank wired him every month that the archaeologist must have been sent to the island to spy for Abdul Hamid.

Having learned all this from Chief Minister Sami Pasha, the Commander invited him to join his meeting with archaeologist Sahir Bey too.

"We haven't been able to pick a name for our son yet, but I did like the names you proposed this time and have decided to use them for our city's streets!" said the Commander, speaking like an overlord who has quickly learned that part of his job consisted of rewarding his subordinates and encouraging them with praise. "But sadly, I must say we were not quite satisfied with what you wrote about the history of the Mingherian people."

"In what sense?"

"You have looked to Asia and all the way to the Aral Sea to find the roots of the Mingherian nation. There was no such lake in the fairy tales I used to hear a child, nor were Asians ever mentioned. In these difficult times, when Mingherians have been abandoned by the world and left to deal with the plague on their own, when they have nothing to rely on but their own sense of self-worth, you at least might spare us the story of how we supposedly 'came to this island from somewhere else.'"

"I hadn't thought of it that way!" Sahir Bey replied. "Though I'm afraid such is the consensus among France and Germany's most celebrated archaeologists and specialists in ancient languages."

"But right now the people of Mingheria will not want to hear that their true home is somewhere far away, or that there was someone else living here on this island before them, and they will especially not want to hear it from scholars like you."

"No one admires your extraordinary achievements more than I do, *commandant*. But no amount of historical scholarship can alter the truth about the origins of the Mingherian people."

"The people of Mingheria are not children. They like to address me as their 'commander' now. This is the greatest honor of my life! Yet here you are, saying the word in French as if to make a mockery of it all."

Sami Pasha could tell from the way the Commander was haranguing the archaeologist and refusing to let the matter go that this young man was filled with an immeasurable anger, and that without that anger, there could have been no nationalist fervor either.

"You must know that the age of kings and sultans is over now," the Commander continued. "Why would you seek to take a statue that belongs to the Mingherian people and put it in the Sultan's museum in Istanbul?"

"The sunken sculpture is a statue of the Queen of the Batanis, one of the oldest of all the ancient Mingherian tribes. Taking it to Istanbul would be a wonderful opportunity to introduce the world to Mingherian culture."

"On the contrary, the moment it got to Istanbul, they would attribute it to Alexander the Great or to some other empire. They'd find some other civilization more favored by the French. Besides, why should the statue of a Mingherian queen go to Istanbul anymore? You will extract the sculpture using whatever resources we have here, and place it on top of the clock tower. You have a month."

CHAPTER 60

One way in which Commander Kâmil liked to test the names people (including his own mother) had been suggesting for his unborn son was by whispering them three times toward the baby in Zeynep's womb. As soon as his son recognized one of the names as his own, he was bound to kick out or do a somersault. The Commander could not stop looking at his wife's pregnant belly (though it was still completely flat), her beautiful round breasts, and her strawberry-colored nipples, and kept finding excuses to "examine" her. He would rest his nose somewhere on her sweet-smelling skin—on her stomach, for instance—and move his head around like a bird trying to dig out buried treasure with its beak. Zeynep would contribute to these childish amusements with jokes and inventive games of her own, and afterward they would happily make love.

One afternoon two days later, the President went up to their rooms to see his wife. The death rate still wasn't falling, and he was feeling troubled. Wanting to cheer him up, Zeynep pulled her husband toward the bed, and the Commander followed her lead. He kissed her for a little while, then began as usual to "examine" her beautiful body. After a joyful inspection of her back, her neck, and her armpits, he looked below her stomach and found a suspicious, slightly hardened redness in her groin. There had been so many mosquito stings, weird insect bites, and numerous other unexplained blemishes that had appeared and disappeared overnight on his wife's healthy, lustrous skin, that there was probably no need to dwell too much on this latest discovery, yet the moment he saw the mark, his heart gave two heavy thumps, like when a person tries to look away from something they're not supposed to see. It did not resemble all the other red marks he had found on her before.

But since his wife never left their rooms, and there were no rats in the hotel either, Commander Kâmil told himself it couldn't be the plague. He touched the hardness with the tip of his finger, pressing gently at first, and then more firmly. When Zeynep did not react, he concluded that it must be an insect bite. A plague bubo would have hurt when he had prodded it. Not wishing to ruin his wife's mood with his misgivings, the Commander decided to forget about the mark.

The British consul George had sent a letter requesting a meeting with the Commander and with his old friend Chief Minister Sami Pasha. With all the other consuls still in hiding, Sami Pasha interpreted the British consul's overture as a positive sign. The British, in their typically wily way, were probably planning to pre-empt everyone else by making the newly created state some kind of offer, but Sami Pasha could not figure out what that offer might consist of, and once he had shared his thoughts with the Commander, they spent some time going over all the topics they might discuss with the consul.

After all this preparation, they were rather surprised to realize that the consul had actually come to tell them that the archaeologist Selim was a kindhearted, well-meaning man who loved the island and all Min-gherians. Consul George also noted that the archaeologist and his wife were less afraid of being sent to the Castle's isolation facility as plague suspects than they were of being made to "quarantine" in the Maiden's Tower with those Turkish officials who had sided with the Ottomans. Selim Sahir Bey feared that these officials who had been confined to the Maiden's Tower because of their loyalty to Istanbul would never be sent back to the capital, but be used for political leverage instead. There was no way the ancient Mingherian queen's statue could be retrieved under these circumstances. All that Selim and his wife wanted now was to be allowed to remain on the island.

"Did he send you here?"

"He told me you have been researching old Mingherian names. He thought I might have some suggestions too."

"The consul is very fond of Mingheria," Sami Pasha interjected. "He's been collecting books about our island for years, and using them to research his own."

"Since you feel our island is important enough to write a book about it, please tell us this," said the Commander. "Do you think the home of the Mingherian people is on this island, or elsewhere?"

"It is here that Mingherians have become Mingherians."

"You shall write our history better than anyone else will!" said the Commander. But he did not go on. He was looking at a strange light that had appeared over the sea. There was a silence . . .

"The government of Mingheria would like to ask the representative of the United Kingdom: what must we do for you to lift this blockade?" Sami Pasha boldly resumed.

"I have no idea what my government or the British ambassador in Istanbul might be saying about the current situation. But when the outbreak stops, the blockade will be lifted."

"The outbreak will not slow no matter what we do!" said Sami Pasha.

"Picking fights with the lodges as if they were the enemy has made matters worse," said the consul.

"It breaks my heart to hear such words from a true friend like you. What does the British government suggest we do to stop the plague?"

"The telegraph lines are down, there is a blockade, and we are under quarantine. From where I stand, I can only speculate as to what the British government might say."

"So what do you think?"

"You have a distinguished guest here," George Bey began delicately. "Princess Pakize is an important personage within the Ottoman royal family. As the daughter of a sultan, she is of some diplomatic value."

"In the Ottoman tradition, descendants from the female line of the dynasty have no connection to the throne, and the people would never accept such a claim."

"Thanks to you, Commander, this is no longer an Ottoman island!" George Bey replied, weighing his words. "And its people are a different people now."

Once George Bey had left, the Commander—taking the consul's warnings as seriously as Sami Pasha always did—decided he would attend a quarantine meeting and take an interest not only in what was going on with the lodges, but also in the various problems the city's neighborhood representatives were reporting from the capital's outermost reaches.

Vangelis Effendi from Flizvos told them that a Muslim "outlaw" who had been squatting in one of the neighborhood's empty homes had died there two days ago, after which his corpse had begun to smell. The Quarantine Regiment had received a tip-off about this particular house—which belonged to the Seferidis family from Thessaloniki—only a week ago, and having broken in through the back door to check, they had nailed every door and shutter closed from the inside and sprayed the whole house with Lysol again before exiting from the same door they'd walked through. The corpse whose smell had revealed its whereabouts yesterday must therefore have belonged to someone who'd hidden there after the Quarantine Regiment's inspection. These people who broke into vacant homes with the excuse of fleeing the plague posed a serious threat to the authority of the state, as they would often use the empty buildings they occupied as bases and meeting points for criminal activities.

This was the first quarantine meeting Apostolos Effendi—representing the steep hills, rocky cliffs, and beautiful views of Dantela neighborhood—had attended since the foundation of the new state, and his first request was to be paid his overdue wages from when the island had still been under Ottoman control. He did not want to be a neighborhood representative anymore. Dantela was a calm, remote, and by now nearly empty Greek neighborhood. Apostolos Effendi was suffering from loneliness. He had told them once that he had encountered the plague demon roaming around empty gardens at night—though according to Sami Pasha, it wasn't plague demons he had seen, but smugglers and boatmen working together in the darkness to sneak people off the island. With so many policemen and government clerks having abandoned their duties, the presence of the state in the city's smaller and more secluded neighborhoods had become almost nonexistent. These zones of dangerous lawlessness, situated predominantly around large, wealthy mansions in semideserted Greek neighborhoods, attracted all kinds of destitute drifters and opportunistic criminals from the Muslim neighborhoods on the other side of the creek. People had also been coming down from the north of the island to rob and loot the capital. Among the different types of gangs proliferating in these areas, there was also a band of orphaned children everyone kept talking about but which very few people had seen. Based on stories about the lives of these gangs of runaway children during the plague, the Mingherian national poet Salih Riza's romantic children's novel *Mother Is in the Forest of the Night* would convert me, at the age of ten, into a fanatical Mingherian nationalist.

The neighborhood representative bringing news from Hrisopolitissa Square reported that over the last two days, fresh rat corpses had begun to appear again along the walls and inside people's gardens. Little by little, these neighborhood representatives, whose primary duties were to ensure restrictions were obeyed, reveal where plague patients were being hidden from the authorities, point out which homes needed to be evacuated, and show the Lysol pump crews which houses and streets they should disinfect, had also taken on the role of intermediaries conveying people's frustrations with the quarantine to those in government. But that day the Commander rebuked a foolish and irresponsible "representative" who complained that a farrier from the Kofunya neighborhood had been sent to the Castle's isolation area even though he wasn't sick. "Where were you when the mistake was made?" the Commander told him. "Your job is to stop people breaking quarantine—not to come here and criticize us."

But if the neighborhood representatives had been spared any widespread rage, it was largely thanks to the presence of the Quarantine Regiment, who were themselves familiar figures, native to the island, and far more prominently involved in the quarantine effort. As a result, people tended to direct their anger at them first. Ever since the new state had been set up, the Quarantine Regiment had become even stricter, drawing increasingly inflamed reactions from the public. The fact that the number of deaths wasn't falling had also exacerbated people's fury. "Everything we have been put through, all that torment and browbeating, it was all for nothing," residents of the city's Muslim neighborhoods could often be heard saying.

The representative from Upper Turunçlar, on the other hand, noted that there was hardly anyone left in his neighborhood to complain about the Quarantine Regiment. Those who used to live close to the incineration pit were all gone, driven away by the smell. People in the part of the neighborhood that overlooked the New Muslim Cemetery had become angry and distressed; the sound of funeral processions never seemed to abate. But even more than the constant stream of people coming and going to the cemetery, the locals were upset about the street dogs who were digging up grave sites at night. The dogs would often get into fights, and sometimes they would pick human remains or dead rats up with their fangs and carry them around, spreading the disease. There was also a rumor that a ship with a red sail would come and save everyone. But nothing too unusual had happened in the neighborhood except for the recent death of a quiltmaker who'd lived on his own.

Once the neighborhood representatives from Vavla, Germe, and Çite had also delivered their reports, it became clear to those in charge of the new government and quarantine measures, and indeed to the Commander himself, that any optimism they might still have carried in their hearts was completely misplaced. The increasingly deadly course of the disease through Vavla—in the streets around the Army Middle School, the Hamidiye Hospital, and the Blind Mehmet Pasha Mosque—was damaging the authority and reputation of the state and of the quarantine effort in their new incarnations as much as it had in the old. Upon Sami Pasha's insistence, and with the doctors' agreement, it was ruled that in order to combat the disease in this most prominent of neighborhoods, quarantine soldiers would be deployed to patrol people's back gardens, some of its streets would be placed behind long-term sanitary cordons, and vacant homes (of which there were only a few) would be boarded shut with the thickest nails to keep thieves, loiterers, and plague sufferers out. The new government had reached the decision early in its reign to burn down any houses and rubbish dumps that were too infected to save, but it had taken a whole week for this policy to be implemented, and the process had drawn the ire of these neighborhoods' inhabitants. Now Sami Pasha wanted the Commander to issue more incineration orders.

As the debate in the meeting hall continued, the Commander looked out of the window at the Hotel Splendid peeking through the rooftops, and wished he could run back to his waiting wife. He was the only one who knew about the red mark on her groin. If he could just hurry home to her now, if they could just get into bed and hold each other and forget about everything else, then maybe he would also be able to forget that the red spot he had found on her body could be the beginnings of a plague bubo.

If Zeynep got the plague, he would probably get it too. Even if he didn't, he would still have to be separated from his wife. That was something he could never do. The more he thought about these things, the harder the Commander found it to follow the debate going on around him. Normally, he had as little patience for people whose agitation and fear of death in the face of the plague led them to making misguided decisions as he did for soldiers who panicked under the enemy's sudden onslaught. Yet here he was behaving just as they did. He must remain calm.

Despite the scale of the outbreak and the prospect of imminent death, there were still large segments of both the Christian and the Muslim population who had maintained their composure, and whose sense of humanity remained intact. While some people thought only of saving themselves, there were many others ready to put their lives at risk to visit neighbors who'd lost their loved ones and bring relief to patients writhing in pain, and a few good-natured souls could even be found trying to console the lunatics who roamed the streets of Arkaz crying, "What has become of us? We have plunged into Hell!" There were still plenty who had not yet lost their sense of community, fellowship, and fraternity.

These people—twenty to twenty-five of whom were dying in the outbreak every day—were constantly paying each other condolence visits. They formed a significant presence in the city. Although they did not go out as much as they used to do before quarantine measures were introduced, their attachment to their families, their neighbors, and the wider community—the fact, in other words, that they were good people—meant that they would often form well-meaning gatherings in mourners' homes, mosque courtyards, and at funeral processions, and spread the disease even farther. In late July, the streets of the Mingherian capital were not completely deserted as those of Bombay or Hong Kong had been in the throes of the third plague pandemic. For somewhere along one of the city's sloping roads, there was bound to be a crowd of thoughtful Muslim men rushing from one funeral or house visit to the next.

The Commander understood from the stories he was hearing that the state and its officials no longer had any status or authority left in the neighborhood of Çite. Yesterday, six people had died there, but rather than focusing on these deaths, the local representative's report centered on the question of "permit slips." The hostility between the unemployed Cretian youths who had come from Taşçılar to settle in Çite and engage in all sorts of misdemeanors, and the neighborhood's original inhabitants, who generally worked as coachmen, farmers, and shopkeepers, showed no signs of subsiding. The neighborhood's pious and impoverished local families believed that the disease had been brought into Çite by these thuggish, defiant youths, and demanded that the impious migrants be banished from their neighborhood altogether.

While the island was still under Ottoman control, Sami Pasha had set up a system of "permits" to deal with these sorts of problems (which occurred in other neighborhoods too). Under this system, access to certain streets and areas was restricted to people equipped with special permits issued by the Quarantine Authority. With this measure, the Governor Pasha had hoped both to trap the rootless, jobless Cretian migrants within a single neighborhood, and create a register of their presence—a plan which had initially succeeded. But when quarantine clerks and permit slip holders began trading these documents for money, the Pasha's innovation took on a completely unintended turn. As both government clerks and neighborhood locals stood to profit from this trade, and as it still served, if only in a limited way, as a form of sanitary cordon, neither the Governor Pasha nor the Prince Consort had wished to forgo the permit slips altogether. But at the same time, their ready availability increased the amount of movement within the city. The neighborhood representative reported that the relatives of two permit holders who had died of the plague yesterday had immediately sold their papers to a shop in the Old Market nearby. In theory, whenever people lost a parent or a sibling or any other family member to the plague, and were therefore evacuated from their infected homes and placed in quarantine, any permits they might have held should have been revoked, but in practice their papers were quickly put to use by others. The latest problem, as the Commander could see through the clouds gathering inside his mind, was that after the foundation of the new state, some clerks had been canceling old permits (or stamping them afresh), and demanding a tax to reissue them on behalf of the new government. As these papers were essential for commerce, everyone was willing to pay the tax, but there had been a few complaints already. The neighborhood representative, who also happened to be a treasury clerk, told the Commander that although there wasn't that much money in it, some people had already begun collecting permit slips in case they might one day be able to sell them for profit.

CHAPTER 61

The Commander soon found he could think of nothing else but the swollen red mark on his wife's groin. She could well be suffering from headaches and fever right now, all alone in her room upstairs in the Splendid Hotel.

He could not stop the terrible scenes forming in his imagination. He left in the middle of the meeting and returned from the State Hall to the Splendid Hotel, followed by his bodyguards. There were very few people out on the streets. A woman walking with a parcel in her hand and a timid little child carrying a small basket both noticed the Commander, though most of the others they encountered did not recognize him. Only a boy with light brown hair spotted the Commander walking past his house; he called out to someone inside, and his father soon joined him at the window. He had light brown hair too. "Long live the Commander!" the child cried.

The Commander was delighted. He waved at the boy. He wanted nothing more than to be the brown-haired child's heroic commander, and to save him and his family from this damned plague. But if Zeynep became unwell, he wouldn't be able to do any of that. If the mark on Zeynep's groin turned out to be a plague bubo, surely he would fall ill too. But the Commander didn't feel sick at all.

The guards and quarantine soldiers stationed at the entrance of the Splendid Palace stood to attention when they saw him. By the time he was climbing up the stairs, Commander Kâmil had already decided he would not speak of the mark to Zeynep. First he would study her from a distance. If she had the plague, there would be other signs of it anyway, such as a fever or a headache. But if she didn't have the plague, mentioning the red mark would only make her worry for no reason. The Commander had seen too many people stricken by misplaced fears and anxieties. They would make life hell for themselves and for everyone around them, at least until it became clear they were not infected after all. But people usually tried to ignore the early symptoms. Everyone knew that if one of their own got sick, they too—as members of the same household—were likely to be infected, or at least be put in isolation, so nobody ever liked to mention the first red marks, the first headaches, or the first signs of fever unless they were sure of what was causing them.

When he walked into their room, the Major found his wife pacing about in a huff, and felt relieved; she did not look like someone whose strength was being sapped by the plague. Should he mention his worries after all, and perhaps make a joke of them?

"My mother gave me a comb from my niece, with pearls on it . . . ," said Zeynep. "It's been right here for the past three days . . ."

"Did your mother come three days ago?"

"No, I went home to her," Zeynep replied. "With the bodyguards, of course!" She glanced at her husband with the smile of someone expecting to be forgiven for their little transgression.

"If even the Commander's own wife won't follow quarantine rules, how can we expect the people to?" said Commander Kâmil, stalking out of the room.

The shock and anger he felt at his wife's failure to obey his instructions far surpassed any fear of dying. His first wife Aysha had not been like this, so whenever Zeynep went against his wishes, the Commander never knew what to do, and would usually just leave the room and wait until his rage had waned.

Downstairs, an informant sent by Sami Pasha was updating Mazhar Effendi on the latest news regarding Sheikh Hamdullah and his condolence visitors. For the first three days, and to avoid antagonizing the Halifiye sect more than it already had, the government had refrained from dispersing the crowds gathering at the lodge to pay their respects in the wake of Ramiz's hanging. But when long queues began to form outside the main door of the lodge, Sami Pasha had suggested that entry into the street itself should be regulated, ostensibly as a quarantine measure. This had resulted in visitors trying to sneak into the lodge through one of the entrances to its back garden. When soldiers from the Quarantine Regiment were deployed to stand guard at these entryways, people started climbing the garden wall where it was low enough, or using secret passages hidden behind briars and blackberry bushes and known to the sect's younger disciples. Even after waiting patiently for their turn, most of the visitors who made it inside the lodge never got to see the sheikh anyway, and once they had dropped off the gifts or the food they had brought, they would hang around for a little longer before eventually going home. Of the nearly two hundred people who lived on the grounds of the lodge, only Nimetullah Effendi with the felt hat and a handful of others knew the location to which His Holiness the Sheikh had retreated. Mazhar Effendi's spies had been working assiduously to locate where exactly the sheikh might be hiding. Sami Pasha planned to extract the sheikh from the lodge and take him somewhere else.

At first the Commander had felt this move would be unnecessarily disrespectful, but after hearing one of their informants report on how people had been rejecting quarantine measures and sympathizing with Ramiz, he too had agreed that the sheikh should be removed. The informant was not exactly sure where the sheikh had gone to hide, but he did have a theory. He believed the sheikh must be in one of two buildings concealed by linden and pine trees on the side of the lodge near Çite, where disciples would stay when they wished to "withdraw" or when it was felt that they needed "moral edification." Both these buildings were usually empty, but for the past few days, they had been surrounded by a detachment of burly, truculent disciples.

The long-planned raid was a complete success. Ten soldiers selected from among the Quarantine Regiment's brawniest recruits and from a particularly tough contingent who was known to mistrust all sheikhs and holy men, as well as a team of six policemen sent by the Chief Minister, formed two separate squads and used two separate ladders to quickly climb over the wall and reach the two houses. Based on intelligence received from another informant, they broke into the first house and found a room with an empty sofa and three more doors. Behind the first door, a dervish who'd been keeping watch woke up when they arrived and was quickly detained. When they opened the second door, they saw Sheikh Hamdullah lying on a bed on the floor. The third room was empty.

As previously planned, an officer disguised as a scribe, wearing a frock coat and a new pair of expensive shoes from the Dafni store, stepped forward to greet the sheikh and kiss his hand. The sheikh's loose white robe hung over him like a ghost. His hair and beard seemed even whiter than usual, and he looked like he wasn't quite awake yet. His vast, dark, eaglelike shadow flickering on the empty wall in the yellow light of the candlelit room was ten times more terrifying than the man himself.

The clerk with the expensive shoes told the sheikh—who was still struggling to wake up (or at any rate pretending to)—that they had been sent by the office of the Chief Minister to secure the sheikh's safety against a probable and imminent assassination attempt. The sheikh had seen the other soldiers standing behind the clerk. It was then that he spoke those famous words that would be used against him for many years to come.

"Is there something going on? Are these His Royal Highness's men? Show me the Sultan's seal, or a signed edict."

As the experienced clerk respectfully and repeatedly assured him that they had indeed come under official orders, that he would be much safer in the place they were about to take him to, and that they would explain everything in greater detail once they got there, two soldiers from the Quarantine Regiment took hold of the sheikh's arms, at which point the sheikh asked to be allowed to bring some of his books and belongings with him. He gathered his two favorite, irreplaceable nightgowns, some shirts and underclothes, the medicinal preparations he mostly bought from Nikiforos's pharmacy, and a few books on Hurufism that he had inherited from his grandfathers, who had been sheikhs in Istanbul. He also suggested that his deputy Nimetullah with the felt hat should come with him, but this request was denied.

The nearest door in the lodge's back garden had been quietly propped open, and just as planned, the Chief Minister's coachman, Zekeriya, was waiting behind it with the armored landau. As soon as the compliant sheikh stepped into the carriage, he recognized the smell of its leather seats, and realized that he had been in this landau before.

Recently, before going to sleep at night, the sheikh had been consulting Ibn Zerhani's writings on the causes of the plague and how to protect from it. Over the last few days, he had read Ibn Zerhani's translation of *Obscuri Libri* and pored over several key passages from his *Exegesis*. The sheikh's brain was teeming with Hurufi secrets, which ascribed new meanings to every word, every number, and most of all, of course, to every letter of the alphabet. When you read as many of these books as he had, your mind would do what the sheikh's was doing now, and begin of its own accord to find clues and words embedded in every corner of the universe.

It was a calm summer evening, with no wind in the air. The endless chirping of the crickets and the light pouring out from the numberless stars into the dark and deep blue sky enhanced the sheikh's state of Hurufi intoxication. Life and meaning, signs and objects, darkness and absence, made up the universe of clues. Light and Soul, Loneliness and Beauty, Strength and Illusion, composed the poetry of the heart. And so the union of Love and God followed a trail of ink winding through the stars, the branches, the scent of flowers, the sound of birds (owls and crows), and the scuttling march of the hedgehogs in the plague-struck night. As the swaying landau slowly made its way through the street by the now nearly vacated Kadiri lodge and the grounds of the Rifai lodge, the sheikh saw two sentries standing guard in the night with torches in hand and was struck by what he interpreted as a sign of the new government's proficiency.

If the new government was as powerful as it seemed to be, he would probably be confined to some other location upon the island. Though of course that wouldn't really work, as all of his disciples, his fans, and his many well-wishers would eventually find out where he was and flock to his door once more. But if the island was still under Ottoman control, or if these scoundrels who'd kidnapped him without even a word of explanation were actually the Empire's men, the sheikh assumed he would be taken somewhere very far from Mingheria, exiled to Arabia or Siirt or some other distant land beyond reach. Whenever sect leaders became too much of a burden, or caused too many headaches, or seemed too eager to exercise their own political influence, it was a time-honored Ottoman tradition to separate them from their congregations and banish them to places it took six months to travel to. In his youth, Sheikh Hamdullah had witnessed some of the sheikhs who'd drawn the ire of governor pashas and Istanbul bureaucrats and been exiled from their homes and lodges having to teach Koran lessons in remote provincial towns so that they could make ends meet. Sometimes it was pride that led these sheikhs, whose only crime was their faith, to make those mistakes that angered Istanbul. Or perhaps they would go a step too far in their attempts to prove to their acolytes just how powerful they were. Sheikh Hamdullah had been very careful, especially under Sami Pasha's rule, to avoid this kind of thing happening to him, though ultimately he had not succeeded.

The carriage crossed a street overlooking the tents and cots crammed in the Hamidiye Hospital's back garden. Then it veered to the left, climbed another slope, passed biscuit maker Zofiri's bakery, and turned into Hamidiye Avenue at the corner where the barber Panagiotis had his shop. The streets were totally dark and completely empty. On his way to his exile, the sheikh saw the city he had lived in for seventeen years as an abandoned, forgotten, and starkly desolate place. The starlight bathed the Castle and the pale pink stone houses in a strange and singular hue. Wherever it was that they were taking him now, he knew he would miss this light. He kept picturing a cold, miserable eastern city without any trees or even any windows, somewhere he'd never been before, like Erzurum or Van. If the sheikh was banished to a place like that, out of reach of any railways, nobody would be able to follow him there, especially not with plague and quarantine still to contend with. Nimetullah Effendi with the felt hat would no doubt find some people to fire up and send off to retrieve the sheikh, but when he inevitably encountered traitors at every step of the way, he too would learn how cowardly human beings could become in defeat.

As the landau drove down Hamidiye Avenue and across the bridge, the sheikh thought it must be taking him to the old State Hall. But when it reached the square outside the former State Hall and current Ministerial Headquarters, the carriage weaved its way through the soldiers and policemen stationed there and continued to Hrisopolitissa Square, past the Theodoropoulos Hospital, and on toward Flizvos bay. On the way to the coast, the sheikh breathed in the smell of kelp and sea, floating in through the carriage's half-open window.

The best thing about living in this city and on this island was that even on the worst days and in the direst of times, there was always a view of the sea and a trace of its scent somewhere nearby to lift the soul and make life seem worth living again. Already the sheikh was dreading the prospect of being sent away from these warm, gentle, mild climes to some snow-covered or drought-ridden place where he would have to wait for the money his disciples sent to him in the post, and live among people so poor that they had to shelter in caves. He would have to introduce himself to a whole new community and a whole new tribe who had no idea of his reputation as an eminent sheikh, and he would be forced to perform Koran recitations and deliver sermons to try and make a living. As the armored landau advanced along the coast, Sheikh Hamdullah kept imagining that soon a boat would come to pick him up and row him out to sea to hand him over to the waiting *Mahmudiye,* and so his years of exile would begin, perhaps with a little mistreatment at the hands of the Ottoman soldiers aboard the warship. As the landau climbed down a steep, hard slope, he listened to the metallic clink of the horses' shoes on the ground and fell into a curious stupor of fantasy and regret: oh, how he wished he could stay here . . .

Yet after it had climbed down to the shore, the carriage didn't stop at Pebble Cove either, but continued northward. The sheikh was glad that none of Abdul Hamid's boats had appeared to take him from the island and off to exile. A strange chill came from the forest, and afterward he heard a rustling sound and the wail-like singing of a bird. To the right of the landau was the swash of low waves against the coast, the cliffs, and the sandy beaches. Sheikh Hamdullah concluded that there was nobody around and no movement at all here, and that even the smugglers' boats must have stopped their activities.

Contrary to his fearful suppositions, nobody was going to send the sheikh to some godforsaken corner of the Ottoman Empire. Sami Pasha had located the owner and the chef of the Constanz Hotel northeast of Arkaz and had them ready this old villa nobody really knew about for the sheikh's "exile." The Pasha and Consul George used to meet up and have lunch there sometimes when the Hotel Regard à l'Ouest was closed for the season, or when they wanted a change.

Though it had just been cleared of squatters and plague sufferers, the creaking, rattling, rickety old building was still infested with djinns and fairies, but Sheikh Hamdullah did not feel at all uneasy. He was so relieved to be staying on the island that he performed his ablutions in his little room and started praying right away, his eyes clouding with tears as he thanked Allah again and again for heeding his humble servant's prayers and keeping him in Mingheria. For he was sure that it would not be long before he would be able to return to his own beloved bed back home in the lodge.

CHAPTER 62

Commander Kâmil did not leave the Ministerial Headquarters until the raid on Sheikh Hamdullah's lodge had been concluded. When messengers later brought the news that the sheikh had been successfully captured and was now being detained at the Constanz Hotel, the Commander and his retinue of guards went out into the night and walked back to the Hotel Splendid. As he strode through the desolate streets, climbing down sloping roads and listening to his own footsteps, the Commander was troubled and upset to notice once again just how abandoned the city looked.

Nearly half a day had passed after he had stormed out of the room and slammed the door shut behind him upon discovering that Zeynep had gone to visit her mother and been outside without his permission, and he had not seen his wife since. He told himself this was because he could not let his mind be "poisoned with worries about the plague" just when his political endeavors were enabling him to put his long-held ideals into practice. But he had also been avoiding their living quarters because he knew that if he returned to find that his wife had indeed caught the plague, that moment of realization would be more than he could bear. Besides, he had been dispatching clerks throughout the day with various messages for his wife. If Zeynep really did have the plague, its early symptoms and headaches would have grown bad enough over the course of the day that they would have become impossible to hide, and surely the clerks would have said something by now.

The Commander was therefore optimistic when he walked into the hotel at midnight. But as he climbed up the staircase, his confidence dwindled. He thought of the red swelling on Zeynep's silky skin. What would it look like now? He resolved not to ask his wife anything about it.

Sami Pasha had stationed a guard at their door, though it was not clear for what purpose. When the Commander turned his key in the lock and went inside, the room was dark, and he could not see his wife. If everything was fine, Zeynep would be asleep by now. But in the dim light coming through the window, the Commander could tell that his wife was not in bed.

He picked up a nearby candle, his hands shaking as he lit it, and when he held up the small brass candlestick, he spotted the pearly comb that had gone missing, then noticed his wife sitting close by, a few steps away from the window.

"Zeynep," he called out.

When his wife didn't reply, Commander Kâmil began to feel anxious, but he still held back. The candlestick in his hand was drawing arabesques with the shadows in the room. He walked up to his wife, and now that her face was properly illuminated, he noticed that she looked pale and forlorn.

"We've taken Sheikh Hamdullah from the lodge and hidden him somewhere outside the city . . . ," he said, his tone almost apologetic.

But he could see that his wife was not interested. Was she annoyed that he'd complained and slammed the door as he'd left, and that he'd disappeared for so long? Or was she scared because she had been all alone just as she began to realize she might be falling sick?

Zeynep started to cry, her tears like those of a fretful child with a deep and private grievance she can't quite articulate. Commander Kâmil tried to comfort her, hugging her, stroking her, holding her in his arms, and whispering tenderly in her ear.

They lay in bed without changing into their bedclothes. The Commander assumed the position he'd learned over the course of their brief married life, and which they both enjoyed: he hugged her from behind, resting his lips against the nape of her neck and wrapping his arms tightly around her belly, right where the baby was. They had spent many nights asleep in this manner.

The Commander touched Zeynep's body, her stomach, her arms, but did not let his hands go near the place on her groin where he suspected she might have developed a plague bubo. The most important thing was that his wife did not have a temperature. But neither did she seem to want to make love like she usually did. The Commander didn't want to either.

Zeynep started crying again. The Commander couldn't bring himself to ask her why. He kept holding her, saying nothing. But didn't his silence effectively signify his acceptance that something terrible was happening?

Wanting desperately to fall asleep, they fell asleep. Much later, somewhere between sleep and wakefulness, they heard shouting from the docks. But they had both been having such strange and terrifying dreams that they assumed the screaming must be part of the inferno inside their minds.

As the noise faded, the Commander thought he might die of sorrow. After years of toil, of running from one city to the next and fighting on one battlefront after the other, his happiness had lasted just two and a half months. Oh, God! Was this it? If his wife really was sick, that would mean the end of everything. Not only would his wife and their unborn child die, he would probably die too. That might even mean the Mingherian nation itself was finished! There were people shouting again, but the scenes going through the Commander's mind were so fateful and so fearsome that he could not arrange any of those outside sounds into a coherent thought, and soon fell asleep again. Or perhaps he convinced himself that he was sleeping.

When his wife began to shiver in his arms, he woke up. He had seen and heard of the violent shaking that would start when patients first developed a fever. He hugged his wife with all the strength he had, as if holding her tighter might stop her from shaking so much. This made it harder for them both to hide the fact of Zeynep's illness from each other.

Through the haze of his thoughts, he also managed to find a moment to feel angry with his wife; it seemed incredible that she should have left her room and the hotel to visit her mother when there had been no real need to do so.

"You have sacrificed all the happiness we've shared, our son's life, our country's future—all for the sake of a little outing!" he wanted to tell her. But he also realized that if he did say that, they would end up arguing before the doctors even arrived. More important, instead of concerning himself with past mistakes, he must now decide what to do next. Yet the problem before him was so monstrous that the Commander didn't even know what to think.

Zeynep cried again in silent, pitiful tears. Her husband still couldn't ask her anything. She went through two more spells of shivering, though her body did not feel unusually warm. The Commander did not know what to do, did not want to get out of bed, and wished that morning would never come, that his wife's illness would not get any worse, that time would simply stop. But the day dawned as it always did, bringing with it a strange pink-and-yellow-tinted glow. The shouting from the docks was growing louder too . . .

The crowd assembled at the docks and along the jetty were mostly angry dervishes from the Halifiye lodge. They were furious about the abduction of their sheikh. In an unpremeditated move, they had walked out of the front door of the lodge in the middle of the night to look for the sheikh, marching through the streets of Kadirler and Vavla on their way down to the docks. They had no slogans or resolutions; they weren't praying or invoking the name of Allah either. All they did was walk silently toward their destination. The tenacious disciples had seemed ready and determined to march all night to find where their sheikh had been taken and bring him back home. Everyone was following the person in front of them. By morning, a large group of people including forty to fifty young acolytes of the Halifiye sect had thus walked from the lodge straight toward Vavla, down to the Old Stone Jetty, along the crescent arc of the bay, and through the port until they reached the Customhouse, at which point, faced with a wall of Quarantine Regiment soldiers lined up at the corner where Istanbul Street meets the docks, they had come to a halt.

This spontaneous rally may have been fueled by the anger of Sheikh Hamdullah's Halifiye sect devotees. Yet the crowd's behavior that day also signaled an instinctive desire to leave Arkaz and flee the plague, and if the new government and its new system were to succeed, it would have made sense to funnel the protesters toward the city gates and allow them to go if they wished to. But by this point the city was ruled by miscommunication and suspicion rather than facts and logic, and following the orders they kept receiving from the Ministerial Headquarters, the Quarantine Regiment stopped the angry Halifiye disciples at the docks.

Barred from leaving the city, the crowd of pious disciples, angry troublemakers, and young dervishes from the Halifiye lodge began to raise their voices. It was here, in our view, that the second phase of the Mingherian Revolution began, brought about by this gathering of people for whom the idea of the nation consisted of the daily bowl of soup and loaf of bread they got from their lodge. It was these Halifiye dervishes—and the assorted rabble-rousers who had joined them on their march—who were responsible for initiating the atmosphere of anarchy and cataclysmic chaos that would erupt that day in Arkaz. As the Commander looked out of the window of the Splendid Hotel, the Quarantine Regiment fired several warning shots into the air. Three rounds of gunfire echoed across the city.

When he stepped away from the window and turned toward the bed, Commander Kâmil noticed that his wife was crying again. As he approached her, Zeynep steeled herself, got to her feet, and lifted her dress, showing him the swelling in her groin.

In just a day, the hardness there had turned into a boil. It was not a fully developed bubo yet. But it would become one soon, and before long, his wife would be writhing in agony. The Commander could see it already, right there in his wife's eyes and in the expression on her face. He knew that Zeynep would soon be delirious from the pain, and he understood that the blissful life they had shared in this room had come to an end.

A blissful life indeed! It was all finished now, all of it! The Commander had reached the end of his own life too. He was so sure of this now that he felt proud of his clear-sightedness, and did not try to trick himself like a coward would do. Yet even this burst of ruthless realism did not last long.

The Commander sat beside his wife and gently touched the boil in her groin. "Does that hurt?" he asked. The boil was not completely swollen yet, and not that painful. But within a day, the pain would increase, and at that point a doctor would have to pierce the bubo to relieve his wife's agony. When he had still been guarding Doctor Nuri and following him around the city's hospitals, Commander Kâmil had seen many patients in that state, and felt sorry for them as he watched them thrash about in pain.

Zeynep lay back down. The Commander could see the shock and disappointment on her face, and understood the guilt she was feeling—as if it were her own fault this had happened.

"We should go to Theodoropoulos Hospital!" said the Commander. "It's better to have the boil pierced and drained early on."

"I don't want to go to the hospital!" said Zeynep. "I don't want to leave this room either."

The Commander gathered his wife in his arms, sensing that it was what she expected. They lay in bed for a long time, quietly hugging each other as tightly as they could. As he listened to her breathing and her thumping heartbeat, and felt the inner movements of her body against his fingertips, the Commander ached with misery, thinking of their two and a half months together, of his wife's irrepressible personality, and of how much they had laughed.

"Come on, darling, let's go to the hospital!" he said a little later.

"Aren't you the Sultan of this place now?" his wife replied. "Let them come here."

The Commander could see her point. The treatment could just as easily take place in their room, which was the largest in the hotel. He also knew that piercing a partially developed bubo on someone's groin could not really be considered a treatment. Given that the patient in question was the Commander's wife, everybody would act as if they were doing something very useful and as if this intervention would save Zeynep's life, but in reality, piercing a bubo—whether it was still relatively small and not yet hardened, or swollen and protruding visibly from someone's neck—did not cure the plague, and its only benefit was that it brought (limited) relief from the pain. But even this was a rumor. The more demonstrable fact they had all learned from experience was that a large majority of patients who developed buboes was destined to die. The Commander had often overheard Prince Consort Nuri hastily debating these matters with the island's Greek doctors in a mixture of Turkish and French.

But now, unless he wanted to go mad, he must forget everything that he had observed or learned from eavesdropping on the doctors and start believing that plague patients with buboes could still be cured. Yet any doctor he summoned to treat his wife would immediately remind him of quarantine regulations and try to separate them from each other. The only way he could prevent this was by quarantining with her.

The Commander could also foresee that any rumors about him having caught the plague too, or being placed under cordon, or shutting himself away in isolation, would not weaken just the quarantine effort but the new government too. People would not mind too much that the Commander's wife hadn't gone to the hospital. But if even their mighty commander couldn't avoid the plague, how was he supposed to save them all, and who was he to teach them the old language and the old Mingherian names they'd forgotten?

At the same time, he did not want the crying and the shaking and the hiccuping wails to begin before he had persuaded Zeynep to leave the room and go to the hospital. His wife did not know what the experience of a plague patient was like. It was his duty to tell her the truth now.

But the only thing Zeynep wanted was for her husband to hold her in his arms and convince her, if only in *that moment,* that nothing bad was going to happen to her. Every time he hugged her, it also made Zeynep think that he was not afraid of catching the disease from her—which could only mean that he truly loved her. Then she would start weeping again, terrified of what was to come.

They lay like that for a long time, holding each other close. The morning light was seeping into the room through the shutters and between the curtains. The Commander watched the particles of dust floating in the beam of light, listened carefully to his wife as she breathed, and tried to make sense of the noises coming from the street.

The discontent caused by Sheikh Hamdullah's abduction from his lodge had continued to grow. Sheikhs from other lodges had also begun to declare their support for this "revolt of the sectarians." There was no organized structure or leadership behind it; it had emerged of its own accord. The Commander was a born Mingherian who knew his people well, and even as he embraced his wife and tried not to succumb to grief and melancholy, he could still guess what was happening in the city from the noises that were drifting in: the combative troops of his own Quarantine Regiment were fighting the rebellious "sectarians" on the streets. No blood had been spilled yet, but both in Vavla and by the docks, the soldiers had already fired a few warning shots in the air—or, according to some, directly at the "sectarians" themselves. While all of this was going on, the Commander was lying in bed with his arms around his wife.

Sometime later, Mazhar Effendi knocked on the door. When the Commander didn't reply, Mazhar Effendi left him a note and went away. The Commander had understood that there was some kind of revolt taking place against the Quarantine Regiment, and he would have liked to go and lead his soldiers on the field. But he also knew that as soon as he walked out of there, he would not be able to hide his wife's illness anymore, and they would immediately have to be parted. Besides, if it became known that his wife was sick, it would also be harder for him to lead the regiment directly.

Toward midday, Zeynep threw up twice in quick succession, then fell onto the bed in exhaustion. Her heart was beating fast, she was sweating, and she was in pain. She was convinced that if any doctors came, they would separate her from her husband, so every time he went anywhere near the door, she would start weeping.

In the afternoon, Zeynep's fever got worse, and she became delirious. "I never got to see Istanbul!" she said, causing the Commander immense distress. He promised her again and again that he would take her there.

"We'll go and see the palace in Beşiktaş where Princess Pakize was imprisoned, we'll visit the Sublime Porte where the government sits, and I'll take you to the Imperial Bacteriology Institute in Nişantaşı!" said the Commander. His wife cried again—and yes, the Commander's eyes filled with tears too.

Eight hours later, Zeynep would die of the plague in their room in the Splendid Hotel. Death had come even faster for her than it had for her father, prison guard Bayram Effendi, who had been killed by the same disease ninety-five days earlier.

CHAPTER 63

At first, the anger displayed by the disciples of the Halifiye sect and by their supporters from other rebellious lodges after the kidnapping of Sheikh Hamdullah did not seem serious enough to cause any great concern. Some of the protesters had been carrying sticks, but most of them were unarmed, and to demonstrate that they had no intention of fighting, they hadn't even picked up any loose branches on the way. Sami Pasha had no doubt that the Quarantine Regiment could easily overpower this aimless mob.

Most historians agree, on the other hand, that the revolt which began in the prisons that evening would dramatically alter the course of Mingheria's history. That said, we do not share some commentators' view that if the Commander had left his sick wife's bedside and immediately taken charge of his troops, events would have taken a completely different turn, and many deaths could have been avoided. For by the time the riot in the Castle's prison had grown to the unexpectedly significant proportions it would soon acquire, and reached a degree of severity that required the Commander's military and political genius, the horse had long since bolted, and the state was already far too weak to intervene.

Furious with the rough treatment they had been receiving from the wardens, and about the spread of the plague through the prison, the inmates of Dormitory Three, also known as the novices' dormitory, had been biding their time for an opportunity to revolt. The atmosphere of "anarchy" that seemed to have taken over the streets of the city after Sheikh Hamdullah's abduction, as well as the animosity that sect leaders, some shopkeepers, and a number of habitual agitators were encouraging against the Quarantine Regiment, provided the prisoners with the excuse and the inspiration they had been waiting for. The whole city was enveloped in an aura of catastrophe, and the angry convicts could sense that their time had come.

But what had most inflamed everyone's tempers was what had happened after the arrival of the plague in Dormitory Three ten days ago. The prison management's only response had been to put the entire dormitory in isolation. With prisoners no longer being allowed to go outside for their daily exercise, their rage had only accumulated. Those who broke out in plague buboes were sent to the Hamidiye Hospital (whose name hadn't changed yet). But no one who went there was ever heard from again, so nobody ever wanted to go. Every day the dormitory doors would open and two spray-pump operators would walk in, flanked by guards, to spray the frightened and subdued prisoners and every corner of their dormitory with disinfectant, but the next day two more would wake up with buboes on their bodies and get sent to their deaths in the Hamidiye Hospital.

It was during one such disinfection operation that one of the prisoners threw himself off the bed pretending to be struck by a bout of feverish plague delirium, and in the ensuing commotion, the other inmates managed to seize one of the guards and take his key. After a brief scuffle, the other guards also surrendered. Very soon, before the Chief Warden had even realized there was a riot going on, the rebels had taken over the whole building. The effects of the plague had also played their part in enabling this easy victory; for a variety of reasons, including fear and funerals, the number of prison clerks and guards turning up for work every day had greatly diminished. Some guards had stopped coming altogether after the first rumors that the plague had spread to the prison too.

By that same evening, the rioters had taken over the rest of the Castle, meeting very little resistance. They had neither planned nor dreamed of such a thing. In fact there wasn't anything particularly organized about their insurrection. But as soon as he saw that the central building, dating back to the Byzantine era, had fallen into the rebels' hands too, the Chief Warden withdrew his men from the Venetian Tower and the administrative offices. For those who argue that the warden acted with excessive caution, we will note the following: whenever they had come across anyone they deemed to be suspicious, or didn't like, or who tried to stand in their way, the delinquent inmates of Dormitory Three had

beaten them to a pulp and left them for dead. Three of the convicts had
burned down the same kitchen building where they had been tortured,
had their feet whipped, and been branded with hot coals. Other fires too
would burn in Arkaz that night. The warden had been right to abandon
the prison.

But this administrative vacuum also left the enterprising thugs of
Dormitory Three with responsibilities they had not anticipated. The
Castle was in their hands now. Would they set the other inmates free?
Any governor, Ottoman or otherwise, would be at a loss to know what
to do about a swarm of newly liberated criminals roaming the streets.
Sami Pasha's guards didn't seem to be around either. There was also some
talk among the rioting prisoners of going to the hospital to retrieve their
comrades who had been sent there with the plague. Meanwhile the prisoners in those dormitories whose doors had remained locked were howling like madmen, shouting "Let us out!" and shaking the metal bars of
their cells. There was a new smell of rust, mold, and smoke in the air.

By morning, all the cellblocks had been emptied. The Castle's spacious grounds became a kind of playground for liberated prisoners. Some
joyfully hugged and congratulated one another. Others had already left
the Castle and walked out into the city. The plague seemed to have been
forgotten. There were no quarantine soldiers or policemen around. It
might be said that the structures of the state, already considerably weakened by the death of the Commander's wife in the Splendid Palace, had
now definitively collapsed.

In her final moments—just like her father the prison guard before
her—Zeynep had seemed to recover a little, and this had given everyone
hope. Seeing the color come back to his wife's cheeks, the Commander
had ignored every precaution and sat next to her, feeling the baby in her
womb. He'd embraced her and told her that everything would be fine,
that the quarantine would work. If she looked out of the window toward
the sea and into that special Mingherian blue, she would know just how
beautiful life could be.

As Zeynep lay dying, tormented with pain, drifting in and out of
consciousness or raving incoherently, her husband Kâmil was right by
her side.

It was decided that there would be no ceremony for Zeynep's funeral,
and that her body would be washed in lime and buried the next morn-

ing. Commander Kâmil could not stop looking at the expression of surprise on his dead wife's ashen face, and felt an immeasurable guilt. He
sat by his wife and held her cooling hand, and did not move until Hadid
dragged him away.

Everyone agreed that the fact the Commander's wife had died of
plague should remain a secret. Accordingly, she was buried without any
religious ritual, in a fresh grave dug especially for her in the New Muslim
Cemetery. Apart from the usual funeral hearse, the gravediggers, and a
few seagulls and crows, only the Commander was present at the burial.
To avoid drawing attention, he had dressed like a villager, with loose
trousers, a wide sash, thick cowhide shoes, and an old-fashioned fez on
his head.

We might conclude that the Commander, reeling from the loss of
his wife and unborn child, had found comfort in daydreams, picturing
himself as an archetypal Mingherian villager, and Zeynep as the village
girl heroine of a "pastoral" Mingherian fairy tale. It still awes and amazes
us today to think that amid all the momentous events which took place
on that twenty-seventh of July 1901, the Commander was able to re-
imagine his grievous loss as a piece of Mingherian mythology.

That day, in the same well-meaning and heartfelt nationalistic vein,
the Commander supplied two journalists—one Greek and the other
Turkish—with a statement about Zeynep. This "interview," which
would later be published in the *Neo Nisi* and the *Arkata Times,* dated
his first meeting with Zeynep all the way back to their childhood. (In
truth there had been a fourteen-year age gap between them.) Zeynep
had been a very bright and very determined little girl who would insist,
despite her teachers' objections, on speaking the traditional Mingherian
language at school and with her friends. The bond between Zeynep and
Kâmil had been formed then. Whenever they felt the urge to talk in
Mingherian, they would seek each other out, and when they spoke, the
colors of their souls would be revealed in all their mysterious lyricism. It
was on Zeynep's sweet little face that the Commander had first begun to
witness the true grace of the Mingherian language, and he had immediately started thinking of what could be done to liberate it, and shield it
from the assault of French, Greek, Arabic, and Turkish.

Every Mingherian citizen today would be able to recite these words
almost entirely from memory, and we too share the view that they con-

stitute the most poetic expression there has ever been of the spirit of Mingherian nationalism and of the Mingherian Revolution, as articulated by the very man who stood at their heart and source. It is perhaps somewhat surprising that the Commander should have been able to dictate a text like this on such a difficult day, and right before his wife's funeral too. Some have suggested that the Commander's deputy, Mazhar Effendi, and various literary figures on the island must have secretly put their pens and quills to work to shape the statement into its final form. The winners of the National Anthem Poetry Competition, to be announced six months later, would also take inspiration from this foundational text.

The statement also contained various reflections on the similarity of sound between the Mingherian words for water, God, and self, and on the shadows cast by the mysterious connections that link objects to their meanings. Painted seven years later, Alexandros Satsos's oil painting of the Commander praying alone at the New Muslim Cemetery as his wife was being buried, is at least as well known among Mingherians today as the poetic interview we have just discussed. The eminent painter's greatest skill was his unique ability in capturing the Commander's inner dilemmas.

The painting shows the Commander as a heroic figure staring brokenheartedly into the fresh grave of his pregnant wife (with crows perching in the distant background) while also exercising every fiber of his will in the knowledge that he must be strong, resilient, and calm for the sake of his nation's future. The painting, whose dominant hue is a misty yellow, captivates us with its atmosphere too. Traces of blue flames rising from the city and from the incineration pit add to the drama of the scene. But the most affecting element of it all is the sense of "homeland" and belonging evoked by the sight of Mingheria's hills, plains, and rugged peaks stretching far away into the distance.

CHAPTER 64

The rulers of the new Mingherian state had mostly been busy dealing with lofty questions around the teaching of Mingherian in primary schools, the history of Mingheria, and Mingherian names and fairy tales. Concentrating on their personal preoccupations, they seemed to have withdrawn from the world, and could neither understand nor grasp the severity of what was happening in the city. Another reason for this was that many government officials, spies, municipal clerks, and soldiers had stopped reporting for work or kept finding excuses to abscond. Two soldiers of the Quarantine Regiment had been attacked by a group of so-called sectarian youths while patrolling the streets of Turunçlar, and although one of them had managed to run away, the other had been viciously beaten, suffering permanent damage to his ruptured eye. The incident had both alarmed the Quarantine Regiment and left them eager for vengeance. Sami Pasha was therefore reluctant to let them roam around the city too freely.

The moment that would truly change the course of history was when the prisoners who'd taken control of the Castle gave the matter some thought and decided that they would open the metal gate of the isolation facility—the only area within the Castle grounds that they had not yet unlocked. As a result of this incredible event, nearly three hundred confirmed or suspected plague patients were set free.

What were the prisoners thinking as the isolation area emptied out? Had they acted under the simple, primitively anarchic logic that since they'd let everyone else go, they might as well "set this lot free" as well? Or had they thought, "Serves them right," knowing that if they let these potentially infected people loose, the whole city would be paralyzed and the plague would spread faster than ever before? We may never know (though there have been plenty of theories in this regard). Perhaps they too believed what the quarantine officials all secretly believed, which was that quarantine was a serious but ineffective and perhaps even futile exercise. (But in any case, the people in the isolation facility had been put there for no good reason. Freeing them was a righteous deed!)

The rioters might have broken the lock on the isolation facility, but they never bothered to tell the people inside, "You're free." They were afraid to go in and risk catching the plague, and no one seemed willing to take on the responsibility, so it was a while before anyone inside realized they could just walk out if they wished to. The Castle's isolation area therefore emptied much more slowly than the cellblocks had. But the news that it had been breached the morning after the prison riot moved much faster and had spread across Arkaz within half a day. Of course this scandal would never have occurred if the guards and quarantine officials hadn't all fled!

The emptying of the prison and the isolation facility—and thus, effectively, of the whole Castle—changed the atmosphere inside the city completely. It became entirely commonplace to run into people who had broken out of isolation, walked through the Castle-Moat neighborhood, and gone back to their homes. Their fellow citizens might wish them well when they crossed paths on the street, just as they did with the newly escaped prisoners, but they were afraid of them too. Neither the government's guards nor its quarantine officials were doing anything to round them up.

Those who were infected and visibly sick when they left the isolation facility did not tend to be well received when they returned to their own homes. Some were devastated to discover upon their arrival that their families had dispersed, their loved ones had died, and their houses had been taken over by strangers. A few would get caught in arguments and squabbles with these new arrivals or with their own relatives who'd let them into the family home. Others would not even be allowed to come inside, lest they should bring illness and plague with them too. A judicious uncle might perhaps tell them that they ought to go back to the Castle and stay there until they had completed their mandatory period of isolation. Those who had predicted that they would be subjected to this kind of treatment, and thought they might not even find the daily bowl of soup and piece of bread they could at least rely on here, had decided not to leave the isolation facility at all. These people had immediately taken over the best beds and spaces vacated by their former neighbors. But it would not be entirely accurate either to suggest that they had stayed put for the sake of a little soup and bread—for over the last week, the amount of flour made available to the bakeries, and the loaves of bread distributed across the city and the isolation area, had fallen to half their usual quantity.

As some commentators have noted, this was a time of anarchy, dereliction, and governmental failure, and this aura of uncertainty kept growing and spreading at pace. Less than a month after the foundation of the new state, the streets were swarming with hardened criminals, rapists, murderers, and plague-infested prisoners, as well as those who were suspected of having caught the disease.

This last category was composed of those who had been put into isolation unfairly. People had indeed been known to be banished to the Castle for insolence against the Quarantine Regiment, for failing to do as they were told, and for flagrant disregard of quarantine regulations. There was no medical justification for their confinement. They should probably have been sent to prison instead, but the authorities knew that isolation could be a harsher and more persuasive punishment, and the Quarantine Regiment thought it was important to be as strict as possible and make an example of those louts who kept ignoring restrictions for no reason. But now that same group were determined to exact revenge on the Quarantine Regiment, whose actions had caused many previously healthy people to catch the plague. Objecting not only to the Quarantine Regiment, but to quarantine rules, doctors, and isolation measures in general, these people liked to claim that it was the doctors, the Christians, and the quarantine officials who'd brought the disease to the island in the first place. Sami Pasha knew it was impossible to gather this growing crowd together and force them back into the isolation facility.

It did not take long for the runaways from the isolation facility to notice that there was a power vacuum in Arkaz. The people who had already been scared to leave their homes after the plague, the revolution, and the public executions had now stopped going out entirely, deterred by the sight of bandits and plague carriers who'd escaped from the prison and the isolation facility freely roaming the streets. Following

Sami Pasha's warning, the Quarantine Regiment was also nowhere to be seen.

One reason why the hotheads who had escaped isolation were able to gain a degree of acceptance in the city was that they were seen as providing some form of protection for shopkeepers and homeowners against the perpetrators of the prison riot and the others who'd escaped with them. Some of the former inmates who'd managed to flee the Castle prison and dungeons in the wake of the riot had already set their sights on certain houses they liked in the city, and were planning to break in, or at least find some corner or back garden to settle into. These criminals were emboldened by the absence of any policemen or soldiers around to maintain law and order. A group of the more ignorant, brazen, and ruthless among them had descended upon the docks in search of a boat that could take them to Smyrna, and here they had clashed with the Quarantine Regiment and with some of the former inmates of the isolation facility. The first serious skirmish had occurred at the foot of Donkey's Bane Hill between a pair of escaped prisoners and the owner of a grocery store which sold figs, walnuts, cheese, and other goods sourced from the villages. One prisoner had been wolfing down the figs on display while another had slipped a piece of cheese into his knapsack, when the grocer and his family staged a counterattack. They could tell that these two were ordinary criminals, rather than plague-infested fugitives from the isolation area, so they were not afraid. The grocer had been joined by one of his brothers and a few friends, all of whom had just spent five days in isolation after being "unfairly" identified as being infected, and had now excitedly come together to celebrate their newfound freedom; they got involved in the fight too. Five minutes and several swings of clubs and sticks later, this clash between escaped prisoners and furious isolation runaways was already over, but it quickly gave rise to the rumor that the "infected" could be relied upon to guard shopkeepers from vicious criminals.

Chief Minister Sami Pasha was following everything closely from the office he'd occupied for the last five years. The Commander's deputy, Mazhar Effendi, and the Doctor and Prince Consort joined him there for a meeting that same evening. They did not have enough soldiers or policemen to safeguard the state from all the fugitives and mischief-makers roaming the city's streets, or against former isolation inmates and sect devotees angling for revenge. After a string of unfortunate clashes and confrontations, the soldiers of the Quarantine Regiment had retreated to their homes, and less than half of them were reporting to the garrison every morning. They'd heard that the Commander's wife had died of the plague, and this had been a blow to their morale. Sami Pasha himself only had enough security forces and gendarmes at his command to guard the Ministries building and square. It was these gendarmes who had chased away a group of hostile convicts who'd sought to break into the Ministerial Headquarters and spend the night in there. There were also rumors that some gangs had taken up residence in various homes across the city, and were making plans to raid government buildings. It was imperative to make peace between the Quarantine Regiment and the people who'd escaped from the Castle's isolation facility, but the men assembled in Sami Pasha's office that evening could not figure out how.

To help secure the ministerial building and the Commander's quarters at the Splendid Hotel, Sami Pasha had asked the garrison to send a small platoon from the Arab division who could be relied upon to understand and follow orders. But the requested soldiers had yet to come down. Mazhar Effendi, who'd been handling these negotiations, had wanted to update the Commander about the situation on the streets and the expanding influence of the isolation fugitives, and ask for his advice. The Commander, grieving the loss of his wife and son, had locked himself inside his room at the top of the Splendid Palace, and would not come out. But in the meantime, a band of escaped convicts had burned down a house in the Kadirler neighborhood, generating a plume of smoke that had been visible from across the city. The Commander should have been wondering what was going on, and asked to be informed. He must have heard the yelling and shouting and the occasional gunshot coming from the city at night.

This seems a suitable moment in which to make one or two remarks upon the role of the individual in history. Had Commander Kâmil's wife Zeynep not caught the plague, would the many other events that resulted from this fact never have occurred, and would history have taken a completely different course? Or would the inevitable developments that history had reserved for the island of Mingheria have come to pass regardless? These are complicated questions to answer. But it is true that under the prevailing mood of anarchy and disorder, the Commander's single-minded preoccupation with his wife and with the Mingherian language only served to worsen the chaotic, disorderly atmosphere that reigned in the city, and more important, it also led to the rapid dissolution of any hope and optimism that the new government had brought with it.

As they assembled before the map of Arkaz the next morning, they saw thirty-two new deaths marked upon it. By now it was almost impossible to keep burying victims individually, but funeral processions were still taking place and breaching quarantine in some of the outer neighborhoods. The new unruly crowd that had taken over the streets of the city had turned defiance of quarantine rules into a matter of course.

Sami Pasha could see better than everybody else that the only way for the government to restore its authority was for the Commander to emerge from the room where he'd been mourning the loss of his wife and take charge of his Quarantine Regiment once more, for nothing else would work now, and if they delayed any further, it might mean the end of everything. The next day, Sami Pasha, Mazhar Effendi, and their guards climbed up the stairs to the third floor of the Splendid Palace, and knocked on the Commander's door. The thick, white, wooden door stayed shut. They waited for quite a long time, then knocked again. When the door still wouldn't open, they took out a letter they'd prepared beforehand, describing all the latest political developments and the urgency of the situation, and slipped it halfway through the gap under the door.

They came back an hour later to find that the letter had been retrieved. Mazhar Effendi pointed out that the doorknob seemed to have moved. The Commander must have woken up. The door wasn't locked. After knocking once more and waiting for a while, they thought it would be appropriate for Prince Consort Nuri to join them too before they went inside, and sent a messenger to the old State Hall building.

Half an hour later, Sami Pasha gently pushed the door open, with Doctor Nuri standing behind him.

Still hearing nothing, Sami Pasha, Doctor Nuri, and Mazhar Effendi walked inside, where they found Commander Kâmil sitting at a walnut writing desk next to one of the hotel's wide-shuttered windows. The Commander had noticed someone come in, but had not shifted his position. Doctor Nuri could sense, as he approached him, that there was something unusual going on.

The Commander had put on his military uniform and was wearing his boots too, though there was no need for those in summer. For a moment, Doctor Nuri thought he must have finally resolved to go out and lead his soldiers into battle, but it appeared the opposite was true: Commander Kâmil looked like he hardly had the strength to breathe, let alone fight anyone. His forehead was slick with sweat, and he was panting.

Doctor Nuri realized that the Commander was following them with his eyes, as if he were sitting in a barber's chair and couldn't move his head. Then his own gaze fell onto the Commander's neck. A huge and extremely conspicuous plague bubo had emerged on the right-hand side of the Commander's neck.

In that historic moment, the three men realized that the founder of the new state and revolutionary hero Commander Kâmil Pasha had caught the plague. They recognized that he had been acting this way because he couldn't bring himself to complain about being sick, or felt that he shouldn't. Sami Pasha also sensed that the Commander would refuse to talk, like a sulking child. Doctor Nuri, on the other hand, remembered that in some cases the plague could affect patients' ability to speak, and cause others to shiver and stammer.

What would happen now? The three men could tell that the Commander was thinking of the fate of the nation and of the island above all else, and that he too, like them, did not wish for news of his illness to be made public. But the Commander was able to see only to the end of his own life. The other three were thinking anxiously of what might happen after that.

CHAPTER 65

Shortly after showing the island's three other political leaders the boil on his neck, Commander Kâmil Pasha abandoned the pose he'd taken, slowly pushed himself off the wicker chair he'd been sitting on, and fell shakily onto the bed he and his late wife had happily shared for two and a half months.

It still amazes us today, as we try to make sense of all these events, that the other three men in the room—Sami Pasha, Mazhar Effendi, and Doctor Nuri—should have been able to think of anything other than fleeing that hotel room right away, returning to the former State Hall and current Ministerial Headquarters, and doing everything they could to save their own and their wives and children's lives. But in their attempt to keep the ship of state afloat, Sami Pasha and Mazhar Effendi were trying to behave as if there were a platoon of soldiers with them, waiting to do their government's bidding.

Some historians have suggested that Commander Kâmil's illness marked the beginning of a Mingherian counterrevolution, and a return to the previous order. If the revolution is understood as a movement for independence and the rejection of Ottoman rule, then that is incorrect; for the island continued on the path of independence even after the Commander was struck by the plague. But if we consider the revolution as a force for secularism and modernization, then these historians' observations might be accurate. What we can definitely agree on is that within two days, it became clear that no matter how hard the doctors and bureaucrats worked, the new government was going to struggle to cling to power. Sami Pasha's web of spies and informants had gone quiet too, as if even they were still trying to understand what was going on. The city was in the grips of indiscipline, disorder, and mayhem now, in a state of what the West might have termed "chaos" and "anarchy." There was not a single person inside the Ministerial Headquarters who had fully understood what was happening outside their door.

In the afternoon, Doctor Nuri and Doctor Nikos made an incision in the Commander's bubo. They gave him an injection to reduce his fever, and to help cool him further, they arranged for a male nurse to gently wipe his body down under their supervision. They did not get too close to the ailing commander. Doctor Nuri would later tell his wife that on the first day, the Commander had hidden his illness like everyone else did, and on the second day he'd begun to behave like a child. Mingherian schoolbooks tell us that despite his illness, the Commander was not "afraid," and persisted in his efforts to fight the outbreak and establish a modern quarantine system. At times he would descend into lengthy silences, grappling with headaches that battered his forehead like sledgehammers, suffering extended bouts of shivering, and withdrawing from the world. But in other moments he would look like he had overcome his fever, try to get out of bed as soon as he woke up, and behave as if there were some other place he had to rush to.

An hour after the bubo in his neck was drained, the Commander gathered his remaining strength and got up to look out of the main window at the city and the docks below. Suffused in its characteristic blue, pink, and white-tinted glow, the bay looked glorious. As if the sight of that glow had confirmed some kind of knowledge he'd been imparted from above and that he'd been pondering ever since, the Commander then declared that the people of Mingheria were the noblest, truest, and most regal in the world, and would remain forever so. A jewel was still a jewel even if it had only ever graced the fingers of greedy, wicked, grasping people, and lost none of its worth for being abused and mistreated by Italians, Greeks, and Turks. Mingheria too was just as valuable as ever. No one could understand or advance Mingheria better than Mingherians themselves. This was what they would use their Mingherian language for. Anyone who said "I am Mingherian" was Mingherian. For centuries, Mingherians had been forbidden from saying "I am Mingherian," but from now on, embracing this most beautiful of declarations would be deemed as sacred as an act of prayer, and be all that was ever asked of a person.

Those same words, he argued, were not just the beginning of their brotherhood with the rest of humanity; they were the beginning of everything. The look on the Commander's face was that of a man out on the streets, walking among his people. In describing these moments to his wife, the Doctor and Prince Consort would say that "it was as if an outpouring of love, passion, and enthusiasm were rushing out of the Commander and spreading all over the city!" Someday the Mingherian people would achieve great things, and change the history of the world! Sadly, these bursts of energy were followed by long periods of exhaustion, during which the Commander would lie in bed raving incoherently and drifting in and out of sleep.

Mazhar Effendi had dispatched a young clerk to the Commander's sickbed to record everything he said. Doctor Nuri's accounts to his wife and the clerk's notes tend to corroborate each other. In his final spells of delirium, the Commander spoke about seeing the warships in the naval blockade, the importance of ensuring his wife did not leave their quarters, and of how his son must go to a Mingherian school to learn how to read and write. At one point, the Commander also pointed out a cloud in the sky that looked exactly like the rose on the flag of Mingheria. This incident would acquire a particular significance in Mingherian culture, and especially in its schoolbooks, so that children would often be taught about it in their drawing classes, and each year at the start of August, the day after the anniversary of the Commander's death, the whole island would celebrate the Rose and Cloud holiday.

Aware of how desperate the situation had become, Sami Pasha and Deputy Mazhar Effendi thought they might try to form an alliance with Sheikh Hamdullah—if only, they reasoned, to prevent any more unnecessary deaths. They sent a messenger to the Constanz Hotel, but received no response from the sheikh.

When he woke up again at midnight, the feverish commander told the young clerk sitting in his room the tale of the Mingherian fox who had gone looking for its mate. This was a story his grandmother had told him once when he was a little boy. Later that same night, the Commander remembered another of his grandmother's old Mingherian stories. Long before the city of Arkaz even existed, there was a boat that crashed onto some rocks out in the bay, and the people who came out of that boat were the forefathers of today's Mingherians. They liked this island, and soon came to see its cliffs, springs, forests, and sea as their new home. Back then Mingheria's rivers teemed with green mullet fish and ancient, red-spotted crabs, its forests were populated by garrulous parrots and stealthy tigers, and its skies were full of pink storks and blue swallows that migrated to Europe in the summer. Zeynep had found each and every one of these creatures its own home on the island, a nest upon a tree, a cave to shelter in. This little Mingherian girl had befriended them all. Her father had been an official in the court of the king. The Commander told the clerk that someone should write a book about Zeynep's friendship with these animals in ancient Mingheria for primary-school children to learn how to read, then started dictating in Turkish what would become the first chapter of *Zeynep's Book*. As he spoke, the Commander walked up to the window, asked through labored breaths for the shutters to be opened, and looked out at the nighttime view of Arkaz. It was as if his grandmother's fairy tales were coming to life in the dark and silent streets below. The Commander's expression was alight with the exhilarating pleasure of mixing memories with the future, and ancient myths with things that were happening today. He understood in that moment, before collapsing onto the bed in agony, that seeing the present in the past was the same thing as imagining the future.

The next morning, after learning that the Commander's condition had deteriorated even further, and that the number of deaths had risen to forty-eight, Sami Pasha exclaimed: "We can only turn to God now!"

Yet within the hour, they had agreed with Mazhar Effendi that it might be helpful for Sami Pasha to pay a visit to the Maiden's Tower, if only as a "last resort." At noon that day, a little rowboat that used to belong to the Governor's Office, and that—readers might recall—had also picked Bonkowski Pasha up from the *Aziziye* one morning at the start of our book, sailed out toward the Maiden's Tower with Sami Pasha on board. Given all the political turmoil and the rising number of deaths, there were no more ferries coming and going from the island anymore, scheduled or otherwise, so by this point the only people still in the Maiden's Tower were that group of government officials who had remained "loyal to Istanbul." Sami Pasha was somewhat hesitant to talk to them, lest they should start making veiled remarks about treason. So he only met with Hadi, deputy to the new governor who had been killed before he could even take office, and after pointing out that everything he'd done had been for the health of the citizens and subjects of the Sultan, the Pasha moved on to the main subject, explaining that the situation on the island was dire, and that he was considering putting Hadi and the other Turkish bureaucrats on a ship to Crete so that they could make their way back from there to Istanbul. But in return, he carefully noted, the Commander asked for Istanbul to lift the blockade and send military reinforcements to help stop the plague.

Hadi would later wryly recount in his memoirs, *From the Islands to the Motherland,* that this had felt less like a meeting between two Ottoman officials than an encounter between a hostage and the pirate holding him to ransom. In any event, Sami Pasha's demands were not realistic; even if they did manage to find a boat willing to make the journey from the Maiden's Tower to Crete, and even if the boat successfully slipped through the blockade, there was no reason why anybody in Istanbul would take instructions from a band of dubious Ottoman officials from Mingheria. Besides, it would take them at least a week to reach Istanbul. Eventually, Sami Pasha himself seemed to realize the absurdity of his proposal, and hastily terminated the meeting (as if he'd suddenly thought of something else he had to do), sailing back to the port in his rowboat.

As Sami Pasha approached the docks, he found the sight of Arkaz unbearably bleak. There was no one around, and not even a hint of activity. It was a cloudy day, the city had taken on a leaden hue, and there seemed to be no life left in it at all. Two columns of blue smoke rising into the sky—nothing more! The boatman was pulling at his oars with resignation. The sea was dark and frightening. One day this outbreak would of course be over, and life, color, and beauty would return to the island. Until then, Sami Pasha thought, he would rather not look at the city at all than see it in this funereal guise.

Sami Pasha was still on the boat when Commander Kâmil Pasha, founder of the state of Mingheria, died of the plague in his room on the top floor of the Splendid Palace, four days after his wife. There was nobody else in the room except for the young clerk who had been recording the Commander's words. Doctor Nuri had been waiting on the second floor of the hotel.

The clerk reported that during the last two hours of his life, Commander Kâmil had uttered a total of two thousand words in Turkish and one hundred and twenty-nine words in Mingherian. Identified as the Commander's words, these Mingherian terms have since been widely reproduced in both Turkish and Mingherian, and utilized in a variety of contexts, including on signs on the walls of government offices, on posters and postage stamps, in the teaching of telegraph systems and the alphabet, and in works of literature. The first Mingherian dictionary even set the Commander's one hundred and twenty-nine words in a different font from the rest. To this day, they are still so prominently displayed in the capital that a visitor to Arkaz who has never heard a word of Mingherian before could probably learn them all within three days, and without even having to try too hard.

Among the words the Commander spoke during his last hours, some (fire, dream, mother) reveal his poetic sensitivities; others (dark, sorrow, lock) point to the great man's emotions; others still (door, towel, glass) suggest that he was lucid throughout this time, but might have occasionally needed some practical assistance.

As for the Commander's mentions of boots and warships, some biographers, historians, and politicians have interpreted them as proof that during the last moments of his life, when he barely had any strength left to speak, the founder of the nation was thinking of summoning his preferred boatman and sailing out with the Quarantine Regiment to attack the Great Powers' warships.

When he returned to his office with Coachman Zekeriya, who'd come to pick him up at the Old Stone Jetty, Sami Pasha found the ministers in a state of agitation. Mazhar Effendi, who'd left the Commander in Doctor Nuri's care, was also present, and the news was startling: it seemed Sheikh Hamdullah had escaped from the Constanz Hotel the night before.

Or perhaps he had been kidnapped (though that part was not yet clear), but in any case there had been no signs of a struggle. Could the sheikh simply have strolled out of the place? That was impossible, and besides, Sami Pasha was sure the sheikh would never do anything like that. For the time being, this was all the information they had. Nobody had yet come out and claimed responsibility for the sheikh's abduction. But the kidnappers could easily beat, torture, and kill the sheikh just as they'd done with Bonkowski Pasha, and in that case the blame might well end up falling on Chief Minister Sami Pasha.

The other problem the authorities faced was the growing popularity of a new gang of isolation fugitives based around the shops and shopkeepers' neighborhoods north of Hamidiye Avenue. Using their extensive network of friends, family, and shopkeepers from the local community to establish themselves as "quarantine victims" and secure the shopkeepers' support against the escaped prisoners roaming the city, most of the forty-odd members of this gang had since settled down in the neighborhood of Hagia Triada. Now they were spreading the disease in this area too. They could see that the Quarantine Regiment was in no state to challenge them, and as their main motivation was revenge, they were constantly looking for ways to draw the soldiers into a fight. Sami Pasha's spies also reported that the gang were inflaming anti-quarantine (and not just anti-isolation) sentiments among the general populace, and that they had encouraged a grocer from their own village to open his shop behind the Customhouse again, exhorting him to stock and sell whatever he wished.

Sami Pasha had just been thinking of sharing all this new information with Doctor and Prince Consort Nuri when the doctor himself showed up at the Pasha's office just before sunset to announce that Commander Kâmil had passed away. Sami Pasha was not surprised to hear this; he had only expected the bad news to arrive a little later than it did.

Upon learning that the Commander and founder of the nation had died, some people began to weep. Sami Pasha considered going to the hotel to look at the corpse, but decided not to, so as to avoid news of the Commander's death spreading any further. He was thinking now that he would surely be expected to take charge of the new state at this difficult time. With all these emotions and yearnings and dreams coursing through him, he knew he would find it difficult to sleep that night, so he had already sent word to Marika. He took the landau to Petalis, then walked the rest of the way to her house through the neighborhood's empty, misty streets. He was surprised to see a flag of Mingheria (if only a small one) hanging at the door of a hotel on the way.

As he entered the house, he had the feeling he always experienced of having walked into some kind of dangerous dream. Like all his favorite dreams, Marika's home was also "forbidden." A nearby torch which had been illuminating the street, the walls, the trees, and their leaves suddenly went out, and all the shadows and happy memories vanished with its light, leaving nothing behind but a feeling of loneliness and dread that made the hollowness of the world seem palpable.

Marika told him a long story about how the plague had spread all over the city, and about the neighbors who had been hiding their dead. Sami Pasha was still on his feet and finding it difficult to concentrate on her account, a fact which Marika soon noticed.

"You look half dead yourself," she said.

Sami Pasha felt grateful to her for knowing how he felt just by looking at his face. He sat down to rest for a while, then made love to Marika, hoping to disappear into his passion and forget everything else, but nothing seemed to alleviate the pangs of horror and despair piercing his stomach.

Marika was still taking some of the new government's pronouncements seriously. "You must get rid of this ban on mosques and churches!" she said. "Otherwise it will only cause you and the quarantine trouble. The people, the nation will turn their backs on you if they are not allowed inside their mosques and churches."

"What exactly is this nation you speak of? We are responsible for *everyone's* safety here—the whole population's."

"A people without their mosques, their churches, and their faith is no nation at all, Pasha."

"It isn't mosques or churches that make this nation, but the fact that we live here. We are the people of this island."

"But Pasha, even if the Greek community were to accept this idea of a nation, would the Muslims do so too? The ringing of our church bells doesn't just remind us that we must pray and that Christ will save us all; it also brings us comfort in the knowledge that there are many others like us all over the city, suffering, fearful, and just as desperate as we are. Death looms larger where there are no bells or calls to prayer, my Pasha."

Chief Minister Sami Pasha listened sullenly. Marika then began to list all the newest rumors. A headless skeleton had been found inside a haunted house in Flizvos which children's gangs used as their nighttime hiding place. The medicines, canned goods, quilt covers, and bedsheets that had arrived with the relief ship *Sühandan* were being sold in secret in Pharmacist Kotzias's store and by some Muslim shopkeepers in the Old Market. One of the soldiers of the Quarantine Regiment had taken a bribe in exchange for hiding a plague-infected mother and son from the quarantine doctors.

"Well, it's good to know there are still some quarantine soldiers around!" said Sami Pasha, then abruptly decided to leave and return to the Ministerial Headquarters.

The building from which he had governed the island he had been living on for the past five years was completely empty. He saw a couple of lone sentries standing guard on the staircases and in the corridors, but no one else. Most of the torches weren't lit. Sami Pasha gave orders for more sentries to be sent before making his way to the living quarters at the back of the building, and it was only half an hour later that he finally managed to retreat to his room, sealing both locks and pulling the latch shut before settling down for a night of fitful, broken sleep.

CHAPTER 66

The next morning, Sami Pasha, the Prince Consort, and Doctor
Nikos congregated as usual before the map of the city, where
they found out that more than forty people had died the previous day. Wary of possible encounters with bands of fugitives from the
Castle's isolation facility or with angry sect disciples, the Quarantine
Regiment had stopped sending men to help enforce isolation measures
and evacuations even in neighborhoods like Bayırlar and Tuzla, where
death rates had been soaring. Meanwhile, Sami Pasha—whose primary
instinct was to protect the Ministerial Headquarters—had been rounding up any new recruits and unoccupied quarantine soldiers he could
find, and keeping them firmly by his side in the Ministries building.

It has not escaped the notice of cultural historians that even in that
moment of calamity and hopelessness, several hours were spent debating and permanently settling the details of how the father of the nation
should be entombed. The grave of the founder of the state of Mingheria
was to be situated in an elevated plot of land in the neighborhood of
Turunçlar, halfway between the New Muslim Cemetery (set aside for
plague victims) and the house where the Major had been born and
raised. This spot was clearly visible from all over the city and from the
Castle, as well as from any ships approaching the island from the south
and east. At the suggestion of the elderly Doctor Tassos, who dabbled in
cultural and archaeological studies and had happened to leave his house
that day, it was also decreed that the design of the mausoleum would
show traces of Roman, Byzantine, Ottoman, and Arab architectural
influences. Thirty-two years later, his vision would finally be realized.

Sami Pasha and his clerks spent nearly the whole day trying to come
up with a way of transporting the Commander's corpse—currently still

in his room in the Splendid Palace—to the grave site without drawing attention to the fact or anyone realizing whom the body belonged to, but it was no use. The streets of the city were rife with gangs who had made a habit of stopping and questioning anyone who crossed their paths, including funeral processions, villagers coming to sell their wares, and escaped prisoners. But even if these hoodlums could somehow be avoided, there would inevitably be a great deal of speculation about the identity of the individual who was being buried on the hill.

But what most unnerved Sami Pasha and the Mingherian government, and weakened their resolve, was a letter brought in by Mazhar Effendi. Composed by a clerk on behalf of the former inmates of the isolation facility, this missive respectfully announced that a group of forty-two people who had unjustly been put in isolation by the Quarantine Regiment and had since been freed now wished to visit the Chief Minister in person to deliver a letter of complaint listing the names and misdeeds—including coercion and corruption—of various members of that same regiment. According to Mazhar Effendi, these people had also rather audaciously requested to conduct a search of the Ministerial Headquarters, on the basis of information they had received suggesting that a number of soldiers who had grievously mistreated the public were now hiding out in there.

It was clear to Sami Pasha that these people were looking for an excuse to start some kind of trouble. He sent Mazhar Effendi to the garrison to request that a detachment of forty to fifty men be sent down in case of a possible attack. Every now and then he would look out of the window at the Splendid Palace, whose upper floors he could see from where he stood, and recall with tearful sorrow that the body of the founder of the state of Mingheria lay there still. But by now he had realized that there was no way they could bury the Commander in the daylight without attracting notice, and without risking or indeed provoking a clash with any of the gangs that had sprung up all over the city. He therefore decided, in consultation with Minister for Public Health Doctor Nikos, that the body of their heroic commander should be taken from his room in the Splendid Hotel after midnight and buried under cover of darkness and in accordance with quarantine regulations.

Half an hour later, Chief Minister Sami Pasha turned up with a retinue of clerks and guards at Princess Pakize and the Prince Consort's door. He entered their quarters alone, and looked genuinely disconsolate as he told the Prince Consort, who'd stood up to greet him, that the Commander would have to be buried after midnight without even his own mother being present. The Pasha seemed to be speaking especially to Princess Pakize, who was listening from the other end of the room.

"Whatever we have done, we have done it to save the lives of the Sultan's subjects!" said Sami Pasha. "Unfortunately, we cannot claim to have achieved any success in this endeavor. But I am pleased to report our humble victory in bringing another matter His Highness the Sultan had tasked you with to a comprehensive and satisfactory conclusion. We have identified Bonkowski Pasha and his assistant Doctor Ilias's killers. It is all in here—the Sherlock Holmes way, and the Turkish way!" said Sami Pasha, putting down a file full of documents.

"I have brought in more guards to protect the main entrance. It is a pity they keep running away . . . I would not be surprised if the rebel prisoners were to try and attack this building, but they will not get their way. Lock your door twice and bolt it shut. Remember, you are here as our honored guests under the protection of the state. Perhaps we could move you to a different location."

"Why would you do that, Pasha?"

"So they wouldn't know where you are . . . ," replied Chief Minister Sami Pasha. "Perhaps the danger is not so great, though you should still stay inside. I will station guards at your door too," he said as he walked out of the room.

That was the last time Princess Pakize and Doctor Nuri ever saw Sami Pasha. It would turn out to be the unhappiest and most frightening night they had spent on the island. They were shaken by Zeynep's death and by the Major's impending funeral, and like everyone else around them, they had begun to understand that they might die too. There was probably nowhere on the island better equipped with traps and poison to protect against rats than the Ministerial Headquarters, yet even Doctor Nuri, who had attended so many international plague and quarantine conferences, had now begun to fear, just as people used to do in the old days, that the plague could be spreading through the very air they breathed, with no need for rats or fleas. Now there was the added risk of being murdered by insurgents and prison fugitives.

They had a few walnuts and some freshly salted fish left. They ate this with a little bit of bread from the garrison. There was now even less bread available in the city than before, meaning that those who had been subsisting on these loaves must be gradually approaching starvation. Before going to sleep, they pushed a small cupboard up against the door. Princess Pakize's letters provide a compelling account of the atmosphere on the island that night, of her feelings, of the mildewy smell drifting in from the port and the deep blue sea, and of the light from the few solitary torches that still burned here and there across the city. When she describes how she and her husband held each other in terror as they lay in bed, and how they couldn't sleep from straining their ears for every sound from the city and every wave in the sea, readers can understand what it must have felt like to be wide awake and crying through the night in fear of the plague.

Shortly after midnight, they heard gunshots from the square and from the main entrance of the building. Some of the shots sounded like they had been fired very close by, and the noise echoed around the square. Feeling agitated, they got out of bed, but walked around the room in a crouch, and made sure not to go near the window.

That night's battle between the insurgents and Sami Pasha's security forces lasted until the morning. Chief Minister Sami Pasha bravely stood his ground until the last moment. Seven of the rebel "hooligans" and two of the Pasha's guards died. Sami Pasha escaped from the back entrance with two of his men, and the former State Hall fell into the rebels' hands.

The shooting stopped in the morning and the battle seemed to end, then briefly picked up again before coming to a definitive stop. After an interval of absolute silence, Doctor Nuri and Princess Pakize heard people running across the square, footsteps on the stairs, and the sound of someone talking. But nobody came to their door. They sat and waited, unable to muster the courage to open the door and check if the guard was still there.

When Doctor Nuri eventually got dressed and stepped out of the room, he saw that there was a different guard outside. The new guard clumsily pointed his gun at them, so they closed the door again and bolted it shut from the inside. They went to the window to see if they could figure out what was happening outside.

An hour later, there was a knock on the door. The visitors were two secretaries Doctor Nuri recognized, some clerks, and an old man dressed like a dervish.

They took Doctor and Prince Consort Nuri to a large office on the same floor. This was the same room our readers have come to know since the start of this book as Sami Pasha's office. Nearly every day since he had first come to the island precisely ninety-eight days ago, Doctor Nuri had gone to examine the map inside the Outbreak Room right next to this office. Sami Pasha had always come with him. But this time there was someone else sitting at the Pasha's desk. Doctor Nuri recognized the man now standing up from Sami Pasha's chair immediately. It was Regent Nimetullah Effendi with the felt hat, though he wasn't wearing his hat now. Once the usual pleasantries had been exchanged, the Regent said: "There has been a battle, the government has fallen, and Sami Pasha has run away. I have humbly taken over the position of Chief Minister. But most of the old ministers remain in place. They will retain their duties. His Holiness the Sheikh has returned to the lodge, peacefully and without ceremony. Everyone agrees that quarantine must be lifted!"

Doctor Nuri understood then that Sheikh Hamdullah had used a group of fugitives from the isolation facility, as well as a motley group of sect devotees, holy men, and quarantine-averse shopkeepers, to drive away the handful of guards that had remained loyal to Sami Pasha, and effectively put himself in charge. Sami Pasha must have managed to flee after the battle, but it was only a matter of time before he was caught. A new de facto government had been formed.

Mosque and church services would resume, church bells and calls to prayer would be heard once more, and the obligation to wash corpses in lime would be lifted. Nimetullah Effendi also noted that the practice of washing corpses in mosques before burial would immediately be reinstated. These were clearly the most urgent matters at hand.

"But, Your Excellency, if you do this there will be so many dead bodies that you will struggle to find enough people to wash them," said Doctor Nuri. "Things will get even worse than they already are!"

The new Chief Minister did not even bother to respond. By now the widespread view among those in favor of ending quarantine was that the measures were of no use anyway, as the number of deaths only kept increasing. The idea that the disease had been brought by quarantine officials in the first place also remained as popular as ever.

Chief Minister Nimetullah Effendi reminded Doctor Nuri that since quarantine had been abolished, he was now released from his duties and free to go. If he wished, he could visit the hospitals and see if he could find a way to help the sick. But any soldiers, doctors, and government officials who had misused their influence and authority would face the consequences of their actions. Nimetullah Effendi then proceeded to explain with tactful care that Doctor Nuri and his wife the former sultan's daughter were still officially guests of the Mingherian government and could always count on the protection of its guards. As Doctor Nuri was about to leave the room, the Regent asked about Sami Pasha's possible whereabouts, but Doctor Nuri replied that he had no idea.

On his return to the guesthouse, Doctor Nuri brought Princess Pakize up to date on all that had happened, noting that Nimetullah Effendi was the Chief Minister now, but that they would not be treated badly.

Not long after this, feeling too restless to sit still and wanting to see what was going on with his own eyes, Doctor Nuri thought he would venture outside, but found that he was stopped at the door. Doctor Nuri understood that the new government did not even want him treating patients in the city's hospitals. Husband and wife had already suspected in some corner of their minds that they would probably be confined to the guesthouse. Now, what had always been a fact of life for Princess Pakize would be the norm for the Prince Consort too.

For the next sixteen days, neither of them left the room. We have therefore based our account of the felt-hatted dervish Nimetullah's tenure as Chief Minister during this period—which some historians have termed the Sheikh Hamdullah Era—on sources beyond Princess Pakize's letters.

The most characteristic feature of the Sheikh Hamdullah Era was that, despite the plague, mosques and churches as well as lodges and monasteries were once again open to worshippers. Even the decision to allow shops, restaurants, and barbers, as well as flea markets and junk dealers, to resume trading did not cause as much damage as the lifting of the ban on mosque and church attendance did. In the eyes of the more ill-informed and indifferent segments of the population, the fact that the government had opened up these places of worship was yet another persuasive argument in support of the view that quarantine was pointless. The decision gave further strength to that pious, fatalistic, defeatist outlook that saw no alternative but to take refuge in Allah. Widely regarded as the source of all cholera outbreaks in Mediterranean cities over the course of the previous half century, most of the island's wickerworkers, kilim weavers, junk dealers, and fruit vendors were Greek shopkeepers who supported quarantine measures. These people were not convinced by Sheikh Hamdullah allowing commercial activities to resume and still wouldn't open their shops. Larger stores and the majority of the city's best-known restaurants also kept their doors shut, as did hotel restaurants and "clubhouses."

The barbershops and diners that did resume their activities were mostly based in smaller backstreets and more distant neighborhoods. Unbeknownst to quarantine officials, these businesses had been surreptitiously breaking quarantine all along, handing out their wares to their usual customers directly from their storerooms, or arranging in advance to open their hidden back doors at a certain time every day and conducting much of their trade during those intervals. More than half of the tradesmen and apprentices working in these kinds of small diners and grocery stores would catch the plague and die before Sheikh Hamdullah's rule was over.

Yet very few people took any notice of this appalling tragedy. Nobody suggested putting precautions in place to stop the apprentices from dying because nobody could really see what was going on anymore. With the abolition of quarantine, the clerks who had kept a tally of the dead in the cemeteries, those who'd been counting hearses, and most important the officials who had then recorded all of this information with color-coded marks on the streets and buildings shown on the big epidemiology map in the Outbreak Room, had all been relieved of their duties. In other words, there was nobody on the island who knew how many people had died on any given day. Those in power probably did not wish to know.

Felt-hatted Nimetullah Effendi became aware of the inconceivable rise in the number of deaths within the first ten days of his reign, and the overwhelming, alarming incompatibility between His Holiness Sheikh

Hamdullah's demands and the reality of what was happening around him seemed to leave him altogether paralyzed. Banning cemeteries from disinfecting corpses with lime, and enforcing His Holiness the Sheikh's express wishes that people should wash their dead in mosque mortuaries instead, urging them to follow the appropriate rituals and recite all the required prayers, had caused the spread of the disease to accelerate, as had all the people frequenting the newly reopened shops, the resumption of a number of Koran classes, and the return of former inmates of the isolation facility to the city and their homes.

Despite the lifting of quarantine measures, the streets had not filled up. There might be the odd sect member roaming around who did not believe in the need for quarantine and did not take the outbreak seriously, and there were still a few villagers left who were brave enough to come down to Arkaz to try and sell their produce. But as Princess Pakize noted, the sounds of carriage bells and wheels and the clatter of their horses' hooves were still rarely heard even now that restrictions had been removed. Although quarantine was over, although the church bells were ringing again and calls to prayer had resumed, the deathly hush covering the port, the bay, and the whole of the city had not faded. Instead, the calls to prayer and the tolling of the church bells had been transformed in the stillness and silence of the city into omens that reminded everyone of the terrifying prospect of death.

The only success registered during the Sheikh Hamdullah Era was that, with the city on the verge of famine, the government was able to hand out six thousand loaves of fresh, warm bread every day. This was made possible by the confiscation of the flour that had been stored in the garrison's depots. The loaves were baked in the garrison's kitchens, then transported in the municipality's carriages and distributed to the public from neighborhood squares.

The government in Istanbul had sent these sacks of flour, beans, and other provisions as a precautionary measure in case there was a revolt against the garrison in the wake of the Pilgrim Ship Mutiny, or if the garrison was besieged or blockaded by foreign armies (as had effectively happened), and in theory they were not supposed to be used under any other circumstances. For years the sheikh had been visiting the garrison under one pretext or another, befriending the Arab soldiers who supported the Halifiye sect and knew about his lodge, and thus getting the chance to practice his Arabic and talk in the language of the Holy Koran, and it was through his conversations with these men that he had managed to discover where that secret trove of food and flour had been hidden.

CHAPTER 67

The other defining feature of the Sheikh Hamdullah Era was its use of trials, executions, and imprisonments in what was, to all intents and purposes, a campaign of "state terror." The terror was of course political, but there was a personal element to it too.

After an initial exchange of gunfire, Sami Pasha had realized that he was the main target of the raid, and sometime after midnight, he had fled the Ministerial Headquarters and gone to hide in Marika's home (they made love), before leaving this well-known location too after a couple of hours and letting his men guide him through the backstreets and out of the city. Deputy Mazhar's spies and informants were all on the former governor's side, and the new sectarian government—which only seemed to know how to give out bread for free—might never have been able to find the old governor.

Sami Pasha was hiding out in an empty cottage in the village of Dumanlı, to which he had brought telegraph lines from Arkaz during his time as governor, and whose wealthier residents—including Ali Talip, owner of the farm the Pasha's hideout was on—had always been fond of the Pasha. Surrounded on all sides by stone walls, and with Ali Talip's armed watchmen stationed at the entrance and patrolling its environs, the farm was a safe location. The prison and isolation fugitives, plague sufferers, criminals, hoodlums, and rabble-rousers who had made a habit during those nights of plague of forcing their way into derelict, deserted buildings, and even into homes where people still lived, would never be able to break in here. The guards in this distant village were all recent migrants from Crete, and did not recognize the old governor's face. Sami Pasha thought they probably had no idea who the Governor of Mingheria was.

Feeling quite safe, Sami Pasha soon began to venture out of the farm for walks across the tall peaks of the Albros Mountains. During one of these excursions, he came across three middle-aged men who had been living in the mountains ever since they'd fled the plague in Arkaz, and one of the men worked out that the weary, animated figure before them was the island's governor. As they knew nothing of the declaration of freedom and independence, of the foundation of the new state, or of the Commander's or even Sheikh Hamdullah's rule, the three plague fugitives wondered what the Governor could possibly be doing there. Afterward, they mentioned their encounter to a few acquaintances. Two days later, they saw Sami Pasha again on a different mountain path with an equally magnificent view.

The next day, under orders from felt-hatted Nimetullah's government, a group of plainclothes policemen from the capital turned up at the cottage to arrest Sami Pasha, bring him back to Arkaz, and take him to the Castle prison, where they locked him up in the Venetian Tower's darkest, dankest cell on the side of the building closest to the sea. Ali Talip's men did not try to stop them.

Sami Pasha was familiar with this cavelike, crab-infested cell, for he had once used it to lock up the bearded lead actor of a Greek theater troupe who had come to Arkaz for a production of *Oedipus Rex* and visited the prisoner—whom he suspected of being a spy—the next evening. The darkness inside the cell concentrated the darkness of Sami Pasha's thoughts. He kept blaming himself for how everything had gone wrong. Instead of accepting his removal from the post of governor of Mingheria, and moving on to the new province he had been assigned to, he had acted like a spoiled child and shamelessly clung to his old role, trying and of course failing to carry on as normal. Clearly his refusal to accept his new appointment had been his biggest mistake. Why had he made this error? As the blue glow of the sea flooded into his cell, his answer to this question always seemed to be the same: because he loved Mingheria! A moment later, the thing he loved so much would morph in his mind from Mingheria to Marika. He had never been able to separate the two anyway. Marika had been so brave and resolute the night he'd escaped from Arkaz, putting herself at risk for the sake of her dear Sami Pasha.

Now Sami Pasha couldn't think of anyone else he could trust and ask for help. Would the Doctor and Prince Consort risk his own life to get Sami Pasha out of prison? Perhaps Princess Pakize might pity him. But with these rampaging sheikhs now in charge of the government, the doctor and the Princess were nothing more than a pair of hostages in the hands of the new regime, no better than all those hapless Turkish bureaucrats being held in the Maiden's Tower. The Governor Pasha thought his old friend the British consul might be able to put some pressure on Sheikh Hamdullah to set him free and decided to write George Bey a letter. But first he must find a pen and some paper.

Before he'd even had the chance to alert anyone on the island that he was being held prisoner in the Castle, Sami Pasha was carried off to court. By that Monday, the twelfth of August, the plague had spread so thoroughly across the island, and everyone was so preoccupied with their own survival and so indifferent to anything else that might be happening around them, that we must consider the fact this trial could even take place as a triumph for the government administered by Nimetullah Effendi and supervised by Sheikh Hamdullah.

Sami Pasha had no doubt that he was going be punished in exemplary fashion for the hanging of Sheikh Hamdullah's brother and knew that the sheikh would arrange this through the courts on some completely unrelated pretext. The Pasha had assumed the trial would be based on cases brought by people who had been cruelly and unfairly put into isolation during the quarantine era despite not being infected, or by those whose homes had been taken from them on the pretext that they had caught the plague. He might even be accused of spying for Abdul Hamid or of acting as his puppet. What had never crossed his mind was the possibility that the case of the Pilgrim Ship Mutiny would be opened again three years after the fact, so that when he sat in his freshly varnished chair inside the courtroom, he was astonished to see the families of the slain pilgrims gathered before him, along with the quarantine officials who had been on duty back then.

The villagers of Nebiler and Çifteler, who had been involved in the Pilgrim Ship Mutiny and were allied with Ramiz and his men, had rejoiced when the news reached their village that Sheikh Hamdullah and his felt-hatted regent had taken over the government of the island, and within two days, unaware of how grievous the outbreak of plague in Arkaz had become (not that they would have cared even if they had known), they had descended upon the capital to meet with Chief Minister Nimetullah Effendi and demand a fresh trial after the courts had unjustly thwarted their previous attempt three years ago to obtain compensation for the deaths of their fathers and brothers killed by the quarantine-enforcing gendarmes.

The new government's judge, who was close to the Halifiye lodge, could have easily thrown the case out on the grounds that the incident took place under Ottoman rule and the new state had no jurisdiction over the matter, but instead he agreed to try it, and since most of the gendarmes who had opened fire on the pilgrims had long since left for other parts of the Ottoman Empire, the trial began—most probably at Sheikh Hamdullah's suggestion—with Sami Pasha charged as the sole individual responsible for the massacre in question.

All the scenes that had haunted Sami Pasha's worst nightmares for the past few years now came to life before his eyes: the dead pilgrims' sons and daughters tearfully blamed him for everything that had happened. Governor Sami Pasha's telegrams to Mazhar Effendi (whom the new government had also put in prison), retrieved from the latter's files and recommending that there should be no mercy for those who had hijacked the ship, were read out in court. An old man with a white beard stood up and shouted accusingly, "Where's your conscience, mighty Governor?" The father and son from Nebiler who had led the mutiny and whom the Governor had so doggedly pursued had come to the trial after being released from prison and were denouncing the actions of the "cruel governor" to his face. The two daughters, two sons, and twelve grandchildren of another pilgrim who'd been shot by the gendarmes were all in the courtroom too, ignoring the outbreak. It frightened Sami Pasha to see how meticulously every aspect of the trial had been staged, and he began to lose hope. At one point he even feared that the father and son might try to take a swing at him right there in court.

Having anticipated that the trial would attract notice in Istanbul and Europe, the new rulers of the state of Mingheria had furnished the courtroom with a bench for the judge to sit on, a desk, and separate chairs for the prosecutor, lawyers, members of the press, and other spectators, and had even hurriedly arranged for robes to be sewn for the judge and lawyers from lengths of fabric in Islamic green embroidered with Mingherian roses the same color as the one which adorned the flag of the nation. (One hundred and sixteen years later, these unsightly robes have regrettably established themselves as a particularly gaudy fixture of the Mingherian justice system and are still proudly and solemnly worn today by all practitioners of the legal profession, including the members of the island's Constitutional Court and other high courts.)

"Yes, I was the Governor back then—however . . . ," Sami Pasha began as he sought to counter the allegations against him, explaining that he had not personally given the order to shoot at the pilgrims and had only found out several days after the fact that the gendarmes had used their weapons in this way, but in the midst of all the accusations, the shouting, and the tears in the courtroom that day, the only part of his statement anyone would remember were the words "I was the Governor back then," if only because they could be interpreted to mean "I am culpable; I am to blame."

As the trial hastened to its conclusion, another fact that compounded Sami Pasha's despair was the impossibility of arguing for the necessity of quarantine provisions inside a courtroom run by a government (some might say a gang) that was so firmly opposed to those measures in the first place. It was with this difficulty in mind that Sami Pasha had declared that the only reason he had put those venerable pilgrims in quarantine was to keep the people of Mingheria safe from disease, and certainly not to submit to the brazen demands of the Great Powers. In spite of this, the consensus among the island's four newspapers and all its inhabitants soon became that Sami Pasha was a man who'd had innocent pilgrims murdered so that the tyrant Abdul Hamid could continue to rule undisturbed from his Yıldız Palace, and the European powers would have no excuse to trouble the Sultan's peace.

At the end of the two-hour trial, Sami Pasha learned from the judge that he had been sentenced to death. Even as one part of his mind reasoned that this was the outcome he had been expecting all along, the other part couldn't believe what he had heard and could not accept what was happening. An intensely sharp pain that felt as if he were being pierced with pins began to spread from the bottom-right corner of his stomach all the way through the rest of his body.

Sami Pasha realized right away that he would not be able to sleep at all until the decision was reversed. He worried for a moment that his eyes might be watering, but not a single teardrop had appeared, and no one else had noticed a thing.

Sami Pasha still remembered the pleasant, sunny, bright yellow June morning three years ago when he'd appointed the "judge" who had now sentenced him to death. Claiming to be well versed in the Holy Koran and in Sharia law, the man had secured this government job through the intercession of the wealthy and highly regarded Hajji Fehmi Effendi, a great supporter of the construction of new telegraph lines on the island, and the Governor had taken the fact that the new judge was a regular at the Halifiye lodge as a positive sign, for it must mean he was "an honorable and God-fearing individual." Sami Pasha couldn't comprehend how that same unassuming, unremarkable figure had now decided that the Pasha should be executed. He went to see the judge, who had summoned him to his office.

The judge could see that the soon-to-be-executed Sami Pasha was looking at him with the bewildered expression of a man who could scarcely understand what was happening around him. "You have been sentenced to death, Your Excellency!" he said, as if he were offering words of consolation. "In olden days, these kinds of decisions used to be referred to the Istanbul courts for review. Too sentimental to stomach the thought of an execution, Abdul Hamid would commute them to exile or life imprisonment, never hanging anyone at all in fear of what the foreign ambassadors might say. But we are in sovereign Mingheria now, and your death sentence will not be sent to the high courts in Istanbul, nor would it be sensible to expect a pardon from Sultan Abdul Hamid."

"What exactly do you mean?"

"This might be your last night on earth, Governor Pasha," the judge replied. "Neither Istanbul nor the Great Powers have the authority to change the Mingherian government's mind."

Realizing that he was going to be executed to show the world that nobody could interfere in the affairs of independent Mingheria, Sami Pasha shivered.

Just as he could not believe the judge's ruling, Sami Pasha was also aware that the tingle spreading from the pins in his stomach to his back and all the way down to his legs had paralyzed his mind and soul, that he could no longer think clearly, and that his fear had grown so great that he could neither see the world around him nor hear and understand what people were saying. In a further blow to his pride and morale, he was transported back to his cell like an animal, locked in a windowless prison wagon that was bolted shut from the outside. But worst of all were the curious glances he kept receiving now that he had been condemned to death, the pitiful looks, the people staring at him as if he were some strange creature. His sentence had only just been issued, but Sami Pasha assumed everyone must know about it already.

As the prison wagon passed through the Castle's main entrance and slowly made its way toward the Venetian Tower, Sami Pasha peered out of an air vent and saw several rows of bodies in front of the west-facing Ottoman-era building where the largest and wealthiest dormitories were situated, and where the prison riot had first begun. After counting twenty-six corpses and feeling no emotion at all, he saw the mattresses, blankets, and other belongings of dead prisoners and former inmates of the isolation facility burning in a corner, the fire smothering the courtyard in a thick, blue, foul-smelling smoke. Since the clerks and soldiers who used to man the city's incineration pit had been dismissed from their posts after Sheikh Hamdullah's supporters had lifted quarantine, anyone who wanted to burn infected materials had been handling the matter themselves, just as the prison management seemed to be doing now.

A little farther on from the neat rows of dead bodies waiting to be picked up by the wagon that evening lay several people who were still alive but clearly on the verge of death. The Pasha saw seven or eight of these suffering, vomiting, wailing plague victims curled up on mattresses or bedsheets, or stretched out on the Castle's stone floor. The thing everyone had been most afraid of had finally come to pass, and the outbreak had spread through the whole prison and every building in the Castle. Sami Pasha was experienced enough to realize that these dying patients must have been brought down to the courtyard now to save time in the evening, when the corpse wagon would come to take all the other dead bodies away too.

Sami Pasha had spotted a few clerks and guards loyal to Sheikh

Hamdullah stationed at the entrance to the Castle's prison complex. But there were no uniformed prison wardens patrolling the courtyard itself; they had all run away.

The wagon briefly stopped when its path was blocked, and two prisoners who had taken over the courtyard came to stand mere inches from Sami Pasha, arguing in a language he couldn't understand. Once the wagon was on its way again, Sami Pasha thought to himself that the situation on the island was so dire now that realistically, if those two hoodlums had noticed that the old governor was right there beside them, so close that he could smell them and hear their labored breathing, they would have pulled him out of the wagon and hanged him themselves before Sheikh Hamdullah's men had their chance. As the wagon approached the Venetian Tower, Sami Pasha saw four more rows of dead plague victims—sixteen in total—laid out on the ground with that same surprising sense of symmetry, and grimly realized that he was incapable of feeling any sorrow at the sight.

His death sentence had made him thoroughly selfish. Though perhaps the sight of other people dying did not upset him unduly because it seemed a sign that the afterlife was real, and that he would not be alone when he got there. The only thought in his mind now, and the source of his selfishness, was this: stay alive! When he returned to his cell, he must get hold of a pen and a piece of paper and write Consul George a letter.

But as soon as he was back in his cell, which seemed to have turned a strange shade of seawater blue in his absence, Sami Pasha began to cry, his body shaking with heaving, hiccuping sobs. He hoped nobody would see him in that state. Afterward he lay down on a pile of straw in the corner and managed by some divine miracle to sleep for about ten minutes. He dreamed that he was walking with his mother in his aunt Atiye's back garden, and in this garden he saw daisies, a soft golden light, and a well. In the dream he was holding his mother's warm hand while she pointed at the windlass on the well. There was an enormous lizard rattling noisily across the windlass, but the creature seemed friendly rather than frightening.

When he woke up, Sami Pasha realized that the rattling sound had been coming from a large crab that was wandering around among the cracks, boulders, and rocks near the wall of the cell that faced the sea, and thinking that this must be a sign, he felt a little better, telling himself that he would not be hanged after all, that he would be freed soon, and that if they had really meant to execute him they would not have brought him back here after the trial but taken him straight to the State Hall.

According to the Mingherian constitution, whose principal clauses Sami Pasha himself had drafted, no executions could be carried out until the Chief Minister—in this case Nimetullah Effendi with the felt hat—had approved the order. Nimetullah Effendi would of course act in accordance with Sheikh Hamdullah's wishes. At that point the Pasha's old friend Sheikh Hamdullah, with whom they'd had so many conversations about poetry and literature when the Pasha had first arrived on the island, would surely quash his rage and resentment and issue a pardon, allowing Sami Pasha to walk right out of the Castle and make his leisurely way back to his quarters. He wouldn't rush on his way back home through the city. Nimetullah Effendi would come to visit him, and Sami Pasha would thank him for the pardon and make sure to mention the sheikh's poetry collection *Aurora*. If they really meant to hang him, they would not have put him in this cell, and this thoughtful, charming crab wouldn't have come all the way out of the sea to visit him.

Sami Pasha felt cheered when he thought of his wife and two daughters in Istanbul. He was still angry with his wife, whose endless prevarications—"I'll be on the next ferry over" or "My father is unwell"—had left him alone in Mingheria for the last five years, and who clearly felt that as the daughter of a pasha she could treat him whichever way she wanted, yet for some reason he could not stop picturing her and their two daughters idling in the sun on the beach at Üsküdar. In this scene, it was as if Marika were in Istanbul too.

When Sheikh Hamdullah pardoned him, Sami Pasha would make peace with his old enemies, revive his friendships with the island's consuls, extricate himself from every troublesome situation, and marry Marika, settling down for a quiet, uneventful life in a white house on that road in Ora that meandered down toward the sea with heavenly views at every turn, or perhaps even a little farther away in Dantela. Why hadn't he done this before? He was full of remorse now for not having treated Marika better. One night, after a few glasses of cognac, he had summoned Coachman Zekeriya and taken Marika out for a moonlit drive in the armored landau, an experience which she had clearly found to be altogether enchanting. Yet even though she would beg him to take her again every month when the full moon was out, he had been so worried about what people might say that he had never done so, and now he was angry at himself for refusing her.

The cell door opened without warning. Sami Pasha emerged from his reverie to greet Sheikh Hamdullah, but when he saw instead the familiar faces of certain prison officers he had known for a long time, he understood what was to come.

"I would like to pray," he said with a calmness even he was surprised to feel. "I must perform my ablutions."

Both the Castle's own mosque and the prayer room inside the prison were closed because of the outbreak. As he waited for a fountain and a prayer mat to be located for his use, picked a spot for his prayers, and recited verses he only half remembered, Sami Pasha was able to forget his pain for a while, if only because he was busy doing something else.

At dusk, they put him back in the same prison wagon as before, which had now come to take him from the tower. As it lurched forward, Sami Pasha saw that the dark, sinister corpse wagon had already arrived at the courtyard and was being loaded with the bodies he had noticed earlier, still laid out in a tidy row, but now stark naked after their clothes had been stripped off and incinerated. Hundreds of crows that had gathered on the chestnut tree in the courtyard began cawing frantically. There were corpses in front of the former Janissaries' building too, piled up in a disorderly heap. The air did not smell of death, but of wet grass. The Chief Warden had ordered the dead prisoners' bedding, mattresses, and blankets to be burned, though as this practice was now technically banned, they were calling it a "cleaning operation" rather than a quarantine measure. Those four or five lucky souls walking around the courtyard now, talking, resting, loading corpses, would still be here upon this world, looking up at this same sky, when the sun rose tomorrow morning—but Sami Pasha would be gone.

He banged his fists against the wooden walls of the wagon and shouted as loud as he could, but nobody noticed he was there. When his fingers began to hurt, and he felt too furious and too helpless to continue, he slumped to the floor and wept for a little while, then willed himself back to his feet and brought his eye right up to the air vent to look out at the streets of the city he had ruled for five years, and so sincerely loved. But it was too dark to see.

When he caught the smell of earth, grass, and seaweed in the air, he recognized the island's characteristic scent and sank back to the floor of the wagon, tearfully praying for Allah to save him. He was full of regret now. There was no anger left in him, nor any pride or dreams of heroic redemption. All he felt was regret at his own stupidity. Which of his mistakes did he regret the most? Once again, former governor and former Chief Minister Sami Pasha told himself that he had wasted too much time on Ramiz, that he had taken things too seriously, that he should have accepted his transfer to another province as soon as the order had arrived. When the wheels of the prison wagon began to make a completely different kind of noise, he realized they must be on Hamidiye Bridge and sprang to his feet to look through the air vent again, staring at the majestic Castle he had just come out of, now bathed in a mysterious glow, and realizing that this was the last time he would ever set eyes on that glorious building.

We do not often find ourselves loving or hating the individuals who populate the pages of a history book. But we do tend to feel these emotions when we read novels. To avoid any further distress to our readers who may have grown fond of Sami Pasha (however few of them there may be), we shall refrain from entering here into a detailed account of how he sat in the cell inside the State Hall hoping either Sheikh Hamdullah or Nimetullah Effendi would come to pardon him, of the agony he suffered as he listened to the imam who had come to console him, of his mournful musings, and of his fear of death.

Until the very last moment, Sami Pasha clung to a hopeful and innocent belief that Sheikh Hamdullah would pardon him. Even when he saw the executioner, he was able to convince himself for a time that it must all be a ruse designed to scare him even more than he already was, and hide the fact that he was going to be pardoned.

Sami Pasha loathed the executioner Şakir because he was a thief and a drunk, and willing to hang people for money. He was so furious at the thought that his life was about to end at this man's hands that he felt he might choke with it. With his arms bound in front of him, he landed a blow to the executioner's back. He fought as hard as he could to get away, but Şakir quickly caught him by the neck.

"You must be strong, Your Excellency," he said. "That is what befits you."

Sami Pasha could feel the presence of the despicable villains who had come to watch his execution, hiding in the dark where they couldn't be seen. He told himself that it didn't matter what these cowards thought of him before he died. Life and the universe were more important. He managed to pull himself together.

But as he approached the gallows, his knees gave away and he fell to the floor, and Şakir—his breath reeking with wine—spoke to him with surprising tenderness. "Hang in there, Pasha!" he said. "Not long to go now—you're nearly done!"

His voice was as soothing as if he were speaking to a child. And so, wearing his white execution gown, and with the noose wrapped around his neck, Sami Pasha bravely leaped into the void, crying, "Mother, I am coming!" Just before he died, the image of an enormous black crow with giant wings flashed in front of his eyes.

CHAPTER 68

As the wind blew across the newly rechristened Mingheria Square, a few people came by to look at Sami Pasha's corpse swinging somberly in its white gown: children unafraid of death or of the outbreak, youths who'd run away from home, various enemies of the Pasha, Greek and Mingherian nationalists, and some of the journalists he'd sent to prison. Ramiz's vengeful relatives from Nebiler village stood by the gallows to gloat and give thanks to Allah and were reprimanded by the police. Tarksis Effendi, whom Sami Pasha had locked up for four years on an accurate but unproven suspicion that he was smuggling historical artifacts out of the island, claimed that the body hanging in the square was not the Pasha's, but was ushered away by the guards when he tried to check.

Those who had been fond of Sami Pasha, including Marika and the more prominent members of Arkaz's Muslim and Greek communities, had locked themselves up in their homes and were waiting, as if petrified, to see what would happen next. Meanwhile, the theory that the plague could probably also be passed through the air had also begun to spread.

But this did not slow the pace of what historians have called state terror. Two days later, Sami Pasha's corpse was lowered from the gallows and buried in a bed of Mingherian roses in Narlık Cemetery. In the early hours of the next day, while it was still dark, Bonkowski Pasha's old friend Pharmacist Nikiforos was hanged in the same spot as Sami Pasha.

Şakir, the executioner, was far harsher and less sympathetic in his treatment of Pharmacist Nikiforos than he had been with Sami Pasha, berating the elderly pharmacist when his legs buckled in fear and responding to the old man's desperate pleas with callous retorts like

"It's too late now" and "You should have thought about it sooner," but Şakir's behavior had nothing to do with the time he had been kicked out of Nikiforos's pharmacy for stealing (of course no one had dared call the police on an executioner), nor with how much he'd had to drink the previous evening, and was instead a consequence of the fact that the wave of "state terror" we have spoken of had slowly turned into a movement against the island's Greeks. Like all its predecessors, Nimetullah Effendi and Sheikh Hamdullah's government too had soon begun to use the outbreak to subjugate and drive away the Greek population, and stop those who had already fled from ever returning, so that Muslims would come to constitute the majority of the island's population. Some Greeks believed this was the real reason why the Telegraph Office still hadn't been opened; if the ferry services resumed, Greeks would soon outnumber Muslims again.

But apart from wanting to alter the composition of the island's population, Sheikh Hamdullah and his government officials' ill treatment of the Greeks was also motivated by a sincere and deeply entrenched fear of Christians and unbelievers. Like mosques and lodges, churches and monasteries too were now free to resume their functions, but while most of the temporary "hospitals" that had been set up inside the grounds of many lodges had since been cleared, those in the monasteries remained in use, and patients were regularly carried out of the lodges in their hospital beds and relocated to green and spacious monastery gardens. Sheikh Hamdullah briefly even considered arranging a population exchange between the island's Greeks and the Muslims who lived in Crete and Rhodes. Only Muslims were being offered government jobs now (despite there being no money left in the treasury), and Turks who were not native to the island could sometimes be given a rough treatment too, if not as bad as the Greeks. Nor was the new government in any hurry to evict all the people who had broken into empty homes in wealthy Greek neighborhoods like Ora, Flizvos, and Dantela, and illegally taken up residence there.

But on the surface of things, these were not the factors which led to the Greek pharmacist Nikiforos's death sentence and immediate execution. Nikiforos had been condemned to the noose by confessions extracted from other suspects through the traditional torture method of bastinado. Princess Pakize and Doctor Nuri had read through the file Sami Pasha had given them before he fled the State Hall during his last night in the city, and studied all the evidence collected therein. Forbidden from leaving their guesthouse rooms, they'd had plenty of time on their hands, and largely unaware of the horrors unfolding in the city, they had spent their days engaging in playful and carefree conjecture.

After the poisoning and death of Doctor Ilias, the authorities arrested the eight soldiers and the captain who worked in the garrison kitchens, and had their feet whipped, and when all the blows delivered, the pain caused, and the blood spilled failed to yield any results, some more foot whipping was swiftly arranged, directed this time at the five soldiers who had laid out the table for the Quarantine Regiment's swearing-in ceremony, as well as the garrison's Cretian provisions master and his two fair-haired assistants.

While Doctor Nuri was busy going around pharmacies and herbalists' shop inquiring about ratsbane sales and any other suspicious activity in such precise and exhaustive detail that Sherlock Holmes himself would have been proud, the state's investigators and their bastinado team had just begun, at the Chief Scrutineer's insistence, to spatter blood everywhere with a second round of foot whipping that targeted the same suspects in the same order as before, when suddenly, just before it was his turn again, the most innocent and naïve-looking of the first group of eight soldiers from the kitchens burst into tears and admitted his guilt, prompted by his terror of more foot whipping to confess to everything he had done, and in order to convince the white-bearded prosecutor and his mustachioed clerks that he was telling the truth and had poisoned the biscuits himself, he had shown them how, while everyone was out praying on the Friday before the swearing-in ceremony, he had snuck into the kitchens with a bag of poison and mixed it into the baking flour. The other kitchen workers, whose feet were sometimes dipped into buckets of brine to stem the flow of blood and stop it from staining the floor, and who would probably have passed out from the agony or be left permanently injured if the scarcely healed wounds on their soles had burst open again under a renewed bout of torture, were delighted by the news of their colleague's confession, for it meant their feet would not be tied up and beaten again after all.

The Chief Scrutineer and Governor Sami Pasha were understandably gratified by the green-eyed, cherubic sixteen-year-old's confession. But until they found out who had given the soft and friendly faced young man his bag of arsenic, and why they had done so, quarantine doctors would continue to be killed. Yet every time the interrogator who was known to swing his stick the hardest would ask the young man this question, holding a candle to his face in the dark, the repentant youth would either just start crying again, or fix his eyes on the flame and make no sound at all.

The Chief Scrutineer was seasoned enough to know that if they subjected him to another round of bastinado in order to find the answer to the second and more vital question of who had given him the rat poison or which pharmacy or herbalist he had bought it from, the baby-faced young man might lie, or be maimed, or even die from his injuries, so he instructed the interrogators to put their efforts on hold until he had reviewed the situation with Sami Pasha. Together they decided that before they started interrogating the young man again and tortured him into revealing how and where he'd obtained the poison, they would wait for the lacerations on his feet to heal completely. In the meantime they would track down every single member of the traitorous fool's family, find out who his friends were, and give them all a foot whipping too if need be.

Having closely read Sami Pasha's report, Princess Pakize could understand what state of mind the Governor Pasha must have been in, and delighted in discussing this topic with her husband: "Sami Pasha must have been so elated to have discovered poor Doctor Ilias's killer before you did, and to have done it in his own way," she began.

"If only they hadn't waited to get that boy's second confession, perhaps this gang of unrepentant assassins would have been rounded up before they got the chance to kill Majid!" said Doctor Nuri.

"But Sami Pasha was not in a hurry, and neither was my uncle. The Pasha knew you were visiting all the pharmacists and the herbalists, assumed you would not be able to reach any definitive conclusion, and thought he would take the opportunity to teach you a lesson. He wanted to show both you and my uncle, who is sadly in thrall to all those murder mysteries his servants read out to him at night, that the Sherlock Holmes method stands no chance in the Orient or anywhere in the Ottoman Empire. I expect my uncle would not have taken kindly to a governor like Sami Pasha forcing him to recognize his mistakes."

"You also believe that Sami Pasha is absolutely loyal to your uncle."

"I have no doubt about that," said Princess Pakize. "That is why I have never felt truly safe here with him living but four rooms away. Don't forget, the biscuits that killed Doctor Ilias were also meant for you."

"But those biscuits were offered to Governor Sami Pasha too."

"Yet he did not eat a single one," said Princess Pakize, staring intently into her husband's eyes.

By this point, the couple were deriving the same pleasure from their perusal of Sami Pasha's file as Abdul Hamid did from his crime novels, and as they applied Sherlock Holmes's logic to the evidence that the Chief Scrutineer's men had collected through bastinado and other similar methods, they could feel that they were edging closer and closer to the truth.

While husband and wife were debating these matters between them, Sami Pasha was hiding in Ali Talip's farm near the village of Dumanlı. Princess Pakize and the Prince Consort were worried about the former governor, and talked about him often. Why had Sami Pasha chosen to come into their room just as he was fleeing Arkaz for his life—and therefore with little time to spare—and hand them this file full of sensitive information on suspects, witness statements, and interrogation reports?

"Because Sami Pasha thinks we are spying for my uncle. He wants us to go back to Abdul Hamid and tell him, 'Your governor Sami Pasha is very capable indeed; he has done a splendid job of uncovering this gang of murderers and catching them all in one fell swoop, just as you ordered!' He thinks my uncle might still forgive him."

"He is the Sultan's faithful servant. All he wants is for the Sultan to know about the investigation he has brought to such a successful conclusion," said Doctor Nuri.

"Do you believe that by identifying all these killers, the Governor Pasha has succeeded in his task?"

"I do," the Prince Consort admitted. "The information I have seen in this file, and the reports drawn up for the Pasha's review, have done enough to persuade me."

"Me, too . . ."

They were quiet for a time.

"Unfortunately this means the Sherlock Holmes method has not succeeded," said Doctor Nuri.

"Perhaps my uncle was not sufficiently serious about this Sherlock Holmes question, just as he never was about the political reforms he introduced at Europe's insistence. If a sultan wishes to embrace and imitate European ways, his people must be equally enthusiastic and willing to accept whatever it is their sultan is doing. I would therefore suggest that you do not trouble yourself further with regard to this matter."

"I would insist—with your permission—that your uncle is completely serious about the philosophy of Sherlock Holmes. He has intuited that the choice here is between the individual and the community. Every big hospital Abdul Hamid builds, every new school, courtroom, military base, train station, and square, is an attempt to sever individuals from their communities so that he can reach out to them directly, and so that they can learn to fear the state and its courts. Not their neighbors down the road."

"Or maybe my uncle just really loves Sherlock Holmes," said Princess Pakize with an impish smile.

A significant portion of the file Sami Pasha had given them was devoted to the investigating judge's remarks on the inquiry. But the lengthiest sections were those containing the statements given by the tortured suspects. ("Governor Sami Pasha couldn't possibly have read them all!" thought the Princess and Prince Consort, but there were detailed notes in the Pasha's hand penciled in the margins.) An official who was ranked somewhere between the investigating judge and the Chief Scrutineer had also provided the Governor with a daily report on how the interrogations—with their beatings and foot whippings—were progressing. These reports provided a clear indication of who was genuinely guilty, and who had only been labeled as such for political reasons.

As they waited for the soles of the well-meaning kitchen boy's feet to heal, the Chief Scrutineer's men began investigating his family and friends. They discovered that the young man lived with his family in one of those ramshackle houses that had been built over the last three years—and with Sami Pasha's tacit blessing—on unclaimed land in the hills behind the incineration pit. His circle included a number of Cretian migrants, as well as plenty of fanatical youths, unemployed idlers, and devoted mosque-goers. He was also friends with the rebellious, combative young men who lived in the Taşçılar neighborhood, and his father, who had assumed his son must have been taken to the Castle's isolation facility after catching the plague in the garrison kitchens, and therefore suspected nothing, told the investigators that he had always tried to keep his son away from his good-for-nothing friends down at the docks, then proceeded to list the names of all the ones who had ever come up the hill to visit.

Many among this group of friends were promptly rounded up and arrested in the days of the outbreak that preceded the revolution. Some were innocent and had their feet whipped for no reason, but others were confirmed to be collaborating with Ramiz's entourage and with those who had come down to Arkaz from Nebiler village to keep the resistance against quarantine measures going. It had taken more than a month for all of this evidence to be gathered. During this time, the Chief Scrutineer was able to extract various confessions under torture and gather letters, telegrams, and handwritten notes from raids on several households, which together demonstrated the incontrovertible links between the village of Nebiler and the angry mob which had become involved in the Pilgrim Ship Mutiny and proved that Ramiz had been the movement's undeclared leader. Governor Sami Pasha and Mazhar Effendi had approached every aspect of this matter, from the principal issues down to the tiniest details, as if they expected their efforts to be shown to students one day as a perfect example of "how to conduct an investigation" and had perhaps regarded this file of documents as their means of proving to Abdul Hamid and the palace just how accomplished a pair of bureaucrats they were.

Once his informants had ascertained the names of each and every one of the angry, pious youths and zealots in Ramiz's entourage, and of the members of the righteous mob who had sworn to take revenge for the Pilgrim Ship Affair, the Chief Scrutineer had arranged for his spies to follow them around, but stopped short of arresting the whole gang. (This oversight would later cost Majid his life.) Sami Pasha, who was still governor at the time, must have balked at the thought of all the anger against quarantine measures that would result from putting so many sect devotees in prison.

What the documents in Sami Pasha's folder also clearly showed was that, as our readers may have already surmised, there had been a significant element of chance in the circumstances surrounding the abduction and murder of Bonkowski Pasha. That is not to say that there weren't plenty of people in Arkaz in those days who would have gladly slaughtered any Christian trying to impose quarantine measures upon the island, as well as the Governor Pasha himself. The assassins' original plan had been to use the poisoned biscuits to kill Bonkowski Pasha and his assistant Ilias simultaneously. But when a devotee of the Terkapçılar lodge in the village of Nebiler who had survived the mutiny aboard the pilgrim ship three years ago, and now lived in Arkaz, had unexpectedly encountered Bonkowski Pasha on the street, he had recognized the famed Royal Chemist from his bearing and appearance, and having come up, in a moment of inspiration, with the lie that he had a sick patient at home, he had used this excuse to lead the Pasha straight to his associates. The Chief Scrutineer's clerks and spies had managed to identify every single one of the men who had tortured and tormented Bonkowski Pasha during his last hours, coldly and ruthlessly strangled him to death, and disposed of his corpse in Hrisopolitissa Square.

"But Mazhar Effendi decided not to arrest them yet because some of them were involved in Ramiz's plot to attack the meeting at the State Hall and put the new governor in charge. The Chief Scrutineer had been supervising the progress and outcome of that operation on Sami Pasha's behalf, so that they could set the trap that would allow them to catch Ramiz and his men red-handed and sentence them immediately. You will recall the Governor had initially thought he would be able to quietly arrest the raiders as they filed out of the back door of the Outbreak Room . . ."

"How clever you are, my lady," said the Doctor and Prince Consort, concurring with his wife's assessment. "Verily, your uncle should have appointed you, not me, as his Sherlock Holmes–style detective."

"But that is exactly what he did!" quick-witted Princess Pakize proudly replied. "Finally we understand why my uncle put me on the *Aziziye* and sent me to Mingheria with you: he knew that you would only be able to solve this mystery with the help of someone who has read the kinds of novels my father reads—someone like me."

"It seems you do appreciate the Sultan's brilliance after all . . ."

"But you mustn't forget that my uncle himself is behind all of these murders you have been trying to solve."

"Do you really believe that?" said Doctor Nuri. "If you are truly convinced that your uncle is as wicked as you suggest, then you must have also concluded that there is no hope of us ever returning to Istanbul."

Sometimes, when the subject of Istanbul came up, they would walk up to the window and peer at the horizon as if they had spotted a ferry from the capital. The Mediterranean Sea seemed livelier than usual, but Arkaz was as quiet and still as a graveyard.

CHAPTER 69

If your uncle had really wanted Bonkowski Pasha assassinated, it would have been much easier for him to arrange it while the Pasha was still in Istanbul. Instead he sent him away to deal with the plague in this distant, isolated land where events could have spun out of control at any moment."

"As indeed they did!" said Princess Pakize. "But that is precisely what my uncle wants. Whenever my uncle wishes to arrange an assassination, he will have it take place in some remote location he does not have full control over, so that nobody will notice his hand in it. After that most accomplished and European-minded of Ottoman viziers, Mithat Pasha, was sentenced to death by the Yıldız Palace Court for his leading role in the political conspiracy and coup that removed and killed Abdul Hamid's uncle Sultan Abdülaziz, my uncle could have simply signed his execution order and had him hanged in Istanbul. But as usual, the sly and 'tenderhearted' Abdul Hamid pretended to be moved by humane considerations and commuted Mithat Pasha's sentence to life imprisonment, sending him away to the prison fortress of Ta'if. They say that place is even worse than the dungeons here in Mingheria. Soon after that, he had Mithat Pasha assassinated in Ta'if, but under such mysterious circumstances that most people didn't even realize it had been Abdul Hamid's idea all along. This is exactly what my uncle has done with Bonkowski Pasha."

"Mithat Pasha was part of the group that removed your father from the throne and replaced him with your uncle. Do you have any concrete evidence to indicate that Abdul Hamid ordered his assassination?"

"My uncle would never leave enough evidence behind to satisfy Sherlock Holmes. That is why he reads Sherlock Holmes novels in the first place. I believe my uncle, just like the rest of the world, reads murder mysteries so that he can learn how to commit murder without leaving any trace and learn about all the latest European methods in this regard. So although I do not have any proof of the many murders my uncle has committed, I have more than enough suspicions."

"Your uncle regarded Mithat Pasha's popularity with the public and the considerable force of his personality as a threat to his own political position."

"I must correct you there, for Mithat Pasha was certainly not as loved as you seem to think he was by this public which you speak of."

"But Bonkowski Pasha, whom your uncle was so fond of, and who served him loyally for so many years, posed no threat to the Sultan—unlike Mithat Pasha."

"Bonkowski Pasha was an expert on poisons. That alone was threat enough. You yourself reminded me of the treatise he prepared for my uncle twenty years ago on the toxic plants growing in the gardens of the Yıldız Palace, and on poisons that kill without leaving a trace. All it would take would be for some informant somewhere to send Abdul Hamid a false report claiming 'Bonkowski Pasha plans to poison His Supreme Highness.'"

"In other words you have no proof that your uncle sent Bonkowski Pasha to Mingheria so that he could have him killed, but you have suspicions."

"We have been arguing about this for days now!" Princess Pakize patiently replied. "The single most reasonable explanation we have been able to arrive at is this: for some reason we are not privy to, my uncle decided he needed to be rid of Bonkowski Pasha—to destroy him, even. His clerks at the palace must have concluded that the best way to do this would be through Pharmacist Nikiforos. Someone in the palace, perhaps Tahsin Pasha, must have remembered and reminded the Sultan about Nikiforos and Bonkowski's long-standing friendship and the campaign they had run through the Pharmacists' Guild, and pointed out that the royal concession the Sultan issued all those years ago had left Nikiforos feeling embarrassed and guilty before Bonkowski. It is these palace clerks' job to remind my uncle about everyone's weaknesses and fears. We have both seen in Sami Pasha's file the encrypted telegrams Nikiforos got from Istanbul, and that Bonkowski too received from

Istanbul and Smyrna. Perhaps Nikiforos thought, after the revolution, that he could use the discussions on the Mingherian vernacular and on Mingherian names for plants, herbs, and medicines as an excuse to befriend the Commander and draw him into Abdul Hamid's sphere of influence too."

"I am not quite convinced, though that does seem to have been Mazhar Effendi's theory."

"Everything in this file is Mazhar Effendi's theory."

While reading through the file, the Princess and Prince Consort had grown increasingly impressed with Mazhar Effendi's fastidious reports, his meticulously categorized and carefully cross-referenced incident logs, and the delicate, lacelike handwriting with which he had noted everything down. The industrious Mazhar Effendi had also penned a series of reports on several other matters that bore no relation to the murders, but were nevertheless of interest to the new Mingherian state. Why had Sami Pasha decided to put those in the file too?

One incident that Mazhar Effendi had investigated and detailed at great length concerned a matter neither the Princess nor the Prince Consort had previously been aware of. During the Telegraph Raid, why had Major Kâmil, future commander of the state of Mingheria, ordered Hamdi Baba to fire at the Theta clock on the Post Office wall? Was there any significance to the fact that the brand of the clock was Theta? Had he targeted the Theta symbol (Θ) because it was a Greek letter, or had there been some meaningful word in his mind that began with the same letter? Another document in the file discussed how the Major behaved when he came to drop Princess Pakize's letters off at the Post Office, noting that he would always read the signs on the walls, and that he seemed particularly interested in the Theta clock.

As the Princess and Prince Consort discussed the various questions raised by the documents in Sami Pasha's file, around forty people were dying in the city every day. These were, without a doubt, the most painful, harrowing days ever experienced in the whole history of the island and of the nation of Mingheria. Any remaining trust in the authority of the state had vanished, and people had even lost their usual instinct to look for a savior they could follow and thus forget about their tribulations. Princess Pakize and Doctor Nuri understood just how far out of joint everything had fallen when they learned that Sami Pasha had been caught and executed. The image of Sami Pasha hanging from the gallows did not leave their minds for a long time. They lost the ability to laugh for a while, and experienced a long spell of despair during which they hardly spoke to each other and didn't eat any food. The Prince Consort was desperate to go out and see what was going on, and what people were doing now that quarantine had been lifted. When the same demonic, inauspicious crow came to tap at their window again two days later, they were horrified to realize that this time Nimetullah Effendi with the felt hat must have had Pharmacist Nikiforos hanged.

"We need to go back to Istanbul now, whatever the cost!" Princess Pakize told her husband. Then she wept for a while, clinging to his embrace. "I do not know if you realize it, but I believe it may be our turn next."

"On the contrary, after all the savage acts they have committed so far, they will be too worried about how the rest of the world might react . . . ," Doctor Nuri confidently replied. "Your trepidations are for naught. They will do the very opposite of what you fear: they will treat us even better than before! For soon they will have no choice but to bring quarantine measures back." There was a casual ease in the Prince Consort's tone now, as if he were lying to his wife to reassure her. "Don't worry, I will ask the clerks and find out why Pharmacist Nikiforos was hanged," he added.

The late Sami Pasha's file also told them that the island's secret police had found answers to questions the Princess and the Prince Consort had either never thought to ask, or thought about but quickly forgotten. For example, according to a number of different reports the Chief Scrutineer had received, the mythical gang of Greek and Turkish children who had lost their families and fled their homes during the plague, and survived on the mountains by picking fruit, eating plants, and catching fish in the creeks, was actually real. But nobody knew which particular cave they might be sheltering in, or which abandoned farm they might have taken over.

The amulet necklace that Bonkowski Pasha had taken from Zeynep's father Bayram Effendi's corpse, meanwhile, had been found during a raid on a residence in Upper Turunçlar, where several of Ramiz's unmarried henchmen had been living. This was incontrovertible proof of their guilt and would have been enough to condemn the killers of the Chief

Inspector of Public Health to the gallows. (We know that during the Sheikh Hamdullah Era, the members of this gang were either released or quietly allowed to escape.)

The file also indicated that Pharmacist Nikiforos had been sending information back to Abdul Hamid. The Sultan had issued Nikiforos with a codebook (just as he had done with the Chief Scrutineer), and Nikiforos had consequently been accused of taking orders from the Sultan's men in Istanbul. Under Abdul Hamid's reign, this would have been something of an honor. But after the declaration of freedom and independence, it was a fact that could be twisted and used against a person, if not quite something to be ashamed of. The Princess and Prince Consort were also able to conclude that although Nikiforos had not supplied the kitchen boy with poison from his own shop, he had secretly "coached" the young man on how to procure ratsbane from other shops and herbalists' stores, all while keeping his own identity hidden. Princess Pakize was convinced that it must have been Abdul Hamid who had given Nikiforos this idea. (Neither they nor we know what Nikiforos might have confessed under torture before his execution.)

In a completely unexpected turn of events, Pharmacist Nikiforos had also been accused of insulting the Mingherian flag, an offense which seemed to magnify his other crimes too. The pharmacist was elated to have played some role in the creation of the flag that Commander Kâmil had waved from the State Hall balcony when he announced the Mingherian Revolution to the world. After the revolution, Nikiforos had used his shopwindow to proudly exhibit some of the other flaglike advertising banners he had made. Needless to say, his intention had never been—as several informants wrongly alleged—to ridicule the flag he himself had come up with, and if anything, he had meant to do the opposite, for he had wholeheartedly supported the island's independence and gloried in the Mingherian flag. But with forty-five to fifty deaths being counted every day, the only people who even bothered to protest at how cruel, groundless, and unjust it had been to sentence him to death on this basis were a few members of the island's Greek community. Yet again, they regretted their decision not to flee the island before the first quarantine measures were announced. They felt thoroughly disheartened now and locked their doors more firmly than ever.

Just as the Chief Scrutineer had finally figured out the pattern and the thinking behind the killings, the Commander had died, and before any further action could be taken, the Sheikh Hamdullah Era had begun and Mazhar Effendi too had been arrested. According to the Chief Scrutineer, the rabble-rousers who opposed quarantine measures and Governor Sami Pasha's rule—in other words, Ramiz and his men—had planned to assassinate the Governor, the garrison Commander, the quarantine doctors, and the island's other notables all at once by feeding them poisoned biscuits when they came to the garrison. (They had briefly considered poisoning the coffee instead.) There was no evidence to prove that Abdul Hamid had known or approved of this daring plan, nor would it have been plausible to argue as much, but it was a fact that the Sultan had occasionally sent telegrams to Pharmacist Nikiforos, who knew better than anyone else on the island where to go and which shops to visit if you were looking for ratsbane.

The incident that changed the course of events and swung the country's political direction toward the path to independence was Bonkowski Pasha's impulsive decision to walk out of the back door of the Post Office that day and thus unwittingly disrupt everyone's plans, slipping away from the municipal guards and plainclothes policemen who had been following him, and falling shortly thereafter into the hands of a group of agitators who were hostile to quarantine and to the Greek community, and who had come to Arkaz to take revenge on the Governor. If it really had been Abdul Hamid's aim to dispatch his Royal Chemist without the act being traced back to him, then this had been achieved. There was no reason to bother with the poisoned-biscuit scheme anymore when the Governor came to the garrison! Yet even though Bonkowski Pasha was already dead, the biscuits were still poisoned, the bold and even-somewhat-brazen plot was carried out regardless, and Doctor Ilias too was killed.

The week before the start of the Mingherian Revolution, the Chief Scrutineer and the public prosecutors decided that it was time to resume their interrogation of the baby-faced kitchen apprentice who had put the poison in the biscuits, for the scabs on the soles of his feet had finally fallen off, and all his wounds had completely healed. The kitchen boy soon realized he would not be able to endure the same pain again, and resolved to tell them everything he knew. No one had given him the big bag of rat poison he had poured into the biscuit flour; he had bought it all with his own money, procuring small amounts at a time from different shops all over Arkaz. How much money did he have, and which shops had he bought the poison from? All kinds of shops—from traditional herbalists and from the new pharmacies! If they were to take him to some of those shops now, would the shopkeepers he'd bought the poison from be able to recognize him? Maybe they would and maybe they wouldn't, for he had only bought a little poison from each, so the shopkeepers might not have taken notice of the transaction or of the buyer, and could easily have forgotten. It had been clever of him to buy the poison in small amounts and from many different shops instead of just the single one, and thus ensure he wasn't recognized. Whose idea had that been?

"Do you think that young kitchen boy might have been reading the adventures of Sherlock Holmes, or any of those French novels?"

"Perhaps there was somebody else on the island who was doing so, and could give him suggestions accordingly. For instance, it is perfectly possible that Pharmacist Nikiforos had been reading them!"

"My uncle is the first person in Istanbul and in the whole of the Ottoman Empire who reads those books!" said Princess Pakize with a firmness and a strange dash of Ottoman pride that put an end to the conversation.

The government's investigative team had decided to subject the kitchen boy to another round of foot whipping until he told them exactly how he had got ahold of the poison. But in the wake of the island's independence, the clerks' and investigators' time had soon been taken up by other matters, such as the raid on the State Hall, Ramiz's trial, and later the inquiry into the attempted assassination of the Commander, which had resulted in the death of Majid instead. The attempt on the Commander's life and the killing of Majid had bolstered Sami Pasha's determination to hang Ramiz, and encouraged the state's investigators and torturers to redouble their efforts, but as the youth who had shot the Commander had refused to speak until he had been left maimed by his injuries, a lot of time had gone by before it could be established that his father had been one of the men from Nebiler who had died during the events of the Pilgrim Ship Mutiny, and that the boy nurtured an immeasurable rage against all Christians and quarantine measures.

By the time Princess Pakize and the Prince Consort had exhausted the topics in Sami Pasha's file, the atmosphere of lawlessness known as "plague anarchy" had become so ubiquitous, and the death rate had increased so quickly, that even though there were now four carts in the city dedicated to the retrieval of corpses, they still couldn't finish their rounds at night, and would often have to keep working until after the early morning prayers. Every day, and especially in the evenings, the gardens of all the lodges, including those of the Halifiye, the Rifai, and the Kadiri sects, would fill up with rows of corpses like those lined up in the courtyard of the Castle prison.

CHAPTER 70

Every time they heard the wheels of these corpse carts rattling through the city streets at night, their drivers muttering obsceni-ties (sometimes in Mingherian) as they went by, Princess Pak-ize and Doctor Nuri, like many others in Arkaz, would despair of ever finding a way out of the quagmire they were in, and lie in bed with their arms wrapped around each other in fear. (Two days ago the carts had collected a corpse from the Ministerial Headquarters too.) After the hanging of Sami Pasha, followed almost immediately by that of Phar-macist Nikiforos, the likelihood of being killed for political reasons sud-denly seemed greater than that of dying from the plague (especially for Doctor Nuri, even though he kept telling his wife the opposite).

On the sixteenth of August 1901—a rainy, windy Friday—fifty-one people died. Princess Pakize was writing her sister a letter when there was a knock on the door, and, thinking it must be the janitor or the parlormaid that the new government had assigned to their service, she did not rise from her writing desk when her husband went to answer. But when she heard the sounds of a whispered conversation taking place at the door, she got up and moved closer.

"They're calling me as a witness!" said Doctor Nuri, looking abashed. "I am to go downstairs and give a statement to the prosecutor."

Doctor Nuri then explained that there had been various accusations put forward against some of the soldiers of the Quarantine Regiment, including blackmail and willfully sending healthy people into isolation. There had allegedly been more serious crimes too, such as the rape and abduction of women, unlawful expropriations, and murder, but the Doctor and Prince Consort had been called as a witness on one specific incident only. One of the accused soldiers had claimed that the order to evacuate a particular house had come from Doctor Nuri. Now Doctor Nuri had been called upon to defend his actions—no longer in the guise of a quarantine doctor, but only as a friend of the Mingherian nation.

"Of course you must go and give your statement, but please do not say anything that might antagonize these delinquents. It would be all too easy for them to harm you. I beg you, please do not keep me waiting here for the sake of lecturing these people on the importance of science, medicine, and quarantine when they have no interest in hearing it, nor any wish to learn. Know that if you are delayed, you will make me the most miserable woman in the world."

"To cause you misery . . . I cannot even imagine it, my lady!" said Doctor Nuri. His admiration for his wife's wit as they debated the latest turn of events, and the enthusiasm with which she wrote to her sister, grew with each passing day. "I will absolutely not be delayed!"

But Doctor Nuri did not return that day. At dusk, Princess Pakize went to sit at her desk, but found she couldn't write a single word. An arrow cursed with a mixture of curiosity, pain, and dread had lodged itself into the gap between her heart and her lungs, and she couldn't breathe. Her attention was so fixed on the noises around her that she could hear every footstep, every shout, and even the softest creaks echoing between the walls of the Ministerial Headquarters, yet there seemed to be no trace of the intimately familiar sound of her husband's shoes. By nightfall, tears had begun to fall from her eyes onto the piece of paper in front of her.

Convinced that if she stood up from her desk before her husband returned, her husband would *never* return, Princess Pakize sat there until midnight, doing nothing at all.

She fell asleep for a while with her head resting on the table, but she could tell she would not be able to rest until Doctor Nuri was back at her side, safe and well. Just before morning prayers—the time when all the recent executions had been carried out—she opened the door and stepped outside. As usual, there was someone guarding the door, a soldier from Damascus who did not speak any Turkish. He had fallen asleep in his chair; he woke with a start and pointed his rifle at Princess Pakize, looking flustered. Princess Pakize went back inside and locked the door, then sat at her desk, petrified, until the day had properly dawned.

Finally she went to bed, having managed to convince herself that no gallows had been erected in the State Hall Square, for if they had been, that sinister crow would have come and perched at her window by now.

The next day brought more waiting, an agony of interrupted sleep, tears, and nightmares. Whether she was dozing at her desk or in bed, Princess Pakize often saw Doctor Nuri in her dreams. In one dreamlike fantasy, her husband was sitting on the prow of the *Aziziye* on his way to China while she awaited his return by her father's side in Istanbul.

But even as the sleepless nights, the nightmares, and the weeping continued, still her husband did not return. During this time Princess Pakize attempted several times to leave the guesthouse and make her way to Sami Pasha's old office. She screamed and railed at the guards loud enough for her voice to be heard all over the Ministerial Headquarters. Thankfully the inauspicious crow was nowhere to be seen.

When a clerk came to the door five days after her husband had left, and informed her that she was expected at the Chief Minister's office in an hour, she calmed herself by reasoning that this must mean her husband was still alive. Given that she was about to go into a meeting with people who had used religion to take over the state, she wore the most modest outfit she could muster, put a shawl around her neck that covered her all the way up to her chin, and wrapped a scarf around her head too.

The janitor and parlormaid who had been bringing her a little bread, walnuts, salted fish, and dried figs every day came along too, acting as her "chaperones." The Chief Minister's office, on the same floor as the guesthouse, had previously been Sami Pasha's office. Princess Pakize had scarcely had a moment to spare a sorrowful thought for the late Sami Pasha when Chief Minister Nimetullah stood up from the old governor's chair and gestured at a large sofa nearby, but Princess Pakize refused to sit. She kept her distance, glaring at everyone. There was also a pair of young clerks sitting in a corner of the room.

The Chief Minister began to speak, telling Princess Pakize that she was the Mingherian state's foremost guest of honor, and that the whole island was immensely proud of the fact that the only royal princess in history to ever leave Istanbul had come here to Mingheria on her first trip. Mingherians were "especially" fond of the Princess and of her unjustly deposed father, former sultan Murad V, because of the persecution they had suffered at the hands of the tyrant Abdul Hamid. But regrettably the island's view of the Princess's husband was not quite so positive. For the cruel sultan had done to her what he had already done to her sisters before, separating her from her father and arranging for her to marry one of his own loyal officials whom he could rely on to spy for him too. Under the pretext of enforcing quarantine rules, the Doctor and Prince Consort had sowed discord upon the island and pitted the army against their people. He was in court right now, about to be sentenced.

Princess Pakize shivered.

But, the Chief Minister indicated, there might be a solution: at this lonely and difficult time, the Mingherian state had no desire for a new confrontation with Abdul Hamid. Accordingly, the government and everyone else who loved this island had been contemplating a plan that was sure to bring all disagreements to an amicable conclusion, cause the international community to take an interest in the island, and even to protect it in some measure. If Princess Pakize were to accept this proposal, she would be doing the people of Mingheria a great service in their time of need.

"If the contribution expected of me lies within my capabilities, then I shall not hesitate to do whatever I can to help this island."

"Your day-to-day life in the safety of your guesthouse room will remain unaltered. You may still write letters all day, if you wish. Indeed, his Excellency the Prince will be returned to the guesthouse as soon as the photograph is taken—should you deem it appropriate, of course."

Nimetullah Effendi proceeded to outline the solution they had come up with. If the Princess agreed, the plan was to arrange a marriage of convenience between her and Sheikh Hamdullah, and take a photograph of them together. The purpose of this scheme was to show the world that the daughter of the previous Ottoman sultan and caliph of Islam was marrying into the Mingherian state. A marriage between the Princess and His Holiness the Sheikh, president of the Mingherian state, was bound to help make their new country much better known, especially if one considered the spread of Islam in the world, the institution of the caliphate, and all the Muslims who gathered yearly in the Hejaz in ever-increasing numbers. Obviously Sheikh Hamdullah did not expect this marriage to constitute a true union. On the contrary, it was the sheikh's express wish that Doctor Nuri should return to the guesthouse and to his spouse's side as soon as possible.

"What does Doctor Nuri think?"

Even though it was to be a marriage of convenience, the Princess would still have to divorce Doctor Nuri to marry the sheikh. There were two ways to arrange this: either the Prince Consort himself could do it by saying "I divorce you!" three times, or Princess Pakize could file for divorce in the Mingherian courts if her husband remained imprisoned for longer than four years.

"I was not even aware that Doctor Nuri was in prison."

"He is about to be sentenced, but he will be pardoned by His Holiness the Sheikh immediately thereafter, and presented with a First-Class Medal of the State of Mingheria."

"It is rather difficult for me to reach a conclusion on this matter without a letter from Doctor Nuri advising on what the most appropriate course of action would be."

The letter arrived later that same day, with Doctor Nuri writing that he was comfortable enough in the Castle prison (he had requested clean underwear, woolen socks, and two fresh shirts too), and indicating that it would be better for Princess Pakize to make this important decision herself without being swayed by her husband's opinion. Princess Pakize was thankful that her husband had not sought to coerce her in any way, not even to save his own life.

But it was not true that her husband was comfortable and safe in his cell. Knowing that the plague had spread to every corner of the Castle, and that there was no time to lose, Princess Pakize did not get the chance to negotiate the details of the wedding and photograph as she would have liked to do.

"Who will give me away?" was all that she could muster. "I should like to say 'I do' myself!"

Princess Pakize was also determined to choose her own wedding dress. Sheikh Hamdullah's entourage wanted her to use the same white dress and the same jewelry she had worn during her wedding at the Yıldız Palace five months ago, which Abdul Hamid had also attended, but Princess Pakize insisted on a traditional and characteristically Mingherian red wedding gown similar to the one she had seen Zeynep wear at her wedding with the Major, and ultimately her request was accepted.

On Thursday, the twenty-second of August, half an hour after midday prayers, the armored landau carrying the President of Mingheria Sheikh Hamdullah Effendi arrived in Mingheria Square, formerly known as the State Hall Square. Chief Minister Nimetullah Effendi had placed sentries on the President's route from the Halifiye lodge to the Ministerial Headquarters, and there were numerous guards inside the Ministries building too. Mousetraps had also been laid out in every corner, underneath stairways, and along the walls.

When she was informed that the sheikh had arrived, Princess Pakize stepped out of her room, where she had been waiting in her red bridal gown and with her head carefully covered. The parlormaid who had helped the Princess into her simple, tasteful dress, had changed into a clean outfit of her own, and followed behind the Princess.

According to Reşit Ekrem Adıgüç, the most charming and entertaining of Mingheria's popular historians, it took a grand total of nine minutes for Princess Pakize to make the trip to the floor below, get married, have her photograph taken, and return to her guesthouse room. In her letter to her sister, Princess Pakize devoted only a single page to those nine minutes, and seemed to take neither the event itself nor the pomp around it particularly seriously. She had nodded in polite greeting at the witnesses, the sheikh, and the imam of the Blind Mehmet Pasha Mosque, who would be performing the ritual, and spent the duration of the ceremony with her eyes lowered like a bashful little girl, only speaking when it was strictly necessary.

What made the whole affair so strange, distasteful, and objectionable was that the seventy-two-year-old Sheikh Hamdullah was fifty years older than his bride. As for the bride herself, she considered the sheikh to be an opportunist with an unseemly habit of exploiting Islam for his political ends (much as her own uncle did sometimes). Princess Pakize detested the sheikh, who had sentenced Governor Sami Pasha, Pharmacist Nikiforos, and many others to death purely to consolidate his hold on power and spread fear among his people.

But she was still surprised to find the sheikh even older, wearier, and more "featureless" than she had imagined. The sheikh tried to catch her eye and smile at her, but Princess Pakize averted her gaze. They sat a little apart in the spot indicated by Vanyas, the photographer assigned to the ceremony, and another photographer sent by the *Arkata Times,* and posed like a pair of tired but happy newlyweds.

Their hands were resting on a pair of dainty tea tables which had been placed in front of them. There was still some distance between them, but at the two photographers' cheerful insistence, Sheikh Hamdullah shifted a little closer to the Princess. Then, upon further exhortation from the photographers, the sheikh placed his hand on Princess Pakize's for a moment, before quickly withdrawing it. Princess Pakize would later write to her sister Hatice that she had found the gesture abhorrent.

CHAPTER 71

The photographs were published on the front pages of the island's four newspapers, including its official gazette, in special issues printed expressly for the purpose. Princess Pakize was so embarrassed that she couldn't even look at the pictures. She spent the day after the wedding crying silently in her room in helpless fury, for her husband had still not been released, and she had begun to think she must have been tricked. Her husband might not even know what had happened. She did not want anyone to see her tears, and she couldn't write letters either. Most upsetting of all was the thought that her father might see the photographs in the newspapers too.

But the next morning brought both the dawn of a clear, sunny day, and the joyful return of Doctor and Prince Consort Nuri, who had finally been graced with the sheikh's pardon. Doctor Nuri laughed and joked as if nothing had happened. They embraced, holding each other for a long time. Princess Pakize cried tears of happiness. Her husband's face looked pale, and he had lost weight, but he had managed to avoid the plague that had spread through the Castle by staying in his cell and not getting too close to anyone.

They closed the shutters and lay in bed in their underwear and night-clothes, wrapped in each other's arms. For a while, Doctor Nuri could not stop shaking, moved by a mixture of excitement, fear, and elation. Princess Pakize and the Prince Consort did not get out of bed all day, and for the first time, they began to plan how they might escape from the island. Now that quarantine had been lifted, the Doctor and Prince Consort was no longer needed. More important, nobody would even be thinking about them now, or even notice they were there. The government was in disarray, and there was nobody left in the Ministerial Headquarters except for Nimetullah Effendi with the felt hat, and a handful of Sheikh Hamdullah's loyal devotees. This group of five or six people was trying valiantly to keep the ship of state afloat, though they had no experience at all in such matters.

The next day the parlormaid did not turn up. The small loaf of bread and two pieces of dried fish that were periodically delivered to the little table outside their door were no longer enough to feed them, and they were beginning to feel their strength wilting. When a clerk came to their door in the afternoon to announce that Chief Minister Nimetullah was expecting Doctor Nuri in his office, they welcomed what they thought might be a sliver of hope. Princess Pakize was feeling more positive now that she had begun writing her letters again, and eagerly set about telling her sister everything her husband had experienced in prison before she forgot the details.

Doctor Nuri returned before half an hour had passed, and said that he had to go and examine Sheikh Hamdullah, who had caught the plague.

"Has he developed any buboes?" asked Princess Pakize, and understood from her husband's expression that the answer was yes. "Don't go; he can't be saved now. You might catch it too!" said Princess Pakize.

"I cannot bear the thought of all these people suffering and dying in vain because of this pack of fools."

"I beg you, please do not go out. Let that stupid, villainous sheikh writhe and perish in the grip of the plague he himself has so blithely encouraged."

"Don't say that, for that is probably what will happen, and then you will feel sorry about it. I have taken an oath, and as a doctor, I am obliged to attend wherever my help is needed."

"He's the one who had the Governor hanged. He's the one who had Pharmacist Nikiforos hanged too."

"And Sami Pasha hanged his brother Ramiz!" said Doctor Nuri, before leaving the room.

Since he was going to walk all the way to the Halifiye lodge, he took two guards with him, but as he strode down Hamidiye Avenue—whose name had not yet been changed—he realized there was no need for any protection at all: even on Arkaz's worst day, he would not have been able to walk the length of its principal thoroughfare without crossing paths with at least eight to ten people, but that day, the avenue was completely deserted. There were no policemen left by the Post Office, and he saw corpses strewn on the stairway that led to the Greek Middle School's lower entrance. Perhaps the area was empty because of all the executions that had taken place. As he crossed the Hamidiye Bridge, he stopped to lean his elbows on the parapet and look out at the city. All the hotels—including the Splendid, the Majestic, and the Levant—were closed. There wasn't a single carriage out on the streets, and as there were no boats about either, the surface of the sea was like glass. The Doctor and Prince Consort had been informed by the new Chief Prison Warden that Barber Panagiotis and his whole family had died over the course of three days. He remembered this fact when he saw that the barber's shop was closed. When he looked up from the foot of Donkey's Bane Hill, he saw a funeral convoy of around ten people slowly climbing its way to the top.

"Prince Consort, Prince Consort!" cried a wan, frail, white-haired Greek woman sitting nearby, her Turkish accented but fluent. "What does the Sultan's daughter make of our lot?"

"The Sultan's daughter writes letters to her sister . . ."

"Let her write, let the darling girl write! Let her tell the world of our wretched predicament," the old woman continued in her richly textured Turkish. "I'm from Istanbul too!" she called out to Doctor Nuri as he walked away.

Even those parts of the city that would have normally been the busiest were steeped in the kind of melancholy typical of small towns where everyone leaves at the end of summer or during harvest season. The city's cats, who had been the first to sense this mood, trotted all the way out to front doors and garden gates to meow at Doctor Nuri as he walked by. Two stray dogs, one male and one female, followed behind him for a while, before disappearing into the thriving, leafy garden of the big house next to Zofiri's bakery, sniffing at each other as they went.

As he approached the Blind Mehmet Pasha Mosque, it seemed to Doctor Nuri that the city's entire population had amassed here. Muslims had been banned from burying their dead until they'd had the body washed in this mosque in accordance with Islamic ritual, and could present a signed and stamped certificate to prove it. But afraid of catching the plague in one of the queues building up around the mosque courtyard and mortuary, people had begun to leave corpses by the side of the road for the corpse cart to pick up at night, or even to conduct their burials themselves in whatever spot they could find.

The rising number of deaths had effectively forced even the most conservative and reckless of the island's Muslims to start embracing some quarantine regulations of their own accord, avoiding crowds and not leaving their homes unless they had to. While a few old men still regularly attended prayers five times a day, the crowd of worshippers turning up for Friday prayers had shrunk to less than half its usual size. Within a fortnight, the new government's anti-quarantine policies had made the devastation two and a half to three times worse than it had been before, and after all these deaths, Sheikh Hamdullah's stance against quarantine was being rejected by his own most devoted followers.

The gardens of the Hamidiye Hospital were crammed all the way to the wall with beds (a gap of four or five meters separating each patient). Adjoining the hospital wall was the equally crowded backyard of the Rifai lodge. Sometimes there weren't enough bed frames and mattresses to go round, so people would be laid out on bedsheets, kilims, and straw mats. As he walked past the lodges, Doctor Nuri peered over the walls and saw that the scene was the same wherever he looked. Those with the most faith and confidence in Sheikh Hamdullah were also those who had suffered the greatest loss and pain.

As he was about to reach the Halifiye lodge, a window swung open on the second floor of someone's house.

"So, Doctor Effendi! What do you think? Are you pleased with your handiwork?" asked a man with a low forehead.

Doctor Nuri wasn't sure whether it was quarantine itself that was being denounced, or its unsuccessful implementation in Mingheria. Soon the critic with the low forehead spotted his guards. "You doctors wouldn't be able to set foot on these streets if it wasn't for your sentries and bodyguards!" he spat.

But what happened was the exact opposite: two youthful dervishes waiting for Doctor Nuri at the entrance to the Halifiye lodge greeted his arrival with respectful and elaborately choreographed salutations. If this place he had first visited two months ago had then been a haven of sorts, Doctor Nuri could see that it had now turned into a kind of hell, and that life at the lodge was falling apart. Dead bodies were piled up outside the various buildings, dormitories, and cells on its grounds, ready to be loaded onto the corpse wagon and taken to the mortuary. Doctor Nuri was walking with his head bowed, as if the scale of the suffering all around him were too mortifying to witness, but he could still see that the whole courtyard was packed with beds, just as much if not more than all the other lodges' grounds.

The door of a little building close to the garden wall opened up, and Doctor Nuri looked inside to see a half-conscious Sheikh Hamdullah lying on a mattress on the floor. He understood immediately that the sheikh's condition was desperate, and that he would not recover.

He pierced the enormous and thoroughly hardened bubo on the sheikh's neck, and drained out the pus. Doctor Nuri wasn't even sure whether the same sheikh whom he'd heard dispensing all those quips and double entendres two months ago had even noticed he was there this time. During that first visit, he had felt as if everyone were looking at him, as if every pair of eyes in the lodge had been fixed upon him. Yet now, even though his patient was technically the "President" of the state, nobody seemed to be paying Doctor Nuri any attention. There was still plenty of activity in the lodge, with people walking or running past and even stopping to look sometimes, but it was as if any sense of spiritual solidarity had dissolved, and everyone was concentrating on saving themselves.

"I have not forgotten my promise to read to you from my poetry collection *Aurora*," said Sheikh Hamdullah when he became fleetingly aware of the Prince Consort's presence. A bout of coughing and copious perspiration left him shivering and convulsing where he lay. Doctor Nuri had taken a few steps back to avoid becoming infected. After a little rest, the sheikh spoke again, but rather than reciting any lines from *Aurora,* he began doing what everyone else seemed to be doing those days and started quoting from the Koran's Resurrection *surah* until finally he passed out once more.

The armored landau had been sent to take Doctor Nuri back. As he looked out of the carriage window at the desolate view of Arkaz Castle beneath a cloak of leaden clouds, the Prince Consort's mind was on how he and his wife might be able to escape this place. Back at the Chief Minister's office, he was honest with Nimetullah Effendi—who, for whatever reason, had not joined Doctor Nuri on his trip to the lodge—and told him that there was no hope for the sheikh. Chief Minister Nimetullah Effendi turned his palms up and uttered a quick prayer.

The next day Princess Pakize and her husband did not leave their room. They both agreed that the most sensible thing to do would be to find some excuse to get in the armored landau, then flee to the north of the island. They could hide out there for a while until they found a boat and smugglers who could guide them on to Crete.

CHAPTER 72

On the morning of Monday, the twenty-sixth of August, after a long spell of pounding headaches and feverish delirium, Sheikh Hamdullah fell asleep. Or perhaps he fainted from the pain and fatigue. The young disciples and other sheikhs who had tearfully clustered at his bedside, unafraid of catching the disease, now assumed—in keeping with their instinctively optimistic interpretation of most events—that their sheikh was simply resting. Indeed when the sheikh woke up from his sleep just before midday prayers, he seemed revived and reinvigorated. He looked energized; he was cheerful; he dispensed witticisms to his audience, recited a little poetry he happened to recall, laughed about the recently drained but already scabbing boil on his neck with those who had been eyeing it in fear, and asked whether the ships that were blockading the island were still there.

But before long, the pain was back, so agonizing that he fell unconscious again, and died soon after. The Greek doctor Tassos, who was a friend of the lodge, confirmed the sheikh's passing, and as he carefully disinfected his hands with Lysol, the group gathered inside the room began to weep. Sheikh Hamdullah had already decided three years ago, persuading everyone then, that he would be succeeded as the leader of the lodge by his dear and faithful regent with the felt hat, the man he had recently appointed as the nation's Chief Minister.

Princess Pakize and her husband learned of Sheikh Hamdullah's death from Doctor Nikos, who came to visit them that same afternoon. Health Minister Doctor Nikos gave the impression that he knew a whole lot of other things too, and perhaps that was why he rushed out of the room so fast, so that he would not let anything slip. Soon after that, a clerk came to the guesthouse to inform them that Chief Minister

Nimetullah wished to see both the Doctor and Prince Consort and the Princess and had asked to be received in their quarters.

The couple looked at each other, wondering what was going to happen next. It was of course more appropriate that they should meet with the Chief Minister in his office, rather than see him in their own rooms. Princess Pakize got dressed and covered her head. When they walked together into the room that used to belong to the Governor and was now the Chief Minister's office, they both realized how much they hated this man whose influence had led to the execution of Governor Sami Pasha.

Chief Minister Nimetullah could sense their hatred, but he ignored it. Once he had settled them in the room's most comfortable seats, his manner thoroughly deferential, he told them quickly and without further ado that the sheikh had died of the plague. As the sheikh had technically been her husband, if only on paper, the Chief Minister offered the Princess his condolences. But he said this casually and did not labor the point. They had been hiding the unhappy news from the city, the journalists, and the rest of the world because the situation in Arkaz, in the nation, and among the people was already catastrophic enough, and now this man whom everyone had placed their faith in, and who had, in essence, been acting as the head of state, had also died. Unless they put the necessary contingencies in place, the rupture caused by this kind of news could easily lead to despair, panic, and anarchy.

So before the news was announced, several Mingherian notables had convened to confer and discuss what might be done next to guide the island through this disaster, and made several important decisions, constituting a road map of sorts. On behalf of the Mingherian people, the Chief Minister now wished to bring these decisions to the Princess and Prince Consort's attention, and solicit their views.

But first the Chief Minister explained who these "Mingherian notables" were: the committee was composed of Bishop Constantinos Effendi, head of the Greek congregation; Nimetullah Effendi himself; the former Chief Scrutineer, currently under house arrest; several wealthy Greek and Muslim elders; two aging journalists, one of whom was Greek; Nikos Bey; a few doctors; and three foreign consuls, including the British consul George Bey.

"What everybody agrees on is that the lifting of quarantine measures has been calamitous for the Mingherian nation," said Chief Minister Nimetullah Effendi, beginning with the most important point of all. "If this disaster continues unabated, we shall all be destroyed . . . and those warships will keep us imprisoned here until we are all dead. There will be no Mingherian nation left to speak of. Mingheria's notables would like Doctor Nuri to return to the helm of our quarantine campaign, and solve this problem once and for all."

Meanwhile, Hamdi Baba would rally the Quarantine Regiment. Curfews, martial law, and all sorts of severe punishments were essential. Nobody knew that better than Doctor Nuri!

"It's too late now," said Doctor Nuri. "Besides, you yourself were opposing quarantine until yesterday."

"It would be unbecoming to speak of ourselves at such a parlous turning point, and with the fate of an entire nation at stake," said Chief Minister Nimetullah Effendi. "I regret the mistakes that have been made, and I will resign my position to return to the lodge."

He pointed at the chair and desk where the late Governor Sami Pasha used to sit. "This will be yours now! You will be the Chief Minister. You will decide the fate of the Mingherian people, and what needs to be done to battle the plague. I assure you that this is what the whole island wants—Greeks and Muslims, doctors and shopkeepers. According to the official count, there were forty-eight deaths yesterday."

Prince Consort Nuri and Princess Pakize had understood what was being proposed, but as they couldn't quite believe it at first, and wanted to make sure, they went through the details of the offer in greater detail.

Nimetullah Effendi would give up his post "in the provincial government"—those were the words he used to refer to the position of Chief Minister—as he had only assumed the role in his capacity as steward and regent to the sheikh anyway. His seat would be taken by Doctor and Prince Consort Nuri, should he wish to accept the offer. The committee of notables was also particularly hopeful that Princess Pakize—already known among the people as the Queen—might take on the symbolic position of head of state that had just been left vacant by the death of His Holiness Sheikh Hamdullah.

"Just as Mingheria's notables wish to see the harshest quarantine measures established once more," said Nimetullah Effendi, "they have also unanimously concluded that it is essential for Princess Pakize to step forward as a true queen in the eyes of the world."

According to Nimetullah Effendi, if Princess Pakize was officially made queen, international public opinion would start paying attention to what was happening in Mingheria, and the nations of Europe would wish to find a just solution to the political turbulence on the island. Faced with the fact of the Queen's presence, and seeing her determination, Abdul Hamid might even withdraw his *Mahmudiye* warship so as not to strengthen the Western powers' hand, and the blockade would thus be broken.

Once they had overcome their initial shock, Princess Pakize and her husband received only positive responses to their questions. The death of the sheikh marked the end of their enforced sojourn on the island; if they wished, they could get on a smuggler's boat and leave whenever they wanted. Both "Queen" Pakize and the Doctor and Prince Consort had been living a life of captivity for twenty-four days now, ever since Sheikh Hamdullah had first taken power.

Noticing Princess Pakize's hesitation, and wishing accordingly to emphasize the symbolic nature of the position of queen, Chief Minister Nimetullah said: "You would not have to leave the guesthouse at all, if you preferred!"

Princess Pakize's response was a memorable one: "On the contrary, good sir, I shall take the throne as queen so that nobody may ever lock me up in a room again, and so that I may go out and walk upon the streets whenever I wish to do so."

"And I would be glad to make this my office!" said Doctor Nuri.

Like Sami Pasha before him, the regent with the felt hat had made no changes at all to this office Doctor Nuri used to visit daily for his meetings with Sami Pasha until just twenty-five days ago. Yet now the Governor's old office looked to Doctor Nuri like a completely different place.

Nimetullah Effendi had also had some boxes and envelopes brought in; he now proceeded to hand Doctor Nuri various official seals and several sets of keys dangling from gold and silver chains, all of which the former Ottoman Governor Sami Pasha had ordered in his excitement at being made the country's first-ever Chief Minister. Finally, and with all the solemnity of an Ottoman bureaucrat, the departing Chief Minister began to list the foremost concerns afflicting the state of Mingheria, starting with the disappearance of most government employees. In our view the most urgent and alarming of these matters was the prospect of famine, which would have been addressed under the category of the supply of food provisions to Arkaz. But the old and the new Chief Minister spent more time discussing Sheikh Hamdullah's funeral arrangements, the future of the Halifiye sect and lodge, and the emblems of the Queen.

At one point during the meeting, the former Chief Minister began, with all the confidence of a man who was sure everyone would want to know, to describe a dream he'd had the week before, and which explained why he had "suddenly" decided to resign from as prestigious a post as that of the Chief Minister of Mingheria. His true aim in telling them about this dream was to give the impression that it had been his decision to step down. But in our view, given the catastrophic situation on the island, and his government's many administrative failures, it would have been rather difficult for Nimetullah Effendi to remain in power. He had taken over the government so that he could abolish quarantine. But by now everyone on the island had grasped that the only thing left to do was to bring back those early quarantine regulations.

By the end of this handover ceremony, which had lasted less than ten minutes in total, the new Chief Minister, Doctor Nuri, agreed that the old Chief Minister, Nimetullah Effendi, should receive financial support from the government for the running of the Halifiye sect and lodge, but firmly refused his request for Sheikh Hamdullah to be given a state funeral, with the funeral prayers recited in the Blind Mehmet Pasha Mosque.

CHAPTER 73

As soon as the departing Chief Minister had left the room, Doctor Nuri gave orders for the armored landau and the guards' carriage to be readied. During their confinement in the guesthouse, the Prince Consort and Princess Pakize had received very limited information on what was happening in the city, and even that had come in dribs and drabs. Now they would be able to see everything with their own eyes.

Chief Minister Doctor Nuri sat beside his wife and directed Coachman Zekeriya toward Hrisopolitissa. To their right, in an area shaded by pine and palm trees and rising into a rocky slope toward the back of the park the old governor Sami Pasha had built, they noticed several people who had sat around blankets and kilims and appeared to be waiting for something. They saw more of these people again near the dusty, copper-colored road that sloped down toward Saint Anthony's Church. They all looked like they were dressed the same, in red and blue. There were also a few men and families sitting and waiting in the shade of the pine trees that lined the dusty road. Doctor Nuri rightly surmised that these—like the people they had seen in the Parc du Levant earlier—must be villagers who had just arrived in Arkaz.

After quarantine was lifted, and travel to and from the city allowed to resume, many villagers who had been trying to survive by herding goats in the island's mountainous north had decided to come down to Arkaz. Some were fleeing the lawlessness that had taken over since the plague had spread to their villages; others had been driven away by hunger and unemployment; others still had come to sell walnuts, cheese, dried figs, and pine honey at inflated prices. Villagers had already been called to the capital during the late Sami Pasha's reign as Chief Minister, and the invitation had continued to be issued under Nimetullah Effendi's regime too, always with the same aim of securing new employees for rapidly emptying government offices or for the craftsmen in the Old Market whose apprentices had run away. Thanks to their acquaintances in the city, the individuals or families who embarked on these journeys were usually able to find somewhere to stay within a couple of days of their arrival, particularly in the Christian neighborhoods, so Doctor Nuri and Princess Pakize concluded that the people they had seen today must still be searching for some kind of shelter or hiding place.

Princess Pakize saw closed doors, crooked, crumbling walls, lush green trees, flat yellow plains, and pink and purple flowers. Everything was charming, beautiful, and fascinating to her. She saw a broken chimney, a child in a garden running away from his mother, and a woman wiping tears from her eyes with the edge of her headscarf, and she knew that she would write to her sister about it all, describing everything in her own words. There was a man with dark clothes and a hat walking alone in purposeful strides, a pair of lazy cats—one black, the other a tabby—drowsing in a corner, a bearded grandfather and his grandson (she would not have realized that they were beggars if her husband hadn't told her) sitting cross-legged in a narrow alleyway, and an old man sleeping on a hammock. She saw an endless procession of faces peering out from behind bay windows whose frames had fallen off, glancing curiously at the passing landau.

The landau moved slowly onward while they looked out of its windows at empty lots, burned-down homes, and Mingheria's famous verdant gardens. They saw people swaying and swerving like drunks as they walked, women calling out to each other in Greek, and a couple arguing as they searched for something they'd lost. They could not figure out who the three masked men they saw walking out of the back entrance of Hagia Yorgos Church might be. A hunchbacked man was banging furiously against someone's front door while being yelled at with equal fury from the floor above. As the landau advanced along the alleyways below the hilly neighborhoods of Hora and Kofunya, Princess Pakize looked through people's open windows to see their families gathered inside, their men dozing on daybeds in the corner, and every single trinket, table, lamp, vase, and mirror they owned, and hoped the landau would stay on these kinds of backstreets for the rest of its journey.

In an empty lot between the Greek Middle School and the Old Bridge, they came across one of the small markets that had emerged in various neighborhoods of Arkaz over the past three weeks ever since people had been allowed to travel in and out of the city again. Noticing the curiosity in his wife's eyes as she looked out of the window, Doctor Nuri told Coachman Zekeriya to stop. Once the carriage with the guards had caught up with them, the Princess and Prince Consort stepped out, intrigued by the scene before them. There were eleven vendors in total, all men, and all dressed in traditional rural garments. Two of the men were father and son. The villagers had laid out their wares on boxes or upturned baskets, which they were using as makeshift tables. The visitors saw cheeses, walnuts, dried figs, jugs of olive oil, and basketfuls of fresh strawberries, plums, and cherries. One vendor was selling a rusty lamp, a vase, and a ceramic dog figurine. Another man, who smiled at them as they walked past, had put out a broken table clock, a pair of long-handled pincers, two funnels (one small and the other large), and a jar full of dried pink and orange fruits. Everyone was being cautious, and no one was getting too close to anyone else.

As the landau advanced along the Arkaz Creek, they saw people dangling fishing rods into the water from the windows of their houses on the bank. Inspired by the children's gangs that had formed during the outbreak, Mingherians had now discovered that they could eat the fish that lived in the island's freshwater streams. The landau veered left before they reached the Old Bridge and passed a row of gardens enclosed by squat walls. Suddenly a small barefoot child leaped out of the bushes like a monkey and hopped onto the landau's mudguard, bringing his face right against the Queen's window. Queen Pakize screamed. But before the guards could get there, the child had already flittered out of sight like a butterfly. The people in these neighborhoods recognized their old Governor Pasha's armored landau. As the carriage weaved through the cramped backstreets, its passengers smelled the scent of roses and linden from people's gardens, and wherever they went, they heard the sound of someone crying.

Hamidiye Avenue, that special place that was at once the most European and the most Ottoman part of the city, was quiet now. Doctor Nuri stopped the carriage on the Hamidiye Bridge so that his wife could step out and admire the city's most beautiful vista. The moment when Princess Pakize—who would be announced as queen the following day with a gun salute to mark the occasion—stepped out of the armored landau to look at the view with her husband would be described many years later by the son of the Bazaar du Île's Kiryakos Effendi in an interview he gave the newspaper *Acropolis* on the fortieth anniversary of the plague. Every two days Kiryakos Effendi's son would set off from the Dantela neighborhood with a small basket of food his mother had cooked and drop it off on the ground-floor windowsill of his grandfather's little house on Donkey's Bane Hill, which the old man refused to leave.

As they approached the side streets leading to the Blind Mehmet Pasha Mosque, the Princess and Prince Consort began to see more and more people outside. "Within a month of the outbreak, nearly one out of every three houses around here was already infected; how bad must things be now?" thought Doctor Nuri.

He told Princess Pakize that all the people inside the mosque courtyard were waiting to have their dead washed in accordance with the prescribed rituals. Doctor Nuri was deeply troubled by this practice, which had so clearly hastened the spread of the outbreak.

When they entered the poor Muslim neighborhoods between the Army Middle School and the Old Stone Jetty, the locals who recognized the Governor Pasha's armored landau—which had not been seen in those parts for some time—were intrigued by its arrival. Some people cursed and shouted as it passed by, but the Cretian migrants who lived here knew that there was another carriage behind it, full of guards. Probably every house in Vavla, Taşçılar, and near the old jetty was contaminated now. Around fifteen people were dying every day in this part of the city, yet the Princess and Prince Consort were surprised to see so many people outside, walking down the street in groups of two or three.

As the landau passed through the Vavla neighborhood, Doctor Nuri understood that over the course of his eight days locked up in the Castle prison, and the sixteen days he had spent in the guesthouse with his wife, many parts of the Arkaz he had come to love had undergone a profound transformation. Many of these changes he could easily identify: the lifting of quarantine measures, the greater numbers out on the streets, the absence of children, the many faces staring out of the windows, and the haunted look in people's eyes.

A dark and fathomless dejection ruled the city now, its companion a silent despair. Back in the early days of the outbreak, the city's prominent Muslims and wealthy Greeks had reacted to the belated introduction of quarantine measures with a mixture of anger, pride, and even indifference. As the late Governor Sami Pasha would often say, people in those kinds of neighborhoods blamed the plague "squarely" on the Governor and the Ottoman state's incompetence. After quarantine was introduced, they had not only sought to flee the plague, but their "despotic and idiotic" governor too. Their anger had given them hope, and proven restorative enough to allow them to make plans for their escape and survival. But now it seemed to Doctor Nuri that even the hope in people had been extinguished by the plague's merciless and implacable advance. Personal bonds had weakened, friendships had suffered, and the compulsion to learn more about what was going on, and to find new rumors to rage at, had also begun to fade. People had enough fear, pain, and anguish of their own to contend with. They wouldn't even notice if their neighbor died anymore.

In the back garden of the Kadiri lodge, they saw white washing hung up to dry. There was a man lying in a corner, naked from the waist up, though they couldn't immediately tell whether he was ill or not. There were dervishes sitting under trees or in other secluded corners, immersed in solitary prayer or contemplation. A man in his nightclothes lying outside on a carefully made bed was looking up at the sky as if he were in a dream, and they only realized he was dead when they saw all the people weeping around him.

When they passed through Çite, another area where the disease was rampant, Princess Pakize was left profoundly moved by the sight of the neighborhood's impoverished streets, its wooden houses so crooked they looked like they might topple over at any moment, its crumbling roof tiles, chimneys, and window frames, and its weeping mothers. As the landau climbed up a steep, narrow street in Bayırlar, they saw that a wagon sealed on all four sides and guarded by soldiers was blocking their way, so that they were forced to stop and turn around. Had Coachman Zekeriya not told them this was a "bread van," they would have never known. The bread vans had been the greatest success of the Sheikh Hamdullah government. They were the main reason the public had never revolted against his regime in spite of all the senseless and misguided policies it had introduced. Every day, six thousand loaves of bread were baked in the garrison kitchens and distributed across the city's neighborhoods in wagons watched over by guards.

The Bektaşi lodge in Gülerenler, which was being used as a hospital, had fallen into a pitiful state. Its elders had all been moved out under Commander Kâmil's rule. Some of the younger dervishes had stayed behind to help nurse patients and try to keep an eye on their lodge. But the lodge-cum-hospital had been a victim of the wars between the city's sects that had continued throughout the Sheikh Hamdullah Era, causing its resources to be stripped under various pretexts, and leading it to receive less assistance and fewer supplies and doctors than anywhere else.

When they reached the end of the lodge's ivy-covered wall, and looked into its lush, spacious gardens, Princess Pakize was enchanted. Tiny figures of all sorts of colors and sizes were gathered in little groups and scattered over a bright green floor, just like in the Indian miniatures she had seen inside an old book she had found in the palace. The most youthful and most numerous group were those wearing white. The older people wore purple and brown. Who were the people dressed in red? In the farthest background, the small buildings and the hospital beds spilling into the lodge's garden looked strange and improbable, and once again, Princess Pakize was reminded of ancient miniatures.

The landau did not slow down, and before the Queen and the Chief Minister could work out what might be happening at the lodge, they had reached the leafy streets of Bayırlar. They glanced into people's backyards and saw women holding each other as they cried, dogs and children running around, corpses laid out on the ground, people hanging their laundry up to dry, and beds, tables, and large jugs of water. In one garden, Princess Pakize saw a patch of blooming pink and purple wildflowers. Someone had brought out an assortment of wooden tables, gold-colored wall clocks, and immaculate white wardrobes. In another garden, there were people standing forlornly in little groups, and yellow and seashell-colored doors that had been removed from their hinges and propped up against tree trunks, but before they could understand what might be going on there, the carriage had already moved on.

When they reached the Zaimler lodge and began to crawl up the rocky, potholed road that came down from the Stone Quarry, the wheels of their carriage shaking with every spin, they stared in wonder at a purple railing covered in myriads of perching crows. They saw red cherries growing on the trees. As the landau wound its way through the quiet, sleepy streets of Upper Turunçlar, they came across a corpse wagon.

According to a measure introduced toward the end of Commander Kâmil's reign and maintained throughout the Sheikh Hamdullah Era, corpses were meant to be collected at night, as doing so during the day damaged the public's morale. While there had only been one corpse wagon in operation under Commander Kâmil's rule, their number—with help from the garrison's carpenters—had since risen to four. But with daily deaths increasing, and the drivers and three-person corpse collection teams assigned to each cart constantly having to be replaced because they had either caught and died of the plague themselves, or had abandoned their duties and fled, even four corpse wagons were no longer enough to keep up with the task at hand. Many bodies were still being hidden from the collection carts—to avoid revealing the location of an infected home, perhaps, if not out of laziness, spite, or wickedness. As they climbed one of the sloping roads leading toward Upper Turunçlar, the passengers of the landau spotted a plume of smoke rising from a fire behind a cluster of trees and houses in the distance, and when they reached the top of the hill, their sweat-drenched horses huffing and puffing along the way, they saw that a barn and a small chicken coop were aflame. At the opposite end of the same field, two Muslim men in long white robes and a man in a frock coat and fez were arguing about something, apparently oblivious or otherwise completely indifferent to the growing fire. Both the Princess and Prince Consort had noticed the strangeness of the situation, and Princess Pakize asked her husband if Coachman Zekeriya might call out to the men. But they were also aware that the three men in the distance seemed not to have noticed the landau at all, and to have no intention of doing so either. As if in a dream, the sensitive Princess was seized in that moment by an overwhelming feeling of abandonment.

Afterward the landau entered the twisting streets of the Arpara neighborhood and passed behind the house (now a museum) where Commander Kâmil's mother, Satiye Hanım, lived with a housekeeper paid for by the state. When the spectacular view from the top of Donkey's Bane Hill appeared at the carriage window, "Queen" Pakize realized that the sense of loneliness and abandonment she had perceived had come from the city, from the Castle of Mingheria, and from the waters of the Eastern Mediterranean itself. The city and the plague frightened her now, and all she wanted to do was go back to her desk and describe her impressions to Hatice. They returned immediately to the Ministerial Headquarters. On the eve of her coronation, Princess Pakize wrote her sister another letter.

CHAPTER 74

After a thorough disinfection at the Theodoropoulos Hospital, Sheikh Hamdullah's corpse was hastily buried at dawn in a small graveyard on the grounds of the lodge. The grave had been quietly dug the night before in a spot shaded by a grand old linden tree in a part of the cemetery reserved for paupers and undistinguished commoners, rather than in the section where former sheikhs were normally laid to rest. Mazhar Effendi, whose advice was frequently solicited in this new era, had arranged for the disinfection procedure to be photographed, both to ensure there was a historical record of the fact that Sheikh Hamdullah's corpse had been washed with lime before burial, and to have something to use against the Halifiye lodge should they ever need to be humiliated into submission. The dark clouds hanging over the city, the colors of the dawning day, and the mysterious aura of the Eastern Mediterranean Sea are a tangible presence in this set of black-and-white photographs. The images also convey a sense of dread and of the loneliness of death during an outbreak of plague.

What is even more interesting about these photographs is that they show Doctor Nikos and two soldiers of the Quarantine Regiment wearing masks. This measure had been swiftly introduced by Chief Minister Doctor Nuri in response to some observations he had made during the long carriage ride he had taken with his wife the previous afternoon. Doctor Nuri had begun to suspect that the plague must have reached the pneumonic stage, so that it could spread not only through rats, but also through particles suspended in the air. He believed that the cause of the exponential increase in the death rate was not just the abolition of quarantine, but also a change in the manner and speed of the microbe's spread. Former Quarantine Master Doctor Nikos, whom Doctor Nuri had met again for the first time in twenty-five days, also agreed with this assessment. What this meant was that the disease could spread much more easily now, and was almost impossible to control.

But Chief Minister Doctor Nuri's instincts told him that before he and Doctor Nikos began to discuss how to reinstate quarantine measures in these dire circumstances and ensure that they were respected, everyone would be heartened—however briefly—by the coronation of the new queen.

One hour later, the island's customary twenty-five-gun salute of blank but earth-shattering shells fired from the garrison by Sergeant Sadri's artillery squad announced Princess Pakize as the Queen and third head of state of independent Mingheria. As the shots were slowly being fired, the news spread like a spell across the shopping district's open stores, through the city's makeshift markets, among the fishermen, and from one household to the next. Apart from the adherents of the Halifiye sect and the followers of its deceased sheikh, everyone was pleased.

But those within the Halifiye lodge who couldn't believe the sheikh was dead, or abide the thought that his corpse had been defiled with lime solution, were ready to revolt. The former Chief Minister had not yet been formally installed as the new sheikh, but he was keeping the lodge's angry young devotees in check. Historians have spent a great deal of time discussing the enduring outrage nursed by these disciples and by the members of their allies in other sects about the disinfection of the sheikh's body before burial. They have argued that the Halifiye sect were being goaded by Ottoman and Turkish factions who wished to see riots break out and for Abdul Hamid to send his warships to bomb the island and its capital, but these are all exaggerations. As the more accurate and entertaining historical facts we are about to reveal will show, things were not quite as bleak as that.

As the cannon announcing Princess Pakize's coronation was being fired from the garrison hill on the morning of Tuesday, the twenty-seventh of August, a day when fifty-three people died of the plague, Doctor Nuri stepped out of the Chief Minister's office, walked over to the guesthouse on the same floor, and kissed his wife's cheeks in congratulations.

"I am full of gladness," the Queen told her husband. "I wonder if my father will find out?"

"The news is bound to soon be heard all over the world!" her husband replied.

Unlike most of their predecessors, and especially Commander Kâmil, neither Queen Pakize nor Doctor Nuri were particularly interested in the impressive ranks and titles which they had now acquired. Doctor Nuri asked Doctor Nikos what needed to be done to establish a new and effective Quarantine Committee. Doctor Nikos pointed out that it would not be easy to restore order to the island, his anger and frustration evident from his tone. "If Sheikh Hamdullah hadn't succumbed to the plague, nobody would have been able to say let's bring quarantine back, put new restrictions in place, and get the isolation facility running again. And if Nimetullah Effendi's so-called ministers—that rabble of shopkeepers who could never understand what it means to serve one's country—hadn't been threatened into submission, Nimetullah Effendi would never have agreed to retreat to his lodge in the first place."

Doctor Nuri and Doctor Nikos sat side by side on the edge of the long meeting table and began to nominate the new Council of Ministers. "We are not an Ottoman province's ordinary Quarantine Committee anymore!" said Doctor Nikos. "As we are all aware, matters of intelligence and national security are of paramount importance in a sovereign state, so someone like Mazhar Effendi would be indispensable in any Quarantine Committee."

"Then you should be quarantine minister again!" said Doctor Nuri. "Mazhar Effendi should be made minister too and resume his activities as Chief Scrutineer."

Doctor Nuri instructed his clerks to summon Mazhar Effendi for a meeting. In the early days of Commander Kâmil's presidency, Mazhar Effendi, soon to be appointed the Commander's deputy, had been at the center of the late Sami Pasha's intelligence operation against the growing influence of those lodges, big and small, that opposed quarantine measures, and the "holy men" giving out consecrated prayer sheets against the plague. Of course the final decision on which lodges should be turned into hospitals and which sheikhs should be targeted and coerced into compliance had rested with the Great Commander Kâmil and Chief Minister Sami Pasha. But it was thanks to the Chief Scrutineer's web of spies and his meticulously well-organized files of information that they had even known what was happening inside those sects and lodges. All those sheikhs who had been banished into exile, whose lodges had been emptied, whose pride and income had been dented, knew perfectly well that it was the Chief Scrutineer who had denounced them to the government's upper echelons, and therefore hated Mazhar Effendi as much as they hated Governor Sami Pasha. The trial that had resulted in Sami Pasha's execution had thus been expected to result in the same fate for Mazhar Effendi too, but at the last moment, his sentence had been commuted to life imprisonment. In our view this relatively lenient treatment resulted from Mazhar Effendi's ingenious gambit of using falsified documents to present himself to the island's public opinion as being Mingherian by birth. Of the three Ottoman bureaucrats on the island who, like Sami Pasha, had decided to support the island's struggle for freedom and independence at the expense of their ties with Istanbul, Mazhar Effendi was the only one who'd had the foresight to do something like this. The fact that his wife was Mingherian had no doubt played its part.

When Sheikh Hamdullah and his felt-hatted regent Nimetullah Effendi took power after Commander Kâmil's death, one of their aims had been to catch and quell the island's Greek nationalist insurgents. As no one on the island had kept track of these rebels' activities as closely as Mazhar Effendi had (originally as a department head under Governor Sami Pasha, and later as deputy to the President), they decided to make use of his experience. So Mazhar Effendi, who had just been given a life sentence, was let go from the dungeons and sent home to serve the rest of his term beside his wife and children. Soon his spies began to visit him at home. It was thanks to Mazhar Effendi, whom they had first jailed and subsequently released, that Nimetullah Effendi's government was able to find out more about the Greek guerrillas coming to the island on smugglers' boats, and learn that the Greek consul, the haberdasher Fedonos, and the jeweler Maximos had been donating money to their cause. Following these efforts, Mazhar Effendi's archives—the newspaper clippings he had assiduously collected over the years, all the letters he had received from his informants (he would always pay more for written intelligence than he did for oral evidence) and filed in their own separate categories, as well as hundreds of telegrams—were moved from their former location in the old State Hall and current Ministerial Headquarters to Mazhar Effendi's home. What turned this ordinary stone-built house down the street from Zofiri's bakery into a veritable intelligence center were the countless folders Mazhar Effendi had compiled in accordance with his own singular and unconventional filing methods, focusing on Mingherian separatists while the island was governed by the Ottomans, before switching to Ottoman, Turkish, and Greek nationalists. In later years, Mazhar Effendi's stone-built house would become the headquarters of the MIA (the Mingherian Intelligence Agency), before finally being turned into a museum.

Mazhar Effendi was confident that just like previous governments, any new government would also wish to avail itself of his knowledge, his services, and his spies. So when he learned that Sheikh Hamdullah was about to die, he began sending letters out to consuls and quarantine doctors to discuss what could be done to save the island. Once he received confirmation of the sheikh's death (well in advance of the firing of the garrison cannon to announce the new head of state), he believed it was only a matter of time before the members of the current government—or more precisely the committee that was ruling the island at the time—resigned their posts and were replaced by people willing to bring quarantine rules back. Unable to sit at home with his thoughts for a moment longer, Mazhar Effendi had all but sprinted to the Ministerial Headquarters so that he could observe or perhaps even "involve" himself in the latest developments. Some have suggested that he might have been looking for an opportunity to sneak into his beloved archive room, while others claim he aspired to the post of Chief Minister. Right outside the entrance to the State Hall, he ran into Health Minister Doctor Nikos, and immediately began to talk of "the wretched state of the island" and the "incompetent fools" who had caused all this, adding that he was personally ready to "take on the challenge" and do "whatever it took" to stop the outbreak.

Faced once again with this outwardly unremarkable government official who had served under the late Sami Pasha, Doctor Nuri was reminded of all the horrors of the past few weeks.

"Were we locked up in the Castle prison at the same time?" he asked, seeking to establish a degree of comradeship.

"They sent me home five days after Governor Sami Pasha's execution!" Mazhar Effendi replied. "But it is you and the quarantine doctors that I should like to serve—not them. The Mingherian nation can only be saved through quarantine now."

"Then you must join the Quarantine Committee—or rather, the Council of Ministers!" said Doctor Nuri, correcting himself.

"But I am still a prisoner. Technically, I am forbidden from leaving my house!" said Mazhar Effendi with a humble smile. He had always been adept at playing the lovable victim.

"The Queen shall soon declare a wide-ranging amnesty," said Doctor Nuri. "We would welcome your thoughts on whose release would be most conducive to the successful restoration of quarantine measures, most helpful in defeating the outbreak, and most beneficial to the people of Mingheria. Don't forget to add yourself to the list too!"

Rather than enumerating the new ministers' names and all the quarantine provisions they agreed to introduce, we shall begin with their decision to bring in an all-day curfew, a decree so momentous that it made every other measure seem inconsequential. Though Doctor Nikos and Doctor Nuri had already separately come to the conclusion that a curfew of this sort was the only possible solution, they had also assumed that it would be simply too difficult to impose, and had refrained from mentioning the subject until the new Minister of Scrutinia, Mazhar Effendi, brought it up.

"If we were to announce quarantine measures today and start boarding up houses and cordoning streets, nobody would pay us any heed," said Doctor Nuri. "There is no trust or respect left in the state and its soldiers. People have lost all hope in the outbreak being stopped, and feel they can only rely on themselves for survival."

"You are very pessimistic!" said Doctor Nikos, pronouncing the word in a French accent. "If that is the case, they won't respect a curfew either."

"They might," said Mazhar Effendi. "If they do not, that will be the end of the state of Mingheria. We would have anarchy on our hands!"

"Either the Ottomans would return, or Greece would invade," said Doctor Nikos.

"No. If the state collapses, it will definitely be the British who take over," said Doctor Nuri.

"There can be no nation without a state," said Mazhar Effendi. "Eventually the island would go back to being slave and colony to some other great power. There is no alternative but to arm the Arab soldiers and tell them to shoot anyone who ventures outside. If the curfew does not take hold, that will be the end of us all. I was thinking about this in prison too."

"Your former master Sami Pasha was hanged for having soldiers shoot people under the pretext of quarantine rules!" said Doctor Nikos. "We wouldn't want to end up the same way."

"What else can we do? We have neither the time nor the men to go knocking on every door in search of the sick, nor can we hope for volunteers. There are so many deaths and so many people hiding that we would never be able to keep up anyway . . . With everyone fighting for their lives, would people even listen if we announced quarantine measures and told them not to walk in pairs?"

So the leaders of the new government agreed to introduce a curfew. As it would take some time to ready the Arab division in the garrison, they decided not to rush.

Most historians are not aware of the desperation which had taken hold that day among the people whose actions were steering the fate of the Mingherian state and nation, and no nationalist historian today would be willing to hear about the agitation underlying the new government's rulings. Yet we would argue that if it hadn't been for that desperation, and the level of resolve required for them to consider turning their soldiers' guns against their own people, it would have been impossible to get anyone to obey quarantine rules again twenty-five days after they had been lifted. Although it took another two days before the curfew and other quarantine regulations were announced to the public through printed posters, town criers, and wagons sent around to spread the news, this time the delay was down to an excess of caution rather than any negligence.

In the meantime, one of the island's two Turkish-language dailies and the state's semiofficial gazette, the *Arkata Times,* reported that the Queen had declared an amnesty. As well as thieves, rapists, and murderers, numerous other prisoners were also set free—including Greek nationalists who had been locked up in the Castle dungeons under Sheikh Hamdullah's rule, Ottoman spies, members of the Quarantine Regiment, opponents of the government, people who'd been caught trying to flee the island, travel agents who'd sold too many tickets, and every kind of fanatic and troublemaker, all in an atmosphere of widespread jubilation. The convicts released under this amnesty would carry the plague that had scythed through the prison dormitories all the way back to their homes and families. But the opposite could also be true. When a soldier of the Quarantine Regiment who had resigned himself to rotting away in a damp Castle cell for the rest of his life had suddenly been released, he had run all the way back to his house in the Tatlısu neighborhood with tears of joy in his eyes, only to find that his mother and father and two of his children had died, and that his wife and surviving son had run away. All this he discovered from talking to the people who seemed to have settled into his house in his absence.

These men who had come from the northwestern seaside village of Kefeli and taken over his house now assumed a menacing air, and told the former Quarantine Regiment soldier—who was already feeling rather buffeted by this onslaught of bad news—that they lived here now, that it wouldn't be fair for him to live on his own in a house like this at a time when everyone was looking for somewhere to shelter, and that he would be better off going away to look for his hapless wife and child.

By then these kinds of transgressions had become commonplace. Had the man whose house had been taken over not been a member of the Quarantine Regiment, and not known he had someone in government—the Minister of Scrutinia—he could turn to for support, he would never have been able to rectify the injustice he had suffered, and his uncertainty over whether to go in search of his wife and son or stay and exact revenge on the thugs who had broken into his home would have probably driven him mad. During those nights of plague, this state of constant misery and indecision would often seep into people's dreams, and this too—along with the headaches, the stinging buboes, and the fear of death—would turn sleep into a veritable ordeal. The Minister of Scrutinia avenged the quarantine soldier by sending guards to his home in Tatlısu, whereupon the family of trespassers was removed from the property and became the first people in twenty-five days to be thrown to the Castle's isolation area as potential plague carriers. The isolation facility, whose courtyards and cramped and interwoven quarters anyone who stepped foot in instantly knew they would never forget until the day they died, had been thoroughly cleaned and disinfected in readiness for the new arrivals.

As the Arab soldiers might not suffice, Mazhar Effendi decided, with Doctor Nuri's approval, to mobilize the Quarantine Regiment once more. Some of these soldiers had been taken to court during the Sheikh Hamdullah Era and found guilty of beating innocent people up, indiscriminately sending uninfected individuals into isolation, causing death, and abusing their power to decide who should be put in quarantine by taking bribes. The courts had not sentenced all of the accused soldiers, managing by and large to differentiate between the guilty and the innocent. One of the latter group was the ever-popular Hamdi Baba. Upon his acquittal, he had immediately returned to his ancestral home in a village surrounded by rocks and cypress trees two hours from Arkaz. At first Hamdi Baba didn't want to return to Arkaz to take charge of the Quarantine Regiment again. Too many quarantine soldiers had been unnecessarily strict, behaved improperly, and lost their people's trust. But then Mazhar Effendi suggested that he could recruit a new Quarantine Regiment under the same name, and eventually managed—with a combination of flattery and the promise of a badge (the Pakize Medal)—to reassure the Sergeant and win him over.

There were numerous differences in aims and methods between the first and second Quarantine Regiments, but this was also the same glorious army that the Mingherian Major and Commander had come all the way from Istanbul to lead, back in the days of Ottoman rule, and which had been instrumental in the foundation of the state of Mingheria. Before the curfew came into effect, Mazhar Effendi assigned the Quarantine Regiment a larger and more central building in the garrison. One hundred and sixteen years later, that same building continues to operate as the Headquarters of the Mingherian Armed Forces.

After the official announcement of quarantine and before the curfew began, the people of Arkaz thronged to the city's makeshift street markets and to those shops that were still open for a few hours every day, paying large sums of money to take home whatever goods were left. As they hardly left their houses anymore, many people had already stocked up on food before, but with the outbreak showing no signs of ending, they had begun to run out of supplies.

The next day, as declared, the total curfew began, with no exceptions allowed under any circumstances. That morning, before the sun had even risen, the detachment of nervous but stern Arab soldiers from Damascus were accompanied by approximately forty soldiers of the Quarantine Regiment.

Although he had allowed the Turkish-speaking officers who'd been sent to the garrison from the army headquarters to return to Istanbul, the Major had kept the Arab division on the island as a potential bargaining chip for diplomatic negotiations, but he had never involved them in Mingheria's day-to-day political disputes. Throughout his twenty-four-day reign, Sheikh Hamdullah had paid four visits to the garrison, the first of which we have previously recounted. During this time, he had not only delighted in the pleasures of reading the Koran and conversing in Arabic, but also taken the opportunity to remove the existing garrison Commander from his post and replace him with an illiterate young Mingherian officer who had been frequenting the Halifiye lodge for many years, and whom the sheikh had now promoted to the rank of Pasha.

We would argue that the people's compliance with the quarantine measures that had been brought back after a twenty-seven-day interval, and more important with the strict curfew that had also been introduced, represents a turning point in our story. Like all sensible commentators, we too would attribute this success primarily to the high death rate on the island (a total of one hundred and thirty-seven people were known to have died in the three days before the curfew) and the terror and hopelessness that everyone was experiencing. The second reason was the absence of an influential sheikh to encourage "flippancy"—as the late Sami Pasha would have termed it—and disdain toward quarantine measures, and the fact that events had shown Sheikh Hamdullah to be just as vulnerable to the plague as anyone else, with his death teaching all the "fatalists," scornful skeptics, and the perennial doubters whom Europeans would call "cynics" a valuable lesson. Those who favored the use of force, on the other hand, believed that the true reason for the success of the curfew was that the Arab soldiers and the Quarantine Regiment were willing to shoot anyone who happened to step outside, including women, children, and the elderly.

Two kids who had gone out in Bayırlar had to hurry back inside when they heard the sound of warning shots. A lunatic who had been walking around Donkey's Bane Hill as if there were no curfew at all was quickly seized after a couple of rounds of shooting, and the walls and shutters of a house in Taşçılar were left covered in bullet holes after the people who lived there had pelted the Arab soldiers with rocks. Later that day, the Quarantine Regiment pushed the door down and arrested the three young Cretian migrants who were living there, sending them to the Castle prison. In all three episodes, the sound of gunfire had echoed through the preternatural silence that had descended upon the city ever since the beginning of curfew, and realizing that the soldiers were taking a firmer stance this time, most people gladly concluded that quarantine would finally take hold.

CHAPTER 75

Princess Pakize kept going back and forth between the guesthouse and the Chief Minister's office to follow the hourly progress of Arkaz's "disciplined" submission to the curfew. Every time a sentry or a clerk came in to report that people were still staying at home, that only the Arab soldiers and the Quarantine Regiment had been seen out on the streets, and that there had been no incidents of note, the Queen would feel even more elated than the men around her, though rather than expressing her emotions in the Chief Minister's office itself, she would return to her guesthouse room and put them in a letter to her sister instead.

When the state had first started distributing bread loaves (in what was at the time a one-horse cart), the bread van would stop at one or two locations in each neighborhood, and people would queue up to pick up their rations under the supervision of their neighborhood representatives and the quarantine soldiers. The bread would be handed out to each male head of household in accordance with the size of his family. This simple system depended on everyone in these neighborhoods knowing each other. But with the plague causing some homes to be evacuated and others to be taken over by new occupants, arguments had soon begun to erupt. People would often turn up in groups, browbeat the rest of the queue into submission, and leave with everyone else's allowance too. This kind of hostile and objectionable behavior occurred mostly at the hands of those who were still demanding that Ramiz's death be avenged, or felt that the island's Rumelian Greeks who remained loyal to Greece, and its Turks who maintained their allegiance to the Ottomans, should all be collectively punished.

Now that they had suffered the humiliation of seeing Sheikh Hamdullah's corpse disinfected with lime, this collection of religious fanatics, sect acolytes, and Mingherian nationalists would have no choice but to moderate their aggression. But in the end this shift would not even be necessary, for Queen Pakize had already come up with a new method of bread distribution which would ensure no one could bully their way to the front of the queue, and had managed to persuade her husband the Chief Minister and the rest of the government to adopt it. From then on, where possible, the bread vans and the guards who protected them would deliver their loaves to each individual household, leaving them in people's back gardens or at their kitchen windows and front doors. The return of the Quarantine Regiment would help ensure it was safe for the bread vans to deliver their cargo door to door.

The Queen provided a detailed and earnest—if slightly overblown—account of her small contribution to this simple matter in a letter to her sister. Right from the start, and moved by a growing sense of responsibility, Queen Pakize had taken what might have been expected to be a symbolic, ceremonial role very seriously indeed. She would join the meetings that took place every morning in the Outbreak Room, which had been given a fresh coat of paint and had the bullet holes in its walls and furniture covered up. She would wear clothes that might have seemed a little too European for a Muslim lady but were nevertheless wholly demure, wrap a shawl around her like a headscarf, and sit at the back of the room.

Once the ministers were gone and she was left alone with her husband, she would start questioning him about everything she had heard, and ask him to explain why he had taken a particular decision. The lengthy descriptions and discussions of the government's policies readers will find in Princess Pakize's letters show that just as the Mingherian constitution intended, the head of state was scrutinizing her husband's work with the utmost care.

Doctor Nuri greeted all of his wife's ideas with unfeigned respect, and most of the Queen's arguments ended up being with the Minister of Scrutinia. After the first two days of the successful curfew (with fifty-nine and fifty-one deaths respectively), Mazhar Effendi told the Queen that for the garrison's bread vans to be able to visit every street and knock on every door, all of Arkaz's streets and houses would have to be named and numbered, and the requisite signs would need to be put up. Everybody knew how important this issue had been to Commander Kâmil, who would always turn up whenever the Committee for Street Names was meeting in the State Hall to show them his own poetic suggestions listed for their perusal in his neat and elegant handwriting. Thirty-five days later, some of Commander Kâmil's street names had already been embraced and adopted by the public, and many of them—such as Dwarf's Fountain Street, Blind Judge Road, Lion's Den Street, and Cross-Eyed Cat Road, among others—are still remembered and in some cases still used by the people of Arkaz today, one hundred and sixteen years on. But this ambitious and poetic project, which the city's postmen were especially eager to see concluded, had been interrupted by the death of Commander Kâmil, the increasing severity of the plague outbreak, and by everyone's terror of dying.

So it was that her attempts as queen of the island to solve the problem of bread distribution made it immediately clear to Princess Pakize just how formidable a figure the Minister of Scrutinia could be.

"You must not indulge that toad!" she told her husband when they were alone one day.

"Our job here is to stop the plague," the Chief Minister replied. "Let him deal with the politics!"

Readers of her correspondence with her sister will note that Murad V's daughter and Abdul Hamid II's niece Queen Pakize was possessed of much finer and more wide-ranging political instincts than both her witless father, who had inexplicably chosen to become a Freemason while he was next in line to the throne, and her husband, whose only political criterion seemed to be "tolerance."

The Queen took great pleasure in joining her husband in the armored landau every day for reconnaissance trips around the empty streets of Arkaz, and considered this an important task. Ever since their first excursion, this activity had become both a habit and a vital opportunity to monitor the efficacy of quarantine measures. As she often wrote to her sister, Princess Pakize was enthralled by the sight of the city's streets, squares, and bridges emptied out by the curfew.

The experience had reminded Princess Pakize of the way she used to feel when she was still imprisoned in the palace in Çırağan with her father and sisters, and would look out at its empty gardens nobody was ever allowed to enter. Gazing at the deserted Hrisopolitissa Square, she had felt as if time were flowing backward. When Coachman Zekeriya had driven the landau past the boatmen's jetties in the empty port, she'd thought despairingly that no ferry would ever come to this island again. As the landau had neared the edges of the city, passing through the vacant lots and collapsing houses near the abandoned Stone Quarry, she'd shivered, and for the first time, she had been afraid. When they had come across a five-year-old girl crying alone in the unpeopled streets of the Tatlısu neighborhood, she too had cried, and would have climbed out of the carriage if her husband hadn't restrained her.

The emotions aroused by these early expeditions would mingle in Princess Pakize's letters with the satisfaction of witnessing the public complying with the curfew. The people of Arkaz did not leave their homes for the next three days either. The only exception was an attempt by a group of Rifai dervishes, whose lodge (where they still lived) had been partially converted into a small field hospital, to sprint to the Blind Mehmet Pasha Mosque down the road for Friday prayers. Forewarned by his spies, the Minister of Scrutinia had sent guards to the scene, and the faithful, wrathful dervishes—who presented a rather striking picture in their strange purple gowns—were all arrested and sent away to the Castle's isolation facility.

To illustrate the magnitude of the calamity the city and its people were facing, we shall now outline the situation at the Hamidiye Hospital on the thirtieth of August, three days after the coronation of the Queen: According to our calculations, there were approximately one hundred and seventy-five patients in the Hamidiye Hospital and the makeshift sick wards (they could hardly be called hospitals) which had been set up on the grounds of various lodges nearby—including the Rifai and the Kadiri. The main buildings, their surroundings, and the gardens were crammed with tents and beds. There was only a meter separating each patient, and sometimes even less than that. The only treatment they received was when the doctors, male nurses, and white-aproned janitors gave them injections to reduce their fever or hurriedly lanced their buboes and cleaned them out. These procedures didn't even serve the purpose of prolonging patients' lives. Time and time again, the Queen had heard her husband describe the heroic and futile efforts of these doctors marching from bed to bed to deliver the same "treatment" to forty or fifty patients at a time, all while trying to shield their faces from the coughing, sneezing, vomiting mouths of the sick.

The Queen had been intensely affected by the sense of doom conveyed by the contrast between the emptiness of the city's streets and the many-hued throngs spread across the green and yellow ground in the gardens of the Hamidiye Hospital. The bodies of the patients who died in the hospital would also be collected at night by the corpse wagons. Five days after the introduction of curfew, Queen Pakize's heart filled with an equally intense joy at the first notable decrease (to thirty-nine deaths) in the daily mortality rate.

The next day the armored landau carrying the Queen and the Chief Minister concluded its journey through the city in the neighborhood of Flizvos. Vacated by the wealthy Greek families who used to live there before the outbreak, the mansions in this area were now populated either by the butler's acquaintances from his ancestral village or by whoever was willing to pay the butler what he'd asked for or by anyone who happened to have a gun to threaten the butler with. As for the poorer Greek quarters the armored landau traversed, the Queen might have thought they were completely abandoned, had it not been for all the people she spotted eyeing the carriage from their second-floor windows, the children playing among themselves in their backyards, and the dogs gaily trotting along the garden walls in pursuit of the landau, just as they used to do in the old days.

It was during this period that the Queen ordered every empty street and square in Arkaz to be photographed. The descriptions you have been reading in this book are based on the photographs Vanyas took of all the city's main squares and roads over the course of the following three days. Much like the Queen herself, we too are moved to tears every time we peruse this poignant collection of eighty-three black-and-white images, where the occasional solitary human figure also appears.

During those same three days, the death rate continued to steadily decrease, until the officials meeting every morning in the Outbreak Room finally began to believe that quarantine measures might have taken hold after all, and that the curfew and the closing of the city gates had yielded the desired effect.

Another development that pleased everyone on the island, and caused those who had campaigned for Princess Pakize to be crowned queen to rejoice that their primary aim had finally been achieved, was the publication of a new article in *Le Figaro,* the same newspaper that had first announced the nation's independence to the world.

> *A Queen for Mingheria (Devenue Reine de Minguère)*
> After declaring independence and breaking away from the Ottoman Empire, Mingheria's nationalists have chosen a princess from the Ottoman royal family as their queen and head of state. In a move that has caught Istanbul and the world by surprise, Princess Pakize, third daughter of the former sultan Murad V, has been crowned queen of Mingheria. Princess Pakize was recently married to an Ottoman quarantine doctor sent from Istanbul to stop the outbreak on the island. But with the outbreak continuing unabated, and communications with the new government severed, the island remains blockaded by British, French, and Russian warships.

The suggestion that the authorities in Istanbul were "surprised" was a detail imagined by the British intelligence services, at whose instigation the article had been written. Doctor Nuri hoped, among other things, to restore the Post Office's telegraph services, "normalize" the island's political situation, and improve relations with the European nations enough for the blockade to be lifted, and was constantly discussing how these aims might be achieved with the Queen and with the other doctors he had brought into the government.

Seeing how glad his wife was about the falling death rate, Doctor Nuri told her the same thing he told everyone else: "As corpses are collected at night, and funerals are banned, the public is not aware of this happy development. Should they find out, they would be just as pleased as you are, but unlike you, they would all be out on the streets the next day, walking around arm in arm. If we are to end the outbreak, the people must remain afraid, and we must not relent."

Doctor Nuri could tell from her frown and the look she gave him that his "Ottoman" wife was displeased with this warning, though he did not dwell too much on her reaction. But while the article in *Le Figaro* was viewed by the island's leading figures as a potential opportunity for political maneuvering, to Princess Pakize it was nothing less than a source of pride. Although she was perfectly aware—as noted in her letters—that she had been made queen purely to attract the attention of the press and thus increase the world's awareness of the island's new government, its flag, and its independence, she took her duties more seriously than ever, sitting with her husband in his office every day, and writing to her sister about the scenes she witnessed during their excursions in the landau. Another reason for the fall in the number of deaths, and one that other historians have largely ignored, was that the city's rats had all mysteriously vanished. For the past week, the children's gangs had stopped handing any dead rats in to the authorities.

It was around this time that the Queen and her husband the Chief Minister began to drop in on ordinary Mingherians living in the capital's more distant, isolated neighborhoods to deliver gifts and parcels of food. These visits were a continuation of the couple's previous outings in the landau. But the Queen's clerks would identify the chosen house in advance. They would make sure the family who lived there were true supporters of the Queen, and that they respected quarantine regulations. The Queen and the Chief Minister never went inside. The Queen, wearing modest but European-style clothes, would enter the garden and announce that she had brought gifts for the children. The family would not go outside, but they would greet their visitors from the window. Usually the Queen would leave the gifts in the garden without saying a word, and wave at the people upstairs like a little girl.

Contrary to what dissenters and jealous detractors claimed, it is fair to say that these house visits proved effective, and gave people confidence. An old man in the Taşçılar neighborhood responded to his visitors' words of reassurance by asking when the ferries would start running again. Meanwhile, Grocer Mihail had deliberately locked himself in by nailing his front door shut from the inside. So far his food had regularly been delivered to him in a basket left outside his window. But he hadn't been able to get ahold of any for the last three days, what with all the changing rules. Might the Chief Minister be able to intervene in some manner? One day, Coachman Zekeriya took them in the landau to the home of the late Governor Sami Pasha's mistress Marika. They left her some biscuits and cheese while she stood weeping at her window. They also visited the Commander's grieving mother and later assigned a clerk to record her tales of the great savior's boyhood for a book to be entitled

Kâmil's Childhood. On a separate trip to the Castle-Moat neighborhood, supporters of the Queen slipped through their backyards and flouted every rule in existence to come within touching distance of their queen, prompting Doctor Nikos to frankly remark to Doctor Nuri that these visits might be compromising proper adherence to quarantine regulations. In response the Queen had reminded them all that the death rate was falling by the day, and rightly pointed out that her neighborhood visits were actually encouraging Mingherians to follow quarantine rules.

The Queen summoned Arkaz's most renowned female dressmaker, Freckled Eleni, to the guesthouse, studied the fabric samples and sketches the woman had brought with her, and allowed her measurements to be taken for three new dresses in the European fashion (though still altogether demure). Just like a European queen, Princess Pakize also had Vanyas photograph her in "profile"—alone and with her husband—for a series of stamps that the new Post Minister had suggested should be issued to mark her coronation. Noticing straightaway how much the Queen had enjoyed these portraits, the Minister of Scrutinia arranged for an initial set of twenty-four copies to be framed and hung in various government departments—such as recruitment offices, the land registry, and charitable public trusts—as well as any banks that were still open. During one of her carriage rides with her husband, the Queen noticed one of these photographs hanging in the large, empty entrance hall of the Ottoman Bank (soon to become the Bank of Mingheria), and later wrote to her sister of how glad their father would have been if he had seen it.

Many people petitioned their local representatives to have the Queen and her husband's landau come to their neighborhoods. For soon the rumor had begun to spread that the plague never struck in those homes where the Queen had visited and dropped off presents and provisions.

CHAPTER 76

From Friday, the thirteenth of September, onward, the fall in the daily death toll became even more pronounced, and a feeling of optimism began to establish itself upon the island. What exactly had caused the outbreak to slow, and its severity to diminish? This is a question that historians have always dwelt on, for the organization of quarantine measures was the reason the eternal state of Mingheria came into being.

In our view, the willingness to have soldiers shoot people in order to enforce the rules, Sheikh Hamdullah's death by the plague, and the fact that between fifty and sixty people had been dying every day, were all factors which ultimately led to the success of the new quarantine measures. There are also some natural and medical factors we do not have definitive information on—such as the disappearance of the rats or a possible reduction in the virulence of the plague microbe—which may also have contributed to this happy ending. But here we will focus specifically on the results of the quarantine effort.

In the early days of the outbreak of plague, the body of any Muslim who died in Arkaz would be washed in the mortuary of the Blind Mehmet Pasha Mosque by a tall, wiry man who was known as the barber. First the barber—who was not a barber at all—would carefully clean the corpse as the rules dictated, wiping its lips, nostrils, and navel with a cloth wrapped tightly around his finger. Then he would wash the body with soap made from olives grown on the island, and copious amounts of water. The old lady who performed the same rituals for female corpses would add a handful of delicate, fragrant rose petals to the water if you gave her a small tip. As Doctor Nikos had regularly sent spray-pump operators to disinfect the mortuary, these corpse washers had managed to avoid being infected when the plague first began to spread. In fact, as they sought to keep up with the increasing demand for their services, they had brought in assistants and apprentices to help them, and begun to wash bodies more hastily and with less care.

Doctor Nuri had gained some experience of these matters from cholera outbreaks in the Hejaz, where there would often be arguments between local Arabs wanting to bury their dead, and the French, Greek, and Turkish doctors representing the Ottoman Empire, and just as he had done then, here too he had initially chosen not to address the issue directly. Rather than letting the debate get out of hand and generate endless discussions on Islamic ritual and quarantine policies, it was much better to slip the corpse washers a little cash to persuade them to perform the rites in a much-more-casual and perfunctory manner than they normally would. The barber and the other corpse washers were already aware of the mortal danger they were in, and having long since given up on cleaning the bodies in accordance with traditional methods, they had sped the process up considerably.

For some time thereafter, the washing of corpses came to consist of little more than pouring boiled water over the victim's body, with the corpse washers hardly even touching the frighteningly grotesque and sometimes already reeking corpses they were given—covered in vomit, phlegm, and buboes. The naked corpses would then be laid out in the mosque's inner courtyard (often frequented by stray cats) to dry under the sun on washing stands or on the floor, and shortly after that, they would be wrapped in shrouds. Within two weeks from the start of quarantine, the practice of enshrouding corpses had also been abandoned. This development had come as the number of unclaimed corpses found on the street had continued to increase, and the dead had begun to be buried as soon as they had been disinfected with lime.

Yet in spite of all this and of regular disinfection operations, the death of an apprentice at the mortuary (who may have caught the plague back in his neighborhood) during the final days of Ottoman rule upon the island, followed soon after the declaration of independence by the death of the barber (whom the whole of Arkaz knew), prompted the Commander and Doctor Nuri to ban corpse washing altogether. But instead of making an official announcement of this decision, the government had simply locked the mortuary doors shut, leading to all sorts of arguments and objections and to the protests of those who were not willing to renounce their customs and believed that if their loved ones were buried without being washed properly first, they would carry all their sins into the afterlife.

After Nimetullah Effendi became the Chief Minister and the Quarantine Committee was dismissed, Muslim corpses were no longer allowed to be buried until they had been bathed by corpse washers who had performed their own ablutions too, and carried out all the rites and recited all the prayers that the funeral rituals prescribed. According to our estimations, this decision alone caused the deaths of more than twenty corpse washers. Within a week into the Sheikh Hamdullah Era, it became clear that when no precautions were taken and corpses continued to be washed in full accordance with religious precepts, the disease spread much faster, and after three corpse washers became infected, the others—who couldn't keep up with the work anyway—all ran away.

Knowing how important this issue was to Sheikh Hamdullah, Nimetullah Effendi enlisted the help of local mayors and religious functionaries to bring in "volunteers" from the island's other cities to work as corpse washers in Arkaz. More than half of these volunteers—some of whom had embraced the task in a genuine spirit of piety, brotherhood, and self-sacrifice—would go on to catch the plague and die. With the whole island soon realizing how dangerous it was to wash corpses in the traditional way, it became increasingly difficult to find willing "volunteers" for the task, and after two of the three soldiers that Sheikh Hamdullah's government had brought in from the garrison to help also died, the authorities tried to keep up with the increasing demand for corpse-washing services by using prisoners the police had snatched from the streets of their villages, or otherwise deemed to be suspicious, as the new mortuary "volunteers." A murderer and a rapist who had been caught and locked up after the prison riot, and could not recite a single prayer between them, had thus also ended up working as corpse washers for a time, before they too had died of the plague.

The hecatomb of the mortuary "volunteers" has rightly been identified by historians and politicians as a demonstration of the excesses and absurdities of the period during which Sheikh Hamdullah and the Halifiye sect ruled over the island. During his brief tenure as Chief Minister, Regent Nimetullah Effendi with the felt hat would also forcibly "appoint" a number of volunteers from sects that were hostile to the Halifiye lodge, or that the sheikh considered to be "heretics," to work as corpse washers. According to some historians, the fact that these people would go on to catch the plague and die like most other corpse washers before them was not a result of any kind of ignorance or fanciful thinking, but should be considered instead as the outcome of an act of outright malevolence, and a calculated massacre.

But in our view the true massacre took place when all of these "volunteer" corpse washers started spreading the disease across the city and the rest of the island. Returning to their lodges to sleep after a day spent washing dead plague victims, these men would soon pass the disease on to their fellow disciples. For a while, the death rate in neighborhoods with a high concentration of religious sects and in those lodges which had been partly converted into hospitals rose exponentially, yet nobody dared speak of the perfectly evident reasons for this increase.

In truth, many sect disciples, including those who didn't believe in microbes and quarantine, were aware in some corner of their minds of the tragic situation they faced, yet for some mysterious reason, they continued to wash corpses with unwavering adherence to the rules. The historian of Mingherian public health Nuran Şimşek has found data to demonstrate that some corpse washers, particularly those from the Rifai sect, must have reinfected their lodge and the patients who were recovering in the improvised "hospital" in its gardens. Sheikh Hamdullah probably caught the microbe that killed him from one of these faithful, pious corpse washers too, for just a few steps away from the modest single-room residence in the grounds of the Halifiye lodge where the sheikh himself lived (and which did not at all resemble the home of a head of state), there was a small stone-built construction where three of these corpse washers—two of them young, the other old and overweight—came to sleep every night.

By the end of the twenty-four days of Sheikh Hamdullah and Nimetullah Effendi's rule, the state of "plague anarchy" that had taken over the lodge gardens, empty land, burned-down lots, and city streets was such that it would be impossible to determine today who was spreading the disease, and where. Already the high number of deaths and the general atmosphere of hopelessness had pushed many young sect devotees to leave their lodges and flee Arkaz for the mountains and fields outside of the city, where they foraged for figs and walnuts to survive.

Chief Minister Doctor Nuri's order to ban corpse washing on the island as soon as he took power, and have the cemeteries and anywhere else the corpse cart went liberally doused with Lysol, were both determining factors in the slowing of the outbreak. In our view, resuming the disinfection of corpses with lime must also have contributed to this outcome.

Though the fact was never publicly announced, the people of Arkaz could sense that the outbreak was subsiding. A feeling of optimism was beginning to suffuse the city, though restrictions continued to be obeyed, and there wasn't much activity on the streets. By the twenty-fourth of September, the number of deaths had fallen to twenty. No one was more ecstatic about this figure than Doctor Nuri himself. The Chief Minister summoned the British consul George Bey to his office.

Like all the other consuls, Monsieur George had also kept to himself under the previous government, worried about possible attacks from the lodges or that he might be accused of being a foreign spy. But as Doctor Nuri knew, George Bey was one of the people regularly consulted by the committee of notables who had been at the forefront of political developments on the island in the wake of Sheikh Hamdullah's death and Nimetullah Effendi's departure from the position of Chief Minister.

The British consul diplomatically congratulated Doctor Nuri on his new role as Chief Minister. But as had always been the case whenever he had found himself in these kinds of situations after the foundation of the new state, there was something in his manner which he would have termed "ironic," and which we would describe as "teasing." On the other hand, his demeanor also made it clear that he took the new government utterly seriously.

Minister of Scrutinia Mazhar Effendi was in attendance too. Just then, the Queen had also entered the shadows of the Chief Minister's office. For a moment, it was as if the spirit of the late Sami Pasha were wandering among them, and they all felt a strange surge of guilt. They seemed to be on the verge of mentioning him, but instead they kept quiet. The Ottoman maps and Abdul Hamid's seal had been taken off the walls and been replaced by a flag of Mingheria and a portrait of

Commander Kâmil. Several landscapes of Mingheria and of Istanbul that Sami Pasha had hanged on the walls, various Ottoman-era edicts, and a photograph of Istanbul's Üsküdar Square remained in place in their original frames.

"The outbreak is waning!" Doctor Nuri began, addressing British consul George Cunningham in a measured tone. "The state of Mingheria now expects His Majesty's government to lift the blockade and send medical supplies and additional doctors in assistance."

"The blockade is the reason the island's independence endures," said the consul. "If the European warships were to leave, Abdul Hamid would not hesitate to punish the presumptuous rebels who slaughtered his new governor and dared speak of revolution. The Sultan would be the first to send either the *Mahmudiye* or the *Orhaniye* over and have them bomb Arkaz with the new Krupp guns he has just had them fitted with in Marseille."

"Then he would land soldiers in Kalar Cove and take full control," said the Minister of Scrutinia, joining the conversation. "Is His Majesty's government prepared to stand and watch as the Bloody Sultan butchers the people of Mingheria?"

"According to international law, the island of Mingheria remains a possession of the Ottoman Empire."

"Yet your warships surround the island, and sink any boat that tries to leave. Is that in accordance with international law?" Everyone in the room was reminded that beneath his amiable exterior, reminiscent of someone's benevolent, pot-bellied uncle, the soft-spoken Minister of Scrutinia was a tough negotiator indeed.

"It is in accordance with international law, as this blockade has been established at the behest of the Ottoman Empire," the British consul replied.

"Then His Majesty's government must recognize the new state of Mingheria. The people of Mingheria would be honored if the United Kingdom and Prime Minister Gascoyne-Cecil's government were the first to formally acknowledge their existence. If the United Kingdom recognizes the state of Mingheria, Abdul Hamid will not be able to bombard Arkaz. But if Istanbul were to undertake an operation of this sort, you and the other consuls would also be attacked. In fact the consuls would probably be the first to die, as was the case in Thessaloniki."

"Our own lives, our own interests are immaterial!" said Monsieur George. "I am ready to do anything I can for this island. But like everyone else here, I find myself cut off from the world."

"I am sure you of all people could easily predict what kind of offer the British government might be willing to accept, and what the Mingherian state would need to do in order to secure Britain's protection against the Ottoman Empire. Should you not have an answer at the ready, you may of course come back to us with a written response in the next couple of days."

"We know you have already been communicating with the British government!" was the unspoken message in the Minister of Scrutinia's tone. But this contention was false.

Everyone in the room had assumed the British consul would accept the suggestion and request some time to prepare a response in writing. But instead the consul shared his thoughts straightaway.

"All of His Majesty's governments, no matter the party in power, have been perturbed over the past twenty-five years by Abdul Hamid's aspirations to gather the world's Muslims under a single political union and challenge British authority. By now about half the foreign office has understood that Abdul Hamid's Pan-Islamist politics are destined to fail. They can sense that far from joining forces, Muslims throughout the world are separating into their own groups—Arabs, Albanians, Kurds, Circassians, Turks, Mingherians—and growing further and further apart, so that the idea of an Islamic union is nothing but an illusion, a kind of masquerade. Unfortunately the British government is still headed today by anti-Muslim politicians like the former conservative prime minister Gladstone." Consul George paused after this remark and turned to look at the Queen. "The torment Abdul Hamid has subjected your sisters, your family, and your father to is well known. Your uncle has inflicted the same treatment upon the Young Turks, the opposition, the Bulgarians, the Serbs, the Rumelian Greeks, the Armenians, and the Mingherians. If Her Majesty the Queen, a member of the Ottoman royal family, were to openly denounce Abdul Hamid's oppressive ways and his Islamist politics, I expect it would not just be the British but the French and the Germans too who would be roused into offering the island and its noble people their protection against the Ottoman sultan."

"I agree with the consul," said the Minister of Scrutinia. "But with this blockade still in place, the question is how to find a journalist who will carry her words to Europe. If she were to speak to Greek reporters and Cretian or Athenian newspapers, that would give the wrong impression."

"There are more than enough newspapers in London and Paris that would be interested in the particulars of an Ottoman sultan's daughter's life in captivity with her father and sisters," said Consul George. "The Queen's coronation was widely reported by the international press."

"But her marriage to the sheikh was not."

"That is because they could tell it was only a marriage of convenience," said the consul. "I am sure Her Majesty the Queen will be glad of the opportunity to express her truest feelings on her cruel and dictatorial uncle Abdul Hamid. Her words will be shaped by her disapprobation of autocratic rulers—a sentiment she has been paying the price for every day of her life. Robert Gascoyne-Cecil's government will understand this sentiment, and there will be people within it who will wish to protect this beautiful island against Abdul Hamid."

The history pages of Istanbul journals and newspapers like *Orhun* and *Tanrıdağ*, which would greet Hitler's conquests in the Balkans forty-two years later with such enthusiasm, have portrayed Consul George's well-meaning proposal as part of some kind of vast and diabolical anti-Turkish conspiracy. (Their theory is that the Ottoman Empire lost its Arab territories because of one spy—Lawrence of Arabia—and the little island of Mingheria through the machinations of another spy—Consul George.) But the consensus among the participants in this historic meeting at the Chief Minister's office that morning of the twenty-fourth of September 1901 was that allowing a European country to establish a mandate or a protectorate over their island would offer some form of security against attacks by Abdul Hamid or other foreign rulers, and with this in mind, they all watched out of the corner of their eyes to see what their queen would say.

"I will decide myself how to articulate my feelings against my uncle!" said Princess Pakize, with a determination that filled her husband with love and pride. "But first I must ponder the matter and determine what would be most beneficial to the people of Mingheria."

CHAPTER 77

Queen Pakize's words seemed to convince all the men gathered in the Chief Minister's office that she would indeed issue a statement criticizing Abdul Hamid. As this was the only hope any of them had for the island's political future, we would argue that their conviction in this regard also served to fortify the feeling of renewed optimism that had begun to establish itself upon the island. But as it turned out, Princess Pakize would never speak publicly against Abdul Hamid or his policies—not with any "foreign" newspapers, nor with any Mingherian or Turkish journalists.

"All you need to do is tell the things you've already told me to some reporter from Europe," Doctor Nuri had once remarked.

"I fear that would be rather unbecoming!" the Queen had replied. Her eyes were wide open, imbuing her face with an expression of utmost innocence. "Those conversations with my sisters and my father are my most precious, most private memories. Must I tell the whole world about them only because my uncle happened to be cruel to us? I wish I knew what my father would say about all this."

"You are a queen now. This is a matter of international diplomacy."

"I am not a queen because I want to be, but only to help quarantine measures hold, end the outbreak, and save people's lives," Princess Pakize had replied. Then she had begun to cry, and as he held her in his arms and stroked her auburn hair, her husband had reminded her that since there were no new ships coming to the island anyway, there were no journalists who could interview her either.

Readers of her correspondence with her sister Hatice through to the end of that September will discover how difficult the Queen was finding it to decide what she was going to say about Abdul Hamid, and will be just as surprised as she was to realize that the time she had spent with her father, her mother, and her sisters in the Çırağan Palace had been the best days of her life. Even after she became queen of Mingheria, Princess Pakize—who was twenty-one years old when the plague broke out—still missed her old life in the palace, playing the piano with her father, reading novels with her sisters, laughing with the elderly harem ladies, and running around from room to room. She would quietly cry about it sometimes, making sure her husband didn't see her tears.

As these feelings of melancholy and longing intensified, there were times when the Queen didn't even want to get out of bed, let alone the guesthouse. But meanwhile the plague was retreating, people were beginning to step outside, and the swaying of the fishing boats and all the other vessels in the harbor (like those that belonged to the army, or the rowboat at the Maiden's Tower, which could be glimpsed from the guesthouse window) seemed to be shaking the city awake from its slumber, just like the autumn's first stormy, southwesterly *lodos* winds, and the passage of warm, kelp-scented breezes.

On a rainy, cloudy, gloomy day at the start of October, when the number of deaths recorded fell to eleven, and the duration of the daily curfew was shortened (the Minister of Scrutinia wanted to see it lifted altogether), the meeting convened in the Outbreak Room to discuss these latest developments was attended by Queen Pakize too, whose contribution led directly to the introduction of several new measures. With some people now falling sick or even dying from malnutrition, it was decided that the villagers' markets that had previously populated the city should be opened again, with the timing of the curfew adjusted accordingly. Although this provision would slow the decline in the city's death rate, the optimism that now characterized the island's political leadership did not dissipate. The representatives of the ferry companies had been arguing that the port must open again soon, and demanding to be allowed to return to their offices so that they could prepare for the return of the first ships and for the resumption of regular ferry services, both of which they claimed to be imminent. As most of these agencies were owned by the local consuls, Chief Minister Doctor Nuri was thus able to infer that it would not be long before the Great Powers' warships left and the blockade was lifted.

"If the British and French withdraw their warships, the *Mahmudiye* will be here bombing Arkaz well before any ordinary ferry journeys can resume!" said the Minister of Scrutinia.

In that moment, everyone thought again that if Mingheria was to maintain its "independence," either the blockade would have to remain in place, or the island would have to become a protectorate of one of the world's Great Powers.

During these meetings, Princess Pakize would often try to picture what her father would do in her position. Sometimes she would imagine that she herself was her father, and as she wrote in a letter to her sister, this would help her think more comfortably, more thoroughly, and more patiently about matters of state. As she sat at her writing desk, she would rub her forehead as her father used to do, or knit her brows, or rest her head against the back of the chair and stare at the ceiling in contemplation. Whenever she did any of these things, Princess Pakize felt that she both was just like her father and could continue to be herself, a state of mind she earnestly described in one of her letters to her sister.

Princess Pakize and Doctor Nuri dutifully continued to take the armored landau to a different neighborhood of Arkaz every day. With the outbreak now receding, these excursions had now become a kind of cautious celebration. The people of Arkaz didn't just love their queen for the bread, walnuts, prunes, and other provisions she brought them, but also because her visits seemed to have forced the plague into a retreat.

Whether they were visiting places like Turunçlar and Bayırlar, where Commander Kâmil had been especially popular, or Greek quarters like Dantela and Petalis, the occasional Mingherian flag would appear as soon as the armored landau arrived at the neighborhood square, and the women would all come to their windows to take a closer look at the Queen, lifting their children up so that she could see them too. It was said that any child the Queen touched or even smiled and waved at from afar would be blessed with good fortune. But there were all sorts of other rumors too, such as the one about her pomegranate colored headscarf, which supposedly augured a good year and meant the plague was bound to end; or that her eyes were always wet with tears even if it seemed from a distance that she was smiling; or about why her husband wasn't handsome (a fact usually blamed on Abdul Hamid's ill will).

The curfew was lifted from morning until the time for evening prayers. The decision to set the timings of the curfew against the call to prayer rather than the time on a clock was not—as some have claimed—a political decision influenced by religious considerations. Rather, most Muslim men on the island did not have a working pocket watch they could rely on, and had in fact been feeling somewhat disoriented ever since the Doctor and Prince Consort had banned church bells and calls to prayer again earlier in his reign. The first call to prayer to be heard on the island in thirty-five days was thus not a call to prayer at all, but a way of announcing to the city that the nighttime curfew was about to begin. Echoing between the cliffs, the call reminded everyone how quiet the port and the city streets had been for all that time. Two days later, on Friday, the fourth of October, the ban on entering mosques, churches, and other religious structures was also lifted.

The gradual return of those sounds that nobody had forgotten, but that most had probably despaired of ever hearing again, seemed to signal to everyone that their old life was slowly returning. At first, many people couldn't even believe it was happening. The greatest delight came from hearing carriage wheels turning, their bells ringing, the clacking of their horses' hooves. The coachmen who had died in the outbreak had been replaced by new ones who were just as kind to their horses as their predecessors had been, coaxing the animals up the steepest sloping roads with nothing but gentle words of encouragement and the occasional flick of the whip. Princess Pakize gave her sister a joyful account of how much it cheered her to hear the coachmen click their tongues or smack their lips and shout "Whoa" at their horses.

The cries of the seagulls, the crows, the doves, and all the other birds had never really subsided, but now they were joined by the calls of the first hawkers returning to the streets, the shouts of children playing outside, and the voices of people emerging from their homes to repair a door, a chimney, a crumbling wall. Princess Pakize listened to the thudding sound of women preparing for the arrival of winter by pounding the dust out of the carpets, kilims, and woven mats they had dangled out of their windows or brought out into the garden. Whether they were Muslim or Greek, they had begun to sing again as they hung their laundry up to dry.

As they traversed the city in the landau, the Princess and Prince Consort could tell from the sounds of the coppersmiths' hammers and the clink of the knife grinders' wheel that the market too must be coming back to life. Not all of the shops had opened yet, but many traders had already come out to sell eggs, cheese, apples, and other similar goods, compelled by the force of habit to advertise their wares as loudly as they would have done if the alleyways of the Old Market had been teeming with people. But in truth, although the mortality rate had now fallen to five or six a day, the streets remained mostly empty, and after all the suffering and death they had witnessed, people were still not quite at ease.

Around noon three days later (once again there had been about half a dozen deaths), during a spell of rain which had brought thunder and black clouds over the city, the Minister of Scrutinia Mazhar Effendi knocked on the Chief Minister's door, and following a rather intricate assortment of bows and other expressions of respect, he reminded Doctor Nuri of the statement Princess Pakize was supposed to issue on the subject of the tyrant Abdul Hamid. Once the outbreak had fully abated, the Great Powers' warships would of course leave, having accomplished their purpose of stopping the disease from infecting Europe. At that point Abdul Hamid's own soldiers and warships would arrive. In addition to the islands of the Dodecanese (including Kos, Symi, and Kastellorizo), several other islands across the Mediterranean Sea had gone back and forth in this way between Greece and the Ottoman Empire. Time and time again the flags hoisted upon their castles would change color, warships would bomb their cities and neighborhoods flat, people would die, and there would be a whole lot of needless suffering. The time had come to make a decision.

"The Queen is considering every possibility!" said Doctor Nuri, silencing Mazhar Effendi before he said anything else it wasn't his place to comment on. But before the rain had stopped, he went to the guesthouse on the same floor and told his wife—who was busy writing a letter—exactly what the Minister of Scrutinia had said.

"That man is plotting against us!" said Queen Pakize in a burst of intuition.

Doctor Nuri too could see how the Minister of Scrutinia had been working to bring every one of the state's returning employees under his own control. Government clerks, soldiers, and the newly restored Quarantine Regiment loved humble and hardworking Mazhar Effendi—who meanwhile no longer seemed to have any hesitation in disagreeing with Doctor Nuri and the Queen. He wished to see the ferry services resume, for instance, but was opposed to restoring the telegraph service, claiming that it would enable Abdul Hamid to interfere in the affairs of the island. In an effort to allow the port to open, the Minister of Scrutinia had also loosened a number of quarantine and isolation measures without consulting Doctor Nuri first. When Princess Pakize and Doctor Nuri had rebuked him for it, he had deflected their criticism with an elaborate display of modesty and deference. By this point they did not believe in his "sincerity" anymore.

Yet there were some matters on which Minister of Scrutinia Mazhar Effendi's views and the Queen's were aligned. They both nurtured a heartfelt affection and regard for the memory of Commander Kâmil, founder of the state, and his wife Zeynep. The Minister of Scrutinia's feelings on the subject might have been motivated by political imperatives. Mingherians were deeply grateful to Commander Kâmil for having freed the island from Ottoman control. As for the Queen, she felt there was something terribly romantic in the couple's love story, in the way the young Ottoman army officer had fallen for this stubborn, argumentative girl who had only recently refused to be someone else's second wife, married her, and started a revolution—all in a few short weeks. Throughout the course of more than one hundred years of the island's subsequent history, Kâmil and Zeynep's mythologized love and all of the various fictions created around it have served as a "cement" which has held the Mingherian nation together. Those who have expressed reservations about these myths, suggested they might be contrived, or even simply joked about their exaggerations, have often ended up in prison.

"If it weren't for the genius, valour, and determination of Commander Kâmil, the people of Mingheria would still be slaves to some other nation today," the Minister of Scrutinia would say. "Imagine—a whole nation slowly forgetting its language, then disappearing into nothing."

It was agreed to set funds aside for two new elementary and middle schools in Arkaz that would focus on Mingherian-language skills. Children in these schools would be taught Mingherian through simplified rewritings of the island's legends and history—from Homer to the romance between Commander Kâmil and Zeynep—collected in the textbook *Our Alphabet*. The Commander's and his wife Zeynep's childhoods would also be told in schoolbooks, recast as fairy tales. The girls' school would be called Zeynep's School, and the boys' school would be known as Kâmil's School. But after they got to middle school, the Queen suggested, boys and girls should be taught together. This somewhat-childish and unenforceable idea was of course far too "advanced" for its time, but it was at least agreed that the middle schools would be named Kâmil-Zeynep schools. At the Queen's insistence, the same name was also given to the Greek school with yellow shutters and pink walls in Eyoklima. Most of the Greek families who used to live in this leafy, shaded, and now deserted neighborhood had long since fled the island, replaced by prison and isolation fugitives and various other squatters.

A cut-and-paste image showing the Commander and Zeynep side by side would be used to illustrate the new Mingherian stamps and banknotes soon to be ordered from a printer in Paris. Meanwhile one thousand five hundred copies of the Commander's portrait were printed in the printing press of the *Arkata Times* and distributed by carriage and men on horseback to every government office on the island.

The Queen did not want any sort of confrontation with the island's Muslim and conservative areas. But she did have certain grievances she couldn't let go of. "How can a woman living in a free and independent nation still be entitled to less of an inheritance than her male peers?" she told her husband one day. "When religious precepts stipulate that a woman's testimony in court is worth only half of a man's, how is that anything but bigotry in disguise?"

Chief Minister Doctor Nuri agreed with his wife's observations, and when he relayed them to the Minister of Scrutinia, he did not meet with any objections. Nor did the minister resort to any of those arguments—"What do women know about commercial law anyway!"—that aging sect leaders and holy men would often make. Two days later, on the ninth of October (when only three deaths were recorded), the new rights granted to women were summarized in dry legal language in an announcement published in the *Arkata Times*—now also serving as the state's official gazette. There was no mention anywhere in the newspaper to indicate that these "reforms" had been introduced upon the will and instigation of the Queen. This was how the notion of "secularism," which would remain a subject of debate among Mingherian Muslims for the next one hundred and sixteen years, first entered the island's history.

On the sixteenth of October, there were no plague deaths on the island. As the island's effective ruler, Mazhar Effendi was rather nervous, for this meant that the blockade would soon be lifted. Whenever they went out in the armored landau, the Queen and the Chief Minister were greeted in every neighborhood with an excitement bordering on rapture. The streets were filling up again, the shops had opened, and the people who'd fled Arkaz had started to come back. The swallows and starlings—who, according to Princess Pakize, could tell that the outbreak had ended—flittered about with ecstatic, exuberant chirrups. Fights kept breaking out between people returning to their homes and the squatters who'd taken over in their absence, or between furious traders whose shops had been looted and the villagers who'd come to settle in the city during the plague, and there were simply not enough policemen or Quarantine Regiment soldiers left to even attempt to intervene. But none of these problems could even begin to overshadow the feeling of euphoria that had brought the smiles back to everyone's faces, got children gamboling again, and had frail old men with one foot in the grave still skipping with joy—nor could anything dampen people's realization that the outbreak was coming to an end, and they would soon be able to return to their old lives.

CHAPTER 78

Before life on the island could truly go back to the way it had been before the plague, the ferries would have to start running again, and of course for that to happen, the Post Office would have to reinstate its telegraph services. On the nineteenth of October, a well-attended meeting Doctor Nuri had been chairing on this very subject was interrupted by the loud, shrill, and resonant sound of a ship's horn heard all over Arkaz.

Several ministers and consuls who had been sitting at the large table where the Quarantine Committee had previously gathered now leaped to their feet. Two people ran to the window. Some were trying to see if they could spot the ship without getting up from their seats when the horn went off again, this time in two longer blasts.

All the people gathered in the room next to the late Governor Sami Pasha's office were now filled with a great sense of anticipation. What ship was this? How had it got through the blockade? For every optimistic consul cheerfully trading bets to see who could guess the name of the ship and ferry company from the sound of its horn, there was another talking apprehensively of enemy invaders and impending massacres. There had been plenty of imperialist governments in the world that had sent vessels disguised as friendly freight ships but carrying armed and frenzied murderers tasked with slaughtering the rebellious natives of some distant colony. But surely a ship that had repeatedly blown its whistle to signal its approach, in a tune so melodious to the ear, couldn't possibly be hostile.

As the sound of the horn echoed between the cliffs of Arkaz, Princess Pakize was on the ground floor of the Ministerial Headquarters (the former State Hall), about to witness an altercation between two elderly lunatics known to everyone in the city—Chained Servet and the Greek madman Dimitrios. Ever since the end of the outbreak three days ago, people had started coming to the State Hall to visit the Queen, present her with gifts and petitions, or even just kiss her hand (some believed it was solely thanks to this twenty-one-year-old woman that the plague demon had finally been banished). Rather than have the municipal guards turn them away, the Queen had arranged instead for a dusty archive room that faced the inner courtyard to be cleared out, furnished with couches, chairs, and a walnut desk, and turned into a chamber where she could receive visitors, consider complaints and petitions, and meet her admirers.

Queen Pakize would spend two hours every day meeting her subjects in this room decorated with photographs of Commander Kâmil and Zeynep and a map of Mingheria. She would listen to people whose families had disappeared during the plague, who couldn't get the squatters out of their homes, who demanded to know where their relatives had disappeared to after being put in isolation, who had come to beg for help, money, or a job. Crotchety Süleyman Effendi wanted the never-ending land and water supply dispute he was embroiled in to finally be resolved. Some would show her sores and injuries they hadn't been able to talk to their doctors about during the plague, while others would request boats or even tickets to take them off the island as soon as possible. People would ask for their telegrams to be sent or their unpaid taxes to be written off, and some—like a cantankerous old lady from Turunçlar—even expected her to help them find their daughters a decent husband. The Queen, they had all collectively decided, was selfless, good-natured, and sincere.

Some of the people queuing up to meet their queen were what we might call "pure and genuine" fans. They did not want anything in particular, except to lay eyes on Princess Pakize, pay their respects to their queen, or hand her the figs and walnuts they'd harvested from their own gardens. The older of two young sisters who had come with their mother had blushed scarlet when she had seen the Queen and hadn't been able to get a single word out. The island's two elderly madmen fell into this category of fan too. After spending the whole summer at home and surviving the outbreak with the help of their families and grandchildren, they had finally, cautiously stepped outside, and rather than starting to argue as soon as they ran into each other, they had begun chatting like old friends, chuckling with relief at having made it through alive.

Like many others in the city, the two lunatics had gone to the State Hall to present the Queen—who was young enough to be their granddaughter—with poems they had written in Turkish, Greek, and Mingherian, and a wicker basket full of figs and walnuts they had picked from their own gardens. But as they waited in line, they had already begun surreptitiously elbowing each other, exchanging curses in three different languages. Some have suggested they must have been egged on by the people around them, while others have noted that it was through these exchanges of blows and profanities that they had endeared themselves to society to begin with, and so they simply did not know how else to behave.

The ferry had first sounded its horn just as the friction between the two old lunatics had begun to degenerate, to the Queen's great displeasure, into a loud and foul-mouthed squabble. When the Queen spoke to them, the two old men beamed at her "like two little boys," and glanced fleetingly at the blue sky as if they'd heard an incantation. Then the ship blew its horn a second and third time, and without saying a word to anyone, the Queen got up, walked up the wide, carpeted staircase followed by clerks, guards, and porters bearing gift baskets, and returned to her room, where she stood at the window to see if she could spot the ship.

The *Enas* was a small rust-red cargo-and-passenger ship from Crete. Operating mostly along the Crete–Thessaloniki–Smyrna triangle, it only rarely came to Mingheria. As soon as she saw the ship, which despite its small, squat captain's cabin, and its short, plump chimney, still struck a rather majestic and imposing figure, the Queen felt that same aching sorrow she had always experienced when gazing out of the windows of the Çırağan Palace at the boats sailing down the Bosphorus and the passenger ferries traveling from the Black Sea to the Mediterranean Sea: life as it was meant to be lived was not inside these rooms she was confined to, but in some other realm she could reach if only she could get on a ship and sail to it.

But at least when she was looking at the ships from the palace windows in Istanbul, her father would be nearby, or she would be surrounded by his possessions and be able to smell his scent in the air. As she pined for Istanbul and her father, she sought to distract herself by starting a new letter to her sister, in which she also wrote that she was aware of the immense responsibility she bore toward Mingheria, and that she felt gratified about how much "the natives" loved her. The Queen thought it unfair that Muslim men could have as many as four wives and divorce any one of them at any time just by saying "I divorce you!" thrice. Her plan, as she wrote to her sister, was to rectify this too at the first opportunity. She was sure that her father would be proud of her if he knew the things she had done and still intended to do.

The rust-colored ship Princess Pakize had watched as it slowly neared the harbor had been guaranteed safe passage past the Great Powers' warships thanks to arrangements made by the British consul in Crete. The ship was carrying belated medical supplies, tents, and hospital beds, three doctors (two of whom were Muslims), and around forty Mingherians—most of them Greeks—who had fled to Crete at the start of the outbreak.

Interpreting the arrival of the *Enas* as proof that the plague was definitely over, many people stopped whatever they had been doing and gathered at the docks in a celebratory mood. The Queen watched closely as the rusty vessel dropped anchor and two rowboats set out from the docks toward it. The crowds gathered at the shore immediately began trading rumors about the precise nature of the vessel and how it had managed to reach the island, and the prevailing theory soon became that the blockade must have been lifted long ago.

It was only three hours after the first passengers had made it ashore that Chief Minister Doctor Nuri was able to speak to his queen and tell her that the ship was "friendly," and that it had been able to reach the island in light of a temporary agreement between her uncle and the British government. (He could see in her expression that this mention of her uncle had not evoked anger in her, but only a longing for Istanbul.)

As arranged by the Minister of Scrutinia, the ship's most significant passenger was a jolly French journalist with an enormous nose whose efforts had been instrumental in the publication of the various articles about Mingheria that had recently appeared in the French and British press. The plan was for this man to conduct the interview the Queen had previously been asked to give on the subject of how Abdul Hamid had imprisoned her father, her sisters, and her whole family, and of course on how she had since become—by some fortuitous historical accident—the queen of a sovereign state. Both *Le Figaro* and the London *Times* would feature this interview prominently, and according to the Minister of Scrutinia, this would prepare the ground for the British to protect the island from Abdul Hamid. Consul George had also suggested that the Queen be reminded once more of her well-known distaste for religious fanaticism and any practices that discriminated against women.

"Tell me, sir, why did we come to this island?"

"We still do not know why your uncle put us in the delegation to China!"

"But we were sent here after the murder of poor Bonkowski Pasha—may he rest in peace!—with orders from my uncle to rescue the island from the plague and solve the mystery of Bonkowski's killing, were we not?" said the Queen, addressing her husband in a tone that may have been slightly condescending, but was also edifying and full of tenderness.

"Indeed, and by the grace of God we succeeded in our aim, which is why the people of this island have chosen you for their queen."

"I have yet to fully comprehend why they made me queen. But what I do know, my lord, is that we were not sent here to tear this land away from Ottoman rule and hand it over to the British. I also know that if we were to do that, I could no longer even dream of returning to Istanbul and seeing my beloved sisters and my dear father ever again."

"Even now it would be difficult for us to return."

"I am well aware of that," said the Queen. "Though everything we have done here has been to stop the outbreak. Let us stay for a little longer. We have a moral obligation to these people who have taken me into their hearts and made me their queen! Far from gossiping about my uncle with some French journalist, all I want to do right now is to sit in the ironclad with you"—that was how they referred to the landau in private—"and go to Dikili, Kofunya, and Upper Turunçlar to help all those people there who need our assistance."

The big-nosed French journalist whose arrival to the island had been arranged via telegraph through the joint efforts of Mazhar Effendi and Consul George assumed the Queen was simply being coy. While he waited for her to come round, he immediately began gathering material for all the other articles he planned to write on the history and attractions of the island, the Castle and its famous dungeons, and of course on the plague itself. When he found out that the Ottoman officials who had been sent to the Maiden's Tower on the pretext of quarantine measures had been held there, and in rather harsh conditions, for the last one hundred and ten days, the journalist asked for the Queen's permission to go and visit those "Turks." The Queen accepted his request and decided she would go to the Maiden's Tower too, so that she could see for herself what was happening there.

Two hours later, in the middle of the afternoon, Princess Pakize and Doctor Nuri arrived at the Maiden's Tower in a convoy of three row-boats. News of the Queen and Chief Minister's visit had been conveyed in advance, yet when they reached their destination, nobody came to greet them apart from the elderly Greek clerk who was in charge of the place, and his boxer dog. Of the sixty or so government officials (some-times referred to as "the Turks") who had remained loyal to Istanbul and the Sultan after the declaration of independence one hundred and thir-teen days before, and been sent to the Maiden's Tower from Arkaz and from villages all over the island for refusing to collaborate with the new Mingherian government, more than half had perished. All those officials who had been hoodwinked, during the island's early days of "Freedom," by Sami Pasha's assurances that "the Mingherian state was fair!" into rejecting the sizable salaries they were being offered, and openly admit-ting their wish to return to Istanbul, had soon been made to pay the price for their candor.

Initially their punishment had consisted of being confined—allegedly for quarantine purposes—to that small, rocky islet, barred from return-ing to Istanbul, and with nothing to do but sit and wither away on its narrow, sunbaked cliffs. But as more and more officials loyal to Istanbul started to arrive from other parts of Mingheria, and the plague began to spread, this tiny quarantine island soon transformed into a kind of hell. The only reason why half of its inmates were able to survive being crammed together at such close quarters was because the other half had died (their corpses nudged from a rocky crag into the currents of the Mediterranean Sea). It was during this dreadful time that the impris-oned officials learned that the Mingherian authorities were planning to use them as bargaining chips in their efforts to reach a settlement with Abdul Hamid.

A few of the "hostages" in the Maiden's Tower had thought of seizing the rowing boat that kept coming and going from the islet and using it to escape. The rest preferred to stay put, hoping that the Ottoman warship *Mahmudiye*, which was participating in the naval blockade, would soon come to their rescue. But in the meantime, they kept dying, struck down by plague, hunger, and heat, worn out from fighting and arguing among each other, and by the terrible conditions they were having to endure. Many experienced Ottoman officials who had stayed true to Abdul Hamid—including Mayor Rahmetullah Effendi and the Chief of Charitable Trusts Nizami Bey, a pair Sami Pasha had particularly disliked—had thus lost their lives en masse during the first week of Sheikh Hamdullah's reign.

The only person who had survived this massacre with his health and sanity intact was Hadi, the deputy of the new governor who had been killed before he could take office. In his memoirs, Hadi wrote about the Queen and her husband's visit to the Maiden's Tower in that same condescending, contemptuous tone that the founders of the modern Turkish Republic would employ when referring to the last Ottoman sultans, to Ottoman princes and royal consorts, and to the Ottoman dynasty as a whole. In Hadi's view, Princess Pakize and Doctor Nuri were nothing but a pair of stuck-up, oblivious snobs whom palace life had left completely detached from reality, and who had become pawns in the hands of foreign powers.

Most of the people who had been locked away in the Maiden's Tower and died there before they could make it back to Istanbul had spent their last breaths on earth cursing the old governor Sami Pasha who had imprisoned them there and taken the island away from Ottoman rule.

Like any responsible queen would have done in her place, Princess Pakize felt guilty and ashamed as she listened to the accounts of the suffering these Ottoman "martyrs" had experienced. She wrote to her sister that as soon as she saw these hostages loyal to Istanbul, these prisoners who had been reduced to skin and bones by hunger and squalor, their eyes bulging out of their sockets, all she wanted to do was plead with the French journalist not to "embarrass Mingherians and Turks alike" by reporting on their conditions. Back when he was still only a prince, her father Murad V had impressed many a European journalist with his fluent French. But Princess Pakize was unsure about her own French. Nor could she really tell the big-nosed journalist "Don't write about what you've seen in the Maiden's Tower and the wretched conditions endured by the Turkish government officials" when she had just rejected his request for an interview on "the Sultan and his daughters held captive in the harem." As she wrestled with these conflicting emotions, the Queen fell silent. She understood that she was caught between the sense of duty she felt toward the island and her hopes of returning to Istanbul one day, and perhaps that was why she was feeling so ashamed.

As they were walking toward the rowing boat that would take them back to the city, the Queen turned toward her husband the Chief Minister and, within hearing distance of all those present, issued the following order:

"Before it sets sail, the rusty Cretian vessel about to weigh anchor from the waters off of the Castle shall stop by the Maiden's Tower first to pick up any passengers wishing to go back home to Istanbul!"

CHAPTER 79

As the rowboat made its way back from the Maiden's Tower to the port, Princess Pakize's eyes roamed of their own accord over the Ministerial Headquarters—the former State Hall whose guesthouse she had been living in—until they found the window where she had sat writing her letters every day. In that moment, she felt as if she were seeing herself from the outside, and discovering how narrow and limited her view of the world had been over the past one hundred and seventy-six days (she had counted them all).

Even more surprising was that she realized only *now*, as she sat in that rowboat, that the island's steep, sheer crags and the monumental White Mountain had been right there behind her all that time. Surely it was impossible for a person not to be influenced by the proximity of such a colossal presence—whether or not they could see it! The Queen had just begun to wonder how the White Mountain might have affected her letters when she was overcome by the sight of that same mountain reflected in the calm mirror of the sea. Just like the day she had first arrived on the island, she could see the rocks at the bottom of the sea, the swift, spiky, fist-sized fish, the aging, absentminded crabs, and star-shaped strands of green and blue seaweed.

Back at the guesthouse, Princess Pakize could not seem to emerge from that feeling of sadness she had been nursing. When the rust-tinged Cretian boat weighed anchor an hour later, then dropped it again in the waters near the Maiden's Tower to pick up the Ottoman officials there, her husband the Chief Minister walked into the room. Together they peered into the distance to see if they could glimpse the last of the tired, haggard Ottoman clerks preparing to make their way back to Istanbul as their bundles, their bedraggled suitcases, and all their remaining possessions were loaded onto the vessel to Crete.

"The Ottoman Empire loses another territory, and its officials withdraw from this island too!" Doctor Nuri observed impassively. "Would you have liked to be on that boat to Istanbul?"

"As long as my uncle remains on the throne, it will be difficult for us to return to Istanbul."

So it was that the question of "treason," which would trouble and torment them until the end of their lives, took on the new form and the more benign designation of "returning to Istanbul."

"Istanbul will no doubt applaud you for your role in allowing these poor men to finally be reunited with their families!" said Doctor Nuri. "But Abdul Hamid and the Ottoman state's enemies here will never stop troubling you."

"When you say Istanbul, you mean my uncle . . . ," said the Queen. "But we did not set the imprisoned clerks free to do my uncle or the Great Powers a favor! We did it because after the injustice they have suffered, it was our human duty to send these brave, steadfast Ottoman subjects back to their homes! It is thanks to these loyal, selfless subjects that the Ottoman state founded by my forefathers has endured for six hundred years."

Stirred by the weight of these words, they were quiet for a time. Once the Cretian ship mooring in the waters by the Maiden's Tower far away in the distance had finished boarding all its passengers, it blew its horn three times, just as it had done when it had first arrived. Doctor Nuri saw that the Queen's yearning for Istanbul had brought tears to her eyes, and he tried to comfort her.

"Even if we could return to Istanbul, we would be your uncle's prisoners there, just like everybody else," he said. "But here, we are still the Queen and her Chief Minister, and we can continue to be of service to this beautiful island and its noble people."

"But as soon as the plague is gone, so too will be the blockade!" said the Queen. "I wonder what will happen then." As if to avoid thinking of the answer to her own question, she then suggested the very thing she most wanted to do in that moment. "Let's get in the ironclad and go on a trip to Dantela and Flizvos!"

Perhaps the Queen could sense that these were to be their last outings in the landau, for her letters from this period often spoke of the children playing hide-and-seek in the lush green gardens of Hora; of the delicate, lacelike streets of Germe; and of the drinking water in Tatlısu, sweeter than in the Beykoz and Çırçır springs near Istanbul. She wrote about the spectacular view from the meadow set aside in Turunçlar for the Commander's mausoleum; the cats combing their fur for fleas as they sunbathed on the steep steps that led from the Kadirler neighborhood down to the sea; the vases of roses that adorned the colorful tables spilling out onto the pavements from the coffeehouses, restaurants, and pastry shops along Istanbul Avenue; and the mullet and mackerel they saw following their horses all along the harbor under the flat surface of the sea outside the landau, each charming scene lovingly described as if she wished to make sure she would never forget it.

On the fifteenth of November, the *Arkata Times*—controlled by the Minister of Scrutinia—reported to the public on the Queen and the Chief Minister's landau trips in an article that took up half of the newspaper's front page. The piece praised the courageous queen who was willing to go all the way to people's doorsteps to bring them gifts and hear about their troubles and had even been prepared to brave the perils of the plague to do so. The tone of the article was admiring and respectful, but toward the end, it also betrayed a touch of disappointment: the Queen had been giving out gifts and parcels of salted fish and crackers during a stop in Arpara one day, but although the neighborhood children had desperately wanted to talk to her, they had not been able to do so, for she did not speak Mingherian. A woman had carried her blue-eyed daughter to her beloved queen's lap so that she might stroke the child's hair for a little while, and after tearfully explaining that she was still waiting for the compensation payment she had been promised for the damage that had been done to her home when her husband had died during the outbreak, that she was alone in the world, and that she had nobody else to turn to but her queen, the poor woman had been heartbroken to realize that because she had been talking in Mingherian, the Queen—who did not speak the language—hadn't understood a word she'd said. The article also noted that the Queen had a heart of gold, that the public was understandably saddened when they realized that despite all the affection they had shown her, she did not speak the people's language, and that this in turn explained why most of the Queen's excursions over the past few weeks had been limited to streets and neighborhoods where people spoke Turkish, Greek, and even French—to those parts of the city, in other words, that were comparatively wealthier.

As he read the article out to his wife inside the Chief Minister's office, Doctor Nuri did not hide his displeasure, and suggested that the Minister of Scrutinia must be behind this. But with her characteristic innocence and hopefulness, the Queen told her husband that the criticism was constructive and justified, and that from now on, it would be more appropriate for them to focus their visits to poorer neighborhoods where Mingherian was more widely spoken.

The next day, they changed their plans (informing guards and photographers accordingly) and went to the Kadirler neighborhood instead. This visit was a success, thanks to the Queen's conscientious and convincing efforts to use the handful of old Mingherian words she had hurriedly learned, and to the antics of two lovable neighborhood boys who managed to make everybody laugh with their pitch-perfect imitations (down to the noises they made) of a nearby horse cart and its driver.

But the day after that, they had just stepped off their carriage in Turunçlar when two young men in their early twenties who had somehow found their way through the well-coached crowd came within earshot of the journalists, shouted "Mingheria belongs to the Mingherians!" twice, and ran away. Later, when they saw how forlorn the Queen looked as she listlessly handed out the gifts she'd brought, the women of the neighborhood tried to comfort the old sultan's daughter by telling her not to mind those rascals, but even so the crestfallen queen couldn't help taking the matter seriously and wrote a long passage to her sister Hatice in which she explained just how unfair the pair of youths had been: she had memorized twenty new Mingherian words a day ever since she'd become queen. She supported the Commander and Zeynep's love and their exalted ideals. Moreover, the fact that she had been born in Istanbul and was not yet entirely acquainted with the island's history, its culture, and the political dispositions and traits of its various tribes and populations was surely an element to be considered in Princess Pakize's favor, not vice versa. Precisely because her ancestry was "different from everybody else's," she could maintain an equal distance from everyone around her and make the most "objective" (she used the French term here), most appropriate decisions for every circumstance. Her forefathers had turned the Ottoman Empire into the world's greatest and most powerful empire thanks to how different they were from—not similar to!—the peoples and populations they ruled over.

"But my lady," her husband the Chief Minister had said one day, "perhaps it is also down to that same reason—to the fact that your ancestors were so unlike the populations they governed, and belonged to a different nation from all the people who lived under their rule—that the Ottoman Empire is now losing all its nations and islands one after the other."

Two days later, another article authored by the journalist Manolis and published this time in the Greek-language daily *Neo Nisi* picked up in a more critical tone on the points which had been made toward the end of the piece in the *Arkata Times* four days before: "As the Great Commander had already proven," the article argued, "the people of Mingheria are more than capable of governing themselves, and unlike those tiny, pitiful colonies in Asia or the Far East, they have no need for overlords who do not even speak their people's language, nor for any 'sultan's daughters'—especially not one whose father takes his orders from the international cabal of the Freemasons." Manolis's article also alluded to the Queen's popularity, but argued that the locals' fascination with her need not be given undue consideration, for "a sultan's daughter who has lived for years like a captive slave" would have been a topic of interest in any part of the world. The other thing to remember was this: "The Ottoman world, where women are confined to harems like caged birds and treated as slaves to their men or at best as graceful ornaments, and where everyone is subject to the will of Abdul Hamid, can never serve as a model for the Mingherian nation's shining future, for at long last, the people of Mingheria and the women of Mingheria are free!"

"This Manolis insults both me and my darling father!" said Princess Pakize. "You must please put a stop to it. I am neither a bird in a harem, nor a slave in a cage, but a queen. I will not allow for even one more person to see this article."

"Believe me, my princess, if I were to have this newspaper nobody reads confiscated from those three sellers who happen to stock it, it would only draw more attention to the matter, and soon people would be talking of nothing else. This must clearly have been written on Mazhar Effendi's behest, and nobody would be happier than he."

"I am the Queen of this country, and I have been granted that title by its people!" said Princess Pakize. "But if my orders are not to be heeded, then I shall not hold this position for a moment longer."

"Your foremost duty is to follow your husband's orders and defer to his will, as the rules of Islam dictate!" said Doctor Nuri, smiling at her.

Princess Pakize was incensed by her husband's toothy smirk, making light of the situation when his own wife was being slandered. But what she really couldn't abide was the realization that she couldn't even get her husband to follow her instructions. They had a long argument, after which they refused to speak to each other for a while and didn't go anywhere for two days. The Minister of Scrutinia had been handling most government business anyway. On the third day, the Queen—who had always relished their excursions in the landau—suggested they plan a trip to the most charming little seafront street in the calm, safe, and serene neighborhood of Dantela. Clerks, government officials, guards, and journalists were duly informed.

But just as they were about to get into the armored landau the next day, they were stopped by the Minister of Scrutinia Mazhar Effendi, who told them that there had been a report of a potential assassination attempt involving explosives. It would be best if they put their trips on hold for a time—no matter which neighborhood they'd decided to visit.

After Mazhar Effendi had left, the Queen told her husband that she did not believe this man—whose sole concern was the advancement of his political career—and that they had no obligation to do as he said.

"I have thought about this question at great length, my lady," said Doctor Nuri. "Should we ever be faced—God forbid—with a situation of danger or urgent need, we would be able to count on at least part of the civilian population to stand with us, but in terms of armed troops, we would probably have to rely on the heroic efforts of forty to fifty men at most. But one word from Mazhar Effendi and he would have a whole army at his disposal—the Quarantine Regiment, the municipal guards, the soldiers in the garrison, their reserves, and all the new recruits they've signed up."

"So are you saying that we are back to living as prisoners?" said Princess Pakize.

"Indeed, but you must not forget that you are still the Queen of Mingheria, and as long as that remains the case, the world shall gradually come to recognize you as the head of this sovereign state, and kneel before you. Already you have taken your place in history as the Queen who was able to stop Mingheria's fearsome plague before it could spread to Europe. In truth, Europe should be grateful to you."

Princess Pakize understood that those days of freedom during which she had been able to leave her room at will, walk around the city as she wished, and travel in her carriage to any neighborhood, observing the people, the houses, and everything else there was to see, had sadly come to an end. Soon there were guards at the guesthouse door again, just like under Sheikh Hamdullah's rule. This time there were always six or seven of them stationed there. Unlike their predecessors, these sentries did not nervously raise their rifles whenever the Queen and the Chief Minister tried to leave the room; they simply stood to attention and blocked their passage with their bodies. It seemed clear now that the island was effectively being ruled by Mazhar Effendi and the other ministers.

In the twelve days that followed, they never left their rooms. As the Queen did not see anything new during this period, she rarely wrote to her sister. But her mind and her soul were with the island's people and its far-flung neighborhoods. In a letter she took a whole five days to finish, she wrote to Hatice that she had suddenly become very curious about the murder mysteries their uncle Abdul Hamid had been reading for years. Might Hatice's husband, who used to stand behind a folding screen and read out novels to the Sultan, now make a list of those novels and their titles for Pakize's perusal?

As they sat in their rooms, they kept talking about how they might someday return to Istanbul, but could think of no other solution except to wait for Princess Pakize's uncle to forgive them. In the meantime, Mingherian newspapers continued to publish scornful, derogatory articles about the couple. (Some of the words and phrases more frequently used in these pieces included "courtier," "Ottoman," "harem dweller," "cage," "prisoner," "Turk," "colony," and "Freemason's daughter.")

On the fifth of December, one and a half months after the waning of the outbreak, Minister of Scrutinia Mazhar Effendi came into the guesthouse in the late afternoon to apprise them of what he deemed to be an "emergency": it seemed that the Great Powers, determined to lift the blockade, had come to an agreement with Abdul Hamid . . . There was a possibility that British and French ships might land in Arkaz that same evening, and that a battle might ensue. Of course nobody at the Ministerial Headquarters wished to see their esteemed guests fall victim to this sort of international skirmish. Accordingly, as soon as darkness began to fall, they would be taken to a secret location—whose whereabouts even they would not be told—north of Arkaz, unknown to any foreign powers and impossible for them to find.

First the armored landau and its retinue of guards would take them to Andin, and here they would be put on a boat which would carry them to their new home on the island. They must gather their belongings and be waiting at the entrance to the Ministerial Headquarters within two hours.

Princess Pakize would later write to her sister that it had taken them only an hour to get ready. They had been terrified. Their initial worry had been that they might be captured by the British (or the French), but when they saw no signs of unusual activity or any additional military presence in the Ministerial Headquarters and out on the streets of Arkaz, they realized that the threat must have been exaggerated. The landau, guided at a leisurely pace by Coachman Zekeriya, passed Pebble Cove and drove north in the night all along the eastern shore of the island.

The bumpy road rose and fell over the hills, curved toward sandy beaches, and looped between orchards. Through the windows of the carriage, they heard the thrumming of the trees, the ripple of a fountain, the patter of a hedgehog's paws. Then a full, silver moon appeared between the clouds, and they felt as if they were no longer in this world at all, but in some other, mysterious realm up above the black clouds.

A small cove appeared before them. The moon was reflected in silver shimmers over the calm surface of the sea. The carriage stopped, and for a moment, its passengers felt the boundless silence of the world.

A few sentries and boatmen and the guards in the carriage behind the landau emerged from the night to assist them. The Queen and the Chief Minister climbed down a narrow ledge to board a little rowboat that had been readied for them by the rocks at the edge of the seashell-and-kelp-scented cove, and after sailing out into the low waves for a short while, they were moved onto another, slightly larger vessel which had been waiting for them with their luggage on board. In this second rowboat, they noticed in the dark the figure of the Minister of Scrutinia Mazhar Effendi's secretary, sitting behind the oarsmen as he awaited their arrival.

As the boat sailed toward the open sea, the secretary gestured at the unbroken darkness and informed them that the *Aziziye* had arrived just before nightfall, and dropped anchor right over there.

Yes, he had indeed said "the *Aziziye*." The very same *Aziziye* that had brought them to Mingheria instead of China, and where they had seen Bonkowski Pasha. They stared at each other in silence, caught in a state of dreamlike confusion between fear, curiosity, and anticipation. As Princess Pakize would describe in her letters, they both suddenly felt like children again, about to be taken somewhere without anyone asking them whether they wanted to go.

Moments later, the dark silhouette of the *Aziziye* surfaced in the moonlight. The rowboat picked up speed and reached the platform at the foot of the white ladder hanging from the ship.

For a time, the shadow of the ship covered everything in darkness. Then Doctor Nuri saw their suitcases being lifted up onto the ship. Princess Pakize was just about to step onto the ladder when the Minister of Scrutinia's secretary stood up on the swaying rowboat and called out to them with a ceremonious air.

"Your Majesty! Your Excellency!" he began. "The *Aziziye* shall resume its travels from Alexandria, where you had left off, and continue on its journey to China." When the moon briefly illuminated their figures, he bowed to them in deferential greeting. "The people of Mingheria are in your debt!" he added, looking mostly at the Queen rather than at Doctor Nuri.

With these gratifying words, the Queen climbed the ladder and boarded the ship. The familiar Russian captain with his familiar solemn bearing had come out to greet them, and smiled when he saw them. The torches in the other cabins and in the guest hall where they'd had dinner with Bonkowski Pasha had all been lit, as if in reminder that this place was a realm of its own. As they were settling into the same mahogany paneled room with the gilded mirror and the smell of dust and leather where Princess Pakize and her husband had spent many a happy hour before, the ship began to move. The Princess stopped what she was doing and climbed onto the deck. She wanted to look out at the "inimitable" landscape of Mingheria, that same view which travel guides for the Levant have been recommending to their readers throughout the twentieth century.

As the *Aziziye* sailed along the ridge of the Eldost Mountains, stretching north to south across the island, Princess Pakize could see their sharp volcanic peaks. Then the moon slipped back behind the clouds, and everything was dark again. Princess Pakize was gloomily thinking that she would not be able to see Mingheria again when she noticed the pale blinking beam of the Arab Lighthouse in the distance. In that same moment, the moon surfaced from among the clouds, and she saw the Castle's pointed spires with the magnificent form of the White Mountain in the background. But this was only a glimpse, for soon the moon disappeared again. Princess Pakize gazed tearfully into the darkness, hoping she might see Mingheria again for one last time, before finally returning to her cabin.

Many Years Later

A ttentive readers may have noticed that I have been more understanding toward Princess Pakize and Doctor Nuri than anybody else in this book. I am their daughter's granddaughter. I
obtained my doctorate from the University of Cambridge on the subject
of the islands of Crete and Mingheria during the second half of the
nineteenth century, so it is only natural that I have been asked to edit
Princess Pakize's correspondence for publication.

After a stormy twenty-day journey, my great-grandmother Queen
Pakize and great-grandfather Doctor Nuri arrived with a six-month
delay to the port of Tianjin and traveled from there to Peking.

In the meantime, the Boxer Uprising—the reason the Ottoman
Guidance Committee had been sent to China in the first place—had
ended in victory for the Great Powers. The foreign invaders' armies,
assembled from many different nations, had crushed the Chinese people
and their soldiers with bloody force and looted Peking for days. The
Chinese rebels, including Chinese Muslims, who had been murdering
Christians on the streets the year before, were slaughtered in droves
by French, Russian, and German forces. (In the court of international
public opinion, the only open objection to this ruthless bloodshed, and
the savagery displayed by the invading armies to whom Abdul Hamid
himself had lent his symbolic support, had come from the novelist Leo
Tolstoy. "The greatest of novelists," as Virginia Woolf would later call
him, had denounced the Russian czar and the German kaiser Wilhelm
for the massacres committed by their troops and defended the insurgent
Chinese people.) Having exacted the deadly revenge demanded by Kaiser Wilhelm II, victor of the brutal war, the allied forces had invited the
mullahs of the Ottoman Guidance Committee to organize a series of

conferences instructing China's Muslims on Islamic history and culture, and on Islam's inherent pacifism.

Aware of all that had transpired on the island of Mingheria, of Abdul Hamid's reaction, and of the possibility that Princess Pakize and her husband the doctor might be accused of treason, the British had taken care to ensure that these two distinguished figures who had belatedly arrived to join the Guidance Committee wouldn't cross paths with the other Ottoman delegates, who had meanwhile begun to prepare for the return journey from China to Istanbul. Doctor Nuri was invited to various regions of China with Muslim populations to deliver a series of lectures on the subject of quarantine and Islam. Princess Pakize's lively letters from Yunan, Kansu, and Sinkiang contain many observations that would be of interest today to historians of East Asian culture.

The British and French doctors who heard about Doctor Nuri's lecture series, and remembered him from the international conferences they had all attended, invited him to join them in Hong Kong. Back then, the hospitals and laboratories the British had set up in these colonies were some of the world's most influential and innovative institutions in the global battle against the plague—both on the bacteriological front, and in terms of quarantine methods. In 1901, Alexandre Yersin was in Indochina, working on behalf of the Institut Pasteur in Paris to try and produce a serum which could be used as a vaccine (he would not succeed), but it had been in Hong Kong that he had first identified the plague microbe seven years before, and not in a British hospital—which, as a French citizen, he wasn't allowed to enter anyway—but in a much-more-improvised establishment. The plague microbe which struck Mingheria in 1901 had already killed hundreds of thousands of people in China since 1894. Many of the problems faced by Tung Wah Hospital, where Doctor Nuri soon began to work, were similar to those that had afflicted the Theodoropoulos and Hamidiye Hospitals too, and were also mostly caused by the public's ignorance (many local Chinese, no matter how sick they were, refused to even set foot in this hospital purely because it was run by the British), but there were some differences too, particularly in the understanding of quarantine measures.

The Princess and the Prince Consort rented one floor of an apartment building in Hong Kong's Victoria district, in a neighborhood inhabited mostly by British and European expatriates, and with a

near-perpendicular view over the sea—just like the view of the Bosphorus from Istanbul's Çamlıca Hill, as Princess Pakize would note in
the first letter she ever wrote from this apartment. They would end up
living in this place—which Princess Pakize had initially assumed would
serve as a "temporary" residence until their return to Istanbul—for a full
twenty-five years.

The only person in Mingheria Doctor Nuri remained in touch with
was the island's former quarantine master and current health minister, the goateed Doctor Nikos, whom Doctor Nuri had first met nine
years before during an outbreak of head lice in the Ottoman garrison
in Sinope. In a telegram they received from Nikos around this time,
they learned that the Queen and the Chief Minister's departure had
been kept secret from the people of the island and from the general
public for quite a while. The announcement had probably been delayed
in the hopes of securing some kind of protection from the British in the
meantime.

On the sixth of December, former Chief Scrutineer Mazhar Effendi
declared himself president of Mingheria with twenty-five blank shells
fired by Artillery Sergeant Sadri. At noon the next day, seven thousand
people gathered in Mingheria Square, formerly known as the State Hall
Square, for the most meticulously organized political pageant to have
ever taken place in the island's history. Joyous crowds watched a procession of high-school students waving tiny flags as they went, Mingherian
shopkeepers and the exceptionally well-drilled Quarantine Regiment
saluting the new president, and village girls from the mountainous
north performing folkloristic dances in traditional costumes. Stepping
out onto the balcony, President Mazhar declared that the republic was a
way of life, with liberty its nourishment and the sole and common goal
of all those who had gathered that day in Mingheria Square.

In those years, it was a habitual occurrence for kings and queens to
be overthrown in military-bureaucratic coups and for republics to be
declared straight afterward, but it was rare for an event of this sort to
unfold so quietly and with so little bloodshed. Mingherian historians of
the nationalist or "Marxist" persuasion have sought to add some drama
to this transition by characterizing it as a "democratic bourgeois revolution." But we can be sure that none of the developments which later took
place under President Mazhar's regime can be considered "democratic."

The new president and former Minister of Scrutinia, Mazhar Effendi, remained wholeheartedly committed to implementing the nationalist reforms introduced by the late Commander Kâmil, founder of the Mingherian state. During his first month in power, he arranged for a committee composed of the archaeologist Selim Sahir and the island's Greek and Muslim middle- and high-school teachers to standardize the Mingherian alphabet, which would start being taught in schools straightaway. Official documents prepared in the Mingherian script were to be given priority treatment in all government offices. (In practice, this was very difficult to achieve.) When a baby had been given one of the Commander's preferred Mingherian names, the Registry Office would issue their birth certificate immediately, while those who chose Greek or Turkish names for their child would encounter difficulties. President Mazhar had ordered every storefront to put up a sign with the shop's name spelled out in the new script. Greece and the Western nations had not paid too much attention to these reforms, but they did object to the harsh treatment President Mazhar meted out to the island's Greek and Rumelian nationalists. Soon after he took power, nearly forty Rumelian "luminaries," as well as twelve Muslim intellectuals who spoke Turkish at home and possessed extensive personal libraries, were accused of separatism and locked up in the Castle prison.

As a complement to this policy of Mingherianization, thousands of photographs of Commander Kâmil and Zeynep were printed and displayed with renewed enthusiasm all over the country. The Commander and Zeynep's meeting, their courtship, and the story of how they had finally been able to get married despite the many obstacles in their way, and all thanks to the Mingherian language, became the basis of elementary- and middle-school teaching. *The Mingherian Alphabet* and *Zeynep's Reading Book* were also very popular. Throughout all these cultural and political schemes, President Mazhar never sought to erase the memory of Princess Pakize's reign as queen and, on the contrary, Mingherian-history schoolbooks gave Queen Pakize's rule the humble and respectable position it deserved. To this date, every Mingherian is proud of the fact that the daughter of a sultan was once "queen" of the island and involved, however fleetingly, in its freedom and independence movement.

Not long after losing her throne to a coup just like the one that had ended her father's reign, Princess Pakize sat at her panoramic desk in Hong Kong and began penning a rather sorrowful letter to her sister Hatice. Having noted that her father Murad V's sultanate had lasted for ninety-three days, while she had been queen for one hundred and one days (from the twenty-seventh of August to the fifth of December 1901), Princess Pakize told her sister that she was curious to know whether her father knew about this, and that she missed them all very much. She should have been "perfectly content" in Hong Kong, where she could live as she wished to and walk freely all over the city, but she missed her sisters, her father, and Istanbul so much that she couldn't be happy and was able to alleviate her sense of longing only by writing these letters.

A year later, Princess Pakize would come to feel even lonelier in Hong Kong following a scandal her sister Hatice became embroiled in. Back in Istanbul, Hatice had been having an affair with Mehmed Kemalettin Pasha, the handsome husband of Abdul Hamid's favorite daughter, Princess Naime (Hatice's cousin), when the love letters they had been tossing each other over the garden wall had fallen into Abdul Hamid's hands. The Sultan had immediately separated his young, dashing son-in-law Kemalettin Pasha (who also happened to be the son of Gazi Osman Pasha, hero of the 1877–78 Russo-Turkish War) from his daughter Naime, stripped him of his rank, and exiled him to Bursa. (As this was also an important political development, the news even made it into the *New York Times,* and Pierre Loti wrote about it too.) Back then, Istanbul society was even more "rigid" than it is today, and rumors of the romantic rivalry between Princess Hatice and her cousin Princess Naime (whom the more spiteful gossips would often openly describe as "ugly" or "hunchbacked"), the two sultans' daughters whose waterside mansions in Ortaköy neighbored each other, quickly spread all over the city. House arrest in Bursa was of course a lighter sentence compared with conditions in the Ta'if fortress where Mithat Pasha had been sent, or the prisons of Sinope or Mingheria. The Sultan did not punish Princess Hatice, whom he had always been especially fond of ever since she had been a child, but he did keep her under close scrutiny for a time, during which it became much harder to correspond with her.

Rumors of the "scandal" did not reach Princess Pakize from Hatice but through other sources. After the foundation of the Turkish Republic, Istanbul newspapers would write that Princess Hatice had purposely arranged for the love letters to be handed to Abdul Hamid so that she could avenge her father by upsetting her uncle. Another theory put forward in this period was that Hatice had been sourcing rat poison from several different pharmacies and passing it to the Rumelian kitchen staff in her cousin's mansion next door so that she could have Naime poisoned and marry her husband. This gossip must have reminded Sultan Abdul Hamid once more that it was possible to use arsenic-laced ratsbane to poison people "without leaving a trace."

By now Princess Pakize knew that she would not be able to return to Istanbul until her uncle had forgiven her. But as she wrote to her sister some time later, there was one crucial difference between them: when Abdul Hamid had first met Princess Hatice, his own much-loved firstborn daughter Princess Ulviye had just died (accidentally setting herself on fire while playing with matches—a new invention at the time), and as he had not yet taken the throne, he had consoled himself by playing with his older brother's newborn daughter Hatice. But since Princess Pakize had been born after her father's confinement to the Çırağan Palace, her uncle Abdul Hamid had not known her as a child, and never even once sat her on his lap and played with her as he had done with Hatice.

Princess Pakize heard of her father's death in August 1904 from her sister. She spent many mournful months thereafter remembering her father's scent, how he would sit and read his books, the look of concentration on his face when he played the piano, and his musical compositions. If grief was one reason why Princess Pakize sent her sister fewer letters over the course of the next two years ("Istanbul is not the same Istanbul without our dear father," she had written on one occasion), the other was the arrival of her daughter Melike (my grandmother) in 1906, which kept her extremely busy. We have therefore based our forthcoming account of the following years largely on archival evidence and memoirs, rather than on her correspondence.

But first I would like to spend a few words on poor Murad V's funeral.

There is probably no episode more piteous in this book than the funeral of Princess Pakize's father, who died after twenty-eight years spent living in captivity. Given that he is one of my ancestors (my great-grandmother's father), I would like to speak now not as an objective historian, but as a sentimental novelist. Murad V's luckless life and his ephemeral and unsuccessful reign had caused a thirty-two-year delay in the introduction of the various constitutional, westernizing, emancipatory, and parliamentarianist reforms that Ottoman bureaucrats and statesmen had sought to introduce in order to secure the survival of the Ottoman state and empire, so that by the time these new freedoms were finally adopted, it was far too late, and the damage had long since been done. Murad's reformist father Abdulmejid had hoped to make him the Crown Prince, skipping Murad's uncle Abdülaziz in the line of succession, and had always nurtured high hopes for this "hapless" son of his, teaching him French and having the Italian pashas Lombardi and Guatelli give him music lessons. But as recounted by a harem lady whose recollections we have relied upon, Murad Effendi was struck at the age of fourteen by an illness which would leave his mind and memory permanently affected, and although he eventually recovered, its effects would still resurface from time to time.

The Neapolitan doctor Capoleone, who had come to treat the patient (and establish some fresh political ties too), recommended wine and cognac, and set up a "cellarette" in the young prince's mansion in Kurbağalıdere. Murad Effendi would end up drinking for the rest of his life. The dinners and musical entertainments he hosted in this Kurbağalıdere residence were attended by freedom-loving constitutionalist and parliamentarianist poets, journalists, and writers like Ibrahim Şinasi, Ziya Pasha, and Namık Kemal. In London, where he had momentarily feared that he had been poisoned, he had "befriended" Prince Edward, and when the British heir to the throne invited him to kiss Queen Victoria's hand when they next met, Murad had done so without fear of what his uncle might say. The young prince wrote letters pledging cooperation to Napoleon III and other notable figures he had met during this trip to Europe. He believed that the "nations" of Europe had vanquished their kings, and those kings had taken a step back. Ottoman sultans should do the same. But when he suddenly became sultan himself, those same things that would later also make his brother Abdul Hamid so anxious—conspiracies, attempted coups, and the memory of the assassination of their uncle Abdülaziz—had driven Murad mad. As a result, the government's bureaucrats had decided unanimously that he should be deposed. In the Yıldız Palace, where Abdul Hamid had initially confined him, Murad had leaped fully clothed into a pond. Another time, he had tried to flee by jumping out of a window. For years afterward, he would try to persuade his doctors that he had regained his sanity, and seek ways to take back the throne, but these ambitions and his attempts to escape would only serve to tighten the conditions of his twenty-eight-year captivity. Lords and pashas sent from the Yıldız Palace would barge into his bedroom at night, torch in hand, and once they had made sure he was exactly where he was supposed to be, they would bow before the former sultan and admit just as they were leaving that they'd hurried over to check he was still there after Abdul Hamid had received reports that Murad V had been sighted in Beyoğlu. Seeing danger everywhere, the deposed sultan was constantly changing the location of his bedroom. But bearing in mind that he was surrounded at all times by sixty or seventy enslaved concubines striving for his attention, we who live in our modern world—as Henry James wrote—cannot realistically be expected to understand him, let alone feel sorry for him. His diabetes had worsened in his final years, and he had been worn out by his daughter Hatice's scandalous romantic entanglements—which he still couldn't quite believe—as well as by the intermediaries Abdul Hamid would constantly send over to ask, "How should I punish your daughter?" (He never did punish her.) Upon Abdul Hamid's orders, the former sultan's death was announced with a small statement in the newspapers. The people of Istanbul who had gathered on Galata Bridge and at Sirkeci Station to attend the funeral were not allowed to approach the New Mosque. The former sultan's body was transported from the Çırağan in the steamboat *Nahit* and hastily buried next to his mother, whom he had visited every morning to pay his respects and talk about politics, and who had always called him "my lion!" With so many rumors going around that Murad V wasn't dead at all, but that he was going to be disinterred immediately after the burial, smuggled out to Europe, and put back on the throne, Abdul Hamid—who had already told all his ministers to attend the funeral—had also sent his own "personal" aide to the ceremony. This aide "whose name would forever live in infamy" had boldly stepped up to the corpse, dug his finger into its hair, and pulled as hard as he could, only letting go when he had made sure that the old sultan was definitely dead.

On the third Friday of July 1905, a large bomb placed inside a car which had been parked near the route Abdul Hamid always took during his public appearances for Friday prayers at the Yıldız Palace exploded with a bang that was heard all over Istanbul, and even as far as Üsküdar. The Sultan had just slowed down to talk to the Ottoman Empire's chief Islamic scholar, the Shaykh al-Islam, who had asked him a question, and with his passage thus delayed, he escaped the explosion unscathed. The metal shrapnel flung out in the conflagration killed twenty-six people, and wounded many more, including several diplomats and the curious crowds who would come every Friday to look at the Sultan. The driver of the car containing the bomb and shrapnel was also killed in the explosion.

Within a week, Abdul Hamid's policemen and torturers had discovered that the assassination plot was the work of revolutionary Armenian separatists who had been preparing explosives in France and Bulgaria for quite some time. The torturing investigators had also swiftly identified the adventurous Belgian anarchist Edward Joris, who had been hiding the bombs in his house. This romantic anarchist who had worked on the main street in Beyoğlu in the first-ever Singer shop, and had devised successful sales strategies that had brought the sewing machine to the Ottoman Empire's remotest mountain villages, was thus sentenced to death, but the Belgian king put so much pressure on Abdul Hamid that the execution was never carried out. After two years in prison, Joris was pardoned by Abdul Hamid and returned to Europe as the Sultan's spy.

While composing these closing pages of our book, we have often been seized by the impression that many of the defining political developments that took place in the Ottoman Empire after 1901 carried the traces and influences of the Mingherian Revolution. Perhaps we have allowed ourselves to get so carried away by the rich history of our little island that we have begun to see Mingheria wherever we look.

Once the British, French, and Russian ships that had been surrounding the island had sailed away, and with no other nation formally recognizing the Mingherian state, Abdul Hamid could have followed the example of the British in Alexandria and sent the warship *Mahmudiye* to bomb the garrison, the Ministerial Headquarters, and the whole of Arkaz, yet he did not do this. On paper, Mingheria was still an Ottoman province, and before any foreign nation—such as the French, say—could think of landing their troops on the island, they would need to make a pact with the British first, and be willing to risk an armed conflict with the Ottoman Empire. Nor did Abdul Hamid, or indeed the Ottoman fleet, have any great desire to bombard the island, send soldiers in, and install a new governor. Any resistance the Ottoman navy and army might encounter in Mingheria could easily become a pretext (just as the plague had been) for the Great Powers to invade the island or for the British to take over as they had done in Cyprus, all in the name of protecting the island's Christian population.

President Mazhar's policy of maintaining good relations with nearby states, including the Ottomans, was influential in the preservation of the island's "independence" after the lifting of the blockade. Also significant were the "reforms" with which he transformed the Quarantine Regiment into a modern army. Two years of compulsory military service were introduced, and within four years, the regiment numbered twenty-five hundred new recruits. Formed of people who spoke Mingherian at home, as well as Greeks and Muslims who had proven their loyalty to the new state, this army's spiritual foundations rested on the vivid, poetic Mingherian nationalism espoused by the Commander and spread with great creativity across the island by Mazhar Effendi.

The twenty-eighth of June, the date when the Commander stood on the State Hall balcony and started the Mingherian Revolution, was chosen as Independence Day (and declared a public holiday). The yearly celebrations would begin with the Quarantine Regiment parading from the garrison to Mingheria Square with traditional postmen's flat caps on their heads and mailbags over their shoulders, singing "The Commander Is Here!" and some of Mingheria's other newly composed marches. For an hour, the entire Mingherian army would file past the balcony where President Mazhar would sit (on a well-concealed, tall-legged chair) and watch their progress. This would be followed by a much-enjoyed and highly anticipated display from high-school students (described with great relish by Western newspapers too), and anthropologists today agree that their performances were a vital component not just of Independence Day celebrations but of a sense of Mingherian identity too.

The performance would begin with one hundred twenty-nine high schoolers walking out into the square, each carrying a big white sign made of cloth and embroidered with a word spelled out in large Mingherian letters. These were the same one hundred twenty-nine Mingherian words the father of the nation, the immortal Commander Kâmil, had spoken in his room in the Hotel Splendid during the last two hours of his life, as recorded by the clerk who was with him at the time. As soon as the high-school girls and boys, all wearing their school uniforms, had taken up their positions in the square, there would be a round of applause, quickly followed by an expectant silence. What marvelous sentences would the students compose, and which of the Commander's wondrous final words, those phrases he had uttered ("My Mingheria is my paradise and your soul"; "Mingheria belongs to the Mingherians"; "My heart is in Mingheria always!") like lines of poetry descended from God, would they remind their audience of this year? As they strode around the square, switching places and forming new sentences with the words they carried, the young students would be cheered on by the spectators, and the President, sitting on the balcony with his wife, would watch them with tears in his eyes. Meanwhile, around two hundred people (one hundred and fifty Greeks, and sixty Muslims) who had regrettably not quite embraced this nationalist, republican spirit and remained stubbornly attached to Greece or to the Ottoman Empire, had been placed in an educational camp near the town of Andin. Others had decided they would prefer to work on the construction of roads and bridges rather than face the education camp. President Mazhar had imposed heavy taxes on those wealthy residents (mostly Greeks) who, having fled to Athens and Smyrna after the revolution, had yet to return, while the rich who had stayed on the island themselves but kept defying the government by banking their money in Athens or Smyrna had been forced for a time to work on roadbuilding projects—until the publication of several articles about "forced labor in Mingheria!" in the Greek and European press led to this particular policy being abandoned.

During this time, in one of life's strange symmetries, Arthur Conan Doyle—creator of Sherlock Holmes—had just got married again and come to honeymoon in Egypt, the Greek islands, and Istanbul, where many of the events in our book have taken place. In Istanbul, Abdul Hamid presented him with a badge of the Order of Mecidiye, while his wife was given a less prestigious award. The British admiral Henry Woods (also known as Woods Pasha), who served for a time as the Sultan's aide-de-camp, would later write in his memoirs that he had witnessed the medal ceremony during which the Sultan finally met the great writer he so deeply admired, but this was not true. When he found out about Doyle's interest in visiting the Yıldız Palace, and how insistent the writer had been in this request, the Sultan had begun to worry that his palace might become the setting for the next Sherlock Holmes novel, and although he would award the visitors their badges anyway, he had canceled the ceremony at the last minute, using the holy month of Ramadan as his excuse.

During the days of plague, Princess Pakize would often compose as many as three or four long letters a week, but in 1907 Princess Pakize wrote from Hong Kong to her sister Hatice just twice, and only once in 1908, the year her second child Süleyman was born. She had a maid at home, and an English-speaking male servant to run her errands, but with two sickly children to look after, her ties with the world outside her home had all but severed. In one of her letters she wrote that Doctor Nuri would go on inspections to distant neighborhoods sometimes, but that the pace of the outbreak in Hong Kong had slowed, and there were far fewer people dying now than there had been three or four years ago.

A topic that was mentioned in each of the three letters from those two years was Princess Pakize's determination to read her way through her sister's lists of "Abdul Hamid's favorite" crime stories and novels (starting with the Sherlock Holmes mysteries), which she would borrow from the English library in Hong Kong. In her 1908 letter to Hatice, she did not tell her sister why she was doing this (it was to see if she could understand how Doctor Ilias's killer had thought to conceal the pharmacies and herbalists he had bought the poison from) quite as openly as she had spoken to Doctor Nuri about it. This reticence was probably due to how close Hatice had grown to their uncle Abdul Hamid, who had not only forgiven her, but also made sure she was invited to palace functions—as if to indicate to society at large that his niece had been entirely blameless in the scandal. After the death of their father, Princess Pakize might have sought to take advantage of Hatice's rapport with the Sultan, but not once did she write to her sister to ask if she could mediate on her own and her husband's behalf to help clear them of the charge of treason. Perhaps she did not think Hatice was close enough to Abdul Hamid to demand such a thing; another possibility is that she did not feel she could trust Abdul Hamid even if he did "forgive" her, and that welcoming such a pardon would be a betrayal of her father's memory.

Princess Pakize heard about Abdul Hamid's restoration of the constitution, the reconvening of the Chamber of Deputies, the Thirty-First of March Incident, and the Action Army landing from Thessaloniki to depose her uncle (Abdul Hamid) and replace him with her younger uncle Reşat, all from the English newspapers she read in Hong Kong. Neither Princess Pakize nor her husband had the slightest difficulty in picturing the angry, organized mobs streaming out of Istanbul mosques to butcher freedom-loving, reformist, and westernized writers on the streets; the artillery and machine-gun battles between the Action Army from Thessaloniki and the soldiers stationed in the Maçka Barracks near the Imperial Bacteriology Institute and in the barracks near Taksim Square; the three ringleaders of the rebellious "Sharia fanatics" dressed in white execution gowns and hanged from modern three-legged gallows in the always busy Eminönü Square, where they would be left to swing in the breeze for three days as an example to the whole of Istanbul; and the chants of "Liberty, equality, fraternity"—with the addition of "justice"—ringing in the air.

The introduction of new freedoms, the removal of Abdul Hamid, and the amnesty for political prisoners had made the idea of "returning to Istanbul" seem once more like a reasonable proposition. If they were to go back to Istanbul, would they be in trouble for what had happened in Mingheria? In those days the officials of the swiftly unraveling and severely indebted Ottoman Empire were operating in a state of such uncertainty that a friend Doctor Nuri had sent letters and telegrams to in search of an answer to this very question, and indeed to find out what might be happening behind the scenes, had in turn heard from his own friend at the Ministry of Justice that perhaps the most suitable course of action was for the pair to return "without saying anything to anyone"—for these kinds of cautious inquiries were often seen by registry clerks and department heads as opportunities to extract prodigious bribes, or interpreted as the misguided actions of guilty malefactors foolishly alerting the authorities to their imminent arrival.

But the idea of returning to Istanbul unprepared—and quite out of the blue—did not sit well with either of them. Of course Princess Pakize owned property in the city (including her mansion on the shore of the Bosphorus), and Doctor Nuri had his marriage allowance and his government salary waiting for him in the treasury coffers, as well as other sources of revenue, but on the other hand, the idea that they had committed "treason" may well have etched itself into their enemies' minds. They could claim their rightful assets whenever they chose to return to Istanbul. But in the meantime, Doctor Nuri's uncommon abilities had secured him a considerable income both from the British colonial administration in Hong Kong, and from his work with local hospitals as a consultant on quarantine measures. Besides, the thought of getting on a ship with their three-year-old daughter and their surly, irascible one-year-old son for a journey that might last for several weeks (they might even have to quarantine at some point!) was more than they could face.

Princess Pakize might not have said as much in any of her letters, but my intuition also tells me this: she loved her husband, their rowdy children, and the life they led in their home, which smelled permanently of food, steam, and soiled nappies. Had she been in Istanbul, she would have ended up the same as everyone else around her, standing in a corner like a faded rose, and living a seemingly more glamorous but ultimately less vibrant life. Princess Pakize had realized long ago that her husband was not like the other princes and royal consorts who would be satisfied with attending receptions for the rest of his life (going to those parties that were arranged to raise money for charities and public health institutions). In truth they were both content with the sheltered "bourgeois existence" they conducted in Hong Kong, far from everyone else and with servants attending to their needs, and even though Istanbul had been "liberated," and Abdul Hamid removed from the throne, they did not feel safe enough to return.

In the eleven short letters she sent to her sister during the five years between 1909 and 1913, Princess Pakize always wrote about the same things, telling her sister that all was well with her and the children in Hong Kong, that her husband was working very hard, and that she was busy doing housework and reading novels. From the questions she asked in her letters, we can surmise that Princess Pakize was not aware of what was happening in Istanbul and in Arkaz.

We shall therefore look to other sources for a brief overview of some of the events that took place in Istanbul and Arkaz during those five years.

The story of the last ten years of the Ottoman Empire is also the story of the vertiginous rate at which it lost all the territories, the countries, and the islands that had been shown on the map of the Empire hanging in the *Aziziye's* main cabin.

In the days after the fall of Abdul Hamid, the word most commonly heard in Istanbul was "freedom." The moment all these new "freedoms" were introduced, the first thing Princess Pakize's sister Hatice did was to pay a sizable sum in "compensation" to separate from the man her uncle had arranged for her to marry (and who had been drawing up all those lists of the murder mysteries Abdul Hamid had read at his sister-in-law Princess Pakize's request). Fifty years later, the conservative commentator Nahit Sırrı Örik would pen a series of columns in the magazine *History World* on the subject of Murad V's son and daughters (excluding Princess Pakize) in which he would imply—based on the various rumors that had been floating around the palace at the time, and which Örik had heard from his father—that the "freedom" they had all been waiting for had done Murad V's children not much good at all.

Nahit Sırrı Örik writes that when Prince Mehmet Selahattin, the eldest of the siblings, finally found freedom after spending twenty-eight years imprisoned in the same palace, he wandered around the streets, ferries, docks, and bridges of Istanbul for days, introducing himself to everyone he met—including young Örik himself, who was thirteen at the time. The Prince's main preoccupation was how he might go about writing and producing a stage play on the subject of the injustices his deposed father had suffered. Örik, who was rather partial to malicious gossip, would argue instead that the half-mad but exceptionally clever and cultured prince planned to approach Sultan Reşat to claim the "arrears" of revenue owed to his late father Murad V without giving his sisters their rightful share, but that even his half-witted uncle Reşat wouldn't take him seriously.

The new era of "freedom" was most evident in the wealth and breadth of books, newspapers, and magazines that came to be published in this period. This was how the people of Istanbul first discovered that some of the French novels they had bought and read while they had all still been living in the age of "despotism" had actually been translated at Abdul Hamid's behest. It was around this time that the note "translated for Abdul Hamid" began to appear in certain books, a practice which became more widely adopted after the foundation of the Turkish Republic.

In our view, there are three explanations for the question—an important one for our book too—of why these novels were still being published in their censored versions "even in the age of freedom": (1) laziness; (2) the fact that many of those old translators had stopped working in the intervening years, and their draft translation had gone missing; (3) and that the same kinds of topics which had so displeased Abdul Hamid, such as any criticisms of Islam and the Turks, were equally irksome to those who came to power after the nation's "liberation" from absolutism. We should also note that the custom of gunning journalists and writers down on the street with the tacit backing of the state—a tradition that has now persisted for more than a hundred years—was first born under the new regime of "freedom."

The collapse of the Empire was hastened by the Italians, who, having made a deal with the British and French, declared war on the Ottomans in 1911 in order to take Libya. (Though in truth, the new Ottoman government would have been just as willing as Abdul Hamid's to take their flag down and hand Libya over to Italy without a fight!) As part of their military strategy, the Italian navy—which must have been seven or eight times stronger than the Ottoman fleet—invaded more than twenty Ottoman islands of various shapes and sizes, including Rhodes. Due to the way the Turks administered these territories, of all the islands in the Dodecanese (what the Ottomans called the Twelve Islands), it was the Ottoman division stationed in Rhodes that put up the greatest resistance against the invaders. In Mingheria, meanwhile, the astute President Mazhar played his cards right and managed—without fighting a single battle—to secure a new treaty for the island guaranteeing its independence.

The Rumelian Greeks, who constituted the vast majority of the population on all of the islands Italy had occupied, did not object to their new situation, for it seemed preferable to be governed by the Italians rather than the crumbling Ottoman state, which had failed to establish law and order and still continued, even years after the Tanzimat-era reforms, to find all kinds of pretexts to impose higher taxes on its Christian subjects (such as the levy collected from non-Muslims wishing to avoid compulsory military service). As it was too far out in the east, the tiny island of Kastellorizo had not been invaded, but its 98 percent Greek population drew up a petition inviting the Italian navy to the island, and declaring their wish to become part of Italy.

The war, which was the first in history to feature aerial bombardments, ended in a swift victory for the Kingdom of Italy. The parties then signed the Treaty of Ouchy, which ceded Libya to the Italians. As for the Mediterranean islands which remained under Italian occupation, perhaps they could be handed back to the Ottomans after the Balkan Wars. For in the meantime, having realized that the Ottoman Empire was falling apart, and witnessed how easily its armies were being defeated, the Balkan nations—having first agreed with one another on who would be entitled to which land—had declared war on the Ottomans. In other words, Greece and the Ottoman Empire were at war once more. The Ottoman state had emerged from the Italo-Turkish War (known in Turkish history books as the Tripolitanian War) with yet another defeat, and its bureaucratic cadres were so sure that they were going to lose the Balkan Wars too that it seemed likely the Ottoman islands would all end up joining Greece. That being the case, perhaps it was better for these islands to remain in Italian hands for the time being—on the understanding that they would eventually be returned to the Ottomans. So the Ottomans withdrew from Libya, and hinted at the Italians that they could keep their soldiers stationed on the islands of the Dodecanese.

Around the same time, in September 1912, President Mazhar signed a "secret" treaty with Italy known as the Chania Accord. Over the course of his thirty-one-year rule, the President would use prisons, labor camps, and other similar methods to subjugate the island's liberals, its pro-Turkish and pro-Greek factions, and various other dissenting voices, and he would also put together a powerful army. Twice a year he would stand on the balcony of the Ministerial Headquarters—the former Governor's Residence and State Hall—and salute each and every one of this army's soldiers, no matter how long it took. Photographs, paintings, and sculptures of the Commander and Zeynep adorned every corner of the island, from lottery tickets to banknotes, from shoeboxes to the labels on alcoholic drinks, from dried-fig cartons to bus stops.

Aboard the Mingherian navy's only warship, which was taking him to Crete to sign the treaty the British had also facilitated, President Mazhar was telling everyone around him that after eleven years the nation's independence was finally going to be recognized by the rest of the world . . . His second-in-command, Hadid, had worked long and hard to persuade people—especially those "authentic" Mingherians who spoke Mingherian at home—to accept the conditions of this treaty.

In October 1912, Italy formally recognized Mingheria's independence. In practice this was a kind of semi-independence, as an Italian flag now also billowed beside the flag of Mingheria hanging from the old State Hall. President Mazhar's job now was to silence those Mingherian nationalists who objected to the presence of the Italian flag, but this was not a particularly substantial contingent. Most people were simply relieved that the Ottomans were not going to send their warships to bomb the island.

With the Balkan Wars also ending in defeat, the Union and Progress Party staged a coup to overthrow the government that had lost the war. There are many aspects of this incident, known colloquially as the Raid on the Sublime Porte, which are reminiscent of the history of Mingheria and its so-called era of quarantine governments. Soldiers and party henchmen attacked a government meeting in broad daylight, shot one of the ministers dead, and forced the government to resign. The "hero of freedom" Enver Bey, the main organizer of this coup, quickly rose to the rank of Pasha, and married Sultan Abdulmejid's granddaughter Princess Naciye.

Five months later, Mahmut Şevket Pasha, Commander of the Action Army and the man whom the plotters of the coup against Abdul Hamid had appointed as the head of the new government, was shot and killed in Istanbul's Divanyolu Street while waiting in traffic in his cabriolet. The bullet-ridden car, which was completely unarmored, is displayed today in the Military Museum in Istanbul's Harbiye district, as are the guns used by the assassins, who were all caught and hanged, and the novelist and history enthusiast Orhan Pamuk has told me of how he would obsessively visit the exhibit once a week during a period in the 1980s when he lived in a house in Nişantaşı at five minutes' walking distance from the museum.

In autumn 1913, a high-ranking functionary of the British government in Hong Kong made an appointment to meet with Doctor Nuri in Tung Wah Hospital. Doctor Nuri had assumed he would be discussing Hong Kong's sewage and quarantine troubles with the green-eyed and fair-haired colonial official, but instead found himself debating the outcome of the Balkan Wars, which he had read about in the local newspapers.

The Ottoman Empire had now lost every last one of the territories it had held in the Balkans for the past four hundred years. The Albanians too had staged a nationalist uprising. Albania's independence movement had been less concerned with fighting Abdul Hamid and the Ottomans than with the need to repel the Great Powers who would seek to take over when the Ottomans were gone. Eventually the foreign nations consented to the foundation of an "independent" Albanian state which they themselves would govern. (There was no doubt in anyone's mind that the Ottoman Empire was finished, but the question now was how the territories it had left behind should be distributed among all the other nations, big and small.) It was decided that Albania would be ruled by a delegation to which six countries would each send a representative, and the head of state would be a prince selected by the Great Powers.

"Everyone wants their own prince to rule Albania," said the British official, a note of exasperation in his manner. There were even some Albanians who thought the best protection they would ever get was from the British, and hoped Queen Victoria's son Prince Arthur, Duke of Connaught and Governor-General of Canada, might come to rule them. The Germans had someone from the Hohenzollern dynasty in mind. A Romanian prince had also surfaced, as well as a pasha from the Egyptian Khedivate who was using forged documents to claim Albanian ancestry.

By now Doctor Nuri had sensed where the conversation was heading, but he still put on a solemn look and asked why he was being told of all these developments.

The official gave him some more information. The Ottoman Minister of Foreign Affairs Gabriel Noradunkyan had told the British that considering the population of Albania was 80 percent Muslim, the monarch chosen for the country should probably be an Ottoman prince. The princes who were near the front of the line of succession and still hoped they might become Ottoman sultans one day had rejected the Union and Progress Party's offer of the Albanian throne. But even the idle, witless princes who were nowhere near inheriting the Ottoman throne (including Abdul Hamid's beloved son and composer Prince Burhanettin Effendi, whom we spoke of at the start of our novel) had turned their noses up at the prospect of being crowned prince of Albania, most probably because all the other princes had also said no. The next candidates to be considered for the role were prominent Ottoman pashas of Albanian origins. The green-eyed colonial official paused for a moment, before noting that the United Kingdom did not have much of a vested interest in Albania. But if the chosen sovereign was to be a distinguished Muslim who was worthy of this charming new nation, and someone the West approved of, the British government might perhaps suggest that Princess Pakize and Doctor Nuri be offered the position, rather than some mediocre princeling. Should this proposal be accepted, it would also solve the Albanian principate's problems with infectious diseases.

Doctor Nuri reiterated the same point he had made to Consul George in Mingheria twelve years before, noting just as earnestly as he had back then that a sultan's daughter—in other words a female descendant of the ruling dynasty—could never wield any political authority in a Muslim country.

The British official replied that Princess Pakize's reign as queen of Mingheria had been successful, and that the foreign office of the United Kingdom had no doubt she would win the affections of the Albanian people.

"We had a very special reason to do what we did in Mingheria . . . ," said the Prince Consort. "We wanted to enforce quarantine measures against the plague."

The high-ranking British functionary clarified that he was not making the Doctor and Princess Pakize a formal offer anyway, and that for the British government to officially be able to make such a proposal, Doctor Nuri and Princess Pakize must first indicate that they were interested in going to Albania to begin with.

The last letter Princess Pakize ever wrote to her sister, and which is included in the correspondence we have inherited, discussed this very topic, so we shall now devote some time to examining its mood and tone. The letter clearly tells us that Princess Pakize took the offer seriously, and discussed it at length—and only partly in jest—with her husband and their children at the dinner table. But what did Hatice think?

In our view, Princess Pakize meant this question less as a boast, and more as an attempt to find out "what Istanbul might say" if something like this came to pass. In this last letter, Princess Pakize also noted that she did not speak Albanian, and did not wish to make the same mistake she had made in Mingheria. Even so, she did still wonder what it might be like, and even made time to visit the library one day to consult the 1911 edition of the *Encyclopaedia Britannica* which had only just arrived from New York, where she read in the first of two brief entries devoted to the country that Albania was not an island, that its terrain was mountainous, and that—according to the ancient Greek geographer and historian Strabo—its people were tall, tough, and honest, and (in the second entry) that the nation was part of the "Empire of the Turks." Her daughter Melike, who was seven at the time, later recalled how her mother would joke with her about becoming an Albanian princess, all while dealing with the housework and complaining about the laziness of her maid. In any event, before they could make a decision, they learned from the newspapers that a German prince (Wilhelm of Wied) had been appointed as Albania's new head of state. (He would be toppled six months later following a Muslim uprising and coup.) So they did not get to indulge for too long in this diverting fantasy.

We do not know for sure why Princess Pakize never wrote to her sister Hatice again. For whatever reason, she must have stopped trusting Hatice, who had meanwhile married again and was living with her new husband in her old waterside mansion, giving birth to two children in quick succession. It is also possible that one or two of Princess Pakize's letters, which were already less than frequent, might have been lost before they could reach Princess Hatice.

When the First World War (known in Istanbul as the General War) broke out one year later, the couple found themselves living with two small children in the enemy territory of Hong Kong. We assume that after ten years there, they must have obtained British passports. The British administration had made all the necessary arrangements for their esteemed Ottoman guests to feel as safe and comfortable as possible.

Princess Pakize, Doctor Nuri, and their children remained in Hong Kong throughout the war, cut off from their connections at the Istanbul court. Whether they were prisoners of the British, or of their own fears and guilty thoughts, we cannot know, but at any rate, with Istanbul occupied by foreign powers after the Armistice of Mudros, they did not wish to risk being perceived as collaborating with the British. (That was how Princess Pakize's second-oldest sister Princess Fehime had come to be seen by the people of Istanbul after she had started throwing parties at her Bosphorus mansion for the officers of the occupying British army.) But the notion of collecting the allowances they must have accumulated, and of reclaiming their waterside home in Ortaköy—the thought, in other words, of returning to Istanbul—was always on their mind.

In November 1918, the warships of the allied British, French, Italian, and Greek forces who had won the First World War entered Istanbul and dropped anchor right in front of the royal palaces on the Bosphorus. Having thus surrendered Istanbul itself, the six-hundred-year-old Ottoman Empire—which had been steadily shrinking with each nation and every island it gave away—had finally come to an end. HMS *Centurion*, the British navy's colossal dreadnought, moored across from the Çırağan Palace where Princess Pakize had spent her whole life. I would often wonder (when I read Turkish high-school textbooks) if it was only a coincidence that in all the photographs from those trying times for Istanbul's Muslim population, the sky is always veiled with black clouds. With the Great Powers' warships anchored outside his window, the last Ottoman sultan (Mehmed VI) was now a prisoner in his own palace, just as his brother Murad V had been. When Mustafa Kemal (Atatürk) chased the Greek troops out of western Anatolia, the last sultan boarded a British warship and fled his palace and Istanbul.

In March 1924—after the proclamation of the Turkish Republic in Ankara in October 1923, and the abolition of the Ottoman caliphate a few months later—the Ottoman royal family was banished from the country. In just three days, one hundred and fifty-six people who had been close to the throne and right at the top of that rarefied palace world Princess Pakize used to inhabit were plucked out of their lives in Istanbul and put on trains taking them into exile in some unknown destination in the West. These one hundred and fifty-six top-tier members of the Ottoman dynasty were also told they must immediately sell off any property and assets they might have in Turkey and were barred from entering Turkish borders, even in transit. As Princess Pakize and the Prince Consort were part of this group of one hundred and fifty-six notables too, they now found themselves stripped of their Turkish citizenship and with no chance of returning to Istanbul. Now that they had been banned from crossing the border to Turkey, it was unclear when the Ottoman royals would ever be able to return.

Princess Hatice, who had divorced from her second husband too during the last year of the war, did not join the rest of the Ottoman royal family in France. She took her two children and her sister's letters and moved to Beirut. For many years, she lived on the alimony she received from her second husband. When he got in trouble with the law for smuggling historical artifacts, the alimony payments stopped, but although Hatice and her two children spent several difficult, penniless years in Beirut, for some reason she never contacted Princess Pakize again.

In our view, there are two reasons why Princess Pakize and her family decided a couple of years later to leave Hong Kong behind and move to France. The first is that they identified and indeed sympathized with those one hundred and fifty-six Ottoman royals who had been banished abroad, and the five or six hundred lesser members of the dynasty who had joined them in voluntary exile. The other reason is that they hoped one of the exiled princelings might make a suitable match for their daughter Melike (my grandmother).

Princess Pakize's correspondence does not touch upon these matters, and I shall keep my account of the family's life after their move from Hong Kong to France in the summer of 1926 fairly brief (as it has no bearing on the history of Mingheria anyway). My grandmother's father, the Doctor and "Prince Consort" Nuri, found work in a hospital in Marseille, where he would later set up his own clinic too. This kept the family at a safe distance from the rest of the Ottoman dynasty—who had settled in and around Nice—and from any gossip. They were also able to avoid the spies of the Turkish consulate in Nice, which had been established solely to keep track of the exiled Ottoman princes and princesses and find out if they became politically active. My grandmother Melike was married to a prince descended from Abdul Hamid's bloodline, and very far removed from the throne.

My mother, born in 1928, was the only child born of that dull, joyless marriage. To escape the confrontational, liquor-soaked family home, this sultan's great-granddaughter did what most Ottoman princesses used to do, and after the end of the Second World War, at the age of eighteen, she entered into an arranged marriage with a wealthy man of Muslim origins. My father, who lived in London, was the son of a wealthy Arab (Iraqi) merchant and a Scottish mother. His hope was that having an Ottoman princess for a bride would impress the London "high" society he was trying to break into. Six months into their arranged marriage, for which she had received a multitude of gifts and jewelry, my mother returned from London to her parents' home in Marseille. Sometime later, my father followed her to Marseille and persuaded her to come back to London with him.

During these tempestuous years, my mother began to develop a "fascination"—or what she would later call a "great fondness"—for Mingheria. As a little girl, she had listened to her grandmother Princess Pakize describe the island as if it were some fairy-tale realm, and talk in half-wistful, half-teasing tones of when she used to be its queen, but to my mother's mother—my grandmother Melike—Mingheria had never been a subject of any particular interest. In my grandmother's mind, her most notable ancestor was never her mother but her grandfather, the Ottoman sultan Murad V, descendant of a six-hundred-year dynasty. My grandmother Melike also used to say that if only she could have left her husband, she would have gone back to Istanbul after 1952. Women in her position had been allowed to return to Turkey after that date.

My mother's "Mingherian fascination" was also encouraged by her longing to distance herself from the Ottoman exiles in Nice and from my father's "Middle Eastern" coterie in London, and live with her husband in a private world of their own. Another reason was that in 1947, Mingheria's independence was made official and formally recognized by the United Nations, with newspapers' society pages and children's supplements devoting ample room to the story of one of the world's smallest independent states. My own Mingherian "nationalism" was also influenced by these charming reports.

After the end of Ottoman rule in Mingheria, the Ottoman flag hanging from the old State Hall had been replaced from 1901 to 1912 by the Mingherian flag; from 1912 to 1943 by the Mingherian and Italian flags; from 1943 to 1945 by the German flag; from 1945 to 1947 by the British flag; and after 1947 by the same Mingherian flag originally designed by the painter Osgan Kalemciyan. (Together with more than two thousand other Armenian intellectuals living in Istanbul, our painter was taken from his home one night in April 1915—ostensibly as an emergency war-time measure ordered by Grand Vizier and "hero of freedom" Talaat Pasha—and never seen or heard from again.)

But the many different flags flying over the island did not bring about much variety in the way people led their day-to-day lives, nor any cultural transformations, because throughout the half century between 1901 and 1952, President Mazhar (1901–32), President Hadid (1932–43), and every other so-called president, half president, and governor that followed would all pursue—in collaboration with the Italians and the Germans—the same policy of Mingherianization, forbidding the teaching of the island's Ottoman and Greek history, sending a number of brave Turkish and Rumelian dissenters to labor camps, and Mingherianizing every aspect of life. We have examined this period in further detail—and at great personal cost—in our book *Mingherianization and Its Consequences,* which was banned from the island for twenty years, and later had several passages censored.

In the summer of 1947, two years before I was born, my mother and father—who had separated for a time—reunited in Marseille. My mother was finally able to persuade my father that they should live in Mingheria for a period. (I owe my Mingherian birth to her success in this endeavor.) Before the summer was over, they had traveled to Arkaz via Crete and settled in the Splendid Palace, in the very room—according to the stories my mother told me, and to the letters my grandmother's mother wrote—where the Commander and Zeynep had died of the plague forty-six years before. A plaque at the entrance of the Splendid Palace notes that the father of the nation had been staying in this hotel the day he declared the island's freedom and independence, but anyone wishing to find out more will be taken to the second-floor meeting hall and be shown a set of photographs taken by Vanyas and by the anonymous photographer of the *Arkata Times,* as well as the desk at which Mazhar Effendi had sat when he was acting as the Commander's deputy.

My father bought my mother a large house with a view of the sea in the neighborhood of Filizler (formerly Flizvos), and throughout the 1950s, my mother—thoroughly bored with sitting at home all day—would take me out on late summer afternoons to the Splendid Palace's Rome gelateria. Sometimes we would sit at a table in the cool shade of linden trees in the garden of the ice-cream shop. At the end of these visits, once we had finished eating our ice cream and I had wiped my hands on my mother's napkin, I would often beg her to take me again to that tiny museum on the hotel's second floor. (This fondness for museums is another interest I share with the novelist Pamuk.)

Those photographs of the day of the revolution, of the people gathered on the Governor's balcony, of the figures who had secured the island's independence, had all bewitched me, as had the inkpot and the set of pens that had belonged to the Commander—whose portrait hung in Arkaz everywhere I looked. Perhaps I could already feel in my child's heart the presence of the profound and mysterious links that exist between history and objects, and nations and writing.

I was born in Mingheria, and even when I have been away from the island, it has never faded from my imagination. If anything, my memories have only been sharpened by distance. After our trips to the Hotel Splendid's ice-cream shop, my mother and I would sometimes walk all the way back home along Commander Kâmil Boulevard (the former Hamidiye Avenue), looking at the storefronts we passed and doing a little shopping as we went. Or we would turn into Istanbul Street and stroll through its refreshingly shady porticoes—past the London Toy Shop, the Island Bookstore, and the Bank of Mingheria—until we reached the shore.

I preferred this second route, for I would always get ten minutes to examine the ships moored to the docks or anchored in the open sea, and read and think about their names, and on the way back home, we would always take a carriage. Sometimes I would walk a little farther to the slipway near the coffee shop next to the new jetty and try to touch the water with my hand, and my mother would say, "Be careful, you'll get your shoes wet!" My shoes, my socks, the skirt and blazer I wore to school, and the rest of my clothes were all well made and came from Europe. Before I had even started going to school, I had already realized that my mother took greater care over my clothes than the other children's mothers did, and I could also see that this was related to some romantic, idealized vision of Ottoman family life.

Then as now, I loved walking among the crowds in the docks, and feeling the bustle of people running to catch the ferry, the elation of arriving passengers coming through customs, and the shadow of the

White Mountain spanning the length of the bay, and like every other Mingherian child, I was afraid of the Castle, and convinced that it was populated by bandits, murderers, and all manner of bloodcurdling creatures. Like most Mingherians who can't really picture the Castle as anything but a sinister, tenebrous void, I have only ever been inside it once, and even then for a very short time. More than the Castle itself, I liked the image of its reflection in the still waters of the bay.

My mother might have enjoyed acting like a princess, but even so, as we climbed onto the carriage on our way back home, she would always ask, "How much to Filizler?" addressing the coachman in Mingherian (though all the coachmen spoke at least a little bit of Turkish). If she thought the price was acceptable, she would say no more, but if it was a lot higher than the usual amount, my mother would point out the fare chart written in Mingherian, and while some of the more impertinent coachmen would argue back, most of them would quickly agree to the fare on the chart.

The tourists who would start thronging Arkaz in the 1990s and make summers in the city unbearable had not yet arrived thirty years before, so the coachmen hadn't become quite so "presumptuous" (as my mother would say), and most of the island's population took pleasure—though they might not speak as openly of it as we are doing now—in the pungent smell of horse dung that hung in the air and especially near carriage stops, perhaps even missing it a little whenever they were away from the island. In 2008, despite being a major tourist attraction, these horse carriages were banned from Arkaz by government decree, as it was too difficult to clean the mess they left behind, and the coachmen had become too numerous and ill disciplined.

My mother and I spoke Turkish at home. My parents spoke to each other in English, but my father was away most of the time, either in London or elsewhere. We addressed the maids, the gardeners, and the watchmen in Mingherian (except for one servant we spoke to in Turkish). Over the course of repeated stays on the island, my mother had managed to teach herself the same language her grandmother had not spoken a word of when she had first arrived on the island, and although I had picked up some Mingherian myself from hearing it spoken at home or outside (mainly in the shops), my mother still wanted to make sure I learned it properly, so when I was four years old, she bought me copies of *The Mingherian Alphabet* and *Zeynep's Reading Book,* taught me how to read and write, and helped me with my Mingherian vocabulary.

Finally, when I was five years old, I began spending time with another little girl called Rina, who was my age, spoke fluent Mingherian, and had my mother's approval (meaning, in other words, that she was from a respectable family). But these plans to have me learn Mingherian through conversation had to be interrupted when Rina started asking what my father did for a living, if he was a spy, which desk he worked at, and whether its drawers were locked—making my mother feel understandably rather uncomfortable. My father had opened a large haberdashery, furniture, and home appliances store on Istanbul Street (he was the first person to bring British refrigerators to the island), and after countless hours whiled away across various government offices, he had also managed to set up a trading company to start buying and selling rosewater, but as neither of these ventures had proven to be particularly successful (and perhaps because he also happened to be a British citizen who had come to the island after the British had withdrawn their troops), he was often suspected of being a spy.

I will take this opportunity to note that at my mother's insistence, my father's housewares store also stocked Consul George's book on Mingheria (finally published in 1932), though no one apart from the occasional tourist paid much attention to this volume, which had been a true labor of love. For sixty years, George Cunningham's *Mingherian History: From Antiquity to the Present*—partly responsible for my decision to become a historian—was shamelessly plundered by the Mingherian state and its historians, usually without any acknowledgment of the source. Having thus been savagely exploited for six decades with the calculated aim of crafting a sense of national identity (based on clothing, cuisine, landscapes, and history), this balanced, informative, and elegant volume was belittled, over the next fifteen years, by a new generation of readers for being too "Orientalist," in Edward Said's negatively inflected sense of the word, and its author—who had made such significant contributions to Mingherian culture—was accused of working for the cause of British imperialism, and harboring all sorts of exotic prejudices. Had the archaeological artifacts, ancient figurines, Mingherian rocks, fossils, jugs, oil landscapes, watercolors, seashells, maps, and books that filled

Monsieur George's house not been put on a British warship and smuggled off the island at some point during the chaotic, embattled years that followed the publication of his book, all of these items—like so many other similar collections and historic homes upon the island—would have been lost, and rather than being safely preserved at the British Museum as they currently are, a whole host of old Mingherian objects and landscapes would have disappeared. Today, the lovely house where Monsieur George used to live with his Mingherian wife is a branch of an international restaurant chain specializing in fried chicken, and its small botanic garden devoted to Mingherian flora has been turned into a parking lot.

Until I started primary school in 1956, I learned most of my Mingherian from playing with the other children on the sands of Flizvos Beach (whose name hadn't changed) down the road from our house. In Mingheria, beach season and plague season both run from late April to late October, and during these months, one of my mother's favorite activities was to go down to the beach in her chic, black, and very demure one-piece bathing suit, and lie like a movie star or a wealthy European lady on a towel draped over the sand and in the shade of an umbrella, where she would spend hours poring over old film magazines my father sent from London (we would collect the parcels from the Post Office together). Her elegant straw bag contained the Nivea sunscreen she would occasionally take out and apply, a pair of black sunglasses she never wore, and a pink bonnet for when she finally decided, hours later, to go into the water, and in which she would meticulously gather every strand of her hair so as not to spoil her hairdresser Flatros's work.

On our way home from the docks, my mother would put her bags on the carriage seat opposite, and I would sit next to her and wait for her to put her hand on my shoulder, reminding her if she forgot. As the carriage climbed up Istanbul Street, my mother might break one of the biscuits she had bought from Zofiri's shop in half, and we would eat it together as we watched pedestrians jostling along the pavements, the newsstands, the teahouses, and the people milling about in front of the travel agencies. One of the reasons I love Mingheria so much is that it is the kind of place where two Muslim women can sit in a carriage on their own and happily eat their biscuits without having to worry about what anyone might think.

When the carriage reached the top of the slope and turned right, following the row of government offices and palm and pine trees that lined Commander Kâmil Boulevard all the way to the Prime Minister's offices, we would make sure to look away when we were about to pass in front of the Mingherian land registry and the Mingherian Ministry of Justice, where my parents had wasted so much of their time in their early years in Mingheria, only to be disappointed at every turn. At this point I should probably note the following: my mother's love for Mingheria was genuine and true, but there was also a more pragmatic side to it relating to property and financial considerations.

My parents were in possession of a number of documents—some with maps and title plans attached—attesting my great-grandfather Doctor Nuri and my grandmother's mother Princess Pakize's ownership of several vast tracts of land which they had obtained during his service as quarantine minister and Chief Minister, and her three and a half months as queen of the island. Some of these deeds, signed by the Commander himself, were "gifts" he had handed out when he had founded the new state (much like new sultans upon their accession to the throne), while others were formal certificates bearing the seal of the state and the signature of Queen Pakize, drawn up by bureaucrats who had worked out precisely how much she was owed for her services as monarch, and presented to her as her rightful dues. As these documents bore the autograph of the father of the nation, as well as one of the earliest official seals of the state, the bureaucrats, department heads, judges, and ministers of Mingheria would always handle them with reverence, and never even think of questioning their authenticity or their validity.

But for my mother—and the various uncles and nephews and distant relations who had optimistically given her power of attorney on the matter—to truly possess this land, to be able to sell it or come and live on it if they wished to, they had to have the significance of those historical documents assessed by a judge, the judge's ruling had to be conveyed to whichever land registry office held jurisdiction over a given plot, the responses received from these local departments had to be reviewed (usually, the land would turn out to have been registered under someone else's name in the meantime), and the new owners as well as any previous owners each had to be told "It's my land, actually!" and sued for the deed in the courts of the nearest Mingherian city.

The locals who had fought all sorts of gangs off of those lands forty years ago and taken up residence there themselves, obtaining official ownership under one of the state's politically motivated property schemes and enlivening the area with the houses they built for their families, couldn't just accept the claim that their land wasn't theirs after all but supposedly belonged to a bunch of people the Great Commander had gifted it to around the time of the foundation of the state (and who didn't even speak Mingherian), and so they fought the lawsuits tooth and nail, and the cases dragged on with no resolution. Moreover, before they could even file these kinds of lawsuits, the holders of those historical documents—which were sometimes referred to as "accession deeds" or as "licenses"—had to prove that they were the rightful heirs of the person named on the original license, and this could not be done through the courts of the country they lived in but only at their local Mingherian embassy (in what was inevitably a lengthy and laborious procedure), or by coming to the island in person and going through the Mingherian courts. One day in Nice, my great-uncle Prince Süleyman Effendi—who had spent a great deal of time thinking about these matters, and "squandered" a lot of money on the lawyers he'd hired to tackle the Istanbul courts—told my grandmother that "in the Republic of Turkey, forbidding the members of the Ottoman royal family from returning to the country has made it much easier to indirectly and surreptitiously seize their assets," an argument which my grandmother had then relayed to my mother. "But in Mingheria, all the Ottomans except for our mother Princess Pakize had already been expelled. So they forgot they should probably ban one other person from returning to the island: you. I would suggest you utilize this fact to your advantage!"

Fifty years after the Mingherian Revolution, the question of how they might "take advantage" of that lapse was one that my parents would always talk and argue about every time my father came to the island. These early arguments, which I was far too young to make sense of at the time, eventually turned into full-blown marital fights, and caused me so much distress that I paid no attention to "those properties" until I was at least thirty years old. Today I sometimes wish I hadn't taken any interest in these family assets after I turned thirty either—for it meant that those who could not comprehend my heartfelt passion for Mingherian history and culture, or the strength of my love for the island, soon began to claim that the real reason I kept visiting Arkaz was to try and claim ownership of that land.

Having resolved not to bring personal polemic into this book, I must now speak of what has been one of my life's greatest woes. In the twenty-one years between 1984 and 2005, I was forbidden from entering Mingheria. The Mingherian embassy in London would not renew the Mingherian passport I was "automatically" entitled to by birth. That same London embassy rejected the visa application I made with my British passport, which I held thanks to my father, and the Mingherian embassy in Paris rejected the application I made there with the French passport I held through my mother's citizenship. For twenty-one years, the impossibility of seeing the island and breathing its air, of spending summers on its beaches with my husband and our children, of strolling through the backstreets of Arkaz, and, of course, of using the Mingherian state archives for my research would be a source of crushing anguish and heartache. A few friends who were well versed in these matters, and had connections in the Mingherian secret service, suggested that I was being punished for the book I'd written, for having put my signature on public statements protesting the military regime that ruled the island in the 1980s, for my criticism of the policy of locking intellectuals, leftists, and religious sectarians up in the Castle prison, and for publishing several articles (deemed to be derogatory of the Mingherian people) on the subject of the historic dungeons of the Castle of Mingheria. But those who were familiar enough with the intricacies of the deep state to know that it did not begin and end with the secret police told me quite candidly that the real reason for my banishment had to do with my great-grandmother's inheritance—meaning, in other words, that it was all a question of money and land.

I had known many foreign scholars of Ottoman history who had spent years patiently sifting through the Ottoman archives to research the massacres of the Empire's Armenian, Greek, and Kurdish populations and other similarly unpleasant topics, or had proven that some of those nationalistic campaigns of the past had not really unfolded in quite the way they had previously been described, and I had seen how distraught they would become when the permits which had allowed them to work in the archives in Istanbul were suddenly and mysteriously revoked. But although I had witnessed so many of my brave and honorable colleagues being ruthlessly punished by the Turkish state for their honesty, I still felt lonely and guilty when the same punishment was inflicted on me by the Mingherian state for twenty years.

By 2008, when Mingheria was declared a candidate for membership of the European Union, it had become harder for the state to silence its opponents—not just moderates like me, but those far-more-vociferous dissenters it had jailed, the leftist militants, and anyone who had ever objected to the criminal seizure of the assets of local Greek and Turkish charitable trusts. Once I was finally able to procure a new Mingherian passport—thanks to several letters of complaint I sent to the European Union, and the intercession of some of the more "liberal" Mingherian government ministers whose families we were acquainted with (in my country, a favor from an influential friend has always offered far-greater protection than any notion of human rights ever could)—I got on the first plane to Arkaz, but the moment I walked out of Commander Kâmil Airport, I realized that every step I took was going to be watched by the secret police. After 2005, when I started writing the introduction which would later turn into this book, I would stay at my friends' houses and in hotels in Mingheria, and constantly find that my suitcases and other possessions had been searched while I was out. What upset me most of all were not even the overt references to my supposedly being a "spy" for Turkey or the United Kingdom (the latter because of my father) that kept appearing in the newspapers of a country which aspired to join the European Union, but the fact that whenever we got together on the island in the summer, it would only take a glass of Arkazian wine before those same Mingherian friends whom I would host whenever they came to London, Paris, or Boston (where I taught as a professor) started repeating those very same accusations, and making crass jokes on the subject.

At an academic conference, I had been complaining about the primitive, mean-spirited jokes my Mingherian friends had been making at my expense when a Dutch professor of Middle Eastern and "Levantine" history whom I had always admired replied with this sardonic remark: "How terribly unjust! If your friends knew you well enough, they would see that you are the staunchest Mingherian nationalist there is."

I regret today that I was not able to give that Orientalist professor—who no doubt thought he was being funny—the response he deserved. But I will indulge in a quick digression now to remind him and my Mingherian friends, as well as all of my readers too, of this important fact: in the twenty-first century, with the era of traditional empires and colonies long since behind us, the word "nationalist" has become a label almost always employed to lend prestige to the behavior of people who tend to agree with everything their government says, have no other aim but to curry favor with those in power, and lack the courage to stand up to authority. But in the age of our revered "Major" Kâmil, "nationalism" was a noble term, reserved for those brave, heroic patriots who rose up in revolt against their colonizers and ran headfirst, flags aloft, toward the invaders' relentless machine guns.

A further consequence of my being banished from the island for twenty-odd years was that just as they were about to reach the age when they might start talking, my two wonderful, strapping boys were barred from spending any time on the island, so that—far from becoming fluent in Mingherian—they never learned a single word of this magical language. Every time I insisted that they should "learn their mother tongue," or tried reproachfully to teach them some Mingherian myself, they would remind me that nobody else in our family (except for my mother and I) knew any Mingherian, not even the Queen, and that even I only ever spoke to their grandmother in Turkish, pointing out with knowing smiles that their mother tongue was actually English, if not Turkish. My sons' teasing and occasional mockery of my attachment to Mingheria, and—as I also explained to the lawyer—their father's persistent refusal to take my side, would eventually lead to my marriage ending in divorce.

While we are on the subject of nationalism and language, I will also touch upon another of my life's saddest days. When a 2012 UEFA European Football Championship qualifying match played in Istanbul between Mingheria—whose population hadn't yet reached half a million—and Turkey ended with a (perhaps) dubious penalty kick which handed Mingheria a last-minute 1–0 victory and knocked Turkey out of the competition, that sensation I'd always had of being divided between my beloved Turkish and my beloved Mingherian transformed into a veritable agony. Furious supporters rampaged through Istanbul breaking the windows of Mingherian restaurants, Mingherian bakeries (which sold the same kind of biscuits that had killed Doctor Ilias), and any other stores which had "Mingheria" in their names, damaging their displays, looting their stock, and occasionally even setting fire to their premises. For the rest of that week, I avoided the journalists and hid myself away, deciding—as I am doing now—that the best course of action was to forget about it all.

While preparing Princess Pakize's letters for publication, I have often wondered what all those people who were living in Arkaz in 1901, trying to dodge the deadly threats of plague and political violence, would think if they could see the Arkaz my mother and I knew in the 1950s. I expect they would have been gladdened by the sight of the Commander's spectacular mausoleum—finally completed in 1933—which we respectfully acknowledged every time our hired carriage crossed Commander Kâmil Bridge (formerly known as Hamidiye Bridge), as by the statues of the Commander and the Commander with Zeynep, which had been placed in each of the city's five most important locations, and by the flags of Mingheria, which we could always see wherever we looked. They would probably also have been impressed by the new jetty—made out of Mingherian stone—where even the bigger ships could now dock, the tall and sturdy new breakwater in the harbor, the Zeynep-Kâmil Hospital and all its modern equipment, the enormous Broadcasting House, constructed in the style of traditional wooden Mingherian homes but using concrete and Mingherian stone instead, all the buildings of the Commander Kâmil University, the small and charming Arkaz Opera House, and the Mingherian Archaeological Museum. But I suspect they would have been somewhat alarmed by the tall apartment blocks that had appeared on Commander Kâmil Boulevard and on the hills that overlooked the sea, by the Mingherian Park Hotel, which resembled a giant white concrete box, and by the enormous blue and pink neon signs spelling out the names of hotels and rosewater brands from the top of the tallest roofs so that they could be seen from approaching passenger ferries.

Completed long after the Mingherian Revolution, the much-delayed clock tower originally commissioned to mark the twenty-fifth anniversary of Abdul Hamid's accession to the throne had ended up with no clock at all, but carried instead the statue of the Goddess Mina (which had almost been named the Marble Zeynep due to its striking resemblance to the Commander's wife) retrieved by the archaeologist Selim Sahir, and shortly after the Italian occupation, people had begun to call it the Memorial of Mingheria—the name still used for it today.

In the 1950s, as we sat on the phaeton taking us home, Commander Kâmil's monumental mausoleum would hover to our left like a tangible presence dominating the city from above, though my mother and I would never talk about him—not on the carriage itself, nor when we got home. But in the Kâmil-Zeynep Primary School—which I began to attend in 1956, and which also happened to be on the carriage's route—the Commander was constantly mentioned, and his image was in every classroom, hanging on the walls and printed in our textbooks.

Before I'd even started primary school, I had already memorized the one hundred twenty-nine Mingherian words the Commander had specifically emphasized, and all the sentences that could be composed with them. This meant that in the first grade, I very quickly learned how to pronounce the letters of the Mingherian alphabet—and consequently how to read as well. By the end of that first school year, and with some help from the pocket dictionary my mother had bought me, I had learned another two hundred and fifty Mingherian words, none of which I had ever heard from the other children on the beach or from Rina. Meanwhile, more than half of my classmates were still busy trying to work their way through the alphabet.

In autumn of 1957, when I got to second grade, the teacher realized that my vocabulary—particularly in Mingherian—was far more advanced than everyone else's, so she made me sit at the front and let me spend the day leafing through my pocket dictionary (a more comprehensive one had yet to be written). When the school inspector came in unannounced one morning for her customary yearly visit, the teacher called me to the blackboard and asked me about all the new words I had learned. I recited some of the oldest Mingherian words I knew and explained what they meant: "darkness," "gazelle," "icy mountain," "spout," "shoe," and "futile." I suspect there were some words whose meanings were obscure even to the teacher and the lady inspector with the bleached blonde hair.

Yet when the inspector asked me to make a sentence with some of those words, I was struck dumb. All I could picture was the excitement of those high-school students who would run around during Independence Day celebrations and stand side by side in the square to form different sentences. Feeling mortified, I looked up at the photographs of Commander Kâmil and Zeynep hanging above the blackboard. How young and beautiful they were! They had spoken this language in that unlit kitchen and had thus rescued both the language and the nation from oblivion. I was ashamed of myself, and grateful to them for saving the Mingherian people.

But unfortunately I still couldn't think in Mingherian, and I would always dream in Turkish. (That is also why I wrote this book in Turkish.) When she saw that I had begun to stammer, the inspector turned to the teacher and said, "Why don't you try?" But although the teacher did begin a sentence in Mingherian, she couldn't seem to complete it, and soon fell silent. She glanced at the inspector in the hopes she might finish the sentence for her, but the inspector struggled too, and couldn't do it either.

Undeterred by this hiccup, the inspector began to ask me questions. "Who was the second president of Mingheria?" "Sheikh Hamdullah!" "What was the first word Zeynep and Kâmil remembered in the kitchen?" "*Akva*—'water'!" "When was the declaration of freedom and independence?" "On the twenty-eighth of June 1901." "Who made the painting of the armored landau traveling through the empty streets that night?" "The artist Tacettin. But it was the people of Mingheria who pictured it first!" The inspector was so moved by this answer that she called me over and gave me a kiss on the forehead. "My dear girl," she said, her voice full of emotion, "if our Great Commander Kâmil and Zeynep could see you now, they would be so gratified and so proud of you, and they would know that the Mingherian language and the Mingherian people live on." (There was no intention of being dismissive in the way she had referred to Zeynep; in the 1950s, Mingherians would always call the Commander's wife by her name alone, as if she were the heroine of some mythical tale.)

The lady inspector had been gazing at the photographs of the Commander and his wife which hung in every classroom in Mingheria. When she turned to look at me, she said: "Queen Pakize would have been proud of this little Mingherian too!"

I realized then that just like the majority of the island, the inspector thought my grandmother's mother, Queen Pakize, was dead and also had no idea that I was her granddaughter's daughter.

At home, my mother had smiled as I relayed this story, then said: "You mustn't tell anyone at school about your great-granny Pakize in France!" This was just one of the many enigmatic pronouncements my mother would make, and whose mystery I was never able to solve no matter how many years I spent puzzling over them. I would sometimes think of these as "metaphysical" riddles, though I understood the political worries and fears that must have lain behind them after 2005, when my luggage, handbag, documents, and files would be given at least one rough search (designed to make sure that when I came back to the room, I knew exactly what had happened) every time I visited the island. By 2005 I had given up on trying to convert the old accession licenses into proper deeds and claim ownership of the Mingherian land that should have been inherited by the Queen's heirs, yet these searches did not stop, and several documents were stolen from my bag and my desk over the years. I am sure that many of the pages in the book you are holding now must have been read before you by the agents of the Mingherian Intelligence Agency, founded by President Mazhar early in his career.

Toward the end of 1958, the teacher called my mother to school one day to tell her that I was a very bright and talented student, and that I should probably be sent abroad to Europe to continue my studies. My mother, who hoped I would be a Mingherian through and through, could have chosen not to mention the teacher's advice to my father. But far from wanting to keep it a secret, she too agreed that I should be educated outside of Mingheria. It was thus decided that rather than going to London, I should move (with my mother) to live with my grandmother in Nice and finish primary school there, where I could also learn French. (I had already more or less figured English out from hearing it spoken at home.) It was around this time that I began to hear my mother and father mention not just my grandmother Melike but my great-grandmother Pakize too—whom they would either call

Great-Granny or lovingly and respectfully refer to as the Queen—and her husband, Doctor Nuri.

My father, who had always been an entertaining and outgoing man, wrote to the Queen and the Doctor to tell them that their great-granddaughter was "a Mingherian they would be proud of." One day, we received a fresh envelope from Marseille containing seven blank postcards showing scenes from the island in the 1900s. Great-Granny Pakize had sent her little Mingherian the postcards she had taken with her when she left the island. As I would later find out, she had also posted many of these to her sister Hatice. That year, I went to each and every location depicted on those postcards and used the simple camera my father had bought me to take black-and-white pictures of those same spots as they looked in late 1958, having the film developed at the Vanyas Photo Studio.

But before I even got the chance to post the photographs back, my father—with his characteristic generosity and ingenuity—made full use of an opportunity which happened to arise in that same period, and having obtained everyone's approval, he arranged for us all to meet in Geneva. The World Health Organization had decided to award my great-grandfather Doctor Nuri, who had retired twenty-five years ago, a Distinguished Service Award. While the Queen and Doctor Nuri were in Geneva, looked after by my grandmother Melike, I was to stay there too. My father had booked us two panoramic rooms at the Hotel Beau Rivage for a week.

In my mind, the city of Geneva in August 1959 was an enchanted place. Like most couples who are always fighting and splitting up only to get back together again, my mother and father had been delighted to be able to leave me in safe hands and had quickly disappeared, but I did not mind too much, for my grandmother Princess Melike had clearly resolved to be happy and enjoy her time with me. Following the death of her husband (and my grandfather) Prince Sait Effendi in a plane crash five years before, she too would have liked my mother and me to move to Nice and be closer to her.

In the mornings, my grandmother Princess Melike and I would sit in our hotel room until nine o'clock, waiting until the moment the water from Geneva's famous fountain (which was turned off at night) began soaring into the air, and afterward we would go out for long walks. My grandmother would gather her light brown hair into a bun held in place by a silver hairpin, and she had a pair of black sunglasses which—unlike my mother—she always wore. Sometimes we would hold hands and take the tram across the bridge to the opposite side of the city to visit the markets and department stores there. I would always assume my grandmother was either comparing prices or looking for something. Every now and then we would sit at a coffee shop or feed bread to the white swans swimming on the lake or stare at the even-uglier and more peculiar shapes of the boats floating on the water or pass the time in one of the city's parks. I remember my grandmother trying to get me to talk about my parents—and specifically about how often they argued. A few times, she mentioned what a strange and distant city I lived in, then smiled and told me about her own childhood in Hong Kong. One day we went to an eleven o'clock matinee of a film that was "suitable" for me (Jacques Tati's *Mon Oncle*). Another time, we sat on a boat and went on a very leisurely tour of Lac Léman. Right from the first day, I knew that we were doing these things to pass the time until my grandmother Melike's mother and father were ready to receive us.

Were it not for the twenty hours I spent (according to my calculations) with my great-grandmother Queen Pakize and my great-grandfather Doctor and Prince Consort Nuri over the course of that week, I doubt I would have ever had the strength to turn that editor's introduction I started with into the book you are about to finish reading.

They both smiled at me when I walked in. They were staying in an identical room (with the same view of Mont Blanc and the fountain) two floors below ours, yet theirs had its own completely distinctive scent of soap and eau de cologne. Even as a ten-year-old, I could tell that they were far happier and jollier than my grandmother, and the reason for this was the unique sense of companionship and trust that endured between them.

"Mummy," said my grandmother, addressing my great-grandmother the Queen, "Mîna has brought you a present from Mingheria!"

"Has she really? How sweet of her! Go on then, show us what you've brought your great-granny and great-granddaddy."

I had been gripped by a strange shyness, and although it would soon dissipate, I felt as if I were in a dream where I had swallowed my tongue and could no longer speak.

"She has photographed the villages from your postcards the way they look now!"

To hear my grandmother Melike—who had never been to Mingheria in her life or shown any interest in the island—refer to these views of Arkaz as "village" scenes was deeply upsetting to me and also caused a great deal of confusion for the Queen and her doctor husband. Addressing them both in the formal style, my grandmother spent a little time trying to describe what the photographs showed.

"This must have taken a lot of work, my little Mingherian!" said Doctor Nuri. My great-grandfather was covered in wrinkles, and his skin whiter than white. He was sitting on an armchair in front of the window, his eyes firmly on the snowy peaks of Mont Blanc. Occasionally he would turn toward us, but most of the time he hardly moved his head at all, as if he had a crick in his neck.

Eventually I managed to gather my courage and handed my gift to the Queen. I was as timid as a self-conscious diplomat. Princess Pakize took the envelope from my hands, put it to one side, then pulled me toward her, kissing me on both cheeks before sitting me on her lap and pressing me to her bosom. She was eighty years old, and she looked thin and frail, but her arms and her chest were strong and solid.

"Is it my turn now?" said Doctor Nuri a short while later.

As I climbed off the Queen's lamp to approach him, I realized that I'd forgotten to kiss my great-grandfather and great-grandmother's hands, which my mother had told me again and again that I must do as soon as I saw them. But I suppose they hadn't exactly behaved as if they had been expecting me to do that. Doctor Nuri's face was so crinkled, and his hairy ears were so enormous, that I shivered a little as I walked up to him, but I would soon come to feel perfectly safe and comfortable in the shelter of his arms too.

Now that I had relaxed, my grandmother Melike walked out of the room, leaving me alone with them. I will now relay the things we talked about with Queen Pakize and the Prince Consort that week, not in any chronological order, but in the way I've remembered them ever since—that is to say, grouped by subject matter.

Me. Through our conversations, I got to know myself better. Was I happy with my life? (I was!) Did I have friends? (I did.) What language did I speak with them? (Turkish—which was true—and Mingherian, which was something of an exaggeration.) Did I know how to swim? (Yes.) How did I know how to take photographs? (My father had taught me.) Where had I got my camera? (My father had brought it from London.) From my answer to this last question, and to some of the other questions which followed it, they understood that although my father was a wealthy London businessman, I had never actually been to London, and for a moment, they fell silent. Was this something I had already known and then forgotten because I didn't really want to think about it, or was it thanks to them that I had first realized my father had been avoiding my mother and me?

Postcards and Photographs. Except for the day Doctor Nuri was presented with his award, we spent most of our time discussing the postcards and photographs. I would sit in the middle of the sofa at the foot of the big bed, the Queen and her Chief Minister on either side of me, and we would spread the postcards and the photographs on a cushion on my lap so that we could study them together. They particularly enjoyed looking at those images in the style of the *vue générale de la baie,* showing a broad view of the city from the former Hamidiye Bridge, and they would reminisce fondly about the old Arkaz. "Do you remember this?" they would ask each other, pointing at a building or a bridge, and suddenly it would all come back to them. But in fact, Doctor Nuri's memory had weakened considerably. One day I would tell him that the big building I had shown him in one of my photographs was the Arkaz Broadcasting House, and the next day he would ask me about it again, looking just as impressed by my response as if he'd heard it for the first time. Within two days, we had gone over every new building in the photographs I had taken. Sometimes I would look at Doctor Nuri's enormous, bony hand—its cracked, wrinkled skin covered in moles and blemishes—and think how strange and even a little eerie it seemed. Even more surprising was when the Queen turned to Doctor Nuri one day and said: "Look! The Mingherian's thumbs are just like yours!" After she said that, I started seeing the resemblance too. Every day that I visited their room, we would look at the photographs for a little while, but we would talk about other things too. One day, after we had finished study-ing the images, the Queen looked over at her husband, then turned to me with a wonderfully kind and gentle manner and said: "Our little Mingherian, we are very grateful to you for bringing these photographs all the way here. Now we have a gift for you too!"

"It's not finished; they're still making it!" said Doctor Nuri.

Mingherian and School. What they really wanted to know was how much of the teaching at school was "actually" in Mingherian. It was true that some of our schoolbooks were written in Mingherian. But I was honest about the fact that most newspapers and books on the island were published in either Greek or Turkish. The blonde school inspec-tor's fantasies of how advanced the teaching of Mingherian at my school had become, and the glowing reports she had prepared for her superiors, must have been inaccurate. That was what I had sensed from my conver-sations with them. But Queen Pakize could tell how nationalistic her lit-tle Mingherian was, and was careful not to hurt my feelings. I made sure not to hurt hers either, telling her that our elementary-school textbooks proudly spoke of her as the Queen who was the daughter of an Ottoman sultan, and the nation's third head of state, and taught us about all the ways in which Queen Pakize had helped the poor during those terrifying days of plague. But the truth was that our schoolbooks didn't talk about any of that, and everyone on the island thought she was dead.

Books and The Count of Monte Cristo. Another question—like "Do you have friends?"—which I would never forget for the rest of my life was when Doctor Nuri asked me: "Do you read books?"

At first I thought he must mean whether I had learned how to read yet, how quickly I could do it, and the kinds of things we read in class. When they understood from my response that I had clearly not yet dis-covered the pleasures of reading, I could see from the expression on their faces that they felt sorry for me (just as they had done when they had realized that my father had never taken me to London). Doctor Nuri told me that just as she used to do as a little girl, my great-granny now preferred to sit at home and read novels all day, rather than go outside.

"I'm afraid that is absolutely untrue, for of course I take great plea-sure in being out and about," said Princess Pakize.

Doctor Nuri felt his wife was being a little petulant, and in his eagerness to introduce the little Mingherian to the merits of reading, he showed me a thick and frayed pocket book that sat on Great-Granny's bedside table: it was *The Count of Monte Cristo*! "Do you know it?"

I remembered the name of the author, and told them that *The Three Musketeers* had been screened at the Majestic Cinema in Arkaz this winter, but that my mother had gone to see it and deemed it not appropriate for my age. If my mother liked a film and thought it would be suitable for me, she would go to see the same film twice so that I could watch it too.

"All these years after the fact, Princess Pakize has managed to solve the mystery of a murder her uncle Abdul Hamid ordered in Arkaz just by reading *The Count of Monte Cristo*!" said Doctor Nuri.

"But you are embellishing, my darling!" said the Queen. "Mine is mere supposition."

"I have no doubt that your supposition is correct!" said Doctor Nuri, turning his head with a little difficulty and giving his wife a loving smile.

Many years later, I was proud and overjoyed to discover while preparing her letters for publication that Princess Pakize's hypothesis had indeed been right. But first I'd had to trawl through Istanbul's antiquarian bookshops to find the six-volume Turkish translation of *The Count of Monte Cristo* published in the Arabic script three years after Abdul Hamid was deposed. The novel was originally published when Abdul Hamid was just two years old, and in its fifty-second chapter, entitled "Toxicology," its author Alexandre Dumas reflects at length through the voice of the Count on how rat poison can be used to kill humans without leaving a trace and even makes comparisons between the East and West. The novel also suggests that malefactors who want their deeds to go undetected would do well to obtain their rat poison from several different sources, rather than a single grocer or herbalist. (Though of course this could also increase the number of pharmacists and shopkeepers who might eventually testify against him!)

When I eagerly leafed through the thick, yellow, fragrant pages of the third volume of the edition of *The Count of Monte Cristo* printed in 1912 by the Bedrosyan Press, and found that chapter 52 was missing, I was filled with renewed admiration for my beloved great-grandmother and rejoiced in the knowledge that all the years I had devoted to preparing her letters for publication had been worth the effort.

The volume didn't even carry a note to say "This chapter has been removed." So to my mind, the promotional note at the beginning of the novel indicating that it had been translated for Abdul Hamid took on the significance of one of Sherlock Holmes's clues. My heart raced with exhilaration.

But I did not know any of this on that day nearly sixty years before, and the only thing I could think of to say was this:

"When we were walking with Grandmother the other day, we saw Abdul Hamid's name written in a watchmaker's window!"

"Did you hear that, my dear?"

"Where did you see Abdul Hamid's name?" they said, looking visibly animated.

This exchange had taken place on our last day. But to better talk about that unforgettable day, I must introduce another subject first.

Live Television. "It's too hot outside!" Princess Pakize would say to explain why they never left the hotel. "Doctor Nuri is a little tired, anyway!"

Toward the end of the week, my great grandfather (who would pass away eight months later) spent some time in the hotel lobby every afternoon except for their last Sunday there watching the boat races being broadcast on the black-and-white television. The races took place between two bridges in the choppy waters where the River Rhône flows into Lac Léman. The jovial spectators gathered on both bridges would watch the oarsmen battling against the powerful currents, and falling into the water when their boats capsized. When we crossed the first bridge with my grandmother Princess Melike in the mornings, we would see them too, and stop to watch.

But what was even more fun, and felt to me like a metaphysical experience, was coming off the bridge only to see the same scene being broadcast live on the television screens of the city's coffeehouses, which were always switched on. What I wanted to do was to wave at the television cameras so that my great-grandparents could see me on their screens in real time. But I did not yet have the words to articulate this childish yearning, and in any case, even if they had understood my wish to wave at them from the television, they would not have been able to help me fulfill it. Not to mention that I really did not want to tell them that we did not yet have televisions in Arkaz.

So on that last afternoon, as I sat in their hotel room and opened my great-grandfather's gift, my mind was on the rich and ineffable links between reality and projection.

I excitedly unwrapped the gift to discover a book (as thick as the one you are holding now), and when I lifted its cover, it turned into a children's pop-up, transforming into a three-dimensional reproduction of Mingheria. How glorious, how lovely, how real it was! The city I had lived in all my life was laid out before me now, in carefully trimmed and exceptionally detailed rows of cardboard cutouts.

I could tell straightaway that this was not the Arkaz where I had grown up, but the city as it must have been in 1901. The new apartment blocks, concrete hotels, and "ministries" were all missing. But everything else was perfectly realistic and precisely where it should be. Yet there was some quality to this marvelous landscape, in the puffs of cloud in the sky, in the red of its roofs and the green of its trees, and in the spires of the Castle, that made you feel at once as if it were your home, and some place out of a fairy tale.

I have always carried Doctor Nuri's beautiful present with me. I wrote the novel you are about to finish with one eye constantly on that three-dimensional fairy tale. To those who might say that this has caused my book to read too much like a fairy tale, I would like to point out my other main source of inspiration in writing this novel: the eighty-three somber, black-and-white photographs of the mostly empty streets of Arkaz, which the Queen had commissioned from the Vanyas Photo Studio at the start of September 1901, and whose influence lies at the heart of this book's "realism." Only when Mingheria officially became a candidate for European Union membership in 2008, and after my childhood friend Rina was named Minister for Culture, was I was finally allowed to return to the state archives whose doors had previously been closed to me.

In the hotel room, my great-grandmother gestured at her husband to look at the Castle situated on the cardboard Arkaz. Back then, the Castle—whose shadow still hangs over me today, and where the history of the city and the whole island first began—was a place I saw every day of my life, so it troubled me that I couldn't quite understand what the Doctor and the Queen were so animatedly discussing.

When I read Princess Pakize's letters years later, I finally understood what they had talked about that day, and what they had remembered. Princess Pakize drew her husband's attention to Hrisopolitissa Square, to the place where Pharmacist Nikiforos had his shop, and to the spot where Bonkowski Pasha's corpse had been found. The lodges of the Halifiye, Rifai, and Gülerenler sects, all of which I have mentioned in this book, had also been re-created in the cardboard-sculpted landscape in meticulous detail, down to the trees that grew in their gardens.

"Have you ever visited this lodge?" said the Queen, looking at me.

These places, secreted behind their walls, were of no interest to my mother, and at the time I hadn't even been aware that they existed. I did not feel any embarrassment when I replied: "I haven't!"

They kept talking, studying the perfectly placed reproductions of Donkey's Bane Hill, Hamidiye Bridge, the garrison, and the Customhouse. My parents would sometimes talk to each other in a strange sort of whispered English, so that I couldn't understand what they were saying, and I would always get upset when they did that and worry that they might be about to have another one of their fights. Seized now by that same fear of loneliness, I went to sit next to Doctor Nuri.

The Queen had placed the cardboard landscape on the coffee table in front of her husband. As they had been talking about the Splendid Palace, I pointed out that it wasn't the best hotel on the island (my mother's words), and that there were better hotels in Mingheria, then noted that the island's best ice-cream parlor was the Splendid's Rome gelateria, and told them about the little Museum of the Commander on the hotel's second floor.

They had not heard about this museum before. They asked me many questions about it, and had me describe its small display in lengthy detail. Now that the conversation had turned to our Heroic Commander—a subject I knew very well indeed—I showed them the house where the Great Savior was born and grew up, and where the real Museum of the Commander was situated. Then I told them about all the things I had seen there.

Noticing how impressed they seemed by my knowledge of the Commander's life, I told them about the Commander's mausoleum, where the teacher would take our whole class on a school trip twice a year (there were checks to make sure), and which did not appear on the post-cards or on the cardboard landscape. I told them that the year before, I had written a homework assignment on this tomb using the *Encyclopaedia Mingheriana* for reference and recited Aşkan the Elder's poems "Oh Commander, Great Commander" and "I Am Mingherian."

"Make sure you go to Istanbul too at the first opportunity!" said Doctor Nuri cryptically.

"Why would you say that?" said the Queen. "We mustn't discourage our little Mingherian. She has been paying attention to her studies, and knows so many things."

I was thrilled by this praise. It helped that we were talking about the Great Commander, the topic I knew best.

"If it hadn't been for our Great Commander, we would still have been prisoners of the Greeks, the Turks, and maybe even the Italians!" I said. "The Commander declared Mingheria free and independent, bringing us and lifting us into the fold of civilized nations."

"Well done!" said Princess Pakize. "Now show us where he did that!"

I suddenly felt very shy, just as I had before the blonde-haired inspector. I wasn't even sure what the question was.

"Look over here, see? This is the balcony of the Governor's Residence," my great-granny said. "What did the Commander do there?"

Now that I had understood the question, I was delighted, for I knew the answer by heart.

"There were thousands of people down in the square, Mingherians of all ages, who had bravely gathered from the farthest reaches of the island!" I intoned. "The Commander told them, 'Long live Mingheria!' "

But in my excitement, I had left out some of the Commander's words, which were quoted in every schoolbook. "And also . . . ," I continued, stammering a little. "He was holding a flag of Mingheria sewn by some village girls."

"Have some of this water, my little Mingherian!" said my great-granny. She gave me a glass of water from the coffee table, and picked up the small tablecloth beneath it, holding it like a flag. "Perhaps if we go out onto the balcony, you'll feel the words and remember them better."

After my great-granny kissed her little Mingherian on both cheeks, I felt relieved and contented. Of course I remembered what the Commander had said, those words I'd gone over thousands of times.

With my great-grandmother Queen Pakize still holding the flag, we went out onto the hotel room's balcony, whose door was always left open. Filled with the same profound, unshakable conviction with which I write those same words down today, we waved our flag in the air and shouted together:

"Long live Mingheria! Long live Mingherians! Long live liberty!"

2016–2021